ALMANAC
of the
50 STATES
Basic Data Profiles
with
Comparative Tables

2002 EDITION

Louise L. Hornor
Editor

information
publications

ISSN 0887-0519
ISBN 0-931845-72-6 (paper)
ISBN 0-931845-73-4 (library)

Information Publications
3790 El Camino Real, PMB 162
Palo Alto, CA 94306
408-286-4449
www.InformationPublications.com

ALMANAC
of the
50 STATES

Basic Data Profiles
with
Comparative Tables

Table of Contents

vi

Introduction

The Almanac of the Fifty States has been created in order to provide a comprehensive, easy to use, state statistical reference book. It presents a general overview of every state, along with tables of comparative ranking.

The book is divided into two parts. The first, State Profiles, is comprised of 52 individual profile sections: one for each of the 50 states, one for the District of Columbia, and one for the US in summary. Each of these profiles is eight pages long, each utilizes the same format organized into 13 subject categories, and each has been compiled from the same sources of information. The result is a set of basic data profiles which are readable, understandable, and provide a strong basis for comparative analysis.

The individual profiles are the heart of the book. Information selected for the profiles has been chosen to include those items which have the greatest general appeal to the broadest cross-section of users. The information comes from the latest reports of federal government agencies, augmented with data from business and trade organizations. No new surveys or original material is included, as the objective is to provide the most vital and significant information about each state, from the most reliable and respected collectors of data. A complete review of the profiles is provided below.

The second part of the book, Comparative Tables, is composed of tables of ranking. The 54 tables each list the states in rank order for a selected characteristic chosen from the state profiles. The purpose here has been to provide straightforward tabular data on how states compare in regard to a given characteristic.

The overall goal of the Almanac of the 50 States is to bring together into a single volume a wide variety of diverse information and present it, state by state, in a clear, comprehensible format. It is not intended as a detailed research tool, but rather as a ready reference source, the first place to turn to answer basic questions about the states.

For readers requiring more depth of coverage or a different focus, it goes without saying that the full range of federal government resources should be examined. Not only Statistical Abstract (and its supplements City and County Data Book, and State and Metropolitan Area Data Book), but the annual reports and serial publications of individual departments and agencies merit attention as well. The federal government is the largest publishing enterprise in the United States, and once the initial hurdle of access is overcome, the researcher is well rewarded: its materials cover a wider range of topics in greater depth and detail than could be imagined.

Additionally, the publications of various trade and professional associations are an excellent source of state information. Most of these organizations produce monographs and annual reports which provide statistical information that is not available elsewhere. Such publications have been useful in compiling this book, and the most pertinent of proprietary information has been reprinted here with permission.

Finally, state governments themselves are publishers of note. Frequently they bring together and make available valuable information on a state and regional level. Most of their material is collected and made available by the respective state libraries.

In order to continue to meet its goals, Almanac of the 50 States is revised and updated on an annual basis. The best suggestions for improvement in a ready-reference source such as this come from the regular users of the work. Therefore, your comments and ideas are actively solicited. If you know how this book can become more useful to you, please contact us.

The Editors
Almanac of the 50 States
Information Publications
3790 El Camino Real, PMB 162
Palo Alto, CA 94306

The profiles

All information in the profiles has been selected from federal government reports and publications, or from materials published by business and trade organizations. The use of such sources ensures an internal consistency and reliability of data that just would not have been available otherwise. Additionally, it enables the users of this book to go back to the more detailed original source materials and use the two in combination.

To enhance this consistency, all headings and terms used in the profiles have been carried over as they appear in the original sources. Those unfamiliar with government terminology may at times be puzzled by either the meaning of a specific term , or why the data was gathered in a certain way. Unclear terms are defined (as the data collection agency uses them) in the next section, The Categories, Headings & Terms. Additionally, the source of origin for each item of information is presented. This allows readers to refer to the original sources themselves which often contain more detailed definitions, and fuller explanations of data collection procedures.

In preparing the format for the profiles, the design has been structured to enable each profile to stand alone. The headings are clear, abbreviations have been avoided whenever possible, and indents have been used to indicate subgroups of the main heading. However, because of the ease of reading, users are cautioned to keep in mind the wording of a heading, and to note whether a dollar amount, median (midway point), mean (average), or percent is being provided. Additionally, it should be pointed out that not all subgroups add to the total shown. This may be due to rounding, or the fact that only selected subgroups are displayed.

The Categories, Headings & Terms

A review of the 13 categories which make up each of the profiles appears below. In addition to citing the source of origin, the paragraphs contain a brief identification of terms and some background methodology on the data collection.

State Summary

All information in this box is taken from the other 12 categories, and individual sources are identified below.

Geography & Environment

General coastline data represents the length of the outline of the coast. Tidal shoreline data represents the shoreline of the outer coast, off-shore islands, sounds, bays, rivers, and creeks to the head of the tidewater. The original source of this information is The Coastline of the United States, 1975.

National parks information comes from State and Metropolitan Area Data Book. Federally owned land data comes from Summary Report of Real Property Owned, published by the U.S. General Services Administration. All other items in this section are from Statistical Abstract.

Demographics & Characteristics of the Population

All 1970, 1980, 1990, and 2000 items are from the 1970, 1980, 1990, and 2000 Censuses of Population, respectively, conducted by the Bureau of the Census. Data from the 2000 U.S. Census is being released between March, 2001 and September, 2002. The information in this book is the latest available at the time this book went to press in January, 2002. The Census Bureau states, "Constraints with staffing and budget, federal guidelines regarding the tabulation of data by race and ethnicity, data processing, or other considerations may result in changes to the types of data products prepared or the timing of their release. For more information on Census 2000 data products, please call Customer Services at 301-457-4100." The release dates for all Census 2000 products are also available online at www.census.gov.

Metropolitan area population data comes from the Bureau of the Census. The metropolitan area population consists of all persons living in Metropolitan Areas (MAs) in the state. An MA is defined by the Bureau of the Census by fairly complicated criteria, but basically consists of a large population nucleus, together with adjacent communities which have a high degree of economic and social integration with that nucleus. Each MA must include at least: (a) one place with 50,000 or more inhabitants, or (b) a Census Bureau-defined urbanized area and a total MA population of at least 100,000 (75,000 in New England). Non-metropolitan area population is everyone not included in metropolitan area population of the state.

Change in population was calculated from data provided by the Bureau of the Census.

Racial statistics are provided, although they are a highly sensitive subject. It is important to recognize that the breakdown represents the self-identification of respondents in regard to pre-set census categories. It does not in any way denote any scientific of biological notion of race. Hispanic origin is not racial group as defined by the Bureau, and persons may be of any race and be of Hispanic origin as well.

A household is defined as the person or persons occupying a housing unit. A housing unit is defined below, under Housing & Construction. Briefly, a housing unit is a separate set of living quarters such as a house, apartment, mobile home, etc. A family is a type of household and consists of a householder and one or more other persons living in the same household who are related to the householder by birth, marriage, or adoption. Married couples, and female heads of household with dependent children and no husband present, are subgroups, or types of families.

Population and age distribution projections are from the Bureau of the Census' World Wide Web site, www.census.gov.

Immigration and naturalization data is from the Statistical Yearbook, a publication of the US Immigration and Naturalization Service.

Vital Statistics & Health

Birth, death, marriage, and divorce data comes from the Monthly Vital Statistics Report, a publication of the Department of Health & Human Services.

Abortion information comes from Family Planning Perspectives, a publication of the Alan Guttmacher Institute, and is reprinted here with permission.

Data for physicians are counts of active, non-federally employed practitioners. Physicians exclude doctors of osteopathy. This information comes from the Health Resources and Services Administration, Department of Health and Human Services, reprinted in Statistical Abstract.

Information on nurses is from the U.S. Department of Health and Human Services, Health Resourses and Services Administration and appears in Statistical Abstract.

Average lifetime data comes from Statistical Abstract.

Hospital data comes from Statistical Abstract. Data reflects AHA member hospitals only. The average daily census refers to the average total number of in-patients receiving treatment each day, excluding newborns. The occupancy rate is the ratio of the average daily census to every 100 beds. Cost per day and cost per stay represent cost to hospital per day and per stay.

Education

Educational attainment data comes from the U.S. Bureau of the Census.

Most of the other education data is from Digest of Education Statistics 2000, compiled by the National Center for Educational Statistics, U.S. Department of Education. Finance data and public school teacher data was taken from Statistical Abstract.

Social Insurance & Welfare Programs

All items here have been obtained from Statistical Abstract and its supplements. It should be noted that detail is provided for three major Social Security programs: those for the retired; for the survivors of enrollees; and for the disabled covered under the program. The original source of Social Security information is the Social Security Administration's Bulletin and the Bulletin's Annual Statistical Supplement. Medicare and Medicaid data are produced by the U.S. Health Care Financing Administration and are also from Statistical Abstract.

Housing & Construction

The Bureau of the Census conducts a decennial Census of Housing which is almost as extensive as its Census of Population. The selection of housing information here, taken from the 2000 Census of Housing, represents just a small portion of what is available.

The Bureau defines some key terms as follows: a housing unit is house, apartment, mobile home or trailer, group of rooms, or single room occupied as separate living quarter or, if vacant, intended as a separate living quarter. Separate living quarters are those in which occupants live and eat separately from any other persons in the building and which have direct access from the outside of the building or from a common hall.

Data for new privately owned housing units and existing home sales comes from Statistical Abstract.

Government and Elections

Names of State officials and current party in majority have been obtained from telephone confirmations from the office of the Governor or Secretary of State of the respective states. Information about the governorship and legislative structure of each state was obtained from respective legislative manuals and annual election reports.

State employees is from Public Employment, 2000, an annual publication of the Bureau of the Census. Figures represent March, 2000, totals for full and part-time employees, along with March payroll data.

Information on local governments comes from the 1997 Census of Governments (conducted by the Bureau of the Census). Readers are cautioned that the data provided concerns governmental units as opposed to geographic entities. For example, in Connecticut there are eight counties, but no county governments, hence a zero appears in the county space in the Connecticut profile.

Voting age population information comes from Current Population Reports, published by the Bureau of the Census. Vote for president is also from Statistical Abstract.

Information on women holding public offices comes from press releases provided by the Center for American Women and Politics at the Eagleton Institute of Rutgers University, and is reprinted with permission.

Data concerning black elected officials are from the Joint Center for Political & Economic Studies, Washington, DC, reprinted in Statistical Abstract.

Hispanic public officials information is from the National Association of Latino Elected and Appointed Officials, Washington, DC, reprinted in Statistical Abstract.

Names of Senators come from the federal website, www.senate.gov, and the number of Representatives by party comes from clerkweb.house.gov.

Governmental Finance

Revenue, expenditure and debt information comes from State Government Finance: 1999. Federal government grants information comes from Federal Aid to States for Fiscal Year 2000. Both are publications of the Bureau of the Census and are available on their website, www.census.gov.

Crime, Law Enforcement & Courts

Information on crime, crime rates, police agencies, and arrests comes from Crime in the US, 2000. Information on number of persons under sentence of death comes from Sourcebook of Criminal Justice Statistics, 2000. Information on prisoners comes from Prisoners in 2000. These sources are publications of the U.S. Department of Justice. Readers are cautioned that crime information is based on crimes known to police.

State court information comes from the legislative manuals of the respective states.

Labor & Income

All civilian labor force data comes from Geographic Profiles of Employment and Unemployment, 1998 and 2000, published by the Department of Labor. The civilian labor force includes all civilians who are either employed or unemployed. Generally, employed persons are those who: 1) did any work as a paid employee; or 2) worked 15 hours or more as an unpaid employee in a family enterprise; or 3) had jobs but were not working due to illness, vacation, etc. Unemployed persons are those who: 1) had no paid employment and were both available for and looking for work; or 2) were waiting to be recalled to a job; or 3) were waiting to report to a new job. A full-time employee is one who works at least 35 hours per week.

Unemployed persons are grouped into four categories: a job loser is someone whose employment has ended involuntarily; a job leaver is someone whose employment ended voluntarily; a reentrant is someone who has previously worked, but was out of the labor force prior to seeking employment; and a new entrant is someone who has never worked before and is now seeking employment.

Hours and earnings data comes from Employment & Earnings, May, 2001, a monthly publication of the Department of Labor.

Average annual pay comes from NEWS, a bulletin put out by the Bureau of Labor Statistics, and includes the pay of workers who are covered by state unemployment insurance laws, and federal civilian workers covered by federal unemployment. This represents approximately 89% of total civilian employment. It excludes members of the armed forces, elected officials in most states, railroad employees, most self-employed persons, and some others. Pay includes bonuses, the cash value of meals and lodging, and tips and other gratuities.

Labor union membership comes from Statistical Abstract.

Household income and poverty information comes from the P-60 Series of the U.S. Bureau of the Census, both published on the Census' website, www.census.gov.

Personal income figures come from Survey of Current Business, a monthly publication of the Department of Commerce, reprinted in Statistical Abstract.

Federal tax data are from Statistics of Income Bulletin, Spring, 2001, a quarterly report of the Internal Revenue Service.

Economy, Business, Industry & Agriculture

Fortune 500 companies come from a count of listed corporations found in the annual directory issue of Fortune.

Business incorporation and failure data comes from proprietary information compiled by Dun & Bradstreet. It is reprinted here with permission.

Business firm ownership is from the U.S. Bureau of the Census' 1997 Economic Census Reports, the most recent Economic Census to have released data on ownership by race at press time.

Gross state product is taken from Survey of Current Business, a publication of the Department of Commerce, Bureau of Economic Analysis, published on the Bureau of the Census' website, www.census.gov. The industries represented are major categories under the U.S. Standard Industrial Classification (SIC) system, which is being phased out. All other industries represented in this section are categories under the North American Industry Classification System (NAICS). NAICS is replacing the SIC system and will reshape the way we view our changing economy. NAICS was developed jointly by the U.S., Canada, and Mexico to provide new comparability in statistics about business activity across North America. For more information on NAICS and to understand the correspondence between NAICS and SIC, please visit the U.S. Bureau of the Census website, www.census.gov, and search for NAICS.

Establishment and payroll data are from the 1999 edition of County Business Patterns, a 52 volume report issued annually by the Bureau of the Census.

Agricultural data comes from the Department of Agriculture, and was republished in Statistical Abstract.

Data on federal economic activity comes from Federal Expenditures by State for Fiscal Year 1999, and reprinted in Statistical Abstract.

Department of Defense information comes from the department and was reprinted in Statistical Abstract.

Fishing data are from <u>Fisheries of the United States, 2000,</u> a publication of the National Oceanic and Atmospheric Administration.

Mining information is from the U.S. Bureau of Mines; construction information is from <u>Statistical Abstract</u>; finance information originates with the Federal Deposit Insurance Corporation and <u>Statistical Abstract</u>. Establishments, receipts/sales/value of shipments, annual payroll and paid employee data come from the 1997 Economic Census, following NAICS classifications.

Communication, Energy & Transportation

The count of daily newspapers and percentages of households with telephones, computers and internet access are from <u>Statistical Abstract</u>.

All energy information comes from <u>State Energy Data Report,</u> and <u>Electric Power Annual,</u> both published by the U.S. Energy Information Administration and American Gas Association <u>Gas Facts</u> and reprinted from <u>Statistical Abstract</u>.

All transportation information comes from <u>Highway Statistics, 2000,</u> an annual publication of the Department of Transportation.

The Profiles

STATE SUMMARY

Capital City .... Montgomery

Governor .... Don Siegelman

Address .... STATE CAPITOL
          MONTGOMERY, AL 31630
          334 242-7200

Admitted as a state 1819

Area (square miles) 52,423

Population, 1980 3,893,800

Population, 1990 4,040,587

Population, 2000 4,447,100

Persons per square mile, 2000 .... 87.6

Largest city .... Birmingham
     population, 2000 243,000

Personal income per capita, 2000
     (in current dollars) $23,471

Gross state product ($mil), 1999 ..... $115,071

Leading industries, 1999 (by payroll)
          Manufacturing
          Health care/Social assistance
          Retail trade

Leading agricultural commodities, 1999
          Broilers, cattle, chicken eggs, greenhouse

GEOGRAPHY & ENVIRONMENT

Area, 1990 (square miles)
total 52,423
   land 50,750
   water (includes territorial water) 1,673

Federally owned land, 2000 .... 4.1%

Highest point
name .... Cheaha Mountain
elevation (feet) 2,405

Lowest point
name .... Gulf of Mexico
elevation (feet) .... sea level

General coastline (miles) 53

Tidal shoreline (miles) 607

Capital city .... Montgomery
population, 2000 202,000

Largest city .... Birmingham
population, 2000 243,000

Number of cities with over 100,000 population
   1980 4
   1990 4
   2000 4

State parks and Recreation areas, 2000
area (acres) 50,000
number of visitors 5,878,000
revenues $25,213,000

Natl. forest system land, 1999 (acres) 665,000

National park acreage, 1984 6,600

DEMOGRAPHICS & CHARACTERISTICS OF THE POPULATION

Population
1970 3,444,354
1980 3,893,800
1990 4,040,587
2000 4,447,100
2015 (projection) 4,956,000
2025 (projection) 5,224,000

Metropolitan area population
1970 2,169,000
1980 2,462,000
2000 3,109,000

Non-metropolitan area population
1970 1,275,000
1980 1,432,000
2000 1,338,000

Change in population, 1990-2000
number 406,513
percent 10.06%

Persons per square mile, 2000 .... 87.6

Persons by age, 2000
under 5 years 295,992
18 and over 3,323,678
21 and over 3,124,317
65 and over 579,798
85 and over 67,301

Alabama 2

Persons by age, 2025 (projected)
under 5 years 300,000
5 to 17 years 838,000
65 and over 1,069,000

Median age, 2000 ....35.8

Race, 2000
One race
White 3,162,808
Black or African American 1,155,930
American Indian and Alaska Native 22,430
Asian Indian 6,900
Chinese 6,337
Filipino 2,727
Japanese 1,966
Korean 4,116
Vietnamese 4,628
Native Hawaiian and other Pacific Islander 1,409
Two or more races 44,179

Race, 2025 (projected)
White 3,780,000
Black 1,364,000

Persons of Hispanic origin, 2000
total Hispanic or Latino 75,830
  Mexican 44,522
  Puerto Rican 6,322
  Cuban 2,354
  Other Hispanic or Latino 22,632

Persons of Hispanic origin, 2025 (proj.) ... 63,000

Persons by sex, 2000
male 2,146,504
female 2,300,596

Marital status, 1990
males
  15 years & older 1,488,017
    single 406,140
    married 925,748
      separated 26,921
    widowed 40,619
    divorced 115,510
females
  15 years & older 1,676,275
    single 348,728
    married 933,898
      separated 41,081

  widowed 235,648
  divorced 158,001

Households & families, 2000
households 1,737,080
persons per household 2.49
  families 1,215,968
  persons per family 3.01
    married couples 906,916
    female householder, no husband
      present 246,466
    one person households 453,898
households with persons under 18 years . 626,857
households with persons over 65 years ... 418,608

Nativity, 1990
number of persons born in state 3,067,607
percent of total residents 75.9%

Immigration & naturalization, 1998
immigrants admitted 1,608
persons naturalized 658
refugees granted resident status 48

VITAL STATISTICS & HEALTH
Births
1999
  with low birth weight 9.3%
  to teenage mothers 14.2%
  to unmarried mothers 33.3%
Birth rate, 1999 (per 1,000) 14.2
Birth rate, 2000 (per 1,000) 14.4

Abortions, 1996
total 15,000
rate (per 1,000 women age 15-44) 15.6

Deaths
1998 43,989
1999 44,806
2000 45,075

Infant deaths
1998 621
1999 571
2000 597

Average lifetime, by race, 1989-1991
total .... 73.64 years
  white .... 75.01 years
  black .... 69.23 years

Marriages
1998 49,893
1999 47,700
2000 44,998

Divorces
1998 26,274
1999 25,885
2000 23,529

Physicians, 1999
total 8,733
rate (per 1,000 persons) 2.00

Nurses, 1999
total 33,680
rate (per 1,000 persons) 7.71

Hospitals, 1998
number 110
beds (x 1,000) 17.0
average daily census (x 1,000) 10.0
patients admitted (x1,000) 644
average cost per day to hospital, 1995 ... $819
average cost per stay to hospital, 1995 ... $5,028

EDUCATION

*Educational attainment of all persons
25 years and older, 1990*
less than 9th grade 348,848
high school graduates 749,591
bachelor's degree 258,231
graduate or professional degree 140,997

2000
high school graduate or more 77.5%
college graduate or more 20.4%

Public school enrollment, Fall, 1998
total 747,970
Kindergarten through grade 8 542,340
grades 9 through 12 205,630

Public School Teachers, 2000
total 47,000
elementary 28,500
secondary 18,500
average salaries
elementary $36,700
secondary $36,700

*State receipts & expenditures for public
schools, 2000*
revenue receipts ($mil) $5,140

*State receipts & expenditures for public
schools, 2000 (continued)*
expenditures
total ($mil) $4,441
per capita $1,016
per pupil $5,118

*Graduating high school seniors,
public high schools, 2000 (est.)* 37,893

SAT scores, 2001
verbal 559
math 554
percent graduates taking test 9%

Institutions of higher education, 1999
total 78
public 48
private 30

*Enrollment in institutions of higher
education, Fall, 1998*
total 216,268
full-time men 64,880
full-time women 82,390
part-time men 28,682
part-time women 40,316

*Minority enrollment in institutions of higher
education, Fall, 1997*
Black, non-Hispanic 53,622
Hispanic 1,696
Asian/Pacific Islander 2,506

Earned degrees conferred, 1998
Bachelor's 20,335
First professional 1,095
Master's 6,318
Doctor s 569

SOCIAL INSURANCE &
WELFARE PROGRAMS

Social Security beneficiaries & benefits, 2000
beneficiaries
total 827,000
retired and dependents 516,000
survivors 146,000
disabled & dependents 165,000
annual benefit payments ($mil)
total $6,942
retired and dependents $4,186
survivors $1,483
disabled & dependents $1,272

Alabama 4

Medicare, 2000
enrollment (x1,000) 677
payments ($mil) $3,885

Medicaid, 1998
recipients (x1,000) 527
payments ($mil) $1,902

Federal public aid
Temporary Assistance for Needy Families
(TANF), 2000
   Recipients (x1,000) 56
   Families (x1,000) 19
Supplemental Security Income
   total recipients, 1999 (x1,000) 160

Food Stamp Program
   participants, 2000 (x1,000) 396

HOUSING & CONSTRUCTION

Total housing units, 2000 1,963,711
   seasonal or recreational use 47,205
   occupied 1,737,080
   owner occupied 1,258,705
   renter occupied 478,375

New privately owned housing units uthorized, 2000
number (x1,000) 17.4
value ($mil) $1,718

New privately owned housing units
started, 2000 (est.) (x1,000) 21.2

Existing home sales, 2000 (x1,000) 75.9

GOVERNMENT & ELECTIONS

State officials, 2002
  Governor (name/party/term expires)
       DON SIEGELMAN
       Democrat - 2002
Lt. Governor .... Steve Windom
Sec. of State .... Jim Bennett
Atty. General .... Bill Pryor
Chief Justice .... Roy Moore

Governorship
minimum age 30
length of term .... 4 years
number of consecutive
   terms permitted 2
who succeeds .... Lt. Governor

State legislature
name .... Legislature
  upper chamber
    name .... Senate
    number of members 35
    length of term .... 4 years
    party in majority, 2000 .... Democratic
  lower chamber
    name .... House of Representatives
    number of members 105
    length of term .... 4 years
    party in majority, 2000 .... Democratic

State employees March, 2000
total 94,254
March payroll $216,753,028

Local governments, 1997
total 1,131
   county 67
   municipal 446
   township 0
   school districts 127
   special districts 491

Voting age population, November, 2000, projected
Total 3,333,000
   male 1,565,000
   female 1,768,000

Vote for president
2000
   Gore 693,000
   Bush 941,000
1996
   Clinton 662,000
   Dole 769,000
   Perot 92,000

Federal representation, 2002 (107th Congress)
Senators (name/party/term expires)

       JEFF SESSIONS
       Republican - 2003
       RICHARD SHELBY
       Republican - 2005

Representatives, total 7
   Democrats 2
   Republicans 5
   other 0

Women holding public office, 2001
U.S. Congress 0
statewide elected office 3
state legislature 11

Black elected officials, 1999
total 725
   US and state legislatures 36
   city/county/regional offices 540
   judicial/law enforcement 53
   education/school boards 96

Hispanic public officials, 2000
total . . . . NA
   state executives & legislators . . . . NA
   city/county/regional offices . . . . NA
   judicial/law enforcement . . . . NA
   education/school boards . . . . NA

GOVERNMENTAL FINANCE

State government revenues, 1999 ($per capita)
total revenue $3,547.27
   total general revenue $2,996.26
    intergovernmental revenue $979.83
    taxes $1,380.42
    current charges $454.36
    miscellaneous $181.66

State government expenditures, 1999 ($per capita)
total expenditure $3,364.39
   total general expenditure $3,041.08
    education $1,316.29
    public welfare $731.16
    health $134.61
    hospitals $235.19
    highways $210.91
    police protection $26.02
    correction $64.64
    natural resources $46.44
    governmental administration $76.95
    interest on general debt $45.30

State debt, 1999 ($per capita) $1,022.25

Federal government grants to state & local government, 2000 (x$1,000)
total $4,569,788
   Dept. of Education $498,991
   Environmental Protection Agency $49,903
   Health Care Financing Admin. $1,964,643
   Dept. Housing & Urban Devel. $427,481
   Dept. of Labor $81,588
   Highway trust fund $472,652

CRIME, LAW ENFORCEMENT & COURTS

Crime, 2000 (all rates per 100,000 inhabitants)
total crimes 202,159
overall crime rate 4,545.9
   property crimes 180,539
    burglaries 40,331
    larcenies 127,399
    motor vehicle thefts 12,809
   property crime rate 4,059.7
   violent crimes 21,620
    murders 329
    forcible rapes 1,482
    robberies 5,702
    aggravated assaults 14,107
   violent crime rate 486.2

Number of police agencies, 2000 214

Arrests, 2000
total 162,906
   persons under 18 years of age 11,684

Prisoners under state & federal jurisdiction, 2000
total 26,225
percent change, 1999-2000 . . . . NA%
   sentenced to more than one year
   total 24,123
   rate per 100,000 residents 549

Persons under sentence of death, 4/1/2001 . . . 190

State's highest court
name . . . . Supreme Court
number of members 9
length of term . . . . 6 years
intermediate appeals court? . . . . yes

Alabama 6

LABOR & INCOME

Civilian labor force, 2000

total	2,154,000
men	1,124,000
women	1,030,000
persons 16-19 years	125,000
white	1,585,000
black	551,000

Civilian labor force as a percent of civilian non-institutional population, 2000

total	63.3%
men	70.7%
women	56.9%
persons 16-19 years	NA%
white	63.8%
black	61.8%

Employment, 2000

total	2,055,000
men	1,074,000
women	981,000
persons 16-19 years	101,000
white	1,532,000
black	505,000

Full-time/part-time labor force, 1998

full-time labor force	1,788,000
working part-time for economic reasons	24,000
part-time labor force	365,000

Unemployment rate, 2000

total	4.6%
men	4.5%
women	4.8%
persons 16-19 years	18.6%
white	3.3%
black	8.3%

Unemployed by reason for unemployment (as a percent of total unemployment), 1998

job losers or completed temp jobs	44.0%
job leavers	12.1%
reentrants	34.1%
new entrants	8.8%

Experienced civilian labor force, by occupation, 1998

executive/administrative/managerial	261,000
professional/specialty	270,000
technicians & related support	68,000
sales	311,000
administrative support/clerical	290,000
service occupations	239,000
precision production/craft/repair	272,000
machine operators/assemblers	189,000
transportation/material moving	94,000
handlers/helpers/laborers	94,000
farming/forestry/fishing	55,000

Experienced civilian labor force, by industry, 1998

construction	132,000
manufacturing	406,000
transportation/communication	83,000
wholesale/retail trade	444,000
finance/real estate/insurance	109,000
services	447,000
government	313,000
agriculture	NA

Average annual pay, 1999	$28,069
change in average annual pay, 1998-1999	3.8%

Hours and earnings of production workers on manufacturing payrolls, 2000

average weekly hours	41.9
average hourly earnings	$12.94
average weekly earnings	$542.19

Labor union membership, 2000	180,800

Household income (in 2000 dollars)

median household income, three year average, 1998-2000	$33,105

Poverty

persons below poverty level, three year average, 1998-2000	14.6%

Personal income ($per capita)
2000 (prelim.)

in current dollars	$23,471
in constant (1996) dollars	$21,862

1999 (preliminary)

in current dollars	$22,946
in constant (1996) dollars	$21,941

Federal income tax returns, 1999

returns filed	1,898,392
adjusted gross income ($1,000)	$70,232,698
total income tax paid ($1,000)	$9,571,394

ECONOMY, BUSINESS, INDUSTRY & AGRICULTURE

Fortune 500 companies, 2000 7

Business incorporations, 1998
total 7,559
change, 1997-1998 .... -2.4%

Business failures, 1998 546

Business firm ownership, 1997
Hispanic owned firms 2,919
Black owned firms 19,077
women owned firms 69,515
Asian & Pacific Islander owned firms 3,315
American Indian & Alaska
   native owned firms 3,513

Shopping centers, 2000 651

Gross state product, 1999 ($mil)
total $115,071
  agriculture services, forestry, fisheries .. $2,280
  mining $1,527
  construction $5,397
  manufacturing--durable goods $11,768
  manufacturing--nondurable goods $10,118
  transportation, communication &
    public utilities $9,971
  wholesale trade $7,542
  retail trade $11,927
  finance/real estate/insurance $16,945
  services $19,447
  federal, state & local government $18,149

Establishments, by major industry group, 1999
total 100,507
  forestry, fishing & agriculture 1,240
  mining 267
  construction 9,839
  manufacturing 5,336
  transportation & warehousing 3,161
  wholesale trade 6,226
  retail trade 19,867
  finance & insurance 5,817
  professional/scientific/technical 8,148
  health care/social assistance 8,522
  information 1,502
  accommodation/food services 6,975

Payroll, by major industry group, 1999
total ($1,000) $42,453,530
  forestry, fishing & agriculture $222,034
  mining $336,014
  construction $2,772,472
  manufacturing $10,631,025
  transportation & warehousing $1,328,974
  wholesale trade $2,745,582
  retail trade $3,939,356
  finance & insurance $2,699,726
  professional/scientific/technical $2,834,005
  health care/social assistance $5,825,271
  information $1,432,975
  accommodation/food services $1,253,146

Agriculture
number of farms, 2000 47,000
farm acreage, 2000 9,000,000
acres per farm, 2000 191
value of farms, 1997 ($mil) $14,356
farm income, 1999 ($mil)
  net farm income $1,450
  debt/asset ratio 12.5%
farm marketings, 1999 ($mil)
total $3,438
  crops $662
  livestock $2,777
principal commodities, in order by marketing
receipts, 1999
    Broilers, cattle, chicken eggs, greenhouse

Federal economic activity in state
expenditures, 2000
  total ($mil) $29,217
  per capita $6,570
  defense ($mil) $5,534
  non-defense ($mil) $23,683
defense department, 2000
  contract awards ($mil) $3,298
  payroll ($mil) $2,376
  civilian employees (x1,000) 20.2
  military personnel (x1,000) 11.1

Fishing, 2000
catch (thousands of pounds) 29,931
value ($1,000) $63,275

Mining, 2000 ($mil; preliminary)
total non-fuel mineral production $1,070

Alabama 8

Construction, 1999 ($mil)
total contracts (including
   non-building) $5,482
     residential $2,368
     non-residential $2,055

Construction industries, 1997
establishments 9,398
receipts ($1,000) $12,613,807
annual payroll ($1,000) $2,453,249
paid employees 94,525

Manufacturing, 1997
establishments 6,480
value of shipments ($1,000) $69,694,695
annual payroll ($1,000) $10,497,421
paid employees 364,887

Transportation industries, 1997
establishments 4,829
receipts ($1,000) $16,482,640
annual payroll ($1,000) $3,040,979
paid employees 88,048

Wholesale trade, 1997
establishments 7,476
sales($1,000) $43,345,729
annual payroll ($1,000) $2,665,198
paid employees 90,151

Retail trade, 1997
establishments 25,586
sales($1,000) $37,614,376
annual payroll ($1,000) $4,039,301
paid employees 342,835

Finance industries
establishments, 1997 8,411
receipts ($1,000), 1997 .... $NA
annual payroll ($1,000), 1997 .... $2,696,398
paid employees, 1997 86,105
commercial banks, 2000
   number 158
     assets ($bil) $181.5
     deposits ($bil) $129.9

Service industries, 1997 (non-exempt firms only)
establishments 26,576
receipts ($1,000) $19,417,250
annual payroll ($1,000) $7,660,797
paid employees 319,408

COMMUNICATION, ENERGY & TRANSPORTATION

Communication
daily newspapers, 2000 24
households with
   telephones, 1998 .... 93.6%
   computers, 2000 .... 44.2%
   internet access, 2000 .... 35.5%

Energy
consumption, 1999
total (trillion Btu) 2,005
per capita (million Btu) 459
by source of production (trillion Btu)
   coal 855
   natural gas 345
   petroleum 551
   nuclear electric power 328
   hydroelectric power 80
by end-use sector (trillion Btu)
   residential 341
   commercial 226
   industrial 977
   transportation 461
electric energy, 1999
   production (billion kWh) 113.9
   net summer capability (million kW) 21.5
gas utilities, 1999
   customers 832,000
   sales (trillion Btu) 103
nuclear plants, 1999 5

Transportation, 2000
public road & street mileage
total 94,311
   urban 20,672
   rural 73,639
   interstate 906
vehicle miles of travel (mil) 56,534
total motor vehicle registrations 3,960,149
   automobiles 1,961,806
   motorcycles 54,359
licensed drivers 3,521,444
   per 1,000 driving age population 1,020
deaths from motor vehicle
   accidents 995

STATE SUMMARY

Capital City ....Juneau

Governor .... Tony Knowles

Address .... STATE CAPITOL
JUNEAU, AK 99811
907 465-3500

Admitted as a state 1959

Area (square miles) 656,424

Population, 1980 401,851

Population, 1990 550,043

Population, 2000 626,932

Persons per square mile, 2000 .... 1.1

Largest city .... Anchorage
population, 2000 260,000

Personal income per capita, 2000
(in current dollars) $30,064

Gross state product ($mil), 1999 .... $26,353

Leading industries, 1999 (by payroll)
Health care/Social assistance
Transportation & Warehousing
Retail trade

Leading agricultural commodities, 1999
Greenhouse, dairy products, potatoes, hay

GEOGRAPHY & ENVIRONMENT

Area, 1990 (square miles)
total 656,424
   land 570,374
   water (includes territorial water) 86,051

Federally owned land, 2000 .... 60.4%

Highest point
name .... Mt. McKinley
elevation (feet) 20,320

Lowest point
name .... Pacific Ocean
elevation (feet) .... sea level

General coastline (miles) 6,568

Tidal shoreline (miles) 33,904

Capital city ....Juneau
population, 2000 30,711

Largest city .... Anchorage
population, 2000 260,000

Number of cities with over 100,000 population
  1980 1
  1990 1
  2000 1

State parks and Recreation areas, 2000
area (acres) 3,291,000
number of visitors 3,888,000
revenues $2,012,000

Natl. forest system land, 1999 (acres) ..21,974,000

National park acreage, 1984 52,106,400

DEMOGRAPHICS & CHARACTERISTICS OF THE POPULATION

Population
1970 302,583
1980 401,851
1990 550,043
2000 626,932
2015 (projection) 791,000
2025 (projection) 885,000

Metropolitan area population
1970 126,000
1980 174,000
2000 260,000

Non-metropolitan area population
1970 176,000
1980 227,000
2000 367,000

Change in population, 1990-2000
number 76,889
percent 13.98%

Persons per square mile, 2000 .... 1.1

Persons by age, 2000
under 5 years 47,591
18 and over 436,215
21 and over 410,474
65 and over 35,699
85 and over 2,634

Alaska 2

Persons by age, 2025 (projected)
under 5 years 82,000
5 to 17 years 194,000
65 and over 92,000

Median age, 2000 .... 32.4

Race, 2000
One race
White 434,534
Black or African American 21,787
American Indian and Alaska Native 98,043
Asian Indian 723
Chinese 1,464
Filipino 12,712
Japanese 1,414
Korean 4,573
Vietnamese 814
Native Hawaiian and other Pacific Islander 3,309
Two or more races 34,146

Race, 2025 (projected)
White 558,000
Black 39,000

Persons of Hispanic origin, 2000
total Hispanic or Latino 25,852
  Mexican 13,334
  Puerto Rican 2,649
  Cuban 553
  Other Hispanic or Latino 9,316

Persons of Hispanic origin, 2025 (proj.) ... 59,000

Persons by sex, 2000
male 324,112
female 302,820

Marital status, 1990
males
  15 years & older 212,540
    single 67,827
    married 119,985
      separated 4,146
    widowed 2,541
    divorced 22,187
females
  15 years & older 187,691
    single 40,938
    married 115,317
      separated 4,455

widowed 9,082
divorced 22,354

Households & families, 2000
households 221,600
persons per household 2.74
  families 152,337
  persons per family 3.28
    married couples 116,318
  female householder, no husband
    present 23,937
  one person households 52,060
households with persons under 18 years .. 95,129
households with persons over 65 years 26,349

Nativity, 1990
number of persons born in state 186,887
percent of total residents 34.0%

Immigration & naturalization, 1998
immigrants admitted 1,008
persons naturalized 995
refugees granted resident status 26

VITAL STATISTICS & HEALTH

Births
1999
  with low birth weight 5.8%
  to teenage mothers 16.1%
  to unmarried mothers 33.2%
Birth rate, 1999 (per 1,000) 16.1
Birth rate, 2000 (per 1,000) 16.1

Abortions, 1996
total 2,000
rate (per 1,000 women age 15-44) 14.6

Deaths
1998 2,480
1999 2,708
2000 2,911

Infant deaths
1998 53
1999 53
2000 64

Average lifetime, by race, 1989-1991
total .... NA years
  white .... NA years
  black .... NA years

Marriages
1998 5,948
1999 5,373
2000 5,564

Divorces
1998 3,212
1999 2,647
2000 2,718

Physicians, 1999
total 1,054
rate (per 1,000 persons) 1.70

Nurses, 1999
total 7,350
rate (per 1,000 persons) 11.86

Hospitals, 1998
number 17
beds (x 1,000) 1.2
average daily census (x 1,000) 1.0
patients admitted (x1,000) 41
average cost per day to hospital, 1995 .... $1,341
average cost per stay to hospital, 1995 .... $8,282

EDUCATION

*Educational attainment of all persons
25 years and older, 1990*
less than 9th grade 16,621
high school graduates 92,925
bachelor's degree 48,617
graduate or professional degree 25,880

2000
high school graduate or more 90.4%
college graduate or more 28.1%

Public school enrollment, Fall, 1998
total 135,373
Kindergarten through grade 8 96,979
grades 9 through 12 38,394

Public School Teachers, 2000
total 7,900
elementary 5,300
secondary 2,600
average salaries
elementary $47,300
secondary $47,300

*State receipts & expenditures for public
schools, 2000*
revenue receipts ($mil) $1,342

*State receipts & expenditures for public
schools, 2000 (continued)*
expenditures
total ($mil) $1,319
per capita $2,129
per pupil $10,711

*Graduating high school seniors,
public high schools, 2000 (est.)* 6,975

SAT scores, 2001
verbal 514
math 510
percent graduates taking test 51%

Institutions of higher education, 1999
total 8
public 4
private 4

*Enrollment in institutions of higher
education, Fall, 1998*
total 27,652
full-time men 5,020
full-time women 6,369
part-time men 5,948
part-time women 10,315

*Minority enrollment in institutions of higher
education, Fall, 1997*
Black, non-Hispanic 1,033
Hispanic 836
Asian/Pacific Islander 975

Earned degrees conferred, 1998
Bachelor's 1,479
First professional 0
Master's 484
Doctor's 68

SOCIAL INSURANCE & WELFARE PROGRAMS

Social Security beneficiaries & benefits, 2000
beneficiaries
total 55,000
retired and dependents 35,000
survivors 10,000
disabled & dependents 10,000
annual benefit payments ($mil)
total $465
retired and dependents $291
survivors $94
disabled & dependents $80

Alaska 4

Medicare, 2000
enrollment (x1,000) 40
payments ($mil) $189

Medicaid, 1998
recipients (x1,000) 75
payments ($mil) $330

Federal public aid
Temporary Assistance for Needy Families
(TANF), 2000
  Recipients (x1,000) 25
  Families (x1,000) 8
Supplemental Security Income
  total recipients, 1999 (x1,000) 8

Food Stamp Program
  participants, 2000 (x1,000) 38

HOUSING & CONSTRUCTION

Total housing units, 2000 260,978
  seasonal or recreational use 21,474
  occupied 221,600
    owner occupied 138,509
    renter occupied 83,091

New privately owned housing units uthorized, 2000
number (x1,000) 2.1
value ($mil) $333

New privately owned housing units
  started, 2000 (est.) (x1,000) 2.1

Existing home sales, 2000 (x1,000) 18.9

GOVERNMENT & ELECTIONS

State officials, 2002
  Governor (name/party/term expires)
    TONY KNOWLES
    Democrat - 2002
Lt. Governor .... Fran Ulmer
Sec. of State .... (no secretary of state)
Atty. General .... Bruce Botelho
Chief Justice .... Dana Fabe

Governorship
minimum age 30
length of term .... 4 years
number of consecutive
  terms permitted 2
who succeeds .... Lt. Governor

State legislature
name .... Legislature
  upper chamber
    name .... Senate
    number of members 20
    length of term .... 4 years
    party in majority, 2000 .... Republican
  lower chamber
    name .... House of Representatives
    number of members 40
    length of term .... 2 years
    party in majority, 2000 .... Republican

State employees March, 2000
total 26,388
March payroll ...., ... $85,564,374

Local governments, 1997
total 175
  county 12
  municipal 149
  township 0
  school districts 0
  special districts 14

Voting age population, November, 2000, projected
Total 430,000
  male 227,000
  female 203,000

Vote for president
2000
  Gore 79,000
  Bush 167,000
1996
  Clinton 80,000
  Dole 123,000
  Perot 26,000

Federal representation, 2002 (107th Congress)
Senators (name/party/term expires)

TED STEVENS
Republican - 2003
FRANK H. MURKOWSKI
Republican - 2005

Representatives, total 1
  Democrats 0
  Republicans 1
  other 0

Women holding public office, 2001
U.S. Congress 0
statewide elected office 1
state legislature 13

Black elected officials, 1999
total 3
   US and state legislatures .... NA
   city/county/regional offices 2
   judicial/law enforcement .... NA
   education/school boards 1

Hispanic public officials, 2000
total .... NA
   state executives & legislators .... NA
   city/county/regional offices .... NA
   judicial/law enforcement .... NA
   education/school boards .... NA

GOVERNMENTAL FINANCE

State government revenues, 1999 ($per capita)
total revenue $11,804.51
  total general revenue $9,589.97
   intergovernmental revenue $1,973.84
   taxes $1,461.07
   current charges $506.84
   miscellaneous $5,648.22

State government expenditures, 1999 ($per capita)
total expenditure $9,912.12
  total general expenditure $8,994.24
   education $2,139.22
   public welfare $1,275.24
   health $257.33
   hospitals $35.68
   highways $932.25
   police protection $98.77
   correction $247.23
   natural resources $415.47
   governmental administration $511.26
   interest on general debt $351.68

State debt, 1999 ($per capita) $6,312.48

Federal government grants to state & local government, 2000 (x$1,000)
total $2,260,169
  Dept. of Education $226,938
  Environmental Protection Agency $88,408
  Health Care Financing Admin. $347,657
  Dept. Housing & Urban Devel. $206,817
  Dept. of Labor $39,243
  Highway trust fund $335,588

CRIME, LAW ENFORCEMENT & COURTS

Crime, 2000 (all rates per 100,000 inhabitants)
total crimes 26,641
overall crime rate 4,249.4
  property crimes 23,087
   burglaries 3,899
   larcenies 16,838
   motor vehicle thefts 2,350
  property crime rate 3,682.5
  violent crimes 3,554
   murders 27
   forcible rapes 497
   robberies 490
   aggravated assaults 2,540
  violent crime rate 566.9

Number of police agencies, 2000 28

Arrests, 2000
total 36,718
  persons under 18 years of age 5,953

Prisoners under state & federal jurisdiction, 2000
total 4,173
percent change, 1999-2000 .... 5.7%
  sentenced to more than one year
   total 2,128
   rate per 100,000 residents 341

Persons under sentence of death, 4/1/2001 ...NA

State's highest court
name .... Supreme Court
number of members 5
length of term .... 10 years
intermediate appeals court? .... yes

Alaska 6

LABOR & INCOME

Civilian labor force, 2000

total	322,000
men	172,000
women	150,000
persons 16-19 years	22,000
white	257,000
black	10,000

Civilian labor force as a percent of civilian non-institutional population, 2000

total	73.5%
men	79.3%
women	67.8%
persons 16-19 years	NA%
white	74.9%
black	76.8%

Employment, 2000

total	301,000
men	160,000
women	141,000
persons 16-19 years	18,000
white	243,000
black	9,000

Full-time/part-time labor force, 1998

full-time labor force	259,000
working part-time for economic reasons	5,000
part-time labor force	57,000

Unemployment rate, 2000

total	6.6%
men	7.2%
women	6.0%
persons 16-19 years	16.7%
white	5.4%
black	8.5%

Unemployed by reason for unemployment (as a percent of total unemployment), 1998

job losers or completed temp jobs	50.0%
job leavers	16.7%
reentrants	33.3%
new entrants	5.6%

Experienced civilian labor force, by occupation, 1998

executive/administrative/managerial	49,000
professional/specialty	48,000
technicians & related support	11,000
sales	39,000
administrative support/clerical	44,000
service occupations	44,000
precision production/craft/repair	36,000
machine operators/assemblers	7,000
transportation/material moving	16,000
handlers/helpers/laborers	13,000
farming/forestry/fishing	10,000

Experienced civilian labor force, by industry, 1998

construction	21,000
manufacturing	10,000
transportation/communication	26,000
wholesale/retail trade	58,000
finance/real estate/insurance	11,000
services	65,000
government	76,000
agriculture	NA

Average annual pay, 1999	$34,034
change in average annual pay, 1998-1999	0.6%

Hours and earnings of production workers on manufacturing payrolls, 2000

average weekly hours	44.3
average hourly earnings	$12.45
average weekly earnings	$551.54

Labor union membership, 2000	56,800

Household income (in 2000 dollars)

median household income, three year average, 1998-2000	$50,746

Poverty

persons below poverty level, three year average, 1998-2000	8.3%

Personal income ($per capita)

2000 (prelim.)	
in current dollars	$30,064
in constant (1996) dollars	$28,003
1999 (preliminary)	
in current dollars	$28,523
in constant (1996) dollars	$27,274

Federal income tax returns, 1999

returns filed	327,510
adjusted gross income ($1,000)	$13,047,086
total income tax paid ($1,000)	$2,008,015

ECONOMY, BUSINESS, INDUSTRY & AGRICULTURE

Fortune 500 companies, 2000 0

Business incorporations, 1998
total 995
change, 1997-1998 .... -6.4%

Business failures, 1998 177

Business firm ownership, 1997
Hispanic owned firms 1,385
Black owned firms 876
women owned firms 16,633
Asian & Pacific Islander owned firms 1,816
American Indian & Alaska
   native owned firms 6,820

Shopping centers, 2000 68

Gross state product, 1999 ($mil)
total $26,353
   agriculture services, forestry, fisheries $449
   mining $5,301
   construction $1,225
   manufacturing--durable goods $226
   manufacturing--nondurable goods $888
   transportation, communication &
      public utilities $4,392
   wholesale trade $791
   retail trade $1,867
   finance/real estate/insurance $2,671
   services $3,419
   federal, state & local government $5,124

Establishments, by major industry group, 1999
total 18,433
   forestry, fishing & agriculture 328
   mining 130
   construction 2,293
   manufacturing 505
   transportation & warehousing 982
   wholesale trade 765
   retail trade 2,762
   finance & insurance 689
   professional/scientific/technical 1,592
   health care/social assistance 1,625
   information 376
   accommodation/food services 1,740

Payroll, by major industry group, 1999
total ($1,000) $7,108,281
   forestry, fishing & agriculture $87,825
   mining $612,066
   construction $717,983
   manufacturing $360,940
   transportation & warehousing $735,317
   wholesale trade $281,842
   retail trade $772,364
   finance & insurance $297,439
   professional/scientific/technical $465,932
   health care/social assistance $1,143,756
   information $253,452
   accommodation/food services $349,893

Agriculture
number of farms, 2000 1,000
farm acreage, 2000 1,000,000
acres per farm, 2000 1,586
value of farms, 1997 ($mil) .... $NA
farm income, 1999 ($mil)
   net farm income $20
   debt/asset ratio 3.5%
farm marketings, 1999 ($mil)
total $48
   crops $19
   livestock $29
principal commodities, in order by marketing
receipts, 1999
   Greenhouse, dairy products, potatoes, hay

Federal economic activity in state
expenditures, 2000
   total ($mil) $5,953
   per capita $9,496
   defense ($mil) $1,712
   non-defense ($mil) $4,242
defense department, 2000
   contract awards ($mil) $831
   payroll ($mil) $902
   civilian employees (x1,000) 4.8
   military personnel (x1,000) 15.7

Fishing, 2000
catch (thousands of pounds) 4,465,987
value ($1,000) $956,990

Mining, 2000 ($mil; preliminary)
total non-fuel mineral production $1,140

Alaska 8

Construction, 1999 ($mil)
total contracts (including
   non-building) $1,353
     residential $426
     non-residential $449

Construction industries, 1997
establishments 1,994
receipts ($1,000) .... $NA
annual payroll ($1,000) $562,975
paid employees 13,911

Manufacturing, 1997
establishments 588
value of shipments ($1,000) $3,760,829
annual payroll ($1,000) $422,169
paid employees 13,402

Transportation industries, 1997
establishments 1,470
receipts ($1,000) $4,998,865
annual payroll ($1,000) $908,872
paid employees 20,489

Wholesale trade, 1997
establishments 951
sales($1,000) .... $NA
annual payroll ($1,000) .... $NA
paid employees .... NA

Retail trade, 1997
establishments 4,090
sales($1,000) $6,598,019
annual payroll ($1,000) $837,287
paid employees 46,235

Finance industries
establishments, 1997 1,200
receipts ($1,000), 1997 .... $NA
annual payroll ($1,000), 1997 .... $335,222
paid employees, 1997 9,842
commercial banks, 2000
  number 6
    assets ($bil) $6.2
    deposits ($bil) $4.1

Service industries, 1997 (non-exempt firms only)
establishments 5,233
receipts ($1,000) $3,204,653
annual payroll ($1,000) $1,133,062
paid employees 38,822

COMMUNICATION, ENERGY & TRANSPORTATION

Communication
daily newspapers, 2000 7
households with
  telephones, 1998 .... 95.7%
  computers, 2000 .... 64.8%
  internet access, 2000 .... 55.6%

Energy
consumption, 1999
total (trillion Btu) 695
per capita (million Btu) 1,122
by source of production (trillion Btu)
  coal 11
  natural gas 420
  petroleum 253
  nuclear electric power .... NA
  hydroelectric power 9
by end-use sector (trillion Btu)
  residential 48
  commercial 63
  industrial 386
  transportation 198
electric energy, 1999
  production (billion kWh) 4.6
  net summer capability (million kW) ... 1.7
gas utilities, 1999
  customers 121,000
  sales (trillion Btu) 43
nuclear plants, 1999 .... na

Transportation, 2000
public road & street mileage
total 12,823
  urban 1,809
  rural 11,014
  interstate 1,083
vehicle miles of travel (mil) 4,613
total motor vehicle registrations 594,399
  automobiles 244,305
  motorcycles 16,063
licensed drivers 465,256
  per 1,000 driving age population 1,016
deaths from motor vehicle
  accidents 103

STATE SUMMARY

Capital City . . . . Phoenix

Governor . . . . Jane Dee Hull

Address . . . . STATE CAPITOL
PHOENIX, AZ 85007
602 542-4331

Admitted as a state 1912

Area (square miles) 114,006

Population, 1980 2,718,215

Population, 1990 3,665,228

Population, 2000 5,130,632

Persons per square mile, 2000 . . . . 45.1

Largest city . . . . Phoenix
population, 2000 1,321,000

Personal income per capita, 2000
(in current dollars) $25,578

Gross state product ($mil), 1999 . . . . . $143,683

Leading industries, 1999 (by payroll)
Manufacturing
Health care/Social assistance
Retail trade

Leading agricultural commodities, 1999
Cattle, dairy products, lettuce, cotton

GEOGRAPHY & ENVIRONMENT

Area, 1990 (square miles)
total 114,006
land 113,642
water (includes territorial water) 364

Federally owned land, 2000 . . . . 44.5%

Highest point
name . . . . Humphrey's Peak
elevation (feet) 12,633

Lowest point
name . . . . Colorado River
elevation (feet) 70

General coastline (miles) 0

Tidal shoreline (miles) 0

Capital city . . . . Phoenix
population, 2000 1,321,000

Largest city . . . . Phoenix
population, 2000 1,321,000

Number of cities with over 100,000 population
1980 4
1990 6
2000 9

State parks and Recreation areas, 2000
area (acres) 59,000
number of visitors 2,371,000
revenues $6,934,000

Natl. forest system land, 1999 (acres) . . 11,255,000

National park acreage, 1984 2,666,600

DEMOGRAPHICS & CHARACTERISTICS OF THE POPULATION

Population
1970 1,775,399
1980 2,718,215
1990 3,665,228
2000 5,130,632
2015 (projection) 5,808,000
2025 (projection) 6,412,000

Metropolitan area population
1970 1,323,000
1980 2,040,000
2000 4,527,000

Non-metropolitan area population
1970 453,000
1980 678,000
2000 604,000

Change in population, 1990-2000
number 1,465,404
percent 39.98%

Persons per square mile, 2000 . . . . 45.1

Persons by age, 2000
under 5 years 382,386
18 and over 3,763,685
21 and over 3,536,279
65 and over 667,839
85 and over 68,525

Arizona 2

Persons by age, 2025 (projected)
under 5 years 445,000
5 to 17 years 1,130,000
65 and over 1,368,000

Median age, 2000 .... 34.2

Race, 2000
One race
White 3,873,611
Black or African American 158,873
American Indian and Alaska Native 255,879
Asian Indian 14,741
Chinese 21,221
Filipino 16,176
Japanese 7,712
Korean 9,123
Vietnamese 12,931
Native Hawaiian and other Pacific Islander 6,733
Two or more races 146,526

Race, 2025 (projected)
White 5,599,000
Black 285,000

Persons of Hispanic origin, 2000
total Hispanic or Latino 1,295,617
  Mexican 1,065,578
  Puerto Rican 17,587
  Cuban 5,272
  Other Hispanic or Latino 207,180

Persons of Hispanic origin, 2025 (proj.) . 2,065,000

Persons by sex, 2000
male 2,561,057
female 2,569,575

Marital status, 1990
males
  15 years & older 1,384,911
    single 409,976
    married 817,459
      separated 24,512
    widowed 32,270
    divorced 125,206
females
  15 years & older 1,447,361
    single 313,652
    married 816,198
      separated 32,513

widowed 150,231
divorced 167,280

Households & families, 2000
households 1,901,327
persons per household 2.64
  families 1,287,367
  persons per family 3.18
    married couples 986,303
    female householder, no husband
      present 210,781
    one person households 472,006
households with persons under 18 years . 673,926
households with persons over 65 years ... 465,062

Nativity, 1990
number of persons born in state 1,252,645
percent of total residents 34.2%

Immigration & naturalization, 1998
immigrants admitted 6,211
persons naturalized 4,105
refugees granted resident status 106

VITAL STATISTICS & HEALTH

Births
1999
  with low birth weight 6.9%
  to teenage mothers 17.0%
  to unmarried mothers 38.8%
Birth rate, 1999 (per 1,000) 17.0
Birth rate, 2000 (per 1,000) 17.5

Abortions, 1996
total 19,000
rate (per 1,000 women age 15-44) 19.8

Deaths
1998 38,502
1999 40,050
2000 40,524

Infant deaths
1998 619
1999 550
2000 571

Average lifetime, by race, 1989-1991
total .... 76.10 years
  white .... 76.42 years
  black .... 70.84 years

Marriages
1998 37,936
1999 41,174
2000 38,716

Divorces
1998 25,798
1999 22,983
2000 21,593

Physicians, 1999
total 9,714
rate (per 1,000 persons) 2.03

Nurses, 1999
total 36,660
rate (per 1,000 persons) 7.67

Hospitals, 1998
number 64
beds (x 1,000) 10.9
average daily census (x 1,000) 6.6
patients admitted (x1,000) 495
average cost per day to hospital, 1995 .... $1,191
average cost per stay to hospital, 1995 .... $5,613

EDUCATION

*Educational attainment of all persons
25 years and older, 1990*
less than 9th grade 207,509
high school graduates 601,440
bachelor's degree 306,554
graduate or professional degree 160,319

2000
high school graduate or more 85.1%
college graduate or more 24.6%

Public school enrollment, Fall, 1998
total 848,262
Kindergarten through grade 8 622,747
grades 9 through 12 225,515

Public School Teachers, 2000
total 44,500
elementary 34,300
secondary 10,200
average salaries
elementary $35,700
secondary $35,700

*State receipts & expenditures for public
schools, 2000*
revenue receipts ($mil) $4,922

*State receipts & expenditures for public
schools, 2000 (continued)*
expenditures
total ($mil) $4,894
per capita $1,024
per pupil $4,866

*Graduating high school seniors,
public high schools, 2000 (est.)* 42,369

SAT scores, 2001
verbal 523
math 525
percent graduates taking test 34%

Institutions of higher education, 1999
total 65
public 25
private 40

*Enrollment in institutions of higher
education, Fall, 1998*
total 302,123
full-time men 69,298
full-time women 75,262
part-time men 66,453
part-time women 91,110

*Minority enrollment in institutions of higher
education, Fall, 1997*
Black, non-Hispanic 10,006
Hispanic 44,614
Asian/Pacific Islander 9,503

Earned degrees conferred, 1998
Bachelor's 18,381
First professional 438
Master's 7,753
Doctor's 788

SOCIAL INSURANCE &
WELFARE PROGRAMS

Social Security beneficiaries & benefits, 2000
beneficiaries
total 791,000
retired and dependents 575,000
survivors 106,000
disabled & dependents 111,000
annual benefit payments ($mil)
total $7,163
retired and dependents $5,026
survivors $1,187
disabled & dependents $950

Arizona 4

Medicare, 2000
enrollment (x1,000) 658
payments ($mil) $2,938

Medicaid, 1998
recipients (x1,000) 508
payments ($mil) $1,644

Federal public aid
Temporary Assistance for Needy Families
(TANF), 2000
   Recipients (x1,000) 83
   Families (x1,000) 33
Supplemental Security Income
   total recipients, 1999 (x1,000) 79

Food Stamp Program
  participants, 2000 (x1,000) 259

HOUSING & CONSTRUCTION

Total housing units, 2000 2,189,189
  seasonal or recreational use 141,965
  occupied 1,901,327
    owner occupied 1,293,556
    renter occupied 607,771

New privately owned housing units uthorized, 2000
number (x1,000) 61.5
value ($mil) $7,158

New privately owned housing units
  started, 2000 (est.) (x1,000) 60.0

Existing home sales, 2000 (x1,000) 180.3

GOVERNMENT & ELECTIONS

State officials, 2002
Governor (name/party/term expires)
      JANE DEE HULL
      Republican - 2002
Lt. Governor .... (no Lt. Governor)
Sec. of State .... Betsey Bayless
Atty. General .... Janet Napolitano
Chief Justice .... Stanley Feldman

Governorship
minimum age 25
length of term .... 4 years
number of consecutive
  terms permitted 2
who succeeds .... Sec. of State

State legislature
name .... Legislature
  upper chamber
    name .... Senate
    number of members 30
    length of term .... 2 years
    party in majority, 2000 .... Republican
  lower chamber
    name .... House of Representatives
    number of members 60
    length of term .... 2 years
    party in majority, 2000 .... Republican

State employees March, 2000
total 78,964
March payroll $189,315,959

Local governments, 1997
total 637
  county 15
  municipal 87
  township 0
  school districts 231
  special districts 304

Voting age population, November, 2000, projected
Total 3,625,000
  male 1,771,000
  female 1,853,000

Vote for president
2000
  Gore 685,000
  Bush 782,000
1996
  Clinton 653,000
  Dole 622,000
  Perot 112,000

Federal representation, 2002 (107th Congress)
Senators (name/party/term expires)

      JON KYL
      Republican - 2007
      JOHN McCAIN
      Republican - 2005

Representatives, total 6
  Democrats 1
  Republicans 5
  other 0

Women holding public office, 2001
U.S. Congress 0
statewide elected office 4
state legislature 32

Black elected officials, 1999
total 13
   US and state legislatures 2
   city/county/regional offices 1
   judicial/law enforcement 4
   education/school boards 6

Hispanic public officials, 2000
total .... NA
   state executives & legislators .... NA
   city/county/regional offices .... NA
   judicial/law enforcement .... NA
   education/school boards .... NA

GOVERNMENTAL FINANCE

State government revenues, 1999 ($per capita)
total revenue $3,164.68
   total general revenue $2,736.83
     intergovernmental revenue $766.44
     taxes $1,578.53
     current charges $162.67
     miscellaneous $229.20

State government expenditures, 1999 ($per capita)
total expenditure $2,988.15
   total general expenditure $2,747.23
     education $991.11
     public welfare $515.05
     health $154.39
     hospitals $13.92
     highways $341.29
     police protection $31.62
     correction $154.94
     natural resources $31.60
     governmental administration $95.84
     interest on general debt $31.46

State debt, 1999 ($per capita) $570.31

Federal government grants to state & local government, 2000 (x$1,000)
total $4,500,535
   Dept. of Education $577,390
   Environmental Protection Agency $46,118
   Health Care Financing Admin. $1,618,842
   Dept. Housing & Urban Devel. $336,961
   Dept. of Labor $74,379
   Highway trust fund $435,976

CRIME, LAW ENFORCEMENT & COURTS

Crime, 2000 (all rates per 100,000 inhabitants)
total crimes 299,092
overall crime rate 5,829.5
   property crimes 271,811
     burglaries 51,902
     larcenies 176,705
     motor vehicle thefts 43,204
   property crime rate 5,297.8
   violent crimes 27,281
     murders 359
     forcible rapes 1,577
     robberies 7,504
     aggravated assaults 17,841
   violent crime rate 531.7

Number of police agencies, 2000 71

Arrests, 2000
total 299,846
   persons under 18 years of age 57,491

Prisoners under state & federal jurisdiction, 2000
total 26,510
percent change, 1999-2000 .... 2.0%
   sentenced to more than one year
     total 25,412
     rate per 100,000 residents 515

Persons under sentence of death, 4/1/2001 ... 125

State's highest court
name .... Supreme Court
number of members 5
length of term .... 6 years
intermediate appeals court? .... yes

Arizona 6

LABOR & INCOME

Civilian labor force, 2000
total 2,347,000
  men 1,271,000
  women 1,076,000
  persons 16-19 years 147,000
  white 2,139,000
  black 90,000

Civilian labor force as a percent of
civilian non-institutional population, 2000
total 64.7%
  men 73.6%
  women 56.6%
  persons 16-19 years .... NA%
  white 64.4%
  black 70.6%

Employment, 2000
total 2,256,000
  men 1,227,000
  women 1,029,000
  persons 16-19 years 134,000
  white 2,055,000
  black 87,000

Full-time/part-time labor force, 1998
full-time labor force 1,872,000
  working part-time for
    economic reasons 19,000
part-time labor force 402,000

Unemployment rate, 2000
total 3.9%
  men 3.5%
  women 4.4%
  persons 16-19 years 8.3%
  white 4.0%
  black 2.5%

Unemployed by reason for unemployment
(as a percent of total unemployment), 1998
job losers or completed temp jobs 36.2%
job leavers 14.9%
reentrants 43.6%
new entrants 6.4%

Experienced civilian labor force, by occupation,
1998
executive/administrative/managerial 322,000
professional/specialty 321,000
technicians & related support 76,000

sales 298,000
administrative support/clerical 328,000
service occupations 341,000
precision production/craft/repair 255,000
machine operators/assemblers 90,000
transportation/material moving 72,000
handlers/helpers/laborers 83,000
farming/forestry/fishing 80,000

Experienced civilian labor force, by industry, 1998
construction 172,000
manufacturing 267,000
transportation/communication 115,000
wholesale/retail trade 492,000
finance/real estate/insurance 146,000
services 545,000
government 293,000
agriculture 70,000

Average annual pay, 1999 .... $30,523
change in average annual pay,
  1998-1999 .... 4.1%

Hours and earnings of production workers
on manufacturing payrolls, 2000
average weekly hours 40.4
average hourly earnings $12.77
average weekly earnings $515.91

Labor union membership, 2000 129,700

Household income (in 2000 dollars)
median household income,
  three year average, 1998-2000 .... $41,456

Poverty
persons below poverty level,
  three year average, 1998-2000 .... 13.6%

Personal income ($per capita)
2000 (prelim.)
  in current dollars $25,578
  in constant (1996) dollars $23,825
1999 (preliminary)
  in current dollars $25,307
  in constant (1996) dollars $24,199

Federal income tax returns, 1999
returns filed 2,087,966
adjusted gross income ($1,000) $91,092,052
total income tax paid ($1,000) $13,407,041

ECONOMY, BUSINESS, INDUSTRY & AGRICULTURE

Fortune 500 companies, 2000 5

Business incorporations, 1998
total 11,499
change, 1997-1998 . . . . 2.1%

Business failures, 1998 1,225

Business firm ownership, 1997
Hispanic owned firms 28,894
Black owned firms 3,582
women owned firms 88,780
Asian & Pacific Islander owned firms 7,145
American Indian & Alaska
   native owned firms 5,510

Shopping centers, 2000 1,062

Gross state product, 1999 ($mil)
total $143,683
   agriculture services, forestry, fisheries . . $2,138
   mining $1,214
   construction $8,327
   manufacturing--durable goods $17,332
   manufacturing--nondurable goods $3,374
   transportation, communication &
      public utilities $10,516
   wholesale trade $9,620
   retail trade $15,359
   finance/real estate/insurance $26,845
   services $31,573
   federal, state & local government $17,385

Establishments, by major industry group, 1999
total 112,545
   forestry, fishing & agriculture 230
   mining 201
   construction 12,333
   manufacturing 4,903
   transportation & warehousing 2,484
   wholesale trade 6,724
   retail trade 16,616
   finance & insurance 6,990
   professional/scientific/technical 11,758
   health care/social assistance 10,809
   information 1,910
   accommodation/food services 9,120

Payroll, by major industry group, 1999
total ($1,000) $52,954,561
   forestry, fishing & agriculture $45,246
   mining $511,479
   construction $4,793,874
   manufacturing $7,580,902
   transportation & warehousing $2,073,124
   wholesale trade $3,341,454
   retail trade $5,125,832
   finance & insurance $4,076,461
   professional/scientific/technical $4,005,161
   health care/social assistance $5,893,548
   information $2,057,039
   accommodation/food services $2,296,387

Agriculture
number of farms, 2000 8,000
farm acreage, 2000 27,000,000
acres per farm, 2000 3,560
value of farms, 1997 ($mil) $14,868
farm income, 1999 ($mil)
   net farm income $708
   debt/asset ratio 4.7%
farm marketings, 1999 ($mil)
   total $2,178
   crops $1,191
   livestock $987
principal commodities, in order by marketing
receipts, 1999
   Cattle, dairy products, lettuce, cotton

Federal economic activity in state
expenditures, 2000
   total ($mil) $29,244
   per capita $5,700
   defense ($mil) $6,585
   non-defense ($mil) $22,659
defense department, 2000
   contract awards ($mil) $4,547
   payroll ($mil) $1,995
   civilian employees (x1,000) 8.2
   military personnel (x1,000) 21.3

Fishing, 2000
catch (thousands of pounds) . . . . NA
value ($1,000) . . . . $NA

Mining, 2000 ($mil; preliminary)
total non-fuel mineral production $2,550

Arizona 8

Construction, 1999 ($mil)
total contracts (including
   non-building) $13,500
     residential $8,270
     non-residential $3,476

Construction industries, 1997
establishments 10,663
receipts ($1,000) .... $NA
annual payroll ($1,000) .... $NA
paid employees 129,315

Manufacturing, 1997
establishments 5,001
value of shipments ($1,000) $44,093,719
annual payroll ($1,000) $6,957,158
paid employees 199,959

Transportation industries, 1997
establishments 4,208
receipts ($1,000) $15,471,090
annual payroll ($1,000) $2,916,595
paid employees 92,711

Wholesale trade, 1997
establishments 7,708
sales($1,000) $49,465,094
annual payroll ($1,000) $3,117,675
paid employees 93,586

Retail trade, 1997
establishments 23,469
sales($1,000) $44,916,454
annual payroll ($1,000) $5,130,701
paid employees 363,999

Finance industries
establishments, 1997 11,366
receipts ($1,000), 1997 .... $NA
annual payroll ($1,000), 1997 .... $3,658,873
paid employees, 1997 110,539
commercial banks, 2000
   number 45
     assets ($bil) $61.8
     deposits ($bil) $30.7

Service industries, 1997 (non-exempt firms only)
establishments 35,277
receipts ($1,000) $28,864,397
annual payroll ($1,000) $11,106,296
paid employees 488,055

COMMUNICATION, ENERGY & TRANSPORTATION

Communication
daily newspapers, 2000 16
households with
   telephones, 1998 .... 92.9%
   computers, 2000 .... 53.5%
   internet access, 2000 .... 42.5%

Energy
consumption, 1999
total (trillion Btu) 1,220
per capita (million Btu) 255
by source of production (trillion Btu)
   coal 404
   natural gas 163
   petroleum 497
   nuclear electric power 323
   hydroelectric power 104
by end-use sector (trillion Btu)
   residential 279
   commercial 267
   industrial 222
   transportation 453
electric energy, 1999
   production (billion kWh) 83.1
   net summer capability (million kW) 15.1
gas utilities, 1999
   customers 852,000
   sales (trillion Btu) 81
nuclear plants, 1999 3

Transportation, 2000
public road & street mileage
total 55,195
   urban 18,206
   rural 36,989
   interstate 1,168
vehicle miles of travel (mil) 49,768
total motor vehicle registrations 3,794,538
   automobiles 2,163,141
   motorcycles 164,279
licensed drivers 3,433,995
   per 1,000 driving age population 879
deaths from motor vehicle
   accidents 1,036

STATE SUMMARY

Capital City .... Little Rock

Governor .... Mike Huckabee

Address .... STATE CAPITOL
LITTLE ROCK, AR 72201
501 682-2345

Admitted as a state 1836

Area (square miles) 53,182

Population, 1980 2,286,435

Population, 1990 2,350,725

Population, 2000 2,673,400

Persons per square mile, 2000 .... 51.3

Largest city .... Little Rock
population, 2000 183,000

Personal income per capita, 2000
(in current dollars) $22,257

Gross state product ($mil), 1999 ...... $64,773

Leading industries, 1999 (by payroll)
Manufacturing
Health care/Social assistance
Retail trade

Leading agricultural commodities, 1999
Broilers, rice, soybeans, cotton

GEOGRAPHY & ENVIRONMENT

Area, 1990 (square miles)
total 53,182
land 52,075
water (includes territorial water) 1,107

Federally owned land, 2000 .... 10.1%

Highest point
name .... Magazine Mountain
elevation (feet) 2,753

Lowest point
name .... Ouachita River
elevation (feet) 55

General coastline (miles) 0

Tidal shoreline (miles) 0

Capital city .... Little Rock
population, 2000 183,000

Largest city .... Little Rock
population, 2000 183,000

Number of cities with over 100,000 population
1980 1
1990 1
2000 1

State parks and Recreation areas, 2000
area (acres) 51,000
number of visitors 6,643,000
revenues $13,502,000

Natl. forest system land, 1999 (acres) ...2,579,000

National park acreage, 1984 99,600

DEMOGRAPHICS & CHARACTERISTICS OF THE POPULATION

Population
1970 1,923,322
1980 2,286,435
1990 2,350,725
2000 2,673,400
2015 (projection) 2,922,000
2025 (projection) 3,055,000

Metropolitan area population
1970 730,000
1980 885,000
2000 1,321,000

Non-metropolitan area population
1970 1,193,000
1980 1,401,000
2000 1,352,000

Change in population, 1990-2000
number 322,675
percent 13.73%

Persons per square mile, 2000 .... 51.3

Persons by age, 2000
under 5 years 181,585
18 and over 1,993,031
21 and over 1,873,359
65 and over 374,019
85 and over 46,492

Persons by age, 2025 (projected)
under 5 years 163,000
5 to 17 years 463,000
65 and over 731,000

Median age, 2000 36

Race, 2000
One race
White 2,138,598
Black or African American 418,950
American Indian and Alaska Native 17,808
Asian Indian 3,104
Chinese 3,126
Filipino 2,489
Japanese 1,036
Korean 1,550
Vietnamese 3,974
Native Hawaiian and other Pacific Islander 1,668
Two or more races 35,744

Race, 2025 (projected)
White 2,536,000
Black 468,000

Persons of Hispanic origin, 2000
total Hispanic or Latino 86,866
  Mexican 61,204
  Puerto Rican 2,473
  Cuban 950
  Other Hispanic or Latino 22,239

Persons of Hispanic origin, 2025 (proj.) ... 67,000

Persons by sex, 2000
male 1,304,693
female 1,368,707

Marital status, 1990
males
  15 years & older 868,546
    single 209,851
    married 563,189
      separated 14,658
    widowed 24,977
    divorced 70,529
females
  15 years & older 966,364
    single 169,510
    married 566,806
      separated 20,598

widowed 139,365
divorced 90,683

Households & families, 2000
households 1,042,696
persons per household : 2.49
  families 732,261
  persons per family 2.99
    married couples 566,401
    female householder, no husband
      present 126,561
    one person households 266,585
households with persons under 18 years . 371,331
households with persons over 65 years ... 263,521

Nativity, 1990
number of persons born in state 1,577,038
percent of total residents 67.1%

Immigration & naturalization, 1998
immigrants admitted 914
persons naturalized 244
refugees granted resident status 45

VITAL STATISTICS & HEALTH
Births
1999
  with low birth weight 8.6%
  to teenage mothers 14.4%
  to unmarried mothers 35.2%
Birth rate, 1999 (per 1,000) 14.4
Birth rate, 2000 (per 1,000) 14.8

Abortions, 1996
total 6,000
rate (per 1,000 women age 15-44) 11.4

Deaths
1998 26,817
1999 27,925
2000 28,231

Infant deaths
1998 287
1999 281
2000 295

Average lifetime, by race, 1989-1991
total .... 74.33 years
  white .... 75.20 years
  black .... 68.93 years

Marriages
1998 38,446
1999 39,363
2000 41,127

Divorces
1998 15,376
1999 15,501
2000 17,895

Physicians, 1999
total 4,906
rate (per 1,000 persons) 1.92

Nurses, 1999
total 19,890
rate (per 1,000 persons) 7.80

Hospitals, 1998
number 82
beds (x 1,000) 9.9
average daily census (x 1,000) 5.8
patients admitted (x1,000) 358
average cost per day to hospital, 1995 ...... $704
average cost per stay to hospital, 1995 .... $4,459

EDUCATION

Educational attainment of all persons 25 years and older, 1990
less than 9th grade 227,633
high school graduates 489,570
bachelor's degree 132,712
graduate or professional degree 66,592

2000
high school graduate or more 81.7%
college graduate or more 18.4%

Public school enrollment, Fall, 1998
total 452,256
Kindergarten through grade 8 319,232
grades 9 through 12 133,024

Public School Teachers, 2000
total 28,700
elementary 14,100
secondary 14,600
average salaries
elementary $32,500
secondary $34,300

State receipts & expenditures for public schools, 2000
revenue receipts ($mil) $2,663

State receipts & expenditures for public schools, 2000 (continued)
expenditures
total ($mil) $2,868
per capita $1,124
per pupil $5,625

Graduating high school seniors, public high schools, 2000 (est.) 26,622

SAT scores, 2001
verbal 562
math 550
percent graduates taking test 6%

Institutions of higher education, 1999
total 45
public 33
private 12

Enrollment in institutions of higher education, Fall, 1998
total 113,751
full-time men 32,440
full-time women 42,124
part-time men 15,206
part-time women 23,981

Minority enrollment in institutions of higher education, Fall, 1997
Black, non-Hispanic 17,461
Hispanic 1,251
Asian/Pacific Islander 1,460

Earned degrees conferred, 1998
Bachelor's 9,222
First professional 460
Master's 2,181
Doctor's 162

SOCIAL INSURANCE & WELFARE PROGRAMS

Social Security beneficiaries & benefits, 2000
beneficiaries
total 517,000
retired and dependents 332,000
survivors 86,000
disabled & dependents 100,000
annual benefit payments ($mil)
total $4,250
retired and dependents $2,633
survivors $845
disabled & dependents $772

Arkansas 4

Medicare, 2000
enrollment (x1,000) 436
payments ($mil) $2,083

Medicaid, 1998
recipients (x1,000) 425
payments ($mil) $1,376

Federal public aid
Temporary Assistance for Needy Families
(TANF), 2000
   Recipients (x1,000) 29
   Families (x1,000) 12
Supplemental Security Income
   total recipients, 1999 (x1,000) 88

Food Stamp Program
   participants, 2000 (x1,000) 247

HOUSING & CONSTRUCTION

Total housing units, 2000 1,173,043
   seasonal or recreational use 29,012
   occupied 1,042,696
      owner occupied 723,535
      renter occupied 319,161

New privately owned housing units uthorized, 2000
number (x1,000) 9.2
value ($mil) $859

New privately owned housing units
   started, 2000 (est.) (x1,000) 12.5

Existing home sales, 2000 (x1,000) 54.7

GOVERNMENT & ELECTIONS

State officials, 2002
   Governor (name/party/term expires)
      MIKE HUCKABEE
      Republican - 2002
Lt. Governor . . . . Winthrop Rockefeller
Sec. of State . . . . Sharon Priest
Atty. General . . . . Mark Pryor
Chief Justice . . . . W. H. Arnold

Governorship
minimum age 30
length of term . . . . 4 years
number of consecutive
   terms permitted 2
who succeeds . . . . Lt. Governor

State legislature
name . . . . General Assembly
   upper chamber
      name . . . . Senate
      number of members 35
      length of term . . . . 4 years
      party in majority, 2000 . . . . Democratic
   lower chamber
      name . . . . House of Representatives
      number of members 100
      length of term . . . . 2 years
      party in majority, 2000 . . . . Democratic

State employees March, 2000
total 56,667
March payroll $136,618,804

Local governments, 1997
total 1,516
   county 75
   municipal 491
   township 0
   school districts 311
   special districts 639

Voting age population, November, 2000, projected
Total 1,929,000
   male 913,000
   female 1,017,000

Vote for president
2000
   Gore 423,000
   Bush 473,000
1996
   Clinton 475,000
   Dole 325,000
   Perot 70,000

Federal representation, 2002 (107th Congress)
Senators (name/party/term expires)

      TIM HUTCHINSON
      Republican - 2003
      BLANCHE LINCOLN
      Democrat - 2005

Representatives, total 4
   Democrats 3
   Republicans 1
   other 0

Women holding public office, 2001
U.S. Congress 1
statewide elected office 2
state legislature 18

Black elected officials, 1999
total 504
US and state legislatures 15
city/county/regional offices 297
judicial/law enforcement 65
education/school boards 127

Hispanic public officials, 2000
total .... NA
state executives & legislators .... NA
city/county/regional offices .... NA
judicial/law enforcement .... NA
education/school boards .... NA

GOVERNMENTAL FINANCE

State government revenues, 1999 ($per capita)
total revenue $4,060.95
total general revenue $3,311.56
intergovernmental revenue $968.39
taxes $1,806.45
current charges $340.53
miscellaneous $196.18

State government expenditures, 1999 ($per capita)
total expenditure $3,505.22
total general expenditure $3,281.54
education $1,437.12
public welfare $742.64
health $113.47
hospitals $157.52
highways $273.90
police protection $26.20
correction $88.73
natural resources $64.51
governmental administration $109.36
interest on general debt $45.36

State debt, 1999 ($per capita) $975.25

Federal government grants to state & local government, 2000 (x$1 000)
total $2,657,353
Dept. of Education $264,058
Environmental Protection Agency $17,051
Health Care Financing Admin. $1,207,626
Dept. Housing & Urban Devel. $213,019
Dept. of Labor $52,426
Highway trust fund $277,484

CRIME, LAW ENFORCEMENT & COURTS

Crime, 2000 (all rates per 100,000 inhabitants)
total crimes 110,019
overall crime rate 4,115.3
property crimes 98,115
burglaries 21,443
larcenies 69,740
motor vehicle thefts 6,932
property crime rate 3,670.0
violent crimes 11,904
murders 168
forcible rapes 848
robberies 2,001
aggravated assaults 8,887
violent crime rate 445.3

Number of police agencies, 2000 140

Arrests, 2000
total 206,776
persons under 18 years of age 17,153

Prisoners under state & federal jurisdiction, 2000
total 11,915
percent change, 1999-2000 .... 4.4%
sentenced to more than one year
total 11,851
rate per 100,000 residents 458

Persons under sentence of death, 4/1/2001 40

State's highest court
name .... Supreme Court
number of members 7
length of term .... 8 years
intermediate appeals court? .... yes

Arkansas 6

LABOR & INCOME

Civilian labor force, 2000
total 1,238,000
  men 664,000
  women 575,000
  persons 16-19 years 83,000
  white 1,012,000
  black 210,000

Civilian labor force as a percent of
civilian non-institutional population, 2000
total 62.6%
  men 69.6%
  women 56.1%
  persons 16-19 years ....NA%
  white 62.4%
  black 63.9%

Employment, 2000
total 1,183,000
  men 634,000
  women 549,000
  persons 16-19 years 71,000
  white 979,000
  black 189,000

Full-time/part-time labor force, 1998
full-time labor force 1,019,000
  working part-time for
    economic reasons 21,000
part-time labor force 197,000

Unemployment rate, 2000
total 4.4%
  men 4.4%
  women 4.5%
  persons 16-19 years 14.7%
  white 3.3%
  black 10.0%

Unemployed by reason for unemployment
(as a percent of total unemployment), 1998
job losers or completed temp jobs 40.3%
job leavers 16.4%
reentrants 32.8%
new entrants 10.4%

Experienced civilian labor force, by occupation, 1998
executive/administrative/managerial 131,000
professional/specialty 141,000
technicians & related support 36,000

sales 137,000
administrative support/clerical 154,000
service occupations 182,000
precision production/craft/repair 136,000
machine operators/assemblers 114,000
transportation/material moving 63,000
handlers/helpers/laborers 68,000
farming/forestry/fishing 47,000

Experienced civilian labor force, by industry, 1998
construction 61,000
manufacturing 226,000
transportation/communication 66,000
wholesale/retail trade 255,000
finance/real estate/insurance 50,000
services 235,000
government 164,000
agriculture 45,000

Average annual pay, 1999 .... $25,371
change in average annual pay,
  1998-1999 .... 3.9%

Hours and earnings of production workers
on manufacturing payrolls, 2000
average weekly hours 41.0
average hourly earnings $11.98
average weekly earnings $491.18

Labor union membership, 2000 61,500

Household income (in 2000 dollars)
median household income,
  three year average, 1998-2000 .... $30,293

Poverty
persons below poverty level,
  three year average, 1998-2000 .... 15.8%

Personal income ($per capita)
2000 (prelim.)
  in current dollars $22,257
  in constant (1996) dollars $20,731
1999 (preliminary)
  in current dollars $22,114
  in constant (1996) dollars $21,146

Federal income tax returns, 1999
returns filed 1,108,693
adjusted gross income ($1,000) $37,728,956
total income tax paid ($1,000) $4,984,670

ECONOMY, BUSINESS, INDUSTRY & AGRICULTURE

Fortune 500 companies, 2000 5

Business incorporations, 1998
total 6,029
change, 1997-1998 .... -12.1%

Business failures, 1998 748

Business firm ownership, 1997
Hispanic owned firms 2,586
Black owned firms 6,721
women owned firms 42,581
Asian & Pacific Islander owned firms 1,530
American Indian & Alaska
   native owned firms 2,308

Shopping centers, 2000 381

Gross state product, 1999 ($mil)
total $64,773
   agriculture services, forestry, fisheries .. $2,370
   mining $506
   construction $2,996
   manufacturing--durable goods $7,747
   manufacturing--nondurable goods $6,852
   transportation, communication &
      public utilities $6,815
   wholesale trade $4,293
   retail trade $7,621
   finance/real estate/insurance $7,499
   services $10,083
   federal, state & local government $7,993

Establishments, by major industry group, 1999
total 62,737
   forestry, fishing & agriculture 947
   mining 265
   construction 5,687
   manufacturing 3,294
   transportation & warehousing 2,463
   wholesale trade 3,545
   retail trade 12,236
   finance & insurance 3,568
   professional/scientific/technical 4,700
   health care/social assistance 5,884
   information 890
   accommodation/food services 4,466

Payroll, by major industry group, 1999
total ($1,000) $23,170,883
   forestry, fishing & agriculture $135,024
   mining $104,362
   construction $1,190,821
   manufacturing $6,386,429
   transportation & warehousing $1,231,484
   wholesale trade $1,292,785
   retail trade $2,181,777
   finance & insurance $1,117,856
   professional/scientific/technical $953,206
   health care/social assistance $3,297,383
   information $674,419
   accommodation/food services $680,257

Agriculture
number of farms, 2000 48,000
farm acreage, 2000 15,000,000
acres per farm, 2000 304
value of farms, 1997 ($mil) $14,948
farm income, 1999 ($mil)
   net farm income $1,831
   debt/asset ratio 19.7%
farm marketings, 1999 ($mil)
total $5,259
   crops $1,863
   livestock $3,397
principal commodities, in order by marketing
receipts, 1999
      Broilers, rice, soybeans, cotton

Federal economic activity in state
expenditures, 2000
   total ($mil) $14,828
   per capita $5,546
   defense ($mil) $1,132
   non-defense ($mil) $13,696
defense department, 2000
   contract awards ($mil) $343
   payroll ($mil) $772
   civilian employees (x1,000) 3.6
   military personnel (x1,000) 4.7

Fishing, 2000
catch (thousands of pounds) ....NA
value ($1,000) ....$NA

Mining, 2000 ($mil; preliminary)
total non-fuel mineral production $506

Arkansas 8

Construction, 1999 ($mil)
total contracts (including
   non-building) $3,353
    residential $1,514
    non-residential $983

Construction industries, 1997
establishments 5,321
receipts ($1,000) $5,031,080
annual payroll ($1,000) .... $NA
paid employees .... NA

Manufacturing, 1997
establishments 4,008
value of shipments ($1,000) $46,398,118
annual payroll ($1,000) $5,967,308
paid employees 239,244

Transportation industries, 1997
establishments 3,580
receipts ($1,000) $9,559,575
annual payroll ($1,000) $1,854,003
paid employees 60,704

Wholesale trade, 1997
establishments 4,463
sales($1,000) $29,094,166
annual payroll ($1,000) $1,298,113
paid employees 48,274

Retail trade, 1997
establishments 15,980
sales($1,000) $21,903,527
annual payroll ($1,000) $2,241,624
paid employees 189,643

Finance industries
establishments, 1997 5,338
receipts ($1,000), 1997 .... $NA
annual payroll ($1,000), 1997 .... $1,182,840
paid employees, 1997 40,995
commercial banks, 2000
  number 185
   assets ($bil) $25.7
   deposits ($bil) $21.5

Service industries, 1997 (non-exempt firms only)
establishments 16,021
receipts ($1,000) $9,292,134
annual payroll ($1,000) $3,633,922
paid employees 174,209

COMMUNICATION, ENERGY & TRANSPORTATION

Communication
daily newspapers, 2000 30
households with
  telephones, 1998 .... 88.7%
  computers, 2000 .... 37.3%
  internet access, 2000 .... 26.5%

Energy
consumption, 1999
total (trillion Btu) 1,204
per capita (million Btu) 472
by source of production (trillion Btu)
  coal 267
  natural gas 266
  petroleum 384
  nuclear electric power 137
  hydroelectric power 28
by end-use sector (trillion Btu)
  residential 193
  commercial 124
  industrial 589
  transportation 297
electric energy, 1999
  production (billion kWh) 44.1
  net summer capability (million kW) 9.3
gas utilities, 1999
  customers 626,000
  sales (trillion Btu) 73
nuclear plants, 1999 2

Transportation, 2000
public road & street mileage
total 97,600
  urban 10,626
  rural 86,974
  interstate 656
vehicle miles of travel (mil) 29,167
total motor vehicle registrations 1,840,193
  automobiles 951,243
  motorcycles 24,998
licensed drivers 1,947,867
  per 1,000 driving age population 940
deaths from motor vehicle
  accidents 652

California 1

STATE SUMMARY

Capital City ....Sacramento

Governor .... Gray Davis

Address ....STATE CAPITOL
SACRAMENTO, CA 95814
916 445-2841

Admitted as a state 1850

Area (square miles) 163,707

Population, 1980 23,667,902

Population, 1990 29,760,021

Population, 2000 33,871,648

Persons per square mile, 2000 .... 217.2

Largest city .... Los Angeles
population, 2000 3,695,000

Personal income per capita, 2000
(in current dollars) $32,275

Gross state product ($mil), 1999 ..... $1,229,098

Leading industries, 1999 (by payroll)
Manufacturing
Professional/Scientific/Technical
Health care/Social assistance

Leading agricultural commodities, 1999
Dairy products, grapes, greenhouse, cattle

GEOGRAPHY & ENVIRONMENT

Area, 1990 (square miles)
total 163,707
land 155,973
water (includes territorial water) 7,734

Federally owned land, 2000 .... 47.8%

Highest point
name .... Mt. Whitney
elevation (feet) 14,494

Lowest point
name .... Death Valley
elevation (feet) .... -282

General coastline (miles) 840

Tidal shoreline (miles) 3,427

Capital city .... Sacramento
population, 2000 407,000

Largest city .... Los Angeles
population, 2000 3,695,000

Number of cities with over 100,000 population
1980 26
1990 43
2000 56

State parks and Recreation areas, 2000
area (acres) 1,413,000
number of visitors 98,520,000
revenues $54,926,000

Natl. forest system land, 1999 (acres) ..20,653,000

National park acreage, 1984 4,510,700

DEMOGRAPHICS & CHARACTERISTICS OF THE POPULATION

Population
1970 19,971,069
1980 23,667,902
1990 29,760,021
2000 33,871,648
2015 (projection) 41,373,000
2025 (projection) 49,285,000

Metropolitan area population
1970 19,241,000
1980 22,689,000
2000 32,750,000

Non-metropolitan area population
1970 730,000
1980 979,000
2000 1,121,000

Change in population, 1990-2000
number 4,111,627
percent 13.82%

Persons per square mile, 2000 .... 217.2

Persons by age, 2000
under 5 years 2,486,981
18 and over 24,621,819
21 and over 23,146,248
65 and over 3,595,658
85 and over 425,657

California 2

Persons by age, 2025 (projected)
under 5 years 4,318,000
5 to 17 years 10,191,000
65 and over 6,424,000

Median age, 2000 .... 33.3

Race, 2000
One race
White 20,170,059
Black or African American 2,263,882
American Indian and Alaska Native 333,346
Asian Indian 314,819
Chinese 980,642
Filipino 918,678
Japanese 288,854
Korean 345,882
Vietnamese 447,032
Native Hawaiian and other Pacific Islander116,961
Two or more races 1,607,646

Race, 2025 (projected)
White 36,388,000
Black 3,426,000

Persons of Hispanic origin, 2000
total Hispanic or Latino 10,966,556
Mexican 8,455,926
Puerto Rican 140,570
Cuban 72,286
Other Hispanic or Latino 2,297,774

Persons of Hispanic origin, 2025 (proj.) 21,232,000

Persons by sex, 2000
male 16,874,892
female 16,996,756

Marital status, 1990
males
15 years & older 11,518,004
single 4,034,185
married 6,348,675
separated 252,628
widowed 237,667
divorced 897,477
females
15 years & older 11,642,977
single 2,939,043
married 6,274,255
separated 359,727

widowed 1,148,050
divorced 1,281,629

Households & families, 2000
households 11,502,870
persons per household 2.87
families 7,920,049
persons per family 3.43
married couples 5,877,084
female householder, no husband
present 1,448,510
one person households 2,708,308
households with persons under 18 years 4,569,910
households with persons over 65 years .. 2,570,170

Nativity, 1990
number of persons born in state 13,797,065
percent of total residents 46.4%

Immigration & naturalization, 1998
immigrants admitted 170,126
persons naturalized 154,793
refugees granted resident status 8,309

VITAL STATISTICS & HEALTH

Births
1999
with low birth weight 6.1%
to teenage mothers 15.6%
to unmarried mothers 32.9%
Birth rate, 1999 (per 1,000) 15.6
Birth rate, 2000 (per 1,000) 15.8

Abortions, 1996
total 238,000
rate (per 1,000 women age 15-44) 33.0

Deaths
1998 234,852
1999 229,380
2000 229,535

Infant deaths
1998 3,188
1999 2,710
2000 2,895

Average lifetime, by race, 1989-1991
total .... 75.86 years
white .... 75.92 years
black .... 69.65 years

Marriages
1998 194,108
1999 215,510
2000 196,896

Divorces
1998 . . . . .NA
1999 . . . . .NA
2000 . . . . .NA

Physicians, 1999
total 82,176
rate (per 1,000 persons) 2.48

Nurses, 1999
total 176,360
rate (per 1,000 persons) 5.32

Hospitals, 1998
number 405
beds (x 1,000) 74.5
average daily census (x 1,000) 45.6
patients admitted (x1,000) 3,170
average cost per day to hospital, 1995 . . . . $1,315
average cost per stay to hospital, 1995 . . . . $7,111

EDUCATION

Educational attainment of all persons
  25 years and older, 1990
  less than 9th grade 2,085,905
  high school graduates 4,167,897
  bachelor's degree 2,858,107
  graduate or professional degree 1,508,567

2000
  high school graduate or more 81.2%
  college graduate or more 27.5%

Public school enrollment, Fall, 1998
total 5,925,964
  Kindergarten through grade 8 4,269,853
  grades 9 through 12 1,656,111

Public School Teachers, 2000
total 284,600
  elementary 210,500
  secondary 74,200
average salaries
  elementary $47,600
  secondary $50,000

State receipts & expenditures for public
  schools, 2000
revenue receipts ($mil) $44,621

State receipts & expenditures for public
  schools, 2000 (continued)
expenditures
  total ($mil) $42,517
  per capita $1,283
  per pupil $6,232

Graduating high school seniors,
  public high schools, 2000 (est.) 303,169

SAT scores, 2001
verbal 498
math 517
percent graduates taking test 51%

Institutions of higher education, 1999
total 403
  public 142
  private 261

Enrollment in institutions of higher
  education, Fall, 1998
total 1,970,592
full-time men 437,984
full-time women 520,746
part-time men 431,478
part-time women 580,384

Minority enrollment in institutions of higher
  education, Fall, 1997
Black, non-Hispanic 153,200
Hispanic 406,326
Asian/Pacific Islander 348,222

Earned degrees conferred, 1998
Bachelor's 112,145
First professional 8,611
Master's 40,606
Doctor's 5,388

SOCIAL INSURANCE & WELFARE PROGRAMS

Social Security beneficiaries & benefits, 2000
beneficiaries
total 4,208,000
  retired and dependents 3,046,000
  survivors 598,000
  disabled & dependents 564,000
annual benefit payments ($mil)
total $38,138
  retired and dependents $26,460
  survivors $6,864
  disabled & dependents $4,814

California 4

Medicare, 2000
enrollment (x1,000) 3,837
payments ($mil) $23,621

Medicaid, 1998
recipients (x1,000) 7,082
payments ($mil) $14,237

Federal public aid
Temporary Assistance for Needy Families
(TANF), 2000
    Recipients (x1,000) 1,300
    Families (x1,000) 499
Supplemental Security Income
    total recipients, 1999 (x1,000) 1,066

Food Stamp Program
    participants, 2000 (x1,000) 1,832

HOUSING & CONSTRUCTION

Total housing units, 2000 12,214,549
    seasonal or recreational use 236,857
    occupied 11,502,870
        owner occupied 6,546,334
        renter occupied 4,956,536

New privately owned housing units uthorized, 2000
number (x1,000) 145.6
value ($mil) $23,344

New privately owned housing units
    started, 2000 (est.) (x1,000) 128.2

Existing home sales, 2000 (x1,000) 733.5

GOVERNMENT & ELECTIONS

State officials, 2002
    Governor (name/party/term expires)
                GRAY DAVIS
            Democrat - 2002
Lt. Governor . . . . .Cruz Bustamonte
Sec. of State . . . . Bill Jones
Atty. General . . . . Bill Lockyer
Chief Justice . . . . Ronald George

Governorship
minimum age 18
length of term . . . . 4 years
number of consecutive
    terms permitted 2
who succeeds . . . . Lt. Governor

State legislature
name . . . . Legislature
    upper chamber
        name . . . . Senate
        number of members 40
        length of term . . . . 4 years
        party in majority, 2000 . . . . .Democratic
    lower chamber
        name . . . . Assembly
        number of members 80
        length of term . . . . 2 years
        party in majority, 2000 . . . . .Democratic

State employees March, 2000
total 444,069
March payroll $1,511,189,561

Local governments, 1997
total 4,607
    county 57
    municipal 471
    township 0
    school districts 1,069
    special districts 3,010

Voting age population, November, 2000, projected
Total 24,873,000
    male 12,308,000
    female 12,566,000

Vote for president
2000
    Gore 5,861,000
    Bush 4,567,000
1996
    Clinton 5,120,000
    Dole 3,828,000
    Perot 698,000

Federal representation, 2002 (107th Congress)
Senators (name/party/term expires)

            BARBARA BOXER
            Democrat - 2005
        DIANNE FEINSTEIN
            Democrat - 2007

Representatives, total 52
    Democrats 32
    Republicans 20
    other 0

Women holding public office, 2001
U.S. Congress 19
statewide elected office 2
state legislature 34

Black elected officials, 1999
total 237
US and state legislatures 10
city/county/regional offices 66
judicial/law enforcement 77
education/school boards 84

Hispanic public officials, 2000
total 767
state executives & legislators 33
city/county/regional offices 317
judicial/law enforcement 37
education/school boards 380

GOVERNMENTAL FINANCE

State government revenues, 1999 ($per capita)
total revenue $4,646.74
total general revenue $3,602.57
intergovernmental revenue $1,017.36
taxes $2,183.96
current charges $244.28
miscellaneous $156.97

State government expenditures, 1999 ($per capita)
total expenditure $4,032.96
total general expenditure $3,625.82
education $1,327.66
public welfare $1,011.21
health $209.99
hospitals $88.04
highways $154.87
police protection $32.59
correction $117.50
natural resources $68.24
governmental administration $148.04
interest on general debt $76.67

State debt, 1999 ($per capita) $1,628.43

Federal government grants to state & local government, 2000 (x$1,000)
total $33,157,559
Dept. of Education $3,111,754
Environmental Protection Agency . . . $208,332
Health Care Financing Admin. $12,126,720
Dept. Housing & Urban Devel. $3,443,139
Dept. of Labor $813,628
Highway trust fund $1,967,080

CRIME, LAW ENFORCEMENT & COURTS

Crime, 2000 (all rates per 100,000 inhabitants)
total crimes 1,266,714
overall crime rate 3,739.7
property crimes 1,056,183
burglaries 222,293
larcenies 651,855
motor vehicle thefts 182,035
property crime rate 3,118.2
violent crimes 210,531
murders 2,079
forcible rapes 9,785
robberies 60,249
aggravated assaults 138,418
violent crime rate 621.6

Number of police agencies, 2000 682

Arrests, 2000
total 1,674,882
persons under 18 years of age 265,978

Prisoners under state & federal jurisdiction, 2000
total 163,001
percent change, 1999-2000 . . . . 0%
sentenced to more than one year
total 160,412
rate per 100,000 residents 474

Persons under sentence of death, 4/1/2001 . . . 592

State's highest court
name . . . . Supreme Court
number of members 7
length of term . . . . 12 years
intermediate appeals court? . . . . yes

California 6

LABOR & INCOME

Civilian labor force, 2000
total 17,091,000
  men 9,314,000
  women 7,776,000
  persons 16-19 years 913,000
  white 13,762,000
  black 1,086,000

Civilian labor force as a percent of
civilian non-institutional population, 2000
total 67.1%
  men 75.6%
  women 59.1%
  persons 16-19 years .... NA%
  white 67.7%
  black 63.5%

Employment, 2000
total 16,246,000
  men 8,870,000
  women 7,376,000
  persons 16-19 years 758,000
  white 13,092,000
  black 1,005,000

Full-time/part-time labor force, 1998
full-time labor force 13,244,000
  working part-time for
    economic reasons 201,000
part-time labor force 3,086,000

Unemployment rate, 2000
total 4.9%
  men 4.8%
  women 5.2%
  persons 16-19 years 17.0%
  white 4.9%
  black 7.5%

Unemployed by reason for unemployment
(as a percent of total unemployment), 1998
job losers or completed temp jobs 46.6%
job leavers 9.4%
reentrants 33.8%
new entrants 10.0%

Experienced civilian labor force, by occupation,
1998
executive/administrative/managerial ... 2,438,000
professional/specialty 2,527,000
technicians & related support 510,000

sales 1,963,000
administrative support/clerical 2,201,000
service occupations 2,241,000
precision production/craft/repair 1,662,000
machine operators/assemblers 859,000
transportation/material moving 560,000
handlers/helpers/laborers 661,000
farming/forestry/fishing 606,000

Experienced civilian labor force, by industry, 1998
construction 716,000
manufacturing 2,314,000
transportation/communication 816,000
wholesale/retail trade 3,068,000
finance/real estate/insurance 848,000
services 3,922,000
government 2,165,000
agriculture 608,000

Average annual pay, 1999 .... $37,564
change in average annual pay,
  1998-1999 .... 6.3%

Hours and earnings of production workers
on manufacturing payrolls, 2000
average weekly hours 41.7
average hourly earnings $14.25
average weekly earnings $594.23

Labor union membership, 2000 2,295,100

Household income (in 2000 dollars)
median household income,
  three year average, 1998-2000 .... $46,802

Poverty
persons below poverty level,
  three year average, 1998-2000 .... 14.0%

Personal income ($per capita)
2000 (prelim.)
  in current dollars $32,275
  in constant (1996) dollars $30,062
1999 (preliminary)
  in current dollars $29,819
  in constant (1996) dollars $28,513

Federal income tax returns, 1999
returns filed 14,509,886
adjusted gross income ($1,000) $752,653,853
total income tax paid ($1,000) $126,108,297

ECONOMY, BUSINESS, INDUSTRY & AGRICULTURE

Fortune 500 companies, 2000 55

Business incorporations, 1998
total 46,935
change, 1997-1998 .... -0.3%

Business failures, 1998 17,679

Business firm ownership, 1997
Hispanic owned firms 336,405
Black owned firms 79,110
women owned firms 700,513
Asian & Pacific Islander owned firms ... 316,048
American Indian & Alaska
  native owned firms 26,603

Shopping centers, 2000 6,044

Gross state product, 1999 ($mil)
total $1,229,098
  agriculture services, forestry, fisheries . $22,779
  mining $7,655
  construction $47,264
  manufacturing--durable goods $121,036
  manufacturing--nondurable goods $58,141
  transportation, communication &
    public utilities $89,906
  wholesale trade $82,506
  retail trade $113,360
  finance/real estate/insurance $266,876
  services $288,081
  federal, state & local government ... $131,493

Establishments, by major industry group, 1999
total 784,935
  forestry, fishing & agriculture 2,404
  mining 892
  construction 65,570
  manufacturing 49,330
  transportation & warehousing 16,878
  wholesale trade 58,194
  retail trade 106,864
  finance & insurance 42,115
  professional/scientific/technical 90,038
  health care/social assistance 80,437
  information 19,037
  accommodation/food services 62,466

Payroll, by major industry group, 1999
total ($1,000) $446,547,247
  forestry, fishing & agriculture $783,496
  mining $880,980
  construction $25,977,173
  manufacturing $76,634,173
  transportation & warehousing $13,394,753
  wholesale trade $35,451,534
  retail trade $32,620,675
  finance & insurance $36,219,904
  professional/scientific/technical $49,574,050
  health care/social assistance $40,845,368
  information $32,764,086
  accommodation/food services $14,296,197

Agriculture
number of farms, 2000 88,000
farm acreage, 2000 28,000,000
acres per farm, 2000 318
value of farms, 1997 ($mil) $75,300
farm income, 1999 ($mil)
  net farm income $4,986
  debt/asset ratio 20.3%
farm marketings, 1999 ($mil)
total $24,801
  crops $18,087
  livestock $6,714
principal commodities, in order by marketing
receipts, 1999
  Dairy products, grapes, greenhouse, cattle

Federal economic activity in state
expenditures, 2000
  total ($mil) $175,751
  per capita $5,189
  defense ($mil) $29,256
  non-defense ($mil) $146,495
defense department, 2000
  contract awards ($mil) $18,100
  payroll ($mil) $11,362
  civilian employees (x1,000) 60.8
  military personnel (x1,000) 146.3

Fishing, 2000
catch (thousands of pounds) 641,237
value ($1,000) $139,111

Mining, 2000 ($mil; preliminary)
total non-fuel mineral production $3,350

California 8

Construction, 1999 ($mil)
total contracts (including
    non-building) $45,949
      residential $21,856
      non-residential $16,099

Construction industries, 1997
establishments 58,317
receipts ($1,000) ....$NA
annual payroll ($1,000) ....$NA
paid employees 548,028

Manufacturing, 1997
establishments 49,297
value of shipments ($1,000) $390,321,123
annual payroll ($1,000) $68,097,248
paid employees 1,867,099

Transportation industries, 1997
establishments 27,394
receipts ($1,000) $113,840,815
annual payroll ($1,000) $21,842,880
paid employees 607,177

Wholesale trade, 1997
establishments 63,528
sales($1,000) ....$NA
annual payroll ($1,000) ....$NA
paid employees ....NA

Retail trade, 1997
establishments 159,385
sales($1,000) ....$NA
annual payroll ($1,000) ....$NA
paid employees ....NA

Finance industries
establishments, 1997 73,580
receipts ($1,000), 1997 ....$NA
annual payroll ($1,000), 1997 .... $35,650,883
paid employees, 1997 820,011
commercial banks, 2000
    number 304
    assets ($bil) $320.0
    deposits ($bil) $238.5

Service industries, 1997 (non-exempt firms only)
establishments 262,174
receipts ($1,000) $294,178,094
annual payroll ($1,000) $102,894,027
paid employees 3,285,881

COMMUNICATION, ENERGY & TRANSPORTATION

Communication
daily newspapers, 2000 92
households with
    telephones, 1998 .... 95.1%
    computers, 2000 .... 56.6%
    internet access, 2000 .... 46.7%

Energy
consumption, 1999
total (trillion Btu) 8,375
per capita (million Btu) 253
by source of production (trillion Btu)
    coal 64
    natural gas 2,182
    petroleum 3,383
    nuclear electric power 355
    hydroelectric power 425
by end-use sector (trillion Btu)
    residential 1,416
    commercial 1,237
    industrial 2,824
    transportation 2,899
electric energy, 1999
    production (billion kWh) 87.9
    net summer capability (million kW) 24.3
gas utilities, 1999
    customers 9,491,000
    sales (trillion Btu) 708
nuclear plants, 1999 4

Transportation, 2000
public road & street mileage
total 168,076
    urban 84,648
    rural 83,428
    interstate 2,453
vehicle miles of travel (mil) 306,649
total motor vehicle registrations 27,697,923
    automobiles 17,321,413
    motorcycles 434,257
licensed drivers 21,243,939
    per 1,000 driving age population 830
deaths from motor vehicle
    accidents 3,753

STATE SUMMARY

Capital City .... Denver

Governor .... Bill Owens

Address .... STATE CAPITOL
              DENVER, CO 80203
              303 866-2471

Admitted as a state 1876

Area (square miles) 104,100

Population, 1980 2,889,964

Population, 1990 3,294,394

Population, 2000 4,301,261

Persons per square mile, 2000 .... 41.5

Largest city .... Denver
  population, 2000 555,000

Personal income per capita, 2000
  (in current dollars) $32,949

Gross state product ($mil), 1999 ...... $153,728

Leading industries, 1999 (by payroll)
              Manufacturing
        Health Care/Social assistance
        Professional/Scientific/Technical

Leading agricultural commodities, 1999
        Cattle, corn, dairy products, wheat

GEOGRAPHY & ENVIRONMENT

Area, 1990 (square miles)
total 104,100
  land 103,730
  water (includes territorial water) 371

Federally owned land, 2000 .... 36.3%

Highest point
name .... Mt. Elbert
elevation (feet) 14,433

Lowest point
name .... Arkansas River
elevation (feet) 3,350

General coastline (miles) 0

Tidal shoreline (miles) 0

Capital city .... Denver
population, 2000 555,000

Largest city .... Denver
population, 2000 555,000

Number of cities with over 100,000 population
  1980 5
  1990 4
  2000 8

State parks and Recreation areas, 2000
area (acres) 347,000
number of visitors 10,284,000
revenues $12,127,000

Natl. forest system land, 1999 (acres) .. 14,509,000

National park acreage, 1984 588,200

DEMOGRAPHICS & CHARACTERISTICS OF THE POPULATION

Population
1970 2,209,596
1980 2,889,964
1990 3,294,394
2000 4,301,261
2015 (projection) 4,833,000
2025 (projection) 5,188,000

Metropolitan area population
1970 1,772,000
1980 2,326,000
2000 3,608,000

Non-metropolitan area population
1970 438,000
1980 563,000
2000 694,000

Change in population, 1990-2000
number 1,006,867
percent 30.56%

Persons per square mile, 2000 .... 41.5

Persons by age, 2000
under 5 years 297,505
18 and over 3,200,466
21 and over 3,014,312
65 and over 416,073
85 and over 48,216

Colorado 2

Persons by age, 2025 (projected)
under 5 years 324,000
5 to 17 years 849,000
65 and over 1,044,000

Median age, 2000 .... 34.3

Race, 2000
One race
White 3,560,005
Black or African American 165,063
American Indian and Alaska Native 44,241
Asian Indian 11,720
Chinese 15,658
Filipino 8,941
Japanese 11,571
Korean 16,395
Vietnamese 15,457
Native Hawaiian and other Pacific Islander 4,621
Two or more races 122,187

Race, 2025 (projected)
White 4,621,000
Black 309,000

Persons of Hispanic origin, 2000
total Hispanic or Latino 735,601
Mexican 450,760
Puerto Rican 12,993
Cuban 3,701
Other Hispanic or Latino 268,147

Persons of Hispanic origin, 2025 (proj.) . 1,067,000

Persons by sex, 2000
male 2,165,983
female 2,135,278

Marital status, 1990
males
15 years & older 1,255,439
single 373,157
married 742,483
separated 22,645
widowed 23,473
divorced 116,326
females
15 years & older 1,305,576
single 287,612
married 743,243
separated 29,520

widowed 118,193
divorced 156,528

Households & families, 2000
households 1,658,238
persons per household 2.53
families 1,084,461
persons per family 3.09
married couples 858,671
female householder, no husband
present 158,979
one person households 435,778
households with persons under 18 years . 585,387
households with persons over 65 years ... 292,763

Nativity, 1990
number of persons born in state 1,427,412
percent of total residents 43.3%

Immigration & naturalization, 1998
immigrants admitted 6,513
persons naturalized 3,230
refugees granted resident status 553

VITAL STATISTICS & HEALTH
Births
1999
with low birth weight 8.3%
to teenage mothers 15.3%
to unmarried mothers 25.4%
Birth rate, 1999 (per 1,000) 15.3
Birth rate, 2000 (per 1,000) 15.8

Abortions, 1996
total 18,000
rate (per 1,000 women age 15-44) 20.9

Deaths
1998 26,638
1999 27,114
2000 27,335
Infant deaths
1998 413
1999 396
2000 431
Average lifetime, by race, 1989-1991
total .... 76.96 years
white .... 77.06 years
black .... 72.41 years

Marriages
1998 31,403
1999 34,771
2000 35,636

Divorces
1998 .... NA
1999 .... NA
2000 .... NA

Physicians, 1999
total 9,914
rate (per 1,000 persons) 2.44

Nurses, 1999
total 31,230
rate (per 1,000 persons) 7.70

Hospitals, 1998
number 69
beds (x 1,000) 9.2
average daily census (x 1,000) 5.1
patients admitted (x1,000) 373
average cost per day to hospital, 1995 .... $1,069
average cost per stay to hospital, 1995 ... $6,289

EDUCATION

*Educational attainment of all persons
25 years and older, 1990*
less than 9th grade 118,252
high school graduates 558,312
bachelor's degree 379,150
graduate or professional degree 189,106

2000
high school graduate or more 89.7%
college graduate or more 34.6%

Public school enrollment, Fall, 1998
total 699,135
Kindergarten through grade 8 501,449
grades 9 through 12 197,686

Public School Teachers, 2000
total 40,800
elementary 20,400
secondary 20,400
average salaries
elementary $38,700
secondary $39,000

*State receipts & expenditures for public
schools, 2000*
revenue receipts ($mil) $4,801

*State receipts & expenditures for public
schools, 2000 (continued)*
expenditures
total ($mil) $4,560
per capita $1,124
per pupil $5,695

*Graduating high school seniors,
public high schools, 2000 (est.)* 38,078

SAT scores, 2001
verbal 539
math 542
percent graduates taking test 31%

Institutions of higher education, 1999
total 71
public 28
private 43

*Enrollment in institutions of higher
education, Fall, 1998*
total 257,247
full-time men 66,955
full-time women 72,462
part-time men 50,277
part-time women 67,553

*Minority enrollment in institutions of higher
education, Fall, 1997*
Black, non-Hispanic 8,922
Hispanic 24,728
Asian/Pacific Islander 8,836

Earned degrees conferred, 1998
Bachelor's 20,374
First professional 834
Master's 8,160
Doctor's 851

SOCIAL INSURANCE &
WELFARE PROGRAMS

Social Security beneficiaries & benefits, 2000
beneficiaries
total 535,000
retired and dependents 376,000
survivors 78,000
disabled & dependents 81,000
annual benefit payments ($mil)
total $4,698
retired and dependents $3,148
survivors $882
disabled & dependents $667

Colorado 4

Medicare, 2000
enrollment (x1,000) 458
payments ($mil) $2,338

Medicaid, 1998
recipients (x1,000) 345
payments ($mil) $1,439

Federal public aid
Temporary Assistance for Needy Families
(TANF), 2000
   Recipients (x1,000) 29
   Families (x1,000) 11
Supplemental Security Income
   total recipients, 1999 (x1,000) 55

Food Stamp Program
   participants, 2000 (x1,000) 156

HOUSING & CONSTRUCTION

Total housing units, 2000 1,808,037
   seasonal or recreational use 72,263
   occupied 1,658,238
      owner occupied 1,116,137
      renter occupied 542,101

New privately owned housing units uthorized, 2000
number (x1,000) 54.6
value ($mil) $6,822

New privately owned housing units
started, 2000 (est.) (x1,000) 45.9

Existing home sales, 2000 (x1,000) 157.3

GOVERNMENT & ELECTIONS

State officials, 2002
  Governor (name/party/term expires)
         BILL OWENS
        Republican - 2002
Lt. Governor . . . . Joe Rogers
Sec. of State . . . . Donnetta Davidson
Atty. General . . . . Ken Salazar
Chief Justice . . . . Mary Mullarkey

Governorship
minimum age 30
length of term . . . . 4 years
number of consecutive
   terms permitted 2
who succeeds . . . . Lt. Governor

State legislature
name . . . . General Assembly
  upper chamber
     name . . . . Senate
     number of members 35
     length of term . . . . 4 years
     party in majority, 2000 . . . . Republican
  lower chamber
     name . . . . House of Representatives
     number of members 65
     length of term . . . . 2 years
     party in majority, 2000 . . . . Republican

State employees March, 2000
total 81,536
March payroll $242,331,884

Local governments, 1997
total 1,869
   county 62
   municipal 269
   township 0
   school districts 180
   special districts 1,358

Voting age population, November, 2000, projected
Total 3,067,000
   male 1,503,000
   female 1,564,000

Vote for president
2000
   Gore 738,000
   Bush 884,000
1996
   Clinton 671,000
   Dole 692,000
   Perot 100,000

Federal representation, 2002 (107th Congress)
Senators (name/party/term expires)

       WAYNE ALLARD
       Republican - 2003
  BEN NIGHTHORSE CAMPBELL
       Republican - 2005

Representatives, total 6
Democrats 2
Republicans 4
other 0

Women holding public office, 2001
U.S. Congress 1
statewide elected office 1
state legislature 34

Black elected officials, 1999
total 21
  US and state legislatures 5
  city/county/regional offices 5
  judicial/law enforcement 10
  education/school boards 1

Hispanic public officials, 2000
total 154
  state executives & legislators 11
  city/county/regional offices 92
  judicial/law enforcement 9
  education/school boards 42

GOVERNMENTAL FINANCE

State government revenues, 1999 ($per capita)
total revenue $3,490.55
  total general revenue $2,896.10
    intergovernmental revenue $729.54
    taxes $1,619.32
    current charges $315.31
    miscellaneous $231.93

State government expenditures, 1999 ($per capita)
total expenditure $3,241.60
  total general expenditure $2,884.25
    education $1,135.09
    public welfare $697.33
    health $72.17
    hospitals $38.27
    highways $285.82
    police protection $17.35
    correction $165.52
    natural resources $47.03
    governmental administration $87.90
    interest on general debt $61.79

State debt, 1999 ($per capita) $1,000.65

Federal government grants to state & local government, 2000 (x$1,000)
total $3,272,542
  Dept. of Education $321,528
  Environmental Protection Agency $68,430
  Health Care Financing Admin. $1,105,056
  Dept. Housing & Urban Devel. $434,705
  Dept. of Labor $62,017
  Highway trust fund $296,739

CRIME, LAW ENFORCEMENT & COURTS

Crime, 2000 (all rates per 100,000 inhabitants)
total crimes 171,304
overall crime rate 3,982.6
  property crimes 156,937
    burglaries 27,133
    larcenies 112,843
    motor vehicle thefts 16,961
  property crime rate 3,648.6
  violent crimes 14,367
    murders 134
    forcible rapes 1,774
    robberies 3,034
    aggravated assaults 9,425
  violent crime rate 334.0

Number of police agencies, 2000 142

Arrests, 2000
total 241,572
  persons under 18 years of age 48,636

Prisoners under state & federal jurisdiction, 2000
total 16,833
percent change, 1999-2000 .... 7.4%
  sentenced to more than one year
    total 16,833
    rate per 100,000 residents 403

Persons under sentence of death, 4/1/2001 7

State's highest court
name .... Supreme Court
number of members 7
length of term .... 10 years
intermediate appeals court? .... yes

Colorado 6

LABOR & INCOME

Civilian labor force, 2000
total	2,276,000
men	1,234,000
women	1,041,000
persons 16-19 years	121,000
white	2,120,000
black	78,000

Civilian labor force as a percent of civilian non-institutional population, 2000
total	72.4%
men	79.6%
women	65.5%
persons 16-19 years	NA%
white	72.5%
black	72.9%

Employment, 2000
total	2,213,000
men	1,200,000
women	1,013,000
persons 16-19 years	106,000
white	2,066,000
black	73,000

Full-time/part-time labor force, 1998
full-time labor force	1,836,000
working part-time for economic reasons	22,000
part-time labor force	409,000

Unemployment rate, 2000
total	2.7%
men	2.8%
women	2.7%
persons 16-19 years	12.3%
white	2.5%
black	6.4%

Unemployed by reason for unemployment (as a percent of total unemployment), 1998
job losers or completed temp jobs	37.2%
job leavers	15.1%
reentrants	41.9%
new entrants	5.8%

Experienced civilian labor force, by occupation, 1998
executive/administrative/managerial	388,000
professional/specialty	406,000
technicians & related support	82,000
sales	296,000
administrative support/clerical	293,000
service occupations	262,000
precision production/craft/repair	251,000
machine operators/assemblers	61,000
transportation/material moving	69,000
handlers/helpers/laborers	89,000
farming/forestry/fishing	NA

Experienced civilian labor force, by industry, 1998
construction	146,000
manufacturing	248,000
transportation/communication	123,000
wholesale/retail trade	430,000
finance/real estate/insurance	142,000
services	589,000
government	314,000
agriculture	NA

Average annual pay, 1999 ... $34,192
change in average annual pay, 1998-1999 ... 6.0%

Hours and earnings of production workers on manufacturing payrolls, 2000
average weekly hours	41.7
average hourly earnings	$14.76
average weekly earnings	$615.49

Labor union membership, 2000 ... 173,200

Household income (in 2000 dollars)
median household income, three year average, 1998-2000 ... $48,506

Poverty
persons below poverty level, three year average, 1998-2000 ... 8.5%

Personal income ($ per capita)
2000 (prelim.)
in current dollars	$32,949
in constant (1996) dollars	$30,690

1999 (preliminary)
in current dollars	$31,678
in constant (1996) dollars	$30,291

Federal income tax returns, 1999
returns filed	2,029,929
adjusted gross income ($1,000)	$100,073,435
total income tax paid ($1,000)	$16,281,779

ECONOMY, BUSINESS, INDUSTRY & AGRICULTURE

Fortune 500 companies, 2000 4

Business incorporations, 1998
total 14,392
change, 1997-1998 .... -8.2%

Business failures, 1998 2,483

Business firm ownership, 1997
Hispanic owned firms 20,859
Black owned firms 4,926
women owned firms 114,807
Asian & Pacific Islander owned firms 9,028
American Indian & Alaska
    native owned firms 3,390

Shopping centers, 2000 777

Gross state product, 1999 ($mil)
total $153,728
    agriculture services, forestry, fisheries .. $2,261
    mining $2,400
    construction $9,233
    manufacturing--durable goods $9,479
    manufacturing--nondurable goods $6,144
    transportation, communication &
        public utilities $18,740
    wholesale trade $9,644
    retail trade $15,127
    finance/real estate/insurance $26,869
    services $35,529
    federal, state & local government $18,303

Establishments, by major industry group, 1999
total 133,743
    forestry, fishing & agriculture 268
    mining 895
    construction 16,657
    manufacturing 5,425
    transportation & warehousing 2,709
    wholesale trade 7,452
    retail trade 18,379
    finance & insurance 8,187
    professional/scientific/technical 16,849
    health care/social assistance 10,585
    information 2,953
    accommodation/food services 10,179

Payroll, by major industry group, 1999
total ($1,000) $59,775,138
    forestry, fishing & agriculture $29,498
    mining $588,461
    construction $5,118,515
    manufacturing $6,627,531
    transportation & warehousing $1,809,145
    wholesale trade $4,329,944
    retail trade $5,155,960
    finance & insurance $4,635,265
    professional/scientific/technical $7,155,247
    health care/social assistance $5,562,471
    information $4,617,473
    accommodation/food services $2,372,276

Agriculture
number of farms, 2000 29,000
farm acreage, 2000 32,000,000
acres per farm, 2000 1,090
value of farms, 1997 ($mil) $19,175
farm income, 1999 ($mil)
    net farm income $923
    debt/asset ratio 15.7%
farm marketings, 1999 ($mil)
total $4,354
    crops $1,338
    livestock $3,016
principal commodities, in order by marketing
receipts, 1999
        Cattle, corn, dairy products, wheat

Federal economic activity in state
expenditures, 2000
    total ($mil) $22,918
    per capita $5,328
    defense ($mil) $4,585
    non-defense ($mil) $18,334
defense department, 2000
    contract awards ($mil) $2,214
    payroll ($mil) $2,395
    civilian employees (x1,000) 11
    military personnel (x1,000) 29.1

Fishing, 2000
catch (thousands of pounds) ....NA
value ($1,000) .... $NA

Mining, 2000 ($mil; preliminary)
total non-fuel mineral production $566

Colorado 8

Construction, 1999 ($mil)
total contracts (including
    non-building) $11,775
      residential $6,370
      non-residential $3,825

Construction industries, 1997
establishments 14,152
receipts ($1,000) $19,138,626
annual payroll ($1,000) $3,728,242
paid employees 122,733

Manufacturing, 1997
establishments 5,681
value of shipments ($1,000) $41,931,225
annual payroll ($1,000) $6,634,727
paid employees 186,156

Transportation industries, 1997
establishments 4,861
receipts ($1,000) $20,024,860
annual payroll ($1,000) $4,102,332
paid employees 107,532

Wholesale trade, 1997
establishments 8,532
sales($1,000) $63,481,099
annual payroll ($1,000) $3,658,671
paid employees 101,918

Retail trade, 1997
establishments 26,130
sales($1,000) $42,188,444
annual payroll ($1,000) $5,183,681
paid employees 366,950

Finance industries
establishments, 1997 13,640
receipts ($1,000), 1997 .... $NA
annual payroll ($1,000), 1997 .... $4,392,917
paid employees, 1997 119,331
commercial banks, 2000
    number 181
      assets ($bil) $46.6
      deposits ($bil) $37.3

Service industries, 1997 (non-exempt firms only)
establishments 40,871
receipts ($1,000) $34,286,545
annual payroll ($1,000) $12,523,870
paid employees 457,757

COMMUNICATION, ENERGY & TRANSPORTATION

Communication
daily newspapers, 2000 29
households with
    telephones, 1998 .... 95.4%
    computers, 2000 .... 62.6%
    internet access, 2000 .... 51.8%

Energy
consumption, 1999
total (trillion Btu) 1,156
per capita (million Btu) 285
by source of production (trillion Btu)
    coal 355
    natural gas 318
    petroleum 426
    nuclear electric power .... NA
    hydroelectric power 17
by end-use sector (trillion Btu)
    residential 261
    commercial 255
    industrial 273
    transportation 366
electric energy, 1999
    production (billion kWh) 36.2
    net summer capability (million kW) 7.3
gas utilities, 1999
    customers 1,345,000
    sales (trillion Btu) 224
nuclear plants, 1999 .... na

Transportation, 2000
public road & street mileage
total 85,409
    urban 14,463
    rural 70,946
    interstate 951
vehicle miles of travel (mil) 41,771
total motor vehicle registrations 3,626,012
    automobiles 1,920,757
    motorcycles 98,218
licensed drivers 3,107,258
    per 1,000 driving age population 935
deaths from motor vehicle
    accidents 681

STATE SUMMARY

Capital City .... Hartford
Governor .... John Rowland
Address .... STATE CAPITOL
HARTFORD, CT 06106
860 566-4840

Admitted as a state 1788
Area (square miles) 5,544
Population, 1980 3,107,576
Population, 1990 3,287,116
Population, 2000 3,405,565
Persons per square mile, 2000 .... 702.9
Largest city .... Bridgeport
population, 2000 140,000

Personal income per capita, 2000
(in current dollars) $40,640

Gross state product ($mil), 1999 ...... $151,779

Leading industries, 1999 (by payroll)
Manufacturing
Finance & Insurance
Health care/Social assistance

Leading agricultural commodities, 1999
Greenhouse, dairy products, chicken eggs,
aquaculture

GEOGRAPHY & ENVIRONMENT

Area, 1990 (square miles)
total 5,544
land 4,845
water (includes territorial water) 698

Federally owned land, 2000 .... 0.5%

Highest point
name .... Mt. Frissell (south slope)
elevation (feet) 2,380

Lowest point
name .... Long Island Sound
elevation (feet) .... sea level

General coastline (miles) 0

Tidal shoreline (miles) 618

Capital city .... Hartford
population, 2000 122,000

Largest city .... Bridgeport
population, 2000 140,000

Number of cities with over 100,000 population
1980 4
1990 5
2000 5

State parks and Recreation areas, 2000
area (acres) 183,000
number of visitors 7,567,000
revenues $3,205,000

Natl. forest system land, 1999 (acres) 0

National park acreage, 1984 3,300

DEMOGRAPHICS & CHARACTERISTICS OF THE POPULATION

Population
1970 3,032,217
1980 3,107,576
1990 3,287,116
2000 3,405,565
2015 (projection) 3,506,000
2025 (projection) 3,739,000

Metropolitan area population
1970 2,819,000
1980 2,879,000
2000 3,257,000

Non-metropolitan area population
1970 213,000
1980 228,000
2000 149,000

Change in population, 1990-2000
number 118,449
percent 3.60%

Persons per square mile, 2000 .... 702.9

Persons by age, 2000
under 5 years 223,344
18 and over 2,563,877
21 and over 2,439,461
65 and over 470,183
85 and over 64,273

Connecticut 2

Persons by age, 2025 (projected)
under 5 years 246,000
5 to 17 years 613,000
65 and over 671,000

Median age, 2000 .... 37.4

Race, 2000
One race
White 2,780,355
Black or African American 309,843
American Indian and Alaska Native 9,639
Asian Indian 23,662
Chinese 19,172
Filipino 7,643
Japanese 4,196
Korean 7,064
Vietnamese 7,538
Native Hawaiian and other Pacific Islander 1,366
Two or more races 74,848

Race, 2025 (projected)
White 3,065,000
Black 490,000

Persons of Hispanic origin, 2000
total Hispanic or Latino 320,323
    Mexican 23,484
    Puerto Rican 194,443
    Cuban 7,101
    Other Hispanic or Latino 95,295

Persons of Hispanic origin, 2025 (proj.) .. 574,000

Persons by sex, 2000
male 1,649,319
female 1,756,246

Marital status, 1990
males
    15 years & older 1,269,569
        single 412,921
        married 739,187
        separated 17,931
        widowed 33,892
        divorced 83,569
females
    15 years & older 1,385,814
        single 357,734
        married 742,707
        separated 27,542

        widowed 163,081
        divorced 122,292

Households & families, 2000
households 1,301,670
persons per household 2.53
    families 881,170
    persons per family 3.08
        married couples 676,467
        female householder, no husband
            present 157,411
        one person households 344,224
households with persons under 18 years . 451,411
households with persons over 65 years ... 326,743

Nativity, 1990
number of persons born in state 1,874,080
percent of total residents 57.0%

Immigration & naturalization, 1998
immigrants admitted 7,780
persons naturalized 7,351
refugees granted resident status 169

VITAL STATISTICS & HEALTH

Births
1999
    with low birth weight 7.6%
    to teenage mothers 13.2%
    to unmarried mothers 29.0%
Birth rate, 1999 (per 1,000) 13.2
Birth rate, 2000 (per 1,000) 13.1

Abortions, 1996
total 16,000
rate (per 1,000 women age 15-44) 22.5

Deaths
1998 28,748
1999 29,446
2000 30,237

Infant deaths
1998 279
1999 226
2000 270

Average lifetime, by race, 1989-1991
total .... 76.91 years
    white .... 77.44 years
    black .... 70.84 years

Marriages

1998	19,936
1999	19,748
2000	19,418

Divorces

1998	9,615
1999	5,655
2000	6,455

Physicians, 1999

total	11,859
rate (per 1,000 persons)	3.61

Nurses, 1999

total	32,660
rate (per 1,000 persons)	9.95

Hospitals, 1998

number	33
beds (x 1,000)	6.9
average daily census (x 1,000)	4.8
patients admitted (x1,000)	330
average cost per day to hospital, 1995	$1,264
average cost per stay to hospital, 1995	$7,358

EDUCATION

Educational attainment of all persons 25 years and older, 1990

less than 9th grade	185,213
high school graduates	648,366
bachelor's degree	356,289
graduate or professional degree	241,404

2000

high school graduate or more	88.2%
college graduate or more	31.6%

Public school enrollment, Fall, 1998

total	544,698
Kindergarten through grade 8	399,381
grades 9 through 12	145,317

Public School Teachers, 2000

total	40,400
elementary	28,900
secondary	11,500
average salaries	
elementary	$51,200
secondary	$53,300

State receipts & expenditures for public schools, 2000

revenue receipts ($mil)	$6,118

State receipts & expenditures for public schools, 2000 (continued)

expenditures	
total ($mil)	$6,118
per capita	$1,864
per pupil	$10,286

Graduating high school seniors, public high schools, 2000 (est.)

	29,858

SAT scores, 2001

verbal	509
math	510
percent graduates taking test	82%

Institutions of higher education, 1999

total	41
public	18
private	23

Enrollment in institutions of higher education, Fall, 1998

total	153,336
full-time men	39,508
full-time women	45,628
part-time men	27,056
part-time women	41,144

Minority enrollment in institutions of higher education, Fall, 1997

Black, non-Hispanic	12,188
Hispanic	8,154
Asian/Pacific Islander	6,049

Earned degrees conferred, 1998

Bachelor's	13,578
First professional	884
Master's	7,167
Doctor's	686

SOCIAL INSURANCE & WELFARE PROGRAMS

Social Security beneficiaries & benefits, 2000

beneficiaries	
total	579,000
retired and dependents	436,000
survivors	72,000
disabled & dependents	70,000
annual benefit payments ($mil)	
total	$5,711
retired and dependents	$4,219
survivors	$896
disabled & dependents	$597

Connecticut 4

Medicare, 2000
enrollment (x1,000) 512
payments ($mil) $3,291

Medicaid, 1998
recipients (x1,000) 381
payments ($mil) $2,421

Federal public aid
Temporary Assistance for Needy Families
(TANF), 2000
  Recipients (x1,000) 66
  Families (x1,000) 28
Supplemental Security Income
  total recipients, 1999 (x1,000) 48

Food Stamp Program
  participants, 2000 (x1,000) 165

HOUSING & CONSTRUCTION

Total housing units, 2000 1,385,975
  seasonal or recreational use 23,379
  occupied 1,301,670
    owner occupied 869,729
    renter occupied 431,941

New privately owned housing units uthorized, 2000
number (x1,000) 9.4
value ($mil) $1,425

New privately owned housing units
  started, 2000 (est.) (x1,000) 10.0

Existing home sales, 2000 (x1,000) 53.2

GOVERNMENT & ELECTIONS

State officials, 2002
Governor (name/party/term expires)
        JOHN ROWLAND
        Republican - 2002
Lt. Governor . . . . M. Jodi Rell
Sec. of State . . . . Susan Bysiewicz
Atty. General . . . . Richard Blumenthal
Chief Justice . . . . William Sullivan

Governorship
minimum age 30
length of term . . . . 4 years
number of consecutive
  terms permitted . . . . not specified
who succeeds . . . . Lt. Governor

State legislature
name . . . . General Assembly
  upper chamber
    name . . . . Senate
    number of members 36
    length of term . . . . 2 years
    party in majority, 2000 . . . . Democratic
  lower chamber
    name . . . . House of Representatives
    number of members 151
    length of term . . . . 2 years
    party in majority, 2000 . . . . Democratic

State employees March, 2000
total 74,225
March payroll $247,169,623

Local governments, 1997
total 583
  county 0
  municipal 30
  township 149
  school districts 17
  special districts 387

Voting age population, November, 2000, projected
Total 2,499,000
  male 1,192,000
  female 1,307,000

Vote for president
2000
  Gore 816,000
  Bush 561,000
1996
  Clinton 736,000
  Dole 483,000
  Perot 140,000

Federal representation, 2002 (107th Congress)
Senators (name/party/term expires)

      JOSEPH LIEBERMAN
      Democrat - 2007
    CHRISTOPHER J. DODD
      Democrat - 2005

Representatives, total 6
  Democrats 3
  Republicans 3
  other 0

GOVERNMENTAL FINANCE

State government revenues, 1999 ($per capita)
total revenue $5,008.32
  total general revenue $4,545.98
    intergovernmental revenue $958.82
    taxes $2,932.21
    current charges $305.65
    miscellaneous $349.30

State government expenditures, 1999 ($per capita)
total expenditure $4,635.39
  total general expenditure $4,064.45
    education $1,001.15
    public welfare $921.18
    health $135.91
    hospitals $345.76
    highways $219.19
    police protection $39.10
    correction $159.86
    natural resources $27.43
    governmental administration $238.39
    interest on general debt $313.36

State debt, 1999 ($per capita) $5,333.53

Federal government grants to state & local government, 2000 (x$1,000)
total $3,770,947
  Dept. of Education $274,677
  Environmental Protection Agency $31,179
  Health Care Financing Admin. $1,638,386
  Dept. Housing & Urban Devel. $529,972
  Dept. of Labor $69,734
  Highway trust fund $399,379

CRIME, LAW ENFORCEMENT & COURTS

Crime, 2000 (all rates per 100,000 inhabitants)
total crimes 110,091
overall crime rate 3,232.7
  property crimes 99,033
    burglaries 17,436
    larcenies 68,498
    motor vehicle thefts. 13,099
  property crime rate 2,908.0
  violent crimes 11,058
    murders 98
    forcible rapes 678
    robberies 3,832
    aggravated assaults 6,450
  violent crime rate 324.7

Number of police agencies, 2000 92

Arrests, 2000
total 132,482
  persons under 18 years of age 20,983

Prisoners under state & federal jurisdiction, 2000
total 18,355
percent change, 1999-2000 .... -1.5%
  sentenced to more than one year
    total 13,155
    rate per 100,000 residents 398

Persons under sentence of death, 4/1/2001 7

State's highest court
name .... Supreme Court
number of members 6
length of term .... 8 years
intermediate appeals court? .... yes

Connecticut 6

LABOR & INCOME

Civilian labor force, 2000

total	1,746,000
men	914,000
women	833,000
persons 16-19 years	NA
white	1,493,000
black	201,000

Civilian labor force as a percent of civilian non-institutional population, 2000

total	68.8%
men	75.4%
women	62.9%
persons 16-19 years	NA%
white	68.8%
black	67.3%

Employment, 2000

total	1,707,000
men	896,000
women	811,000
persons 16-19 years	NA
white	1,462,000
black	193,000

Full-time/part-time labor force, 1998

full-time labor force	NA
working part-time for economic reasons	7,000
part-time labor force	NA

Unemployment rate, 2000

total	2.3%
men	2.0%
women	2.6%
persons 16-19 years	NA%
white	2.0%
black	4.2%

Unemployed by reason for unemployment (as a percent of total unemployment), 1998

job losers or completed temp jobs	NA%
job leavers	NA%
reentrants	NA%
new entrants	NA%

Experienced civilian labor force, by occupation, 1998

executive/administrative/managerial	285,000
professional/specialty	290,000
technicians & related support	NA
sales	204,000
administrative support/clerical	249,000
service occupations	221,000
precision production/craft/repair	188,000
machine operators/assemblers	93,000
transportation/material moving	NA
handlers/helpers/laborers	NA
farming/forestry/fishing	NA

Experienced civilian labor force, by industry, 1998

construction	75,000
manufacturing	325,000
transportation/communication	96,000
wholesale/retail trade	277,000
finance/real estate/insurance	142,000
services	464,000
government	187,000
agriculture	NA

Average annual pay, 1999 .... $42,653
change in average annual pay,
1998-1999 .... 4.3%

Hours and earnings of production workers on manufacturing payrolls, 2000

average weekly hours	42.6
average hourly earnings	$15.69
average weekly earnings	$668.39

Labor union membership, 2000 245,800

Household income (in 2000 dollars)
median household income,
three year average, 1998-2000 .... $50,360

Poverty
persons below poverty level,
three year average, 1998-2000 .... 7.6%

Personal income ($per capita)
2000 (prelim.)
in current dollars $40,640
in constant (1996) dollars $37,854
1999 (preliminary)
in current dollars $39,167
in constant (1996) dollars $37,452

Federal income tax returns, 1999

returns filed	1,646,153
adjusted gross income ($1,000)	$106,834,855
total income tax paid ($1,000)	$20,687,918

ECONOMY, BUSINESS, INDUSTRY & AGRICULTURE

Fortune 500 companies, 2000 13

Business incorporations, 1998
total 2,617
change, 1997-1998 .... -22.5%

Business failures, 1998 530

Business firm ownership, 1997
Hispanic owned firms 6,594
Black owned firms 7,251
women owned firms 72,393
Asian & Pacific Islander owned firms 5,904
American Indian & Alaska
    native owned firms 1,311

Shopping centers, 2000 800

Gross state product, 1999 ($mil)
total $151,779
    agriculture services, forestry, fisheries .. $1,038
    mining $113
    construction $4,954
    manufacturing--durable goods $17,033
    manufacturing--nondurable goods $8,015
    transportation, communication &
        public utilities $9,020
    wholesale trade $9,750
    retail trade $12,213
    finance/real estate/insurance $43,623
    services $33,389
    federal, state & local government $12,631

Establishments, by major industry group, 1999
total 92,454
    forestry, fishing & agriculture 104
    mining 74
    construction 9,281
    manufacturing 5,657
    transportation & warehousing 1,550
    wholesale trade 5,179
    retail trade 14,258
    finance & insurance 5,612
    professional/scientific/technical 10,174
    health care/social assistance 9,281
    information 1,666
    accommodation/food services 6,711

Payroll, by major industry group, 1999
total ($1,000) $62,082,551
    forestry, fishing & agriculture $10,482
    mining $32,730
    construction $2,725,582
    manufacturing $11,112,058
    transportation & warehousing $1,019,251
    wholesale trade $4,185,453
    retail trade $4,277,410
    finance & insurance $9,660,600
    professional/scientific/technical $5,016,497
    health care/social assistance $6,869,396
    information $2,575,023
    accommodation/food services $1,301,584

Agriculture
number of farms, 2000 4,000
farm acreage, 2000 ....NA
acres per farm, 2000 92
value of farms, 1997 ($mil) $2,850
farm income, 1999 ($mil)
    net farm income $139
    debt/asset ratio 11.7%
farm marketings, 1999 ($mil)
    total $482
        crops $302
        livestock $180
principal commodities, in order by marketing
receipts, 1999
    Greenhouse, dairy products, chicken eggs,
aquaculture

Federal economic activity in state
expenditures, 2000
    total ($mil) $19,517
    per capita $5,731
    defense ($mil) $2,674
    non-defense ($mil) $16,843
defense department, 2000
    contract awards ($mil) $2,177
    payroll ($mil) $541
    civilian employees (x1,000) 2.6
    military personnel (x1,000) 6.5

Fishing, 2000
catch (thousands of pounds) 19,563
value ($1,000) $31,227

Mining, 2000 ($mil; preliminary)
total non-fuel mineral production $3100

Connecticut 8

Construction, 1999 ($mil)
total contracts (including
    non-building) $4,448
      residential $1,561
      non-residential $2,167

Construction industries, 1997
establishments 8,843
receipts ($1,000) ....$NA
annual payroll ($1,000) ....$NA
paid employees ....NA

Manufacturing, 1997
establishments 5,911
value of shipments ($1,000) $48,699,736
annual payroll ($1,000) $10,862,423
paid employees 262,959

Transportation industries, 1997
establishments 3,117
receipts ($1,000) $14,845,997
annual payroll ($1,000) $2,884,882
paid employees 71,136

Wholesale trade, 1997
establishments 6,091
sales($1,000) ....$NA
annual payroll ($1,000) ....$NA
paid employees ....NA

Retail trade, 1997
establishments 20,606
sales($1,000) $35,832,852
annual payroll ($1,000) $4,263,558
paid employees 264,497

Finance industries
establishments, 1997 8,904
receipts ($1,000), 1997 ....$NA
annual payroll ($1,000), 1997 .... $7,285,415
paid employees, 1997 137,061
commercial banks, 2000
    number 23
      assets ($bil) $3.4
      deposits ($bil) $2.8

Service industries, 1997 (non-exempt firms only)
establishments 29,434
receipts ($1,000) $28,367,270
annual payroll ($1,000) $10,967,404
paid employees 348,287

COMMUNICATION, ENERGY & TRANSPORTATION

Communication
daily newspapers, 2000 17
households with
    telephones, 1998 .... 95.1%
    computers, 2000 .... 60.4%
    internet access, 2000 .... 51.2%

Energy
consumption, 1999
total (trillion Btu) 839
per capita (million Btu) 256
by source of production (trillion Btu)
    coal ....NA
    natural gas 135
    petroleum 440
    nuclear electric power 135
    hydroelectric power 14
by end-use sector (trillion Btu)
    residential 245
    commercial 197
    industrial 162
    transportation 235
electric energy, 1999
    production (billion kWh) 20.5
    net summer capability (million kW) 2.9
gas utilities, 1999
    customers 483,000
    sales (trillion Btu) 97
nuclear plants, 1999 2

Transportation, 2000
public road & street mileage
total 20,845
    urban 11,804
    rural 9,041
    interstate 346
vehicle miles of travel (mil) 30,756
total motor vehicle registrations 2,853,449
    automobiles 2,009,190
    motorcycles 53,742
licensed drivers 2,652,593
    per 1,000 driving age population 1,000
deaths from motor vehicle
    accidents 342

Delaware 1

STATE SUMMARY

Capital City . . . . Dover

Governor . . . . Ruth Ann Minner

Address . . . . LEGISLATIVE HALL
DOVER, DE 19901
302 739-4101

Admitted as a state 1787

Area (square miles) 2,489

Population, 1980 594,338

Population, 1990 666,168

Population, 2000 783,600

Persons per square mile, 2000 . . . . 400.8

Largest city . . . . Wilmington
population, 2000 72,664

Personal income per capita, 2000
(in current dollars) $31,255

Gross state product ($mil), 1999 . . . . $34,669

Leading industries, 1999 (by payroll)
Finance & Insurance
Manufacturing
Health care/Social assistance

Leading agricultural commodities, 1999
Broilers, greenhouse, soybeans, dairy products

GEOGRAPHY & ENVIRONMENT

Area, 1990 (square miles)
total 2,489
  land 1,955
  water (includes territorial water) 535

Federally owned land, 2000 . . . . 1.2%

Highest point
name . . . . Ebright Road (New Castle County)
elevation (feet) 442

Lowest point
name . . . . Atlantic Ocean
elevation (feet) . . . . .sea level

General coastline (miles) 28

Tidal shoreline (miles) 381

Capital city . . . . Dover
population, 2000 32,135

Largest city . . . . Wilmington
population, 2000 72,664

Number of cities with over 100,000 population
1980 0
1990 0
2000 0

State parks and Recreation areas, 2000
area (acres) 21,000
number of visitors 3,910,000
revenues $6,619,000

Natl. forest system land, 1999 (acres) 0

National park acreage, 1984 . . . . .NA

DEMOGRAPHICS & CHARACTERISTICS OF THE POPULATION

Population
1970 548,107
1980 594,338
1990 666,168
2000 783,600
2015 (projection) 832,000
2025 (projection) 861,000

Metropolitan area population
1970 386,000
1980 398,000
2000 627,000

Non-metropolitan area population
1970 162,000
1980 196,000
2000 157,000

Change in population, 1990-2000
number 117,432
percent 17.63%

Persons per square mile, 2000 . . . . 400.8

Persons by age, 2000
under 5 years 51,531
18 and over 589,013
21 and over 553,669
65 and over 101,726
85 and over 10,549

Delaware 2

Persons by age, 2025 (projected)
under 5 years 52,000
5 to 17 years 136,000
65 and over 165,000

Median age, 2000 36

Race, 2000
One race
White 584,773
Black or African American 150,666
American Indian and Alaska Native 2,731
Asian Indian 5,280
Chinese 4,128
Filipino 2,018
Japanese 614
Korean 1,991
Vietnamese 817
Native Hawaiian and other Pacific Islander ..283
Two or more races 13,033

Race, 2025 (projected)
White 633,000
Black 199,000

Persons of Hispanic origin, 2000
total Hispanic or Latino 37,277
  Mexican 12,986
  Puerto Rican 14,005
  Cuban 932
  Other Hispanic or Latino 9,354

Persons of Hispanic origin, 2025 (proj.) ... 48,000

Persons by sex, 2000
male 380,541
female 403,059

Marital status, 1990
males
  15 years & older 251,905
    single 76,997
    married 149,973
      separated 5,339
    widowed 6,760
    divorced 18,175
females
  15 years & older 275,435
    single 68,503
    married 150,309
      separated 7,048

widowed 31,351
divorced 25,272

Households & families, 2000
households 298,736
persons per household 2.54
  families 204,590
  persons per family 3.04
    married couples 153,136
    female householder, no husband
      present 38,986
    one person households 74,639
households with persons under 18 years . 105,833
households with persons over 65 years 71,466

Nativity, 1990
number of persons born in state 334,209
percent of total residents 50.2%

Immigration & naturalization, 1998
immigrants admitted 1,063
persons naturalized 648
refugees granted resident status 23

VITAL STATISTICS & HEALTH

Births
1999
  with low birth weight 8.6%
  to teenage mothers 14.2%
  to unmarried mothers 38.8%
Birth rate, 1999 (per 1,000) 14.2
Birth rate, 2000 (per 1,000) 14.5

Abortions, 1996
total 4,000
rate (per 1,000 women age 15-44) 24.1

Deaths
1998 6,676
1999 6,666
2000 6,862

Infant deaths
1998 110
1999 101
2000 123

Average lifetime, by race, 1989-1991
total .... 74.76 years
  white .... 75.76 years
  black .... 69.26 years

Delaware 3

Marriages
1998 5,028
1999 5,180
2000 5,131

Divorces
1998 3,373
1999 3,647
2000 3,177

Physicians, 1999
total 1,791
rate (per 1,000 persons) 2.38

Nurses, 1999
total 8,440
rate (per 1,000 persons) 11.20

Hospitals, 1998
number 6
beds (x 1,000) 2.0
average daily census (x 1,000) 1.4
patients admitted (x1,000) 84
average cost per day to hospital, 1995 . . . . $1,058
average cost per stay to hospital, 1995 . . . . $7,298

EDUCATION

*Educational attainment of all persons
   25 years and older, 1990*
   less than 9th grade 31,009
   high school graduates 140,030
   bachelor's degree 58,615
   graduate or professional degree 33,107

2000
   high school graduate or more 86.1%
   college graduate or more 24.0%

Public school enrollment, Fall, 1998
total 113,262
   Kindergarten through grade 8 . . . . 79.955
   grades 9 through 12 33,307

Public School Teachers, 2000
total 7,600
   elementary 3,700
   secondary 3,900
average salaries
   elementary $44,300
   secondary $44,600

*State receipts & expenditures for public
   schools, 2000*
revenue receipts ($mil) $1,030

*State receipts & expenditures for public
   schools, 2000 (continued)*
expenditures
   total ($mil) $993
   per capita $1,318
   per pupil $8,653

*Graduating high school seniors,
   public high schools, 2000 (est.)* 6,356

SAT scores, 2001
verbal 501
math 499
percent graduates taking test 67%

Institutions of higher education, 1999
total 10
   public 5
   private 5

*Enrollment in institutions of higher
   education, Fall, 1998*
total 46,260
full-time men 11,865
full-time women 15,875
part-time men 7,053
part-time women 11,467

*Minority enrollment in institutions of higher
   education, Fall, 1997*
Black, non-Hispanic 6,723
Hispanic 999
Asian/Pacific Islander 1,013

Earned degrees conferred, 1998
Bachelor's 4,418
First professional 344
Master's 1,439
Doctor's 172

SOCIAL INSURANCE &
WELFARE PROGRAMS

Social Security beneficiaries & benefits, 2000
beneficiaries
total 135,000
   retired and dependents 96,000
   survivors 19,000
   disabled & dependents 19,000
annual benefit payments ($mil)
total $1,268
   retired and dependents $872
   survivors $229
   disabled & dependents $167

Delaware 4

Medicare, 2000
enrollment (x1,000) 110
payments ($mil) $430

Medicaid, 1998
recipients (x1,000) 101
payments ($mil) $420

Federal public aid
Temporary Assistance for Needy Families
(TANF), 2000
   Recipients (x1,000) 18
   Families (x1,000) 6
Supplemental Security Income
   total recipients, 1999 (x1,000) 12

Food Stamp Program
   participants, 2000 (x1,000) 32

HOUSING & CONSTRUCTION

Total housing units, 2000 343,072
   seasonal or recreational use 25,977
   occupied 298,736
      owner occupied 216,038
      renter occupied 82,698

New privately owned housing units uthorized, 2000
number (x1,000) 4.6
value ($mil) $414

New privately owned housing units
started, 2000 (est.) (x1,000) 5.2

Existing home sales, 2000 (x1,000) 7.7

GOVERNMENT & ELECTIONS

State officials, 2002
   Governor (name/party/term expires)
      RUTH ANN MINNER
      Democrat - 2005
Lt. Governor . . . . John Carney
Sec. of State . . . . Harriet Smith Windsor
Atty. General . . . . M. Jane Brady
Chief Justice . . . . Norman Veasey

Governorship
minimum age 30
length of term . . . . 4 years
number of consecutive
   terms permitted . . 2 max. (not nec. consecutive)
who succeeds . . . . Lt. Governor

State legislature
name . . . . General Assembly
   upper chamber
      name . . . . Senate
      number of members 21
      length of term . . . . 4 years
      party in majority, 2000 . . . . Democratic
lower chamber
      name . . . . House of Representatives
      number of members 41
      length of term . . . . 2 years
      party in majority, 2000 . . . . Republican

State employees March, 2000
total 28,267
March payroll $73,716,938

Local governments, 1997
total 336
   county 3
   municipal 57
   township 0
   school districts 19
   special districts 257

Voting age population, November, 2000, projected
Total 582,000
   male 278,000
   female 303,000

Vote for president
2000
   Gore 180,000
   Bush 137,000
1996
   Clinton 140,000
   Dole 99,000
   Perot 29,000

Federal representation, 2002 (107th Congress)
Senators (name/party/term expires)

      THOMAS CARPER
      Democrate - 2007
      JOSEPH R. BIDEN, JR.
      Democrat - 2003

Representatives, total 1
   Democrats 0
   Republicans 1
   other 0

Women holding public office, 2001
U.S. Congress 0
statewide elected office 3
state legislature 16

Black elected officials, 1999
total 24
  US and state legislatures 4
  city/county/regional offices 16
  judicial/law enforcement 1
  education/school boards 3

Hispanic public officials, 2000
total 3
  state executives & legislators 1
  city/county/regional offices 2
  judicial/law enforcement .... NA
  education/school boards .... NA

GOVERNMENTAL FINANCE

State government revenues, 1999 ($per capita)
total revenue $6,025.50
  total general revenue $5,387.88
    intergovernmental revenue $1,013.67
    taxes $2,695.01
    current charges $713.49
    miscellaneous $965.72

State government expenditures, 1999 ($per capita)
total expenditure $5,229.73
  total general expenditure $4,871.93
    education $1,729.68
    public welfare $667.71
    health $265.19
    hospitals $77.87
    highways $401.13
    police protection $84.08
    correction $267.74
    natural resources $103.94
    governmental administration $399.60
    interest on general debt $311.86

State debt, 1999 ($per capita) $4,926.92

Federal government grants to state & local government, 2000 (x$1,000)
total $817,675
  Dept. of Education $82,932
  Environmental Protection Agency $16,972
  Health Care Financing Admin. $281,484
  Dept. Housing & Urban Devel. $87,584
  Dept. of Labor $17,553
  Highway trust fund $119,731

CRIME, LAW ENFORCEMENT & COURTS

Crime, 2000 (all rates per 100,000 inhabitants)
total crimes 35,090
overall crime rate 4,478.1
  property crimes 29,727
    burglaries 5,216
    larcenies 21,360
    motor vehicle thefts 3,151
  property crime rate 3,793.6
  violent crimes 5,363
    murders 25
    forcible rapes 424
    robberies 1,394
    aggravated assaults 3,520
  violent crime rate 684.4

Number of police agencies, 2000 52

Arrests, 2000
total 36,739
  persons under 18 years of age 7,374

Prisoners under state & federal jurisdiction, 2000
total 6,921
percent change, 1999-2000 .... -0.9%
  sentenced to more than one year
  total 3,937
  rate per 100,000 residents 513

Persons under sentence of death, 4/1/2001 18

State's highest court
name .... Supreme Court
number of members 5
length of term .... 12 years
intermediate appeals court? .... no

Delaware 6

LABOR & INCOME

Civilian labor force, 2000
total 409,000
  men 212,000
  women 197,000
  persons 16-19 years 28,000
  white 315,000
  black 89,000

Civilian labor force as a percent of
civilian non-institutional population, 2000
total 69.6%
  men 76.0%
  women 63.8%
  persons 16-19 years .... NA%
  white 68.3%
  black 74.9%

Employment, 2000
total 393,000
  men 204,000
  women 189,000
  persons 16-19 years 23,000
  white 304,000
  black 84,000

Full-time/part-time labor force, 1998
full-time labor force 325,000
  working part-time for
    economic reasons 3,000
part-time labor force 68,000

Unemployment rate, 2000
total 4.0%
  men 4.0%
  women 4.0%
  persons 16-19 years 16.3%
  white 3.4%
  black 6.0%

Unemployed by reason for unemployment
(as a percent of total unemployment), 1998
job losers or completed temp jobs 46.7%
job leavers 20.0%
reentrants 33.3%
new entrants 6.7%

Experienced civilian labor force, by occupation,
1998
executive/administrative/managerial 60,000
professional/specialty 59,000
technicians & related support 14,000

sales 39,000
administrative support/clerical 64,000
service occupations 57,000
precision production/craft/repair 43,000
machine operators/assemblers 19,000
transportation/material moving 16,000
handlers/helpers/laborers 14,000
farming/forestry/fishing .... NA

Experienced civilian labor force, by industry, 1998
construction 22,000
manufacturing 50,000
transportation/communication 21,000
wholesale/retail trade 76,000
finance/real estate/insurance 43,000
services 95,000
government 53,000
agriculture .... NA

Average annual pay, 1999 .... $35,102
change in average annual pay,
  1998-1999 .... 3.3%

Hours and earnings of production workers
on manufacturing payrolls, 2000
average weekly hours 43.4
average hourly earnings $16.54
average weekly earnings $717.84

Labor union membership, 2000 46,900

Household income (in 2000 dollars)
median household income,
  three year average, 1998-2000 .... $50,154

Poverty
persons below poverty level,
  three year average, 1998-2000 .... 9.8%

Personal income ($per capita)
2000 (prelim.)
  in current dollars $31,255
  in constant (1996) dollars $29,112
1999 (preliminary)
  in current dollars $30,685
  in constant (1996) dollars $29,341

Federal income tax returns, 1999
returns filed 371,029
adjusted gross income ($1,000) $17,304,487
total income tax paid ($1,000) $2,619,386

ECONOMY, BUSINESS, INDUSTRY & AGRICULTURE

Fortune 500 companies, 2000 3

Business incorporations, 1998
total 48,074
change, 1997-1998 .... -7.9%

Business failures, 1998 28

Business firm ownership, 1997
Hispanic owned firms 898
Black owned firms 2,707
women owned firms 13,662
Asian & Pacific Islander owned firms 1,501
American Indian & Alaska
  native owned firms 288

Shopping centers, 2000 149

Gross state product, 1999 ($mil)
total $34,669
  agriculture services, forestry, fisheries $292
  mining $2
  construction $1,486
  manufacturing--durable goods $1,562
  manufacturing--nondurable goods $3,353
  transportation, communication &
    public utilities $1,752
  wholesale trade $1,382
  retail trade $2,455
  finance/real estate/insurance $13,813
  services $5,379
  federal, state & local government $3,194

Establishments, by major industry group, 1999
total 23,381
  forestry, fishing & agriculture 43
  mining 18
  construction 2,352
  manufacturing 696
  transportation & warehousing 648
  wholesale trade 1,001
  retail trade 3,757
  finance & insurance 1,608
  professional/scientific/technical 2,119
  health care/social assistance 1,857
  information 331
  accommodation/food services 1,526

Payroll, by major industry group, 1999
total ($1,000) $12,612,016
  forestry, fishing & agriculture .... $NA
  mining .... $NA
  construction $727,281
  manufacturing $1,777,150
  transportation & warehousing $221,606
  wholesale trade $834,869
  retail trade $959,322
  finance & insurance $1,921,970
  professional/scientific/technical $959,027
  health care/social assistance $1,312,123
  information $352,545
  accommodation/food services $344,414

Agriculture
number of farms, 2000 3,000
farm acreage, 2000 1,000,000
acres per farm, 2000 223
value of farms, 1997 ($mil) $1,791
farm income, 1999 ($mil)
  net farm income $121
  debt/asset ratio 21.7%
farm marketings, 1999 ($mil)
  total $718
  crops $153
  livestock $566
principal commodities, in order by marketing
receipts, 1999
    Broilers, greenhouse, soybeans, dairy products

Federal economic activity in state
expenditures, 2000
  total ($mil) $3,959
  per capita $5,053
  defense ($mil) $425
  non-defense ($mil) $3,534
defense department, 2000
  contract awards ($mil) $95
  payroll ($mil) $329
  civilian employees (x1,000) 1.4
  military personnel (x1,000) 3.7

Fishing, 2000
catch (thousands of pounds) 6,676
value ($1,000) $6,707

Mining, 2000 ($mil; preliminary)
total non-fuel mineral production $312

Delaware 8

Construction, 1999 ($mil)
total contracts (including
   non-building) $1,036
     residential $545
     non-residential $324

Construction industries, 1997
establishments 2,257
receipts ($1,000) .... $NA
annual payroll ($1,000) .... $NA
paid employees 20,070

Manufacturing, 1997
establishments 687
value of shipments ($1,000) $13,516,996
annual payroll ($1,000) $1,505,099
paid employees 41,969

Transportation industries, 1997
establishments 857
receipts ($1,000) $3,101,647
annual payroll ($1,000) $527,204
paid employees 16,490

Wholesale trade, 1997
establishments 1,118
sales($1,000) $13,159,122
annual payroll ($1,000) $685,466
paid employees 15,805

Retail trade, 1997
establishments 5,040
sales($1,000) $8,555,393
annual payroll ($1,000) $980,593
paid employees 69,887

Finance industries
establishments, 1997 4,210
receipts ($1,000), 1997 .... $NA
annual payroll ($1,000), 1997 .... $2,176,527
paid employees, 1997 52,071
commercial banks, 2000
   number 32
     assets ($bil) $151.6
     deposits ($bil) $77.8

Service industries, 1997 (non-exempt firms only)
establishments 6,006
receipts ($1,000) $5,141,411
annual payroll ($1,000) $1,903,778
paid employees 70,912

COMMUNICATION, ENERGY & TRANSPORTATION

Communication
daily newspapers, 2000 2
households with
   telephones, 1998 .... 96.6%
   computers, 2000 .... 58.6%
   internet access, 2000 .... 50.7%

Energy
consumption, 1999
total (trillion Btu) 279
per capita (million Btu) 370
by source of production (trillion Btu)
   coal 36
   natural gas 58
   petroleum 141
   nuclear electric power .... NA
   hydroelectric power .... NA
by end-use sector (trillion Btu)
   residential 56
   commercial 45
   industrial 107
   transportation 71
electric energy, 1999
   production (billion kWh) 6.2
   net summer capability (million kW) 2.3
gas utilities, 1999
   customers 121,000
   sales (trillion Btu) 25
nuclear plants, 1999 .... na

Transportation, 2000
public road & street mileage
total 5,779
   urban 1,984
   rural 3,795
   interstate 41
vehicle miles of travel (mil) 8,240
total motor vehicle registrations 630,446
   automobiles 400,306
   motorcycles 10,952
licensed drivers 556,688
   per 1,000 driving age population 912
deaths from motor vehicle
   accidents 123

STATE SUMMARY

Capital City .... Washington, DC

Governor .... A. Williams (mayor)

Address .... DISTRICT BUILDING
WASHINGTON, DC 20002
202 727-1000

Admitted as a state .... NA

Area (square miles) 68

Population, 1980 638,333

Population, 1990 606,900

Population, 2000 572,059

Persons per square mile, 2000 .... 9,316.90

Largest city .... Washington, DC
population, 2000 572,000

Personal income per capita, 2000
(in current dollars) $37,383

Gross state product ($mil), 1999 .... $55,832

Leading industries, 1999 (by payroll)
Professional/Scientific/Technical
Health care/Social assistance
Information

Leading agricultural commodities, 1999
na

GEOGRAPHY & ENVIRONMENT

Area, 1990 (square miles)
total 68
land 61
water (includes territorial water) 7

Federally owned land, 2000 .... 23.2%

Highest point
name .... Tenleytown
elevation (feet) 410

Lowest point
name .... Potomac River
elevation (feet) .... sea level

General coastline (miles) 0

Tidal shoreline (miles) 0

Capital city .... Washington, DC
population, 2000 572,000

Largest city .... Washington, DC
population, 2000 572,000

Number of cities with over 100,000 population
1980 .... NA
1990 .... NA
2000 1

State parks and Recreation areas, 2000
area (acres) .... NA
number of visitors .... NA
revenues .... $na

Nat. forest system land, 1999 (acres) 0

National park acreage, 1984 6,900

DEMOGRAPHICS & CHARACTERISTICS OF THE POPULATION

Population
1970 756,668
1980 638,333
1990 606,900
2000 572,059
2015 (projection) 594,000
2025 (projection) 655,000

Metropolitan area population
1970 757,000
1980 638,000
2000 572,000

Non-metropolitan area population
1970 .... NA
1980 .... NA
2000 .... NA

Change in population, 1990-2000
number .... -34,841
percent .... -5.74%

Persons per square mile, 2000 .... 9,316.90

Persons by age, 2000
under 5 years 32,536
18 and over 457,067
21 and over 425,229
65 and over 69,898
85 and over 8,975

District of Columbia 2

Persons by age, 2025 (projected)
under 5 years 52,000
5 to 17 years 115,000
65 and over 92,000

Median age, 2000 .... 34.6

Race, 2000
One race
White 176,101
Black or African American 343,312
American Indian and Alaska Native 1,713
Asian Indian 2,845
Chinese 3,734
Filipino 2,228
Japanese 1,117
Korean 1,095
Vietnamese 1,903
Native Hawaiian and other Pacific Islander .. 348
Two or more races 13,446

Race, 2025 (projected)
White 239,000
Black 386,000

Persons of Hispanic origin, 2000
total Hispanic or Latino 44,953
  Mexican 5,098
  Puerto Rican 2,328
  Cuban 1,101
  Other Hispanic or Latino 36,426

Persons of Hispanic origin, 2025 (proj.) ... 80,000

Persons by sex, 2000
male 269,366
female 302,693

Marital status, 1990
males
  15 years & older 232,989
    single 118,273
    married 87,306
      separated 12,860
    widowed 8,428
    divorced 18,982
females
  15 years & older 275,245
    single 123,762
    married 88,488
      separated 16,721

widowed 35,180
divorced 27,815

Households & families, 2000
households 248,338
persons per household 2.16
  families 114,166
  persons per family 3.07
    married couples 56,631
    female householder, no husband
      present 47,032
    one person households 108,744
households with persons under 18 years .. 60,987
households with persons over 65 years 53,369

Nativity, 1990
number of persons born in state 238,728
percent of total residents 39.3%

Immigration & naturalization, 1998
immigrants admitted 2,377
persons naturalized 1,024
refugees granted resident status 188

VITAL STATISTICS & HEALTH

Births
1999
  with low birth weight 13.1%
  to teenage mothers 14.5%
  to unmarried mothers 61.7%
Birth rate, 1999 (per 1,000) 14.5
Birth rate, 2000 (per 1,000) 14.8

Abortions, 1996
total 21,000
rate (per 1,000 women age 15-44) 154.5

Deaths
1998 5,694
1999 6,076
2000 5,957

Infant deaths
1998 76
1999 96
2000 194

Average lifetime, by race, 1989-1991
total .... 67.99 years
  white .... 76.09 years
  black .... 64.44 years

Marriages
1998 2,372
1999 3,752
2000 2,798

Divorces
1998 1,096
1999 2,067
2000 1,548

Physicians, 1999
total 3,935
rate (per 1,000 persons) 7.58

Nurses, 1999
total 8,290
rate (per 1,000 persons) 15.97

Hospitals, 1998
number 12
beds (x 1,000) 3.6
average daily census (x 1,000) 2.7
patients admitted (x1,000) 140
average cost per day to hospital, 1995 .... $1,346
average cost per stay to hospital, 1995 .... $8,632

EDUCATION

*Educational attainment of all persons
25 years and older, 1990*
less than 9th grade 39,107
high school graduates 86,756
bachelor's degree 65,892
graduate or professional degree 70,393

2000
high school graduate or more 83.2%
college graduate or more 38.3%

Public school enrollment, Fall, 1998
total 71,889
Kindergarten through grade 8 56,712
grades 9 through 12 15,177

Public School Teachers, 2000
total 4,800
elementary 3,300
secondary 1,500
average salaries
elementary $47,600
secondary $46,400

*State receipts & expenditures for public
schools, 2000*
revenue receipts ($mil) $719

*State receipts & expenditures for public
schools, 2000 (continued)*
expenditures
total ($mil) $683
per capita $1,317
per pupil $9,933

*Graduating high school seniors,
public high schools, 2000 (est.)* 2,530

SAT scores, 2001
verbal 482
math 474
percent graduates taking test 56%

Institutions of higher education, 1999
total 17
public 2
private 15

*Enrollment in institutions of higher
education, Fall, 1998*
total 72,388
full-time men 21,512
full-time women 27,909
part-time men 10,020
part-time women 12,947

*Minority enrollment in institutions of higher
education, Fall, 1997*
Black, non-Hispanic 20,898
Hispanic 2,940
Asian/Pacific Islander 4,436

Earned degrees conferred, 1998
Bachelor's 7,369
First professional 2,676
Master's 7,006
Doctor's 562

SOCIAL INSURANCE & WELFARE PROGRAMS

Social Security beneficiaries & benefits, 2000
beneficiaries
total 74,000
retired and dependents 52,000
survivors 13,000
disabled & dependents 10,000
annual benefit payments ($mil)
total $579
retired and dependents $384
survivors $112
disabled & dependents $83

District of Columbia 4

Medicare, 2000
enrollment (x1,000) 76
payments ($mil) $784

Medicaid, 1998
recipients (x1,000) 166
payments ($mil) $731

Federal public aid
Temporary Assistance for Needy Families
(TANF), 2000
   Recipients (x1,000) 46
   Families (x1,000) 20
Supplemental Security Income
   total recipients, 1999 (x1,000) 20

Food Stamp Program
  participants, 2000 (x1,000) 81

HOUSING & CONSTRUCTION

Total housing units, 2000 274,845
  seasonal or recreational use 2,207
  occupied 248,338
    owner occupied 101,214
    renter occupied 147,124

New privately owned housing units uthorized, 2000
number (x1,000) 0.8
value ($mil) $54

New privately owned housing units
  started, 2000 (est.) (x1,000) 0.4

Existing home sales, 2000 (x1,000) 12.7

GOVERNMENT & ELECTIONS

State officials, 2002
  Governor (name/party/term expires)
    ANTHONY WILLIAMS (MAYOR)
      Democrat - 2003
Lt. Governor . . . .
Sec. of State . . . .
Atty. General . . . .
Chief Justice . . . .

Governorship
minimum age . . . .
length of term . . . .
number of consecutive
  terms permitted . . . .
who succeeds . . . .

State legislature
name . . . .
  upper chamber
    name . . . .
    number of members . . . .
    length of term . . . .
    party in majority, 2000 . . . .
  lower chamber
    name . . . .
    number of members . . . .
    length of term . . . .
    party in majority, 2000 . . . .

State employees March, 2000
total . . . . NA
March payroll . . . . $NA

Local governments, 1997
total 2
  county 0
  municipal 1
  township 0
  school districts 0
  special districts 1

Voting age population, November, 2000, projected
Total 411,000
  male 189,000
  female 222,000

Vote for president
2000
  Gore 172,000
  Bush 18,000
1996
  Clinton 158,000
  Dole 17,000
  Perot 4,000

Federal representation, 2002 (107th Congress)
Senators (name/party/term expires)

Representatives, total 1
  Democrats 1
  Republicans 0
  other 0

District of Columbia 5

Women holding public office, 2001
U.S. Congress 1
statewide elected office 0
state legislature ....na

Black elected officials, 1999
total 199
  US and state legislatures 52
  city/county/regional offices 192
  judicial/law enforcement ....NA
  education/school boards 5

Hispanic public officials, 2000
total 1
  state executives & legislators ....NA
  city/county/regional offices 1
  judicial/law enforcement ....NA
  education/school boards ....NA

GOVERNMENTAL FINANCE

State government revenues, 1999 ($per capita)
total revenue ....$NA
  total general revenue ....$NA
    intergovernmental revenue ....$NA
    taxes ....$NA
    current charges ....$NA
    miscellaneous ....$NA

State government expenditures, 1999 ($per capita)
total expenditure ....$NA
  total general expenditure ....$NA
    education ....$NA
    public welfare ....$NA
    health ....$NA
    hospitals ....$NA
    highways ....$NA
    police protection ....$NA
    correction ....$NA
    natural resources ....$NA
    governmental administration ....$NA
    interest on general debt ....$NA

State debt, 1999 ($per capita) ....$NA

Federal government grants to state & local government, 2000 (x$1,000)
total $2,962,504
  Dept. of Education $159,088
  Environmental Protection Agency $74,848
  Health Care Financing Admin. $638,965
  Dept. Housing & Urban Devel. $429,051
  Dept. of Labor $39,055
  Highway trust fund $130,733

CRIME, LAW ENFORCEMENT & COURTS

Crime, 2000 (all rates per 100,000 inhabitants)
total crimes 41,626
overall crime rate 7,276.5
  property crimes 33,000
    burglaries 4,745
    larcenies 21,655
    motor vehicle thefts.................. 6,600
  property crime rate 5,768.6
  violent crimes 8,626
    murders 239
    forcible rapes 251
    robberies 3,554
    aggravated assaults 4,582
  violent crime rate 1,507.9

Number of police agencies, 2000 ....na

Arrests, 2000
total ....NA
  persons under 18 years of age ....na

Prisoners under state & federal jurisdiction, 2000
total 7,456
percent change, 1999-2000 .... -13.8%
  sentenced to more than one year
    total 5,008
    rate per 100,000 residents 971

Persons under sentence of death, 4/1/2001 ...NA

State's highest court
name ....Court of Appeals
number of members 9
length of term .... 15 years
intermediate appeals court? ....no

District of Columbia 6

LABOR & INCOME

Civilian labor force, 2000

total 279,000
  men 135,000
  women 144,000
  persons 16-19 years 8,000
  white 112,000
  black 158,000

*Civilian labor force as a percent of
civilian non-institutional population, 2000*

total 67.5%
  men 70.8%
  women 64.7%
  persons 16-19 years .... NA%
  white 77.0%
  black 61.6%

Employment, 2000

total 263,000
  men 127,000
  women 136,000
  persons 16-19 years 5,000
  white 109,000
  black 145,000

Full-time/part-time labor force, 1998

full-time labor force 234,000
  working part-time for
    economic reasons 2,000
part-time labor force 33,000

Unemployment rate, 2000

total 5.8%
  men 5.8%
  women 5.7%
  persons 16-19 years 33.1%
  white 2.5%
  black 8.3%

*Unemployed by reason for unemployment
(as a percent of total unemployment), 1998*

job losers or completed temp jobs 33.3%
job leavers 8.3%
reentrants 50.0%
new entrants 8.3%

*Experienced civilian labor force, by occupation,
1998*

executive/administrative/managerial 52,000
professional/specialty 65,000
technicians & related support 12,000

sales 22,000
administrative support/clerical 40,000
service occupations 46,000
precision production/craft/repair 9,000
machine operators/assemblers .... NA
transportation/material moving 8,000
handlers/helpers/laborers 7,000
farming/forestry/fishing .... NA

Experienced civilian labor force, by industry, 1998

construction 8,000
manufacturing 6,000
transportation/communication 13,000
wholesale/retail trade 34,000
finance/real estate/insurance 12,000
services 105,000
government 69,000
agriculture .... NA

Average annual pay, 1999 .... $50,742
change in average annual pay,
  1998-1999 .... 4.7%

*Hours and earnings of production workers
on manufacturing payrolls, 2000*

average weekly hours 39.6
average hourly earnings $15.57
average weekly earnings $616.57

Labor union membership, 2000 35,900

Household income (in 2000 dollars)
median household income,
  three year average, 1998-2000 .... $38,752

Poverty
persons below poverty level,
  three year average, 1998-2000 .... 17.3%

Personal income ($per capita)
2000 (prelim.)
  in current dollars $37,383
  in constant (1996) dollars $34,820
1999 (preliminary)
  in current dollars $38,228
  in constant (1996) dollars $36,554

Federal income tax returns, 1999
returns filed 273,916
adjusted gross income ($1,000) $14,731,132
total income tax paid ($1,000) $2,630,240

ECONOMY, BUSINESS, INDUSTRY & AGRICULTURE

Fortune 500 companies, 2000 2

Business incorporations, 1998
total 1,353
change, 1997-1998 .... -7.5%

Business failures, 1998 75

Business firm ownership, 1997
Hispanic owned firms 2,153
Black owned firms 10,909
women owned firms 13,979
Asian & Pacific Islander owned firms 2,422
American Indian & Alaska
  native owned firms 66

Shopping centers, 2000 87

Gross state product, 1999 ($mil)
total $55,832
  agriculture services, forestry, fisheries $17
  mining $21
  construction $468
  manufacturing--durable goods $252
  manufacturing--nondurable goods $1,048
  transportation, communication &
    public utilities $2,853
  wholesale trade $757
  retail trade $1,577
  finance/real estate/insurance $7,294
  services $20,512
  federal, state & local government $21,032

Establishments, by major industry group, 1999
total 19,469
  forestry, fishing & agriculture 4
  mining 3
  construction 315
  manufacturing 186
  transportation & warehousing 212
  wholesale trade 377
  retail trade 1,935
  finance & insurance 889
  professional/scientific/technical 4,170
  health care/social assistance 2,016
  information 685
  accommodation/food services 1,639

Payroll, by major industry group, 1999
total ($1,000) $18,287,742
  forestry, fishing & agriculture .... $NA
  mining .... $NA
  construction $304,785
  manufacturing $92,895
  transportation & warehousing $101,967
  wholesale trade $293,541
  retail trade $396,477
  finance & insurance $1,367,657
  professional/scientific/technical $5,326,746
  health care/social assistance $2,112,843
  information $1,737,383
  accommodation/food services $805,626

Agriculture
number of farms, 2000 .... NA
farm acreage, 2000 .... NA
acres per farm, 2000 .... NA
value of farms, 1997 ($mil) .... $NA
farm income, 1999 ($mil)
  net farm income .... $NA
  debt/asset ratio .... NA%
farm marketings, 1999 ($mil)
  total .... $NA
  crops .... $NA
  livestock .... $NA
principal commodities, in order by marketing
receipts, 1999
    NA

Federal economic activity in state
expenditures, 2000
  total ($mil) $28,254
  per capita $49,391
  defense ($mil) $2,521
  non-defense ($mil) $25,733
defense department, 2000
  contract awards ($mil) $1,899
  payroll ($mil) $1,218
  civilian employees (x1,000) 12.6
  military personnel (x1,000) 13

Fishing, 2000
catch (thousands of pounds) .... NA
value ($1,000) .... $NA

Mining, 2000 ($mil; preliminary)
total non-fuel mineral production .... $na

District of Columbia 8

Construction, 1999 ($mil)
total contracts (including
    non-building) $1,203
       residential $168
       non-residential $785

Construction industries, 1997
establishments 271
receipts ($1,000) .... $NA
annual payroll ($1,000) .... $NA
paid employees .... NA

Manufacturing, 1997
establishments 351
value of shipments ($1,000) $2,443,911
annual payroll ($1,000) $569,906
paid employees 11,906

Transportation industries, 1997
establishments 710
receipts ($1,000) $5,343,223
annual payroll ($1,000) $974,030
paid employees 18,238

Wholesale trade, 1997
establishments 394
sales($1,000) .... $NA
annual payroll ($1,000) .... $NA
paid employees .... NA

Retail trade, 1997
establishments 3,645
sales($1,000) .... $NA
annual payroll ($1,000) .... $NA
paid employees .... NA

Finance industries
establishments, 1997 2,161
receipts ($1,000), 1997 .... $NA
annual payroll ($1,000), 1997 .... $1,699,162
paid employees, 1997 26,621
commercial banks, 2000
   number 6
     assets ($bil) $0.8
     deposits ($bil) $0.6

Service industries, 1997 (non-exempt firms only)
establishments 7,765
receipts ($1,000) $15,305,259
annual payroll ($1,000) $5,779,482
paid employees 130,661

COMMUNICATION, ENERGY & TRANSPORTATION

Communication
daily newspapers, 2000 2
households with
   telephones, 1998 .... 91.0%
   computers, 2000 .... 48.8%
   internet access, 2000 .... 39.6%

Energy
consumption, 1999
total (trillion Btu) 170
per capita (million Btu) 327
by source of production (trillion Btu)
   coal .... NA
   natural gas 33
   petroleum 34
   nuclear electric power .... NA
   hydroelectric power .... NA
by end-use sector (trillion Btu)
   residential 34
   commercial 106
   industrial 4
   transportation 27
electric energy, 1999
   production (billion kWh) ....
   net summer capability (million kW) 0.8
gas utilities, 1999
   customers 139,000
   sales (trillion Btu) 22
nuclear plants, 1999 .... na

Transportation, 2000
public road & street mileage
total 1,425
   urban 1,425
   rural 0
   interstate 13
vehicle miles of travel (mil) 3,498
total motor vehicle registrations 242,081
   automobiles 200,288
   motorcycles 1,127
licensed drivers 348,216
   per 1,000 driving age population 743
deaths from motor vehicle
   accidents 49

Florida 1

STATE SUMMARY

Capital City . . . . .Tallahassee

Governor .J.E. "Jeb" Bush

Address . . . . . . .THE CAPITOL
TALLAHASSEE, FL 32301
850 488-4441

Admitted as a state 1845

Area (square miles) 65,758

Population, 1980 .9,746,324

Population, 1990 12,937,926

Population, 2000 15,982,378

Persons per square mile, 2000 . . . . 296.3

Largest city . . . . Jacksonville
population, 2000 736,000

Personal income per capita, 2000
(in current dollars) $28,145

Gross state product ($mil), 1999 . . . . . . $442,895

Leading industries, 1999 (by payroll)
Health care/Social assistance
Retail trade
Professional/Scientific/Technical

Leading agricultural commodities, 1999
Oranges, greenhouse, sugar cane, dairy products

GEOGRAPHY & ENVIRONMENT

Area, 1990 (square miles)
total 65,758
land 53,997
water (includes territorial water) 11,761

Federally owned land, 2000 . . . . 13.2%

Highest point
name . . . . . Sec. 30 TGN R20W (Walton County)
elevation (feet) 345

Lowest point
name . . . . .Atlantic Ocean
elevation (feet) . . . . .sea level

General coastline (miles) 1,650

Tidal shoreline (miles) 8,426

Capital city . . . . .Tallahassee
population, 2000 151,000

Largest city . . . . Jacksonville
population, 2000 736,000

Number of cities with over 100,000 population
1980 9
1990 9
2000 13

State parks and Recreation areas, 2000
area (acres) 547,000
number of visitors 16,672,000
revenues $28,577,000

Nat'l forest system land, 1999 (acres) . . .1,147,000

National park acreage, 1984 2,145,100

DEMOGRAPHICS & CHARACTERISTICS OF THE POPULATION

Population
1970 6,791,418
1980 9,746,324
1990 12,937,926
2000 15,982,378
2015 (projection) 18,497,000
2025 (projection) 20,710,000

Metropolitan area population
1970 6,213,000
1980 8,885,000
2000 14,837,000

Non-metropolitan area population
1970 578,000
1980 862,000
2000 1,145,000

Change in population, 1990-2000
number 3,044,452
percent 23.53%

Persons per square mile, 2000 . . . . 296.3

Persons by age, 2000
under 5 years 945,823
18 and over 12,336,038
21 and over 11,736,378
65 and over 2,807,597
85 and over 331,287

Florida 2

Persons by age, 2025 (projected)
under 5 years 1,086,000
5 to 17 years 2,894,000
65 and over 5,453,000

Median age, 2000 .... 38.7

Race, 2000
One race
White 12,465,029
Black or African American 2,335,505
American Indian and Alaska Native 53,541
Asian Indian 70,740
Chinese 46,368
Filipino 54,310
Japanese 10,897
Korean 19,139
Vietnamese 33,190
Native Hawaiian and other Pacific Islander 8,625
Two or more races 376,315

Race, 2025 (projected)
White 16,541,000
Black 3,556,000

Persons of Hispanic origin, 2000
total Hispanic or Latino 2,682,715
   Mexican 363,925
   Puerto Rican 482,027
   Cuban 833,120
   Other Hispanic or Latino 1,003,643

Persons of Hispanic origin, 2025 (proj.) . 4,944,000

Persons by sex, 2000
male 7,797,715
female 8,184,663

Marital status, 1990
males
   15 years & older 5,027,000
      single 1,336,469
      married 3,082,684
         separated 104,624
      widowed 156,680
      divorced 451,167
females
   15 years & older 5,498,857
      single 1,046,893
      married 3,084,722
         separated 138,290

widowed 758,011
divorced 609,231

Households & families, 2000
households 6,337,929
persons per household 2.46
   families 4,210,760
   persons per family 2.98
      married couples 3,192,266
      female householder, no husband
         present 759,000
      one person households 1,687,303
households with persons under 18 years 1,986,554
households with persons over 65 years . . 1,943,478

Nativity, 1990
number of persons born in state 3,940,240
percent of total residents 30.5%

Immigration & naturalization, 1998
immigrants admitted 59,965
persons naturalized 30,926
refugees granted resident status 14,093

VITAL STATISTICS & HEALTH

Births
1999
   with low birth weight 8.2%
   to teenage mothers 13.0%
   to unmarried mothers 37.5%
Birth rate, 1999 (per 1,000) 13.0
Birth rate, 2000 (per 1,000) 13.3

Abortions, 1996
total 94,000
rate (per 1,000 women age 15-44) 32.0

Deaths
1998 158,339
1999 163,224
2000 164,401

Infant deaths
1998 1,467
1999 1,447
2000 1,458

Average lifetime, by race, 1989-1991
total .... 75.84 years
   white .... 76.82 years
   black .... 68.77 years

Marriages
1998 139,463
1999 136,889
2000 141,924

Divorces
1998 80,136
1999 81,674
2000 81,861

Physicians, 1999
total 36,760
rate (per 1,000 persons) 2.43

Nurses, 1999
total 131,800
rate (per 1,000 persons) 8.72

Hospitals, 1998
number 204
beds (x 1,000) 49.2
average daily census (x 1,000) 29.7
patients admitted (x1,000) 1,947
average cost per day to hospital, 1995 .... $1,004
average cost per stay to hospital, 1995 .... $6,040

EDUCATION

*Educational attainment of all persons
25 years and older, 1990*
  less than 9th grade 842,811
  high school graduates 2,679,285
  bachelor's degree 1,062,649
  graduate or professional degree 561,756

2000
  high school graduate or more 84.0%
  college graduate or more 22.8%

Public school enrollment, Fall, 1998
total 2,337,633
  Kindergarten through grade 8 1,704,024
  grades 9 through 12 633,609

Public School Teachers, 2000
total 132,600
  elementary 67,700
  secondary 64,900
average salaries
  elementary $36,700
  secondary $36,700

*State receipts & expenditures for public
schools, 2000*
revenue receipts ($mil) $19,320

*State receipts & expenditures for public
schools, 2000 (continued)*
expenditures
  total ($mil) $17,471
  per capita $1,156
  per pupil $6,536

*Graduating high school seniors,
public high schools, 2000 (est.)* 99,930

SAT scores, 2001
verbal 498
math 499
percent graduates taking test 54%

Institutions of higher education, 1999
total 147
  public 39
  private 108

*Enrollment in institutions of higher
education, Fall, 1998*
total 661,312
full-time men 152,783
full-time women 183,116
part-time men 132,981
part-time women 192,432

*Minority enrollment in institutions of higher
education, Fall, 1997*
Black, non-Hispanic 93,337
Hispanic 99,092
Asian/Pacific Islander 20,351

Earned degrees conferred, 1998
Bachelor's 48,463
First professional 2,762
Master's 16,677
Doctor's 1,881

SOCIAL INSURANCE &
WELFARE PROGRAMS

Social Security beneficiaries & benefits, 2000
beneficiaries
total 3,193,000
  retired and dependents 2,381,000
  survivors 414,000
  disabled & dependents 398,000
annual benefit payments ($mil)
total $28,700
  retired and dependents $20,622
  survivors $4,751
  disabled & dependents $3,328

Florida 4

Medicare, 2000
enrollment (x1,000) 2,771
payments ($mil) $19,221

Medicaid, 1998
recipients (x1,000) 1,905
payments ($mil) $5,686

Federal public aid
Temporary Assistance for Needy Families
(TANF), 2000
   Recipients (x1,000) 151
   Families (x1,000) 67
Supplemental Security Income
   total recipients, 1999 (x1,000) 367

Food Stamp Program
   participants, 2000 (x1,000) 882

HOUSING & CONSTRUCTION

Total housing units, 2000 7,302,947
   seasonal or recreational use 482,944
   occupied 6,337,929
      owner occupied 4,441,799
      renter occupied 1,896,130

New privately owned housing units uthorized, 2000
number (x1,000) 155.3
value ($mil) $17,462

New privately owned housing units
   started, 2000 (est.) (x1,000) 148.1

Existing home sales, 2000 (x1,000) 505.4

GOVERNMENT & ELECTIONS

State officials, 2002
   Governor (name/party/term expires)
         J.E. "JEB" BUSH
         Republican - 2002
Lt. Governor . . . . Frank Brogan
Sec. of State . . . . Katherine Harris
Atty. General . . . . Robert Butterworth
Chief Justice . . . . Charles Wells

Governorship
minimum age 30
length of term . . . . 4 years
number of consecutive
   terms permitted 2
who succeeds . . . . Lt. Governor

State legislature
name . . . . Legislature
  upper chamber
     name . . . . Senate
     number of members 40
     length of term . . . . 4 years
     party in majority, 2000 . . . . Republican
  lower chamber
     name . . . . House of Representatives
     number of members 120
     length of term . . . . 2 years
     party in majority, 2000 . . . . Republican

State employees March, 2000
total 207,430
March payroll $568,501,104

Local governments, 1997
total 1,081
   county 66
   municipal 394
   township 0
   school districts 95
   special districts 526

Voting age population, November, 2000, projected
Total 11,774,000
   male 5,618,000
   female 6,155,000

Vote for president
2000
   Gore 2,912,000
   Bush 2,913,000
1996
   Clinton 2,546,000
   Dole 2,243,000
   Perot 484,000

Federal representation, 2002 (107th Congress)
Senators (name/party/term expires)

         BILL NELSON
         Democrat - 2007
         BOB GRAHAM
         Democrat - 2005

Representatives, total 23
   Democrats 8
   Republicans 15
   other 0

Women holding public office, 2001
U.S. Congress 4
statewide elected office 1
state legislature 38

Black elected officials, 1999
total 216
US and state legislatures 23
city/county/regional offices 146
judicial/law enforcement 33
education/school boards 14

Hispanic public officials, 2000
total 90
state executives & legislators 17
city/county/regional offices 57
judicial/law enforcement 11
education/school boards 5

GOVERNMENTAL FINANCE

State government revenues, 1999 ($per capita)
total revenue $3,256.43
total general revenue $2,595.58
intergovernmental revenue $601.59
taxes $1,574.89
current charges $144.16
miscellaneous $274.94

State government expenditures, 1999 ($per capita)
total expenditure $2,809.75
total general expenditure $2,629.50
education $891.72
public welfare $562.43
health $154.11
hospitals $36.53
highways $236.60
police protection $22.69
correction $139.46
natural resources $83.33
governmental administration $117.02
interest on general debt $68.20

State debt, 1999 ($per capita) $1,179.60

Federal government grants to state & local government, 2000 (x$1,000)
total $11,675,656
Dept. of Education $1,154,177
Environmental Protection Agency $88,232
Health Care Financing Admin. $4,713,191
Dept. Housing & Urban Devel. $1,117,059
Dept. of Labor $182,334
Highway trust fund $1,103,923

CRIME, LAW ENFORCEMENT & COURTS

Crime, 2000 (all rates per 100,000 inhabitants)
total crimes 910,154
overall crime rate 5,694.7
property crimes 780,377
burglaries 172,898
larcenies 518,298
motor vehicle thefts 89,181
property crime rate 4,882.7
violent crimes 129,777
murders 903
forcible rapes 7,057
robberies 31,809
aggravated assaults 90,008
violent crime rate 812.0

Number of police agencies, 2000 517

Arrests, 2000
total 881,709
persons under 18 years of age 124,845

Prisoners under state & federal jurisdiction, 2000
total 71,319
percent change, 1999-2000 . . . . 2.5%
sentenced to more than one year
total 71,318
rate per 100,000 residents 462

Persons under sentence of death, 4/1/2001 . . . 383

State's highest court
name . . . . Supreme Court
number of members 7
length of term . . . . 6 years
intermediate appeals court? . . . . yes

Florida 6

LABOR & INCOME

Civilian labor force, 2000
total 7,490,000
  men 4,029,000
  women 3,461,000
  persons 16-19 years 414,000
  white 6,239,000
  black 1,067,000

Civilian labor force as a percent of
civilian non-institutional population, 2000
total 62.6%
  men 70.1%
  women 55.7%
  persons 16-19 years .... NA%
  white 61.4%
  black 69.4%

Employment, 2000
total 7,221,000
  men 3,897,000
  women 3,324,000
  persons 16-19 years 360,000
  white 6,045,000
  black 1,001,000

Full-time/part-time labor force, 1998
full-time labor force 6,120,000
  working part-time for
    economic reasons 68,000
part-time labor force 1,108,000

Unemployment rate, 2000
total 3.6%
  men 3.3%
  women 4.0%
  persons 16-19 years 12.9%
  white 3.1%
  black 6.3%

Unemployed by reason for unemployment
(as a percent of total unemployment), 1998
job losers or completed temp jobs 48.4%
job leavers 11.6%
reentrants 33.2%
new entrants 6.8%

Experienced civilian labor force, by occupation,
1998
executive/administrative/managerial ... 1,033,000
professional/specialty 975,000
technicians & related support 240,000

sales 1,021,000
administrative support/clerical 1,059,000
service occupations 1,114,000
precision production/craft/repair 784,000
machine operators/assemblers 232,000
transportation/material moving 279,000
handlers/helpers/laborers 284,000
farming/forestry/fishing 185,000

Experienced civilian labor force, by industry, 1998
construction 488,000
manufacturing 608,000
transportation/communication 475,000
wholesale/retail trade 1,646,000
finance/real estate/insurance 536,000
services 1,933,000
government 886,000
agriculture 164,000

Average annual pay, 1999 .... $28,911
change in average annual pay,
  1998-1999 .... 2.6%

Hours and earnings of production workers
on manufacturing payrolls, 2000
average weekly hours 41.9
average hourly earnings $12.28
average weekly earnings $514.53

Labor union membership, 2000 433,600

Household income (in 2000 dollars)
median household income,
  three year average, 1998-2000 .... $37,998

Poverty
persons below poverty level,
  three year average, 1998-2000 .... 12.1%

Personal income ($per capita)
2000 (prelim.)
  in current dollars $28,145
  in constant (1996) dollars $26,216
1999 (preliminary)
  in current dollars $28,023
  in constant (1996) dollars $26,796

Federal income tax returns, 1999
returns filed 7,263,531
adjusted gross income ($1,000) $320,842,538
total income tax paid ($1,000) $52,731,941

ECONOMY, BUSINESS, INDUSTRY & AGRICULTURE

Fortune 500 companies, 2000 12

Business incorporations, 1998
total 109,355
change, 1997-1998 .... 1.0%

Business failures, 1998 2,047

Business firm ownership, 1997
Hispanic owned firms 193,902
Black owned firms 59,732
women owned firms 337,811
Asian & Pacific Islander owned firms 33,769
American Indian & Alaska
  native owned firms 10,546

Shopping centers, 2000 3,452

Gross state product, 1999 ($mil)
total $442,895
  agriculture services, forestry, fisheries .. $7,838
  mining $878
  construction $22,406
  manufacturing--durable goods $18,052
  manufacturing--nondurable goods $13,664
  transportation, communication &
    public utilities $38,082
  wholesale trade $33,880
  retail trade $50,610
  finance/real estate/insurance $95,440
  services $108,007
  federal, state & local government $54,039

Establishments, by major industry group, 1999
total 424,089
  forestry, fishing & agriculture 1,201
  mining 234
  construction 38,320
  manufacturing 15,601
  transportation & warehousing 10,534
  wholesale trade 30,816
  retail trade 66,928
  finance & insurance 26,613
  professional/scientific/technical 49,243
  health care/social assistance 40,134
  information 6,786
  accommodation/food services 28,333

Payroll, by major industry group, 1999
total ($1,000) $160,961,646
  forestry, fishing & agriculture $257,222
  mining $268,163
  construction $10,640,995
  manufacturing $13,795,810
  transportation & warehousing $6,101,453
  wholesale trade $11,223,836
  retail trade $16,958,967
  finance & insurance $13,271,178
  professional/scientific/technical $14,439,087
  health care/social assistance $22,045,107
  information $6,614,242
  accommodation/food services $7,382,412

Agriculture
number of farms, 2000 44,000
farm acreage, 2000 10,000,000
acres per farm, 2000 234
value of farms, 1997 ($mil) $23,690
farm income, 1999 ($mil)
  net farm income $2,815
  debt/asset ratio 17.5%
farm marketings, 1999 ($mil)
total $7,066
  crops $5,702
  livestock $1,363
principal commodities, in order by marketing
receipts, 1999
  Oranges, greenhouse, sugar cane, dairy products

Federal economic activity in state
expenditures, 2000
  total ($mil) $92,776
  per capita $5,805
  defense ($mil) $13,460
  non-defense ($mil) $79,317
defense department, 2000
  contract awards ($mil) $6,470
  payroll ($mil) $6,887
  civilian employees (x1,000) 26.4
  military personnel (x1,000) 60.9

Fishing, 2000
catch (thousands of pounds) 120,022
value ($1,000) $212,700

Mining, 2000 ($mil; preliminary)
total non-fuel mineral production $1,920

Florida 8

Construction, 1999 ($mil)
total contracts (including
    non-building) $32,243
      residential $16,866
      non-residential $11,770

Construction industries, 1997
establishments 35,231
receipts ($1,000) .... $NA
annual payroll ($1,000) $8,531,072
paid employees .... NA

Manufacturing, 1997
establishments 16,304
value of shipments ($1,000) $82,022,637
annual payroll ($1,000) $14,199,437
paid employees 463,791

Transportation industries, 1997
establishments 16,797
receipts ($1,000) $55,654,962
annual payroll ($1,000) $9,950,698
paid employees 300,206

Wholesale trade, 1997
establishments 34,936
sales($1,000) $195,495,814
annual payroll ($1,000) $10,641,150
paid employees 333,153

Retail trade, 1997
establishments 89,744
sales($1,000) $158,693,907
annual payroll ($1,000) $17,477,577
paid employees 1,274,403

Finance industries
establishments, 1997 45,027
receipts ($1,000), 1997 .... $NA
annual payroll ($1,000), 1997 .... $NA
paid employees, 1997 .... NA
commercial banks, 2000
    number 265
      assets ($bil) $58.9
      deposits ($bil) $47.7

Service industries, 1997 (non-exempt firms only)
establishments 138,956
receipts ($1,000) $113,230,011
annual payroll ($1,000) $42,934,184
paid employees 1,745,657

COMMUNICATION, ENERGY & TRANSPORTATION

Communication
daily newspapers, 2000 42
households with
    telephones, 1998 .... 92.3%
    computers, 2000 .... 50.1%
    internet access, 2000 .... 43.2%

Energy
consumption, 1999
total (trillion Btu) 3,853
per capita (million Btu) 255
by source of production (trillion Btu)
    coal 672
    natural gas 542
    petroleum 1,912
    nuclear electric power 335
    hydroelectric power 2
by end-use sector (trillion Btu)
    residential 1,018
    commercial 810
    industrial 680
    transportation 1,346
electric energy, 1999
    production (billion kWh) 166.9
    net summer capability (million kW) 36.5
gas utilities, 1999
    customers 633,000
    sales (trillion Btu) 67
nuclear plants, 1999 5

Transportation, 2000
public road & street mileage
total 116,649
    urban 49,227
    rural 67,422
    interstate 1,471
vehicle miles of travel (mil) 152,136
total motor vehicle registrations 11,781,010
    automobiles 7,352,705
    motorcycles 249,276
licensed drivers 12,853,428
    per 1,000 driving age population 1,009
deaths from motor vehicle
    accidents 2,999

Georgia 1

STATE SUMMARY

Capital City .... Atlanta

Governor .... Roy Barnes

Address .... STATE CAPITOL
ATLANTA, GA 30334
404 656-2881

Admitted as a state 1788

Area (square miles) 59,441

Population, 1980 5,463,105

Population, 1990 6,478,216

Population, 2000 8,186,453

Persons per square mile, 2000 .... 141.3

Largest city .... Atlanta
population, 2000 416,000

Personal income per capita, 2000
(in current dollars) $27,940

Gross state product ($mil), 1999 ...... $275,719

Leading industries, 1999 (by payroll)
Manufacturing
Health care/Social assistance
Professional/Scientific/Technical

Leading agricultural commodities, 1999
Broilers, cotton, peanuts, chicken eggs

GEOGRAPHY & ENVIRONMENT

Area, 1990 (square miles)
total 59,441
land 57,919
water (includes territorial water) 1,522

Federally owned land, 2000 .... 5.4%

Highest point
name .... Brasstown Bald
elevation (feet) 4,784

Lowest point
name .... Atlantic Ocean
elevation (feet) .... sea level

General coastline (miles) 100

Tidal shoreline (miles) 2,344

Capital city .... Atlanta
population, 2000 416,000

Largest city .... Atlanta
population, 2000 416,000

Number of cities with over 100,000 population
1980 4
1990 4
2000 5

State parks and Recreation areas, 2000
area (acres) 76,000
number of visitors 16,124,000
revenues $18,172,000

Natl. forest system land, 1999 (acres) 865,000

National park acreage, 1984 40,100

DEMOGRAPHICS & CHARACTERISTICS OF THE POPULATION

Population
1970 4,587,930
1980 5,463,105
1990 6,478,216
2000 8,186,453
2015 (projection) 9,200,000
2025 (projection) 9,869,000

Metropolitan area population
1970 2,807,000
1980 3,403,000
2000 5,667,000

Non-metropolitan area population
1970 1,781,000
1980 2,060,000
2000 2,520,000

Change in population, 1990-2000
number 1,708,237
percent 26.37%

Persons per square mile, 2000 .... 141.3

Persons by age, 2000
under 5 years 595,150
18 and over 6,017,219
21 and over 5,646,535
65 and over 785,275
85 and over 87,857

Georgia 2

Persons by age, 2025 (projected)
under 5 years 628,000
5 to 17 years 1,700,000
65 and over 1,668,000

Median age, 2000 .... 33.4

Race, 2000
One race
White 5,327,281
Black or African American 2,349,542
American Indian and Alaska Native 21,737
Asian Indian 46,132
Chinese 27,446
Filipino 11,036
Japanese 7,242
Korean 28,745
Vietnamese 29,016
Native Hawaiian and other Pacific Islander 4,246
Two or more races 114,188

Race, 2025 (projected)
White 6,282,000
Black 3,322,000

Persons of Hispanic origin, 2000
total Hispanic or Latino 435,227
Mexican 275,288
Puerto Rican 35,532
Cuban 12,536
Other Hispanic or Latino 111,871

Persons of Hispanic origin, 2025 (proj.) .. 346,000

Persons by sex, 2000
male 4,027,113
female 4,159,340

Marital status, 1990
males
15 years & older 2,404,921
single 716,125
married 1,439,894
separated 54,170
widowed 52,429
divorced 196,473
females
15 years & older 2,627,194
single 601,461
married 1,447,597
separated 81,530

widowed 306,707
divorced 271,429

Households & families, 2000
households 3,006,369
persons per household 2.65
families 2,111,647
persons per family 3.14
married couples 1,548,800
female householder, no husband
present 435,410
one person households 710,523
households with persons under 18 years 1,174,114
households with persons over 65 years ... 563,830

Nativity, 1990
number of persons born in state 4,179,861
percent of total residents 64.5%

Immigration & naturalization, 1998
immigrants admitted 10,445
persons naturalized 6,274
refugees granted resident status 769

VITAL STATISTICS & HEALTH
Births
1999
with low birth weight 8.7%
to teenage mothers 16.3%
to unmarried mothers 36.6%
Birth rate, 1999 (per 1,000) 16.3
Birth rate, 2000 (per 1,000) 16.7

Abortions, 1996
total 37,000
rate (per 1,000 women age 15-44) 21.1

Deaths
1998 60,788
1999 62,028
2000 63,980

Infant deaths
1998 1,038
1999 1,058
2000 1,121

Average lifetime, by race, 1989-1991
total .... 73.61 years
white .... 75.24 years
black .... 68.79 years

Marriages
1998 59,763
1999 62,642
2000 56,031

Divorces
1998 35,753
1999 34,227
2000 30,734

Physicians, 1999
total 16,470
rate (per 1,000 persons) 2.11

Nurses, 1999
total 56,680
rate (per 1,000 persons) 7.28

Hospitals, 1998
number 156
beds (x 1,000) 25.2
average daily census (x 1,000) 15.0
patients admitted (x1,000) 822
average cost per day to hospital, 1995 ...... $836
average cost per stay to hospital, 1995 .... $5,618

EDUCATION

*Educational attainment of all persons
25 years and older, 1990*
less than 9th grade 483,755
high school graduates 1,192,935
bachelor's degree 519,613
graduate or professional degree 257,545

2000
high school graduate or more 82.6%
college graduate or more 23.1%

Public school enrollment, Fall, 1998
total 1,401,291
Kindergarten through grade 8 1,029,386
grades 9 through 12 371,905

Public School Teachers, 2000
total 90,700
elementary 53,400
secondary 37,300
average salaries
elementary $40,400
secondary $41,800

*State receipts & expenditures for public
schools, 2000*
revenue receipts ($mil) $10,070

*State receipts & expenditures for public
schools, 2000 (continued)*
expenditures
total ($mil) $10,176
per capita $1,307
per pupil $6,387

*Graduating high school seniors,
public high schools, 2000 (est.)* 66,635

SAT scores, 2001
verbal 491
math 489
percent graduates taking test 63%

Institutions of higher education, 1999
total 103
public 54
private 49

*Enrollment in institutions of higher
education, Fall, 1998*
total 303,685
full-time men 90,497
full-time women 111,299
part-time men 40,415
part-time women 61,474

*Minority enrollment in institutions of higher
education, Fall, 1997*
Black, non-Hispanic 78,736
Hispanic 5,051
Asian/Pacific Islander 9,294

Earned degrees conferred, 1998
Bachelor's 29,408
First professional 2,489
Master's 10,671
Doctor's 1,084

SOCIAL INSURANCE &
WELFARE PROGRAMS

Social Security beneficiaries & benefits, 2000
beneficiaries
total 1,106,000
retired and dependents 712,000
survivors 186,000
disabled & dependents 209,000
annual benefit payments ($mil)
total $9,503
retired and dependents $5,947
survivors $1,872
disabled & dependents $1,683

Georgia 4

Medicare, 2000
enrollment (x1,000) 898
payments ($mil) $4,111

Medicaid, 1998
recipients (x1,000) 1,222
payments ($mil) $3,012

Federal public aid
Temporary Assistance for Needy Families
(TANF), 2000
    Recipients (x1,000) 140
    Families (x1,000) 53
Supplemental Security Income
    total recipients, 1999 (x1,000) 197

Food Stamp Program
    participants, 2000 (x1,000) 559

HOUSING & CONSTRUCTION

Total housing units, 2000 3,281,737
    seasonal or recreational use 50,064
    occupied 3,006,369
      owner occupied 2,029,154
      renter occupied 977,215

New privately owned housing units uthorized, 2000
number (x1,000) 91.8
value ($mil) $8,722

New privately owned housing units
started, 2000 (est.) (x1,000) 81.5

Existing home sales, 2000 (x1,000) 144.5

GOVERNMENT & ELECTIONS

State officials, 2002
  Governor (name/party/term expires)
        ROY BARNES
       Democrat - 2002
Lt. Governor . . . . Mark Taylor
Sec. of State . . . . Cathy Cox
Atty. General . . . . Thurbert Baker
Chief Justice . . . . Robert Benham

Governorship
minimum age 30
length of term . . . . 4 years
number of consecutive
    terms permitted 2
who succeeds . . . . Lt. Governor

State legislature
name . . . . General Assembly
  upper chamber
    name . . . . Senate
    number of members 56
    length of term . . . . 2 years
    party in majority, 2000 . . . . Democratic
lower chamber
    name . . . . House of Representatives
    number of members 180
    length of term . . . . 2 years
    party in majority, 2000 . . . . Democratic

State employees March, 2000
total 142,467
March payroll $339,147,822

Local governments, 1997
total 1,344
  county 156
  municipal 535
  township 0
  school districts 180
  special districts 473

Voting age population, November, 2000, projected
Total 5,893,000
  male 2,818,000
  female 3,075,000

Vote for president
2000
  Gore 1,116,000
  Bush 1,420,000
1996
  Clinton 1,054,000
  Dole 1,081,000
  Perot 146,000

Federal representation, 2002 (107th Congress)
Senators (name/party/term expires)

        MAX CLELAND
       Democrat - 2003
        ZELL MILLER
       Democrat - 2005

Representatives, total 11
  Democrats 3
  Republicans 8
  other 0

Women holding public office, 2001
U.S. Congress 1
statewide elected office 2
state legislature 49

Black elected officials, 1999
total 584
  US and state legislatures 48
  city/county/regional offices 394
  judicial/law enforcement 40
  education/school boards 102

Hispanic public officials, 2000
total 3
  state executives & legislators .... NA
  city/county/regional offices 3
  judicial/law enforcement .... NA
  education/school boards .... NA

GOVERNMENTAL FINANCE

State government revenues, 1999 ($per capita)
total revenue $3,548.75
  total general revenue $2,753.56
    intergovernmental revenue $753.80
    taxes $1,600.08
    current charges $213.85
    miscellaneous $185.83

State government expenditures, 1999 ($per capita)
total expenditure $2,979.25
  total general expenditure $2,770.69
    education $1,271.74
    public welfare $620.63
    health $96.42
    hospitals $85.34
    highways $202.16
    police protection $21.71
    correction $120.73
    natural resources $52.96
    governmental administration $76.67
    interest on general debt $50.25

State debt, 1999 ($per capita) $804.91

Federal government grants to state & local government, 2000 (x$1,000)
total $7,192,114
  Dept. of Education $597,069
  Environmental Protection Agency $55,045
  Health Care Financing Admin. $2,706,371
  Dept. Housing & Urban Devel. $858,430
  Dept. of Labor $138,694
  Highway trust fund $710,134

CRIME, LAW ENFORCEMENT & COURTS

Crime, 2000 (all rates per 100,000 inhabitants)
total crimes 388,949
overall crime rate 4,751.1
  property crimes 347,630
    burglaries 68,488
    larcenies 240,440
    motor vehicle thefts 38,702
  property crime rate 4,246.4
  violent crimes 41,319
    murders 651
    forcible rapes 1,968
    robberies 13,250
    aggravated assaults 25,450
  violent crime rate 504.7

Number of police agencies, 2000 267

Arrests, 2000
total 250,502
  persons under 18 years of age 28,235

Prisoners under state & federal jurisdiction, 2000
total 44,232
percent change, 1999-2000 .... 5.1%
  sentenced to more than one year
    total 44,141
    rate per 100,000 residents 550

Persons under sentence of death, 4/1/2001 ... 132

State's highest court
name .... Supreme Court
number of members 7
length of term .... 6 years
intermediate appeals court? .... yes

Georgia 6

LABOR & INCOME

Civilian labor force, 2000

total	4,173,000
men	2,180,000
women	1,993,000
persons 16-19 years	233,000
white	2,766,000
black	1,334,000

Civilian labor force as a percent of civilian non-institutional population, 2000

total	69.9%
men	77.4%
women	63.3%
persons 16-19 years	NA%
white	69.9%
black	69.6%

Employment, 2000

total	4,019,000
men	2,109,000
women	1,910,000
persons 16-19 years	210,000
white	2,698,000
black	1,249,000

Full-time/part-time labor force, 1998

full-time labor force	3,429,000
working part-time for economic reasons	42,000
part-time labor force	592,000

Unemployment rate, 2000

total	3.7%
men	3.3%
women	4.2%
persons 16-19 years	9.7%
white	2.5%
black	6.4%

Unemployed by reason for unemployment (as a percent of total unemployment), 1998

job losers or completed temp jobs	41.4%
job leavers	14.2%
reentrants	33.1%
new entrants	11.2%

Experienced civilian labor force, by occupation, 1998

executive/administrative/managerial	606,000
professional/specialty	506,000
technicians & related support	114,000
sales	470,000
administrative support/clerical	544,000
service occupations	487,000
precision production/craft/repair	460,000
machine operators/assemblers	337,000
transportation/material moving	215,000
handlers/helpers/laborers	177,000
farming/forestry/fishing	86,000

Experienced civilian labor force, by industry, 1998

construction	221,000
manufacturing	738,000
transportation/communication	312,000
wholesale/retail trade	746,000
finance/real estate/insurance	214,000
services	831,000
government	581,000
agriculture	85,000

Average annual pay, 1999	$32,339
change in average annual pay, 1998-1999	4.8%

Hours and earnings of production workers on manufacturing payrolls, 2000

average weekly hours	41.2
average hourly earnings	$13.01
average weekly earnings	$536.01

Labor union membership, 2000 228,100

Household income (in 2000 dollars)

median household income, three year average, 1998-2000	$42,887

Poverty

persons below poverty level, three year average, 1998-2000	12.6%

Personal income ($per capita)

2000 (prelim.)

in current dollars	$27,940
in constant (1996) dollars	$26,025

1999 (preliminary)

in current dollars	$27,198
in constant (1996) dollars	$26,007

Federal income tax returns, 1999

returns filed	3,555,069
adjusted gross income ($1,000)	$156,404,683
total income tax paid ($1,000)	$23,551,444

ECONOMY, BUSINESS, INDUSTRY & AGRICULTURE

Fortune 500 companies, 2000 15

Business incorporations, 1998
total 28,916
change, 1997-1998 .... -1.4%

Business failures, 1998 800

Business firm ownership, 1997
Hispanic owned firms 11,741
Black owned firms 55,766
women owned firms 145,576
Asian & Pacific Islander owned firms 18,158
American Indian & Alaska
    native owned firms 4,470

Shopping centers, 2000 1,644

Gross state product, 1999 ($mil)
total $275,719
    agriculture services, forestry, fisheries .. $3,697
    mining $1,244
    construction $13,744
    manufacturing--durable goods $19,120
    manufacturing--nondurable goods $27,660
    transportation, communication &
        public utilities $31,476
    wholesale trade $24,967
    retail trade $25,743
    finance/real estate/insurance $42,230
    services $53,029
    federal, state & local government $32,808

Establishments, by major industry group, 1999
total 197,759
    forestry, fishing & agriculture 1,141
    mining 224
    construction 19,985
    manufacturing 8,936
    transportation & warehousing 5,169
    wholesale trade 14,033
    retail trade 33,375
    finance & insurance 12,284
    professional/scientific/technical 21,165
    health care/social assistance 16,205
    information 3,609
    accommodation/food services 14,106

Payroll, by major industry group, 1999
total ($1,000) $103,836,505
    forestry, fishing & agriculture $208,170
    mining $323,346
    construction $6,192,917
    manufacturing $16,872,823
    transportation & warehousing $4,175,160
    wholesale trade $8,581,289
    retail trade $8,592,615
    finance & insurance $7,301,193
    professional/scientific/technical $8,992,432
    health care/social assistance $10,166,565
    information $5,703,926
    accommodation/food services $3,293,245

Agriculture
number of farms, 2000 50,000
farm acreage, 2000 11,000,000
acres per farm, 2000 222
value of farms, 1997 ($mil) $16,874
farm income, 1999 ($mil)
    net farm income $2,099
    debt/asset ratio 16.3%
farm marketings, 1999 ($mil)
total $5,241
    crops $1,907
    livestock $3,334
principal commodities, in order by marketing
receipts, 1999
    Broilers, cotton, peanuts, chicken eggs

Federal economic activity in state
expenditures, 2000
    total ($mil) $42,460
    per capita $5,187
    defense ($mil) $8,499
    non-defense ($mil) $33,961
defense department, 2000
    contract awards ($mil) $3,665
    payroll ($mil) $4,934
    civilian employees (x1,000) 30.4
    military personnel (x1,000) 66

Fishing, 2000
catch (thousands of pounds) 9,694
value ($1,000) $21,331

Mining, 2000 ($mil: preliminary)
total non-fuel mineral production $1,660

Georgia 8

Construction, 1999 ($mil)
total contracts (including
    non-building) $18,592
      residential $9,750
      non-residential $6,514

Construction industries, 1997
establishments 17,280
receipts ($1,000) ....$NA
annual payroll ($1,000) $4,555,191
paid employees 160,111

Manufacturing, 1997
establishments 9,804
value of shipments ($1,000) $126,678,011
annual payroll ($1,000) $16,051,302
paid employees 552,706

Transportation industries, 1997
establishments 7,924
receipts ($1,000) $34,517,369
annual payroll ($1,000) $6,558,196
paid employees 183,540

Wholesale trade, 1997
establishments 16,132
sales($1,000) $169,616,237
annual payroll ($1,000) $8,166,296
paid employees 214,242

Retail trade, 1997
establishments 44,037
sales($1,000) $74,096,020
annual payroll ($1,000) $8,458,918
paid employees 630,376

Finance industries
establishments, 1997 17,992
receipts ($1,000), 1997 .... $NA
annual payroll ($1,000), 1997 .... $7,270,600
paid employees, 1997 190,856
commercial banks, 2000
  number 337
    assets ($bil) $168.1
    deposits ($bil) $109.3

Service industries, 1997 (non-exempt firms only)
establishments 57,434
receipts ($1,000) $51,436,453
annual payroll ($1,000) $19,541,575
paid employees 755,082

COMMUNICATION, ENERGY & TRANSPORTATION

Communication
daily newspapers, 2000 34
households with
  telephones, 1998 .... 91.4%
  computers, 2000 .... 47.1%
  internet access, 2000 .... 38.3%

Energy
consumption, 1999
total (trillion Btu) 2,798
per capita (million Btu) 359
by source of production (trillion Btu)
  coal 790
  natural gas 341
  petroleum 1,044
  nuclear electric power 334
  hydroelectric power 28
by end-use sector (trillion Btu)
  residential 553
  commercial 416
  industrial 957
  transportation 871
electric energy, 1999
  production (billion kWh) 110.5
  net summer capability (million kW) 23.3
gas utilities, 1999
  customers 1,057,000
  sales (trillion Btu) 202
nuclear plants, 1999 4

Transportation, 2000
public road & street mileage
total 114,727
  urban 27,606
  rural 87,121
  interstate 1,244
vehicle miles of travel (mil) 105,010
total motor vehicle registrations 7,155,006
  automobiles 4,066,530
  motorcycles 86,988
licensed drivers 5,550,176
  per 1,000 driving age population 888
deaths from motor vehicle
  accidents 1,541

STATE SUMMARY

Capital City .... Honolulu

Governor .... Ben Cayetano

Address .... STATE CAPITOL
HONOLULU, HI 96813
808 586-0034

Admitted as a state 1959

Area (square miles) 10,932

Population, 1980 964,691

Population, 1990 1,108,229

Population, 2000 1,211,537

Persons per square mile, 2000 .... 188.6

Largest city .... Honolulu
population, 2000 372,000

Personal income per capita, 2000
(in current dollars) $28,221

Gross state product ($mil), 1999 .... $40,914

Leading industries, 1999 (by payroll)
Health care/Social assistance
Accommodation & Food services
Retail trade

Leading agricultural commodities, 1999
Pineapples, sugar, greenhouse, macadamia nuts

GEOGRAPHY & ENVIRONMENT

Area, 1990 (square miles)
total 10,932
land 6,423
water (includes territorial water) 4,508

Federally owned land, 2000 .... 15.6%

Highest point
name .... Mauna Kea
elevation (feet) 13,796

Lowest point
name .... Pacific Ocean
elevation (feet) .... sea level

General coastline (miles) 750

Tidal shoreline (miles) 1,052

Capital city .... Honolulu
population, 2000 372,000

Largest city .... Honolulu
population, 2000 372,000

Number of cities with over 100,000 population
1980 1
1990 1
2000 1

State parks and Recreation areas, 2000
area (acres) 27,000
number of visitors 18,171,000
revenues $771,000

Natl. forest system land, 1999 (acres) 0

National park acreage, 1984 245,000

DEMOGRAPHICS & CHARACTERISTICS OF THE POPULATION

Population
1970 769,913
1980 964,691
1990 1,108,229
2000 1,211,537
2015 (projection) 1,553,000
2025 (projection) 1,812,000

Metropolitan area population
1970 631,000
1980 763,000
2000 876,000

Non-metropolitan area population
1970 139,000
1980 202,000
2000 335,000

Change in population, 1990-2000
number 103,308
percent 9.32%

Persons per square mile, 2000 .... 188.6

Persons by age, 2000
under 5 years 78,163
18 and over 915,770
21 and over 867,329
65 and over 160,601
85 and over 17,564

Hawaii 2

Persons by age, 2025 (projected)
under 5 years 143,000
5 to 17 years 340,000
65 and over 289,000

Median age, 2000 .... 36.2

Race, 2000
One race
White 294,102
Black or African American 22,003
American Indian and Alaska Native 3,535
Asian Indian 1,441
Chinese 56,600
Filipino 170,635
Japanese 201,764
Korean 23,537
Vietnamese 7,867
Native Hawaiian and other Pacific Islander1 13,539
Two or more races 259,343

Race, 2025 (projected)
White 566,000
Black 42,000

Persons of Hispanic origin, 2000
total Hispanic or Latino 87,699
  Mexican 19,820
  Puerto Rican 30,005
  Cuban 711
  Other Hispanic or Latino 37,163

Persons of Hispanic origin, 2025 (proj.) .. 186,000

Persons by sex, 2000
male 608,671
female 602,866

Marital status, 1990
males
  15 years & older 441,420
  single 152,188
  married 248,386
    separated 6,425
    widowed 9,053
    divorced 31,793
females
  15 years & older 428,783
  single 106,715
  married 244,799
    separated 7,539

widowed 38,530
divorced 38,739

Households & families, 2000
households 403,240
persons per household 2.92
  families 287,068
  persons per family 3.42
    married couples 216,077
    female householder, no husband
      present 49,923
    one person households 88,153
households with persons under 18 years . 153,008
households with persons over 65 years ... 110,475

Nativity, 1990
number of persons born in state 621,992
percent of total residents 56.1%

Immigration & naturalization, 1998
immigrants admitted 5,465
persons naturalized 4,493
refugees granted resident status 8

VITAL STATISTICS & HEALTH
Births
1999
  with low birth weight 7.6%
  to teenage mothers 14.4%
  to unmarried mothers 32.8%
Birth rate, 1999 (per 1,000) 14.4
Birth rate, 2000 (per 1,000) 14.9

Abortions, 1996
total 7,000
rate (per 1,000 women age 15-44) 27.3

Deaths
1998 8,011
1999 8,270
2000 8,292

Infant deaths
1998 112
1999 121
2000 138

Average lifetime, by race, 1989-1991
total .... 78.21 years
  white .... 77.92 years
  black ....NA years

Marriages
1998 20,774
1999 22,873
2000 24,994

Divorces
1998 4,810
1999 4,377
2000 4,622

Physicians, 1999
total 3,184
rate (per 1,000 persons) 2.69

Nurses, 1999
total 9,540
rate (per 1,000 persons) 8.05

Hospitals, 1998
number 20
beds (x 1,000) 2.8
average daily census (x 1,000) 2.1
patients admitted (x1,000) 98
average cost per day to hospital, 1995 . . . . . . $956
average cost per stay to hospital, 1995 . . . . $8,445

EDUCATION

Educational attainment of all persons
  25 years and older, 1990
  less than 9th grade 71,806
  high school graduates 203,893
  bachelor's degree 111,837
  graduate or professional degree 50,587

2000
  high school graduate or more 87.4%
  college graduate or more 26.3%

Public school enrollment, Fall, 1998
total 188,069
  Kindergarten through grade 8 134,685
  grades 9 through 12 53,384

Public School Teachers, 2000
total 11,100
  elementary 6,000
  secondary 5,100
average salaries
  elementary $40,600
  secondary $40,600

State receipts & expenditures for public
  schools, 2000
revenue receipts ($mil) $1,508

State receipts & expenditures for public
  schools, 2000 (continued)
expenditures
  total ($mil) $1,421
  per capita $1,198
  per pupil $6,777

Graduating high school seniors,
  public high schools, 2000 (est.) 10,152

SAT scores, 2001
verbal 486
math 515
percent graduates taking test 52%

Institutions of higher education, 1999
total 20
  public 10
  private 10

Enrollment in institutions of higher
  education, Fall, 1998
total 61,681
full-time men 16,057
full-time women 20,204
part-time men 11,519
part-time women 13,901

Minority enrollment in institutions of higher
  education, Fall, 1997
Black, non-Hispanic 1,657
Hispanic 1,429
Asian/Pacific Islander 37,353

Earned degrees conferred, 1998
Bachelor's 4,653
First professional 130
Master's 1,529
Doctor's 168

SOCIAL INSURANCE & WELFARE PROGRAMS

Social Security beneficiaries & benefits, 2000
beneficiaries
total 184,000
  retired and dependents 143,000
  survivors 23,000
  disabled & dependents 18,000
annual benefit payments ($mil)
total $1,628
  retired and dependents $1,230
  survivors $246
  disabled & dependents $152

Hawaii 4

Medicare, 2000
enrollment (x1,000) 162
payments ($mil) $622

Medicaid, 1998
recipients (x1,000) 185
payments ($mil) $507

Federal public aid
Temporary Assistance for Needy Families
(TANF), 2000
    Recipients (x1,000) 44
    Families (x1,000) 15
Supplemental Security Income
    total recipients, 1999 (x1,000) 20

Food Stamp Program
    participants, 2000 (x1,000) 118

HOUSING & CONSTRUCTION

Total housing units, 2000 460,542
    seasonal or recreational use 25,584
    occupied 403,240
        owner occupied 227,888
        renter occupied 175,352

New privately owned housing units uthorized, 2000
number (x1,000) 4.9
value ($mil) $823

New privately owned housing units
started, 2000 (est.) (x1,000) 3.8

Existing home sales, 2000 (x1,000) 22.8

GOVERNMENT & ELECTIONS

State officials, 2002
  Governor (name/party/term expires)
      BEN CAYETANO
      Democrat - 2002
Lt. Governor .... Mazie Hirono
Sec. of State .... (no sec. of state)
Atty. General .... Earl Anzai
Chief Justice .... Ronald Moon

Governorship
minimum age 30
length of term .... 4 years
number of consecutive
    terms permitted 2
who succeeds .... Lt. Governor

State legislature
name .... Legislature
  upper chamber
    name .... Senate
    number of members 25
    length of term .... 4 years
    party in majority, 2000 .... Democratic
  lower chamber
    name .... House of Representatives
    number of members 51
    length of term .... 2 years
    party in majority, 2000 .... Democratic

State employees March, 2000
total 67,750
March payroll $158,645,396

Local governments, 1997
total 19
  county 3
  municipal 1
  township 0
  school districts 0
  special districts 15

Voting age population, November, 2000, projected
Total 909,000
  male 450,000
  female 460,000

Vote for president
2000
  Gore 205,000
  Bush 138,000
1996
  Clinton 205,000
  Dole 114,000
  Perot 27,000

Federal representation, 2002 (107th Congress)
Senators (name/party/term expires)

      DANIEL AKATA
      Democrat - 2007
      DANIEL K. INOUYE
      Democrat - 2005

Representatives, total 2
  Democrats 2
  Republicans 0
  other 0

Women holding public office, 2001
U.S. Congress 1
statewide elected office 1
state legislature 19

Black elected officials, 1999
total .... NA
  US and state legislatures .... NA
  city/county/regional offices .... NA
  judicial/law enforcement .... NA
  education/school boards .... NA

Hispanic public officials, 2000
total 2
  state executives & legislators 1
  city/county/regional offices 1
  judicial/law enforcement .... NA
  education/school boards .... NA

GOVERNMENTAL FINANCE

State government revenues, 1999 ($per capita)
total revenue $5,606.41
  total general revenue $4,736.04
    intergovernmental revenue $1,067.10
    taxes $2,671.17
    current charges $675.97
    miscellaneous $321.81

State government expenditures, 1999 ($per capita)
total expenditure $5,285.32
  total general expenditure $4,766.57
    education $1,499.96
    public welfare $799.75
    health $298.61
    hospitals $155.97
    highways $238.21
    police protection $5.80
    correction $113.29
    natural resources $61.20
    governmental administration $244.45
    interest on general debt $410.62

State debt, 1999 ($per capita) $4,573.03

Federal government grants to state & local government, 2000 (x$1,000)
total $1,221,151
  Dept. of Education $161,548
  Environmental Protection Agency $21,714
  Health Care Financing Admin. $354,655
  Dept. Housing & Urban Devel. $177,411
  Dept. of Labor $36,955
  Highway trust fund $81,507

CRIME, LAW ENFORCEMENT & COURTS

Crime, 2000 (all rates per 100,000 inhabitants)
total crimes 62,987
overall crime rate 5,198.9
  property crimes 60,033
    burglaries 10,665
    larcenies 43,254
    motor vehicle thefts 6,114
  property crime rate 4,955.1
  violent crimes 2,954
    murders 35
    forcible rapes 346
    robberies 1,123
    aggravated assaults 1,450
  violent crime rate 243.8

Number of police agencies, 2000 3

Arrests, 2000
total 57,264
  persons under 18 years of age 11,407

Prisoners under state & federal jurisdiction, 2000
total 5,053
percent change, 1999-2000 .... 3.1%
  sentenced to more than one year
    total 3,553
    rate per 100,000 residents 302

Persons under sentence of death, 4/1/2001 ... NA

State's highest court
name .... Supreme Court
number of members 5
length of term .... 10 years
intermediate appeals court? .... yes

Hawaii 6

LABOR & INCOME

Civilian labor force, 2000
total 595,000
  men 306,000
  women 290,000
  persons 16-19 years 24,000
  white 163,000
  black .... NA

*Civilian labor force as a percent of
civilian non-institutional population, 2000*
total 67.0%
  men 71.7%
  women 62.6%
  persons 16-19 years .... NA%
  white 70.2%
  black .... NA%

Employment, 2000
total 570,000
  men 291,000
  women 279,000
  persons 16-19 years 20,000
  white 157,000
  black .... NA

Full-time/part-time labor force, 1998
full-time labor force 482,000
  working part-time for
    economic reasons 8,000
part-time labor force 115,000

Unemployment rate, 2000
total 4.3%
  men 4.9%
  women 3.7%
  persons 16-19 years 16.5%
  white 3.5%
  black .... NA%

*Unemployed by reason for unemployment
(as a percent of total unemployment), 1998*
job losers or completed temp jobs 48.6%
job leavers 8.1%
reentrants 35.1%
new entrants 10.8%

*Experienced civilian labor force, by occupation,
1998*
executive/administrative/managerial 73,000
professional/specialty 76,000
technicians & related support 15,000

sales 81,000
administrative support/clerical 96,000
service occupations 117,000
precision production/craft/repair 54,000
machine operators/assemblers 16
transportation/material moving 17,000
handlers/helpers/laborers 21,000
farming/forestry/fishing 28,000

Experienced civilian labor force, by industry, 1998
construction 32,000
manufacturing 19,000
transportation/communication 47,000
wholesale/retail trade 127,000
finance/real estate/insurance 35,000
services 153,000
government 108,000
agriculture 25,000

Average annual pay, 1999 .... $29,771
change in average annual pay,
  1998-1999 .... 2.5%

*Hours and earnings of production workers
on manufacturing payrolls, 2000*
average weekly hours 38.3
average hourly earnings $13.58
average weekly earnings $520.11

Labor union membership, 2000 123,500

Household income (in 2000 dollars)
median household income,
  three year average, 1998-2000 .... $48,026

Poverty
persons below poverty level,
  three year average, 1998-2000 .... 10.5%

Personal income ($per capita)
2000 (prelim.)
  in current dollars $28,221
  in constant (1996) dollars $26,286
1999 (preliminary)
  in current dollars $27,842
  in constant (1996) dollars $26,623

Federal income tax returns, 1999
returns filed 558,612
adjusted gross income ($1,000) $22,327,292
total income tax paid ($1,000) $2,989,312

ECONOMY, BUSINESS, INDUSTRY & AGRICULTURE

Fortune 500 companies, 2000 0

Business incorporations, 1998
total 3,792
change, 1997-1998 .... 0.0%

Business failures, 1998 781

Business firm ownership, 1997
Hispanic owned firms 4,153
Black owned firms 638
women owned firms 25,807
Asian & Pacific Islander owned firms 50,634
American Indian & Alaska
native owned firms 458

Shopping centers, 2000 190

Gross state product, 1999 ($mil)
total $40,914
agriculture services, forestry, fisheries $493
mining $43
construction $1,654
manufacturing--durable goods $199
manufacturing--nondurable goods $830
transportation, communication &
public utilities $4,268
wholesale trade $1,539
retail trade $4,456
finance/real estate/insurance $9,481
services $9,023
federal, state & local government $8,928

Establishments, by major industry group, 1999
total 29,569
forestry, fishing & agriculture 47
mining 11
construction 2,328
manufacturing 919
transportation & warehousing 699
wholesale trade 1,812
retail trade 4,903
finance & insurance 1,371
professional/scientific/technical 2,716
health care/social assistance 2,979
information 493
accommodation/food services 3,082

Payroll, by major industry group, 1999
total ($1,000) $11,661,968
forestry, fishing & agriculture $11,525
mining .... $NA
construction $890,361
manufacturing $402,625
transportation & warehousing $762,856
wholesale trade $600,250
retail trade $1,262,964
finance & insurance $789,327
professional/scientific/technical $737,647
health care/social assistance $1,706,595
information $332,321
accommodation/food services $1,581,715

Agriculture
number of farms, 2000 6,000
farm acreage, 2000 1,000,000
acres per farm, 2000 253
value of farms, 1997 ($mil) .... $NA
farm income, 1999 ($mil)
net farm income $63
debt/asset ratio 7.1%
farm marketings, 1999 ($mil)
total $533
crops $447
livestock $86
principal commodities, in order by marketing
receipts, 1999
Pineapples, sugar, greenhouse, macadamia nuts

Federal economic activity in state
expenditures, 2000
total ($mil) $9,015
per capita $7,441
defense ($mil) $3,473
non-defense ($mil) $5,542
defense department, 2000
contract awards ($mil) $1,160
payroll ($mil) $2,537
civilian employees (x1,000) 17.9
military personnel (x1,000) 40.4

Fishing, 2000
catch (thousands of pounds) 32,531
value ($1,000) $68,447

Mining, 2000 ($mil preliminary)
total non-fuel mineral production $91

Hawaii 8

Construction, 1999 ($mil)
total contracts (including
    non-building) $1,837
      residential $576
      non-residential $756

Construction industries, 1997
establishments 2,246
receipts ($1,000) $3,821,698
annual payroll ($1,000) $817,781
paid employees 20,985

Manufacturing, 1997
establishments 893
value of shipments ($1,000) $3,416,655
annual payroll ($1,000) $470,626
paid employees 16,412

Transportation industries, 1997
establishments 1,529
receipts ($1,000) $4,459,645
annual payroll ($1,000) $1,064,737
paid employees 34,443

Wholesale trade, 1997
establishments 2,106
sales($1,000) $7,660,732
annual payroll ($1,000) $636,834
paid employees 20,809

Retail trade, 1997
establishments 7,722
sales($1,000) $12,837,212
annual payroll ($1,000) $1,670,323

paid employees 110,892

Finance industries
establishments, 1997 3,850
receipts ($1,000), 1997 .... $NA
annual payroll ($1,000), 1997 .... $1,135,785
paid employees, 1997 35,201
commercial banks, 2000
    number 8
      assets ($bil) $24.4
      deposits ($bil) $17.5

Service industries, 1997 (non-exempt firms only)
establishments 8,741
receipts ($1,000) $8,795,040
annual payroll ($1,000) $3,102,362
paid employees 120,784

COMMUNICATION, ENERGY & TRANSPORTATION

Communication
daily newspapers, 2000 6
households with
    telephones, 1998 .... 93.2%
    computers, 2000 .... 52.4%
    internet access, 2000 .... 43.0%

Energy
consumption, 1999
total (trillion Btu) 241
per capita (million Btu) 204
by source of production (trillion Btu)
    coal 3
    natural gas 3
    petroleum 214
    nuclear electric power .... NA
    hydroelectric power 1
by end-use sector (trillion Btu)
    residential 23
    commercial 25
    industrial 71
    transportation 122
electric energy, 1999
    production (billion kWh) 6.5
    net summer capability (million kW) 1.6
gas utilities, 1999
    customers 34,000
    sales (trillion Btu) 3
nuclear plants, 1999 .... na

Transportation, 2000
public road & street mileage
total 4,281
    urban 2,104
    rural 2,177
    interstate 55
vehicle miles of travel (mil) 8,543
total motor vehicle registrations 737,551
    automobiles 459,515
    motorcycles 19,772
licensed drivers 769,383
    per 1,000 driving age population 811
deaths from motor vehicle
    accidents 131

STATE SUMMARY

Capital City .... Boise

Governor .... Dirk Kempthorne

Address .... STATE CAPITOL
BOISE, ID 83720
208 334-2100

Admitted as a state 1890

Area (square miles) 83,574

Population, 1980 943,935

Population, 1990 1,006,749

Population, 2000 1,293,953

Persons per square mile, 2000 .... 15.6

Largest city .... Boise
population, 2000 186,000

Personal income per capita, 2000
(in current dollars) $24,180

Gross state product ($mil), 1999 .... $34,025

Leading industries, 1999 (by payroll)
Manufacturing
Health care/Social assistance
Retail trade

Leading agricultural commodities, 1999
Dairy products, cattle, potatoes, wheat

GEOGRAPHY & ENVIRONMENT

Area, 1990 (square miles)
total 83,574
land 82,751
water (includes territorial water) 823

Federally owned land, 2000 .... 62.5%

Highest point
name .... Borah Peak
elevation (feet) 12,662

Lowest point
name .... Snake River
elevation (feet) 710

General coastline (miles) 0

Tidal shoreline (miles) 0

Capital city .... Boise
population, 2000 186,000

Largest city .... Boise
population, 2000 186,000

Number of cities with over 100,000 population
1980 1
1990 1
2000 1

State parks and Recreation areas, 2000
area (acres) 43,000
number of visitors 2,573,000
revenues $3,503,000

Natl. forest system land, 1999 (acres) .. 20,459,000

National park acreage, 1984 86,900

DEMOGRAPHICS & CHARACTERISTICS OF THE POPULATION

Population
1970 713,015
1980 943,935
1990 1,006,749
2000 1,293,953
2015 (projection) 1,622,000
2025 (projection) 1,739,000

Metropolitan area population
1970 112,000
1980 173,000
2000 508,000

Non-metropolitan area population
1970 601,000
1980 771,000
2000 786,000

Change in population, 1990-2000
number 287,204
percent 28.53%

Persons per square mile, 2000 .... 15.6

Persons by age, 2000
under 5 years 97,643
18 and over 924,923
21 and over 860,220
65 and over 145,916
85 and over 18,057

Idaho 2

Persons by age, 2025 (projected)
under 5 years 112,000
5 to 17 years 312,000
65 and over 374,000

Median age, 2000 .... 33.2

Race, 2000
One race
White 1,177,304
Black or African American 5,456
American Indian and Alaska Native 17,645
Asian Indian 1,289
Chinese 2,224
Filipino 1,614
Japanese 2,642
Korean 1,250
Vietnamese 1,323
Native Hawaiian and other Pacific Islander 1,308
Two or more races 25,609

Race, 2025 (projected)
White 1,661,000
Black 17,000

Persons of Hispanic origin, 2000
total Hispanic or Latino 101,690
  Mexican 79,324
  Puerto Rican 1,509
  Cuban 408
  Other Hispanic or Latino 20,449

Persons of Hispanic origin, 2025 (proj.) .. 205,000

Persons by sex, 2000
male 648,660
female 645,293

Marital status, 1990
males
  15 years & older 367,363
    single 91,380
    married 237,525
      separated 4,284
      widowed 7,312
      divorced 31,146
females
  15 years & older 378,964
    single 66,935
    married 236,258
      separated 5,397

widowed 38,831
divorced 36,940

Households & families, 2000
households 469,645
persons per household 2.69
  families 335,588
  persons per family 3.17
    married couples 276,511
    female householder, no husband
      present 40,849
    one person households 105,175
households with persons under 18 years . 181,967
households with persons over 65 years ... 100,742

Nativity, 1990
number of persons born in state 508,992
percent of total residents 50.6%

Immigration & naturalization, 1998
immigrants admitted 1,504
persons naturalized 853
refugees granted resident status 55

VITAL STATISTICS & HEALTH
Births
1999
  with low birth weight 6.2%
  to teenage mothers 15.9%
  to unmarried mothers 21.6%
Birth rate, 1999 (per 1,000) 15.9
Birth rate, 2000 (per 1,000) 16.0

Abortions, 1996
total 2,000
rate (per 1,000 women age 15-44) 6.1

Deaths
1998 9,269
1999 9,579
2000 9,564

Infant deaths
1998 132
1999 128
2000 122

Average lifetime, by race, 1989-1991
total .... 76.88 years
  white .... 76.89 years
  black .... NA years

Marriages
1998 15,524
1999 15,439
2000 13,981

Divorces
1998 7,018
1999 6,780
2000 6,874

Physicians, 1999
total 1,944
rate (per 1,000 persons) 1.55

Nurses, 1999
total 7,520
rate (per 1,000 persons) 6.01

Hospitals, 1998
number 42
beds (x 1,000) 3.4
average daily census (x 1,000) 1.9
patients admitted (x1,000) 115
average cost per day to hospital, 1995 ..... $719
average cost per stay to hospital, 1995 .... $4,686

EDUCATION

*Educational attainment of all persons
25 years and older, 1990*
less than 9th grade 44,219
high school graduates 182,892
bachelor's degree 74,443
graduate or professional degree 31,692

2000
high school graduate or more 86.2%
college graduate or more 20.0%

Public school enrollment, Fall, 1998
total 244,722
Kindergarten through grade 8 168,604
grades 9 through 12 76,118

Public School Teachers, 2000
total 13,600
elementary 7,000
secondary 6,700
average salaries
elementary $35,200
secondary $35,100

*State receipts & expenditures for public
schools, 2000*
revenue receipts ($mil) $1,577

*State receipts & expenditures for public
schools, 2000 (continued)*
expenditures
total ($mil) $1,483
per capita $1,184
per pupil $5,756

*Graduating high school seniors,
public high schools, 2000 (est.)* 15,700

SAT scores, 2001
verbal 543
math 542
percent graduates taking test 17%

Institutions of higher education, 1999
total 15
public 7
private 8

*Enrollment in institutions of higher
education, Fall, 1998*
total 63,085
full-time men 19,788
full-time women 22,684
part-time men 8,188
part-time women 12,425

*Minority enrollment in institutions of higher
education, Fall, 1997*
Black, non-Hispanic 406
Hispanic 1,773
Asian/Pacific Islander 930

Earned degrees conferred, 1998
Bachelor's 4,602
First professional 156
Master's 1,026
Doctor's 91

SOCIAL INSURANCE &
WELFARE PROGRAMS

Social Security beneficiaries & benefits, 2000
beneficiaries
total 194,000
retired and dependents 140,000
survivors 28,000
disabled & dependents 26,000
annual benefit payments ($mil)
total $1,697
retired and dependents $1,176
survivors $310
disabled & dependents $211

Idaho 4

Medicare, 2000
enrollment (x1,000) 161
payments ($mil) $639

Medicaid, 1998
recipients (x1,000) 123
payments ($mil) $425

Federal public aid
Temporary Assistance for Needy Families
(TANF), 2000
 Recipients (x1,000) 2
 Families (x1,000) 1
Supplemental Security Income
 total recipients, 1999 (x1,000) 18

Food Stamp Program
 participants, 2000 (x1,000) 58

HOUSING & CONSTRUCTION

Total housing units, 2000 527,824
 seasonal or recreational use 27,478
 occupied 469,645
  owner occupied 339,960
  renter occupied 129,685

New privately owned housing units uthorized, 2000
number (x1,000) 10.9
value ($mil) $1,359

*New privately owned housing units
started, 2000 (est.) (x1,000)* 11.5

Existing home sales, 2000 (x1,000) 30.4

GOVERNMENT & ELECTIONS

State officials, 2002
Governor (name/party/term expires)
  DIRK KEMPTHORNE
  Republican - 2002
Lt. Governor .... Jack Riggs
Sec. of State .... Pete T. Cenarrusa
Atty. General .... Alan Lance
Chief Justice .... Linda Copple Trout

Governorship
minimum age 30
length of term .... 4 years
number of consecutive
 terms permitted .... not specified
who succeeds .... Lt. Governor

State legislature
name .... Legislature
 upper chamber
  name .... Senate
  number of members 35
  length of term .... 2 years
  party in majority, 2000 .... Republican
lower chamber
  name .... House of Representatives
  number of members 70
  length of term .... 2 years
  party in majority, 2000 .... Republican

State employees March, 2000
total 29,759
March payroll $64,092,790

Local governments, 1997
total 1,147
 county 44
 municipal 200
 township 0
 school districts 114
 special districts 789

Voting age population, November, 2000, projected
Total 921,000
 male 455,000
 female 467,000

Vote for president
2000
 Gore 139,000
 Bush 337,000
1996
 Clinton 165,000
 Dole 257,000
 Perot 63,000

Federal representation, 2002 (107th Congress)
Senators (name/party/term expires)

  LARRY CRAIG
  Republican - 2003
  MIKE CRAPO
  Republican - 2005

Representatives, total 2
 Democrats 0
 Republicans 2
 other 0

Women holding public office, 2001
U.S. Congress 0
statewide elected office 1
state legislature 26

Black elected officials, 1999
total .... NA
  US and state legislatures .... NA
  city/county/regional offices .... NA
  judicial/law enforcement .... NA
  education/school boards .... NA

Hispanic public officials, 2000
total 2
  state executives & legislators .... NA
  city/county/regional offices 2
  judicial/law enforcement .... NA
  education/school boards .... NA

GOVERNMENTAL FINANCE

State government revenues, 1999 ($per capita)
total revenue $3,891.05
  total general revenue $3,073.75
    intergovernmental revenue $767.60
    taxes $1,734.54
    current charges $277.54
    miscellaneous $294.08

State government expenditures, 1999 ($per capita)
total expenditure $3,379.67
  total general expenditure $3,017.39
    education $1,228.07
    public welfare $552.16
    health $78.47
    hospitals $32.60
    highways $337.18
    police protection $29.42
    correction $134.41
    natural resources $100.27
    governmental administration $169.78
    interest on general debt $94.32

State debt, 1999 ($per capita) $1,622.78

Federal government grants to state & local government, 2000 (x$1,000)
total $1,229,225
  Dept. of Education $128,202
  Environmental Protection Agency $27,317
  Health Care Financing Admin. $453,103
  Dept. Housing & Urban Devel. $79,699
  Dept. of Labor $31,225
  Highway trust fund $171,908

CRIME, LAW ENFORCEMENT & COURTS

Crime, 2000 (all rates per 100,000 inhabitants)
total crimes 41,228
overall crime rate 3,186.2
  property crimes 37,961
    burglaries 7,330
    larcenies 28,545
    motor vehicle thefts 2,086
  property crime rate 2,933.7
  violent crimes 3,267
    murders 16
    forcible rapes 384
    robberies 223
    aggravated assaults 2,644
  violent crime rate 252.5

Number of police agencies, 2000 117

Arrests, 2000
total 79,810
  persons under 18 years of age 19,491

Prisoners under state & federal jurisdiction, 2000
total 5,526
percent change, 1999-2000 .... 14.1%
  sentenced to more than one year
    total 5,526
    rate per 100,000 residents 430

Persons under sentence of death, 4/1/2001 20

State's highest court
name .... Supreme Court
number of members 5
length of term .... 6 years
intermediate appeals court? .... yes

Idaho 6

LABOR & INCOME

Civilian labor force, 2000

total	658,000
men	358,000
women	299,000
persons 16-19 years	52,000
white	637,000
black	NA

Civilian labor force as a percent of civilian non-institutional population, 2000

total	69.2%
men	76.7%
women	61.9%
persons 16-19 years	NA%
white	69.1%
black	NA%

Employment, 2000

total	626,000
men	341,000
women	285,000
persons 16-19 years	45,000
white	607,000
black	NA

Full-time/part-time labor force, 1998

full-time labor force	513,000
working part-time for economic reasons	11,000
part-time labor force	140,000

Unemployment rate, 2000

total	4.9%
men	4.8%
women	4.9%
persons 16-19 years	13.2%
white	4.7%
black	NA%

Unemployed by reason for unemployment (as a percent of total unemployment), 1998

job losers or completed temp jobs	51.5%
job leavers	12.1%
reentrants	27.3%
new entrants	6.1%

Experienced civilian labor force, by occupation, 1998

executive/administrative/managerial	74,000
professional/specialty	83,000
technicians & related support	19,000
sales	69,000
administrative support/clerical	79,000
service occupations	94,000
precision production/craft/repair	79,000
machine operators/assemblers	42,000
transportation/material moving	34,000
handlers/helpers/laborers	35,000
farming/forestry/fishing	43,000

Experienced civilian labor force, by industry, 1998

construction	40,000
manufacturing	104,000
transportation/communication	31,000
wholesale/retail trade	123,000
finance/real estate/insurance	24,000
services	118,000
government	104,000
agriculture	41,000

Average annual pay, 1999	$26,042
change in average annual pay, 1998-1999	4.7%

Hours and earnings of production workers on manufacturing payrolls, 2000

average weekly hours	39.2
average hourly earnings	$14.17
average weekly earnings	$555.46

Labor union membership, 2000	40,700

Household income (in 2000 dollars)

median household income, three year average, 1998-2000	$37,462

Poverty

persons below poverty level, three year average, 1998-2000	13.3%

Personal income ($per capita)

2000 (prelim.)

in current dollars	$24,180
in constant (1996) dollars	$22,522

1999 (preliminary)

in current dollars	$23,445
in constant (1996) dollars	$22,418

Federal income tax returns, 1999

returns filed	545,767
adjusted gross income ($1,000)	$20,366,524
total income tax paid ($1,000)	$2,710,287

Idaho 7

ECONOMY, BUSINESS, INDUSTRY & AGRICULTURE

Fortune 500 companies, 2000 3

Business incorporations, 1998
total 2,322
change, 1997-1998 .... -6.7%

Business failures, 1998 441

Business firm ownership, 1997
Hispanic owned firms 2,844
Black owned firms 164
women owned firms 25,763
Asian & Pacific Islander owned firms 1,028
American Indian & Alaska
   native owned firms 1,239

Shopping centers, 2000 168

Gross state product, 1999 ($mil)
total $34,025
   agriculture services, forestry, fisheries .. $1,776
   mining $188
   construction $2,261
   manufacturing--durable goods $5,649
   manufacturing--nondurable goods $1,695
   transportation, communication &
      public utilities $2,667
   wholesale trade $2,183
   retail trade $3,481
   finance/real estate/insurance $4,018
   services $5,545
   federal, state & local government $4,562

Establishments, by major industry group, 1999
total 36,975
   forestry, fishing & agriculture 639
   mining 107
   construction 5,716
   manufacturing 1,649
   transportation & warehousing 1,372
   wholesale trade 2,011
   retail trade 5,896
   finance & insurance 2,275
   professional/scientific/technical 2,860
   health care/social assistance 3,148
   information 597
   accommodation/food services 2,923

Payroll, by major industry group, 1999
total ($1,000) $11,027,126
   forestry, fishing & agriculture $126,642
   mining $93,740
   construction $1,097,253
   manufacturing $2,169,082
   transportation & warehousing $285,560
   wholesale trade $775,360
   retail trade $1,252,387
   finance & insurance $553,136
   professional/scientific/technical $880,874
   health care/social assistance $1,352,717
   information $304,253
   accommodation/food services $413,951

Agriculture
number of farms, 2000 25,000
farm acreage, 2000 12,000,000
acres per farm, 2000 486
value of farms, 1997 ($mil) $12,960
farm income, 1999 ($mil)
   net farm income $874
   debt/asset ratio 19%
farm marketings, 1999 ($mil)
total $3,347
   crops $1,744
   livestock $1,603
principal commodities, in order by marketing
receipts, 1999
   Dairy products, cattle, potatoes, wheat

Federal economic activity in state
expenditures, 2000
   total ($mil) $7,009
   per capita $5,417
   defense ($mil) $625
   non-defense ($mil) $6,384
defense department, 2000
   contract awards ($mil) $213
   payroll ($mil) $399
   civilian employees (x1,000) 1.4
   military personnel (x1,000) 4.2

Fishing, 2000
catch (thousands of pounds) .... NA
value ($1,000) .... $NA

Mining, 2000 ($mil; preliminary)
total non-fuel mineral production $398

105

Idaho 8

Construction, 1999 ($mil)
total contracts (including
    non-building) $2,380
       residential $1,293
       non-residential $746

Construction industries, 1997
establishments 5,221
receipts ($1,000) $5,362,988
annual payroll ($1,000) $1,117,718
paid employees 40,060

Manufacturing, 1997
establishments 2,090
value of shipments ($1,000) $17,608,486
annual payroll ($1,000) $2,231,139
paid employees 71,274

Transportation industries, 1997
establishments 1,871
receipts ($1,000) $3,322,159
annual payroll ($1,000) $592,714
paid employees 20,189

Wholesale trade, 1997
establishments 2,490
sales($1,000) $11,201,238
annual payroll ($1,000) $737,146
paid employees 27,231

Retail trade, 1997
establishments 7,998
sales($1,000) $11,510,569
annual payroll ($1,000) $1,233,031
paid employees 93,090

Finance industries
establishments, 1997 3,009
receipts ($1,000), 1997 .... $NA
annual payroll ($1,000), 1997 .... $534,196
paid employees, 1997 18,741
commercial banks, 2000
   number 18
     assets ($bil) $2.5
     deposits ($bil) $2.1

Service industries, 1997 (non-exempt firms only)
establishments 9,222
receipts ($1,000) $5,506,289
annual payroll ($1,000) $2,038,895
paid employees 88,434

COMMUNICATION, ENERGY & TRANSPORTATION

Communication
daily newspapers, 2000 12
households with
    telephones, 1998 .... 94.1%
    computers, 2000 .... 54.5%
    internet access, 2000 .... 42.3%

Energy
consumption, 1999
total (trillion Btu) 518
per capita (million Btu) 414
by source of production (trillion Btu)
   coal 8
   natural gas 72
   petroleum 170
   nuclear electric power .... NA
   hydroelectric power 140
by end-use sector (trillion Btu)
   residential 96
   commercial 87
   industrial 210
   transportation 126
electric energy, 1999
   production (billion kWh) 12.5
   net summer capability (million kW) 2.6
gas utilities, 1999
   customers 306,000
   sales (trillion Btu) 66
nuclear plants, 1999 .... na

Transportation, 2000
public road & street mileage
total 46,456
   urban 4,082
   rural 42,374
   interstate 611
vehicle miles of travel (mil) 13,534
total motor vehicle registrations 1,177,700
   automobiles 515,266
   motorcycles 42,001
licensed drivers 883,546
   per 1,000 driving age population 912
deaths from motor vehicle
   accidents 276

STATE SUMMARY

Capital City . . . . Springfield

Governor . . . . George Ryan

Address . . . . STATE CAPITOL
SPRINGFIELD, IL 62706
217 782-6830

Admitted as a state 1818

Area (square miles) 57,918

Population, 1980 11,426,518

Population, 1990 11,430,602

Population, 2000 12,419,293

Persons per square mile, 2000 . . . . 223.4

Largest city . . . . Chicago
population, 2000 2,896,000

Personal income per capita, 2000
(in current dollars) $32,259

Gross state product ($mil), 1999 . . . . . . $445,666

Leading industries, 1999 (by payroll)
Manufacturing
Finance & Insurance
Health care/Social assistance

Leading agricultural commodities, 1999
Corn, soybeans, hogs, cattle

GEOGRAPHY & ENVIRONMENT

Area, 1990 (square miles)
total 57,918
land 55,593
water (includes territorial water) 2,325

Federally owned land, 2000 . . . . 1.6%

Highest point
name . . . . Charles Mound
elevation (feet) 1,235

Lowest point
name . . . . Mississippi River
elevation (feet) 279

General coastline (miles) 0

Tidal shoreline (miles) 0

Capital city . . . . Springfield
population, 2000 111,000

Largest city . . . . Chicago
population, 2000 2,896,000

Number of cities with over 100,000 population
1980 4
1990 4
2000 7

State parks and Recreation areas, 2000
area (acres) 305,000
number of visitors 44,484,000
revenues $5,200,000

Natl. forest system land, 1999 (acres) 292,000

National park acreage, 1984 . . . . NA

DEMOGRAPHICS & CHARACTERISTICS OF THE POPULATION

Population
1970 11,110,285
1980 11,426,518
1990 11,430,602
2000 12,419,293
2015 (projection) 12,808,000
2025 (projection) 13,440,000

Metropolitan area population
1970 9,125,000
1980 9,339,000
2000 10,542,000

Non-metropolitan area population
1970 1,986,000
1980 2,088,000
2000 1,878,000

Change in population, 1990-2000
number 988,691
percent 8.65%

Persons per square mile, 2000 . . . . 223.4

Persons by age, 2000
under 5 years 876,549
18 and over 9,173,842
21 and over 8,634,455
65 and over 1,500,025
85 and over 192,031

Illinois 2

Persons by age, 2025 (projected)
under 5 years 964,000
5 to 17 years 2,416,000
65 and over 2,234,000

Median age, 2000 .... 34.7

Race, 2000
One race
White 9,125,471
Black or African American 1,876,875
American Indian and Alaska Native 31,006
Asian Indian 124,723
Chinese 76,725
Filipino 86,298
Japanese 20,379
Korean 51,453
Vietnamese 19,101
Native Hawaiian and other Pacific Islander 4,610
Two or more races 235,016

Race, 2025 (projected)
White 10,504,000
Black 2,176,000

Persons of Hispanic origin, 2000
total Hispanic or Latino 1,530,262
  Mexican 1,144,390
  Puerto Rican 157,851
  Cuban 18,438
  Other Hispanic or Latino 209,583

Persons of Hispanic origin, 2025 (proj.) . 2,275,000

Persons by sex, 2000
male 6,080,336
female 6,338,957

Marital status, 1990
males
  15 years & older 4,282,894
    single 1,395,167
    married 2,474,607
      separated 73,642
    widowed 114,145
    divorced 298,975
females
  15 years & older 4,666,480
    single 1,184,564
    married 2,477,596
      separated 106,037

widowed 581,341
divorced 422,979

Households & families, 2000
households 4,591,779
persons per household 2.63
  families 3,105,513
  persons per family 3.23
    married couples 2,353,892
  female householder, no husband
    present 563,718
  one person households 1,229,807
households with persons under 18 years 1,663,878
households with persons over 65 years .. 1,064,919

Nativity, 1990
number of persons born in state 7,897,755
percent of total residents 69.1%

Immigration & naturalization, 1998
immigrants admitted 33,163
persons naturalized 16,804
refugees granted resident status 1,471

VITAL STATISTICS & HEALTH

Births
1999
  with low birth weight 8.0%
  to teenage mothers 15.0%
  to unmarried mothers 34.1%
Birth rate, 1999 (per 1,000) 15.0
Birth rate, 2000 (per 1,000) 15.2

Abortions, 1996
total 69,000
rate (per 1,000 women age 15-44) 26.1

Deaths
1998 104,153
1999 108,436
2000 106,712

Infant deaths
1998 1,526
1999 1,542
2000 1,486

Average lifetime, by race, 1989-1991
total .... 74.90 years
  white .... 76.16 years
  black .... 67.46 years

Marriages

1998	84,533
1999	85,944
2000	85,517

Divorces

1998	40,549
1999	41,025
2000	39,078

Physicians, 1999

total	31,928
rate (per 1,000 persons)	2.63

Nurses, 1999

total	110,270
rate (per 1,000 persons)	9.09

Hospitals, 1998

number	203
beds (x 1,000)	39.2
average daily census (x 1,000)	23.7
patients admitted (x1,000)	1,466
average cost per day to hospital, 1995	$1,050
average cost per stay to hospital, 1995	$6,584

EDUCATION

Educational attainment of all persons 25 years and older, 1990

less than 9th grade	750,932
high school graduates	2,187,342
bachelor's degree	989,808
graduate or professional degree	545,188

2000

high school graduate or more	85.5%
college graduate or more	27.1%

Public school enrollment, Fall, 1998

total	2,011,530
Kindergarten through grade 8	1,451,579
grades 9 through 12	559,951

Public School Teachers, 2000

total	127,000
elementary	90,000
secondary	37,100
average salaries	
elementary	$44,500
secondary	$51,300

State receipts & expenditures for public schools, 2000

revenue receipts ($mil)	$15,760

State receipts & expenditures for public schools, 2000 (continued)
expenditures

total ($mil)	$14,823
per capita	$1,222
per pupil	$6,720

Graduating high school seniors, public high schools, 2000 (est.) ... 111,230

SAT scores, 2001

verbal	576
math	589
percent graduates taking test	12%

Institutions of higher education, 1999

total	175
public	60
private	115

Enrolment in institutions of higher education, Fall, 1998

total	729,234
full-time men	179,341
full-time women	207,513
part-time men	138,573
part-time women	203,807

Minority enrollment in institutions of higher education, Fall, 1997

Black, non-Hispanic	94,788
Hispanic	67,595
Asian/Pacific Islander	41,294

Earned degrees conferred, 1998

Bachelor's	52,196
First professional	4,508
Master's	25,111
Doctor's	2,690

SOCIAL INSURANCE & WELFARE PROGRAMS

Social Security beneficiaries & benefits, 2000
beneficiaries

total	1,842,000
retired and dependents	1,320,000
survivors	291,000
disabled & dependents	232,000
annual benefit payments ($mil)	
total	$17,530
retired and dependents	$12,060
survivors	$3,477
disabled & dependents	$1,993

Illinois 4

Medicare, 2000
enrollment (x1,000) 1,629
payments ($mil) $7,309

Medicaid, 1998
recipients (x1,000) 1,364
payments ($mil) $6,173

Federal public aid
Temporary Assistance for Needy Families
(TANF), 2000
   Recipients (x1,000) 183
   Families (x1,000) 90
Supplemental Security Income
   total recipients, 1999 (x1,000) 251

Food Stamp Program
   participants, 2000 (x1,000) 779

HOUSING & CONSTRUCTION

Total housing units, 2000 4,885,615
   seasonal or recreational use 29,712
   occupied 4,591,779
      owner occupied 3,088,884
      renter occupied 1,502,895

New privately owned housing units uthorized, 2000
number (x1,000) 51.9
value ($mil) $6,528

New privately owned housing units
started, 2000 (est.) (x1,000) 48.1

Existing home sales, 2000 (x1,000) 239

GOVERNMENT & ELECTIONS

State officials, 2002
   Governor (name/party/term expires)
        GEORGE RYAN
        Republican - 2002
Lt. Governor . . . . Corrine Wood
Sec. of State . . . . Jesse White
Atty. General . . . . Jim Ryan
Chief Justice . . . . Charles Freeman

Governorship
minimum age 25
length of term . . . . 4 years
number of consecutive
   terms permitted . . . . not specified
who succeeds . . . . Lt. Governor

State legislature
name . . . . General Assembly
   upper chamber
      name . . . . Senate
      number of members 59
      length of term . . . . 4 years
      party in majority, 2000 . . . . Republican
   lower chamber
      name . . . . House of Representatives
      number of members 118
      length of term . . . . 2 years
      party in majority, 2000 . . . . Democratic

State employees March, 2000
total 151,173
March payroll $408,845,822

Local governments, 1997
total 6,835
   county 102
   municipal 1,288
   township 1,433
   school districts 944
   special districts 3,068

Voting age population, November, 2000, projected
Total 8,983,000
   male 4,308,000
   female 4,675,000

Vote for president
2000
   Gore 2,589,000
   Bush 2,019,000
1996
   Clinton 2,342,000
   Dole 1,587,000
   Perot 346,000

Federal representation, 2002 (107th Congress)
Senators (name/party/term expires)

        RICHARD DURBIN
        Democrat - 2003
      PETER FITZGERALD
        Republican - 2005

Representatives, total 20
   Democrats 10
   Republicans 10
   other 0

Women holding public office, 2001
U.S. Congress 2
statewide elected office 2
state legislature 47

Black elected officials, 1999
total 627
  US and state legislatures 27
  city/county/regional offices 314
  judicial/law enforcement 56
  education/school boards 230

Hispanic public officials, 2000
total 1,190
  state executives & legislators 7
  city/county/regional offices 34
  judicial/law enforcement .... NA
  education/school boards 21,149

GOVERNMENTAL FINANCE

State government revenues, 1999 ($per capita)
total revenue $3,569.68
  total general revenue $2,942.39
    intergovernmental revenue $772.15
    taxes $1,748.90
    current charges $175.66
    miscellaneous $245.68

State government expenditures, 1999 ($per capita)
total expenditure $3,159.04
  total general expenditure $2,832.85
    education $894.86
    public welfare $776.15
    health $160.58
    hospitals $70.43
    highways $206.66
    police protection $28.01
    correction $96.25
    natural resources $27.99
    governmental administration $93.39
    interest on general debt $141.15

State debt, 1999 ($per capita) $2,191.72

Federal government grants to state & local government, 2000 (x$1,000)
total $11,270,857
  Dept. of Education $1,058,672
  Environmental Protection Agency ... $138,500
  Health Care Financing Admin. $4,164,511
  Dept. Housing & Urban Devel. $1,704,591
  Dept. of Labor $225,950
  Highway trust fund $857,676

CRIME, LAW ENFORCEMENT & COURTS

Crime, 2000 (all rates per 100,000 inhabitants)
total crimes 532,315
overall crime rate 4,286.2
  property crimes 450,748
    burglaries 81,913
    larcenies 312,692
    motor vehicle thefts 56,143
  property crime rate 3,629.4
  violent crimes 81,567
    murders 891
    forcible rapes 4,090
    robberies 25,758
    aggravated assaults 50,828
  violent crime rate 656.8

Number of police agencies, 2000 1

Arrests, 2000
total 253,967
  persons under 18 years of age 45,896

Prisoners under state & federal jurisdiction, 2000
total 45,281
percent change, 1999-2000 .... 1.4%
  sentenced to more than one year
    total 45,281
    rate per 100,000 residents 371

Persons under sentence of death, 4/1/2001 ... 175

State's highest court
name .... Supreme Court
number of members 7
length of term .... 10 years
intermediate appeals court? .... yes

Illinois 6

LABOR & INCOME

Civilian labor force, 2000
total	6,419,000
men	3,402,000
women	3,017,000
persons 16-19 years	396,000
white	5,282,000
black	900,000

Civilian labor force as a percent of civilian non-institutional population, 2000
total	69.8%
men	77.1%
women	63.1%
persons 16-19 years	NA%
white	70.6%
black	65.3%

Employment, 2000
total	6,140,000
men	3,249,000
women	2,891,000
persons 16-19 years	349,000
white	5,111,000
black	801,000

Full-time/part-time labor force, 1998
full-time labor force	5,112,000
working part-time for economic reasons	45,000
part-time labor force	1,112,000

Unemployment rate, 2000
total	4.4%
men	4.5%
women	4.2%
persons 16-19 years	11.9%
white	3.2%
black	11.0%

Unemployed by reason for unemployment (as a percent of total unemployment), 1998
job losers or completed temp jobs	46.6%
job leavers	11.9%
reentrants	35.4%
new entrants	6.5%

Experienced civilian labor force, by occupation, 1998
executive/administrative/managerial	920,000
professional/specialty	910,000
technicians & related support	184,000
sales	792,000
administrative support/clerical	901,000
service occupations	832,000
precision production/craft/repair	617,000
machine operators/assemblers	410,000
transportation/material moving	265,000
handlers/helpers/laborers	267,000
farming/forestry/fishing	107,000

Experienced civilian labor force, by industry, 1998
construction	294,000
manufacturing	1,115,000
transportation/communication	407,000
wholesale/retail trade	1,235,000
finance/real estate/insurance	425,000
services	1,572,000
government	717,000
agriculture	96,000

Average annual pay, 1999 .... $36,279
change in average annual pay, 1998-1999	4.5%

Hours and earnings of production workers on manufacturing payrolls, 2000
average weekly hours	41.5
average hourly earnings	$14.39
average weekly earnings	$597.19

Labor union membership, 2000 1,046,300

Household income (in 2000 dollars)
median household income, three year average, 1998-2000	$46,435

Poverty
persons below poverty level, three year average, 1998-2000	10.5%

Personal income ($per capita)
2000 (prelim.)	
in current dollars	$32,259
in constant (1996) dollars	$30,048
1999 (preliminary)	
in current dollars	$31,278
in constant (1996) dollars	$29,908

Federal income tax returns, 1999
returns filed	5,714,463
adjusted gross income ($1,000)	$283,628,857
total income tax paid ($1,000)	$47,352,772

ECONOMY, BUSINESS, INDUSTRY & AGRICULTURE

Fortune 500 companies, 2000 39

Business incorporations, 1998
total 35,319
change, 1997-1998 .... -2.1%

Business failures, 1998 3,291

Business firm ownership, 1997
Hispanic owned firms 31,010
Black owned firms 41,244
women owned firms 239,725
Asian & Pacific Islander owned firms 36,857
American Indian & Alaska
   native owned firms 3,945

Shopping centers, 2000 2,175

Gross state product, 1999 ($mil)
total $445,666
   agriculture services, forestry, fisheries .. $3,575
   mining $1,151
   construction $20,059
   manufacturing--durable goods $39,760
   manufacturing--nondurable goods $32,803
   transportation, communication &
      public utilities $40,830
   wholesale trade $35,342
   retail trade $36,683
   finance/real estate/insurance $90,755
   services $100,527
   federal, state & local government $44,180

Establishments, by major industry group, 1999
total 306,899
   forestry, fishing & agriculture 384
   mining 605
   construction 29,509
   manufacturing 17,653
   transportation & warehousing 9,091
   wholesale trade 21,764
   retail trade 44,017
   finance & insurance 21,142
   professional/scientific/technical 34,856
   health care/social assistance 26,265
   information 5,452
   accommodation/food services 23,579

Payroll, by major industry group, 1999
total ($1,000) $188,020,334
   forestry, fishing & agriculture $94,352
   mining $437,631
   construction $11,159,074
   manufacturing $33,839,442
   transportation & warehousing $6,831,654
   wholesale trade $16,077,476
   retail trade $12,214,416
   finance & insurance $19,044,069
   professional/scientific/technical $18,173,508
   health care/social assistance $18,657,241
   information $6,746,628
   accommodation/food services $4,833,711

Agriculture
number of farms, 2000 78,000
farm acreage, 2000 28,000,000
acres per farm, 2000 355
value of farms, 1997 ($mil) $61,880
farm income, 1999 ($mil)
   net farm income $1,007
   debt/asset ratio 13.9%
farm marketings, 1999 ($mil)
total $6,757
   crops $5,233
   livestock $1,524
principal commodities, in order by marketing
receipts, 1999
   Corn, soybeans, hogs, cattle

Federal economic activity in state
expenditures, 2000
   total ($mil) $60,008
   per capita $4,832
   defense ($mil) $3,973
   non-defense ($mil) $56,035
defense department, 2000
   contract awards ($mil) $1,609
   payroll ($mil) $2,361
   civilian employees (x1,000) 12.7
   military personnel (x1,000) 32.1

Fishing, 2000
catch (thousands of pounds) 49
value ($1,000) $35

Mining, 2000 ($mil; preliminary)
total non-fuel mineral production $907

Illinois 8

Construction, 1999 ($mil)
total contracts (including
    non-building) $16,823
        residential $6,821
        non-residential $6,419

Construction industries, 1997
establishments 27,240
receipts ($1,000) $39,082,063
annual payroll ($1,000) .... $NA
paid employees .... NA

Manufacturing, 1997
establishments 17,967
value of shipments ($1,000) $205,420,843
annual payroll ($1,000) $32,953,527
paid employees 915,860

Transportation industries, 1997
establishments 13,511
receipts ($1,000) $51,664,629
annual payroll ($1,000) $9,995,630
paid employees 278,347

Wholesale trade, 1997
establishments 24,757
sales($1,000) $284,546,480
annual payroll ($1,000) $14,310,760
paid employees 357,606

Retail trade, 1997
establishments 65,254
sales($1,000) $111,805,925
annual payroll ($1,000) $12,998,071
paid employees 931,248

Finance industries
establishments, 1997 31,193
receipts ($1,000), 1997 .... $NA
annual payroll ($1,000), 1997 .... $18,277,430
paid employees, 1997 401,132
commercial banks, 2000
    number 711
        assets ($bil) $355.5
        deposits ($bil) $249.4

Service industries, 1997 (non-exempt firms only)
establishments 91,748
receipts ($1,000) $89,604,909
annual payroll ($1,000) $33,542,945
paid employees 1,150,231

COMMUNICATION, ENERGY & TRANSPORTATION

Communication
daily newspapers, 2000 68
households with
    telephones, 1998 .... 91.8%
    computers, 2000 .... 50.2%
    internet access, 2000 .... 40.1%

Energy
consumption, 1999
total (trillion Btu) 3,883
per capita (million Btu) 320
by source of production (trillion Btu)
    coal 837
    natural gas 1,058
    petroleum 1,340
    nuclear electric power 868
    hydroelectric power 2
by end-use sector (trillion Btu)
    residential 897
    commercial 722
    industrial 1,273
    transportation 991
electric energy, 1999
    production (billion kWh) 149.8
    net summer capability (million kW) 17
gas utilities, 1999
    customers 3,809,000
    sales (trillion Btu) 527
nuclear plants, 1999 11

Transportation, 2000
public road & street mileage
total 138,372
    urban 36,347
    rural 102,025
    interstate 2,165
vehicle miles of travel (mil) 102,866
total motor vehicle registrations 8,972,584
    automobiles 5,953,984
    motorcycles 195,443
licensed drivers 7,961,046
    per 1,000 driving age population 835
deaths from motor vehicle
    accidents 1,418

STATE SUMMARY

Capital City .... Indianapolis

Governor .... Frank O'Bannon

Address .... STATE HOUSE
INDIANAPOLIS, IN 46204
317 232-4567

Admitted as a state 1816

Area (square miles) 36,420

Population, 1980 5,490,224

Population, 1990 5,544,159

Population, 2000 6,080,485

Persons per square mile, 2000 .... 169.5

Largest city .... Indianapolis
population, 2000 782,000

Personal income per capita, 2000
(in current dollars) $27,011

Gross state product ($mil), 1999 ...... $182,202

Leading industries, 1999 (by payroll)
Manufacturing
Health care/Social assistance
Retail trade

Leading agricultural commodities, 1999
Corn, soybeans, hogs, dairy products

GEOGRAPHY & ENVIRONMENT

Area, 1990 (square miles)
total 36,420
  land 35,870
  water (includes territorial water) 550

Federally owned land, 2000 .... 2.2%

Highest point
name .... Franklin Twp., Wayne County
elevation (feet) 1,257

Lowest point
name .... Ohio River
elevation (feet) 320

General coastline (miles) 0

Tidal shoreline (miles) 0

Capital city .... Indianapolis
population, 2000 782,000

Largest city .... Indianapolis
population, 2000 782,000

Number of cities with over 100,000 population
1980 5
1990 5
2000 5

State parks and Recreation areas, 2000
area (acres) 178,000
number of visitors 18,475,000
revenues $31,355,000

Natl. forest system land, 1999 (acres) 196,000

National park acreage, 1984 9,700

DEMOGRAPHICS & CHARACTERISTICS OF THE POPULATION

Population
1970 5,195,392
1980 5,490,224
1990 5,544,159
2000 6,080,485
2015 (projection) 6,404,000
2025 (projection) 6,546,000

Metropolitan area population
1970 3,551,000
1980 3,719,000
2000 4,390,000

Non-metropolitan area population
1970 1,644,000
1980 1,771,000
2000 1,691,000

Change in population, 1990-2000
number 536,326
percent 9.67%

Persons per square mile, 2000 .... 169.5

Persons by age, 2000
under 5 years 423,215
18 and over 4,506,089
21 and over 4,221,426
65 and over 752,831
85 and over 91,558

Indiana 2

Persons by age, 2025 (projected)
under 5 years 396,000
5 to 17 years 1,095,000
65 and over 1,260,000

Median age, 2000 .... 35.2

Race, 2000
One race
White 5,320,022
Black or African American 510,034
American Indian and Alaska Native 15,815
Asian Indian 14,685
Chinese 12,531
Filipino 6,674
Japanese 5,065
Korean 7,502
Vietnamese 4,843
Native Hawaiian and other Pacific Islander 2,005
Two or more races 75,672

Race, 2025 (projected)
White 5,811,000
Black 615,000

Persons of Hispanic origin, 2000
total Hispanic or Latino 214,536
    Mexican 153,042
    Puerto Rican 19,678
    Cuban 2,754
    Other Hispanic or Latino 39,062

Persons of Hispanic origin, 2025 (proj.) .. 243,000

Persons by sex, 2000
male 2,982,474
female 3,098,011

Marital status, 1990
males
    15 years & older 2,064,662
        single 569,459
        married 1,268,941
            separated 24,707
        widowed 50,574
        divorced 175,688
females
    15 years & older 2,263,865
        single 481,644
        married 1,272,465
            separated 33,317
        widowed 274,357
        divorced 235,399

Households & families, 2000
households 2,336,306
persons per household 2.53
    families 1,602,501
    persons per family 3.05
        married couples 1,251,458
    female householder, no husband
        present 259,372
    one person households 605,428
households with persons under 18 years . 834,826
households with persons over 65 years ... 524,632

Nativity, 1990
number of persons born in state 3,940,076
percent of total residents 71.1%

Immigration & naturalization, 1998
immigrants admitted 3,981
persons naturalized 2,404
refugees granted resident status 394

VITAL STATISTICS & HEALTH
Births
1999
    with low birth weight 7.9%
    to teenage mothers 14.5%
    to unmarried mothers 34.5%
Birth rate, 1999 (per 1,000) 14.5
Birth rate, 2000 (per 1,000) 14.6

Abortions, 1996
total 15,000
rate (per 1,000 women age 15-44) 11.2

Deaths
1998 46,333
1999 55,303
2000 55,848

Infant deaths
1998 404
1999 358
2000 633

Average lifetime, by race, 1989-1991
total .... 75.39 years
    white .... 75.82 years
    black .... 69.80 years

Marriages
1998 34,566
1999 33,913
2000 34,498

Divorces
1998 ....NA
1999 ....NA
2000 ....NA

Physicians, 1999
total 11,753
rate (per 1,000 persons) 1.98

Nurses, 1999
total 49,360
rate (per 1,000 persons) 8.31

Hospitals, 1998
number 111
beds (x 1,000) 19.4
average daily census (x 1,000) 11.2
patients admitted (x1,000) 704
average cost per day to hospital, 1995 ...... $963
average cost per stay to hospital, 1995 .... $5,610

EDUCATION

*Educational attainment of all persons
25 years and older, 1990*
less than 9th grade 297,423
high school graduates 1,333,093
bachelor's degree 321,278
graduate or professional degree 221,663

2000
high school graduate or more 84.6%
college graduate or more 17.1%

Public school enrollment, Fall, 1998
total 988,094
Kindergarten through grade 8 696,832
grades 9 through 12 291,262

Public School Teachers, 2000
total 58,700
elementary 31,500
secondary 27,200
average salaries
elementary $41,900
secondary $41,800

*State receipts & expenditures for public
schools, 2000*
revenue receipts ($mil) $8,442

*State receipts & expenditures for public
schools, 2000 (continued)*
expenditures
total ($mil) $7,942
per capita $1,336
per pupil $7,254

*Graduating high school seniors,
public high schools, 2000 (est.)* 58,364

SAT scores, 2001
verbal 499
math 501
percent graduates taking test 60%

Institutions of higher education, 1999
total 94
public 28
private 66

*Enrollment in institutions of higher
education, Fall, 1998*
total 299,604
full-time men 96,368
full-time women 106,974
part-time men 40,785
part-time women 55,477

*Minority enrollment in institutions of higher
education, Fall, 1997*
Black, non-Hispanic 19,437
Hispanic 6,838
Asian/Pacific Islander 5,362

Earned degrees conferred, 1998
Bachelor's 30,833
First professional 1,499
Master's 7,873
Doctor's 1,115

SOCIAL INSURANCE &
WELFARE PROGRAMS

Social Security beneficiaries & benefits, 2000
beneficiaries
total 994,000
retired and dependents 695,000
survivors 154,000
disabled & dependents 144,000
annual benefit payments ($mil)
total $9,380
retired and dependents $6,336
survivors $1,846
disabled & dependents $1,198

Medicare, 2000
enrollment (x1,000) 845
payments ($mil) $4,720

Medicaid, 1998
recipients (x1,000) 607
payments ($mil) $2,564

Federal public aid
Temporary Assistance for Needy Families
(TANF), 2000
   Recipients (x1,000) 97
   Families (x1,000) 35
Supplemental Security Income
   total recipients, 1999 (x1,000) 88

Food Stamp Program
   participants, 2000 (x1,000) 300

HOUSING & CONSTRUCTION

Total housing units, 2000 2,532,319
   seasonal or recreational use 33,803
   occupied 2,336,306
      owner occupied 1,669,162
      renter occupied 667,144

New privately owned housing units uthorized, 2000
number (x1,000) 37.9
value ($mil) $4,414

New privately owned housing units
started, 2000 (est.) (x1,000) 37.6

Existing home sales, 2000 (x1,000) 126.8

GOVERNMENT & ELECTIONS

State officials, 2002
Governor (name/party/term expires)
      FRANK O'BANNON
      Democrat - 2001
Lt. Governor ....Joe Kernan
Sec. of State .... Sue Ann Gilroy
Atty. General .... Steve Carter
Chief Justice .... Randall T. Shepard

Governorship
minimum age 30
length of term .... 4 years
number of consecutive
   terms permitted 2
who succeeds .... Lt. Governor

State legislature
name .... General Assembly
  upper chamber
    name .... Senate
    number of members 50
    length of term .... 4 years
    party in majority, 2000 .... Republican
  lower chamber
    name .... House of Representatives
    number of members 100
    length of term .... 2 years
    party in majority, 2000 .... Democratic

State employees March, 2000
total 105,837
March payroll $239,059,568

Local governments, 1997
total 3,198
   county 91
   municipal 569
   township 1,008
   school districts 294
   special districts 1,236

Voting age population, November, 2000, projected
Total 4,448,000
   male 2,127,000
   female 2,321,000

Vote for president
2000
   Gore 902,000
   Bush 1,246,000
1996
   Clinton 887,000
   Dole 1,007,000
   Perot 224,000

Federal representation, 2002 (107th Congress)
Senators (name/party/term expires)

      RICHARD G. LUGAR
      Republican - 2007
      EVAN BAYH
      Democrat - 2005

Representatives, total 10
   Democrats 4
   Republicans 6
   other 0

GOVERNMENTAL FINANCE

CRIME, LAW ENFORCEMENT & COURTS

Indiana 6

LABOR & INCOME

Civilian labor force, 2000

total	3,084,000
men	1,701,000
women	1,383,000
persons 16-19 years	166,000
white	2,840,000
black	215,000

Civilian labor force as a percent of civilian non-institutional population, 2000

total	68.1%
men	76.8%
women	59.8%
persons 16-19 years	NA%
white	68.2%
black	69.5%

Employment, 2000

total	2,984,000
men	1,647,000
women	1,336,000
persons 16-19 years	146,000
white	2,760,000
black	197,000

Full-time/part-time labor force, 1998

full-time labor force	NA
working part-time for economic reasons	23,000
part-time labor force	NA

Unemployment rate, 2000

total	3.2%
men	3.1%
women	3.4%
persons 16-19 years	11.9%
white	2.8%
black	8.5%

Unemployed by reason for unemployment (as a percent of total unemployment), 1998

job losers or completed temp jobs	NA%
job leavers	NA%
reentrants	NA%
new entrants	NA%

Experienced civilian labor force, by occupation, 1998

executive/administrative/managerial	403,000
professional/specialty	369,000
technicians & related support	NA
sales	339,000
administrative support/clerical	442,000
service occupations	381,000
precision production/craft/repair	364,000
machine operators/assemblers	326,000
transportation/material moving	145,000
handlers/helpers/laborers	165,000
farming/forestry/fishing	NA

Experienced civilian labor force, by industry, 1998

construction	150,000
manufacturing	774,000
transportation/communication	168,000
wholesale/retail trade	579,000
finance/real estate/insurance	167,000
services	666,000
government	313,000
agriculture	NA

Average annual pay, 1999 .... $30,027
change in average annual pay, 1998-1999 .... 3.2%

Hours and earnings of production workers on manufacturing payrolls, 2000

average weekly hours	42.1
average hourly earnings	$15.83
average weekly earnings	$666.44

Labor union membership, 2000 418,400

Household income (in 2000 dollars)
median household income, three year average, 1998-2000 .... $39,717

Poverty
persons below poverty level, three year average, 1998-2000 .... 8.2%

Personal income ($per capita)
2000 (prelim.)
 in current dollars $27,011
 in constant (1996) dollars $25,159
1999 (preliminary)
 in current dollars $26,092
 in constant (1996) dollars $24,949

Federal income tax returns, 1999

returns filed	2,803,511
adjusted gross income ($1,000)	$115,131,164
total income tax paid ($1,000)	$16,553,207

ECONOMY, BUSINESS, INDUSTRY & AGRICULTURE

Fortune 500 companies, 2000 5

Business incorporations, 1998
total 11,996
change, 1997-1998 .... -5.8%

Business failures, 1998 473

Business firm ownership, 1997
Hispanic owned firms 4,277
Black owned firms 11,107
women owned firms 107,082
Asian & Pacific Islander owned firms 4,854
American Indian & Alaska
    native owned firms 2,898

Shopping centers, 2000 926

Gross state product, 1999 ($mil)
total $182,202
    agriculture services, forestry, fisheries .. $1,820
    mining $761
    construction $9,235
    manufacturing--durable goods $39,502
    manufacturing--nondurable goods $16,792
    transportation, communication &
        public utilities $13,845
    wholesale trade $11,157
    retail trade $16,853
    finance/real estate/insurance $23,744
    services $30,219
    federal, state & local government $18,273

Establishments, by major industry group, 1999
total 146,528
    forestry, fishing & agriculture 260
    mining 333
    construction 16,591
    manufacturing 9,320
    transportation & warehousing 4,520
    wholesale trade 8,788
    retail trade 24,431
    finance & insurance 9,441
    professional/scientific/technical 11,223
    health care/social assistance 12,627
    information 2,161
    accommodation/food services 11,673

Payroll, by major industry group, 1999
total ($1,000) $75,591,951
    forestry, fishing & agriculture $48,269
    mining $272,705
    construction $5,097,320
    manufacturing $24,712,126
    transportation & warehousing $2,790,780
    wholesale trade $4,384,107
    retail trade $6,070,539
    finance & insurance $4,427,830
    professional/scientific/technical $3,066,733
    health care/social assistance $8,724,968
    information $1,563,614
    accommodation/food services $2,188,041

Agriculture
number of farms, 2000 64,000
farm acreage, 2000 16,000,000
acres per farm, 2000 242
value of farms, 1997 ($mil) $31,323
farm income, 1999 ($mil)
    net farm income $421
    debt/asset ratio 15.8%
farm marketings, 1999 ($mil)
total $4,373
    crops $2,792
    livestock $1,581
principal commodities, in order by marketing
receipts, 1999
    Corn, soybeans, hogs, dairy products

Federal economic activity in state
expenditures, 2000
    total ($mil) $28,723
    per capita $4,724
    defense ($mil) $2,506
    non-defense ($mil) $26,218
defense department, 2000
    contract awards ($mil) $1,611
    payroll ($mil) $929
    civilian employees (x1,000) 9.3
    military personnel (x1,000) 1.1

Fishing, 2000
catch (thousands of pounds) ....NA
value ($1,000) ....$NA

Mining, 2000 ($mil; preliminary)
total non-fuel mineral production $729

Indiana 8

Construction, 1999 ($mil)
total contracts (including
    non-building) $10,437
      residential $5,127
      non-residential $3,775

Construction industries, 1997
establishments 15,627
receipts ($1,000) .... $NA
annual payroll ($1,000) .... $NA
paid employees .... NA

Manufacturing, 1997
establishments 9,361
value of shipments ($1,000) $143,606,930
annual payroll ($1,000) $22,476,650
paid employees 637,736

Transportation industries, 1997
establishments 6,662
receipts ($1,000) $24,965,721
annual payroll ($1,000) $4,071,112
paid employees 127,195

Wholesale trade, 1997
establishments 10,612
sales($1,000) $70,169,880
annual payroll ($1,000) $4,170,280
paid employees 129,290

Retail trade, 1997
establishments 34,398
sales($1,000) $59,181,921
annual payroll ($1,000) $6,483,600
paid employees 516,853

Finance industries
establishments, 1997 13,588
receipts ($1,000), 1997 .... $NA
annual payroll ($1,000), 1997 .... $NA
paid employees, 1997 .... NA
commercial banks, 2000
  number 153
    assets ($bil) $84.6
    deposits ($bil) $54.6

Service industries, 1997 (non-exempt firms only)
establishments 38,836
receipts ($1,000) $27,451,336
annual payroll ($1,000) $10,402,214
paid employees 455,626

COMMUNICATION, ENERGY & TRANSPORTATION

Communication
daily newspapers, 2000 68
households with
  telephones, 1998 .... 93.9%
  computers, 2000 .... 48.8%
  internet access, 2000 .... 39.4%

Energy
consumption, 1999
total (trillion Btu) 2,736
per capita (million Btu) 460
by source of production (trillion Btu)
  coal 1,451
  natural gas 577
  petroleum 899
  nuclear electric power .... NA
  hydroelectric power 4
by end-use sector (trillion Btu)
  residential 484
  commercial 301
  industrial 1,306
  transportation 645
electric energy, 1999
  production (billion kWh) 114.2
  net summer capability (million kW) 20.4
gas utilities, 1999
  customers 1,713,000
  sales (trillion Btu) 245
nuclear plants, 1999 .... na

Transportation, 2000
public road & street mileage
total 93,608
  urban 19,944
  rural 73,664
  interstate 1,169
vehicle miles of travel (mil) 70,862
total motor vehicle registrations 5,570,942
  automobiles 3,244,937
  motorcycles 117,331
licensed drivers 3,976,241
  per 1,000 driving age population 849
deaths from motor vehicle
  accidents 875

Iowa 1

STATE SUMMARY

Capital City .... Des Moines

Governor .... Tom Vilsack

Address .... STATE CAPITOL
DES MOINES, IA 50319
515 281-5211

Admitted as a state 1846

Area (square miles) 56,276

Population, 1980 2,913,808

Population, 1990 2,776,755

Population, 2000 2,926,324

Persons per square mile, 2000 .... 52.4

Largest city .... Des Moines
population, 2000 199,000

Personal income per capita, 2000
(in current dollars) $26,723

Gross state product ($mil), 1999 .... $85,243

Leading industries, 1999 (by payroll)
Manufacturing
Health care/Social assistance
Retail trade

Leading agricultural commodities, 1999
Corn, hogs, soybeans, cattle

GEOGRAPHY & ENVIRONMENT

Area, 1990 (square miles)
total 56,276
land 55,875
water (includes territorial water) 401

Federally owned land, 2000 .... 0.6%

Highest point
name ...... Sec. 29 T 100N R 41W (Oscealo Co.)
elevation (feet) 1,670

Lowest point
name .... Mississippi River
elevation (feet) 480

General coastline (miles) 0

Tidal shoreline (miles) 0

Capital city .... Des Moines
population, 2000 199,000

Largest city .... Des Moines
population, 2000 199,000

Number of cities with over 100,000 population
1980 2
1990 2
2000 2

State parks and Recreation areas, 2000
area (acres) 63,000
number of visitors 15,152,000
revenues $3,234,000

Natl. forest system land, 1999 (acres) 0

National park acreage, 1984 1,700

DEMOGRAPHICS & CHARACTERISTICS OF THE POPULATION

Population
1970 2,825,368
1980 2,913,808
1990 2,776,755
2000 2,926,324
2015 (projection) 2,994,000
2025 (projection) 3,040,000

Metropolitan area population
1970 1,154,000
1980 1,223,000
2000 1,326,000

Non-metropolitan area population
1970 1,671,000
1980 1,691,000
2000 1,600,000

Change in population, 1990-2000
number 149,569
percent 5.39%

Persons per square mile, 2000 .... 52.4

Persons by age, 2000
under 5 years 188,413
18 and over 2,192,686
21 and over 2,051,156
65 and over 436,213
85 and over 65,118

Iowa 2

Persons by age, 2025 (projected)
under 5 years 175,000
5 to 17 years 492,000
65 and over 686,000

Median age, 2000 .... 36.6

Race, 2000
One race
White 2,748,640
Black or African American 61,853
American Indian and Alaska Native 8,989
Asian Indian 5,641
Chinese 6,161
Filipino 2,272
Japanese 1,474
Korean 5,063
Vietnamese 7,129
Native Hawaiian and other Pacific Islander 1,009
Two or more races 31,778

Race, 2025 (projected)
White 2,858,000
Black 91,000

Persons of Hispanic origin, 2000
total Hispanic or Latino 82,473
  Mexican 61,154
  Puerto Rican 2,690
  Cuban 750
  Other Hispanic or Latino 17,879

Persons of Hispanic origin, 2025 (proj.) ... 96,000

Persons by sex, 2000
male 1,435,515
female 1,490,809

Marital status, 1990
males
  15 years & older 1,033,960
    single 281,081
    married 656,858
      separated 9,933
    widowed 27,309
    divorced 68,712
females
  15 years & older 1,136,037
    single 232,630
    married 658,571
      separated 13,418

widowed 154,259
divorced 90,577

Households & families, 2000
households 1,149,276
persons per household 2.46
  families 769,684
    persons per family 3
    married couples 633,254
    female householder, no husband
      present 98,270
    one person households 313,083
households with persons under 18 years . 382,455
households with persons over 65 years ... 291,420

Nativity, 1990
number of persons born in state 2,154,669
percent of total residents 77.6%

Immigration & naturalization, 1998
immigrants admitted 1,655
persons naturalized 191
refugees granted resident status 180

VITAL STATISTICS & HEALTH
Births
1999
  with low birth weight 6.2%
  to teenage mothers 13.1%
  to unmarried mothers 27.5%
Birth rate, 1999 (per 1,000) 13.1
Birth rate, 2000 (per 1,000) 13.4

Abortions, 1996
total 6,000
rate (per 1,000 women age 15-44) 9.4

Deaths
1998 27,569
1999 28,411
2000 28,082

Infant deaths
1998 239
1999 243
2000 224

Average lifetime, by race, 1989-1991
total .... 77.29 years
  white .... 77.38 years
  black .... NA years

Iowa 3

Marriages
1998 23,540
1999 22,965
2000 20,256

Divorces
1998 9,546
1999 9,874
2000 9,440

Physicians, 1999
total 5,009
rate (per 1,000 persons) 1.75

Nurses, 1999
total 31,220
rate (per 1,000 persons) 10.88

Hospitals, 1998
number 116
beds (x 1,000) 12.2
average daily census (x 1,000) 6.9
patients admitted (x1,000) 374
average cost per day to hospital, 1995 ...... $702
average cost per stay to hospital, 1995 .... $5,049

EDUCATION

Educational attainment of all persons 25 years and older, 1990
less than 9th grade 163,335
high school graduates 684,368
bachelor's degree 207,269
graduate or professional degree 92,123

2000
high school graduate or more 89.7%
college graduate or more 25.5%

Public school enrollment, Fall, 1998
total 498,214
Kindergarten through grade 8 336,696
grades 9 through 12 161,518

Public School Teachers, 2000
total 33,900
elementary 15,900
secondary 18,000
average salaries
elementary $34,700
secondary $36,500

State receipts & expenditures for public schools, 2000
revenue receipts ($mil) $3,724

State receipts & expenditures for public schools, 2000 (continued)
expenditures
total ($mil) $3,417
per capita $1,191
per pupil $6,386

Graduating high school seniors, public high schools, 2000 (est.) 34,149

SAT scores, 2001
verbal 593
math 603
percent graduates taking test 5%

Institutions of higher education, 1999
total 59
public 20
private 39

Enrollment in institutions of higher education, Fall, 1998
total 181,944
full-time men 59,836
full-time women 65,630
part-time men 21,847
part-time women 34,631

Minority enrollment in institutions of higher education, Fall, 1997
Black, non-Hispanic 5,048
Hispanic 3,044
Asian/Pacific Islander 4,021

Earned degrees conferred, 1998
Bachelor's 17,543
First professional 1,566
Master's 3,589
Doctor's 648

SOCIAL INSURANCE & WELFARE PROGRAMS

Social Security beneficiaries & benefits, 2000
beneficiaries
total 540,000
retired and dependents 396,000
survivors 82,000
disabled & dependents 62,000
annual benefit payments ($mil)
total $4,891
retired and dependents $3,417
survivors $968
disabled & dependents $505

Iowa 4

Medicare, 2000
enrollment (x1,000) 476
payments ($mil) $1,453

Medicaid, 1998
recipients (x1,000) 315
payments ($mil) $1,289

Federal public aid
Temporary Assistance for Needy Families
(TANF), 2000
   Recipients (x1,000) 53
   Families (x1,000) 20
Supplemental Security Income
  total recipients, 1999 (x1,000) 40

Food Stamp Program
  participants, 2000 (x1,000) 123

HOUSING & CONSTRUCTION

Total housing units, 2000 1,232,511
  seasonal or recreational use 16,472
  occupied 1,149,276
    owner occupied 831,419
    renter occupied 317,857

New privately owned housing units uthorized, 2000
number (x1,000) 12.5
value ($mil) $1,333

New privately owned housing units
  started, 2000 (est.) (x1,000) 13.0

Existing home sales, 2000 (x1,000) 53.1

GOVERNMENT & ELECTIONS

State officials, 2002
Governor (name/party/term expires)
            TOM VILSACK
           Democrate - 2002
Lt. Governor . . . . Sally Pedersen
Sec. of State . . . . Chet Culver
Atty. General . . . . Tom Miller
Chief Justice . . . . Louis Lavorato

Governorship
minimum age 30
length of term . . . . 4 years
number of consecutive
  terms permitted . . . . not specified
who succeeds . . . . Lt. Governor

State legislature
name . . . . General Assembly
  upper chamber
    name . . . . Senate
    number of members 50
    length of term . . . . 4 years
    party in majority, 2000 . . . . Republican
  lower chamber
    name . . . . House of Representatives
    number of members 100
    length of term . . . . 2 years
    party in majority, 2000 . . . . Republican

State employees March, 2000
total 66,461
March payroll $187,723,629

Local governments, 1997
total 1,876
  county 99
  municipal 950
  township 0
  school districts 394
  special districts 433

Voting age population, November, 2000, projected
Total 2,165,000
  male 1,038,000
  female 1,127,000

Vote for president
2000
  Gore 639,000
  Bush 634,000
1996
  Clinton 620,000
  Dole 493,000
  Perot 105,000

Federal representation, 2002 (107th Congress)
Senators (name/party/term expires)

           TOM HARKIN
          Democrat - 2003
      CHARLES E. GRASSLEY
         Republican - 2005

Representatives, total 5
  Democrats 1
  Republicans 4
  other 0

Women holding public office, 2001
U.S. Congress 0
statewide elected office 2
state legislature 33

Black elected officials, 1999
total 14
   US and state legislatures 1
   city/county/regional offices 8
   judicial/law enforcement 1
   education/school boards 4

Hispanic public officials, 2000
total 1
   state executives & legislators .... NA
   city/county/regional offices 1
   judicial/law enforcement .... NA
   education/school boards .... NA

GOVERNMENTAL FINANCE

State government revenues, 1999 ($per capita)
total revenue $4,052.75
  total general revenue $3,208.95
   intergovernmental revenue $859.93
   taxes $1,696.69
   current charges $411.38
   miscellaneous $240.95

State government expenditures, 1999 ($per capita)
total expenditure $3,596.73
  total general expenditure $3,325.64
   education $1,336.09
   public welfare $704.57
   health $72.55
   hospitals $201.01
   highways $414.07
   police protection $26.44
   correction $89.08
   natural resources $79.92
   governmental administration $136.80
   interest on general debt $29.64

State debt, 1999 ($per capita) $861.52

Federal government grants to state & local government, 2000 (x$1,000)
total $2,639,454
  Dept. of Education $251,282
  Environmental Protection Agency $45,011
  Health Care Financing Admin. $1,108,960
  Dept. Housing & Urban Devel. $200,129
  Dept. of Labor $37,897
  Highway trust fund $304,606

CRIME, LAW ENFORCEMENT & COURTS

Crime, 2000 (all rates per 100,000 inhabitants)
total crimes 94,630
overall crime rate 3,233.7
  property crimes 86,834
   burglaries 16,342
   larcenies 65,118
   motor vehicle thefts 5,374
  property crime rate 2,967.3
  violent crimes 7,796
   murders 46
   forcible rapes 676
   robberies 1,071
   aggravated assaults 6,003
  violent crime rate 266.4

Number of police agencies, 2000 184

Arrests, 2000
total 113,918
  persons under 18 years of age 23,042

Prisoners under state & federal jurisdiction, 2000
total 7,955
percent change, 1999-2000 .... 10.0%
  sentenced to more than one year
   total 7,955
   rate per 100,000 residents 276

Persons under sentence of death, 4/1/2001 ... NA

State's highest court
name .... Supreme Court
number of members 9
length of term .... 8 years
intermediate appeals court? .... yes

Iowa 6

LABOR & INCOME

Civilian labor force, 2000
total 1,563,000
  men 837,000
  women 726,000
  persons 16-19 years 109,000
  white 1,506,000
  black .... NA

Civilian labor force as a percent of civilian non-institutional population, 2000
total 71.3%
  men 76.9%
  women 65.7%
  persons 16-19 years ....NA%
  white 71.5%
  black .... NA%

Employment, 2000
total 1,522,000
  men 817,000
  women 705,000
  persons 16-19 years 99,000
  white 1,471,000
  black .... NA

Full-time/part-time labor force, 1998
full-time labor force ....NA
  working part-time for
    economic reasons 15,000
part-time labor force ....NA

Unemployment rate, 2000
total 2.6%
  men 2.4%
  women 2.9%
  persons 16-19 years 8.8%
  white 2.3%
  black .... NA%

Unemployed by reason for unemployment (as a percent of total unemployment), 1998
job losers or completed temp jobs .... NA%
job leavers .... NA%
reentrants .... NA%
new entrants .... NA%

Experienced civilian labor force, by occupation, 1998
executive/administrative/managerial 174,000
professional/specialty 206,000
technicians & related support ....NA

sales 195,000
administrative support/clerical 206,000
service occupations 218,000
precision production/craft/repair 179,000
machine operators/assemblers 100,000
transportation/material moving 71,000
handlers/helpers/laborers 68,000
farming/forestry/fishing 92,000

Experienced civilian labor force, by industry, 1998
construction 69,000
manufacturing 260,000
transportation/communication 66,000
wholesale/retail trade 317,000
finance/real estate/insurance 97,000
services 337,000
government 204,000
agriculture 98,000

Average annual pay, 1999 .... $26,939
change in average annual pay,
  1998-1999 .... 3.5%

Hours and earnings of production workers on manufacturing payrolls, 2000
average weekly hours 41.6
average hourly earnings $14.66
average weekly earnings $609.86

Labor union membership, 2000 181,800

Household income (in 2000 dollars)
median household income,
  three year average, 1998-2000 .... $42,993

Poverty
persons below poverty level,
  three year average, 1998-2000 .... 7.9%

Personal income ($per capita)
2000 (prelim.)
  in current dollars $26,723
  in constant (1996) dollars $24,891
1999 (preliminary)
  in current dollars $25,727
  in constant (1996) dollars $24,600

Federal income tax returns, 1999
returns filed 1,345,040
adjusted gross income ($1,000) $52,170,593
total income tax paid ($1,000) $7,087,242

ECONOMY, BUSINESS, INDUSTRY & AGRICULTURE

Fortune 500 companies, 2000 2

Business incorporations, 1998
total 4,173
change, 1997-1998 .... -11.1%

Business failures, 1998 244

Business firm ownership, 1997
Hispanic owned firms 1,343
Black owned firms 1,353
women owned firms 57,527
Asian & Pacific Islander owned firms 1,741
American Indian & Alaska
   native owned firms 949

Shopping centers, 2000 326

Gross state product, 1999 ($mil)
total $85,243
   agriculture services, forestry, fisheries .. $3,000
   mining $218
   construction $3,759
   manufacturing--durable goods $10,747
   manufacturing--nondurable goods $8,311
   transportation, communication &
      public utilities $7,231
   wholesale trade $6,700
   retail trade $7,705
   finance/real estate/insurance $12,865
   services $14,450
   federal, state & local government $10,258

Establishments, by major industry group, 1999
total 81,213
   forestry, fishing & agriculture 271
   mining 189
   construction 8,621
   manufacturing 3,828
   transportation & warehousing 3,198
   wholesale trade 5,256
   retail trade 14,494
   finance & insurance 5,443
   professional/scientific/technical 5,486
   health care/social assistance 7,093
   information 1,563
   accommodation/food services 6,566

Payroll, by major industry group, 1999
total ($1,000) $32,026,668
   forestry, fishing & agriculture $57,426
   mining $68,283
   construction $2,149,404
   manufacturing $8,199,078
   transportation & warehousing $1,103,983
   wholesale trade $2,111,419
   retail trade $3,032,142
   finance & insurance $2,966,595
   professional/scientific/technical $1,167,818
   health care/social assistance $4,350,831
   information $1,186,009
   accommodation/food services $946,528

Agriculture
number of farms, 2000 95,000
farm acreage, 2000 33,000,000
acres per farm, 2000 345
value of farms, 1997 ($mil) $54,780
farm income, 1999 ($mil)
   net farm income $1,450
   debt/asset ratio 18.7%
farm marketings, 1999 ($mil)
total $9,716
   crops $5,004
   livestock $4,712
principal commodities, in order by marketing
receipts, 1999
   Corn, hogs, soybeans, cattle

Federal economic activity in state
expenditures, 2000
   total ($mil) $14,751
   per capita $5,041
   defense ($mil) $896
   non-defense ($mil) $13,855
defense department, 2000
   contract awards ($mil) $621
   payroll ($mil) $272
   civilian employees (x1,000) 1.5
   military personnel (x1,000) 0.4

Fishing, 2000
catch (thousands of pounds) .... NA
value ($1,000) .... $NA

Mining, 2000 ($mil; preliminary)
total non-fuel mineral production $510

Iowa 8

Construction, 1999 ($mil)
total contracts (including
    non-building) $3,825
       residential $1,418
       non-residential $1,333

Construction industries, 1997
establishments 7,822
receipts ($1,000) $8,013,465
annual payroll ($1,000) $1,723,041
paid employees .... NA

Manufacturing, 1997
establishments 3,934
value of shipments ($1,000) $63,640,436
annual payroll ($1,000) $7,849,890
paid employees 244,994

Transportation industries, 1997
establishments 4,637
receipts ($1,000) $10,662,026
annual payroll ($1,000) $1,791,260
paid employees 61,007

Wholesale trade, 1997
establishments 6,755
sales($1,000) $38,422,230
annual payroll ($1,000) $2,118,459
paid employees 75,462

Retail trade, 1997
establishments 19,647
sales($1,000) $26,283,470
annual payroll ($1,000) $2,985,443
paid employees 250,724

Finance industries
establishments, 1997 7,670
receipts ($1,000), 1997 .... $NA
annual payroll ($1,000), 1997 .... $2,749,916
paid employees, 1997 82,571
commercial banks, 2000
    number 431
       assets ($bil) $44.6
       deposits ($bil) $34.3

Service industries, 1997 (non-exempt firms only)
establishments 19,560
receipts ($1,000) $12,056,850
annual payroll ($1,000) $4,375,569
paid employees 210,117

COMMUNICATION, ENERGY & TRANSPORTATION

Communication
daily newspapers, 2000 37
households with
    telephones, 1998 .... 96.0%
    computers, 2000 .... 53.6%
    internet access, 2000 .... 39.0%

Energy
consumption, 1999
total (trillion Btu) 1,122
per capita (million Btu) 391
by source of production (trillion Btu)
    coal 416
    natural gas 236
    petroleum 419
    nuclear electric power 39
    hydroelectric power 10
by end-use sector (trillion Btu)
    residential 223
    commercial 159
    industrial 463
    transportation 278
electric energy, 1999
    production (billion kWh) 37
    net summer capability (million kW) ... 8.4
gas utilities, 1999
    customers 888,000
    sales (trillion Btu) 121
nuclear plants, 1999 1

Transportation, 2000
public road & street mileage
total 113,377
    urban 9,864
    rural 103,513
    interstate 782
vehicle miles of travel (mil) 29,433
total motor vehicle registrations 3,106,223
    automobiles 1,751,690
    motorcycles 126,421
licensed drivers 1,952,508
    per 1,000 driving age population 856
deaths from motor vehicle
    accidents 445

STATE SUMMARY

Capital City .... Topeka

Governor .... Bill Graves

Address .... STATE CAPITOL
TOPEKA, KS 66612
785 296-3232

Admitted as a state 1861

Area (square miles) 82,282

Population, 1980 2,363,679

Population, 1990 2,477,574

Population, 2000 2,688,418

Persons per square mile, 2000 .... 32.9

Largest city .... Wichita
population, 2000 344,000

Personal income per capita, 2000
(in current dollars) $27,816

Gross state product ($mil), 1999 .... $80,843

Leading industries, 1999 (by payroll)
Manufacturing
Health care/Social assistance
Retail trade

Leading agricultural commodities, 1999
Cattle, wheat, corn, sorghum grain

GEOGRAPHY & ENVIRONMENT

Area, 1990 (square miles)
total 82,282
land 81,823
water (includes territorial water) 459

Federally owned land, 2000 .... 1.3%

Highest point
name .... Mt. Sunflower
elevation (feet) 4,039

Lowest point
name .... Verdigris River
elevation (feet) 679

General coastline (miles) 0

Tidal shoreline (miles) 0

Capital city .... Topeka
population, 2000 122,000

Largest city .... Wichita
population, 2000 344,000

Number of cities with over 100,000 population
1930 3
1990 4
2000 4

State parks and Recreation areas, 2000
area (acres) 32,000
number of visitors 7,202,000
revenues $4,242,000

Natl. forest system land, 1999 (acres) 108,000

National park acreage, 1984 700

DEMOGRAPHICS & CHARACTERISTICS OF THE POPULATION

Population
1970 2,249,071
1980 2,363,679
1990 2,477,574
2000 2,688,418
2015 (projection) 2,939,000
2025 (projection) 3,108,000

Metropolitan area population
1970 1,109,000
1980 1,184,000
2000 1,521,000

Non-metropolitan area population
1970 1,140,000
1980 1,180,000
2000 1,167,000

Change in population, 1990-2000
number 210,844
percent 8.51%

Persons per square mile, 2000 .... 32.9

Persons by age, 2000
under 5 years 188,708
18 and over 1,975,425
21 and over 1,847,513
65 and over 356,229
85 and over 51,770

Kansas 2

Persons by age, 2025 (projected)
under 5 years 203,000
5 to 17 years 548,000
65 and over 605,000

Median age, 2000 .... 35.2

Race, 2000
One race
White 2,313,944
Black or African American 154,198
American Indian and Alaska Native 24,936
Asian Indian 8,153
Chinese 7,624
Filipino 3,509
Japanese 1,935
Korean 4,529
Vietnamese 11,623
Native Hawaiian and other Pacific Islander   1,313
Two or more races 56,496

Race, 2025 (projected)
White 2,741,000
Black 249,000

Persons of Hispanic origin, 2000
total Hispanic or Latino 188,252
  Mexican 148,270
  Puerto Rican 5,237
  Cuban 1,680
  Other Hispanic or Latino 33,065

Persons of Hispanic origin, 2025 (proj.) .. 281,000

Persons by sex, 2000
male 1,328,474
female 1,359,944

Marital status, 1990
males
  15 years & older 924,895
    single 244,866
    married 585,864
     separated 9,846
    widowed 22,096
    divorced 72,069
females
  15 years & older 988,835
    single 189,997
    married 581,241
     separated 12,874

  widowed 122,731
  divorced 94,866

Households & families, 2000
households 1,037,891
persons per household 2.51
  families 701,547
  persons per family 3.07
  married couples 567,924
  female householder, no husband
    present 96,661
  one person households 280,387
households with persons under 18 years . 368,875
households with persons over 65 years ... 241,686

Nativity, 1990
number of persons born in state 1,519,904
percent of total residents 61.3%

Immigration & naturalization, 1998
immigrants admitted 3,184
persons naturalized 2,208
refugees granted resident status 136

VITAL STATISTICS & HEALTH
Births
1999
  with low birth weight 7.1%
  to teenage mothers 14.6%
  to unmarried mothers 28.6%
Birth rate, 1999 (per 1,000) 14.6
Birth rate, 2000 (per 1,000) 14.9

Abortions, 1996
total 11,000
rate (per 1,000 women age 15-44) 18.9

Deaths
1998 24,152
1999 24,472
2000 24,720

Infant deaths
1998 279
1999 269
2000 239

Average lifetime, by race, 1989-1991
total .... 76.76 years
  white .... 77.06 years
  black .... 71.22 years

Marriages
1998 20,878
1999 19,004
2000 22,232

Divorces
1998 10,691
1999 10,164
2000 10,580

Physicians, 1999
total 5,424
rate (per 1,000 persons) 2.04

Nurses, 1999
total 23,660
rate (per 1,000 persons) 8.91

Hospitals, 1998
number 129
beds (x 1,000) 10.9
average daily census (x 1,000) 5.9
patients admitted (x1,000) 300
average cost per day to hospital, 1995 ...... $732
average cost per stay to hospital, 1995 .... $5,308

EDUCATION

*Educational attainment of all persons
25 years and older, 1990*
less than 9th grade 120,951
high school graduates 514,177
bachelor's degree 221,016
graduate or professional degree 109,361

2000
high school graduate or more 88.1%
college graduate or more 27.3%

Public school enrollment, Fall, 1998
total 472,353
Kindergarten through grade 8 327,474
grades 9 through 12 144,879

Public School Teachers, 2000
total 33,200
elementary 16,900
secondary 16,300
average salaries
elementary $38,500
secondary $38,500

*State receipts & expenditures for public
schools, 2000*
revenue receipts ($mil) $3,595

*State receipts & expenditures for public
schools, 2000 (continued)*
expenditures
total ($mil) $3,327
per capita $1,254
per pupil $7,149

*Graduating high school seniors,
public high schools, 2000 (est.) 28,964*

SAT scores, 2001
verbal 577
math 580
percent graduates taking test 9%

Institutions of higher education, 1999
total 59
public 33
private 26

*Enrollment in institutions of higher
education, Fall, 1998*
total 177,639
full-time men 47,414
full-time women 50,638
part-time men 32,809
part-time women 46,778

*Minority enrollment in institutions of higher
education, Fall, 1997*
Black, non-Hispanic 8,957
Hispanic 7,999
Asian/Pacific Islander 4,204

Earned degrees conferred, 1998
Bachelor's 14,026
First professional 584
Master's 4,596
Doctor's 487

SOCIAL INSURANCE &
WELFARE PROGRAMS

Social Security beneficiaries & benefits, 2000
beneficiaries
total 440,000
retired and dependents 317,000
survivors 67,000
disabled & dependents 56,000
annual benefit payments ($mil)
total $4,057
retired and dependents $2,821
survivors $789
disabled & dependents $448

Kansas 4

Medicare, 2000
enrollment (x1,000) 389
payments ($mil) $1,915

Medicaid, 1998
recipients (x1,000) 242
payments ($mil) $916

Federal public aid
Temporary Assistance for Needy Families
(TANF), 2000
   Recipients (x1,000) 36
   Families (x1,000) 12
Supplemental Security Income
   total recipients, 1999 (x1,000) 36

Food Stamp Program
participants, 2000 (x1,000) 117

HOUSING & CONSTRUCTION

Total housing units, 2000 1,131,200
   seasonal or recreational use 9,639
   occupied 1,037,891
     owner occupied 718,703
     renter occupied 319,188

New privately owned housing units uthorized, 2000
number (x1,000) 12.5
value ($mil) $1,397

New privately owned housing units
started, 2000 (est.) (x1,000) 15.2

Existing home sales, 2000 (x1,000) 64.2

GOVERNMENT & ELECTIONS

State officials, 2002
   Governor (name/party/term expires)
BILL GRAVES
Republican - 2002
Lt. Governor .... Gary Sherrer
Sec. of State .... Ron Thornburgh
Atty. General ....Carla Stovall
Chief Justice .... Kay McFarland

Governorship
minimum age ....not specified
length of term .... 4 years
number of consecutive
   terms permitted 2
who succeeds .... Lt. Governor

State legislature
name .... Legislature
   upper chamber
     name .... Senate
     number of members 40
     length of term .... 4 years
     party in majority, 2000 .... Republican
   lower chamber
     name .... House of Representatives
     number of members 125
     length of term .... 2 years
     party in majority, 2000 .... Republican

State employees March, 2000
total 52,726
March payroll $123,743,477

Local governments, 1997
total 3,950
   county 105
   municipal 627
   township 1,370
   school districts 324
   special districts 1,524

Voting age population, November, 2000, projected
Total 1,983,000
   male 961,000
   female 1,022,000

Vote for president
2000
   Gore 399,000
   Bush 622,000
1996
   Clinton 388,000
   Dole 583,000
   Perot 93,000

Federal representation, 2002 (107th Congress)
Senators (name/party/term expires)

PAT ROBERTS
Republican - 2003
SAM BROWNBACK
Republican - 2005

Representatives, total 4
   Democrats 1
   Republicans 3
   other 0

Women holding public office, 2001
U.S. Congress 0
statewide elected office 2
state legislature 54

Black elected officials, 1999
total 19
   US and state legislatures 7
   city/county/regional offices 5
   judicial/law enforcement 4
   education/school boards 3

Hispanic public officials, 2000
total 6
   state executives & legislators 2
   city/county/regional offices 4
   judicial/law enforcement .... NA
   education/school boards .... NA

GOVERNMENTAL FINANCE

State government revenues, 1999 ($per capita)
total revenue $3,273.16
   total general revenue $2,862.55
    intergovernmental revenue $710.33
    taxes $1,729.23
    current charges $244.29
    miscellaneous $178.70

State government expenditures, 1999 ($per capita)
total expenditure $3,153.91
   total general expenditure $2,892.80
    education $1,400.90
    public welfare $473.61
    health $129.03
    hospitals $61.43
    highways $361.53
    police protection $17.44
    correction $101.29
    natural resources $63.72
    governmental administration $115.03
    interest on general debt $7.38

State debt, 1999 ($per capita) $558.51

*Federal government grants to state & local
government, 2000 (x$1,000)*
total $2,314,551
   Dept. of Education $261,667
   Environmental Protection Agency $49,484
   Health Care Financing Admin. $929,059
   Dept. Housing & Urban Devel. $164,541
   Dept. of Labor $36,704
   Highway trust fund $304,381

CRIME, LAW ENFORCEMENT & COURTS

Crime, 2000 (all rates per 100,000 inhabitants)
total crimes 118,527
overall crime rate 4,408.8
   property crimes 108,057
    burglaries 21,484
    larcenies 80,077
    motor vehicle thefts 6,496
   property crime rate 4,019.4
   violent crimes 10,470
    murders 169
    forcible rapes 1,022
    robberies 2,048
    aggravated assaults 7,231
   violent crime rate 389.4

Number of police agencies, 2000 .... na

Arrests, 2000
total .... NA
   persons under 18 years of age .... na

Prisoners under state & federal jurisdiction, 2000
total 8,344
percent change, 1999-2000 .... -2.6%
   sentenced to more than one year
    total 8,344
    rate per 100,000 residents 312

Persons under sentence of death, 4/1/2001 4

State's highest court
name .... Supreme Court
number of members 7
length of term .... 6 years
intermediate appeals court? .... yes

Kansas 6

LABOR & INCOME

Civilian labor force, 2000

total	1,411,000
men	731,000
women	680,000
persons 16-19 years	105,000
white	1,278,000
black	90,000

Civilian labor force as a percent of civilian non-institutional population, 2000

total	70.5%
men	75.7%
women	65.7%
persons 16-19 years	NA%
white	70.5%
black	72.2%

Employment, 2000

total	1,359,000
men	703,000
women	655,000
persons 16-19 years	91,000
white	1,238,000
black	81,000

Full-time/part-time labor force, 1998

full-time labor force	1,130,000
working part-time for economic reasons	13,000
part-time labor force	280,000

Unemployment rate, 2000

total	3.7%
men	3.8%
women	3.6%
persons 16-19 years	13.3%
white	3.1%
black	9.9%

Unemployed by reason for unemployment (as a percent of total unemployment), 1998

job losers or completed temp jobs	44.4%
job leavers	16.7%
reentrants	37.0%
new entrants	3.7%

Experienced civilian labor force, by occupation, 1998

executive/administrative/managerial	192,000
professional/specialty	203,000
technicians & related support	45,000
sales	166,000
administrative support/clerical	195,000
service occupations	188,000
precision production/craft/repair	154,000
machine operators/assemblers	89,000
transportation/material moving	53,000
handlers/helpers/laborers	60,000
farming/forestry/fishing	63,000

Experienced civilian labor force, by industry, 1998

construction	65,000
manufacturing	213,000
transportation/communication	73,000
wholesale/retail trade	250,000
finance/real estate/insurance	70,000
services	322,000
government	224,000
agriculture	63,000

Average annual pay, 1999 ... $28,029

change in average annual pay, 1998-1999	4.4%

Hours and earnings of production workers on manufacturing payrolls, 2000

average weekly hours	40.6
average hourly earnings	$14.98
average weekly earnings	$608.19

Labor union membership, 2000 ... 108,500

Household income (in 2000 dollars)

median household income, three year average, 1998-2000	$37,705

Poverty

persons below poverty level, three year average, 1998-2000	10.4%

Personal income ($per capita)

2000 (prelim.)

in current dollars	$27,816
in constant (1996) dollars	$25,909

1999 (preliminary)

in current dollars	$26,633
in constant (1996) dollars	$25,467

Federal income tax returns, 1999

returns filed	1,211,713
adjusted gross income ($1,000)	$50,957,887
total income tax paid ($1,000)	$7,434,908

ECONOMY, BUSINESS, INDUSTRY & AGRICULTURE

Fortune 500 companies, 2000 2

Business incorporations, 1998
total 4,780
change, 1997-1998 .... -1.4%

Business failures, 1998 1,140

Business firm ownership, 1997
Hispanic owned firms 3,547
Black owned firms 3,396
women owned firms 54,638
Asian & Pacific Islander owned firms 2,626
American Indian & Alaska
  native owned firms 2,318

Shopping centers, 2000 493

Gross state product, 1999 ($mil)
total $80,843
  agriculture services, forestry, fisheries .. $2,304
  mining $1,022
  construction $3,711
  manufacturing--durable goods $7,344
  manufacturing--nondurable goods $6,254
  transportation, communication &
    public utilities $10,093
  wholesale trade $6,426
  retail trade $8,318
  finance/real estate/insurance $10,389
  services $14,105
  federal, state & local government $10,876

Establishments, by major industry group, 1999
total 74,486
  forestry, fishing & agriculture 199
  mining 894
  construction 7,648
  manufacturing 3,295
  transportation & warehousing 2,407
  wholesale trade 4,964
  retail trade 12,286
  finance & insurance 5,133
  professional/scientific/technical 6,245
  health care/social assistance 6,440
  information 1,456
  accommodation/food services 5,549

Payroll, by major industry group, 1999
total ($1,000) $30,600,434
  forestry, fishing & agriculture ....$NA
  mining $201,979
  construction $2,130,775
  manufacturing $6,960,734
  transportation & warehousing $1,006,633
  wholesale trade $2,559,720
  retail trade $2,645,944
  finance & insurance $1,960,203
  professional/scientific/technical $1,913,542
  health care/social assistance $3,883,933
  information $1,507,032
  accommodation/food services $901,809

Agriculture
number of farms, 2000 64,000
farm acreage, 2000 48,000,000
acres per farm, 2000 742
value of farms, 1997 ($mil) $27,485
farm income, 1999 ($mil)
  net farm income $1,548
  debt/asset ratio 20.1%
farm marketings, 1999 ($mil)
total $7,616
  crops $2,607
  livestock $5,009
principal commodities, in order by marketing
receipts, 1999
  Cattle, wheat, corn, sorghum grain

Federal economic activity in state
expenditures, 2000
  total ($mil) $14,260
  per capita $5,304
  defense ($mil) $2,048
  non-defense ($mil) $12,212
defense department, 2000
  contract awards ($mil) $891
  payroll ($mil) $1,136
  civilian employees (x1,000) 5.5
  military personnel (x1,000) 15.5

Fishing, 2000
catch (thousands of pounds) ....NA
value ($1,000) ....$NA

Mining, 2000 ($mil; preliminary)
total non-fuel mineral production $624

Kansas 8

Construction, 1999 ($mil)
total contracts (including
    non-building) $4,388
      residential $1,958
      non-residential $1,654

Construction industries, 1997
establishments 7,000
receipts ($1,000) $8,770,376
annual payroll ($1,000) .... $NA
paid employees 61,345

Manufacturing, 1997
establishments 3,471
value of shipments ($1,000) $48,611,181
annual payroll ($1,000) $6,772,450
paid employees 203,303

Transportation industries, 1997
establishments 3,753
receipts ($1,000) $11,749,763
annual payroll ($1,000) $2,138,854
paid employees 61,856

Wholesale trade, 1997
establishments 5,965
sales($1,000) $44,113,075
annual payroll ($1,000) $2,155,061
paid employees 68,008

Retail trade, 1997
establishments 16,629
sales($1,000) $23,080,403
annual payroll ($1,000) $2,651,788
paid employees 214,819

Finance industries
establishments, 1997 7,423
receipts ($1,000), 1997 .... $NA
annual payroll ($1,000), 1997 .... $2,103,069
paid employees, 1997 64,496
commercial banks, 2000
   number 376
     assets ($bil) $37.9
     deposits ($bil) $31.0

Service industries, 1997 (non-exempt firms only)
establishments 19,341
receipts ($1,000) $13,095,658
annual payroll ($1,000) $5,000,164
paid employees 220,599

COMMUNICATION, ENERGY & TRANSPORTATION

Communication
daily newspapers, 2000 45
households with
   telephones, 1998 .... 94.5%
   computers, 2000 .... 55.8%
   internet access, 2000 .... 43.9%

Energy
consumption, 1999
total (trillion Btu) 1,050
per capita (million Btu) 396
by source of production (trillion Btu)
   coal 329
   natural gas 302
   petroleum 437
   nuclear electric power 97
   hydroelectric power .... NA
by end-use sector (trillion Btu)
   residential 201
   commercial 169
   industrial 392
   transportation 288
electric energy, 1999
   production (billion kWh) 42
   net summer capability (million kW) ... 10
gas utilities, 1999
   customers 1,621,000
   sales (trillion Btu) 192
nuclear plants, 1999 1

Transportation, 2000
public road & street mileage
total 134,582
   urban 10,207
   rural 124,375
   interstate 872
vehicle miles of travel (mil) 28,130
total motor vehicle registrations 2,296,135
   automobiles 826,441
   motorcycles 49,548
licensed drivers 1,908,117
   per 1,000 driving age population 927
deaths from motor vehicle
   accidents 461

STATE SUMMARY

Capital City . . . . Frankfort

Governor . . . . Paul Patton

Address . . . . STATE CAPITOL
FRANKFORT, KY 40601
502 564-2611

Admitted as a state 1792

Area (square miles) 40,411

Population, 1980 3,660,777

Population, 1990 3,685,296

Population, 2000 4,041,769

Persons per square mile, 2000 . . . . 101.7

Largest city . . . . Louisville
  population, 2000 256,000

Personal income per capita, 2000
  (in current dollars) $24,294

Gross state product ($mil), 1999 . . . . . . $113,539

Leading industries, 1999 (by payroll)
  Manufacturing
  Health care/Social assistance
  Retail trade

Leading agricultural commodities, 1999
  Horses/mules, tobacco, cattle, broilers

GEOGRAPHY & ENVIRONMENT

Area, 1990 (square miles)
total 40,411
  land 39,732
  water (includes territorial water) 679

Federally owned land, 2000 . . . . 5.7%

Highest point
name . . . . Black Mountain
elevation (feet) 4,139

Lowest point
name . . . . Mississippi River
elevation (feet) 257

General coastline (miles) 0

Tidal shoreline (miles) 0

Capital city . . . . Frankfort
population, 2000 27,741

Largest city . . . . Louisville
population, 2000 256,000

Number of cities with over 100,000 population
  1930 2
  1990 2
  2000 2

State parks and Recreation areas, 2000
area (acres) 44,000
number of visitors 7,792,000
revenues $50,607,000

Natl. forest system land, 1995 (acres) 693,000

National park acreage, 1984 79,300

DEMOGRAPHICS & CHARACTERISTICS OF THE POPULATION

Population
1970 3,220,711
1980 3,660,777
1990 3,685,296
2000 4,041,769
2015 (projection) 4,231,000
2025 (projection) 4,314,000

Metropolitan area population
1970 1,550,000
1980 1,677,000
2000 1,973,000

Non-metropolitan area population
1970 1,671,000
1980 1,984,000
2000 2,069,000

Change in population, 1990-2000
number 356,473
percent 9.67%

Persons per square mile, 2000 . . . . 101.7

Persons by age, 2000
under 5 years 265,901
18 and over 3,046,951
21 and over 2,867,257
65 and over 504,793
85 and over 58,261

Kentucky 2

Persons by age, 2025 (projected)
under 5 years 232,000
5 to 17 years 656,000
65 and over 917,000

Median age, 2000 .... 35.9

Race, 2000
One race
White 3,640,889
Black or African American 295,994
American Indian and Alaska Native 8,616
Asian Indian 6,771
Chinese 5,397
Filipino 3,106
Japanese 3,683
Korean 3,818
Vietnamese 3,596
Native Hawaiian and other Pacific Islander   1,460
Two or more races 42,443

Race, 2025 (projected)
White 3,916,000
Black 343,000

Persons of Hispanic origin, 2000
total Hispanic or Latino 59,939
  Mexican 31,385
  Puerto Rican 6,469
  Cuban 3,516
  Other Hispanic or Latino 18,569

Persons of Hispanic origin, 2025 (proj.) ... 55,000

Persons by sex, 2000
male 1,975,368
female 2,066,401

Marital status, 1990
males
  15 years & older 1,378,871
    single 361,278
    married 871,978
      separated 19,937
    widowed 36,071
    divorced 109,544
females
  15 years & older 1,514,810
    single 293,241
    married 873,810
      separated 28,705

widowed 200,233
divorced 147,526

Households & families, 2000
households 1,590,647
persons per household 2.47
  families 1,104,398
  persons per family 2.97
    married couples 857,944
    female householder, no husband
      present 187,957
    one person households 414,095
households with persons under 18 years . 564,175
households with persons over 65 years ... 363,000

Nativity, 1990
number of persons born in state 2,851,449
percent of total residents 77.4%

Immigration & naturalization, 1998
immigrants admitted 2,017
persons naturalized 586
refugees granted resident status 808

VITAL STATISTICS & HEALTH

Births
1999
  with low birth weight 8.2%
  to teenage mothers 13.7%
  to unmarried mothers 30.4%
Birth rate, 1999 (per 1,000) 13.7
Birth rate, 2000 (per 1,000) 14.1

Abortions, 1996
total 8,000
rate (per 1,000 women age 15-44) 9.6

Deaths
1998 38,224
1999 39,321
2000 39,532

Infant deaths
1998 416
1999 363
2000 340

Average lifetime, by race, 1989-1991
total .... 74.37 years
  white .... 74.65 years
  black .... 70.16 years

Marriages
1998 44,288
1999 43,773
2000 39,671

Divorces
1998 22,369
1999 22,689
2000 21,593

Physicians, 1999
total 8,382
rate (per 1,000 persons) 2.12

Nurses, 1999
total 33,190
rate (per 1,000 persons) 8.38

Hospitals, 1998
number 106
beds (x 1,000) 15.2
average daily census (x 1,000) 8.7
patients admitted (x1,000) 551
average cost per day to hospital, 1995 . . . . . . $795
average cost per stay to hospital, 1995 . . . . $4,838

EDUCATION

*Educational attainment of all persons
25 years and older, 1990*
less than 9th grade 442,579
high school graduates . . . . : 741,012
bachelor's degree 189,539
graduate or professional degree 128,588

2000
high school graduate or more 78.7%
college graduate or more 20.5%

Public school enrollment, Fall, 1998
total 655,687
Kindergarten through grade 8 464,567
grades 9 through 12 191,120

Public School Teachers, 2000
total 40,100
elementary 28,300
secondary 11,800
average salaries
elementary $35,800
secondary $37,700

*State receipts & expenditures for public
schools, 2000*
revenue receipts ($mil) $4,637

*State receipts & expenditures for public
schools, 2000 (continued)*
expenditures
total ($mil) $4,571
per capita $1,154
per pupil $7,053

*Graduating high school seniors,
public high schools, 2000 (est.)* 36,956

SAT scores, 2001
verbal 550
math 550
percent graduates taking test 12%

Institutions of higher education, 1999
total 67
public 22
private 45

*Enrollment in institutions of higher
education, Fall, 1998*
total 180,576
full-time men 53,189
full-time women 69,406
part-time men 21,178
part-time women 36,803

*Minority enrollment in institutions of higher
education, Fall, 1997*
Black, non-Hispanic 12,711
Hispanic 1,354
Asian/Pacific Islander 2,258

Earned degrees conferred, 1998
Bachelor's 14,977
First professional 1,180
Master's 4,773
Doctor's 410

SOCIAL INSURANCE & WELFARE PROGRAMS

Social Security beneficiaries & benefits, 2000
beneficiaries
total 739,000
retired and dependents 438,000
survivors 130,000
disabled & dependents 172,000
annual benefit payments ($mil)
total $6,203
retired and dependents $3,505
survivors $1,324
disabled & dependents $1,373

Kentucky 4

Medicare, 2000
enrollment (x1,000) 615
payments ($mil) $3,153

Medicaid, 1998
recipients (x1,000) 644
payments ($mil) $2,425

Federal public aid
Temporary Assistance for Needy Families
(TANF), 2000
    Recipients (x1,000) 89
    Families (x1,000) 39
Supplemental Security Income
    total recipients, 1999 (x1,000) 172

Food Stamp Program
    participants, 2000 (x1,000) 403

HOUSING & CONSTRUCTION
Total housing units, 2000 1,750,927
    seasonal or recreational use 30,420
    occupied 1,590,647
        owner occupied 1,125,397
        renter occupied 465,250

New privately owned housing units uthorized, 2000
number (x1,000) 18.5
value ($mil) $1,767

New privately owned housing units
started, 2000 (est.) (x1,000) 21.4

Existing home sales, 2000 (x1,000) 71.3

GOVERNMENT & ELECTIONS
State officials, 2002
Governor (name/party/term expires)
PAUL PATTON
Democrat - 2004
Lt. Governor .... Steve Henry
Sec. of State .... John Y. Brown, III
Atty. General .... Ben Chandler, III
Chief Justice .... Joseph E. Lambert

Governorship
minimum age 30
length of term .... 4 years
number of consecutive
    terms permitted 2
who succeeds .... Lt. Governor

State legislature
name .... General Assembly
 upper chamber
    name .... Senate
    number of members 38
    length of term .... 4 years
    party in majority, 2000 .... Democratic
lower chamber
    name .... House of Representatives
    number of members 100
    length of term .... 2 years
    party in majority, 2000 .... Democratic

State employees March, 2000
total 91,622
March payroll $217,909,537

Local governments, 1997
total 1,366
    county 119
    municipal 434
    township 0
    school districts 176
    special districts 637

Voting age population, November, 2000, projected
Total 2,993,000
    male 1,425,000
    female 1,568,000

Vote for president
2000
    Gore 639,000
    Bush 872,000
1996
    Clinton 637,000
    Dole 623,000
    Perot 120,000

Federal representation, 2002 (107th Congress)
Senators (name/party/term expires)

MITCH McCONNELL
Republican - 2003
JIM BUNNING
Republican - 2005

Representatives, total 6
    Democrats 1
    Republicans 5
    other 0

Women holding public office, 2001
U.S. Congress 1
statewide elected office 0
state legislature 15

Black elected officials, 1999
total 62
  US and state legislatures 4
  city/county/regional offices 47
  judicial/law enforcement 5
  education/school boards 6

Hispanic public officials, 2000
total .... NA
  state executives & legislators .... NA
  city/county/regional offices .... NA
  judicial/law enforcement .... NA
  education/school boards .... NA

GOVERNMENTAL FINANCE

State government revenues, 1999 ($per capita)
total revenue $4,254.95
  total general revenue $3,429.59
    intergovernmental revenue $974.44
    taxes $1,857.40
    current charges $342.00
    miscellaneous $255.75

State government expenditures, 1999 ($per capita)
total expenditure $3,730.95
  total general expenditure $3,364.67
    education $1,242.33
    public welfare $904.49
    health $94.45
    hospitals $114.67
    highways $353.80
    police protection $36.50
    correction $87.75
    natural resources $70.08
    governmental administration $148.26
    interest on general debt $111.06

State debt, 1999 ($per capita) $1,873.80

Federal government grants to state & local government, 2000 (x$1,000)
total $4,719,614
  Dept. of Education $422,129
  Environmental Protection Agency $26,292
  Health Care Financing Admin. $2,207,666
  Dept. Housing & Urban Devel. $395,217
  Dept. of Labor $68,483
  Highway trust fund $518,800

CRIME, LAW ENFORCEMENT & COURTS

Crime, 2000 (all rates per 100,000 inhabitants)
total crimes 119,626
overall crime rate 2,959.7
  property crimes 107,723
    burglaries 25,308
    larcenies 73,141
    motor vehicle thefts 9,274
  property crime rate 2,665.2
  violent crimes 11,903
    murders 193
    forcible rapes 1,091
    robberies 3,256
    aggravated assaults 7,363
  violent crime rate 294.5

Number of police agencies, 2000 11

Arrests, 2000
total 15,678
  persons under 18 years of age 1,831

Prisoners under state & federal jurisdiction, 2000
total 14,919
percent change, 1999-2000 .... -2.6%
  sentenced to more than one year
    total 14,919
    rate per 100,000 residents 373

Persons under sentence of death, 4/1/2001 42

State's highest court
name .... Supreme Court
number of members 7
length of term .... 6 years
intermediate appeals court? .... yes

Kentucky 6

LABOR & INCOME

Civilian labor force, 2000
total 1,982,000
  men 1,045,000
  women 936,000
  persons 16-19 years 130,000
  white 1,804,000
  black 161,000

Civilian labor force as a percent of
civilian non-institutional population, 2000
total 64.3%
  men 71.3%
  women 57.9%
  persons 16-19 years .... NA%
  white 64.2%
  black 64.7%

Employment, 2000
total 1,900,000
  men 1,003,000
  women 897,000
  persons 16-19 years 109,000
  white 1,735,000
  black 149,000

Full-time/part-time labor force, 1998
full-time labor force 1,612,000
  working part-time for
    economic reasons 20,000
part-time labor force 313,000

Unemployment rate, 2000
total 4.1%
  men 4.0%
  women 4.2%
  persons 16-19 years 15.8%
  white 3.8%
  black 8.0%

Unemployed by reason for unemployment
(as a percent of total unemployment), 1998
job losers or completed temp jobs 37.1%
job leavers 14.6%
reentrants 39.3%
new entrants 9.0%

Experienced civilian labor force, by occupation,
1998
executive/administrative/managerial 252,000
professional/specialty 271,000
technicians & related support 56,000

sales 219,000
administrative support/clerical 259,000
service occupations 264,000
precision production/craft/repair 230,000
machine operators/assemblers 136,000
transportation/material moving 95,000
handlers/helpers/laborers 84,000
farming/forestry/fishing 50,000

Experienced civilian labor force, by industry, 1998
construction 126,000
manufacturing 319,000
transportation/communication 118,000
wholesale/retail trade 402,000
finance/real estate/insurance 86,000
services 416,000
government 259,000
agriculture 46

Average annual pay, 1999 .... $27,748
change in average annual pay,
  1998-1999 .... 3.9%

Hours and earnings of production workers
on manufacturing payrolls, 2000
average weekly hours 42.1
average hourly earnings $14.82
average weekly earnings $623.92

Labor union membership, 2000 208,000

Household income (in 2000 dollars)
median household income,
  three year average, 1998-2000 .... $37,186

Poverty
persons below poverty level,
  three year average, 1998-2000 .... 12.5%

Personal income ($per capita)
2000 (prelim.)
  in current dollars $24,294
  in constant (1996) dollars $22,629
1999 (preliminary)
  in current dollars $23,161
  in constant (1996) dollars $22,147

Federal income tax returns, 1999
returns filed 1,719,514
adjusted gross income ($1,000) $63,288,305
total income tax paid ($1,000) $8,551,652

ECONOMY, BUSINESS, INDUSTRY & AGRICULTURE

Fortune 500 companies, 2000 4

Business incorporations, 1998
total 7,867
change, 1997-1998 .... -6.3%

Business failures, 1998 270

Business firm ownership, 1997
Hispanic owned firms 1,481
Black owned firms 5,629
women owned firms 65,965
Asian & Pacific Islander owned firms 2,595
American Indian & Alaska
     native owned firms 3,069

Shopping centers, 2000 625

Gross state product, 1999 ($mil)
total $113,539
   agriculture services, forestry, fisheries .. $2,002
   mining $2,433
   construction $5,064
   manufacturing--durable goods $18,586
   manufacturing--nondurable goods $12,689
   transportation, communication &
      public utilities $9,108
   wholesale trade $6,964
   retail trade $10,861
   finance/real estate/insurance $12,404
   services $18,122
   federal, state & local government $15,306

Establishments, by major industry group, 1999
total 89,946
   forestry, fishing & agriculture 343
   mining 624
   construction 9,490
   manufacturing 4,291
   transportation & warehousing 3,053
   wholesale trade 4,986
   retail trade 17,105
   finance & insurance 5,510
   professional/scientific/technical 7,097
   health care/social assistance 8,573
   information 1,408
   accommodation/food services 6,507

Payroll, by major industry group, 1999
total ($1,000) $39,540,856
   forestry, fishing & agriculture $49,448
   mining $880,381
   construction $2,446,107
   manufacturing $10,436,853
   transportation & warehousing $2,339,616
   wholesale trade $2,408,073
   retail trade $3,619,769
   finance & insurance $2,108,990
   professional/scientific/technical $1,682,157
   health care/social assistance $5,391,987
   information $885,205
   accommodation/food services $1,360,081

Agriculture
number of farms, 2000 90,000
farm acreage, 2000 14,000,000
acres per farm, 2000 151
value of farms, 1997 ($mil) $20,155
farm income, 1999 ($mil)
   net farm income $847
   debt/asset ratio 14.9%
farm marketings, 1999 ($mil)
total $3,456
   crops $1,298
   livestock $2,158
principal commodities, in order by marketing
receipts, 1999
      Horses/mules, tobacco, cattle, broilers

Federal economic activity in state
expenditures, 2000
   total ($mil) $24,444
   per capita $6,048
   defense ($mil) $2,683
   non-defense ($mil) $21,761
defense department, 2000
   contract awards ($mil) $910
   payroll ($mil) $1,856
   civilian employees (x1,000) 6.1
   military personnel (x1,000) 35.8

Fishing, 2000
catch (thousands of pounds) ....NA
value ($1,000) ....$NA

Mining, 2000 ($mil; preliminary)
total non-fuel mineral production $497

Kentucky 8

Construction, 1999 ($mil)
total contracts (including
   non-building) $6,676
      residential $2,810
      non-residential $2,696

Construction industries, 1997
establishments 8,727
receipts ($1,000) $9,740,926
annual payroll ($1,000) $1,979,407
paid employees 76,131

Manufacturing, 1997
establishments 4,455
value of shipments ($1,000) $88,437,375
annual payroll ($1,000) $9,416,025
paid employees 296,956

Transportation industries, 1997
establishments 4,439
receipts ($1,000) $17,813,725
annual payroll ($1,000) $2,518,260
paid employees 79,676

Wholesale trade, 1997
establishments 6,215
sales($1,000) $39,671,609
annual payroll ($1,000) $2,342,131
paid employees 80,672

Retail trade, 1997
establishments 22,349
sales($1,000) $34,364,705
annual payroll ($1,000) $3,843,736
paid employees 315,734

Finance industries
establishments, 1997 7,911
receipts ($1,000), 1997 .... $NA
annual payroll ($1,000), 1997 .... $2,133,023
paid employees, 1997 71,664
commercial banks, 2000
   number 233
      assets ($bil) $52.5
      deposits ($bil) $39.5

Service industries, 1997 (non-exempt firms only)
establishments 23,987
receipts ($1,000) $16,666,966
annual payroll ($1,000) $5,898,883
paid employees 279,646

COMMUNICATION, ENERGY & TRANSPORTATION

Communication
daily newspapers, 2000 23
households with
   telephones, 1998 .... 92.9%
   computers, 2000 .... 46.2%
   internet access, 2000 .... 36.6%

Energy
consumption, 1999
   total (trillion Btu) 1,830
   per capita (million Btu) 462
by source of production (trillion Btu)
   coal 885
   natural gas 220
   petroleum 726
   nuclear electric power .... NA
   hydroelectric power 27
by end-use sector (trillion Btu)
   residential 316
   commercial 219
   industrial 851
   transportation 444
electric energy, 1999
   production (billion kWh) 81.7
   net summer capability (million kW) 14.7
gas utilities, 1999
   customers 725,000
   sales (trillion Btu) 96
nuclear plants, 1999 .... na

Transportation, 2000
public road & street mileage
total 79,267
   urban 11,826
   rural 67,441
   interstate 762
vehicle miles of travel (mil) 46,803
total motor vehicle registrations 2,826,403
   automobiles 1,673,926
   motorcycles 43,990
licensed drivers 2,694,469
   per 1,000 driving age population 852
deaths from motor vehicle
   accidents 820

STATE SUMMARY

Capital City .... Baton Rouge

Governor .... Mike Foster

Address .... STATE CAPITOL
BATON ROUGE, LA 70804
225 342-7015

Admitted as a state 1812

Area (square miles) 51,843

Population, 1980 4,205,900

Population, 1990 4,219,973

Population, 2000 4,468,976

Persons per square mile, 2000 .... 102.6

Largest city .... New Orleans
population, 2000 485,000

Personal income per capita, 2000
(in current dollars) $23,334

Gross state product ($mil), 1999 ...... $128,959

Leading industries, 1999 (by payroll)
Manufacturing
Health care/Social assistance
Retail trade

Leading agricultural commodities, 1999
Sugar, cotton, rice, cattle

GEOGRAPHY & ENVIRONMENT

Area, 1990 (square miles)
total 51,843
land 43,566
water (includes territorial water) 8,277

Federally owned land, 2000 .... 4.2%

Highest point
name .... Driskill Mountain
elevation (feet) 535

Lowest point
name .... New Orleans
elevation (feet) .... -8

General coastline (miles) 397

Tidal shoreline (miles) 7,721

Capital city .... Baton Rouge
population, 2000 228,000

Largest city .... New Orleans
population, 2000 485,000

Number of cities with over 100,000 population
1980 2
1990 4
2000 4

State parks and Recreation areas, 2000
area (acres) 36,000
number of visitors 1,715,000
revenues $3,484,000

Natl. forest system land, 1999 (acres) 604,000

National park acreage, 1984 6,300

DEMOGRAPHICS & CHARACTERISTICS OF THE POPULATION

Population
1970 3,644,637
1980 4,205,900
1990 4,219,973
2000 4,468,976
2015 (projection) 4,840,000
2025 (projection) 5,133,000

Metropolitan area population
1970 2,439,000
1980 2,892,000
2000 3,370,000

Non-metropolitan area population
1970 1,205,000
1980 1,314,000
2000 1,099,000

Change in population, 1990-2000
number 249,003
percent 5.90%

Persons per square mile, 2000 . ... 102.6

Persons by age, 2000
under 5 years 317,392
18 and over 3,249,177
21 and over 3,029,001
65 and over 516,929
85 and over 58,676

Louisiana 2

Persons by age, 2025 (projected)
under 5 years 346,000
5 to 17 years 936,000
65 and over 945,000

Median age, 2000 34

Race, 2000
One race
White 2,856,161
Black or African American 1,451,944
American Indian and Alaska Native 25,477
Asian Indian........................ 8,280
Chinese 7,474
Filipino 4,504
Japanese 1,519
Korean 2,876
Vietnamese 24,358
Native Hawaiian and other Pacific Islander 1,240
Two or more races 48,265

Race, 2025 (projected)
White 3,145,000
Black 1,849,000

Persons of Hispanic origin, 2000
total Hispanic or Latino 107,738
  Mexican 32,267
  Puerto Rican 7,670
  Cuban 8,448
  Other Hispanic or Latino 59,353

Persons of Hispanic origin, 2025 (proj.) .. 227,000

Persons by sex, 2000
male............................2,162,903
female 2,306,073

Marital status, 1990
males
  15 years & older 1,503,716
    single 464,285
    married 892,014
      separated 45,440
    widowed 42,270
    divorced 105,147
females
  15 years & older 1,680,787
    single 409,309
    married 905,705
      separated 66,061

widowed 216,577
divorced 149,196

Households & families, 2000
households 1,656,053
persons per household 2.62
  families 1,156,438
  persons per family 3.16
    married couples 809,498
    female householder, no husband
      present 275,075
    one person households 419,200
households with persons under 18 years . 649,314
households with persons over 65 years ... 372,354

Nativity, 1990
number of persons born in state 3,332,542
percent of total residents 79.0%

Immigration & naturalization, 1998
immigrants admitted.................. 2,193
persons naturalized 2,478
refugees granted resident status 219

VITAL STATISTICS & HEALTH
Births
1999
  with low birth weight 10.0%
  to teenage mothers 15.4%
  to unmarried mothers 44.8%
Birth rate, 1999 (per 1,000) 15.4
Birth rate, 2000 (per 1,000) 15.5

Abortions, 1996
total 15,000
rate (per 1,000 women age 15-44) 14.7

Deaths
1998 39,672
1999 41,238
2000 41,150

Infant deaths
1998 636
1999 622
2000 638

Average lifetime, by race, 1989-1991
total .... 73.05 years
  white........................ 74.87 years
  black .... 68.62 years

Marriages
1998 42,157
1999 40,608
2000 40,544

Divorces
1998 . . . . NA
1999 . . . . NA
2000 . . . . NA

Physicians, 1999
total 10,975
rate (per 1,000 persons) 2.51

Nurses, 1999
total 35,370
rate (per 1,000 persons) 8.09

Hospitals, 1998
number 126
beds (x 1,000) 17.8
average daily census (x 1,000) 9.8
patients admitted (x1,000) 638
average cost per day to hospital, 1995 . . . . . . $902
average cost per stay to hospital, 1995 . . . . $5,612

EDUCATION

*Educational attainment of all persons
25 years and older, 1990*
less than 9th grade 372,913
high school graduates 803,328
bachelor's degree 267,055
graduate or professional degree 142,068

2000
high school graduate or more 80.8%
college graduate or more 22.5%

Public school enrollment, Fall, 1998
total 768,734
Kindergarten through grade 8 558,473
grades 9 through 12 210,261

Public School Teachers, 2000
total 49,400
elementary 34,300
secondary 15,100
average salaries
elementary $33,100
secondary $33,100

*State receipts & expenditures for public
schools, 2000*
revenue receipts ($mil) $5,382

*State receipts & expenditures for public
schools, 2000 (continued)*
expenditures
total ($mil) $4,834
per capita $1,106
per pupil $6,039

*Graduating high school seniors,
public high schools, 2000 (est.)* 35,184

SAT scores, 2001
verbal 564
math 562
percent graduates taking test 7%

Institutions of higher education, 1999
total 85
public 62
private 23

*Enrollment in institutions of higher
education, Fall, 1998*
total 221,110
full-time men 69,383
full-time women 90,640
part-time men 23,028
part-time women 38,059

*Minority enrollment in institutions of higher
education, Fall, 1997*
Black, non-Hispanic 59,487
Hispanic 5,271
Asian/Pacific Islander 4,704

Earned degrees conferred, 1998
Bachelor's 18,553
First professional 1,723
Master's 5,674
Doctor's 567

SOCIAL INSURANCE & WELFARE PROGRAMS

Social Security beneficiaries & benefits, 2000
beneficiaries
total 711,000
retired and dependents 429,000
survivors 154,000
disabled & dependents 128,000
annual benefit payments ($mil)
total $5,906
retired and dependents $3,350
survivors $1,562
disabled & dependents $995

Louisiana 4

Medicare, 2000
enrollment (x1,000) 597
payments ($mil) $4,383

Medicaid, 1998
recipients (x1,000) 721
payments ($mil) $2,384

Federal public aid
Temporary Assistance for Needy Families
(TANF), 2000
    Recipients (x1,000) 85
    Families (x1,000) 27
Supplemental Security Income
  total recipients, 1999 (x1,000) 168

Food Stamp Program
  participants, 2000 (x1,000) 500

HOUSING & CONSTRUCTION

Total housing units, 2000 1,847,181
  seasonal or recreational use 39,578
  occupied 1,656,053
    owner occupied 1,125,135
    renter occupied 530,918

New privately owned housing units uthorized, 2000
number (x1,000) 14.7
value ($mil) $1,553

New privately owned housing units
  started, 2000 (est.) (x1,000) 15.8

Existing home sales, 2000 (x1,000) 84.2

GOVERNMENT & ELECTIONS

State officials, 2002
Governor (name/party/term expires)
        MIKE FOSTER
       Republican - 2004
Lt. Governor .... Kathleen Blanco
Sec. of State .... Fox McKeithen
Atty. General .... Richard Ieyoub, Jr.
Chief Justice .... Pascal Calagero, Jr.

Governorship
minimum age 25
length of term .... 4 years
number of consecutive
  terms permitted 2
who succeeds .... Lt. Governor

State legislature
name .... Legislature
  upper chamber
    name .... Senate
    number of members 39
    length of term .... 4 years
    party in majority, 2000 .... Democratic
  lower chamber
    name .... House of Representatives
    number of members 105
    length of term .... 4 years
    party in majority, 2000 .... Democratic

State employees March, 2000
total 112,504
March payroll $258,988,465

Local governments, 1997
total 467
  county 60
  municipal 302
  township 0
  school districts 66
  special districts 39

Voting age population, November, 2000, projected
Total 3,255,000
  male 1,532,000
  female 1,723,000

Vote for president
2000
  Gore 792,000
  Bush 928,000
1996
  Clinton 928,000
  Dole 713,000
  Perot 123,000

Federal representation, 2002 (107th Congress)
Senators (name/party/term expires)

      MARY LANDRIEU
       Democrat - 2003
       JOHN BREAUX
       Democrat - 2005

Representatives, total 7
  Democrats 2
  Republicans 5
  other 0

GOVERNMENTAL FINANCE

CRIME, LAW ENFORCEMENT & COURTS

Louisiana 6

LABOR & INCOME

Civilian labor force, 2000
total 2,030,000
men 1,064,000
women 966,000
persons 16-19 years 133,000
white 1,422,000
black 586,000

*Civilian labor force as a percent of
civilian non-institutional population, 2000*
total 61.7%
men 70.5%
women 54.2%
persons 16-19 years ....NA%
white 63.5%
black 57.8%

Employment, 2000
total 1,917,000
men 1,007,000
women 910,000
persons 16-19 years 112,000
white 1,369,000
black 527,000

Full-time/part-time labor force, 1998
full-time labor force 1,748,000
working part-time for
      economic reasons 27,000
part-time labor force 315,000

Unemployment rate, 2000
total 5.5%
men 5.4%
women 5.7%
persons 16-19 years 15.6%
white 3.7%
black 10.0%

*Unemployed by reason for unemployment
(as a percent of total unemployment), 1998*
job losers or completed temp jobs 39.8%
job leavers 12.7%
reentrants 31.4%
new entrants 16.1%

*Experienced civilian labor force, by occupation,
1998*
executive/administrative/managerial 254,000
professional/specialty 278,000
technicians & related support 65,000

sales 236,000
administrative support/clerical 295,000
service occupations 313,000
precision production/craft/repair 226,000
machine operators/assemblers 107,000
transportation/material moving 124,000
handlers/helpers/laborers 95,000
farming/forestry/fishing 51,000

Experienced civilian labor force, by industry, 1998
construction 116,000
manufacturing 229,000
transportation/communication 112,000
wholesale/retail trade 423,000
finance/real estate/insurance 87,000
services 481,000
government 311,000
agriculture 45

Average annual pay, 1999 .... $27,221
change in average annual pay,
      1998-1999 .... 1.2%

*Hours and earnings of production workers
on manufacturing payrolls, 2000*
average weekly hours 42.8
average hourly earnings $15.57
average weekly earnings $666.40

Labor union membership, 2000 121,900

Household income (in 2000 dollars)
median household income,
      three year average, 1998-2000 .... $30,219

Poverty
persons below poverty level,
      three year average, 1998-2000 .... 18.6%

Personal income ($per capita)
2000 (prelim.)
      in current dollars $23,334
      in constant (1996) dollars $21,734
1999 (preliminary)
      in current dollars $22,792
      in constant (1996) dollars $21,794

Federal income tax returns, 1999
returns filed 1,859,756
adjusted gross income ($1,000) $65,928,921
total income tax paid ($1,000) $9,234,609

ECONOMY, BUSINESS, INDUSTRY & AGRICULTURE

Fortune 500 companies, 2000 1

Business incorporations, 1998
total 9,196
change, 1997-1998 . . . . -17.5%

Business failures, 1998 377

Business firm ownership, 1997
Hispanic owned firms 6,645
Black owned firms 25,782
women owned firms 70,550
Asian & Pacific Islander owned firms 6,490
American Indian & Alaska
   native owned firms 3,230

Shopping centers, 2000 710

Gross state product, 1999 ($mil)
total $128,959
   agriculture services, forestry, fisheries . . $1,232
   mining $15,121
   construction $6,259
   manufacturing--durable goods $5,112
   manufacturing--nondurable goods $14,509
   transportation, communication &
      public utilities $11,897
   wholesale trade $7,573
   retail trade $11,944
   finance/real estate/insurance $16,793
   services $22,653
   federal, state & local government $15,866

Establishments, by major industry group, 1999
total 101,020
   forestry, fishing & agriculture 820
   mining 1,492
   construction 8,479
   manufacturing 3,488
   transportation & warehousing 3,738
   wholesale trade 6,331
   retail trade 17,655
   finance & insurance 7,164
   professional/scientific/technical 9,928
   health care/social assistance 10,028
   information 1,349
   accommodation/food services 7,284

Payroll, by major industry group, 1999
total ($1,000) $41,487,661
   forestry, fishing & agriculture $135,745
   mining $2,037,789
   construction $3,768,558
   manufacturing $6,310,735
   transportation & warehousing $2,064,898
   wholesale trade $2,635,118
   retail trade $3,894,610
   finance & insurance $2,501,928
   professional/scientific/technical $2,629,041
   health care/social assistance $6,008,744
   information $966,199
   accommodation/food services $1,776,660

Agriculture
number of farms, 2000 30,000
farm acreage, 2000 8,000,000
acres per farm, 2000 275
value of farms, 1997 ($mil) $10,455
farm income, 1999 ($mil)
   net farm income $565
   debt/asset ratio 14.9%
farm marketings, 1999 ($mil)
total $1,848
   crops $1,228
   livestock $620
principal commodities, in order by marketing
receipts, 1999
   Sugar, cotton, rice cattle

Federal economic activity in state
expenditures, 2000
   total ($mil) $25,955
   per capita $5,808
   defense ($mil) $3,399
   non-defense ($mil) $22,556
defense department, 2000
   contract awards ($mil) $1,938
   payroll ($mil) $1,403
   civilian employees (x1,000) 8.6
   military personnel (x1,000) 15.5

Fishing, 2000
catch (thousands of pounds) 1,344,913
value ($1,000) $401,095

Mining, 2000 ($mil; preliminary)
total non-fuel mineral production $404

Louisiana 8

Construction, 1999 ($mil)
total contracts (including
    non-building) $5,045
       residential $1,647
       non-residential $2,113

Construction industries, 1997
establishments 7,646
receipts ($1,000) $11,262,360
annual payroll ($1,000) $2,983,765
paid employees 106,314

Manufacturing, 1997
establishments 4,054
value of shipments ($1,000) $81,385,399
annual payroll ($1,000) $6,259,067
paid employees 173,489

Transportation industries, 1997
establishments 5,617
receipts ($1,000) $19,654,813
annual payroll ($1,000) $3,445,825
paid employees 105,779

Wholesale trade, 1997
establishments 7,497
sales($1,000) $49,321,765
annual payroll ($1,000) $2,634,472
paid employees 87,291

Retail trade, 1997
establishments 23,558
sales($1,000) $37,222,865
annual payroll ($1,000) $4,089,854
paid employees 333,931

Finance industries
establishments, 1997 10,009
receipts ($1,000), 1997 .... $NA
annual payroll ($1,000), 1997 .... $2,461,217
paid employees, 1997 81,495
commercial banks, 2000
    number 149
       assets ($bil) $51.7
       deposits ($bil) $41.9

Service industries, 1997 (non-exempt firms only)
establishments 30,455
receipts ($1,000) $25,112,448
annual payroll ($1,000) $8,758,084
paid employees 391,385

COMMUNICATION, ENERGY & TRANSPORTATION

Communication
daily newspapers, 2000 26
households with
    telephones, 1998 .... 91.1%
    computers, 2000 .... 41.2%
    internet access, 2000 .... 30.2%

Energy
consumption, 1999
total (trillion Btu) 3,615
per capita (million Btu) 827
by source of production (trillion Btu)
    coal 228
    natural gas 1,558
    petroleum 1,452
    nuclear electric power 139
    hydroelectric power 8
by end-use sector (trillion Btu)
    residential 325
    commercial 237
    industrial 2,249
    transportation 805
electric energy, 1999
    production (billion kWh) 64.8
    net summer capability (million kW) 16.3
gas utilities, 1999
    customers 737,000
    sales (trillion Btu) 304
nuclear plants, 1999 2

Transportation, 2000
public road & street mileage
total 60,900
    urban 13,941
    rural 46,959
    interstate 894
vehicle miles of travel (mil) 40,849
total motor vehicle registrations 3,556,982
    automobiles 1,964,694
    motorcycles 47,736
licensed drivers 2,759,120
    per 1,000 driving age population 813
deaths from motor vehicle
    accidents 937

Maine 1

STATE SUMMARY

Capital City . . . . .Augusta

Governor . . . . .Angus King

Address . . . . . . .STATE HOUSE
AUGUSTA, ME 04333
207 287-3531

Admitted as a state 1820

Area (square miles) 35,387

Population, 1980 .1,124,660

Population, 1990 .1,227,928

Population, 2000 .1,274,923

Persons per square mile, 2000 . . . . 41.3

Largest city . . . . Portland
population, 2000 64,249

Personal income per capita, 2000
(in current dollars) $25,623

Gross state product ($mil), 1999 . . . . $34,064

Leading industries, 1999 (by payroll)
Manufacturing
Health care/Social assistance
Retail trade

Leading agricultural commodities, 1999
Potatoes, dairy products, chicken eggs,
aquaculture

GEOGRAPHY & ENVIRONMENT

Area, 1990 (square miles)
total 35,387
land 30,865
water (includes territorial water) 4,523

Federally owned land, 2000 . . . . 0.9%

Highest point
name . . . . Mount Katahdin
elevation (feet) 5,267

Lowest point
name . . . . .Atlantic Ocean
elevation (feet) .sea level

General coastline (miles) 228

Tidal shoreline (miles) 3,478

Capital city .Augusta
population, 2000 18,560

Largest city . . . . Portland
population, 2000 64,249

Number of cities with over 100,000 population
1980 0
1990 0
2000 0

State parks and Recreation areas, 2000
area (acres) 95,000
number of visitors 2,265,000
revenues $1,943,000

Natl. forest system land, 1999 (acres) 53,000

National park acreage, 1984 41,100

DEMOGRAPHICS & CHARACTERISTICS OF THE POPULATION

Population
1970 993,722
1980 1,124,660
1990 1,227,928
2000 1,274,923
2015 (projection) 1,362,000
2025 (projection) 1,423,000

Metropolitan area population
1970 365,000
1980 404,000
2000 467,000

Non-metropolitan area population
1970 628,000
1980 720,000
2000 808,000

Change in population, 1990-2000
number 46,995
percent 3.83%

Persons per square mile, 2000 . . . . 41.3

Persons by age, 2000
under 5 years 70,726
18 and over 973,685
21 and over 924,108
65 and over 183,402
85 and over 23,316

Maine 2

Persons by age, 2025 (projected)
under 5 years 76,000
5 to 17 years 213,000
65 and over 304,000

Median age, 2000 .... 38.6

Race, 2000
One race
White 1,236,014
Black or African American 6,760
American Indian and Alaska Native 7,098
Asian Indian 1,021
Chinese 2,034
Filipino 1,159
Japanese 616
Korean 875
Vietnamese 1,323
Native Hawaiian and other Pacific Islander .. 382
Two or more races 12,647

Race, 2025 (projected)
White 1,388,000
Black 8,000

Persons of Hispanic origin, 2000
total Hispanic or Latino 9,360
  Mexican 2,756
  Puerto Rican 2,275
  Cuban 478
  Other Hispanic or Latino 3,851

Persons of Hispanic origin, 2025 (proj.) ... 20,000

Persons by sex, 2000
male 620,309
female 654,614

Marital status, 1990
males
  15 years & older 465,004
    single 126,930
    married 287,910
      separated 5,460
    widowed 12,311
    divorced 37,853
females
  15 years & older 504,117
    single 106,076
    married 286,893
      separated 7,413

widowed 60,977
divorced 50,171

Households & families, 2000
households 518,200
persons per household 2.39
  families 340,685
  persons per family 2.9
    married couples 272,152
    female householder, no husband
      present 49,022
    one person households 139,969
households with persons under 18 years . 167,685
households with persons over 65 years ... 128,137

Nativity, 1990
number of persons born in state 840,930
percent of total residents 68.5%

Immigration & naturalization, 1998
immigrants admitted 709
persons naturalized 544
refugees granted resident status 80

VITAL STATISTICS & HEALTH

Births
1999
  with low birth weight 6.0%
  to teenage mothers 10.9%
  to unmarried mothers 31.3%
Birth rate, 1999 (per 1,000) 10.9
Birth rate, 2000 (per 1,000) 10.8

Abortions, 1996
total 3,000
rate (per 1,000 women age 15-44) 9.7

Deaths
1998 11,496
1999 12,261
2000 12,377

Infant deaths
1998 73
1999 57
2000 63

Average lifetime, by race, 1989-1991
total .... 76.35 years
  white .... 76.35 years
  black .... NA years

Marriages
1998 10,494
1999 10,146
2000 10,488

Divorces
1998 5,132
1999 5,731
2000 5,846

Physicians, 1999
total 2,913
rate (per 1,000 persons) 2.32

Nurses, 1999
total 13,600
rate (per 1,000 persons) 10.85

Hospitals, 1998
number 38
beds (x 1,000) 3.8
average daily census (x 1,000) 2.3
patients admitted (x1,000) 144
average cost per day to hospital, 1995 ...... $916
average cost per stay to hospital, 1995 .... $6,083

EDUCATION

Educational attainment of all persons
  25 years and older, 1990
    less than 9th grade 70,153
    high school graduates 295,074
    bachelor's degree 100,788
    graduate or professional degree 48,564

2000
  high school graduate or more 89.3%
  college graduate or more 24.1%

Public school enrollment, Fall, 1998
total 210,503
  Kindergarten through grade 8 150,860
  grades 9 through 12 59,643

Public School Teachers, 2000
total 15,500
  elementary 10,700
  secondary 4,700
average salaries
  elementary $35,300
  secondary $36,100

State receipts & expenditures for public
  schools, 2000
revenue receipts ($mil) $1,714

State receipts & expenditures for public
  schools, 2000 (continued)
expenditures
  total ($mil) $1,714
  per capita $1,368
  per pupil $8,173

Graduating high school seniors,
  public high schools, 2000 (est.) 12,871

SAT scores, 2001
verbal 506
math 500
percent graduates taking test 69%

Institutions of higher education, 1999
total 34
  public 15
  private 19

Enrollment in institutions of higher
  education, Fall, 1998
total 59,986
full-time men 14,826
full-time women 17,899
part-time men 8,089
part-time women 16,172

Minority enrollment in institutions of higher
  education, Fall, 1997
Black, non-Hispanic 571
Hispanic 376
Asian/Pacific Islander 840

Earned degrees conferred, 1998
Bachelor's 5,442
First professional 183
Master's 1,108
Doctor's 49

SOCIAL INSURANCE & WELFARE PROGRAMS

Social Security beneficiaries & benefits, 2000
beneficiaries
total 251,000
  retired and dependents 170,000
  survivors 34,000
  disabled & dependents 47,000
annual benefit payments ($mil)
total $2,075
  retired and dependents $1,360
  survivors $371
  disabled & dependents $344

Maine 4

Medicare, 2000
enrollment (x1,000) 213
payments ($mil) $793

Medicaid, 1998
recipients (x1,000) 170
payments ($mil) $747

Federal public aid
Temporary Assistance for Needy Families
(TANF), 2000
   Recipients (x1,000) 28
   Families (x1,000) 11
Supplemental Security Income
   total recipients, 1999 (x1,000) 29

Food Stamp Program
   participants, 2000 (x1,000) 102

HOUSING & CONSTRUCTION

Total housing units, 2000 651,901
   seasonal or recreational use 101,470
   occupied 518,200
      owner occupied 370,905
      renter occupied 147,295

New privately owned housing units uthorized, 2000
number (x1,000) 6.2
value ($mil) $723

*New privately owned housing units
started, 2000 (est.) (x1,000)* 5.8

Existing home sales, 2000 (x1,000) 40.7

GOVERNMENT & ELECTIONS

State officials, 2002
Governor (name/party/term expires)
         ANGUS KING, JR.
         Independent - 2002
Lt. Governor . . . . (no Lieutenant Governor)
Sec. of State . . . . Dan Gwadosky
Atty. General . . . . Steve Rowe
Chief Justice . . . . Leigh Saufley

Governorship
minimum age 30
length of term . . . . 4 years
number of consecutive
   terms permitted 2
who succeeds . . . . Pres. of the Senate

State legislature
name . . . . Legislature
   upper chamber
      name . . . . Senate
      number of members 35
      length of term . . . . 2 years
      party in majority, 2000 . . . . Democratic
   lower chamber
      name . . . . House of Representatives
      number of members 151
      length of term . . . . 2 years
      party in majority, 2000 . . . . Democratic

State employees March, 2000
total 25,070
March payroll $58,896,958

Local governments, 1997
total 832
   county 16
   municipal 22
   township 467
   school districts 98
   special districts 229

Voting age population, November, 2000, projected
Total 968,000
   male 465,000
   female 503,000

Vote for president
2000
   Gore 320,000
   Bush 287,000
1996
   Clinton 313,000
   Dole 186,000
   Perot 86,000

Federal representation, 2002 (107th Congress)
Senators (name/party/term expires)

        OLYMPIA SNOWE
        Republican - 2007
        SUSAN COLLINS
        Republican - 2003

Representatives, total 2
   Democrats 2
   Republicans 0
   other 0

Women holding public office, 2001
U.S. Congress 2
statewide elected office 0
state legislature 56

Black elected officials, 1999
total . . . . NA
  US and state legislatures . . . . NA
  city/county/regional offices . . . . NA
  judicial/law enforcement . . . . NA
  education/school boards . . . . NA

Hispanic public officials, 2000
total . . . . NA
  state executives & legislators . . . . NA
  city/county/regional offices . . . . NA
  judicial/law enforcement . . . . NA
  education/school boards . . . . NA

GOVERNMENTAL FINANCE

State government revenues, 1999 ($per capita)
total revenue $4,698.60
  total general revenue $3,875.87
    intergovernmental revenue $1,149.15
    taxes $2,027.53
    current charges $273.97
    miscellaneous $425.21

State government expenditures, 1999 ($per capita)
total expenditure $3,882.46
  total general expenditure $3,500.68
    education $974.61
    public welfare $1,122.76
    health $221.87
    hospitals $35.25
    highways $286.81
    police protection $35.06
    correction $62.60
    natural resources $98.00
    governmental administration $152.44
    interest on general debt $142.09

State debt, 1999 ($per capita) $3,092.55

Federal government grants to state & local government, 2000 (x$1,000)
total $1,849,710
  Dept. of Education $134,319
  Environmental Protection Agency $28,863
  Health Care Financing Admin. $872,072
  Dept. Housing & Urban Devel. $195,235
  Dept. of Labor $24,929
  Highway trust fund $146,453

CRIME, LAW ENFORCEMENT & COURTS

Crime, 2000 (all rates per 100,000 inhabitants)
total crimes 33,400
overall crime rate 2,619.8
  property crimes 32,003
    burglaries 6,775
    larcenies 23,906
    motor vehicle thefts 1,322
  property crime rate 2,510.2
  violent crimes 1,397
    murders 15
    forcible rapes 320
    robberies 247
    aggravated assaults 815
  violent crime rate 109.6

Number of police agencies, 2000 176

Arrests, 2000
total 61,049
  persons under 18 years of age 10,885

Prisoners under state & federal jurisdiction, 2000
total 1,679
percent change, 1999-2000 . . . . -2.2%
  sentenced to more than one year
    total 1,635
    rate per 100,000 residents 129

Persons under sentence of death, 4/1/2001 . . . NA

State's highest court
name . . . . Supreme Court
number of members 7
length of term . . . . 7 years
intermediate appeals court? . . . . no

Maine 6

LABOR & INCOME

Civilian labor force, 2000
total 689,000
  men 361,000
  women 328,000
  persons 16-19 years 37,000
  white 678,000
  black .... NA

Civilian labor force as a percent of
civilian non-institutional population, 2000
total 69.0%
  men 74.4%
  women 63.9%
  persons 16-19 years ....NA%
  white 69.1%
  black .... NA%

Employment, 2000
total 665,000
  men 348,000
  women 317,000
  persons 16-19 years 33,000
  white 655,000
  black .... NA

Full-time/part-time labor force, 1998
full-time labor force 513,000
  working part-time for
    economic reasons 10,000
part-time labor force 138,000

Unemployment rate, 2000
total 3.5%
  men 3.5%
  women 3.5%
  persons 16-19 years 12.0%
  white 3.5%
  black .... NA%

Unemployed by reason for unemployment
(as a percent of total unemployment), 1998
job losers or completed temp jobs 48.3%
job leavers 17.2%
reentrants 31.0%
new entrants 3.4%

Experienced civilian labor force, by occupation,
1998
executive/administrative/managerial 82,000
professional/specialty 91,000
technicians & related support ....NA

sales 79,000
administrative support/clerical 88,000
service occupations 85,000
precision production/craft/repair 87,000
machine operators/assemblers 46,000
transportation/material moving 28,000
handlers/helpers/laborers 23,000
farming/forestry/fishing 26,000

Experienced civilian labor force, by industry, 1998
construction 28,000
manufacturing 106,000
transportation/communication 25,000
wholesale/retail trade 133,000
finance/real estate/insurance 35,000
services 154,000
government 79,000
agriculture ....NA

Average annual pay, 1999 .... $26,887
change in average annual pay,
  1998-1999 .... 3.9%

Hours and earnings of production workers
on manufacturing payrolls, 2000
average weekly hours 41.3
average hourly earnings $14.28
average weekly earnings $589.76

Labor union membership, 2000 78,100

Household income (in 2000 dollars)
median household income,
  three year average, 1998-2000 .... $41,597

Poverty
persons below poverty level,
  three year average, 1998-2000 .... 9.8%

Personal income ($per capita)
2000 (prelim.)
  in current dollars $25,623
  in constant (1996) dollars $23,866
1999 (preliminary)
  in current dollars $24,960
  in constant (1996) dollars $23,867

Federal income tax returns, 1999
returns filed 595,018
adjusted gross income ($1,000) $22,367,024
total income tax paid ($1,000) $3,002,050

ECONOMY, BUSINESS, INDUSTRY & AGRICULTURE

Fortune 500 companies, 2000 0

Business incorporations, 1998
total 2,669
change, 1997-1998 .... -5.5%

Business failures, 1998 259

Business firm ownership, 1997
Hispanic owned firms 545
Black owned firms 257
women owned firms 30,598
Asian & Pacific Islander owned firms 646
American Indian & Alaska
    native owned firms 1,417

Shopping centers, 2000 203

Gross state product, 1999 ($mil)
total $34,064
    agriculture services, forestry, fisheries $674
    mining $5
    construction $1,552
    manufacturing--durable goods $2,262
    manufacturing--nondurable goods $2,999
    transportation, communication &
        public utilities $2,396
    wholesale trade $2,007
    retail trade $4,136
    finance/real estate/insurance $6,401
    services $6,862
    federal, state & local government $4,770

Establishments, by major industry group, 1999
total 38,878
    forestry, fishing & agriculture 725
    mining 23
    construction 4,612
    manufacturing 1,917
    transportation & warehousing 1,266
    wholesale trade 1,739
    retail trade 6,977
    finance & insurance 1,698
    professional/scientific/technical 3,023
    health care/social assistance 3,933
    information 665
    accommodation/food services 3,680

Payroll, by major industry group, 1999
total ($1,000) $12,586,264
    forestry, fishing & agriculture $101,083
    mining .... $NA
    construction $814,811
    manufacturing $2,815,744
    transportation & warehousing $268,473
    wholesale trade $720,444
    retail trade $1,353,044
    finance & insurance $887,666
    professional/scientific/technical $686,648
    health care/social assistance $2,184,337
    information $347,735
    accommodation/food services $540,204

Agriculture
number of farms, 2000 7,000
farm acreage, 2000 1,000,000
acres per farm, 2000 187
value of farms, 1997 ($mil) $1,742
farm income, 1999 ($mil)
    net farm income $98
    debt/asset ratio 21.2%
farm marketings, 1999 ($mil)
total $515
    crops $229
    livestock $286
principal commodities, in order by marketing
receipts, 1999
    Potatoes, dairy products, chicken eggs,
aquaculture

Federal economic activity in state
expenditures, 2000
    total ($mil) $7,849
    per capita $6,157
    defense ($mil) $1,303
    non-defense ($mil) $6,546
defense department, 2000
    contract awards ($mil) $772
    payroll ($mil) $571
    civilian employees (x1,000) 5.8
    military personnel (x1,000) 2.7

Fishing, 2000
catch (thousands of pounds) 226,849
value ($1,000) $275,107

Mining, 2000 ($mil; preliminary)
total non-fuel mineral production $3102

Maine 8

Construction, 1999 ($mil)
total contracts (including
  non-building) $1,653
    residential $590
    non-residential $585

Construction industries, 1997
establishments 4,198
receipts ($1,000) .... $NA
annual payroll ($1,000) .... $NA
paid employees 24,902

Manufacturing, 1997
establishments 2,384
value of shipments ($1,000) $15,184,255
annual payroll ($1,000) $2,755,677
paid employees 88,327

Transportation industries, 1997
establishments 1,988
receipts ($1,000) $3,700,710
annual payroll ($1,000) $615,598
paid employees 20,364

Wholesale trade, 1997
establishments 2,084
sales($1,000) $7,956,976
annual payroll ($1,000) $694,494
paid employees 23,360

Retail trade, 1997
establishments 9,528
sales($1,000) $13,275,829
annual payroll ($1,000) $1,418,745
paid employees 102,614

Finance industries
establishments, 1997 2,816
receipts ($1,000), 1997 .... $NA
annual payroll ($1,000), 1997 .... $906,349
paid employees, 1997 26,289
commercial banks, 2000
  number 15
    assets ($bil) $7.7
    deposits ($bil) $5.4

Service industries, 1997 (non-exempt firms only)
establishments 10,316
receipts ($1,000) $5,340,913
annual payroll ($1,000) $2,001,440
paid employees 87,636

COMMUNICATION, ENERGY & TRANSPORTATION

Communication
daily newspapers, 2000 7
households with
  telephones, 1998 .... 96.5%
  computers, 2000 .... 54.7%
  internet access, 2000 .... 42.6%

Energy
consumption, 1999
total (trillion Btu) 529
per capita (million Btu) 422
by source of production (trillion Btu)
  coal 3
  natural gas 6
  petroleum 250
  nuclear electric power .... NA
  hydroelectric power 81
by end-use sector (trillion Btu)
  residential 98
  commercial 58
  industrial 260
  transportation 113
electric energy, 1999
  production (billion kWh) 1.2
  net summer capability (million kW) 0.1
gas utilities, 1999
  customers 23,000
  sales (trillion Btu) 5
nuclear plants, 1999 .... na

Transportation, 2000
public road & street mileage
total 22,670
  urban 2,634
  rural 20,036
  interstate 367
vehicle miles of travel (mil) 14,190
total motor vehicle registrations 1,024,096
  automobiles 618,283
  motorcycles 28,791
licensed drivers 920,235
  per 1,000 driving age population 911
deaths from motor vehicle
  accidents 169

Maryland 1

STATE SUMMARY

Capital City . . . . Annapolis

Governor . . . . Parris Glendening

Address . . . . STATE HOUSE
ANNAPOLIS, MD 21401
410 974-3901

Admitted as a state 1788

Area (square miles) 12,407

Population, 1980 4,216,975

Population, 1990 4,781,468

Population, 2000 5,296,486

Persons per square mile, 2000 . . . . 541.8

Largest city . . . . Baltimore
population, 2000 651,000

Personal income per capita, 2000
(in current dollars) $33,872

Gross state product ($mil), 1999 . . . . . . $174,710

Leading industries, 1999 (by payroll)
Professional/Scientific/Technical
Health care/Social assistance
Manufacturing

Leading agricultural commodities, 1999
Broilers, greenhouse, dairy products, cattle

GEOGRAPHY & ENVIRONMENT

Area, 1990 (square miles)
total 12,407
land 9,775
water (includes territorial water) 2,633

Federally owned land, 2000 . . . . 2.6%

Highest point
name . . . . Backbone Mountain
elevation (feet) 3,360

Lowest point
name . . . . Atlantic Ocean
elevation (feet) . . . . sea level

General coastline (miles) 31

Tidal shoreline (miles) 3,190

Capital city . . . . Annapolis
population, 2000 35,838

Largest city . . . . Baltimore
population, 2000 651,000

Number of cities with over 100,000 population
1980 1
1990 1
2000 1

State parks and Recreation areas, 2000
area (acres) 259,000
number of visitors 10,004,000
revenues $14,202,000

Natl. forest system land, 1999 (acres) 0

National park acreage, 1984 39,700

DEMOGRAPHICS & CHARACTERISTICS OF THE POPULATION

Population
1970 3,923,897
1980 4,216,975
1990 4,781,468
2000 5,296,486
2015 (projection) 5,862,000
2025 (projection) 6,274,000

Metropolitan area population
1970 3,668,000
1980 3,920,000
2000 4,911,000

Non-metropolitan area population
1970 255,000
1980 287,000
2000 385,000

Change in population, 1990-2000
number 515,018
percent 10.77%

Persons per square mile, 2000 . . . . 541.8

Persons by age, 2000
under 5 years 353,393
18 and over 3,940,314
21 and over 3,736,905
65 and over 599,307
85 and over 66,902

Maryland 2

Persons by age, 2025 (projected)
under 5 years 411,000
5 to 17 years 1,060,000
65 and over 1,029,000

Median age, 2000 36

Race, 2000
One race
White 3,391,308
Black or African American 1,477,411
American Indian and Alaska Native 15,423
Asian Indian 49,909
Chinese 49,400
Filipino 26,608
Japanese 6,620
Korean 39,155
Vietnamese 16,744
Native Hawaiian and other Pacific Islander 2,303
Two or more races 103,587

Race, 2025 (projected)
White 3,755,000
Black 2,073,000

Persons of Hispanic origin, 2000
total Hispanic or Latino 227,916
  Mexican 39,900
  Puerto Rican 25,570
  Cuban 6,754
  Other Hispanic or Latino 155,692

Persons of Hispanic origin, 2025 (proj.) .. 438,000

Persons by sex, 2000
male 2,557,794
female 2,738,692

Marital status, 1990
males
  15 years & older 1,814,522
    single 587,368
    married 1,066,185
      separated 60,311
    widowed 44,219
    divorced 116,750
females
  15 years & older 1,979,591
    single 516,498
    married 1,077,126
      separated 80,567

widowed 216,413
divorced 169,554

Households & families, 2000
households 1,980,859
persons per household 2.61
  families 1,359,318
  persons per family 3.13
    married couples 994,549
    female householder, no husband
      present 279,876
  one person households 495,459
households with persons under 18 years . 739,048
households with persons over 65 years ... 429,316

Nativity, 1990
number of persons born in state 2,383,427
percent of total residents 49.8%

Immigration & naturalization, 1998
immigrants admitted 15,561
persons naturalized 9,615
refugees granted resident status 935

VITAL STATISTICS & HEALTH

Births
1999
  with low birth weight 9.0%
  to teenage mothers 13.9%
  to unmarried mothers 34.9%
Birth rate, 1999 (per 1,000) 13.9
Birth rate, 2000 (per 1,000) 14.2

Abortions, 1996
total 31,000
rate (per 1,000 women age 15-44) 26.3

Deaths
1998 40,792
1999 43,089
2000 43,779

Infant deaths
1998 548
1999 553
2000 452

Average lifetime, by race, 1989-1991
total .... 74.79 years
  white .... 76.30 years
  black .... 69.69 years

Marriages
1998 37,515
1999 39,179
2000 39,986

Divorces
1998 16,397
1999 16,785
2000 16,968

Physicians, 1999
total 19,592
rate (per 1,000 persons) 3.79

Nurses, 1999
total 44,210
rate (per 1,000 persons) 8.55

Hospitals, 1998
number 51
beds (x 1,000) 12.7
average daily census (x 1,000) 8.6
patients admitted (x1,000) 565
average cost per day to hospital, 1995 .... $1,064
average cost per stay to hospital, 1995 .... $5,899

EDUCATION

Educational attainment of all persons 25 years and older, 1990
less than 9th grade 246,505
high school graduates 878,432
bachelor's degree 486,695
graduate or professional degree 339,469

2000
high school graduate or more 85.7%
college graduate or more 32.3%

Public school enrollment, Fall, 1998
total 841,671
Kindergarten through grade 8 606,560
grades 9 through 12 235,111

Public School Teachers, 2000
total 50,500
elementary 28,300
secondary 22,100
average salaries
elementary $43,300
secondary $45,000

State receipts & expenditures for public schools, 2000
revenue receipts ($mil) $7,343

State receipts & expenditures for public schools, 2000 (continued)
expenditures
total ($mil) $7,041
per capita $1,361
per pupil $7,704

Graduating high school seniors, public high schools, 2000 (est.) 48,106

SAT scores, 2001
verbal 508
math 510
percent graduates taking test 65%

Institutions of higher education, 1999
total 59
public 33
private 26

Enrollment in institutions of higher education, Fall, 1998
total 265,173
full-time men 59,623
full-time women 73,815
part-time men 50,464
part-time women 81,271

Minority enrollment in institutions of higher education, Fall, 1997
Black, non-Hispanic 60,582
Hispanic 6,750
Asian/Pacific Islander 15,157

Earned degrees conferred, 1998
Bachelor's 20,809
First professional 1,115
Master's 10,130
Doctor's 995

SOCIAL INSURANCE & WELFARE PROGRAMS

Social Security beneficiaries & benefits, 2000
beneficiaries
total 723,000
retired and dependents 519,000
survivors 115,000
disabled & dependents 89,000
annual benefit payments ($mil)
total $6,622
retired and dependents $4,541
survivors $1,292
disabled & dependents $789

Maryland 4

Medicare, 2000
enrollment (x1,000) 635
payments ($mil) $3,998

Medicaid, 1998
recipients (x1,000) 561
payments ($mil) $2,489

Federal public aid
Temporary Assistance for Needy Families
(TANF), 2000
  Recipients (x1,000) 72
  Families (x1,000) 29
Supplemental Security Income
  total recipients, 1999 (x1,000) 87

Food Stamp Program
  participants, 2000 (x1,000) 219

HOUSING & CONSTRUCTION

Total housing units, 2000 2,145,283
seasonal or recreational use 38,880
occupied 1,980,859
  owner occupied 1,341,751
  renter occupied 639,108

New privately owned housing units uthorized, 2000
number (x1,000) 30.4
value ($mil) $3,232

New privately owned housing units
started, 2000 (est.) (x1,000) 27.9

Existing home sales, 2000 (x1,000) 101

GOVERNMENT & ELECTIONS

State officials, 2002
Governor (name/party/term expires)
PARRIS GLENDENING
Democrat - 2002
Lt. Governor . . . . Kathleen K. Townsend
Sec. of State . . . . John Willis
Atty. General . . . . Joseph Curran
Chief Justice . . . . Robert Bell

Governorship
minimum age 30
length of term . . . . 4 years
number of consecutive
  terms permitted 2
who succeeds . . . . Lt. Governor

State legislature
name . . . . Legislature
  upper chamber
    name . . . . Senate
    number of members 47
    length of term . . . . 4 years
    party in majority, 2000 . . . . Democratic
  lower chamber
    name . . . . House of Delegates
    number of members 141
    length of term . . . . 4 years
    party in majority, 2000 . . . . Democratic

State employees March, 2000
total 97,633
March payroll $297,176,781

Local governments, 1997
total 420
  county 23
  municipal 156
  township 0
  school districts 0
  special districts 241

Voting age population, November, 2000, projected
Total 3,925,000
  male 1,875,000
  female 2,050,000

Vote for president
2000
  Gore 1,141,000
  Bush 814,000
1996
  Clinton 966,000
  Dole 682,000
  Perot 116,000

Federal representation, 2002 (107th Congress)
Senators (name/party/term expires)

PAUL S. SARBANES
Democrat - 2007
BARBARA MIKULSKI
Democrat - 2005

Representatives, total 8
Democrats 4
Republicans 4
other 0

Women holding public office, 2001
U.S. Congress 2
statewide elected office 1
state legislature 55

Black elected officials, 1999
total 185
    US and state legislatures 40
    city/county/regional offices 101
    judicial/law enforcement 33
    education/school boards 11

Hispanic public officials, 2000
total .... NA
    state executives & legislators .... NA
    city/county/regional offices .... NA
    judicial/law enforcement .... NA
    education/school boards .... NA

GOVERNMENTAL FINANCE

State government revenues, 1999 ($per capita)
total revenue $3,792.36
    total general revenue $3,140.17
        intergovernmental revenue $734.40
        taxes $1,837.17
        current charges $293.99
        miscellaneous $274.62

State government expenditures, 1999 ($per capita)
total expenditure $3,401.91
    total general expenditure $3,004.77
        education $998.26
        public welfare $696.13
        health $179.39
        hospitals $65.63
        highways $255.89
        police protection $55.96
        correction $144.57
        natural resources $64.67
        governmental administration $144.95
        interest on general debt $92.03

State debt, 1999 ($per capita) $2,165.92

Federal government grants to state & local government, 2000 (x$1,000)
total $5,538,103
    Dept. of Education $406,660
    Environmental Protection Agency $82,922
    Health Care Financing Admin. $1,697,560
    Dept. Housing & Urban Devel. $681,685
    Dept. of Labor $94,216
    Highway trust fund $378,497

CRIME, LAW ENFORCEMENT & COURTS

Crime, 2000 (all rates per 100,000 inhabitants)
total crimes 255,085
overall crime rate 4,816.1
    property crimes 213,422
        burglaries 39,426
        larcenies 145,423
        motor vehicle thefts 28,573
    property crime rate 4,029.5
    violent crimes 41,663
        murders 430
        forcible rapes 1,543
        robberies 13,560
        aggravated assaults 26,130
    violent crime rate 786.6

Number of police agencies, 2000 144

Arrests, 2000
total 292,169
    persons under 18 years of age 46,630

Prisoners under state & federal jurisdiction, 2000
total 23,538
percent change, 1999-2000 .... 1.9%
    sentenced to more than one year
        total 22,490
        rate per 100,000 residents 429

Persons under sentence of death, 4/1/2001 16

State's highest court
name .... Court of Appeals
number of members 7
length of term .... 10 years
intermediate appeals court? .... yes

Maryland 6

LABOR & INCOME

Civilian labor force, 2000
total	2,805,000
men	1,479,000
women	1,326,000
persons 16-19 years	147,000
white	1,868,000
black	845,000

Civilian labor force as a percent of civilian non-institutional population, 2000
total	69.9%
men	75.7%
women	64.3%
persons 16-19 years	NA%
white	68.3%
black	73.3%

Employment, 2000
total	2,697,000
men	1,418,000
women	1,278,000
persons 16-19 years	125,000
white	1,817,000
black	791,000

Full-time/part-time labor force, 1998
full-time labor force	2,370,000
working part-time for economic reasons	20,000
part-time labor force	387,000

Unemployment rate, 2000
total	3.9%
men	4.1%
women	3.6%
persons 16-19 years	14.8%
white	2.7%
black	6.4%

Unemployed by reason for unemployment (as a percent of total unemployment), 1998
job losers or completed temp jobs	48.0%
job leavers	6.4%
reentrants	39.2%
new entrants	6.4%

Experienced civilian labor force, by occupation, 1998
executive/administrative/managerial	488,000
professional/specialty	548,000
technicians & related support	110,000
sales	295,000
administrative support/clerical	395,000
service occupations	357,000
precision production/craft/repair	272,000
machine operators/assemblers	79,000
transportation/material moving	79,000
handlers/helpers/laborers	82,000
farming/forestry/fishing	NA

Experienced civilian labor force, by industry, 1998
construction	174,000
manufacturing	195,000
transportation/communication	115,000
wholesale/retail trade	464,000
finance/real estate/insurance	204,000
services	737,000
government	624,000
agriculture	NA

Average annual pay, 1999 .... $34,472
change in average annual pay, 1998-1999 .... 3.5%

Hours and earnings of production workers on manufacturing payrolls, 2000
average weekly hours	40.8
average hourly earnings	$14.99
average weekly earnings	$611.59

Labor union membership, 2000 353,300

Household income (in 2000 dollars)
median household income, three year average, 1998-2000 .... $51,695

Poverty
persons below poverty level, three year average, 1998-2000 .... 7.3%

Personal income ($per capita)
2000 (prelim.)
in current dollars	$33,872
in constant (1996) dollars	$31,550
1999 (preliminary)
in current dollars	$32,166
in constant (1996) dollars	$30,757

Federal income tax returns, 1999
returns filed	2,499,237
adjusted gross income ($1,000)	$127,431,167
total income tax paid ($1,000)	$19,394,696

ECONOMY, BUSINESS, INDUSTRY & AGRICULTURE

Fortune 500 companies, 2000 7

Business incorporations, 1998
total 16,714
change, 1997-1998 .... -7.5%

Business failures, 1998 1,283

Business firm ownership, 1997
Hispanic owned firms 11,158
Black owned firms 47,614
women owned firms 115,801
Asian & Pacific Islander owned firms 22,164
American Indian & Alaska
   native owned firms 2,421

Shopping centers, 2000 940

Gross state product, 1999 ($mil)
total $174,710
   agriculture services, forestry, fisheries .. $1,440
   mining $145
   construction $9,451
   manufacturing--durable goods $6,361
   manufacturing--nondurable goods $7,855
   transportation, communication &
      public utilities $13,096
   wholesale trade $10,800
   retail trade $15,677
   finance/real estate/insurance $37,179
   services $42,217
   federal, state & local government $30,491

Establishments, by major industry group, 1999
total 127,431
   forestry, fishing & agriculture 234
   mining 106
   construction 14,713
   manufacturing 3,972
   transportation & warehousing 3,247
   wholesale trade 6,197
   retail trade 19,573
   finance & insurance 7,221
   professional/scientific/technical 16,191
   health care/social assistance 13,014
   information 2,275
   accommodation/food services 8,791

Payroll, by major industry group, 1999
total ($1,000) $64,183,349
   forestry, fishing & agriculture $39,481
   mining $71,860
   construction $5,302,248
   manufacturing $6,385,688
   transportation & warehousing $1,652,691
   wholesale trade $4,273,807
   retail trade $5,642,129
   finance & insurance $4,912,577
   professional/scientific/technical $9,134,232
   health care/social assistance $7,810,040
   information $2,905,497
   accommodation/food services $1,943,138

Agriculture
number of farms, 2000 12,000
farm acreage, 2000 2,000,000
acres per farm, 2000 169
value of farms, 1997 ($mil) $8,400
farm income, 1999 ($mil)
   net farm income $337
   debt/asset ratio 14.9%
farm marketings, 1999 ($mil)
total $1,481
   crops $544
   livestock $937
principal commodities, in order by marketing
receipts, 1999
      Broilers, greenhouse, dairy products, cattle

Federal economic activity in state
expenditures, 2000
   total ($mil) $45,089
   per capita $8,513
   defense ($mil) $8,596
   non-defense ($mil) $36,493
defense department, 2000
   contract awards ($mil) $4,977
   payroll ($mil) $3,726
   civilian employees (x1,000) 32
   military personnel (x1,000) 30.4

Fishing, 2000
catch (thousands of pounds) 48,913
value ($1,000) $53,874

Mining, 2000 ($mil; preliminary)
total non-fuel mineral production $357

Maryland 8

Construction, 1999 ($mil)
total contracts (including
 non-building) $7,659
  residential $2,980
  non-residential $3,531

Construction industries, 1997
establishments 14,166
receipts ($1,000) $20,706,928
annual payroll ($1,000) $4,296,364
paid employees 139,269

Manufacturing, 1997
establishments 4,196
value of shipments ($1,000) $38,281,223
annual payroll ($1,000) $6,220,818
paid employees 174,740

Transportation industries, 1997
establishments 4,988
receipts ($1,000) $16,622,056
annual payroll ($1,000) $3,430,383
paid employees 97,363

Wholesale trade, 1997
establishments 7,433
sales($1,000) $58,060,786
annual payroll ($1,000) $4,045,868
paid employees 105,973

Retail trade, 1997
establishments 27,422
sales($1,000) $48,297,830
annual payroll ($1,000) $5,916,600
paid employees 404,802

Finance industries
establishments, 1997 11,896
receipts ($1,000), 1997 .... $NA
annual payroll ($1,000), 1997 .... $5,467,655
paid employees, 1997 140,830
commercial banks, 2000
 number 74
  assets ($bil) $46.9
  deposits ($bil) $35.6

Service industries, 1997 (non-exempt firms only)
establishments 42,330
receipts ($1,000) $40,050,875
annual payroll ($1,000) $16,348,105
paid employees 557,370

COMMUNICATION, ENERGY & TRANSPORTATION

Communication
daily newspapers, 2000 14
households with
 telephones, 1998 .... 97.2%
 computers, 2000 .... 53.7%
 internet access, 2000 .... 43.8%

Energy
consumption, 1999
total (trillion Btu) 1,378
per capita (million Btu) 267
by source of production (trillion Btu)
 coal 304
 natural gas 201
 petroleum 584
 nuclear electric power 141
 hydroelectric power 15
by end-use sector (trillion Btu)
 residential 359
 commercial 337
 industrial 277
 transportation 405
electric energy, 1999
 production (billion kWh) 49.3
 net summer capability (million kW) ... 11
gas utilities, 1999
 customers 834,000
 sales (trillion Btu) 86
nuclear plants, 1999 2

Transportation, 2000
public road & street mileage
total 30,494
 urban 14,429
 rural 16,065
 interstate 481
vehicle miles of travel (mil) 50,174
total motor vehicle registrations 3,847,538
 automobiles 2,605,816
 motorcycles 49,296
licensed drivers 3,382,451
 per 1,000 driving age population 828
deaths from motor vehicle
 accidents 588

STATE SUMMARY

Capital City . . . . Boston

Governor . . . . Jane Swift

Address . . . . STATE HOUSE
BOSTON, MA 02133
617 727-3600

Admitted as a state 1788

Area (square miles) 10,555

Population, 1980 5,737,037

Population, 1990 6,016,425

Population, 2000 6,349,097

Persons per square mile, 2000 810

Largest city . . . . Boston
population, 2000 589,000

Personal income per capita, 2000
(in current dollars) $37,992

Gross state product ($mil), 1999 . . . . . . $262,564

Leading industries, 1999 (by payroll)
Manufacturing
Finance & Insurance
Health care/Social assistance

Leading agricultural commodities, 1999
Greenhouse, dairy products, cranberries, sweet
corn

GEOGRAPHY & ENVIRONMENT

Area, 1990 (square miles)
total 10,555
land 7,838
water (includes territorial water) 2,717

Federally owned land, 2000 . . . . 1.4%

Highest point
name . . . . Mt. Greylock
elevation (feet) 3,487

Lowest point
name . . . . Atlantic Ocean
elevation (feet) . . . . sea level

General coastline (miles) 192

Tidal shoreline (miles) 1,519

Capital city . . . . Boston
population, 2000 589,000

Largest city . . . . Boston
population, 2000 589,000

Number of cities with over 100,000 population
1980 3
1990 3
2000 5

State parks and Recreation areas, 2000
area (acres) 289,000
number of visitors 12,775,000
revenues $5,725,000

Natl. forest system land, 1999 (acres) 0

National park acreage, 1984 30,900

DEMOGRAPHICS & CHARACTERISTICS OF THE POPULATION

Population
1970 5,689,170
1980 5,737,037
1990 6,016,425
2000 6,349,097
2015 (projection) 6,574,000
2025 (projection) 6,902,000

Metropolitan area population
1970 5,266,000
1980 5,231,000
2000 6,088,000

Non-metropolitan area population
1970 423,000
1980 506,000
2000 261,000

Change in population, 1990-2000
number 332,672
percent 5.53%

Persons per square mile, 2000 810

Persons by age, 2000
under 5 years 397,268
18 and over 4,849,033
21 and over 4,587,935
65 and over 860,162
85 and over 116,692

Massachusetts 2

Persons by age, 2025 (projected)
under 5 years 439,000
5 to 17 years 1,128,000
65 and over 1,252,000

Median age, 2000 .... 36.5

Race, 2000
One race
White 5,367,286
Black or African American 343,454
American Indian and Alaska Native 15,015
Asian Indian 43,801
Chinese 84,392
Filipino 8,273
Japanese 10,539
Korean 17,369
Vietnamese 33,962
Native Hawaiian and other Pacific Islander 2,489
Two or more races 146,005

Race, 2025 (projected)
White 5,694,000
Black 655,000

Persons of Hispanic origin, 2000
total Hispanic or Latino 428,729
  Mexican 22,288
  Puerto Rican 199,207
  Cuban 8,867
  Other Hispanic or Latino 198,367

Persons of Hispanic origin, 2025 (proj.) .. 934,000

Persons by sex, 2000
male 3,058,816
female 3,290,281

Marital status, 1990
males
  15 years & older 2,305,194
    single 832,633
    married 1,273,184
      separated 38,922
      widowed 63,724
    divorced 135,653
females
  15 years & older 2,572,630
    single 765,274
    married 1,287,900
      separated 60,931

widowed 311,956
divorced 207,500

Households & families, 2000
households 2,443,580
persons per household 2.51
  families 1,576,696
  persons per family 3.11
    married couples 1,197,917
    female householder, no husband
      present 289,944
    one person households 684,345
households with persons under 18 years . 804,940
households with persons over 65 years ... 604,481

Nativity, 1990
number of persons born in state 4,134,235
percent of total residents 68.7%

Immigration & naturalization, 1998
immigrants admitted 15,869
persons naturalized 10,568
refugees granted resident status 793

VITAL STATISTICS & HEALTH
Births
1999
  with low birth weight 7.1%
  to teenage mothers 13.1%
  to unmarried mothers 26.5%
Birth rate, 1999 (per 1,000) 13.1
Birth rate, 2000 (per 1,000) 13.2

Abortions, 1996
total 41,000
rate (per 1,000 women age 15-44) 29.3

Deaths
1998 58,364
1999 55,840
2000 56,475

Infant deaths
1998 426
1999 403
2000 385

Average lifetime, by race, 1989-1991
total .... 76.72 years
  white .... 76.90 years
  black .... 72.45 years

Marriages
1998 39,219
1999 39,411
2000 36,999

Divorces
1998 16,524
1999 13,181
2000 18,597

Physicians, 1999
total 26,062
rate (per 1,000 persons) 4.22

Nurses, 1999
total 72,840
rate (per 1,000 persons) 11.80

Hospitals, 1998
number 82
beds (x 1,000) 16.5
average daily census (x 1,000) 11.5
patients admitted (x1,000) 738
average cost per day to hospital, 1995 .... $1,157
average cost per stay to hospital, 1995 .... $7,099

EDUCATION

*Educational attainment of all persons
    25 years and older, 1990*
    less than 9th grade 317,943
    high school graduates 1,178,509
    bachelor's degree 657,161
    graduate or professional degree 421,838

2000
    high school graduate or more 85.1%
    college graduate or more 32.7%

Public school enrollment, Fall, 1998
total 962,317
    Kindergarten through grade 8 704,624
    grades 9 through 12 257,693

Public School Teachers, 2000
total 68,000
    elementary 29,200
    secondary 38,800
average salaries
    elementary $46,300
    secondary $46,300

*State receipts & expenditures for public
    schools, 2000*
revenue receipts ($mil) $9,222

*State receipts & expenditures for public
    schools, 2000 (continued)*
expenditures
    total ($mil) $8,946
    per capita $1,449
    per pupil $9,366

*Graduating high school seniors,
    public high schools, 2000 (est.) 50,537*

SAT scores, 2001
verbal 511
math 515
percent graduates taking test 79%

Institutions of higher education, 1999
total 129
    public 33
    private 96

*Enrollment in institutions of higher
    education, Fall, 1998*
total 415,616
full-time men 121,167
full-time women 145,591
part-time men 59,440
part-time women 89,418

*Minority enrollment in institutions of higher
    education, Fall, 1997*
Black, non-Hispanic 25,129
Hispanic 18,983
Asian/Pacific Islander 26,434

Earned degrees conferred, 1998
Bachelor's 40,727
First professional 3,948
Master's 23,651
Doctor's 2,554

SOCIAL INSURANCE &
WELFARE PROGRAMS

Social Security beneficiaries & benefits, 2000
beneficiaries
total 1,064,000
    retired and dependents 759,000
    survivors 140,000
    disabled & dependents 165,000
annual benefit payments ($mil)
total $9,696
    retired and dependents $6,691
    survivors $1,656
    disabled & dependents $1,350

Massachusetts 4

Medicare, 2000
enrollment (x1,000) 954
payments ($mil) $5,466

Medicaid, 1998
recipients (x1,000) 908
payments ($mil) $4,609

Federal public aid
Temporary Assistance for Needy Families
(TANF), 2000
    Recipients (x1,000) 100
    Families (x1,000) 44
Supplemental Security Income
total recipients, 1999 (x1,000) 167

Food Stamp Program
participants, 2000 (x1,000) 232

HOUSING & CONSTRUCTION

Total housing units, 2000 2,621,989
    seasonal or recreational use 93,771
    occupied 2,443,580
    owner occupied 1,508,052
    renter occupied 935,528

New privately owned housing units uthorized, 2000
number (x1,000) 18
value ($mil) $2,741

New privately owned housing units
started, 2000 (est.) (x1,000) 17.7

Existing home sales, 2000 (x1,000) 94.1

GOVERNMENT & ELECTIONS

State officials, 2002
Governor (name/party/term expires)
JANE SWIFT
Republican - 2002
Lt. Governor . . . . (Vacant)
Sec. of State . . . . William Galvin
Atty. General . . . . Thomas Reilly
Chief Justice . . . . Margaret Marshall

Governorship
minimum age . . . . not specified
length of term . . . . 4 years
number of consecutive
    terms permitted . . . . not specified
who succeeds . . . . Lt. Governor

State legislature
name . . . . General Court
    upper chamber
        name . . . . Senate
        number of members 40
        length of term . . . . 2 years
        party in majority, 2000 . . . . Democratic
    lower chamber
        name . . . . House of Representatives
        number of members 160
        length of term . . . . 2 years
        party in majority, 2000 . . . . Democratic

State employees March, 2000
total 114,124
March payroll $345,257,144

Local governments, 1997
total 861
    county 12
    municipal 44
    township 307
    school districts 85
    special districts 413

Voting age population, November, 2000, projected
Total 4,749,000
    male 2,248,000
    female 2,500,000

Vote for president
2000
    Gore 1,616,000
    Bush 879,000
1996
    Clinton 1,572,000
    Dole 718,000
    Perot 227,000

Federal representation, 2002 (107th Congress)
Senators (name/party/term expires)

EDWARD M. KENNEDY
Democrat - 2007
JOHN F. KERRY
Democrat - 2003

Representatives, total 10
    Democrats 10
    Republicans 0
    other 0

Women holding public office, 2001
U.S. Congress 0
statewide elected office 2
state legislature 49

Black elected officials, 1999
total 31
   US and state legislatures 6
   city/county/regional offices 20
   judicial/law enforcement 2
   education/school boards 3

Hispanic public officials, 2000
total 13
   state executives & legislators 3
   city/county/regional offices 7
   judicial/law enforcement ....NA
   education/school boards 3

GOVERNMENTAL FINANCE

State government revenues, 1999 ($per capita)
total revenue $4,553.70
  total general revenue $4,155.96
   intergovernmental revenue $883.29
   taxes $2,385.65
   current charges $272.70
   miscellaneous $614.32

State government expenditures, 1999 ($per capita)
total expenditure $4,539.20
  total general expenditure $4,181.19
   education $947.55
   public welfare $983.95
   health $222.54
   hospitals $83.91
   highways $365.51
   police protection $69.28
   correction $126.57
   natural resources $35.12
   governmental administration $170.37
   interest on general debt $307.99

State debt, 1999 ($per capita) $5,797.08

Federal government grants to state & local government, 2000 (x$1,000)
total $7,499,910
  Dept. of Education $545,152
  Environmental Protection Agency ... $140,372
  Health Care Financing Admin. $3,381,401
  Dept. Housing & Urban Devel. $1,312,524
  Dept. of Labor $103,550
  Highway trust fund $484,249

CRIME, LAW ENFORCEMENT & COURTS

Crime, 2000 (all rates per 100,000 inhabitants)
total crimes 192,131
overall crime rate 3,026.1
  property crimes 161,901
   burglaries 30,600
   larcenies 105,425
   motor vehicle thefts 25,876
  property crime rate 2,550.0
  violent crimes 30,230
   murders 125
   forcible rapes 1,696
   robberies 5,815
   aggravated assaults 22,594
  violent crime rate 476.1

Number of police agencies, 2000 261

Arrests, 2000
total 138,649
  persons under 18 years of age 19,933

Prisoners under state & federal jurisdiction, 2000
total 10,722
percent change, 1999-2000 .... -5.6%
  sentenced to more than one year
   total 9,479
   rate per 100,000 residents 252

Persons under sentence of death, 4/1/2001 ...NA

State's highest court
name .... Supreme Court
number of members 7
length of term .... to age 70
intermediate appeals court? .... yes

LABOR & INCOME

Civilian labor force, 2000

total	3,237,000
men	1,702,000
women	1,534,000
persons 16-19 years	173,000
white	2,936,000
black	198,000

Civilian labor force as a percent of civilian non-institutional population, 2000

total	67.4%
men	73.8%
women	61.4%
persons 16-19 years	NA%
white	67.5%
black	65.8%

Employment, 2000

total	3,151,000
men	1,659,000
women	1,492,000
persons 16-19 years	156,000
white	2,865,000
black	185,000

Full-time/part-time labor force, 1998

full-time labor force	2,603,000
working part-time for economic reasons	19,000
part-time labor force	671,000

Unemployment rate, 2000

total	2.6%
men	2.6%
women	2.7%
persons 16-19 years	9.4%
white	2.4%
black	6.3%

Unemployed by reason for unemployment (as a percent of total unemployment), 1998

job losers or completed temp jobs	56.0%
job leavers	11.0%
reentrants	26.6%
new entrants	5.5%

Experienced civilian labor force, by occupation, 1998

executive/administrative/managerial	521,000
professional/specialty	582,000
technicians & related support	99,000
sales	371,000
administrative support/clerical	462,000
service occupations	471,000
precision production/craft/repair	349,000
machine operators/assemblers	159,000
transportation/material moving	97,000
handlers/helpers/laborers	112,000
farming/forestry/fishing	NA

Experienced civilian labor force, by industry, 1998

construction	140,000
manufacturing	501,000
transportation/communication	144,000
wholesale/retail trade	622,000
finance/real estate/insurance	217,000
services	965,000
government	374,000
agriculture	NA

Average annual pay, 1999	$40,331
change in average annual pay, 1998-1999	6.8%

Hours and earnings of production workers on manufacturing payrolls, 2000

average weekly hours	41.9
average hourly earnings	$14.65
average weekly earnings	$613.84

Labor union membership, 2000	406,300

Household income (in 2000 dollars)

median household income, three year average, 1998-2000	$46,947

Poverty

persons below poverty level, three year average, 1998-2000	10.2%

Personal income ($per capita)
2000 (prelim.)

in current dollars	$37,992
in constant (1996) dollars	$35,387

1999 (preliminary)

in current dollars	$35,733
in constant (1996) dollars	$34,168

Federal income tax returns, 1999

returns filed	3,048,771
adjusted gross income ($1,000)	$172,449,434
total income tax paid ($1,000)	$30,246,838

ECONOMY, BUSINESS, INDUSTRY & AGRICULTURE

Fortune 500 companies, 2000 13

Business incorporations, 1998
total 11,798
change, 1997-1998 .... -5.1%

Business failures, 1998 1,200

Business firm ownership, 1997
Hispanic owned firms 12,725
Black owned firms 11,834
women owned firms 142,661
Asian & Pacific Islander owned firms 12,729
American Indian & Alaska
  native owned firms 3,428

Shopping centers, 2000 1,008

Gross state product, 1999 ($mil)
total $262,564
  agriculture services, forestry, fisheries .. $1,429
  mining $98
  construction $10,861
  manufacturing--durable goods $24,182
  manufacturing--nondurable goods $12,386
  transportation, communication &
    public utilities $14,833
  wholesale trade $19,560
  retail trade $20,581
  finance/real estate/insurance $64,279
  services $70,462
  federal, state & local government $23,892

Establishments, by major industry group, 1999
total 173,267
  forestry, fishing & agriculture 382
  mining 95
  construction 15,860
  manufacturing 9,329
  transportation & warehousing 3,383
  wholesale trade 9,873
  retail trade 25,924
  finance & insurance 8,867
  professional/scientific/technical 20,614
  health care/social assistance 16,454
  information 3,575
  accommodation/food services 14,586

Payroll, by major industry group, 1999
total ($1,000) $115,269,583
  forestry, fishing & agriculture $21,496
  mining $53,813
  construction $5,074,494
  manufacturing $18,832,530
  transportation & warehousing $2,098,028
  wholesale trade $7,605,741
  retail trade $7,131,729
  finance & insurance $14,079,704
  professional/scientific/technical $13,457,618
  health care/social assistance $13,670,003
  information $6,790,899
  accommodation/food services $3,203,563

Agriculture
number of farms, 2000 6,000
farm acreage, 2000 1,000,000
acres per farm, 2000 93
value of farms, 1997 ($mil) $3,534
farm income, 1999 ($mil)
  net farm income $65
  debt/asset ratio 11.7%
farm marketings, 1999 ($mil)
total $396
  crops $295
  livestock $101
principal commodities, in order by marketing
receipts, 1999
  Greenhouse, dairy products, cranberries, sweet
corn

Federal economic activity in state
expenditures, 2000
  total ($mil) $40,824
  per capita $6,430
  defense ($mil) $5,607
  non-defense ($mil) $35,217
defense department, 2000
  contract awards ($mil) $4,737
  payroll ($mil) $826
  civilian employees (x1,000) 6.9
  military personnel (x1,000) 2.3

Fishing, 2000
catch (thousands of pounds) 187,861
value ($1,000) $288,263

Mining, 2000 ($mil; preliminary)
total non-fuel mineral production $210

Massachusetts 8

Construction, 1999 ($mil)
total contracts (including
    non-building) $8,922
      residential $2,913
      non-residential $4,281

Construction industries, 1997
establishments 14,519
receipts ($1,000) ....$NA
annual payroll ($1,000) ....$NA
paid employees ....NA

Manufacturing, 1997
establishments 9,733
value of shipments ($1,000) $82,603,724
annual payroll ($1,000) $17,445,834
paid employees 441,770

Transportation industries, 1997
establishments 6,100
receipts ($1,000) $26,876,138
annual payroll ($1,000) $4,650,315
paid employees 129,023

Wholesale trade, 1997
establishments 11,423
sales($1,000) $116,391,186
annual payroll ($1,000) $6,954,390
paid employees 161,894

Retail trade, 1997
establishments 38,975
sales($1,000) $62,533,487
annual payroll ($1,000) $7,533,875
paid employees 522,783

Finance industries
establishments, 1997 14,325
receipts ($1,000), 1997 ....$NA
annual payroll ($1,000), 1997 .... $12,728,967
paid employees, 1997 247,872
commercial banks, 2000
  number 44
    assets ($bil) $111.4
    deposits ($bil) $72.6

Service industries, 1997 (non-exempt firms only)
establishments 53,392
receipts ($1,000) $59,619,241
annual payroll ($1,000) $23,414,817
paid employees 703,699

COMMUNICATION, ENERGY & TRANSPORTATION

Communication
daily newspapers, 2000 32
households with
  telephones, 1998 .... 95.5%
  computers, 2000 .... 53.0%
  internet access, 2000 .... 45.5%

Energy
consumption, 1999
total (trillion Btu) 1,569
per capita (million Btu) 254
by source of production (trillion Btu)
  coal 13
  natural gas 356
  petroleum 639
  nuclear electric power 48
  hydroelectric power .,..................15
by end-use sector (trillion Btu)
  residential 412
  commercial 325
  industrial 391
  transportation 441
electric energy, 1999
  production (billion kWh) 4.4
  net summer capability (million kW) 2.2
gas utilities, 1999
  customers 1,325,000
  sales (trillion Btu) 169
nuclear plants, 1999 1

Transportation, 2000
public road & street mileage
total 35,311
  urban 23,101
  rural 12,210
  interstate 566
vehicle miles of travel (mil) 52,796
total motor vehicle registrations 5,265,399
  automobiles 3,673,638
  motorcycles 106,715
licensed drivers 4,489,695
  per 1,000 driving age population 897
deaths from motor vehicle
  accidents 433

Michigan 1

STATE SUMMARY

Capital City . . . . Lansing

Governor . . . . John Engler

Address . . . . STATE CAPITOL
LANSING, MI 48909
517 373-3400

Admitted as a state 1837

Area (square miles) 96,810

Population, 1980 9,262,078

Population, 1990 9,295,297

Population, 2000 9,938,444

Persons per square mile, 2000 . . . . 174.9

Largest city . . . . Detroit
population, 2000 951,000

Personal income per capita, 2000
(in current dollars) $29,612

Gross state product ($mil), 1999 . . . . . . $308,310

Leading industries, 1999 (by payroll)
Manufacturing
Health care/Social assistance
Retail trade

Leading agricultural commodities, 1999
Dairy products, greenhouse, soybeans, corn

GEOGRAPHY & ENVIRONMENT

Area, 1990 (square miles)
total 96,810
land 56,809
water (includes territorial water) 40,001

Federally owned land, 2000 . . . . 11.2%

Highest point
name . . . . Mt. Avron
elevation (feet) 1,979

Lowest point
name . . . . Lake Erie
elevation (feet) 572

General coastline (miles) 0

Tidal shoreline (miles) 0

Capital city . . . . Lansing
population, 2000 119,000

Largest city . . . . Detroit
population, 2000 951,000

Number of cities with over 100,000 population
1980 8
1990 7
2000 8

State parks and Recreation areas, 2000
area (acres) 351,000
number of visitors 27,534,000
revenues $32,347,000

Natl. forest system land, 1999 (acres) . . . 2,857,000

National park acreage, 1984 630,200

DEMOGRAPHICS & CHARACTERISTICS OF THE POPULATION

Population
1970 8,881,826
1980 9,262,078
1990 9,295,297
2000 9,938,444
2015 (projection) 9,917,000
2025 (projection) 10,078,000

Metropolitan area population
1970 7,361,000
1980 7,481,000
2000 8,169,000

Non-metropolitan area population
1970 1,521,000
1980 1,782,000
2000 1,769,000

Change in population, 1990-2000
number 643,147
percent 6.92%

Persons per square mile, 2000 . . . . 174.9

Persons by age, 2000
under 5 years 672,005
18 and over 7,342,677
21 and over 6,914,135
65 and over 1,219,018
85 and over 142,460

Michigan 2

Persons by age, 2025 (projected)
under 5 years 656,000
5 to 17 years 1,763,000
65 and over 1,821,000

Median age, 2000 .... 35.5

Race, 2000
One race
White 7,966,053
Black or African American 1,412,742
American Indian and Alaska Native 58,479
Asian Indian 54,631
Chinese 33,189
Filipino 17,377
Japanese 11,288
Korean 20,886
Vietnamese 13,673
Native Hawaiian and other Pacific Islander 2,692
Two or more races 192,416

Race, 2025 (projected)
White 8,011,000
Black 1,705,000

Persons of Hispanic origin, 2000
total Hispanic or Latino 323,877
   Mexican 220,769
   Puerto Rican 26,941
   Cuban 7,219
   Other Hispanic or Latino 68,948

Persons of Hispanic origin, 2025 (proj.) .. 431,000

Persons by sex, 2000
male 4,873,095
female 5,065,349

Marital status, 1990
males
   15 years & older 3,458,188
   single 1,078,995
   married 2,015,282
      separated 57,534
   widowed 88,226
   divorced 275,685
females
   15 years & older 3,775,938
   single 931,043
   married 2,031,579
      separated 82,215

widowed 433,615
divorced 379,701

Households & families, 2000
households 3,785,661
persons per household 2.56
   families 2,575,699
   persons per family 3.1
      married couples 1,947,710
   female householder, no husband
      present 473,802
   one person households 993,607
households with persons under 18 years 1,347,469
households with persons over 65 years ... 862,730

Nativity, 1990
number of persons born in state 6,958,717
percent of total residents 74.9%

Immigration & naturalization, 1998
immigrants admitted 13,943
persons naturalized 7,100
refugees granted resident status 1,250

VITAL STATISTICS & HEALTH

Births
1999
   with low birth weight 8.0%
   to teenage mothers 13.5%
   to unmarried mothers 33.1%
Birth rate, 1999 (per 1,000) 13.5
Birth rate, 2000 (per 1,000) 13.7

Abortions, 1996
total 49,000
rate (per 1,000 women age 15-44) 22.3

Deaths
1998 86,292
1999 87,232
2000 86,967

Infant deaths
1998 1,110
1999 1,103
2000 1,118

Average lifetime, by race, 1989-1991
total .... 75.04 years
   white .... 76.18 years
   black .... 68.49 years

Marriages
1998 66,089
1999 67,136
2000 66,372

Divorces
1998 38,882
1999 38,017
2000 39,377

Physicians, 1999
total 22,246
rate (per 1,000 persons) 2.26

Nurses, 1999
total 83,370
rate (per 1,000 persons) 8.45

Hospitals, 1998
number 151
beds (x 1,000) 27.2
average daily census (x 1,000) 17.5
patients admitted (x1,000) 1,105
average cost per day to hospital, 1995 . . . . . . $994
average cost per stay to hospital, 1995 . . . . $6,218

EDUCATION

Educational attainment of all persons
   25 years and older, 1990
   less than 9th grade 452,893
   high school graduates 1,887,449
   bachelor's degree 638,267
   graduate or professional degree 375,780

2000
   high school graduate or more 86.2%
   college graduate or more 23.0%

Public school enrollment, Fall, 1998
total 1,720,266
   Kindergarten through grade 8 1,245,299
   grades 9 through 12 474,967

Public School Teachers, 2000
total 96,100
   elementary 49,900
   secondary 46,200
average salaries
   elementary $48,700
   secondary $48,700

State receipts & expenditures for public
   schools, 2000
revenue receipts ($mil) $16,818

State receipts & expenditures for public
   schools, 2000 (continued)
expenditures
   total ($mil) $14,025
      per capita $1,422
      per pupil $8,099

Graduating high school seniors,
   public high schools, 2000 (est.) 100,600

SAT scores, 2001
verbal 561
math 572
percent graduates taking test 11%

Institutions of higher education, 1999
total 112
   public 44
   private 68

Enrollment in institutions of higher
   education, Fall, 1998
total 557,011
full-time men 133,328
full-time women 161,097
part-time men 108,928
part-time women 153,658

Minority enrollment in institutions of higher
   education, Fall, 1997
Black, non-Hispanic 61,698
Hispanic 12,125
Asian/Pacific Islander 16,786

Earned degrees conferred, 1998
Bachelor's 44,186
First professional 2,542
Master's 17,898
Doctor's 1,565

SOCIAL INSURANCE & WELFARE PROGRAMS

Social Security beneficiaries & benefits, 2000
beneficiaries
total 1,645,000
   retired and dependents 1,138,000
   survivors 262,000
   disabled & dependents 245,000
annual benefit payments ($mil)
total $15,892
   retired and dependents $10,585
   survivors $3,151
   disabled & dependents $2,157

Michigan 4

Medicare, 2000
enrollment (x1,000) 1,389
payments ($mil) $6,269

Medicaid, 1998
recipients (x1,000) 1,363
payments ($mil) $4,345

Federal public aid
Temporary Assistance for Needy Families
(TANF), 2000
   Recipients (x1,000) 207
   Families (x1,000) 75
Supplemental Security Income
   total recipients, 1999 (x1,000) 210

Food Stamp Program
   participants, 2000 (x1,000) 611

HOUSING & CONSTRUCTION

Total housing units, 2000 4,234,279
   seasonal or recreational use 233,922
   occupied 3,785,661
      owner occupied 2,793,124
      renter occupied 992,537

New privately owned housing units uthorized, 2000
number (x1,000) 52.5
value ($mil) $6,256

New privately owned housing units
started, 2000 (est.) (x1,000) 50.9

Existing home sales, 2000 (x1,000) 150.8

GOVERNMENT & ELECTIONS

State officials, 2002
   Governor (name/party/term expires)
        JOHN ENGLER
        Republican - 2002
Lt. Governor .... Dick Posthumus
Sec. of State .... Candice Miller
Atty. General .... Jennifer Granholm
Chief Justice .... Elizabeth Weaver

Governorship
minimum age 30
length of term .... 4 years
number of consecutive
   terms permitted 2
who succeeds .... Lt. Governor

State legislature
name .... Legislature
   upper chamber
      name .... Senate
      number of members 38
      length of term .... 4 years
      party in majority, 2000 .... Republican
   lower chamber
      name .... House of Representatives
      number of members 110
      length of term .... 2 years
      party in majority, 2000 .... Republican

State employees March, 2000
total 179,100
March payroll $503,742,494

Local governments, 1997
total 2,775
   county 83
   municipal 534
   township 1,242
   school districts 584
   special districts 332

Voting age population, November, 2000, projected
Total 7,358,000
   male 3,519,000
   female 3,839,000

Vote for president
2000
   Gore 2,170,000
   Bush 1,953,000
1996
   Clinton 1,990,000
   Dole 1,481,000
   Perot 337,000

Federal representation, 2002 (107th Congress)
Senators (name/party/term expires)

      DEBBIE STABENOW
      Democrat - 2007
      CARL LEVIN
      Democrat - 2003

Representatives, total 16
   Democrats 9
   Republicans 7
   other 0

Women holding public office, 2001
U.S. Congress 2
statewide elected office 2
state legislature 33

Black elected officials, 1999
total 338
    US and state legislatures 22
    city/county/regional offices 144
    judicial/law enforcement 54
    education/school boards 118

Hispanic public officials, 2000
total 8
    state executives & legislators 2
    city/county/regional offices 5
    judicial/law enforcement . . . . NA
    education/school boards 1

GOVERNMENTAL FINANCE

State government revenues, 1999 ($per capita)
total revenue $4,736.97
    total general revenue $3,729.95
        intergovernmental revenue $889.10
        taxes $2,215.84
        current charges $376.57
        miscellaneous $248.45

State government expenditures, 1999 ($per capita)
total expenditure $3,933.39
    total general expenditure $3,560.78
        education $1,642.44
        public welfare $635.49
        health $244.15
        hospitals $106.76
        highways $244.15
        police protection $29.76
        correction $153.38
        natural resources $39.71
        governmental administration $82.51
        interest on general debt $90.41

State debt, 1999 ($per capita) $1,641.26

Federal government grants to state & local government, 2000 (x$1,000)
total $9,486,173
    Dept. of Education $916,639
    Environmental Protection Agency . . . $200,933
    Health Care Financing Admin. $3,887,940
    Dept. Housing & Urban Devel. $856,659
    Dept. of Labor $191,073
    Highway trust fund $847,003

CRIME, LAW ENFORCEMENT & COURTS

Crime, 2000 (all rates per 100,000 inhabitants)
total crimes 408,456
overall crime rate 4,109.9
    property crimes 353,297
        burglaries 69,790
        larcenies 227,783
        motor vehicle thefts 55,724
    property crime rate 3,554.9
    violent crimes 55,159
        murders 669
        forcible rapes 5,025
        robberies 13,712
        aggravated assaults 35,753
    violent crime rate 555.0

Number of police agencies, 2000 554

Arrests, 2000
total 333,591
    persons under 18 years of age 47,165

Prisoners under state & federal jurisdiction, 2000
total 47,718
percent change, 1999-2000 . . . . 2.4%
    sentenced to more than one year
        total 47,718
        rate per 100,000 residents 480

Persons under sentence of death, 4/1/2001 . . . NA

State's highest court
name . . . . Supreme Court
number of members 7
length of term . . . . 8 years
intermediate appeals court? . . . . yes

Michigan 6

LABOR & INCOME

Civilian labor force, 2000

total	5,201,000
men	2,815,000
women	2,386,000
persons 16-19 years	406,000
white	4,412,000
black	640,000

Civilian labor force as a percent of civilian non-institutional population, 2000

total	68.9%
men	76.7%
women	61.5%
persons 16-19 years	NA%
white	69.4%
black	65.4%

Employment, 2000

total	5,016,000
men	2,717,000
women	2,299,000
persons 16-19 years	365,000
white	4,276,000
black	596,000

Full-time/part-time labor force, 1998

full-time labor force	4,025,000
working part-time for economic reasons	49,000
part-time labor force	1,004,000

Unemployment rate, 2000

total	3.6%
men	3.5%
women	3.6%
persons 16-19 years	10.3%
white	3.1%
black	6.9%

Unemployed by reason for unemployment (as a percent of total unemployment), 1998

job losers or completed temp jobs	50.0%
job leavers	10.8%
reentrants	31.4%
new entrants	8.2%

Experienced civilian labor force, by occupation, 1998

executive/administrative/managerial	648,000
professional/specialty	695,000
technicians & related support	156,000
sales	572,000
administrative support/clerical	658,000
service occupations	688,000
precision production/craft/repair	619,000
machine operators/assemblers	451,000
transportation/material moving	205,000
handlers/helpers/laborers	218,000
farming/forestry/fishing	102,000

Experienced civilian labor force, by industry, 1998

construction	241,000
manufacturing	1,206,000
transportation/communication	182,000
wholesale/retail trade	1,009,000
finance/real estate/insurance	239,000
services	1,174,000
government	564,000
agriculture	94,000

Average annual pay, 1999 .... $35,734
change in average annual pay, 1998-1999 .... 3.5%

Hours and earnings of production workers on manufacturing payrolls, 2000

average weekly hours	43.6
average hourly earnings	$19.20
average weekly earnings	$837.12

Labor union membership, 2000 938,300

Household income (in 2000 dollars)
median household income, three year average, 1998-2000 .... $46,181

Poverty
persons below poverty level, three year average, 1998-2000 .... 10.2%

Personal income ($per capita)
2000 (prelim.)
in current dollars	$29,612
in constant (1996) dollars	$27,582
1999 (preliminary)
in current dollars	$27,844
in constant (1996) dollars	$26,625

Federal income tax returns, 1999

returns filed	4,556,948
adjusted gross income ($1,000)	$207,142,472
total income tax paid ($1,000)	$31,568,671

ECONOMY, BUSINESS, INDUSTRY & AGRICULTURE

Fortune 500 companies, 2000 19

Business incorporations, 1998
total 28,983
change, 1997-1998 .... -7.3%

Business failures, 1998 1,551

Business firm ownership, 1997
Hispanic owned firms 9,997
Black owned firms 24,954
women owned firms 184,590
Asian & Pacific Islander owned firms 11,677
American Indian & Alaska
   native owned firms 5,802

Shopping centers, 2000 1,056

Gross state product, 1999 ($mil)
total $308,310
   agriculture services, forestry, fisheries .. $2,849
   mining $876
   construction $14,880
   manufacturing--durable goods $59,832
   manufacturing--nondurable goods $20,908
   transportation, communication &
      public utilities $20,280
   wholesale trade $22,630
   retail trade $30,207
   finance/real estate/insurance $43,546
   services $60,402
   federal, state & local government $31,900

Establishments, by major industry group, 1999
total 236,456
   forestry, fishing & agriculture 727
   mining 443
   construction 26,710
   manufacturing 15,790
   transportation & warehousing 4,963
   wholesale trade 13,689
   retail trade 39,262
   finance & insurance 12,816
   professional/scientific/technical 20,991
   health care/social assistance 23,270
   information 3,565
   accommodation/food services 18,541

Payroll, by major industry group, 1999
total ($1,000) $138,301,024
   forestry, fishing & agriculture $93,231
   mining $309,881
   construction $7,961,884
   manufacturing $37,205,538
   transportation & warehousing $3,470,820
   wholesale trade $8,556,148
   retail trade $10,267,842
   finance & insurance $7,241,695
   professional/scientific/technical $9,571,252
   health care/social assistance $14,844,811
   information $4,031,905
   accommodation/food services $3,317,152

Agriculture
number of farms, 2000 52,000
farm acreage, 2000 10,000,000
acres per farm, 2000 200
value of farms, 1997 ($mil) $16,800
farm income, 1999 ($mil)
   net farm income $659
   debt/asset ratio 13.7%
farm marketings, 1999 ($mil)
total $3,470
   crops $2,139
   livestock $1,331
principal commodities, in order by marketing
receipts, 1999
   Dairy products, greenhouse, soybeans, corn

Federal economic activity in state
expenditures, 2000
   total ($mil) $46,823
   per capita $4,711
   defense ($mil) $2,345
   non-defense (Smil) $44,478
defense department, 2000
   contract awards (Smil) $1,446
   payroll ($mil) $867
   civilian employees (x1,000) 7.7
   military personnel (x1,000) 1

Fishing, 2000
catch (thousands of pounds) 12,704
value ($1,000) $8,963

Mining, 2000 (Smil; preliminary)
total non-fuel mineral production $1,670

Michigan 8

Construction, 1999 ($mil)
total contracts (including
   non-building) $14,709
     residential $6,065
     non-residential $5,985

Construction industries, 1997
establishments 24,701
receipts ($1,000) .... $NA
annual payroll ($1,000) .... $NA
paid employees .... NA

Manufacturing, 1997
establishments 16,190
value of shipments ($1,000) $218,202,588
annual payroll ($1,000) $34,937,673
paid employees 850,368

Transportation industries, 1997
establishments 8,279
receipts ($1,000) $36,595,788
annual payroll ($1,000) $5,958,085
paid employees 158,480

Wholesale trade, 1997
establishments 16,060
sales($1,000) $165,291,997
annual payroll ($1,000) $8,338,463
paid employees 213,537

Retail trade, 1997
establishments 55,276
sales($1,000) $96,836,422
annual payroll ($1,000) $10,728,469
paid employees 796,730

Finance industries
establishments, 1997 19,451
receipts ($1,000), 1997 .... $NA
annual payroll ($1,000), 1997 .... $7,888,761
paid employees, 1997 226,680
commercial banks, 2000
  number 168
    assets ($bil) $138.5
    deposits ($bil) $97.7

Service industries, 1997 (non-exempt firms only)
establishments 69,034
receipts ($1,000) $54,177,927
annual payroll ($1,000) $22,254,086
paid employees 819,080

COMMUNICATION, ENERGY & TRANSPORTATION

Communication
daily newspapers, 2000 49
households with
  telephones, 1998 .... 94.9%
  computers, 2000 .... 51.5%
  internet access, 2000 .... 42.1%

Energy
consumption, 1999
total (trillion Btu) 3,240
per capita (million Btu) 328
by source of production (trillion Btu)
  coal 823
  natural gas 930
  petroleum 1,098
  nuclear electric power 155
  hydroelectric power 11
by end-use sector (trillion Btu)
  residential 744
  commercial 568
  industrial 1,083
  transportation 845
electric energy, 1999
  production (billion kWh) 87.9
  net summer capability (million kW) 22.4
gas utilities, 1999
  customers 3,275,000
  sales (trillion Btu) 477
nuclear plants, 1999 4

Transportation, 2000
public road & street mileage
total 121,979
  urban 30,007
  rural 91,972
  interstate 1,241
vehicle miles of travel (mil) 97,792
total motor vehicle registrations 8,435,721
  automobiles 5,023,421
  motorcycles 182,213
licensed drivers 6,925,246
  per 1,000 driving age population 908
deaths from motor vehicle
  accidents 1,382

Minnesota 1

STATE SUMMARY

Capital City . . . . St. Paul

Governor . . . . .Jesse Ventura

Address . . . . STATE CAPITOL
ST. PAUL, MN 55155
651 296-3391

Admitted as a state 1858

Area (square miles) 86,943

Population, 1980 .4,075,970

Population, 1990 .4,375,099

Population, 2000 4,919,479

Persons per square mile, 2000 . . . . 61.8

Largest city . . . . Minneapolis
population, 2000 383,000

Personal income per capita, 2000
(in current dollars) $32,101

Gross state product ($mil), 1999 . . . . . . $172,982

Leading industries, 1999 (by payroll)
Manufacturing
Health care/Social assistance
Finance & Insurance

Leading agricultural commodities, 1999
Dairy products, soybeans, corn, hogs

GEOGRAPHY & ENVIRONMENT

Area, 1990 (square miles)
total 86,943
land 79,617
water (includes territorial water) 7,326

Federally owned land, 2000 . . . . 8.2%

Highest point
name . . . . .Eagle Mountain
elevation (feet) 2,301

Lowest point
name . . . . Lake Superior
elevation (feet) 602

General coastline (miles) 0

Tidal shoreline (miles) 0

Capital city . . . . St. Paul
population, 2000 287,000

Largest city . . . . Minneapolis
population, 2000 383,000

Number of cities with over 100,000 population
1980 2
1990 2
2000 2

State parks and Recreation areas, 2000
area (acres) 256,000
number of visitors 8,496,000
revenues $10,939,000

Natl. forest system land, 1999 (acres) . . .2,838,000

National park acreage, 1984 138,100

DEMOGRAPHICS & CHARACTERISTICS OF THE POPULATION

Population
1970 3,806,103
1980 4,075,970
1990 4,375,099
2000 4,919,479
2015 (projection) 5,283,000
2025 (projection) 5,510,000

Metropolitan area population
1970 2,434,000
1980 2,621,000
2000 3,463,000

Non-metropolitan area population
1970 1,373,000
1980 1,455,000
2000 1,456,000

Change in population, 1990-2000
number 544,380
percent 12.44%

Persons per square mile, 2000 . . . . 61.8

Persons by age, 2000
under 5 years 329,594
18 and over 3,632,585
21 and over 3,414,300
65 and over 594,266
85 and over 85,601

Minnesota 2

Persons by age, 2025 (projected)
under 5 years 343,000
5 to 17 years 922,000
65 and over 1,099,000

Median age, 2000 .... 35.4

Race, 2000
One race
White 4,400,282
Black or African American 171,731
American Indian and Alaska Native 54,967
Asian Indian 16,887
Chinese 16,060
Filipino 6,284
Japanese 3,816
Korean 12,584
Vietnamese 18,824
Native Hawaiian and other Pacific Islander 1,979
Two or more races 82,742

Race, 2025 (projected)
White 4,855,000
Black 279,000

Persons of Hispanic origin, 2000
total Hispanic or Latino 143,382
  Mexican 95,613
  Puerto Rican 6,616
  Cuban 2,527
  Other Hispanic or Latino 38,626

Persons of Hispanic origin, 2025 (proj.) .. 193,000

Persons by sex, 2000
male 2,435,631
female 2,483,848

Marital status, 1990
males
  15 years & older 1,635,377
    single 504,483
    married 985,981
      separated 17,429
    widowed 36,176
    divorced 108,737
females
  15 years & older 1,743,785
    single 420,836
    married 987,634
      separated 22,253

widowed 193,619
divorced 141,696

Households & families, 2000
households 1,895,127
persons per household 2.52
  families 1,255,141
  persons per family 3.09
    married couples 1,018,245
    female householder, no husband
      present 168,782
  one person households 509,468
households with persons under 18 years . 658,565
households with persons over 65 years ... 402,837

Nativity, 1990
number of persons born in state 3,220,512
percent of total residents 73.6%

Immigration & naturalization, 1998
immigrants admitted 6,981
persons naturalized 4,331
refugees granted resident status 1,696

VITAL STATISTICS & HEALTH

Births
1999
  with low birth weight 6.1%
  to teenage mothers 13.8%
  to unmarried mothers 25.9%
Birth rate, 1999 (per 1,000) 13.8
Birth rate, 2000 (per 1,000) 14.0

Abortions, 1996
total 15,000
rate (per 1,000 women age 15-44) 13.9

Deaths
1998 37,252
1999 38,537
2000 37,752

Infant deaths
1998 332
1999 332
2000 373

Average lifetime, by race, 1989-1991
total .... 77.76 years
  white .... 77.97 years
  black .... NA years

Marriages
1998 32,197
1999 33,123
2000 33,355

Divorces
1998 15,319
1999 13,514
2000 14,779

Physicians, 1999
total 12,125
rate (per 1,000 persons) 2.54

Nurses, 1999
total 51,970
rate (per 1,000 persons) 10.88

Hospitals, 1998
number 136
beds (x 1,000) 16.5
average daily census (x 1,000) 11.3
patients admitted (x1,000) 516
average cost per day to hospital, 1995 ...... $736
average cost per stay to hospital, 1995 .... $6,241

EDUCATION

*Educational attainment of all persons
25 years and older, 1990*
less than 9th grade 239,322
high school graduates 913,265
bachelor's degree 431,381
graduate or professional degree 173,203

2000
high school graduate or more 90.8%
college graduate or more 31.2%

Public school enrollment, Fall, 1998
total 855,119
Kindergarten through grade 8 585,553
grades 9 through 12 269,566

Public School Teachers, 2000
total 56,000
elementary 29,500
secondary 26,500
average salaries
elementary $40,600
secondary $39,200

*State receipts & expenditures for public
schools, 2000*
revenue receipts ($mil) $8,033

*State receipts & expenditures for public
schools, 2000 (continued)*
expenditures
total ($mil) $7,991
per capita $1,673
per pupil $8,015

*Graduating high school seniors,
public high schools, 2000 (est.)* 57,603

SAT scores, 2001
verbal 580
math 589
percent graduates taking test 9%

Institutions of higher education, 1999
total 116
public 57
private 59

*Enrollment in institutions of higher
education, Fall, 1998*
total 278,997
full-time men 81,541
full-time women 95,315
part-time men 42,120
part-time women 60,021

*Minority enrollment in institutions of higher
education, Fall, 1997*
Black, non-Hispanic 8,235
Hispanic 3,844
Asian/Pacific Islander 9,330

Earned degrees conferred, 1998
Bachelor's 23,044
First professional 1,666
Master's 7,226
Doctor's 943

SOCIAL INSURANCE & WELFARE PROGRAMS

Social Security beneficiaries & benefits, 2000
beneficiaries
total 739,000
retired and dependents 545,000
survivors 108,000
disabled & dependents 86,000
annual benefit payments ($mil)
total $6,633
retired and dependents $4,673
survivors $1,252
disabled & dependents $708

Minnesota 4

Medicare, 2000
enrollment (x1,000) 648
payments ($mil) $3,109

Medicaid, 1998
recipients (x1,000) 538
payments ($mil) $2,924

Federal public aid
Temporary Assistance for Needy Families
(TANF), 2000
    Recipients (x1,000) 115
    Families (x1,000) 39
Supplemental Security Income
    total recipients, 1999 (x1,000) 64

Food Stamp Program
    participants, 2000 (x1,000) 196

HOUSING & CONSTRUCTION

Total housing units, 2000 2,065,946
    seasonal or recreational use 105,609
    occupied 1,895,127
    owner occupied 1,412,865
    renter occupied 482,262

New privately owned housing units uthorized, 2000
number (x1,000) 32.8
value ($mil) $4,204

New privately owned housing units
    started, 2000 (est.) (x1,000) 30.7

Existing home sales, 2000 (x1,000) 105.5

GOVERNMENT & ELECTIONS

State officials, 2002
    Governor (name/party/term expires)
            JESSE VENTURA
            Reform - 2002
Lt. Governor . . . . Mae Schunk
Sec. of State . . . . Mary Kiffmeyer
Atty. General .Mike Hatch
Chief Justice . . . . Kathleen Blatz

Governorship
minimum age 25
length of term . . . . 4 years
number of consecutive
    terms permitted . . . . not specified
who succeeds . . . . Lt. Governor

State legislature
name . . . . Legislature
    upper chamber
            name . . . . Senate
            number of members 67
            length of term . . . . 4 years
            party in majority, 2000 . . . . .Democratic
    lower chamber
            name . . . . House of Representatives
            number of members 134
            length of term . . . . 2 years
            party in majority, 2000 . . . . .Democratic

State employees March, 2000
total 88,154
March payroll $259,000,626

Local governments, 1997
total 3,501
    county 87
    municipal 854
    township 1,794
    school districts 360
    special districts 406

Voting age population, November, 2000, projected
Total 3,547,000
    male 1,724,000
    female 1,823,000

Vote for president
2000
    Gore 1,168,000
    Bush 1,110,000
1996
    Clinton 1,120,000
    Dole 766,000
    Perot 258,000

Federal representation, 2002 (107th Congress)
Senators (name/party/term expires)

            MARK DAYTON
            Democrat - 2007
            PAUL WELLSTONE
            Democrat - 2003

Representatives, total 8
    Democrats 5
    Republicans 3
    other 0

190

Women holding public office, 2001
U.S. Congress 2
statewide elected office 4
state legislature 58

Black elected officials, 1999
total 16
  US and state legislatures 1
  city/county/regional offices 4
  judicial/law enforcement 6
  education/school boards 5

Hispanic public officials, 2000
total 3
  state executives & legislators 1
  city/county/regional offices 1
  judicial/law enforcement 1
  education/school boards . . . . NA

GOVERNMENTAL FINANCE

State government revenues, 1999 ($per capita)
total revenue $5,253.72
  total general revenue $4,006.15
    intergovernmental revenue $846.95
    taxes $2,613.69
    current charges $255.85
    miscellaneous $289.66

State government expenditures, 1999 ($per capita)
total expenditure $4,269.20
  total general expenditure $3,855.05
    education $1,488.93
    public welfare $1,031.51
    health $89.00
    hospitals $44.73
    highways $281.88
    police protection $25.49
    correction $69.68
    natural resources $98.80
    governmental administration $149.84
    interest on general debt $89.08

State debt, 1999 ($per capita) $1,148.60

Federal government grants to state & local government, 2000 (x$1,000)
total $4,599,300
  Dept. of Education $385,410
  Environmental Protection Agency . . . $110,199
  Health Care Financing Admin. $1,811,447
  Dept. Housing & Urban Devel. $515,284
  Dept. of Labor $70,703
  Highway trust fund $422,597

CRIME, LAW ENFORCEMENT & COURTS

Crime, 2000 (all rates per 100,000 inhabitants)
total crimes 171,611
overall crime rate 3,488.4
  property crimes 157,798
    burglaries 26,116
    larcenies 118,250
    motor vehicle thefts 13,432
  property crime rate 3,207.6
  violent crimes 13,813
    murders 151
    forcible rapes 2,240
    robberies 3,713
    aggravated assaults 7,709
  violent crime rate 280.8

Number of police agencies, 2000 292

Arrests, 2000
total 275,125
  persons under 18 years of age 74,282

Prisoners under state & federal jurisdiction, 2000
total 6,238
percent change, 1999-2000 . . . . 4.5%
  sentenced to more than one year
    total 6,238
    rate per 100,000 residents 128

Persons under sentence of death, 4/1/2001 . . . NA

State's highest court
name . . . . Supreme Court
number of members 9
length of term . . . . 6 years
intermediate appeals court? . . . . no

Minnesota 6

LABOR & INCOME

Civilian labor force, 2000

total	2,739,000
men	1,436,000
women	1,303,000
persons 16-19 years	205,000
white	2,571,000
black	83,000

Civilian labor force as a percent of civilian non-institutional population, 2000

total	75.1%
men	80.1%
women	70.3%
persons 16-19 years	NA%
white	75.5%
black	77.6%

Employment, 2000

total	2,649,000
men	1,381,000
women	1,268,000
persons 16-19 years	186,000
white	2,493,000
black	77,000

Full-time/part-time labor force, 1998

full-time labor force	NA
working part-time for economic reasons	23,000
part-time labor force	NA

Unemployment rate, 2000

total	3.3%
men	3.8%
women	2.7%
persons 16-19 years	8.9%
white	3.0%
black	7.0%

Unemployed by reason for unemployment (as a percent of total unemployment), 1998

job losers or completed temp jobs	NA%
job leavers	NA%
reentrants	NA%
new entrants	NA%

Experienced civilian labor force, by occupation, 1998

executive/administrative/managerial	433,000
professional/specialty	430,000
technicians & related support	NA
sales	294,000
administrative support/clerical	346,000
service occupations	350,000
precision production/craft/repair	286,000
machine operators/assemblers	154,000
transportation/material moving	NA
handlers/helpers/laborers	NA
farming/forestry/fishing	108,000

Experienced civilian labor force, by industry, 1998

construction	116,000
manufacturing	408,000
transportation/communication	130,000
wholesale/retail trade	539,000
finance/real estate/insurance	159,000
services	650,000
government	359,000
agriculture	102,000

Average annual pay, 1999 ... $33,487
change in average annual pay, 1998-1999 ... 4.4%

Hours and earnings of production workers on manufacturing payrolls, 2000

average weekly hours	40.8
average hourly earnings	$14.99
average weekly earnings	$611.59

Labor union membership, 2000 ... 419,000

Household income (in 2000 dollars)
median household income, three year average, 1998-2000 ... $50,865

Poverty
persons below poverty level, three year average, 1998-2000 ... 7.8%

Personal income ($per capita)
2000 (prelim.)

in current dollars	$32,101
in constant (1996) dollars	$29,900

1999 (preliminary)

in current dollars	$30,622
in constant (1996) dollars	$29,281

Federal income tax returns, 1999

returns filed	2,340,604
adjusted gross income ($1,000)	$110,821,428
total income tax paid ($1,000)	$16,597,704

ECONOMY, BUSINESS, INDUSTRY & AGRICULTURE

Fortune 500 companies, 2000 16

Business incorporations, 1998
total 12,481
change, 1997-1998 .... -1.4%

Business failures, 1998 1,711

Business firm ownership, 1997
Hispanic owned firms 3,616
Black owned firms 4,024
women owned firms 108,417
Asian & Pacific Islander owned firms 5,435
American Indian & Alaska
  native owned firms 2,413

Shopping centers, 2000 483

Gross state product, 1999 ($mil)
total $172,982
  agriculture services, forestry, fisheries .. $3,004
  mining $804
  construction $8,585
  manufacturing--durable goods $19,034
  manufacturing--nondurable goods $12,285
  transportation, communication &
    public utilities $13,183
  wholesale trade $14,210
  retail trade $16,310
  finance/real estate/insurance $31,974
  services $35,994
  federal, state & local government $17,599

Establishments, by major industry group, 1999
total 137,305
  forestry, fishing & agriculture 479
  mining 156
  construction 14,661
  manufacturing 8,089
  transportation & warehousing 3,968
  wholesale trade 9,344
  retail trade 20,869
  finance & insurance 8,474
  professional/scientific/technical 14,438
  health care/social assistance 11,118
  information 2,526
  accommodation/food services 9,893

Payroll, by major industry group, 1999
total ($1,000) $75,337,972
  forestry, fishing & agriculture $46,908
  mining $342,269
  construction $4,827,285
  manufacturing $14,368,166
  transportation & warehousing $2,565,117
  wholesale trade $6,091,122
  retail trade $5,534,859
  finance & insurance $6,632,091
  professional/scientific/technical $5,497,173
  health care/social assistance $8,905,920
  information $2,453,287
  accommodation/food services $2,061,342

Agriculture
number of farms, 2000 79,000
farm acreage, 2000 29,000,000
acres per farm, 2000 362
value of farms, 1997 ($mil) $30,992
farm income, 1999 ($mil)
  net farm income $1,257
  debt/asset ratio 20.4%
farm marketings, 1999 ($mil)
total $7,061
  crops $3,513
  livestock $3,548
principal commodities, in order by marketing
receipts, 1999
    Dairy products, soybeans, corn, hogs

Federal economic activity in state
expenditures, 2000
  total ($mil) $22,992
  per capita $4,674
  defense ($mil) $1,927
  non-defense ($mil) $21,065
defense department, 2000
  contract awards ($mil) $1,458
  payroll ($mil) $440
  civilian employees (x1,000) 2.5
  military personnel (x1,000) 0.7

Fishing, 2000
catch (thousands of pounds) 377
value ($1,000) $172

Mining, 2000 ($mil; preliminary)
total non-fuel mineral production $1,570

Minnesota 8

Construction, 1999 ($mil)
total contracts (including
   non-building) $8,775
     residential $3,739
     non-residential $3,345

Construction industries, 1997
establishments 12,709
receipts ($1,000) $18,208,956
annual payroll ($1,000) $3,572,392
paid employees .... NA

Manufacturing, 1997
establishments 8,471
value of shipments ($1,000) $78,725,094
annual payroll ($1,000) $13,759,547
paid employees 399,756

Transportation industries, 1997
establishments 6,124
receipts ($1,000) $16,400,262
annual payroll ($1,000) $3,250,254
paid employees 103,124

Wholesale trade, 1997
establishments 10,915
sales($1,000) $103,287,268
annual payroll ($1,000) $5,479,893
paid employees 147,559

Retail trade, 1997
establishments 28,378
sales($1,000) $48,814,277
annual payroll ($1,000) $5,423,993
paid employees 419,310

Finance industries
establishments, 1997 12,840
receipts ($1,000), 1997 .... $NA
annual payroll ($1,000), 1997 .... $6,232,366
paid employees, 1997 152,750
commercial banks, 2000
  number 492
    assets ($bil) $187.1
    deposits ($bil) $122.6

Service industries, 1997 (non-exempt firms only)
establishments 37,594
receipts ($1,000) $30,489,747
annual payroll ($1,000) $11,925,851
paid employees 468,166

COMMUNICATION, ENERGY & TRANSPORTATION

Communication
daily newspapers, 2000 25
households with
  telephones, 1998 .... 98.0%
  computers, 2000 .... 57.0%
  internet access, 2000 .... 43.0%

Energy
consumption, 1999
total (trillion Btu) 1,675
per capita (million Btu) 351
by source of production (trillion Btu)
  coal 336
  natural gas 346
  petroleum 661
  nuclear electric power 142
  hydroelectric power 59
by end-use sector (trillion Btu)
  residential 340
  commercial 218
  industrial 618
  transportation 500
electric energy, 1999
  production (billion kWh) 44.2
  net summer capability (million kW) 9
gas utilities, 1999
  customers 1,297,000
  sales (trillion Btu) 245
nuclear plants, 1999 3

Transportation, 2000
public road & street mileage
total 132,250
  urban 16,018
  rural 116,232
  interstate 912
vehicle miles of travel (mil) 52,601
total motor vehicle registrations 4,629,940
  automobiles 2,625,595
  motorcycles 142,799
licensed drivers 2,940,789
  per 1,000 driving age population 777
deaths from motor vehicle
  accidents 625

STATE SUMMARY

Capital City .... Jackson

Governor .... Ronnie Musgrove

Address .... STATE CAPITOL
JACKSON, MS 39201
601 359-3100

Admitted as a state 1817

Area (square miles) 48,434

Population, 1980 2,520,638

Population, 1990 2,573,216

Population, 2000 2,844,658

Persons per square mile, 2000 .... 60.6

Largest city .... Jackson
population, 2000 184,000

Personal income per capita, 2000
(in current dollars) $20,993

Gross state product ($mil), 1999 .... $64,286

Leading industries, 1999 (by payroll)
Manufacturing
Health care/Social assistance
Retail trade

Leading agricultural commodities, 1999
Broilers, cotton, aquaculture, soybeans

GEOGRAPHY & ENVIRONMENT

Area, 1990 (square miles)
total 48,434
land 46,914
water (includes territorial water) 1,520

Federally owned land, 2000 .... 5.5%

Highest point
name .... Woodall Mountain
elevation (feet) 806

Lowest point
name .... Gulf of Mexico
elevation (feet) .... sea level

General coastline (miles) 44

Tidal shoreline (miles) 359

Capital city .... Jackson
population, 2000 184,000

Largest city .... Jackson
population, 2000 184,000

Number of cities with over 100,000 population
1980 1
1990 1
2000 1

State parks and Recreation areas, 2000
area (acres) 24,000
number of visitors 4,198,000
revenues $7,266,000

Natl. forest system land, 1999 (acres) ... 1,159,000

National park acreage, 1984 107,500

DEMOGRAPHICS & CHARACTERISTICS OF THE POPULATION

Population
1970 2,216,994
1980 2,520,638
1990 2,573,216
2000 2,844,658
2015 (projection) 3,035,000
2025 (projection) 3,142,000

Metropolitan area population
1970 564,000
1980 716,000
2000 1,024,000

Non-metropolitan area population
1970 1,653,000
1980 1,804,000
2000 1,821,000

Change in population, 1990-2000
number 271,442
percent 10.55%

Persons per square mile, 2000 .... 60.6

Persons by age, 2000
under 5 years 204,364
18 and over 2,069,471
21 and over 1,923,445
65 and over 343,523
85 and over 42,891

Mississippi 2

Persons by age, 2025 (projected)
under 5 years 190,000
5 to 17 years 546,000
65 and over 615,000

Median age, 2000 .... 33.8

Race, 2000
One race
White 1,746,099
Black or African American 1,033,809
American Indian and Alaska Native 11,652
Asian Indian 3,827
Chinese 3,099
Filipino 2,608
Japanese 766
Korean 1,334
Vietnamese 5,387
Native Hawaiian and other Pacific Islander .. 667
Two or more races 20,021

Race, 2025 (projected)
White 1,939,000
Black 1,162,000

Persons of Hispanic origin, 2000
total Hispanic or Latino 39,569
Mexican 21,616
Puerto Rican 2,881
Cuban 1,508
Other Hispanic or Latino 13,564

Persons of Hispanic origin, 2025 (proj.) ... 39,000

Persons by sex, 2000
male 1,373,554
female 1,471,104

Marital status, 1990
males
15 years & older 913,815
single 275,422
married 545,992
separated 22,646
widowed 27,747
divorced 64,654
females
15 years & older 1,038,813
single 245,289
married 554,540
separated 34,234

widowed 150,004
divorced 88,980

Households & families, 2000
households 1,046,434
persons per household 2.63
families 747,159
persons per family 3.14
married couples 520,844
female householder, no husband
present 180,705
one person households 257,708
households with persons under 18 years . 414,602
households with persons over 65 years ... 248,129

Nativity, 1990
number of persons born in state 1,989,265
percent of total residents 77.3%

Immigration & naturalization, 1998
immigrants admitted 701
persons naturalized 378
refugees granted resident status 41

VITAL STATISTICS & HEALTH
Births
1999
with low birth weight 10.3%
to teenage mothers 15.4%
to unmarried mothers 45.9%
Birth rate, 1999 (per 1,000) 15.4
Birth rate, 2000 (per 1,000) 15.8

Abortions, 1996
total 4,000
rate (per 1,000 women age 15-44) 7.2

Deaths
1998 27,850
1999 28,185
2000 28,671
Infant deaths
1998 435
1999 443
2000 421

Average lifetime, by race, 1989-1991
total .... 73.03 years
white .... 74.78 years
black .... 69.41 years

Marriages
1998 20,620
1999 21,944
2000 19,715

Divorces
1998 12,976
1999 15,341
2000 14,355

Physicians, 1999
total 4,533
rate (per 1,000 persons) 1.64

Nurses, 1999
total 21,700
rate (per 1,000 persons) 7.84

Hospitals, 1998
number 96
beds (x 1,000) 13.0
average daily census (x 1,000) 8.1
patients admitted (x1,000) 414
average cost per day to hospital, 1995 . . . . . . $584
average cost per stay to hospital, 1995 . . . . $4,265

EDUCATION

Educational attainment of all persons
  25 years and older, 1990
  less than 9th grade 240,267
  high school graduates 423,624
  bachelor's degree 149,109
  graduate or professional degree 77,838

2000
  high school graduate or more 80.3%
  college graduate or more 18.7%

Public school enrollment, Fall, 1998
total 502,379
  Kindergarten through grade 8 365,497
  grades 9 through 12 136,882

Public School Teachers, 2000
total 30,800
  elementary 17,000
  secondary 13,800
average salaries
  elementary $31,400
  secondary $32,500

State receipts & expenditures for public
  schools, 2000
revenue receipts ($mil) $2,929

State receipts & expenditures for public
  schools, 2000 (continued)
expenditures
  total ($mil) $2,697
  per capita $974
  per pupil $4,905

Graduating high school seniors,
  public high schools, 2000 (est.) 26,375

SAT scores, 2001
verbal 566
math 551
percent graduates taking test 4%

Institutions of higher education, 1999
total 46
  public 31
  private 15

Enrollment in institutions of higher
  education, Fall, 1998
total 132,438
full-time men 42,992
full-time women 55,807
part-time men 12,530
part-time women 21,109

Minority enrollment in institutions of higher
  education, Fall, 1997
Black, non-Hispanic 40,439
Hispanic 759
Asian/Pacific Islander 1,046

Earned degrees conferred, 1998
Bachelor's 10,290
First professional .494
Master's 3,405
Doctor's 351

SOCIAL INSURANCE & WELFARE PROGRAMS

Social Security beneficiaries & benefits, 2000
beneficiaries
total 516,000
  retired and dependents 303,000
  survivors 92,000
  disabled & dependents 121,000
annual benefit payments ($mil)
total $4,101
  retired and dependents $2,364
  survivors $855
  disabled & dependents $883

Mississippi 4

Medicare, 2000
enrollment (x1,000) 414
payments ($mil) $2,248

Medicaid, 1998
recipients (x1,000) 486
payments ($mil) $1,442

Federal public aid
Temporary Assistance for Needy Families
(TANF), 2000
   Recipients (x1,000) 33
   Families (x1,000) 15
Supplemental Security Income
   total recipients, 1999 (x1,000) 131

Food Stamp Program
   participants, 2000 (x1,000) 276

HOUSING & CONSTRUCTION

Total housing units, 2000 1,161,953
   seasonal or recreational use 21,845
   occupied 1,046,434
      owner occupied 756,967
      renter occupied 289,467

New privately owned housing units uthorized, 2000
number (x1,000) 11.3
value ($mil) $918

New privately owned housing units
started, 2000 (est.) (x1,000) 12.8

Existing home sales, 2000 (x1,000) 45.1

GOVERNMENT & ELECTIONS

State officials, 2002
   Governor (name/party/term expires)
      RONNIE MUSGROVE
      Democrat - 2004
Lt. Governor .... Amy Tuck
Sec. of State .... Eric Clark
Atty. General .... Mike Moore
Chief Justice .... Edwin Lloyd Pittman

Governorship
minimum age 30
length of term .... 4 years
number of consecutive
   terms permitted 2
who succeeds .... Lt. Governor

State legislature
name .... Legislature
   upper chamber
      name .... Senate
      number of members 52
      length of term .... 4 years
      party in majority, 2000 .... Democratic
   lower chamber
      name .... House of Representatives
      number of members 122
      length of term .... 4 years
      party in majority, 2000 .... Democratic

State employees March, 2000
total 63,756
March payroll $147,961,612

Local governments, 1997
total 936
   county 82
   municipal 295
   township 0
   school districts 164
   special districts 395

Voting age population, November, 2000, projected
Total 2,047,000
   male 958,000
   female 1,089,000

Vote for president
2000
   Gore 405,000
   Bush 573,000
1996
   Clinton 394,000
   Dole 440,000
   Perot 52,000

Federal representation, 2002 (107th Congress)
Senators (name/party/term expires)

      TRENT LOTT
      Republican - 2007
      THAD COCHRAN
      Republican - 2003

Representatives, total 5
   Democrats 3
   Republicans 2
   other 0

Mississippi 5

Women holding public office, 2001
U.S. Congress 0
statewide elected office 1
state legislature 22

Black elected officials, 1999
total 850
  US and state legislatures 46
  city/county/regional offices 575
  judicial/law enforcement 97
  education/school boards 132

Hispanic public officials, 2000
total ....NA
  state executives & legislators ....NA
  city/county/regional offices ....NA
  judicial/law enforcement ....NA
  education/school boards ....NA

GOVERNMENTAL FINANCE

State government revenues, 1999 ($per capita)
total revenue $3,865.07
  total general revenue $3,240.56
    intergovernmental revenue $1,119.18
    taxes $1,652.02
    current charges $306.34
    miscellaneous $163.01

State government expenditures, 1999 ($per capita)
total expenditure $3,585.47
  total general expenditure $3,276.93
    education $1,148.30
    public welfare $789.15
    health $97.39
    hospitals $156.54
    highways $332.33
    police protection $21.11
    correction $85.87
    natural resources $73.17
    governmental administration $79.77
    interest on general debt $59.56

State debt, 1999 ($per capita) $1,164.63

Federal government grants to state & local government, 2000 (x$1,000)
total $3,420,424
  Dept. of Education $345,483
  Environmental Protection Agency $34,229
  Health Care Financing Admin. $1,583,293
  Dept. Housing & Urban Devel. $266,339
  Dept. of Labor $52,981
  Highway trust fund $271,832

CRIME, LAW ENFORCEMENT & COURTS

Crime, 2000 (all rates per 100,000 inhabitants)
total crimes 113,911
overall crime rate 4,004.4
  property crimes 103,644
    burglaries 26,918
    larcenies 69,758
    motor vehicle thefts 6,968
  property crime rate 3,643.5
  violent crimes 10,267
    murders 255
    forcible rapes 1,019
    robberies 2,703
    aggravated assaults 6,290
  violent crime rate 360.9

Number of police agencies, 2000 84

Arrests, 2000
total 124,995
  persons under 18 years of age 15,741

Prisoners under state & federal jurisdiction, 2000
total 20,241
percent change, 1999-2000 .... 10.9%
  sentenced to more than one year
    total 19,239
    rate per 100,000 residents 688

Persons under sentence of death, 4/1/2001 66

State's highest court
name .... Supreme Court
number of members 9
length of term .... 6 years
intermediate appeals court? ....no

199

Mississippi 6

LABOR & INCOME

Civilian labor force, 2000

total 1,326,000
  men 677,000
  women 649,000
  persons 16-19 years 81,000
  white 876,000
  black 436,000

*Civilian labor force as a percent of
civilian non-institutional population, 2000*

total 63.6%
  men 71.5%
  women 57.0%
  persons 16-19 years .... NA%
  white 64.4%
  black 61.8%

Employment, 2000

total 1,251,000
  men 641,000
  women 610,000
  persons 16-19 years 67,000
  white 849,000
  black 388,000

Full-time/part-time labor force, 1998

full-time labor force 1,099,000
  working part-time for
    economic reasons 17,000
part-time labor force 170,000

Unemployment rate, 2000

total 5.7%
  men 5.4%
  women 6.0%
  persons 16-19 years 18.1%
  white 3.1%
  black 11.0%

*Unemployed by reason for unemployment
(as a percent of total unemployment), 1998*

job losers or completed temp jobs 35.3%
job leavers 11.8%
reentrants 38.2%
new entrants 13.2%

*Experienced civilian labor force, by occupation,
1998*

executive/administrative/managerial 133,000
professional/specialty 187,000
technicians & related support 37,000

sales 134,000
administrative support/clerical 156,000
service occupations 178,000
precision production/craft/repair 156,000
machine operators/assemblers 117,000
transportation/material moving 68,000
handlers/helpers/laborers 51,000
farming/forestry/fishing 42,000

Experienced civilian labor force, by industry, 1998

construction 70,000
manufacturing 244,000
transportation/communication 73,000
wholesale/retail trade 221,000
finance/real estate/insurance 55,000
services 243,000
government 206,000
agriculture 41,000

Average annual pay, 1999 .... $24,392
change in average annual pay,
  1998-1999 .... 2.4%

*Hours and earnings of production workers
on manufacturing payrolls, 2000*

average weekly hours 40.7
average hourly earnings $11.64
average weekly earnings $473.75

Labor union membership, 2000 67,700

Household income (in 2000 dollars)
median household income,
  three year average, 1998-2000 .... $31,528

Poverty
persons below poverty level,
  three year average, 1998-2000 .... 15.5%

Personal income ($per capita)
2000 (prelim.)
  in current dollars $20,993
  in constant (1996) dollars $19,554
1999 (preliminary)
  in current dollars $20,506
  in constant (1996) dollars $19,608

Federal income tax returns, 1999
returns filed 1,171,297
adjusted gross income ($1,000) $37,962,745
total income tax paid ($1,000) $4,800,082

ECONOMY, BUSINESS, INDUSTRY & AGRICULTURE

Fortune 500 companies, 2000 1

Business incorporations, 1998
total 5,003
change, 1997-1998 .... 1.9%

Business failures, 1998 177

Business firm ownership, 1997
Hispanic owned firms 988
Black owned firms 17,617
women owned firms 38,321
Asian & Pacific Islander owned firms 2,518
American Indian & Alaska
    native owned firms 1,088

Shopping centers, 2000 444

Gross state product, 1999 ($mil)
total $64,286
    agriculture services, forestry, fisheries .. $1,687
    mining $638
    construction $2,999
    manufacturing--durable goods $7,528
    manufacturing--nondurable goods $5,713
    transportation, communication &
        public utilities $6,096
    wholesale trade $3,786
    retail trade $7,017
    finance/real estate/insurance $7,347
    services $11,180
    federal, state & local government $10,295

Establishments, by major industry group, 1999
total 59,834
    forestry, fishing & agriculture 926
    mining 327
    construction 5,158
    manufacturing 2,885
    transportation & warehousing 2,315
    wholesale trade 3,137
    retail trade 12,744
    finance & insurance 4,281
    professional/scientific/technical 4,113
    health care/social assistance 4,949
    information 925
    accommodation/food services 4,096

Payroll, by major industry group, 1999
total ($1,000) $22,172,251
    forestry, fishing & agriculture $132,099
    mining $142,856
    construction $1,465,320
    manufacturing $5,919,164
    transportation & warehousing $739,195
    wholesale trade $1,186,970
    retail trade $2,354,595
    finance & insurance $1,111,832
    professional/scientific/technical $863,426
    health care/social assistance $3,348,576
    information $467,475
    accommodation/food services $1,176,240

Agriculture
number of farms, 2000 43,000
farm acreage, 2000 11,000,000
acres per farm, 2000 258
value of farms, 1997 ($mil) $11,875
farm income, 1999 ($mil)
    net farm income $949
    debt/asset ratio 18.7%
farm marketings, 1999 ($mil)
total $3,174
    crops $1,031
    livestock $2,143
principal commodities, in order by marketing
receipts, 1999
    Broilers, cotton, aquaculture, soybeans

Federal economic activity in state
expenditures, 2000
    total ($mil) $18,358
    per capita $6,454
    defense ($mil) $2,943
    non-defense ($mil) $15,416
defense department, 2000
    contract awards ($mil) $1,557
    payroll ($mil) $1,392
    civilian employees (x1,000) 9.5
    military personnel (x1,000) 16.6

Fishing, 2000
catch (thousands of pounds) 217,744
value ($1,000) $58,715

Mining, 2000 ($mil; preliminary)
total non-fuel mineral production $157

Mississippi 8

Construction, 1999 ($mil)
total contracts (including
   non-building) $3,873
     residential $1,252
     non-residential $1,253

Construction industries, 1997
establishments 4,746
receipts ($1,000) $6,040,116
annual payroll ($1,000) $1,144,991
paid employees 47,242

Manufacturing, 1997
establishments 3,729
value of shipments ($1,000) $40,608,792
annual payroll ($1,000) $5,745,062
paid employees 234,764

Transportation industries, 1997
establishments 3,649
receipts ($1,000) $8,011,288
annual payroll ($1,000) $1,448,856
paid employees 46,325

Wholesale trade, 1997
establishments 3,881
sales($1,000) $20,072,266
annual payroll ($1,000) $1,163,509
paid employees 43,026

Retail trade, 1997
establishments 15,786
sales($1,000) $20,923,871
annual payroll ($1,000) $2,257,567
paid employees 194,483

Finance industries
establishments, 1997 5,521
receipts ($1,000), 1997 .... $NA
annual payroll ($1,000), 1997 .... $1,102,195
paid employees, 1997 39,365
commercial banks, 2000
  number 101
   assets ($bil) $34.0
   deposits ($bil) $26.4

Service industries, 1997 (non-exempt firms only)
establishments 14,781
receipts ($1,000) $10,660,675
annual payroll ($1,000) $3,855,275
paid employees 179,905

COMMUNICATION, ENERGY & TRANSPORTATION

Communication
daily newspapers, 2000 23
households with
  telephones, 1998 .... 90.3%
  computers, 2000 .... 37.2%
  internet access, 2000 .... 26.3%

Energy
consumption, 1999
total (trillion Btu) 1,209
per capita (million Btu) 437
by source of production (trillion Btu)
  coal 138
  natural gas 346
  petroleum 483
  nuclear electric power 90
  hydroelectric power .... NA
by end-use sector (trillion Btu)
  residential 203
  commercial 146
  industrial 451
  transportation 409
electric energy, 1999
  production (billion kWh) 32.2
  net summer capability (million kW) 6.8
gas utilities, 1999
  customers 435,000
  sales (trillion Btu) 72
nuclear plants, 1999 1

Transportation, 2000
public road & street mileage
total 73,498
  urban 8,055
  rural 65,443
  interstate 685
vehicle miles of travel (mil) 35,536
total motor vehicle registrations 2,289,411
  automobiles 1,318,648
  motorcycles 31,845
licensed drivers 2,007,746
  per 1,000 driving age population 929
deaths from motor vehicle
  accidents 949

STATE SUMMARY

Capital City . . . . .Jefferson City

Governor . . . . Bob Holden

Address . . . . .STATE CAPITOL
JEFFERSON CITY, MO 65102
573 751-3222

Admitted as a state 1821

Area (square miles) 69,709

Population, 1980 4,916,686

Population, 1990 5,117,073

Population, 2000 5,595,211

Persons per square mile, 2000 . . . . 81.2

Largest city . . . . .Kansas City
   population, 2000 442,000

Personal income per capita, 2000
   (in current dollars) $27,445

Gross state product ($mil), 1999 . . . . . . $170,470

Leading industries, 1999 (by payroll)
   Manufacturing
   Health care/Social assistance
   Retail trade

Leading agricultural commodities, 1999
   Cattle, soybeans, hogs, corn

GEOGRAPHY & ENVIRONMENT

Area, 1990 (square miles)
total 69,709
   land 68,898
   water (includes territorial water) 811

Federally owned land, 2000 . . . . 10.8%

Highest point
name . . . . .Taum Sauk Mountain
elevation (feet) 1,772

Lowest point
name . . . . St. Francis River
elevation (feet) 230

General coastline (miles) 0

Tidal shoreline (miles) 0

Capital city .Jefferson City
population, 2000 39,636

Largest city . . . . .Kansas City
population, 2000 442,000

Number of cities with over 100,000 population
   1980 4
   1990 4
   2000 4

State parks and Recreation areas, 2000
area (acres) 137,000
number of visitors 18,174,000
revenues $6,947,000

Natl. forest system land, 1999 (acres) . . .1,495,000

National park acreage, 1984 62,700

DEMOGRAPHICS & CHARACTERISTICS OF THE POPULATION

Population
1970 4,677,623
1980 4,916,686
1990 5,117,073
2000 5,595,211
2015 (projection) .6,005,000
2025 (projection) .6,250,000

Metropolitan area population
1970 3,170,000
1980 3,226,000
2000 3,795,000

Non-metropolitan area population
1970 1,508,000
1980 1,690,000
2000 1,800,000

Change in population, 1990-2000
number 478,138
percent 9.34%

Persons per square mile, 2000 . . . . 81.2

Persons by age, 2000
under 5 years 369,898
18 and over 4,167,519
21 and over 3,919,855
65 and over 755,379
85 and over 98,571

Missouri 2

Persons by age, 2025 (projected)
under 5 years 381,000
5 to 17 years 1,039,000
65 and over 1,258,000

Median age, 2000 .... 36.1

Race, 2000
One race
White 4,748,083
Black or African American 629,391
American Indian and Alaska Native 25,076
Asian Indian 12,169
Chinese 13,667
Filipino 7,735
Japanese 3,337
Korean 6,767
Vietnamese 10,626
Native Hawaiian and other Pacific Islander 3,178
Two or more races 82,061

Race, 2025 (projected)
White 5,317,000
Black 800,000

Persons of Hispanic origin, 2000
total Hispanic or Latino 118,592
  Mexican 77,887
  Puerto Rican 6,677
  Cuban 3,022
  Other Hispanic or Latino 31,006

Persons of Hispanic origin, 2025 (proj.) .. 172,000

Persons by sex, 2000
male 2,720,177
female 2,875,034

Marital status, 1990
males
  15 years & older 1,896,107
    single 516,097
    married 1,178,576
      separated 32,893
    widowed 50,859
    divorced 150,575
females
  15 years & older 2,112,391
    single 440,593
    married 1,185,687
      separated 45,638

widowed 280,906
divorced 205,205

Households & families, 2000
households 2,194,594
persons per household 2.48
  families 1,476,516
  persons per family 3.02
    married couples 1,140,866
    female householder, no husband
      present 253,760
    one person households 599,808
households with persons under 18 years . 762,492
households with persons over 65 years ... 525,811

Nativity, 1990
number of persons born in state 3,563,820
percent of total residents 69.6%

Immigration & naturalization, 1998
immigrants admitted 3,588
persons naturalized 2,156
refugees granted resident status 516

VITAL STATISTICS & HEALTH

Births
1999
  with low birth weight 7.7%
  to teenage mothers 13.8%
  to unmarried mothers 34.1%
Birth rate, 1999 (per 1,000) 13.8
Birth rate, 2000 (per 1,000) 13.9

Abortions, 1996
total 11,000
rate (per 1,000 women age 15-44) 9.1

Deaths
1998 54,703
1999 55,931
2000 54,880

Infant deaths
1998 590
1999 611
2000 670

Average lifetime, by race, 1989-1991
total .... 75.25 years
  white .... 76.02 years
  black .... 68.81 years

Marriages
1998 43,795
1999 45,314
2000 43,725

Divorces
1998 25,799
1999 24,656
2000 26,464

Physicians, 1999
total 12,695
rate (per 1,000 persons) 2.32

Nurses, 1999
total 53,890
rate (per 1,000 persons) 9.85

Hospitals, 1998
number 122
beds (x 1,000) 20.7
average daily census (x 1,000) 11.9
patients admitted (x1,000) 742
average cost per day to hospital, 1995 ...... $967
average cost per stay to hospital, 1995 .... $6,228

EDUCATION

*Educational attainment of all persons
25 years and older, 1990*
less than 9th grade 380,613
high school graduates 1,090,940
bachelor's degree 383,678
graduate or professional degree 202,083

2000
high school graduate or more 86.6%
college graduate or more 26.2%

Public school enrollment, Fall, 1998
total 912,445
Kindergarten through grade 8 650,545
grades 9 through 12 261,900

Public School Teachers, 2000
total 63,700
elementary 32,800
secondary 30,900
average salaries
elementary $35,000
secondary $36,300

*State receipts & expenditures for public
schools, 2000*
revenue receipts ($mil) $7,326

*State receipts & expenditures for public
schools, 2000 (continued)*
expenditures
total ($mil) $6,191
per capita $1,132
per pupil $6,234

*Graduating high school seniors,
public high schools, 2000 (est.)* 53,500

SAT scores, 2001
verbal 577
math 577
percent graduates taking test 8%

Institutions of higher education, 1999
total 113
public 31
private 82

*Enrollment in institutions of higher
education, Fall, 1998*
total 311,383
full-time men 83,093
full-time women 97,919
part-time men 52,677
part-time women 77,694

*Minority enrollment in institutions of higher
education, Fall, 1997*
Black, non-Hispanic 27,336
Hispanic 5,536
Asian/Pacific Islander 6,989

Earned degrees conferred, 1998
Bachelor's 28,888
First professional 2,394
Master's 11,661
Doctor's 860

SOCIAL INSURANCE &
WELFARE PROGRAMS

Social Security beneficiaries & benefits, 2000
beneficiaries
total 1,005,000
retired and dependents 687,000
survivors 154,000
disabled & dependents 164,000
annual benefit payments ($mil)
total $8,881
retired and dependents $5,876
survivors $1,699
disabled & dependents $1,306

Missouri 4

Medicare, 2000
enrollment (x1,000) 854
payments ($mil) $4,274

Medicaid, 1998
recipients (x1,000) 734
payments ($mil) $2,570

Federal public aid
Temporary Assistance for Needy Families
(TANF), 2000
    Recipients (x1,000) 125
    Families (x1,000) 47
Supplemental Security Income
    total recipients, 1999 (x1,000) 111

Food Stamp Program
    participants, 2000 (x1,000) 420

HOUSING & CONSTRUCTION

Total housing units, 2000 2,442,017
    seasonal or recreational use 66,053
    occupied 2,194,594
        owner occupied 1,542,149
        renter occupied 652,445

New privately owned housing units uthorized, 2000
number (x1,000) 24.3
value ($mil) $2,569

*New privately owned housing units
started, 2000 (est.) (x1,000)* 26.0

Existing home sales, 2000 (x1,000) 118.6

GOVERNMENT & ELECTIONS

State officials, 2002
    Governor (name/party/term expires)
                BOB HOLDEN
                Democrat - 2005
Lt. Governor . . . . Joe Maxwell
Sec. of State . . . . Matt Blunt
Atty. General . . . . Jay Nixon
Chief Justice . . . . William Ray Price, Jr.

Governorship
minimum age 30
length of term . . . . 4 years
number of consecutive
    terms permitted . . 2 max. (not nec. consecutive)
who succeeds . . . . Lt. Governor

State legislature
name . . . . Legislature
    upper chamber
        name . . . . Senate
        number of members 34
        length of term . . . . 4 years
        party in majority, 2000 . . . . Democratic
    lower chamber
        name . . . . House of Representatives
        number of members 163
        length of term . . . . 2 years
        party in majority, 2000 . . . . Democratic

State employees March, 2000
total 109,463
March payroll $236,806,925

Local governments, 1997
total 3,416
    county 114
    municipal 944
    township 324
    school districts 537
    special districts 1,497

Voting age population, November, 2000, projected
Total 4,105,000
    male 1,950,000
    female 2,155,000

Vote for president
2000
    Gore 1,111,000
    Bush 1,190,000
1996
    Clinton 1,026,000
    Dole 890,000
    Perot 217,000

Federal representation, 2002 (107th Congress)
Senators (name/party/term expires)

                JEAN CARNAHAN
                Democrat - 2007
                CHRISTOPHER BOND
                Republican - 2005

Representatives, total 9
    Democrats 4
    Republicans 5
    other 0

Women holding public office, 2001
U.S. Congress 3
statewide elected office 2
state legislature 46

Black elected officials, 1999
total 201
    US and state legislatures 17
    city/county/regional offices 149
    judicial/law enforcement 12
    education/school boards 23

Hispanic public officials, 2000
total 1
    state executives & legislators .... NA
    city/county/regional offices 1
    judicial/law enforcement .... NA
    education/school boards .... NA

GOVERNMENTAL FINANCE

State government revenues, 1999 ($per capita)
total revenue $3,566.84
    total general revenue $2,883.88
        intergovernmental revenue $865.59
        taxes $1,566.03
        current charges $227.71
        miscellaneous $224.55

State government expenditures, 1999 ($per capita)
total expenditure $3,021.92
    total general expenditure $2,806.32
        education $1,048.21
        public welfare $681.37
        health $113.35
        hospitals $96.31
        highways $255.90
        police protection $31.38
        correction $90.02
        natural resources $46.00
        governmental administration $125.31
        interest on general debt $91.37

State debt, 1999 ($per capita) $1,628.12

Federal government grants to state & local government, 2000 (x$1,000)
total $5,671,188
    Dept. of Education $467,931
    Environmental Protection Agency $58,711
    Health Care Financing Admin. $2,533,059
    Dept. Housing & Urban Devel. $498,755
    Dept. of Labor $80,244
    Highway trust fund $669,311

CRIME, LAW ENFORCEMENT & COURTS

Crime, 2000 (all rates per 100,000 inhabitants)
total crimes 253,338
overall crime rate 4,527.8
    property crimes 225,919
        burglaries 41,685
        larcenies 159,539
        motor vehicle thefts 24,695
    property crime rate 4,037.7
    violent crimes 27,419
        murders 347
        forcible rapes 1,351
        robberies 7,598
        aggravated assaults 18,123
    violent crime rate 490.0

Number of police agencies, 2000 141

Arrests, 2000
total 246,187
    persons under 18 years of age 31,553

Prisoners under state & federal jurisdiction, 2000
total 27,323
percent change, 1999-2000 .... 4.5%
    sentenced to more than one year
        total 27,299
        rate per 100,000 residents 494

Persons under sentence of death, 4/1/2001 79

State's highest court
name .... Supreme Court
number of members 7
length of term .... 12 years
intermediate appeals court? .... yes

Missouri 6

LABOR & INCOME

Civilian labor force, 2000

total 2,930,000
  men 1,540,000
  women 1,390,000
  persons 16-19 years 176,000
  white 2,619,000
  black 269,000

*Civilian labor force as a percent of
  civilian non-institutional population, 2000*

total 70.3%
  men 76.8%
  women 64.3%
  persons 16-19 years .... NA%
  white 71.1%
  black 65.5%

Employment, 2000

total 2,828,000
  men 1,492,000
  women 1,336,000
  persons 16-19 years 155,000
  white 2,543,000
  black 245,000

Full-time/part-time labor force, 1998

full-time labor force 2,377,000
  working part-time for
    economic reasons 27,000
part-time labor force 481,000

Unemployment rate, 2000

total 3.5%
  men 3.1%
  women 3.9%
  persons 16-19 years 11.9%
  white 2.9%
  black 8.9%

*Unemployed by reason for unemployment
  (as a percent of total unemployment), 1998*

job losers or completed temp jobs 42.0%
job leavers 12.6%
reentrants 37.8%
new entrants 7.6%

*Experienced civilian labor force, by occupation,
1998*

executive/administrative/managerial 392,000
professional/specialty 430,000
technicians & related support 85,000
sales 358,000
administrative support/clerical 429,000
service occupations 318,000
precision production/craft/repair 322,000
machine operators/assemblers 172,000
transportation/material moving 129,000
handlers/helpers/laborers 120,000
farming/forestry/fishing 90,000

Experienced civilian labor force, by industry, 1998

construction 163,000
manufacturing 409,000
transportation/communication 174,000
wholesale/retail trade 563,000
finance/real estate/insurance 156,000
services 720,000
government 387,000
agriculture 90,000

Average annual pay, 1999 .... $29,958
change in average annual pay,
  1998-1999 .... 3.6%

*Hours and earnings of production workers
  on manufacturing payrolls, 2000*

average weekly hours 41.4
average hourly earnings $14.40
average weekly earnings $596.16

Labor union membership, 2000 337,900

Household income (in 2000 dollars)

median household income,
  three year average, 1998-2000 .... $47,462

Poverty

persons below poverty level,
  three year average, 1998-2000 .... 9.7%

Personal income ($per capita)

2000 (prelim.)
  in current dollars $27,445
  in constant (1996) dollars $25,564
1999 (preliminary)
  in current dollars $26,187
  in constant (1996) dollars $25,040

Federal income tax returns, 1999

returns filed 2,530,205
adjusted gross income ($1,000) $102,312,485
total income tax paid ($1,000) $14,762,516

ECONOMY, BUSINESS, INDUSTRY & AGRICULTURE

Fortune 500 companies, 2000 13

Business incorporations, 1998
total 9,579
change, 1997-1998 .... -6.8%

Business failures, 1998 1,321

Business firm ownership, 1997
Hispanic owned firms 4,107
Black owned firms 13,678
women owned firms 103,626
Asian & Pacific Islander owned firms 4,974
American Indian & Alaska
   native owned firms 4,106

Shopping centers, 2000 903

Gross state product, 1999 ($mil)
total $170,470
   agriculture services, forestry, fisheries .. $1,928
   mining $427
   construction $8,369
   manufacturing--durable goods $17,437
   manufacturing--nondurable goods $15,530
   transportation, communication &
      public utilities $17,199
   wholesale trade $12,621
   retail trade $16,584
   finance/real estate/insurance $26,038
   services $34,888
   federal, state & local government $19,449

Establishments, by major industry group, 1999
total 144,874
   forestry, fishing & agriculture 306
   mining 298
   construction 15,592
   manufacturing 7,465
   transportation & warehousing 4,981
   wholesale trade 9,342
   retail trade 24,023
   finance & insurance 9,240
   professional/scientific/technical 12,062
   health care/social assistance 12,820
   information 2,418
   accommodation/food services 10,980

Payroll, by major industry group, 1999
total ($1,000) $68,536,025
   forestry, fishing & agriculture $27,377
   mining $165,032
   construction $4,846,546
   manufacturing $12,552,395
   transportation & warehousing $2,617,498
   wholesale trade $5,057,334
   retail trade $5,814,566
   finance & insurance $5,219,138
   professional/scientific/technical $4,748,113
   health care/social assistance $8,757,851
   information $3,247,362
   accommodation/food services $2,243,838

Agriculture
number of farms, 2000 109,000
farm acreage, 2000 30,000,000
acres per farm, 2000 275
value of farms, 1997 ($mil) $30,199
farm income, 1999 ($mil)
   net farm income $405
   debt/asset ratio 15.4%
farm marketings, 1999 ($mil)
total $4,256
   crops $1,779
   livestock $2,477
principal commodities, in order by marketing
receipts, 1999
   Cattle, soybeans, hogs, corn

Federal economic activity in state
expenditures, 2000
   total ($mil) $35,687
   per capita $6,378
   defense ($mil) $6,020
   non-defense ($mil) $29,668
defense department, 2000
   contract awards ($mil) $4,508
   payroll ($mil) $1,604
   civilian employees (x1,000) 9.4
   military personnel (x1,000) 16.2

Fishing, 2000
catch (thousands of pounds) ....NA
value ($1,000) ....$NA

Mining, 2000 ($mil; preliminary)
total non-fuel mineral production $1,320

Missouri 8

Construction, 1999 ($mil)
total contracts (including
    non-building) $7,862
     residential $3,133
     non-residential $3,238

Construction industries, 1997
establishments 14,669
receipts ($1,000) ....$NA
annual payroll ($1,000) ....$NA
paid employees 129,183

Manufacturing, 1997
establishments 7,702
value of shipments ($1,000) $96,452,153
annual payroll ($1,000) $12,300,024
paid employees 391,945

Transportation industries, 1997
establishments 7,246
receipts ($1,000) $22,258,343
annual payroll ($1,000) $4,453,538
paid employees 135,632

Wholesale trade, 1997
establishments 11,260
sales($1,000) $96,009,109
annual payroll ($1,000) $5,130,520
paid employees 144,328

Retail trade, 1997
establishments 32,757
sales($1,000) $52,001,235
annual payroll ($1,000) $5,990,982
paid employees 451,894

Finance industries
establishments, 1997 13,688
receipts ($1,000), 1997 ....$NA
annual payroll ($1,000), 1997 .... $5,198,325
paid employees, 1997 149,584
commercial banks, 2000
    number 362
     assets ($bil) $64.5
     deposits ($bil) $52.4

Service industries, 1997 (non-exempt firms only)
establishments 40,064
receipts ($1,000) $31,361,754
annual payroll ($1,000) $11,786,494
paid employees 478,052

COMMUNICATION, ENERGY & TRANSPORTATION

Communication
daily newspapers, 2000 43
households with
    telephones, 1998 .... 96.2%
    computers, 2000 .... 52.6%
    internet access, 2000 .... 42.5%

Energy
consumption, 1999
total (trillion Btu) 1,768
per capita (million Btu) 323
by source of production (trillion Btu)
    coal 686
    natural gas 270
    petroleum 781
    nuclear electric power 91
    hydroelectric power 18
by end-use sector (trillion Btu)
    residential 432
    commercial 334
    industrial 380
    transportation 623
electric energy, 1999
    production (billion kWh) 73.5
    net summer capability (million kW) 16.8
gas utilities, 1999
    customers 1,455,000
    sales (trillion Btu) 181
nuclear plants, 1999 1

Transportation, 2000
public road & street mileage
total 123,039
    urban 16,370
    rural 106,669
    interstate 1,178
vehicle miles of travel (mil) 67,083
total motor vehicle registrations 4,579,629
    automobiles 2,715,215
    motorcycles 60,897
licensed drivers 3,856,271
    per 1,000 driving age population 898
deaths from motor vehicle
    accidents 1,157

STATE SUMMARY

Capital City . . . . .Helena

Governor . . . . Judy Martz

Address . . . . STATE CAPITOL
HELENA, MT 59620
406 444-3111

Admitted as a state 1889

Area (square miles) 147,046

Population, 1980 786,690

Population, 1990 799,065

Population, 2000 902,195

Persons per square mile, 2000 . . . . 6.2

Largest city . . . . Billings
population, 2000 89,847

Personal income per capita, 2000
(in current dollars) $22,569

Gross state product ($mil), 1999 . . . . $20,636

Leading industries, 1999 (by payroll)
Health care/Social assistance
Retail trade
Manufacturing

Leading agricultural commodities, 1999
Cattle, wheat, barley, hay

GEOGRAPHY & ENVIRONMENT

Area, 1990 (square miles)
total 147,046
land 145,556
water (includes territorial water) 1,490

Federally owned land, 2000 . . . . 29.4%

Highest point
name . . . . Granite Peak
elevation (feet) 12,799

Lowest point
name . . . . .Kootenal River
elevation (feet) 1,800

General coastline (miles) 0

Tidal shoreline (miles) 0

Capital city . . . . .Helena
population, 2000 25,780

Largest city . . . . Billings
population, 2000 89,847

Number of cities with over 100,000 population
1980 0
1990 0
2000 0

State parks and Recreation areas, 2000
area (acres) 65,000
number of visitors 1,367,000
revenues $1,652,000

Natl. forest system land, 1999 (acres) . .16,886,000

National park acreage, 1984 1,220,900

DEMOGRAPHICS & CHARACTERISTICS OF THE POPULATION

Population
1970 694,409
1980 786,690
1990 799,065
2000 902,195
2015 (projection) 1,069,000
2025 (projection) 1,121,000

Metropolitan area population
1970 169,000
1980 189,000
2000 306,000

Non-metropolitan area population
1970 525,000
1980 598,000
2000 597,000

Change in population, 1990-2000
number 103,130
percent 12.91%

Persons per square mile, 2000 . . . . 6.2

Persons by age, 2000
under 5 years 54,869
18 and over 672,133
21 and over 631,866
65 and over 120,949
85 and over 15,337

Montana 2

Persons by age, 2025 (projected)
under 5 years 65,000
5 to 17 years 182,000
65 and over 274,000

Median age, 2000 .... 37.5

Race, 2000
One race
White 817,229
Black or African American 2,692
American Indian and Alaska Native 56,068
Asian Indian 379
Chinese 827
Filipino 859
Japanese 885
Korean 833
Vietnamese 199
Native Hawaiian and other Pacific Islander ..470
Two or more races 15,730

Race, 2025 (projected)
White 1,007,000
Black 6,000

Persons of Hispanic origin, 2000
total Hispanic or Latino 18,081
Mexican 11,735
Puerto Rican 931

Cuban 285
Other Hispanic or Latino 5,130

Persons of Hispanic origin, 2025 (proj.) ... 39,000

Persons by sex, 2000
male 449,480
female 452,715

Marital status, 1990
males
15 years & older 299,504
single 79,234
married 186,723
separated 3,584
widowed 7,466
divorced 26,081
females
15 years & older 312,028
single 57,335
married 187,117
separated 4,548

widowed 36,750
divorced 30,826

Households & families, 2000
households 358,667
persons per household 2.45
families 237,407
persons per family 2.99
married couples 192,067
female householder, no husband
present 32,016
one person households 98,422
households with persons under 18 years . 119,550
households with persons over 65 years 83,982

Nativity, 1990
number of persons born in state 470,861
percent of total residents 58.9%

Immigration & naturalization, 1998
immigrants admitted 299
persons naturalized 165
refugees granted resident status 20

VITAL STATISTICS & HEALTH

Births
1999
with low birth weight 6.8%
to teenage mothers 12.2%
to unmarried mothers 30.0%
Birth rate, 1999 (per 1,000) 12.2
Birth rate, 2000 (per 1,000) 12.3

Abortions, 1996
total 3,000
rate (per 1,000 women age 15-44) 15.6

Deaths
1998 7,853
1999 8,128
2000 8,104

Infant deaths
1998 77
1999 72
2000 61

Average lifetime, by race, 1989-1991
total .... 76.23 years
white .... 76.72 years
black .... NA years

Marriages
1998 6,358
1999 6,633
2000 6,568

Divorces
1998 3,351
1999 2,548
2000 2,149

Physicians, 1999
total 1,683
rate (per 1,000 persons) 1.91

Nurses, 1999
total 7,850
rate (per 1,000 persons) 8.89

Hospitals, 1998
number 53
beds (x 1,000) 4.4
average daily census (x 1,000) 3.0
patients admitted (x1,000) 97
average cost per day to hospital, 1995 ...... $493
average cost per stay to hospital, 1995 .... $5,184

EDUCATION

Educational attainment of all persons
25 years and older, 1990
less than 9th grade 41,144
high school graduates 170,070
bachelor's degree 71,610
graduate or professional degree 28,911

2000
high school graduate or more 89.6%
college graduate or more 23.8%

Public school enrollment, Fall, 1998
total 159,988
Kindergarten through grade 8 109,535
grades 9 through 12 50,453

Public School Teachers, 2000
total 10,400
elementary 7,100
secondary 3,300
average salaries
elementary $31,700
secondary $32,900

State receipts & expenditures for public
schools, 2000
revenue receipts ($mil) $1,096

State receipts & expenditures for public
schools, 2000 (continued)
expenditures
total ($mil) $1,086
per capita $1,230
per pupil $6,801

Graduating high school seniors,
public high schools, 2000 (est.) 10,893

SAT scores, 2001
verbal 539
math 539
percent graduates taking test 23%

Institutions of higher education, 1999
total 28
public 18
private 10

Enrollment in institutions of higher
education, Fall, 1998
total 44,150
full-time men 16,528
full-time women 17,438
part-time men 4,007
part-time women 6,177

Minority enrollment in institutions of higher
education, Fall, 1997
Black, non-Hispanic 158
Hispanic 546
Asian/Pacific Islander 362

Earned degrees conferred, 1998
Bachelor's 4,932
First professional 68
Master's 822
Doctor's 98

SOCIAL INSURANCE & WELFARE PROGRAMS

Social Security beneficiaries & benefits, 2000
beneficiaries
total 158,000
retired and dependents 111,000
survivors 24,000
disabled & dependents 23,000
annual benefit payments ($mil)
total $1,376
retired and dependents $926
survivors $267
disabled & dependents $182

Montana 4

Medicare, 2000
enrollment (x1,000) 135
payments ($mil) $575

Medicaid, 1998
recipients (x1,000) 101
payments ($mil) $361

Federal public aid
Temporary Assistance for Needy Families
(TANF), 2000
    Recipients (x1,000) 14
    Families (x1,000) 5
Supplemental Security Income
  total recipients, 1999 (x1,000) 14

Food Stamp Program
  participants, 2000 (x1,000) 59

HOUSING & CONSTRUCTION

Total housing units, 2000 412,633
  seasonal or recreational use 24,213
  occupied 358,667
    owner occupied 247,723
    renter occupied 110,944

New privately owned housing units uthorized, 2000
number (x1,000) 2.6
value ($mil) $235

New privately owned housing units
  started, 2000 (est.) (x1,000) 2.2

Existing home sales, 2000 (x1,000) 19.7

GOVERNMENT & ELECTIONS

State officials, 2002
Governor (name/party/term expires)
    JUDY MARTZ
    Republican - 2005
Lt. Governor .... Karl Ohs
Sec. of State .... Bob Brown
Atty. General .... Mike Magrath
Chief Justice .... Karla Gray

Governorship
minimum age 25
length of term .... 4 years
number of consecutive
  terms permitted .... 8 out of 16 yrs
who succeeds .... Lt. Governor

State legislature
name .... Legislature
  upper chamber
    name .... Senate
    number of members 50
    length of term .... 4 years
    party in majority, 2000 .... Republican
  lower chamber
    name .... House of Representatives
    number of members 100
    length of term .... 2 years
    party in majority, 2000 .... Republican

State employees March, 2000
total 23,226
March payroll $51,034,212

Local governments, 1997
total 1,144
  county 54
  municipal 128
  township 0
  school districts 362
  special districts 600

Voting age population, November, 2000, projected
Total 668,000
  male 328,000
  female 340,000

Vote for president
2000
  Gore 137,000
  Bush 240,000
1996
  Clinton 168,000
  Dole 180,000
  Perot 55,000

Federal representation, 2002 (107th Congress)
Senators (name/party/term expires)

    CONRAD BURNS
    Republican - 2007
    MAX BAUCUS
    Democrat - 2003

Representatives, total 1
  Democrats 0
  Republicans 1
  other 0

Women holding public office, 2001
U.S. Congress 0
statewide elected office 2
state legislature 34

Black elected officials, 1999
total . . . . NA
   US and state legislatures . . . . NA
   city/county/regional offices . . . . NA
   judicial/law enforcement . . . . NA
   education/school boards . . . . NA

Hispanic public officials, 2000
total 1
   state executives & legislators . . . . NA
   city/county/regional offices . . . . NA
   judicial/law enforcement 1
   education/school boards . . . . NA

GOVERNMENTAL FINANCE

State government revenues, 1999 ($per capita)
total revenue $4,219.99
   total general revenue $3,534.88
     intergovernmental revenue $1,304.90
     taxes $1,524.42
     current charges $352.35
     miscellaneous $353.21

State government expenditures, 1999 ($per capita)
total expenditure $3,978.31
   total general expenditure $3,552.04
     education $1,253.60
     public welfare $560.50
     health $224.54
     hospitals $44.11
     highways $456.11
     police protection $43.23
     correction $106.58
     natural resources $182.41
     governmental administration $211.96
     interest on general debt $167.15

State debt, 1999 ($per capita) $2,668.14

Federal government grants to state & local government, 2000 (x$1,000)
total $1,438,862
   Dept. of Education $168,463
   Environmental Protection Agency $31,676
   Health Care Financing Admin. $358,877
   Dept. Housing & Urban Devel. $121,118
   Dept. of Labor $28,095
   Highway trust fund $260,173

CRIME, LAW ENFORCEMENT & COURTS

Crime, 2000 (all rates per 100,000 inhabitants)
total crimes 31,878
overall crime rate 3,533.4
   property crimes 29,707
     burglaries 3,946
     larcenies 23,805
     motor vehicle thefts 1,956
   property crime rate 3,292.7
   violent crimes 2,171
     murders 16
     forcible rapes 301
     robberies 249
     aggravated assaults 1,605
   violent crime rate 240.6

Number of police agencies, 2000 41

Arrests, 2000
total 13,156
   persons under 18 years of age 4,663

Prisoners under state & federal jurisdiction, 2000
total 3,105
percent change, 1999-2000 . . . . 5.2%
   sentenced to more than one year
     total 3,105
     rate per 100,000 residents 348

Persons under sentence of death, 4/1/2001 6

State's highest court
name . . . . Supreme Court
number of members 7
length of term . . . . 8 years
intermediate appeals court? . . . . no

Montana 6

LABOR & INCOME

Civilian labor force, 2000
total 479,000
  men 256,000
  women 223,000
  persons 16-19 years 35,000
  white 449,000
  black .... NA

Civilian labor force as a percent of
civilian non-institutional population, 2000
total 69.3%
  men 74.4%
  women 64.3%
  persons 16-19 years .... NA%
  white 69.9%
  black .... NA%

Employment, 2000
total 456,000
  men 243,000
  women 212,000
  persons 16-19 years 30,000
  white 430,000
  black .... NA

Full-time/part-time labor force, 1998
full-time labor force 354,000
  working part-time for
    economic reasons 7,000
part-time labor force 114,000

Unemployment rate, 2000
total 4.9%
  men 5.2%
  women 4.6%
  persons 16-19 years 16.0%
  white 4.3%
  black .... NA%

Unemployed by reason for unemployment
(as a percent of total unemployment), 1998
job losers or completed temp jobs 42.3%
job leavers 15.4%
reentrants 38.5%
new entrants 3.8%

Experienced civilian labor force, by occupation,
1998
executive/administrative/managerial 58,000
professional/specialty 65,000
technicians & related support 11,000

sales 54,000
administrative support/clerical 60,000
service occupations 76,000
precision production/craft/repair 50,000
machine operators/assemblers 13,000
transportation/material moving 22,000
handlers/helpers/laborers 20,000
farming/forestry/fishing 37,000

Experienced civilian labor force, by industry, 1998
construction 22,000
manufacturing 32,000
transportation/communication 23,000
wholesale/retail trade 97,000
finance/real estate/insurance 16,000
services 97,000
government 81,000
agriculture 34,000

Average annual pay, 1999 .... $23,253
change in average annual pay,
  1998-1999 .... 2.7%

Hours and earnings of production workers
on manufacturing payrolls, 2000
average weekly hours 38.5
average hourly earnings $14.34
average weekly earnings $552.09

Labor union membership, 2000 51,200

Household income (in 2000 dollars)
median household income,
  three year average, 1998-2000 .... $32,045

Poverty
persons below poverty level,
  three year average, 1998-2000 .... 16.0%

Personal income ($per capita)
2000 (prelim.)
  in current dollars $22,569
  in constant (1996) dollars $21,022
1999 (preliminary)
  in current dollars $22,314
  in constant (1996) dollars $21,337

Federal income tax returns, 1999
returns filed 416,951
adjusted gross income ($1,000) $13,413,566
total income tax paid ($1,000) $1,752,889

ECONOMY, BUSINESS, INDUSTRY & AGRICULTURE

Fortune 500 companies, 2000 0

Business incorporations, 1998
total 2,812
change, 1997-1998 .... -12.6%

Business failures, 1998 201

Business firm ownership, 1997
Hispanic owned firms 1,006
Black owned firms 62
women owned firms 22,404
Asian & Pacific Islander owned firms 443
American Indian & Alaska
    native owned firms 1,912

Shopping centers, 2000 97

Gross state product, 1999 ($mil)
total $20,636
    agriculture services, forestry, fisheries $828
    mining $754
    construction $1,158
    manufacturing--durable goods $874
    manufacturing--nondurable goods $671
    transportation, communication &
        public utilities $2,461
    wholesale trade $1,354
    retail trade $2,137
    finance/real estate/insurance $2,818
    services $4,195
    federal, state & local government $3,385

Establishments, by major industry group, 1999
total 31,365
    forestry, fishing & agriculture 393
    mining 272
    construction 3,760
    manufacturing 1,207
    transportation & warehousing 1,052
    wholesale trade 1,555
    retail trade 5,038
    finance & insurance 1,656
    professional/scientific/technical 2,532
    health care/social assistance 2,713
    information 595
    accommodation/food services 3,169

Payroll, by major industry group, 1999
total ($1,000) $6,441,362
    forestry, fishing & agriculture $47,405
    mining $203,926
    construction $577,806
    manufacturing $633,549
    transportation & warehousing $228,833
    wholesale trade $420,361
    retail trade $873,403
    finance & insurance $422,167
    professional/scientific/technical $396,912
    health care/social assistance $1,144,136
    information $211,006
    accommodation/food services $366,882

Agriculture
number of farms, 2000 28,000
farm acreage, 2000 57,000,000
acres per farm, 2000 2,054
value of farms, 1997 ($mil) $18,178
farm income, 1999 ($mil)
    net farm income $482
    debt/asset ratio 13.3%
farm marketings, 1999 ($mil)
total $1,716
    crops $789
    livestock $928
principal commodities, in order by marketing
receipts, 1999
    Cattle, wheat, barley, hay

Federal economic activity in state
expenditures, 2000
    total ($mil) $5,917
    per capita $6,558
    defense ($mil) $390
    non-defense ($mil) $5,527
defense department, 2000
    contract awards ($mil) $87
    payroll ($mil) $290
    civilian employees (x1,000) 1.1
    military personnel (x1,000) 3.5

Fishing, 2000
catch (thousands of pounds) .... NA
value ($1,000) .... $NA

Mining, 2000 ($mil; preliminary)
total non-fuel mineral production $582

Montana 8

Construction, 1999 ($mil)
total contracts (including
  non-building) $927
    residential $346
    non-residential $297

Construction industries, 1997
establishments 3,392
receipts ($1,000) $2,236,830
annual payroll ($1,000) .... $NA
paid employees 17,987

Manufacturing, 1997
establishments 1,485
value of shipments ($1,000) $5,222,699
annual payroll ($1,000) $626,561
paid employees 22,526

Transportation industries, 1997
establishments 1,669
receipts ($1,000) $2,770,535
annual payroll ($1,000) $486,865
paid employees 16,902

Wholesale trade, 1997
establishments 1,939
sales($1,000) $8,249,519
annual payroll ($1,000) $439,090
paid employees 17,417

Retail trade, 1997
establishments 7,387
sales($1,000) $8,014,759
annual payroll ($1,000) $919,324
paid employees 75,840

Finance industries
establishments, 1997 2,574
receipts ($1,000), 1997 .... $NA
annual payroll ($1,000), 1997 .... $NA
paid employees, 1997 .... NA
commercial banks, 2000
  number 84
    assets ($bil) $10.9
    deposits ($bil) $8.8

Service industries, 1997 (non-exempt firms only)
establishments 8,324
receipts ($1,000) $3,283,738
annual payroll ($1,000) $1,131,361
paid employees 59,464

COMMUNICATION, ENERGY & TRANSPORTATION

Communication
daily newspapers, 2000 11
households with
  telephones, 1998 .... 94.7%
  computers, 2000 .... 51.5%
  internet access, 2000 .... 40.6%

Energy
consumption, 1999
total (trillion Btu) 412
per capita (million Btu) 467
by source of production (trillion Btu)
  coal 174
  natural gas 64
  petroleum 174
  nuclear electric power .... NA
  hydroelectric power 143
by end-use sector (trillion Btu)
  residential 62
  commercial 48
  industrial 196
  transportation 107
electric energy, 1999
  production (billion kWh) 27.6
  net summer capability (million kW) 3
gas utilities, 1999
  customers 250,000
  sales (trillion Btu) 32
nuclear plants, 1999 .... na

Transportation, 2000
public road & street mileage
total 69,567
  urban 2,491
  rural 67,076
  interstate 1,191
vehicle miles of travel (mil) 9,882
total motor vehicle registrations 1,026,226
  automobiles 466,659
  motorcycles 26,402
licensed drivers 678,899
  per 1,000 driving age population 968
deaths from motor vehicle
  accidents 237

STATE SUMMARY

Capital City .... Lincoln

Governor ....Mike Johanns

Address .... STATE CAPITOL
LINCOLN, NE 68509
402 471-2244

Admitted as a state 1867

Area (square miles) 77,358

Population, 1980 1,569,825

Population, 1990 1,578,385

Population, 2000 1,711,263

Persons per square mile, 2000 .... 22.3

Largest city .... Omaha
population, 2000 390,000

Personal income per capita, 2000
(in current dollars) $27,829

Gross state product ($mil), 1999 .... $53,744

Leading industries, 1999 (by payroll)
Manufacturing
Health care/Social assistance
Finance & Insurance

Leading agricultural commodities, 1999
Cattle, corn, soybeans, hogs

GEOGRAPHY & ENVIRONMENT

Area, 1990 (square miles)
total 77,358
land 76,878
water (includes territorial water) 481

Federally owned land, 2000 .... 1.3%

Highest point
name ....Johnson Twp. (Kimball County)
elevation (feet) 5,426

Lowest point
name .... southeast corner of state
elevation (feet) 840

General coastline (miles) 0

Tidal shoreline (miles) 0

Capital city .... Lincoln
population, 2000 226,000

Largest city .... Omaha
population, 2000 390,000

Number of cities with over 100,000 population
1980 2
1990 2
2000 2

State parks and Recreation areas, 2000
area (acres) 133,000
number of visitors 9,619,000
revenues $13,706,000

Natl. forest system land, 1999 (acres) 352,000

National park acreage, 1984 5,900

DEMOGRAPHICS & CHARACTERISTICS OF THE POPULATION

Population
1970 1,485,333
1980 1,569,825
1990 1,578,385
2000 1,711,263
2015 (projection) 1,850,000
2025 (projection) 1,930,000

Metropolitan area population
1970 650,000
1980 708,000
2000 900,000

Non-metropolitan area population
1970 835,000
1980 862,000
2000 811,000

Change in population, 1990-2000
number 132,878
percent 8.42%

Persons per square mile, 2000 .... 22.3

Persons by age, 2000
under 5 years 117,048
18 and over 1,261,021
21 and over 1,180,859
65 and over 232,195
85 and over 33,953

Nebraska 2

Persons by age, 2025 (projected)
under 5 years 124,000
5 to 17 years 336,000
65 and over 405,000

Median age, 2000 . . . . 35.3

Race, 2000
One race
White 1,533,261
Black or African American 68,541
American Indian and Alaska Native 14,896
Asian Indian 3,273
Chinese 3,093
Filipino 2,101
Japanese 1,582
Korean 2,423
Vietnamese 6,364
Native Hawaiian and other Pacific Islander . . 836
Two or more races 23,953

Race, 2025 (projected)
White 1,754,000
Black 109,000

Persons of Hispanic origin, 2000
total Hispanic or Latino 94,425
Mexican 71,030
Puerto Rican 1,993
Cuban 859
Other Hispanic or Latino 20,543

Persons of Hispanic origin, 2025 (proj.) . . 111,000

Persons by sex, 2000
male 843,351
female 867,912

Marital status, 1990
males
15 years & older 583,134
single 162,919
married 366,215
separated 5,839
widowed 14,891
divorced 39,109
females
15 years & older 631,861
single 132,954
married 366,625
separated 7,713

widowed 81,161
divorced 51,121

Households & families, 2000
households 666,184
persons per household 2.49
families 443,411
persons per family 3.06
married couples 360,996
female householder, no husband
present 60,343
one person households 183,550
households with persons under 18 years . 229,980
households with persons over 65 years . . . 157,560

Nativity, 1990
number of persons born in state 1,107,280
percent of total residents 70.2%

Immigration & naturalization, 1998
immigrants admitted 1,267
persons naturalized 717
refugees granted resident status 36

VITAL STATISTICS & HEALTH
Births
1999
with low birth weight 6.7%
to teenage mothers 14.3%
to unmarried mothers 25.9%
Birth rate, 1999 (per 1,000) 14.3
Birth rate, 2000 (per 1,000) 14.8

Abortions, 1996
total 4,000
rate (per 1,000 women age 15-44) 12.3

Deaths
1998 15,207
1999 15,579
2000 14,988

Infant deaths
1998 159
1999 148
2000 189

Average lifetime, by race, 1989-1991
total . . . . 76.92 years
white . . . . 77.21 years
black . . . . NA years

Marriages
1998 12,320
1999 12,801
2000 13,020

Divorces
1998 6,376
1999 6,254
2000 6,414

Physicians, 1999
total 3,679
rate (per 1,000 persons) 2.21

Nurses, 1999
total 14,950
rate (per 1,000 persons) 8.97

Hospitals, 1998
number 86
beds (x 1,000) 8.1
average daily census (x 1,000) 4.9
patients admitted (x1,000) 192
average cost per day to hospital, 1995 . . . . . . $661
average cost per stay to hospital, 1995 . . . . $5,880

EDUCATION

Educational attainment of all persons
  25 years and older, 1990
  less than 9th grade 79,925
  high school graduates 345,778
  bachelor's degree 130,172
  graduate or professional degree 58,490

2000
  high school graduate or more 90.4%
  college graduate or more 24.6%

Public school enrollment, Fall, 1998
total 291,140
  Kindergarten through grade 8 199,754
  grades 9 through 12 91,386

Public School Teachers, 2000
total 20,400
  elementary 11,900
  secondary 8,500
average salaries
  elementary $33,300
  secondary $33,300

State receipts & expenditures for public
  schools, 2000
revenue receipts ($mil) $1,912

State receipts & expenditures for public
  schools, 2000 (continued)
expenditures
  total ($mil) $1,905
  per capita $1,143
  per pupil $6,576

Graduating high school seniors,
  public high schools, 2000 (est.) 22,093

SAT scores, 2001
verbal 562
math 568
percent graduates taking test 8%

Institutions of higher education, 1999
total 37
  public 16
  private 21

Enrollment in institutions of higher
  education, Fall, 1998
total 111,123
full-time men 32,472
full-time women 36,761
part-time men 17,739
part-time women 24,151

Minority enrollment in institutions of higher
  education, Fall, 1997
Black, non-Hispanic 3,748
Hispanic 2,387
Asian/Pacific Islander 2,419

Earned degrees conferred, 1998
Bachelor's 10,071
First professional 764
Master's 2,905
Doctor's 429

SOCIAL INSURANCE & WELFARE PROGRAMS

Social Security beneficiaries & benefits, 2000
beneficiaries
total 284,000
  retired and dependents 209,000
  survivors 42,000
  disabled & dependents 33,000
annual benefit payments ($mil)
total $2,533
  retired and dependents $1,778
  survivors $493
  disabled & dependents $262

Nebraska 4

Medicare, 2000
enrollment (x1,000) 252
payments ($mil) $1,225

Medicaid, 1998
recipients (x1,000) 211
payments ($mil) $753

Federal public aid
Temporary Assistance for Needy Families
(TANF), 2000
   Recipients (x1,000) 28
   Families (x1,000) 10
Supplemental Security Income
  total recipients, 1999 (x1,000) 21

Food Stamp Program
  participants, 2000 (x1,000) 82

HOUSING & CONSTRUCTION

Total housing units, 2000 722,668
  seasonal or recreational use 11,912
  occupied 666,184
    owner occupied 449,317
    renter occupied 216,867

New privately owned housing units uthorized, 2000
number (x1,000) 9.1
value ($mil) $830

New privately owned housing units
  started, 2000 (est.) (x1,000) 8.4

Existing home sales, 2000 (x1,000) 31.3

GOVERNMENT & ELECTIONS

State officials, 2002
  Governor (name/party/term expires)
        MIKE JOHANNS
        Democrat - 2003
Lt. Governor . . . . David Heineman
Sec. of State . . . . John Gale
Atty. General . . . . Don Stenberg
Chief Justice . . . . John V. Hendry

Governorship
minimum age 30
length of term . . . . 4 years
number of consecutive
  terms permitted 2
who succeeds . . . . Lt. Governor

State legislature
name . . . . Unicameral Legislature
  upper chamber
    name . . . . NA
    number of members 49
    length of term . . . . 4 year
    party in majority, 2000 . . . . NA
  lower chamber
    name . . . . NA
    number of members . . . . NA
    length of term . . . . NA
    party in majority, 2000 . . . . NA

State employees March, 2000
total 35,852
March payroll $71,305,001

Local governments, 1997
total 2,894
  county 93
  municipal 535
  township 455
  school districts 681
  special districts 1,130

Voting age population, November, 2000, projected
Total 1,234,000
  male 593,000
  female 641,000

Vote for president
2000
  Gore 232,000
  Bush 434,000
1996
  Clinton 237,000
  Dole 363,000
  Perot 71,000

Federal representation, 2002 (107th Congress)
Senators (name/party/term expires)

        BEN NELSON
        Democrat - 2007
        CHARLES HAGEL
        Republican - 2003

Representatives, total 3
  Democrats 0
  Republicans 3
  other 0

Women holding public office, 2001
U.S. Congress 0
statewide elected office 2
state legislature 9

Black elected officials, 1999
total 4
  US and state legislatures 1
  city/county/regional offices 1
  judicial/law enforcement .... NA
  education/school boards 2

Hispanic public officials, 2000
total 3
  state executives & legislators 1
  city/county/regional offices 2
  judicial/law enforcement .... NA
  education/school boards .... NA

GOVERNMENTAL FINANCE

State government revenues, 1999 ($per capita)
total revenue $3,346.60
  total general revenue $3,054.55
    intergovernmental revenue $852.55
    taxes $1,597.87
    current charges $308.35
    miscellaneous $295.78

State government expenditures, 1999 ($per capita)
total expenditure $3,111.36
  total general expenditure $2,978.17
    education $1,144.83
    public welfare $673.51
    health $137.99
    hospitals $92.75
    highways $387.46
    police protection $33.95
    correction $74.70
    natural resources $86.64
    governmental administration $85.44
    interest on general debt $63.84

State debt, 1999 ($per capita) $1,092.50

Federal government grants to state & local government, 2000 (x$1,000)
total $1,682,451
  Dept. of Education $155,504
  Environmental Protection Agency $29,844
  Health Care Financing Admin. $698,287
  Dept. Housing & Urban Devel. $131,785
  Dept. of Labor $23,707
  Highway trust fund $194,818

CRIME, LAW ENFORCEMENT & COURTS

Crime, 2000 (all rates per 100,000 inhabitants)
total crimes 70,085
overall crime rate 4,095.5
  property crimes 64,479
    burglaries 10,131
    larcenies 49,118
    motor vehicle thefts 5,230
  property crime rate 3,767.9
  violent crimes 5,606
    murders 63
    forcible rapes 436
    robberies 1,147
    aggravated assaults 3,960
  violent crime rate 327.6

Number of police agencies, 2000 228

Arrests, 2000
total 105,221
  persons under 18 years of age 19,509

Prisoners under state & federal jurisdiction, 2000
total 3,895
percent change, 1999-2000 .... 5.6%
  sentenced to more than one year
    total 3,816
    rate per 100,000 residents 228

Persons under sentence of death, 4/1/2001 11

State's highest court
name .... Supreme Court
number of members 7
length of term .... 6 years
intermediate appeals court? .... no

Nebraska 6

LABOR & INCOME

Civilian labor force, 2000
total 924,000
  men 482,000
  women 443,000
  persons 16-19 years 73,000
  white 870,000
  black 32,000

Civilian labor force as a percent of
civilian non-institutional population, 2000
total 73.7%
  men 78.6%
  women 69.0%
  persons 16-19 years ....NA%
  white 74.0%
  black 66.4%

Employment, 2000
total 897,000
  men 468,000
  women 428,000
  persons 16-19 years 66,000
  white 846,000
  black 29,000

Full-time/part-time labor force, 1998
full-time labor force ....NA
  working part-time for
    economic reasons 8,000
part-time labor force ....NA

Unemployment rate, 2000
total 3.0%
  men 2.8%
  women 3.2%
  persons 16-19 years 9.7%
  white 2.7%
  black 9.5%

Unemployed by reason for unemployment
(as a percent of total unemployment), 1998
job losers or completed temp jobs .... NA%
job leavers .... NA%
reentrants .... NA%
new entrants .... NA%

Experienced civilian labor force, by occupation,
1998
executive/administrative/managerial 104,000
professional/specialty 118,000
technicians & related support ....NA

sales 113,000
administrative support/clerical 134,000
service occupations 124,000
precision production/craft/repair 82,000
machine operators/assemblers 51,000
transportation/material moving 37,000
handlers/helpers/laborers 36,000
farming/forestry/fishing 83,000

Experienced civilian labor force, by industry, 1998
construction 38,000
manufacturing 106,000
transportation/communication 51,000
wholesale/retail trade 187,000
finance/real estate/insurance 64,000
services 206,000
government 123,000
agriculture 85,000

Average annual pay, 1999 .... $26,633
change in average annual pay,
  1998-1999 .... 4.3%

Hours and earnings of production workers
on manufacturing payrolls, 2000
average weekly hours 41.4
average hourly earnings $12.93
average weekly earnings $535.30

Labor union membership, 2000 64,900

Household income (in 2000 dollars)
median household income,
  three year average, 1998-2000 .... $38,574

Poverty
persons below poverty level,
  three year average, 1998-2000 .... 10.6%

Personal income ($per capita)
2000 (prelim.)
  in current dollars $27,829
  in constant (1996) dollars $25,921
1999 (preliminary)
  in current dollars $27,437
  in constant (1996) dollars $26,235

Federal income tax returns, 1999
returns filed 804,169
adjusted gross income ($1,000) $31,863,507
total income tax paid ($1,000) $4,503,366

ECONOMY, BUSINESS, INDUSTRY & AGRICULTURE

Fortune 500 companies, 2000 5

Business incorporations, 1998
total 3,348
change, 1997-1998 .... -5.0%

Business failures, 1998 383

Business firm ownership, 1997
Hispanic owned firms 1,437
Black owned firms 1,565
women owned firms 33,469
Asian & Pacific Islander owned firms 877
American Indian & Alaska
    native owned firms 799

Shopping centers, 2000 277

Gross state product, 1999 ($mil)
total $53,744
    agriculture services, forestry, fisheries .. $2,606
    mining $79
    construction $2,554
    manufacturing--durable goods $3,871
    manufacturing--nondurable goods $3,661
    transportation, communication &
        public utilities $5,783
    wholesale trade $4,269
    retail trade $4,712
    finance/real estate/insurance $8,332
    services $10,291
    federal, state & local government $7,585

Establishments, by major industry group, 1999
total 48,968
    forestry, fishing & agriculture 205
    mining 122
    construction 5,602
    manufacturing 1,955
    transportation & warehousing 1,983
    wholesale trade 3,090
    retail trade 8,155
    finance & insurance 3,528
    professional/scientific/technical 3,561
    health care/social assistance 3,913
    information 850
    accommodation/food services 3,954

Payroll, by major industry group, 1999
total ($1,000) $19,435,923
    forestry, fishing & agriculture .... $NA
    mining .... $NA
    construction $1,347,219
    manufacturing $3,340,032
    transportation & warehousing $860,851
    wholesale trade $1,329,863
    retail trade $1,743,239
    finance & insurance $1,879,544
    professional/scientific/technical $1,238,286
    health care/social assistance $2,651,597
    information $1,190,086
    accommodation/food services $569,710

Agriculture
number of farms, 2000 54,000
farm acreage, 2000 46,000,000
acres per farm, 2000 859
value of farms, 1997 ($mil) $31,960
farm income, 1999 ($mil)
    net farm income $1,651
    debt/asset ratio 22.3%
farm marketings, 1999 ($mil)
total $8,555
    crops $3,130
    livestock $5,425
principal commodities, in order by marketing
receipts, 1999
    Cattle, corn, soybeans, hogs

Federal economic activity in state
expenditures, 2000
    total ($mil) $9,611
    per capita $5,617
    defense ($mil) $908
    non-defense ($mil) $8,703
defense department, 2000
    contract awards ($mil) $238
    payroll ($mil) $660
    civilian employees (x1,000) 3.2
    military personnel (x1,000) 7.6

Fishing, 2000
catch (thousands of pounds) ....NA
value ($1,000) ....$NA

Mining, 2000 ($mil; preliminary)
total non-fuel mineral production $170

Nebraska 8

Construction, 1999 ($mil)
total contracts (including
    non-building) $2,872
      residential $950
      non-residential $1,179

Construction industries, 1997
establishments 5,107
receipts ($1,000) $5,429,818
annual payroll ($1,000) .... $NA
paid employees 40,127

Manufacturing, 1997
establishments 2,039
value of shipments ($1,000) $28,357,769
annual payroll ($1,000) $3,165,556
paid employees 111,098

Transportation industries, 1997
establishments 2,742
receipts ($1,000) .... $NA
annual payroll ($1,000) .... $NA
paid employees .... NA

Wholesale trade, 1997
establishments 3,894
sales($1,000) $39,737,729
annual payroll ($1,000) $1,344,281
paid employees 48,010

Retail trade, 1997
establishments 11,268
sales($1,000) $16,350,932
annual payroll ($1,000) $1,799,417
paid employees 149,478

Finance industries
establishments, 1997 4,861
receipts ($1,000), 1997 .... $NA
annual payroll ($1,000), 1997 .... $1,781,185
paid employees, 1997 57,400
commercial banks, 2000
    number 276
      assets ($bil) $30.1
      deposits ($bil) $23.7

Service industries, 1997 (non-exempt firms only)
establishments 12,630
receipts ($1,000) $9,746,159
annual payroll ($1,000) $3,663,195
paid employees 157,646

COMMUNICATION, ENERGY & TRANSPORTATION

Communication
daily newspapers, 2000 17
households with
    telephones, 1998 .... 95.8%
    computers, 2000 .... 48.5%
    internet access, 2000 .... 37.0%

Energy
consumption, 1999
total (trillion Btu) 602
per capita (million Btu) 361
by source of production (trillion Btu)
    coal 196
    natural gas 121
    petroleum 246
    nuclear electric power 107
    hydroelectric power 18
by end-use sector (trillion Btu)
    residential 130
    commercial 111
    industrial 166
    transportation 194
electric energy, 1999
    production (billion kWh) 30
    net summer capability (million kW) 5.8
gas utilities, 1999
    customers 515,000
    sales (trillion Btu) 74
nuclear plants, 1999 2

Transportation, 2000
public road & street mileage
total 92,791
    urban 5,186
    rural 87,605
    interstate 482
vehicle miles of travel (mil) 18,081
total motor vehicle registrations 1,618,933
    automobiles 852,481
    motorcycles 20,881
licensed drivers 1,195,219
    per 1,000 driving age population 909
deaths from motor vehicle
    accidents 276

STATE SUMMARY

Capital City . . . . .Carson City

Governor . . . . Kenny Guinn

Address . . . . STATE CAPITOL
CARSON CITY, NV 89710
775 684-5670

Admitted as a state 1864

Area (square miles) 110,567

Population, 1980 800,493

Population, 1990 1,201,833

Population, 2000 1,998,257

Persons per square mile, 2000 . . . . 18.2

Largest city . . . . Las Vegas
population, 2000 478,000

Personal income per capita, 2000
(in current dollars) $30,529

Gross state product ($mil), 1999 . . . . $69,864

Leading industries, 1999 (by payroll)
Accommodation & Food services
Construction
Retail trade

Leading agricultural commodities, 1999
Cattle, dairy products, hay, greenhouse

GEOGRAPHY & ENVIRONMENT

Area, 1990 (square miles)
total 110,567
land 109,806
water (includes territorial water) 761

Federally owned land, 2000 . . . . 83.0%

Highest point
name . . . . .Boundary Peak
elevation (feet) 13,140

Lowest point
name . . . . Colorado River
elevation (feet) 470

General coastline (miles) 0

Tidal shoreline (miles) 0

Capital city . . . . .Carson City
population, 2000 52,457

Largest city . . . . Las Vegas
population, 2000 478,000

Number of cities with over 100,000 population
1980 2
1990 3
2000 4

State parks and Recreation areas, 2000
area (acres) 133,000
number of visitors 3,451,000
revenues $1,903,000

Natl. forest system land, 1999 (acres) . . .5,826,000

National park acreage, 1984 700,200

DEMOGRAPHICS & CHARACTERISTICS OF THE POPULATION

Population
1970 488,738
1980 800,493
1990 1,201,833
2000 1,998,257
2015 (projection) 2,179,000
2025 (projection) 2,312,000

Metropolitan area population
1970 394,000
1980 657,000
2000 1,748,000

Non-metropolitan area population
1970 94,000
1980 144,000
2000 251,000

Change in population, 1990-2000
number 796,424
percent 66.27%

Persons per square mile, 2000 . . . . 18.2

Persons by age, 2000
under 5 years 145,817
18 and over 1,486,458
21 and over 1,411,378
65 and over 218,929
85 and over 16,989

Nevada 2

Persons by age, 2025 (projected)
under 5 years 136,000
5 to 17 years 345,000
65 and over 486,000

Median age, 2000 35

Race, 2000
One race
White 1,501,886
Black or African American 135,477
American Indian and Alaska Native 26,420
Asian Indian 5,535
Chinese 14,113
Filipino 40,529
Japanese 8,277
Korean 7,554
Vietnamese 4,420
Native Hawaiian and other Pacific Islander 8,426
Two or more races 76,428

Race, 2025 (projected)
White 1,933,000
Black 202,000

Persons of Hispanic origin, 2000
total Hispanic or Latino 393,970
  Mexican 285,764
  Puerto Rican 10,420
  Cuban 11,498
  Other Hispanic or Latino 86,288

Persons of Hispanic origin, 2025 (proj.) .. 583,000

Persons by sex, 2000
male 1,018,051
female 980,206

Marital status, 1990
males
  15 years & older 481,852
    single 135,767
    married 268,566
      separated 10,990
    widowed 11,204
    divorced 66,315
females
  15 years & older 466,194
    single 89,055
    married 264,789
      separated 12,211

widowed 42,131
divorced 70,219

Households & families, 2000
households 751,165
persons per household 2.62
  families 498,333
  persons per family 3.14
    married couples 373,201
    female householder, no husband
      present 83,482
    one person households 186,745
households with persons under 18 years . 264,800
households with persons over 65 years ... 159,831

Nativity, 1990
number of persons born in state 261,998
percent of total residents 21.8%

Immigration & naturalization, 1998
immigrants admitted 6,106
persons naturalized 4,414
refugees granted resident status 263

VITAL STATISTICS & HEALTH

Births
1999
  with low birth weight 7.6%
  to teenage mothers 16.2%
  to unmarried mothers 35.7%
Birth rate, 1999 (per 1,000) 16.2
Birth rate, 2000 (per 1,000) 16.4

Abortions, 1996
total 15,000
rate (per 1,000 women age 15-44) 44.6

Deaths
1998 14,241
1999 15,082
2000 15,263
Infant deaths
1998 205
1999 199
2000 190

Average lifetime, by race, 1989-1991
total .... 74.18 years
  white .... 74.44 years
  black .... NA years

Marriages
1998 143,914
1999 159,291
2000 144,300

Divorces
1998 14,818
1999 15,026
2000 18,084

Physicians, 1999
total 3,209
rate (per 1,000 persons) 1.77

Nurses, 1999
total 11,420
rate (per 1,000 persons) 6.31

Hospitals, 1998
number 20
beds (x 1,000) 3.5
average daily census (x 1,000) 2.3
patients admitted (x1,000) 171
average cost per day to hospital, 1995 .... $1,072
average cost per stay to hospital, 1995 .... $6,014

EDUCATION

Educational attainment of all persons
  25 years and older, 1990
  less than 9th grade 47,771
  high school graduates 248,968
  bachelor's degree 79,693
  graduate or professional degree 40,947

2000
  high school graduate or more 82.8%
  college graduate or more 19.3%

Public school enrollment, Fall, 1998
total 311,061
  Kindergarten through grade 8 229,275
  grades 9 through 12 81,786

Public School Teachers, 2000
total 17,500
  elementary 10,600
  secondary 6,900
average salaries
  elementary $39,100
  secondary $39,800

State receipts & expenditures for public
  schools, 2000
revenue receipts ($mil) $2,696

State receipts & expenditures for public
  schools, 2000 (continued)
expenditures
  total ($mil) $2,514
  per capita $1,389
  per pupil $6,283

Graduating high school seniors,
  public high schools, 2000 (est.) 13,922

SAT scores, 2001
verbal 509
math 515
percent graduates taking test 33%

Institutions of higher education, 1999
total 15
  public 6
  private 9

Enrollment in institutions of higher
  education, Fall, 1998
total 83,155
full-time men 13,576
full-time women 16,211
part-time men 23,235
part-time women 30,133

Minority enrollment in institutions of higher
  education, Fall, 1997
Black, non-Hispanic 4,582
Hispanic 7,167
Asian/Pacific Islander 5,258

Earned degrees conferred, 1998
Bachelor's 3,937
First professional 48
Master's 1,301
Doctor's 91

SOCIAL INSURANCE & WELFARE PROGRAMS

Social Security beneficiaries & benefits, 2000
beneficiaries
total 287,000
  retired and dependents 212,000
  survivors 35,000
  disabled & dependents 40,000
annual benefit payments ($mil)
total $2,609
  retired and dependents $1,849
  survivors $402
  disabled & dependents $358

Nevada 4

Medicare, 2000
enrollment (x1,000) 229
payments ($mil) $1,069

Medicaid, 1998
recipients (x1,000) 128
payments ($mil) $462

Federal public aid
Temporary Assistance for Needy Families
(TANF), 2000
Recipients (x1,000) 15
Families (x1,000) 7
Supplemental Security Income
total recipients, 1999 (x1,000) 24

Food Stamp Program
participants, 2000 (x1,000) 61

HOUSING & CONSTRUCTION

Total housing units, 2000 827,457
seasonal or recreational use 16,526
occupied 751,165
owner occupied 457,247
renter occupied 293,918

New privately owned housing units uthorized, 2000
number (x1,000) 32.3
value ($mil) $3,312

New privately owned housing units
started, 2000 (est.) (x1,000) 34.5

Existing home sales, 2000 (x1,000) 56.7

GOVERNMENT & ELECTIONS

State officials, 2002
Governor (name/party/term expires)
KENNY GUINN
Republican - 2002
Lt. Governor . . . . Lorraine Hunt
Sec. of State . . . . Dean Heller
Atty. General . . . . Frankie Sue Del Papa
Chief Justice . . . . William Maupin

Governorship
minimum age 25
length of term . . . . 4 years
number of consecutive
terms permitted 2
who succeeds . . . . Lt. Governor

State legislature
name . . . . Legislature
upper chamber
name . . . . Senate
number of members 21
length of term . . . . 4 years
party in majority, 2000 . . . . Republican
lower chamber
name . . . . State Assembly
number of members 42
length of term . . . . 2 years
party in majority, 2000 . . . . Democratic

State employees March, 2000
total 25,777
March payroll $73,660,819

Local governments, 1997
total 205
county 16
municipal 19
township 0
school districts 17
special districts 153

Voting age population, November, 2000, projected
Total 1,390,000
male 705,000
female 685,000

Vote for president
2000
Gore 280,000
Bush 302,000
1996
Clinton 204,000
Dole 199,000
Perot 44,000

Federal representation, 2002 (107th Congress)
Senators (name/party/term expires)

JOHN ENSIGN
Republican - 2007
HARRY REID
Democrat - 2005

Representatives, total 2
Democrats 1
Republicans 1
other 0

Nevada 5

Women holding public office, 2001
U.S. Congress 1
statewide elected office 3
state legislature 22

Black elected officials, 1999
total 13
US and state legislatures 5
city/county/regional offices 4
judicial/law enforcement 2
education/school boards 2

Hispanic public officials, 2000
total 4
state executives & legislators 1
city/county/regional offices 2
judicial/law enforcement 1
education/school boards .... NA

GOVERNMENTAL FINANCE

State government revenues, 1999 ($per capita)
total revenue $4,185.67
total general revenue $2,770.97
intergovernmental revenue $544.01
taxes $1,895.81
current charges $183.41
miscellaneous $147.74

State government expenditures, 1999 ($per capita)
total expenditure $3,373.31
total general expenditure $2,918.23
education $1,133.81
public welfare $435.64
health $51.86
hospitals $50.63
highways $266.60
police protection $26.52
correction $121.69
natural resources $38.81
governmental administration $142.16
interest on general debt $128.76

State debt, 1999 ($per capita) $1,656.73

Federal government grants to state & local government, 2000 (x$1,000)
total $1,244,481
Dept. of Education $108,452
Environmental Protection Agency $30,605
Health Care Financing Admin. $329,001
Dept. Housing & Urban Devel $145,786
Dept. of Labor $38,650
Highway trust fund $149,191

CRIME, LAW ENFORCEMENT & COURTS

Crime, 2000 (all rates per 100,000 inhabitants)
total crimes 85,297
overall crime rate 4,268.6
property crimes 74,823
burglaries 17,526
larcenies 44,125
motor vehicle thefts 13,172
property crime rate 3,744.4
violent crimes 10,474
murders 129
forcible rapes 860
robberies 4,543
aggravated assaults 4,942
violent crime rate 524.2

Number of police agencies, 2000 34

Arrests, 2000
total 156,398
persons under 18 years of age 26,966

Prisoners under state & federal jurisdiction, 2000
total 10,012
percent change, 1999-2000 .... 5.5%
sentenced to more than one year
total 9,921
rate per 100,000 residents 518

Persons under sentence of death, 4/1/2001 92

State's highest court
name .... Supreme Court
number of members 5
length of term .... 6 years
intermediate appeals court? .... no

231

Nevada 6

LABOR & INCOME

Civilian labor force, 2000
total 986,000
  men 540,000
  women 446,000
  persons 16-19 years 54,000
  white 858,000
  black 58,000

Civilian labor force as a percent of civilian non-institutional population, 2000
total 70.0%
  men 77.2%
  women 63.0%
  persons 16-19 years ....NA%
  white 69.9%
  black 71.1%

Employment, 2000
total 946,000
  men 518,000
  women 428,000
  persons 16-19 years 47,000
  white 824,000
  black 54,000

Full-time/part-time labor force, 1998
full-time labor force 781,000
  working part-time for
    economic reasons 10,000
part-time labor force 138,000

Unemployment rate, 2000
total 4.1%
  men 4.2%
  women 3.9%
  persons 16-19 years 12.9%
  white 3.9%
  black 6.9%

Unemployed by reason for unemployment (as a percent of total unemployment), 1998
job losers or completed temp jobs 50.0%
job leavers 12.5%
reentrants 30.0%
new entrants 5.0%

Experienced civilian labor force, by occupation, 1998
executive/administrative/managerial 129,000
professional/specialty 98,000
technicians & related support 22,000

sales 119,000
administrative support/clerical 119,000
service occupations 211,000
precision production/craft/repair 108,000
machine operators/assemblers 25,000
transportation/material moving 40,000
handlers/helpers/laborers 33,000
farming/forestry/fishing ....NA

Experienced civilian labor force, by industry, 1998
construction 74,000
manufacturing 48,000
transportation/communication 45,000
wholesale/retail trade 171,000
finance/real estate/insurance 49,000
services 338,000
government 105,000
agriculture ....NA

Average annual pay, 1999 .... $31,213
change in average annual pay,
  1998-1999 .... 3.3%

Hours and earnings of production workers on manufacturing payrolls, 2000
average weekly hours 42.4
average hourly earnings $13.84
average weekly earnings $586.82

Labor union membership, 2000 150,900

Household income (in 2000 dollars)
median household income,
  three year average, 1998-2000 .... $44,755

Poverty
persons below poverty level,
  three year average, 1998-2000 .... 10.0%

Personal income ($per capita)
2000 (prelim.)
  in current dollars $30,529
  in constant (1996) dollars $28,436
1999 (preliminary)
  in current dollars $30,351
  in constant (1996) dollars $29,022

Federal income tax returns, 1999
returns filed 912,829
adjusted gross income ($1,000) $43,969,433
total income tax paid ($1,000) $7,274,065

ECONOMY, BUSINESS, INDUSTRY & AGRICULTURE

Fortune 500 companies, 2000 3

Business incorporations, 1998
total 27,571
change, 1997-1998 .... 2.1%

Business failures, 1998 677

Business firm ownership, 1997
Hispanic owned firms 6,565
Black owned firms 2,796
women owned firms 33,311
Asian & Pacific Islander owned firms 5,005
American Indian & Alaska
    native owned firms 1,231

Shopping centers, 2000 382

Gross state product, 1999 ($mil)
total $69,864
    agriculture services, forestry, fisheries $512
    mining $1,519
    construction $7,147
    manufacturing--durable goods $1,720
    manufacturing--nondurable goods $1,165
    transportation, communication &
        public utilities $5,587
    wholesale trade $3,234
    retail trade $7,266
    finance/real estate/insurance $11,803
    services $22,729
    federal, state & local government $7,182

Establishments, by major industry group, 1999
total 46,890
    forestry, fishing & agriculture 46
    mining 219
    construction 4,795
    manufacturing 1,701
    transportation & warehousing 965
    wholesale trade 2,500
    retail trade 6,793
    finance & insurance 3,495
    professional/scientific/technical 5,196
    health care/social assistance 3,933
    information 890
    accommodation/food services 3,879

Payroll, by major industry group, 1999
total ($1,000) $24,391,383
    forestry, fishing & agriculture $3,942
    mining $578,105
    construction $2,879,337
    manufacturing $1,345,766
    transportation & warehousing $766,995
    wholesale trade $1,167,604
    retail trade........................ $2,279,220
    finance & insurance $1,143,530
    professional/scientific/technical $1,609,836
    health care/social assistance $2,126,591
    information $601,763
    accommodation/food services $5,861,453

Agriculture
number of farms, 2000 3,000
farm acreage, 2000 7,000,000
acres per farm, 2000 2,267
value of farms, 1997 ($mil) $3,080
farm income, 1999 ($mil)
    net farm income $65
    debt/asset ratio 8.3%
farm marketings, 1999 ($mil)
total $334
    crops.............................. $118
    livestock $216
principal commodities, in order by marketing
receipts, 1999
    Cattle, dairy products, hay, greenhouse

Federal economic activity in state
expenditures, 2000
    total ($mil) $8,626
    per capita $4,317
    defense ($mil) $1,081
    non-defense ($mil) $7,545
defense department, 2000
    contract awards ($mil) $276
    payroll ($mil) $818
    civilian employees (x1,000) 2
    military personnel (x1,000) 7.7

Fishing, 2000
catch (thousands of pounds) .... NA
value ($1,000) .... $NA

Mining, 2000 ($mil; preliminary)
total non-fuel mineral production $32,800

Nevada 8

Construction, 1999 ($mil)
total contracts (including
   non-building) $5,626
      residential $2,988
      non-residential $1,716

Construction industries, 1997
establishments 4,212
receipts ($1,000) .... $NA
annual payroll ($1,000) $2,233,287
paid employees 68,283

Manufacturing, 1997
establishments 1,648
value of shipments ($1,000) $6,673,683
annual payroll ($1,000) $1,241,068
paid employees 39,954

Transportation industries, 1997
establishments 1,613
receipts ($1,000) $5,723,497
annual payroll ($1,000) $1,104,838
paid employees 35,946

Wholesale trade, 1997
establishments 2,627
sales($1,000) $14,067,392
annual payroll ($1,000) $1,051,407
paid employees 32,203

Retail trade, 1997
establishments 9,002
sales($1,000) $19,019,702
annual payroll ($1,000) $2,224,801
paid employees 137,171

Finance industries
establishments, 1997 5,177
receipts ($1,000), 1997 .... $NA
annual payroll ($1,000), 1997 .... $1,279,439
paid employees, 1997 40,038
commercial banks, 2000
   number 32
      assets ($bil) $37.9
      deposits ($bil) $13.3

Service industries, 1997 (non-exempt firms only)
establishments 14,130
receipts ($1,000) $25,459,043
annual payroll ($1,000) $8,534,541
paid employees 351,412

COMMUNICATION, ENERGY & TRANSPORTATION

Communication
daily newspapers, 2000 8
households with
   telephones, 1998 .... 93.1%
   computers, 2000 .... 48.8%
   internet access, 2000 .... 41.0%

Energy
consumption, 1999
total (trillion Btu) 615
per capita (million Btu) 340
by source of production (trillion Btu)
   coal 180
   natural gas 157
   petroleum 221
   nuclear electric power .... NA
   hydroelectric power 29
by end-use sector (trillion Btu)
   residential 122
   commercial 97
   industrial 198
   transportation 198
electric energy, 1999
   production (billion kWh) 26.5
   net summer capability (million kW) 5.4
gas utilities, 1999
   customers 510,000
   sales (trillion Btu) 46
nuclear plants, 1999 .... na

Transportation, 2000
public road & street mileage
total 37,854
   urban 5,533
   rural 32,321
   interstate 560
vehicle miles of travel (mil) 17,639
total motor vehicle registrations 1,219,725
   automobiles 655,592
   motorcycles 24,445
licensed drivers 1,370,643
   per 1,000 driving age population 891
deaths from motor vehicle
   accidents 323

234

STATE SUMMARY

Capital City . . . . Concord

Governor . . . . Jeanne Shaheen

Address . . . . STATE HOUSE
CONCORD, NH 03301
603 271-2121

Admitted as a state 1788

Area (square miles) 9,351

Population, 1980 920,610

Population, 1990 1,109,252

Population, 2000 1,235,786

Persons per square mile, 2000 . . . . 137.8

Largest city . . . . Manchester
population, 2000 107,000

Personal income per capita, 2000
(in current dollars) $33,332

Gross state product ($mil), 1999 . . . . $44,229

Leading industries, 1999 (by payroll)
Manufacturing
Health care/Social assistance
Retail trade

Leading agricultural commodities, 1999
Greenhouse, dairy products, apples, cattle

GEOGRAPHY & ENVIRONMENT

Area, 1990 (square miles)
total 9,351
land 8,969
water (includes territorial water) 382

Federally owned land, 2000 . . . . 13.2%

Highest point
name . . . . Mt. Washington
elevation (feet) 6,288

Lowest point
name . . . . Atlantic Ocean
elevation (feet) . . . . sea level

General coastline (miles) 13

Tidal shoreline (miles) 131

Capital city . . . . Concord
population, 2000 40,687

Largest city . . . . Manchester
population, 2000 107,000

Number of cities with over 100,000 population
1980 0
1990 0
2000 1

State parks and Recreation areas, 2000
area (acres) 74,000
number of visitors 5,127,000
revenues $12,319,000

Natl. forest system land, 1999 (acres) 827,000

National park acreage, 1984 8,600

DEMOGRAPHICS & CHARACTERISTICS OF THE POPULATION

Population
1970 737,681
1980 920,610
1990 1,109,252
2000 1,235,786
2015 (projection) 1,372,000
2025 (projection) 1,439,000

Metropolitan area population
1970 404,000
1980 511,000
2000 740,000

Non-metropolitan area population
1970 333,000
1980 410,000
2000 496,000

Change in population, 1990-2000
number 126,534
percent 11.41%

Persons per square mile, 2000 . . . . 137.8

Persons by age, 2000
under 5 years 75,685
18 and over 926,224
21 and over 875,763
65 and over 147,970
85 and over 18,231

New Hampshire 2

Persons by age, 2025 (projected)
under 5 years 86,000
5 to 17 years 229,000
65 and over 273,000

Median age, 2000 .... 37.1

Race, 2000
One race
White 1,186,851
Black or African American 9,035
American Indian and Alaska Native 2,964
Asian Indian 3,873
Chinese 4,074
Filipino 1,203
Japanese 877
Korean 1,800
Vietnamese 1,697
Native Hawaiian and other Pacific Islander . . 371
Two or more races 13,214

Race, 2025 (projected)
White 1,389,000
Black 14,000

Persons of Hispanic origin, 2000
total Hispanic or Latino 20,489
　Mexican 4,590
　Puerto Rican 6,215
　Cuban 785
　Other Hispanic or Latino 8,899

Persons of Hispanic origin, 2025 (proj.) ... 34,000

Persons by sex, 2000
male 607,687
female 628,099

Marital status, 1990
males
　15 years & older 422,521
　single 120,673
　married 260,469
　　separated 6,023
　　widowed 9,653
　　divorced 31,726
females
　15 years & older 449,800
　single 101,572
　married 261,146
　　separated 7,629

　　widowed 45,976
　　divorced 41,106

Households & families, 2000
households 474,606
persons per household 2.53
　families 323,651
　persons per family 3.03
　　married couples 262,438
　　female householder, no husband
　　　present 42,952
　　one person households 116,014
households with persons under 18 years . 168,371
households with persons over 65 years ... 101,849

Nativity, 1990
number of persons born in state 488,894
percent of total residents 44.1%

Immigration & naturalization, 1998
immigrants admitted 1,010
persons naturalized 645
refugees granted resident status 86

VITAL STATISTICS & HEALTH

Births
1999
　with low birth weight 6.2%
　to teenage mothers 11.7%
　to unmarried mothers 24.2%
Birth rate, 1999 (per 1,000) 11.7
Birth rate, 2000 (per 1,000) 12.0

Abortions, 1996
total 3,000
rate (per 1,000 women age 15-44) 12.7

Deaths
1998 8,911
1999 9,537
2000 9,703

Infant deaths
1998 63
1999 49
2000 74

Average lifetime, by race, 1989-1991
total .... 76.72 years
　white .... 76.68 years
　black .... NA years

Marriages

1998	7,345
1999	9,676
2000	11,558

Divorces

1998	7,021
1999	6,966
2000	7,106

Physicians, 1999

total	2,813
rate (per 1,000 persons)	2.34

Nurses, 1999

total	10,860
rate (per 1,000 persons)	9.04

Hospitals, 1998

number	28
beds (x 1,000)	2.8
average daily census (x 1,000)	1.8
patients admitted (x1,000)	109
average cost per day to hospital, 1995	$915
average cost per stay to hospital, 1995	$6,188

EDUCATION

Educational attainment of all persons 25 years and older, 1990

less than 9th grade	47,691
high school graduates	226,267
bachelor's degree	117,260
graduate or professional degree	56,681

2000

high school graduate or more	88.1%
college graduate or more	30.1%

Public school enrollment, Fall, 1998

total	204,713
Kindergarten through grade 8	146,722
grades 9 through 12	57,991

Public School Teachers, 2000

total	14,000
elementary	9,600
secondary	4,400
average salaries	
elementary	$37,700
secondary	$37,700

State receipts & expenditures for public schools, 2000

revenue receipts ($mil)	$1,571

State receipts & expenditures for public schools, 2000 (continued)

expenditures	
total ($mil)	$1,469
per capita	$1,223
per pupil	$6,840

Graduating high school seniors, public high schools, 2000 (est.)

	10,383

SAT scores, 2001

verbal	520
math	516
percent graduates taking test	72%

Institutions of higher education, 1999

total	27
public	9
private	18

Enrollment in institutions of higher education, Fall, 1998

total	60,784
full-time men	17,926
full-time women	21,334
part-time men	7,794
part-time women	13,730

Minority enrollment in institutions of higher education, Fall, 1997

Black, non-Hispanic	975
Hispanic	1,120
Asian/Pacific Islander	1,200

Earned degrees conferred, 1998

Bachelor's	7,600
First professional	189
Master's	2,370
Doctor's	147

SOCIAL INSURANCE & WELFARE PROGRAMS

Social Security beneficiaries & benefits, 2000

beneficiaries	
total	200,000
retired and dependents	145,000
survivors	26,000
disabled & dependents	30,000
annual benefit payments ($mil)	
total	$1,849
retired and dependents	$1,298
survivors	$306
disabled & dependents	$245

New Hampshire 4

Medicare, 2000
enrollment (x1,000) 167
payments ($mil) $629

Medicaid, 1998
recipients (x1,000) 94
payments ($mil) $606

Federal public aid
Temporary Assistance for Needy Families
(TANF), 2000
   Recipients (x1,000) 14
   Families (x1,000) 6
Supplemental Security Income
   total recipients, 1999 (x1,000) 11

Food Stamp Program
   participants, 2000 (x1,000) 36

HOUSING & CONSTRUCTION

Total housing units, 2000 547,024
   seasonal or recreational use 56,413
   occupied 474,606
     owner occupied 330,700
     renter occupied 143,906

New privately owned housing units uthorized, 2000
number (x1,000) 6.7
value ($mil) $937

New privately owned housing units
started, 2000 (est.) (x1,000) 6.0

Existing home sales, 2000 (x1,000) 43.5

GOVERNMENT & ELECTIONS

State officials, 2002
   Governor (name/party/term expires)
     JEANNE SHAHEEN
     Democrat - 2001
Lt. Governor ....(no Lieutenant Governor)
Sec. of State .... William H. Gardner
Atty. General ....Philip McLaughlin
Chief Justice .... David A. Brock

Governorship
minimum age 30
length of term .... 2 years
number of consecutive
   terms permitted .... not specified
who succeeds .... Pres. of Senate

State legislature
name .... General Court
   upper chamber
     name .... Senate
     number of members 24
     length of term .... 2 years
     party in majority, 2000 ....Democratic
   lower chamber
     name .... House of Representatives
     number of members ....·.........400
     length of term .... 2 years
     party in majority, 2000 .... Republican

State employees March, 2000
total 24,580
March payroll ....,..........$55,176,689

Local governments, 1997
total 575
   county 10
   municipal 13
   township 221
   school districts 166
   special districts 165

Voting age population, November, 2000, projected
Total 911,000
   male 443,000
   female 468,000

Vote for president
2000
   Gore 266,000
   Bush 274,000
1996
   Clinton 246,000
   Dole 196,000
   Perot 48,000

Federal representation, 2002 (107th Congress)
Senators (name/party/term expires)

     ROBERT SMITH
     Republican - 2003
     JUDD GREGG
     Republican - 2005

Representatives, total 2
   Democrats 0
   Republicans 2
   other 0

Women holding public office, 2001
U.S. Congress 0
statewide elected office 1
state legislature 124

Black elected officials, 1999
total 3
   US and state legislatures 3
   city/county/regional offices .... NA
   judicial/law enforcement .... NA
   education/school boards .... NA

Hispanic public officials, 2000
total 1
   state executives & legislators 1
   city/county/regional offices .... NA
   judicial/law enforcement .... NA
   education/school boards .... NA

GOVERNMENTAL FINANCE

State government revenues, 1999 ($per capita)
total revenue $3,350.39
  total general revenue $2,587.83
    intergovernmental revenue $926.06
    taxes $891.49
    current charges $358.92
    miscellaneous $411.36

State government expenditures, 1999 ($per capita)
total expenditure $2,992.44
  total general expenditure $2,581.51
    education $588.47
    public welfare $788.72
    health $102.35
    hospitals $34.17
    highways $288.34
    police protection $29.30
    correction $65.17
    natural resources $30.16
    governmental administration $137.48
    interest on general debt $283.10

State debt, 1999 ($per capita) $4,517.84

Federal government grants to state & local government, 2000 (x$1,000)
total $1,115,854
  Dept. of Education $92,501
  Environmental Protection Agency $38,517
  Health Care Financing Admin. $458,585
  Dept. Housing & Urban Devel. $117,859
  Dept. of Labor $18,492
  Highway trust fund $122,814

CRIME, LAW ENFORCEMENT & COURTS

Crime, 2000 (all rates per 100,000 inhabitants)
total crimes 30,068
overall crime rate 2,433.1
  property crimes 27,901
    burglaries 4,992
    larcenies 20,761
    motor vehicle thefts 2,148
  property crime rate 2,257.8
  violent crimes 2,167
    murders 22
    forcible rapes 522
    robberies 453
    aggravated assaults 1,170
  violent crime rate 175.4

Number of police agencies, 2000 98

Arrests, 2000
total 33,622
  persons under 18 years of age 6,898

Prisoners under state & federal jurisdiction, 2000
total 2,257
percent change, 1999-2000 .... 0%
  sentenced to more than one year
    total 2,257
    rate per 100,000 residents 185

Persons under sentence of death, 4/1/2001 0

State's highest court
name .... Supreme Court
number of members 5
length of term .... to age 70
intermediate appeals court? .... no

New Hampshire 6

LABOR & INCOME

Civilian labor force, 2000

total	686,000
men	362,000
women	324,000
persons 16-19 years	46,000
white	664,000
black	NA

Civilian labor force as a percent of civilian non-institutional population, 2000

total	73.0%
men	79.8%
women	66.7%
persons 16-19 years	NA%
white	72.9%
black	NA%

Employment, 2000

total	666,000
men	352,000
women	314,000
persons 16-19 years	41,000
white	646,000
black	NA

Full-time/part-time labor force, 1998

full-time labor force	NA
working part-time for economic reasons	4,000
part-time labor force	NA

Unemployment rate, 2000

total	2.8%
men	2.8%
women	2.8%
persons 16-19 years	9.6%
white	2.8%
black	NA%

Unemployed by reason for unemployment (as a percent of total unemployment), 1998

job losers or completed temp jobs	NA%
job leavers	NA%
reentrants	NA%
new entrants	NA%

Experienced civilian labor force, by occupation, 1998

executive/administrative/managerial	99,000
professional/specialty	108,000
technicians & related support	NA
sales	78,000
administrative support/clerical	88,000
service occupations	80,000
precision production/craft/repair	72,000
machine operators/assemblers	47,000
transportation/material moving	NA
handlers/helpers/laborers	NA
farming/forestry/fishing	NA

Experienced civilian labor force, by industry, 1998

construction	NA
manufacturing	133,000
transportation/communication	29,000
wholesale/retail trade	125,000
finance/real estate/insurance	36,000
services	158,000
government	82,000
agriculture	NA

Average annual pay, 1999	$32,139
change in average annual pay, 1998-1999	3.9%

Hours and earnings of production workers on manufacturing payrolls, 2000

average weekly hours	40.8
average hourly earnings	$13.41
average weekly earnings	$547.13

Labor union membership, 2000 59,800

Household income (in 2000 dollars)

median household income, three year average, 1998-2000	$48,928

Poverty

persons below poverty level, three year average, 1998-2000	7.4%

Personal income ($per capita)

2000 (prelim.)

in current dollars	$33,332
in constant (1996) dollars	$31,047

1999 (preliminary)

in current dollars	$30,905
in constant (1996) dollars	$29,552

Federal income tax returns, 1999

returns filed	611,824
adjusted gross income ($1,000)	$30,301,774
total income tax paid ($1,000)	$4,965,632

ECONOMY, BUSINESS, INDUSTRY & AGRICULTURE

Fortune 500 companies, 2000 0

Business incorporations, 1998
total 2,346
change, 1997-1998 .... -15.9%

Business failures, 1998 322

Business firm ownership, 1997
Hispanic owned firms 735
Black owned firms 326
women owned firms 27,265
Asian & Pacific Islander owned firms 1,165
American Indian & Alaska
 native owned firms 1,038

Shopping centers, 2000 229

Gross state product, 1999 ($mil)
total $44,229
 agriculture services, forestry, fisheries $320
 mining $39
 construction $1,822
 manufacturing--durable goods $7,336
 manufacturing--nondurable goods $2,457
 transportation, communication &
  public utilities $2,551
 wholesale trade $2,936
 retail trade $4,361
 finance/real estate/insurance $10,254
 services $8,689
 federal, state & local government $3,466

Establishments, by major industry group, 1999
total 37,180
 forestry, fishing & agriculture 198
 mining 43
 construction 4,023
 manufacturing 2,271
 transportation & warehousing 774
 wholesale trade 2,140
 retail trade 6,607
 finance & insurance 1,681
 professional/scientific/technical 3,794
 health care/social assistance 3,225
 information 741
 accommodation/food services 3,046

Payroll, by major industry group, 1999
total ($1,000) $16,060,229
 forestry, fishing & agriculture $26,536
 mining $23,507
 construction $922,228
 manufacturing $3,624,625
 transportation & warehousing $405,027
 wholesale trade $1,042,636
 retail trade $1,791,616
 finance & insurance $935,458
 professional/scientific/technical $995,083
 health care/social assistance $1,935,534
 information $641,926
 accommodation/food services $566,756

Agriculture
number of farms, 2000 3,000
farm acreage, 2000 .... NA
acres per farm, 2000 135
value of farms, 1997 ($mil) $1,118
farm income, 1999 ($mil)
 net farm income $25
 debt/asset ratio 10.9%
farm marketings, 1999 ($mil)
total $153
 crops $90
 livestock $63
principal commodities, in order by marketing
receipts, 1999
 Greenhouse, dairy products, apples, cattle

Federal economic activity in state
expenditures, 2000
 total ($mil) $5,802
 per capita $4,695
 defense ($mil) $689
 non-defense ($mil) $5,113
defense department, 2000
 contract awards ($mil) $398
 payroll ($mil) $262
 civilian employees (x1,000) 1
 military personnel (x1,000) 0.7

Fishing, 2000
catch (thousands of pounds) 17,160
value ($1,000) $13,951

Mining, 2000 ($mil; preliminary)
total non-fuel mineral production $359

New Hampshire 8

Construction, 1999 ($mil)
total contracts (including
  non-building) $1,666
    residential $760
    non-residential $673

Construction industries, 1997
establishments 3,612
receipts ($1,000) ....$NA
annual payroll ($1,000) ....$NA
paid employees 22,371

Manufacturing, 1997
establishments 2,522
value of shipments ($1,000) $20,196,331
annual payroll ($1,000) $3,461,347
paid employees 102,193

Transportation industries, 1997
establishments 1,388
receipts ($1,000) $3,653,649
annual payroll ($1,000) $749,385
paid employees 23,452

Wholesale trade, 1997
establishments 2,444
sales($1,000) $12,157,681
annual payroll ($1,000) $970,119
paid employees 26,379

Retail trade, 1997
establishments 8,776
sales($1,000) $16,264,348
annual payroll ($1,000) $1,687,429
paid employees 117,518

Finance industries
establishments, 1997 2,881
receipts ($1,000), 1997 ....$NA
annual payroll ($1,000), 1997 .... $1,026,219
paid employees, 1997 28,719
commercial banks, 2000
  number 16
    assets ($bil) $22.4
    deposits ($bil) $16.4

Service industries, 1997 (non-exempt firms only)
establishments 10,928
receipts ($1,000) $6,891,262
annual payroll ($1,000) $2,892,133
paid employees 109,929

COMMUNICATION, ENERGY & TRANSPORTATION

Communication
daily newspapers, 2000 12
households with
  telephones, 1998 .... 95.6%
  computers, 2000 .... 63.7%
  internet access, 2000 .... 56.0%

Energy
consumption, 1999
total (trillion Btu) 335
per capita (million Btu) 279
by source of production (trillion Btu)
  coal 35
  natural gas 21
  petroleum 188
  nuclear electric power 92
  hydroelectric power 25
by end-use sector (trillion Btu)
  residential 82
  commercial 56
  industrial 97
  transportation 101
electric energy, 1999
  production (billion kWh) 13.9
  net summer capability (million kW) 2.3
gas utilities, 1999
  customers 90,000
  sales (trillion Btu) 19
nuclear plants, 1999 1

Transportation, 2000
public road & street mileage
total 15,211
  urban 2,938
  rural 12,273
  interstate 224
vehicle miles of travel (mil) 12,021
total motor vehicle registrations 1,051,751
  automobiles 670,394
  motorcycles 48,651
licensed drivers 929,630
  per 1,000 driving age population 968
deaths from motor vehicle
  accidents 126

STATE SUMMARY

Capital City ....Trenton

Governor .... Christie Whitman

Address ....STATE HOUSE
TRENTON, NJ 08625
609 292-6000

Admitted as a state 1787

Area (square miles) 8,722

Population, 1980 7,364,823

Population, 1990 7,730,188

Population, 2000 8,414,350

Persons per square mile, 2000 .... 1,134.20

Largest city .... Newark
population, 2000 274,000

Personal income per capita, 2000
(in current dollars) $36,983

Gross state product ($mil), 1999 ...... $331,544

Leading industries, 1999 (by payroll)
Manufacturing
Professional/Scientific/Technical
Wholesale trade

Leading agricultural commodities, 1999
Greenhouse, horses/mules, dairy products,
blueberries

GEOGRAPHY & ENVIRONMENT

Area, 1990 (square miles)
total 8,722
land 7,419
water (includes territorial water) 1,303

Federally owned land, 2000 .... 2.6%

Highest point
name .... High Point
elevation (feet) 1,803

Lowest point
name ....Atlantic Ocean
elevation (feet) ....sea level

General coastline (miles) 130

Tidal shoreline (miles) 1,792

Capital city ....Trenton
population, 2000 85,403

Largest city .... Newark
population, 2000 274,000

Number of cities with over 100,000 population
1980 4
1990 4
2000 4

State parks and Recreation areas, 2000
area (acres) 345,000
number of visitors 15,073,000
revenues $7,283,000

Natl. forest system land, 1999 (acres) 0

National park acreage, 1984 34,500

DEMOGRAPHICS & CHARACTERISTICS OF THE POPULATION

Population
1970 7,171,112
1980 7,364,823
1990 7,730,188
2000 8,414,350
2015 (projection) 8,924,000
2025 (projection) 9,558,000

Metropolitan area population
1970 7,171,000
1980 7,365,000
2000 8,414,000

Non-metropolitan area population
1970 ....NA
1980 ....NA
2000 ....NA

Change in population, 1990-2000
number 684,162
percent 8.85%

Persons per square mile, 2000 .... 1,134.20

Persons by age, 2000
under 5 years 563,785
18 and over 6,326,792
21 and over 6,033,473
65 and over 1,113,136
85 and over 135,999

Persons by age, 2025 (projected)
under 5 years 630,000
5 to 17 years 1,589,000
65 and over 1,654,000

Median age, 2000 .... 36.7

Race, 2000
One race
White 6,104,705
Black or African American 1,141,821
American Indian and Alaska Native 19,492
Asian Indian 169,180
Chinese 100,355
Filipino 85,245
Japanese 14,672
Korean 65,349
Vietnamese 15,180
Native Hawaiian and other Pacific Islander 3,329
Two or more races 213,755

Race, 2025 (projected)
White 6,815,000
Black 1,721,000

Persons of Hispanic origin, 2000
total Hispanic or Latino 1,117,191
   Mexican 102,929
   Puerto Rican 366,788
   Cuban 77,337
   Other Hispanic or Latino 570,137

Persons of Hispanic origin, 2025 (proj.) . 1,861,000

Persons by sex, 2000
male 4,082,813
female 4,331,537

Marital status, 1990
males
  15 years & older 2,964,562
   single 970,980
   married 1,747,960
    separated 65,293
   widowed 86,408
   divorced 159,214
females
  15 years & older 3,258,962
   single 842,911
   married 1,760,170
    separated 94,224

   widowed 412,403
   divorced 243,478

Households & families, 2000
households 3,064,645
persons per household 2.68
  families 2,154,539
  persons per family 3.21
   married couples 1,638,322
  female householder, no husband
   present 387,012
  one person households 751,287
households with persons under 18 years 1,122,728
households with persons over 65 years ... 793,781

Nativity, 1990
number of persons born in state 4,232,369
percent of total residents 54.8%

Immigration & naturalization, 1998
immigrants admitted 35,091
persons naturalized 21,301
refugees granted resident status 826

VITAL STATISTICS & HEALTH

Births
1999
  with low birth weight 8.2%
  to teenage mothers 14.0%
  to unmarried mothers 28.5%
Birth rate, 1999 (per 1,000) 14.0
Birth rate, 2000 (per 1,000) 14.0

Abortions, 1996
total 63,000
rate (per 1,000 women age 15-44) 35.8

Deaths
1998 66,021
1999 73,981
2000 75,681

Infant deaths
1998 680
1999 720
2000 704

Average lifetime, by race, 1989-1991
total .... 75.42 years
  white .... 76.46 years
  black .... 68.47 years

Marriages

1998 48,400
1999 65,632
2000 50,360

Divorces

1998 25,295
1999 25,181
2000 25,576

Physicians, 1999

total 24,525
rate (per 1,000 persons) 3.01

Nurses, 1999

total 65,730
rate (per 1,000 persons) 8.07

Hospitals, 1998

number 83
beds (x 1,000) 26.4
average daily census (x 1,000) 18.6
patients admitted (x1,000) 1,083
average cost per day to hospital, 1995 ...... $962
average cost per stay to hospital, 1995 .... $7,007

EDUCATION

Educational attainment of all persons 25 years and older, 1990

less than 9th grade 486,210
high school graduates 1,606,555
bachelor's degree 826,887
graduate or professional degree 457,130

2000

high school graduate or more 87.3%
college graduate or more 30.1%

Public school enrollment, Fall, 1998

total 1,268,996
Kindergarten through grade 8 936,428
grades 9 through 12 332,568

Public School Teachers, 2000

total 94,400
elementary 59,400
secondary 35,000
average salaries
elementary $51,200
secondary $54,200

State receipts & expenditures for public schools, 2000

revenue receipts ($mil) $12,820

State receipts & expenditures for public schools, 2000 (continued)

expenditures
total ($mil) $12,861
per capita $1,579
per pupil $10,504

Graduating high school seniors, public high schools, 2000 (est.) 68,946

SAT scores, 2001

verbal 499
math 513
percent graduates taking test 81%

Institutions of higher education, 1999

total 58
public 33
private 25

Enrollment in institutions of higher education, Fall, 1998

total 325,898
full-time men 84,855
full-time women 98,180
part-time men 57,374
part-time women 85,489

Minority enrollment in institutions of higher education, Fall, 1997

Black, non-Hispanic 38,614
Hispanic 33,498
Asian/Pacific Islander 23,146

Earned degrees conferred, 1998

Bachelor's 25,056
First professional 1,785
Master's 8,889
Doctor's 959

SOCIAL INSURANCE & WELFARE PROGRAMS

Social Security beneficiaries & benefits, 2000

beneficiaries
total 1,352,000
retired and dependents 1,000,000
survivors 188,000
disabled & dependents 165,000
annual benefit payments ($mil)
total $13,521
retired and dependents $9,712
survivors $2,319
disabled & dependents $1,489

New Jersey 4

Medicare, 2000
enrollment (x1,000) 1,195
payments ($mil) $6,767

Medicaid, 1998
recipients (x1,000) 813
payments ($mil) $4,219

Federal public aid
Temporary Assistance for Needy Families
(TANF), 2000
  Recipients (x1,000) 131
  Families (x1,000) 52
Supplemental Security Income
  total recipients, 1999 (x1,000) 146

Food Stamp Program
participants, 2000 (x1,000) 345

HOUSING & CONSTRUCTION

Total housing units, 2000 3,310,275
  seasonal or recreational use 109,075
  occupied 3,064,645
    owner occupied 2,011,473
    renter occupied 1,053,172

New privately owned housing units uthorized, 2000
number (x1,000) 34.6
value ($mil) $3,376

New privately owned housing units
started, 2000 (est.) (x1,000) 31.2

Existing home sales, 2000 (x1,000) 134.4

GOVERNMENT & ELECTIONS

State officials, 2002
  Governor (name/party/term expires)
        JAMES MCGREEVY
        Democrat - 2005
Lt. Governor .... (no Lieutenant Governor)
Sec. of State .... DeForest Soaries
Atty. General .... John Farmer
Chief Justice .... Deborah Poritz (Actg.)

Governorship
minimum age 30
length of term .... 4 years
number of consecutive
  terms permitted 2
who succeeds .... Pres. of Senate

State legislature
name .... Legislature
  upper chamber
      name .... Senate
      number of members 40
      length of term .... 4 years
      party in majority, 2000 .... Republican
  lower chamber
      name .... General Assembly
      number of members 80
      length of term .... 2 years
      party in majority, 2000 .... Republican

State employees March, 2000
total 150,177
March payroll $528,149,790

Local governments, 1997
total 1,421
  county 21
  municipal 324
  township 243
  school districts 522
  special districts 281

Voting age population, November, 2000, projected
Total 6,245,000
  male 2,972,000
  female 3,272,000

Vote for president
2000
  Gore 1,789,000
  Bush 1,284,000
1996
  Clinton 1,652,000
  Dole 1,103,000
  Perot 262,000

Federal representation, 2002 (107th Congress)
Senators (name/party/term expires)

        JON CORZINE
        Democrat - 2007
        BOB TORRICELLI
        Democrat - 2003

Representatives, total 13
  Democrats 7
  Republicans 6
  other 0

Women holding public office, 2001
U.S. Congress 1
statewide elected office 0
state legislature 18

Black elected officials, 1999
total 239
US and state legislatures 16
city/county/regional offices 133
judicial/law enforcement 1
education/school boards 89

Hispanic public officials, 2000
total 77
state executives & legislators 6
city/county/regional offices 46
judicial/law enforcement . . . . NA
education/school boards 25

GOVERNMENTAL FINANCE

State government revenues, 1999 ($per capita)
total revenue $4,807.57
total general revenue $3,648.16
intergovernmental revenue $874.36
taxes $2,078.54
current charges $370.81
miscellaneous $324.45

State government expenditures, 1999 ($per capita)
total expenditure $3,936.73
total general expenditure $3,172.00
education $1,045.54
public welfare $655.53
health $85.82
hospitals $118.42
highways $198.04
police protection $37.06
correction $135.42
natural resources $34.96
governmental administration $141.44
interest on general debt $144.44

State debt, 1999 ($per capita) $3,430.00

Federal government grants to state & local government, 2000 (x$1,000)
total $8,212,241
Dept. of Education $634,688
Environmental Protection Agency $80,672
Health Care Financing Admin. $3,570,538
Dept. Housing & Urban Devel. $1,361,787
Dept. of Labor $152,693
Highway trust fund $588,337

CRIME, LAW ENFORCEMENT & COURTS

Crime, 2000 (all rates per 100,000 inhabitants)
total crimes 265,935
overall crime rate 3,160.5
property crimes 233,637
burglaries 43,924
larcenies 155,562
motor vehicle thefts 34,151
property crime rate 2,776.6
violent crimes 32,298
murders 289
forcible rapes 1,357
robberies 13,553
aggravated assaults 17,099
violent crime rate 383.8

Number of police agencies, 2000 541

Arrests, 2000
total 430,502
persons under 18 years of age 73,582

Prisoners under state & federal jurisdiction, 2000
total 29,784
percent change, 1999-2000 . . . . -5.4%
sentenced to more than one year
total 29,784
rate per 100,000 residents 362

Persons under sentence of death, 4/1/2001 18

State's highest court
name . . . . Supreme Court
number of members 7
length of term . . . . 7 years
intermediate appeals court? . . . . yes

New Jersey 6

LABOR & INCOME

Civilian labor force, 2000
total	4,188,000
men	2,255,000
women	1,933,000
persons 16-19 years	207,000
white	3,367,000
black	595,000

Civilian labor force as a percent of
civilian non-institutional population, 2000
total	66.6%
men	75.5%
women	58.4%
persons 16-19 years	NA%
white	66.2%
black	67.9%

Employment, 2000
total	4,030,000
men	2,176,000
women	1,854,000
persons 16-19 years	180,000
white	3,266,000
black	544,000

Full-time/part-time labor force, 1998
full-time labor force	3,453,000
working part-time for economic reasons	24,000
part-time labor force	703,000

Unemployment rate, 2000
total	3.8%
men	3.5%
women	4.0%
persons 16-19 years	12.7%
white	3.0%
black	8.6%

Unemployed by reason for unemployment
(as a percent of total unemployment), 1998
job losers or completed temp jobs	51.6%
job leavers	7.8%
reentrants	30.7%
new entrants	9.9%

Experienced civilian labor force, by occupation, 1998
executive/administrative/managerial	656,000
professional/specialty	668,000
technicians & related support	144,000
sales	530,000
administrative support/clerical	645,000
service occupations	557,000
precision production/craft/repair	376,000
machine operators/assemblers	202,000
transportation/material moving	163,000
handlers/helpers/laborers	152,000
farming/forestry/fishing	44,000

Experienced civilian labor force, by industry, 1998
construction	186,000
manufacturing	562,000
transportation/communication	289,000
wholesale/retail trade	797,000
finance/real estate/insurance	313,000
services	1,168,000
government	546,000
agriculture	39,000

Average annual pay, 1999 .... $NA
change in average annual pay,
1998-1999 .... NA%

Hours and earnings of production workers
on manufacturing payrolls, 2000
average weekly hours	41.9
average hourly earnings	$15.47
average weekly earnings	$648.19

Labor union membership, 2000 762,000

Household income (in 2000 dollars)
median household income,
three year average, 1998-2000 .... $51,032

Poverty
persons below poverty level,
three year average, 1998-2000 .... 8.1%

Personal income ($per capita)
2000 (prelim.)
in current dollars	$36,983
in constant (1996) dollars	$34,448
1999 (preliminary)
in current dollars	$36,106
in constant (1996) dollars	$34,525

Federal income tax returns, 1999
returns filed	3,987,660
adjusted gross income ($1,000)	$231,282,999
total income tax paid ($1,000)	$40,450,521

ECONOMY, BUSINESS, INDUSTRY & AGRICULTURE

Fortune 500 companies, 2000 22

Business incorporations, 1998
total 29,282
change, 1997-1998 .... -14.8%

Business failures, 1998 2,024

Business firm ownership, 1997
Hispanic owned firms 36,116
Black owned firms 26,500
women owned firms 155,345
Asian & Pacific Islander owned firms 41,432
American Indian & Alaska
native owned firms 2,375

Shopping centers, 2000 1,279

Gross state product, 1999 ($mil)
total $331,544
agriculture services, forestry, fisheries .. $1,749
mining $257
construction $12,627
manufacturing--durable goods $11,722
manufacturing--nondurable goods $27,614
transportation, communication &
public utilities $31,534
wholesale trade $30,757
retail trade $25,461
finance/real estate/insurance $78,417
services $77,836
federal, state & local government $33,570

Establishments, by major industry group, 1999
total 231,823
forestry, fishing & agriculture 210
mining 121
construction 22,767
manufacturing 11,448
transportation & warehousing 6,676
wholesale trade 17,436
retail trade 34,582
finance & insurance 12,134
professional/scientific/technical 29,419
health care/social assistance 21,874
information 3,819
accommodation/food services 16,387

Payroll, by major industry group, 1999
total ($1,000) $133,445,676
forestry, fishing & agriculture $17,566
mining $112,290
construction $6,514,547
manufacturing $16,851,056
transportation & warehousing $5,231,723
wholesale trade $13,826,891
retail trade $9,238,380
finance & insurance $12,249,298
professional/scientific/technical $13,910,472
health care/social assistance $13,565,390
information $6,847,305
accommodation/food services $4,091,136

Agriculture
number of farms, 2000 10,000
farm acreage, 2000 1,000,000
acres per farm, 2000 86
value of farms, 1997 ($mil) $6,881
farm income, 1999 ($mil)
net farm income $127
debt/asset ratio 8.6%
farm marketings, 1999 ($mil)
total $740
crops $554
livestock $187
principal commodities, in order by marketing
receipts, 1999
Greenhouse, horses/mules, dairy products,
blueberries

Federal economic activity in state
expenditures, 2000
total ($mil) $43,469
per capita $5,166
defense ($mil) $4,405
non-defense ($mil) $39,064
defense department, 2000
contract awards ($mil) $2,944
payroll ($mil) $1,518
civilian employees (x1,000) 14.2
military personnel (x1,000) 8.5

Fishing, 2000
catch (thousands of pounds) 171,804
value ($1,000) $107,163

Mining, 2000 ($mil; preliminary)
total non-fuel mineral production $286

New Jersey 8

Construction, 1999 ($mil)
total contracts (including
  non-building) $9,574
    residential $3,697
    non-residential $4,632

Construction industries, 1997
establishments 21,595
receipts ($1,000) .... $NA
annual payroll ($1,000) .... $NA
paid employees 140,900

Manufacturing, 1997
establishments 11,530
value of shipments ($1,000) $101,328,913
annual payroll ($1,000) $16,479,211
paid employees 432,049

Transportation industries, 1997
establishments 10,288
receipts ($1,000) $40,677,410
annual payroll ($1,000) $10,408,595
paid employees 250,768

Wholesale trade, 1997
establishments 19,595
sales($1,000) $233,041,288
annual payroll ($1,000) $12,558,945
paid employees 287,964

Retail trade, 1997
establishments 49,551
sales($1,000) $81,672,814
annual payroll ($1,000) $9,316,914
paid employees 585,436

Finance industries
establishments, 1997 18,869
receipts ($1,000), 1997 .... $NA
annual payroll ($1,000), 1997 .... $11,960,496
paid employees, 1997 251,453
commercial banks, 2000
  number 81
    assets ($bil) $100.8
    deposits ($bil) $80.0

Service industries, 1997 (non-exempt firms only)
establishments 75,780
receipts ($1,000) $70,211,335
annual payroll ($1,000) $26,407,488
paid employees 833,102

COMMUNICATION, ENERGY & TRANSPORTATION

Communication
daily newspapers, 2000 19
households with
  telephones, 1998 .... 95.1%
  computers, 2000 .... 54.3%
  internet access, 2000 .... 47.8%

Energy
consumption, 1999
total (trillion Btu) 2,589
per capita (million Btu) 318
by source of production (trillion Btu)
  coal 68
  natural gas 641
  petroleum 1,236
  nuclear electric power 308
  hydroelectric power 37347
by end-use sector (trillion Btu)
  residential 540
  commercial 541
  industrial 645
  transportation 863
electric energy, 1999
  production (billion kWh) 38.9
  net summer capability (million kW) 12.1
gas utilities, 1999
  customers 2,415,000
  sales (trillion Btu) 569
nuclear plants, 1999 4

Transportation, 2000
public road & street mileage
total 36,022
  urban 24,184
  rural 11,838
  interstate 420
vehicle miles of travel (mil) 67,446
total motor vehicle registrations 6,390,031
  automobiles 4,450,719
  motorcycles 111,430
licensed drivers 5,654,973
  per 1,000 driving age population 864
deaths from motor vehicle
  accidents 731

New Mexico 1

STATE SUMMARY

Capital City .... Santa Fe

Governor .... Gary Johnson

Address .... STATE CAPITOL
SANTA FE, NM 87503
505 827-3000

Admitted as a state 1912

Area (square miles) 121,598

Population, 1980 1,302,894

Population, 1990 1,515,069

Population, 2000 1,819,046

Persons per square mile, 2000 15

Largest city .... Albuquerque
population, 2000 449,000

Personal income per capita, 2000
(in current dollars) $22,203

Gross state product ($mil), 1999 .... $51,026

Leading industries, 1999 (by payroll)
Health care/Social assistance
Retail trade
Professional/Scientific/Technical

Leading agricultural commodities, 1999
Cattle, dairy products, hay, pecans

GEOGRAPHY & ENVIRONMENT

Area, 1990 (square miles)
total 121,598
land 121,365
water (includes territorial water) 234

Federally owned land, 2000 .... 34.2%

Highest point
name .... Wheeler Peak
elevation (feet) 13,161

Lowest point
name .... Red Bluff Reservoir
elevation (feet) 2,842

General coastline (miles) 0

Tidal shoreline (miles) 0

Capital city .... Santa Fe
population, 2000 62,203

Largest city .... Albuquerque
population, 2000 449,000

Number of cities with over 100,000 population
1980 1
1990 1
2000 1

State parks and Recreation areas, 2000
area (acres) 91,000
number of visitors 4,639,000
revenues $4,320,000

Natl. forest system land, 1999 (acres) ... 9,327,000

National park acreage, 1984 250,300

DEMOGRAPHICS & CHARACTERISTICS OF THE POPULATION

Population
1970 1,017,055
1980 1,302,894
1990 1,515,069
2000 1,819,046
2015 (projection) 2,300,000
2025 (projection) 2,612,000

Metropolitan area population
1970 456,000
1980 609,000
2000 1,035,000

Non-metropolitan area population
1970 562,000
1980 694,000
2000 784,000

Change in population, 1990-2000
number 303,977
percent 20.06%

Persons per square mile, 2000 15

Persons by age, 2000
under 5 years 130,628
18 and over 1,310,472
21 and over 1,227,546
65 and over 212,225
85 and over 23,306

251

New Mexico 2

Persons by age, 2025 (projected)
under 5 years 196,000
5 to 17 years 516,000
65 and over 441,000

Median age, 2000 .... 34.6

Race, 2000
One race
White 1,214,253
Black or African American 34,343
American Indian and Alaska Native 173,483
Asian Indian 3,104
Chinese 3,979
Filipino 2,888
Japanese 1,964
Korean 1,791
Vietnamese 3,274
Native Hawaiian and other Pacific Islander 1,503
Two or more races 66,327

Race, 2025 (projected)
White 2,192,000
Black 89,000

Persons of Hispanic origin, 2000
total Hispanic or Latino 765,386
Mexican 330,049
Puerto Rican 4,488
Cuban 2,588
Other Hispanic or Latino 428,261

Persons of Hispanic origin, 2025 (proj.) . 1,241,000

Persons by sex, 2000
male 894,317
female 924,729

Marital status, 1990
males
15 years & older 552,408
single 161,891
married 327,955
separated 8,651
widowed 12,842
divorced 49,720
females
15 years & older 584,092
single 131,144
married 328,570
separated 11,879

widowed 58,273
divorced 66,105

Households & families, 2000
households 677,971
persons per household 2.63
families 466,515
persons per family 3.18
married couples 341,818
female householder, no husband
present 89,622
one person households 172,181
households with persons under 18 years . 261,684
households with persons over 65 years ... 151,722

Nativity, 1990
number of persons born in state 783,311
percent of total residents 51.7%

Immigration & naturalization, 1998
immigrants admitted 2,199
persons naturalized 649
refugees granted resident status 102

VITAL STATISTICS & HEALTH
Births
1999
with low birth weight 7.7%
to teenage mothers 15.6%
to unmarried mothers 45.1%
Birth rate, 1999 (per 1,000) 15.6
Birth rate, 2000 (per 1,000) 15.6

Abortions, 1996
total 5,000
rate (per 1,000 women age 15-44) 14.4

Deaths
1998 13,410
1999 13,676
2000 13,488

Infant deaths
1998 180
1999 188
2000 193

Average lifetime, by race, 1989-1991
total .... 75.74 years
white .... 76.08 years
black .... NA years

Marriages

1998	13,379
1999	14,506
2000	14,462

Divorces

1998	8,039
1999	8,258
2000	9,203

Physicians, 1999

total	3,717
rate (per 1,000 persons)	2.14

Nurses, 1999

total	12,600
rate (per 1,000 persons)	7.24

Hospitals, 1998

number	36
beds (x 1,000)	3.5
average daily census (x 1,000)	1.9
patients admitted (x1,000)	158
average cost per day to hospital, 1995	$1,073
average cost per stay to hospital, 1995	$5,358

EDUCATION

Educational attainment of all persons 25 years and older, 1990

less than 9th grade	105,362
high school graduates	264,943
bachelor's degree	111,957
graduate or professional degree	76,379

2000

high school graduate or more	82.2%
college graduate or more	23.6%

Public school enrollment, Fall, 1998

total	328,753
Kindergarten through grade 8	232,485
grades 9 through 12	96,268

Public School Teachers, 2000

total	20,300
elementary	14,300
secondary	6,000
average salaries	
elementary	$32,300
secondary	$33,200

State receipts & expenditures for public schools, 2000

revenue receipts ($mil)	$2,190

State receipts & expenditures for public schools, 2000 (continued)

expenditures	
total ($mil)	$2,134
per capita	$1,227
per pupil	$6,513

Graduating high school seniors, public high schools, 2000 (est.) 17,254

SAT scores, 2001

verbal	551
math	542
percent graduates taking test	13%

Institutions of higher education, 1999

total	44
public	27
private	17

Enrollment in institutions of higher education, Fall, 1998

total	109,002
full-time men	25,640
full-time women	31,805
part-time men	20,007
part-time women	31,550

Minority enrollment in institutions of higher education, Fall, 1997

Black, non-Hispanic	2,822
Hispanic	36,516
Asian/Pacific Islander	1,916

Earned degrees conferred, 1998

Bachelor's	6,582
First professional	185
Master's	2,564
Doctor's	307

SOCIAL INSURANCE & WELFARE PROGRAMS

Social Security beneficiaries & benefits, 2000

beneficiaries	
total	281,000
retired and dependents	191,000
survivors	46,000
disabled & dependents	43,000
annual benefit payments ($mil)	
total	$2,303
retired and dependents	$1,508
survivors	$456
disabled & dependents	$338

New Mexico 4

Medicare, 2000
enrollment (x1,000) 229
payments ($mil) $854

Medicaid, 1998
recipients (x1,000) 329
payments ($mil) $862

Federal public aid
Temporary Assistance for Needy Families
(TANF), 2000
   Recipients (x1,000) 71
   Families (x1,000) 24
Supplemental Security Income
   total recipients, 1999 (x1,000) 46

Food Stamp Program
   participants, 2000 (x1,000) 169

HOUSING & CONSTRUCTION

Total housing units, 2000 780,579
   seasonal or recreational use 31,990
   occupied 677,971
      owner occupied 474,445
      renter occupied 203,526

New privately owned housing units uthorized, 2000
number (x1,000) 8.9
value ($mil) $1,073

New privately owned housing units
   started, 2000 (est.) (x1,000) 8.1

Existing home sales, 2000 (x1,000) 30.6

GOVERNMENT & ELECTIONS

State officials, 2002
   Governor (name/party/term expires)
      GARY JOHNSON
      Republican - 2002
Lt. Governor .... Walter Bradley
Sec. of State .... Rebecca Vigil-Giron
Atty. General .... Patricia Madrid
Chief Justice .... Patricio Serna

Governorship
minimum age 30
length of term .... 4 years
number of consecutive
   terms permitted 2
who succeeds .... Lt. Governor

State legislature
name .... Legislature
   upper chamber
      name .... Senate
      number of members 42
      length of term .... 4 years
      party in majority, 2000 .... Democratic
   lower chamber
      name .... House of Representatives
      number of members 70
      length of term .... 2 years
      party in majority, 2000 .... Democratic

State employees March, 2000
total 57,900
March payroll $131,019,668

Local governments, 1997
total 881
   county 33
   municipal 99
   township 0
   school districts 96
   special districts 653

Voting age population, November, 2000, projected
Total 1,263,000
   male 611,000
   female 652,000

Vote for president
2000
   Gore 287,000
   Bush 286,000
1996
   Clinton 273,000
   Dole 233,000
   Perot 32,000

Federal representation, 2002 (107th Congress)
Senators (name/party/term expires)

      JEFF BINGAMAN
      Democrat - 2007
      PETE V. DOMENICI
      Republican - 2003

Representatives, total 3
   Democrats 1
   Republicans 2
   other 0

Women holding public office, 2001
U.S. Congress 1
statewide elected office 3
state legislature 35

Black elected officials, 1999
total 4
US and state legislatures 1
city/county/regional offices . . . . NA
judicial/law enforcement 2
education/school boards 1

Hispanic public officials, 2000
total 618
state executives & legislators 48
city/county/regional offices 316
judicial/law enforcement 74
education/school boards 180

GOVERNMENTAL FINANCE

State government revenues, 1999 ($per capita)
total revenue $5,033.14
total general revenue $4,115.69
intergovernmental revenue $1,190.58
taxes $1,985.49
current charges $365.27
miscellaneous $574.35

State government expenditures, 1999 ($per capita)
total expenditure $4,649.50
total general expenditure $4,272.94
education $1,609.87
public welfare $769.35
health $157.87
hospitals $191.00
highways $537.71
police protection $40.28
correction $119.61
natural resources $68.54
governmental administration $171.74
interest on general debt $97.67

State debt, 1999 ($per capita) $1,815.37

Federal government grants to state & local government, 2000 (x$1,000)
total $2,773,983
Dept. of Education $381,099
Environmental Protection Agency $31,988
Health Care Financing Admin. $943,656
Dept. Housing & Urban Devel. $175,520
Dept. of Labor $46,026
Highway trust fund $262,524

CRIME, LAW ENFORCEMENT & COURTS

Crime 2000 (all rates per 100,000 inhabitants)
total crimes 100,391
overall crime rate 5,518.9
property crimes 86,605
burglaries 21,339
larcenies 57,925
motor vehicle thefts 7,341
property crime rate 4,761.0
violent crimes 13,786
murders 135
forcible rapes 922
robberies 2,499
aggravated assaults 10,230
violent crime rate 757.9

Number of police agencies, 2000 35

Arrests, 2000
total 78,113
persons under 18 years of age 10,611

Prisoners under state & federal jurisdiction, 2000
total 5,342
percent change, 1999-2000 . . . . 4.3%
sentenced to more than one year
total 4,887
rate per 100,000 residents 279

Persons under sentence of death, 4/1/2001 5

State's highest court
name . . . . Supreme Court
number of members 5
length of term . . . . 8 years
intermediate appeals court? . . . . yes

New Mexico 6

LABOR & INCOME

Civilian labor force, 2000

total 833,000
  men 435,000
  women 398,000
  persons 16-19 years 56,000
  white 721,000
  black 20,000

Civilian labor force as a percent of
civilian non-institutional population, 2000

total 63.2%
  men 69.8%
  women 57.2%
  persons 16-19 years .... NA%
  white 63.3%
  black 64.3%

Employment, 2000

total 792,000
  men 413,000
  women 380,000
  persons 16-19 years 47,000
  white 689,000
  black 19,000

Full-time/part-time labor force, 1998

full-time labor force 663,000
  working part-time for
    economic reasons 9,000
part-time labor force 168,000

Unemployment rate, 2000

total 4.9%
  men 5.2%
  women 4.5%
  persons 16-19 years 17.0%
  white 4.5%
  black 2.8%

Unemployed by reason for unemployment
(as a percent of total unemployment), 1998

job losers or completed temp jobs 45.1%
job leavers 11.8%
reentrants 35.3%
new entrants 9.8%

Experienced civilian labor force, by occupation,
1998

executive/administrative/managerial 111,000
professional/specialty 130,000
technicians & related support 30,000

sales 92,000
administrative support/clerical 103,000
service occupations 126,000
precision production/craft/repair 102,000
machine operators/assemblers 28,000
transportation/material moving 39,000
handlers/helpers/laborers 33,000
farming/forestry/fishing 31,000

Experienced civilian labor force, by industry, 1998

construction 47,000
manufacturing 53,000
transportation/communication 42,000
wholesale/retail trade 160,000
finance/real estate/insurance 36,000
services 184,000
government 169,000
agriculture 30,000

Average annual pay, 1999 .... $26,270
change in average annual pay,
  1998-1999 .... 2.2%

Hours and earnings of production workers
on manufacturing payrolls, 2000

average weekly hours 38.2
average hourly earnings $13.34
average weekly earnings $509.59

Labor union membership, 2000 56,200

Household income (in 2000 dollars)
median household income,
  three year average, 1998-2000 .... $35,254

Poverty
persons below poverty level,
  three year average, 1998-2000 .... 19.3%

Personal income ($per capita)
2000 (prelim.)
  in current dollars $22,203
  in constant (1996) dollars $20,681
1999 (preliminary)
  in current dollars $22,063
  in constant (1996) dollars $21,097

Federal income tax returns, 1999
returns filed 776,902
adjusted gross income ($1,000) $26,532,301
total income tax paid ($1,000) $3,470,985

ECONOMY, BUSINESS, INDUSTRY & AGRICULTURE

Fortune 500 companies, 2000 0

Business incorporations, 1998
total 2,763
change, 1997-1998 .... -5.3%

Business failures, 1998 585

Business firm ownership, 1997
Hispanic owned firms 28,285
Black owned firms 1,132
women owned firms 38,706
Asian & Pacific Islander owned firms 2,548
American Indian & Alaska
    native owned firms 6,838

Shopping centers, 2000 311

Gross state product, 1999 ($mil)
total $51,026
    agriculture services, forestry, fisheries .. $1,049
    mining $4,281
    construction $2,022
    manufacturing--durable goods $7,690
    manufacturing--nondurable goods $837
    transportation, communication &
        public utilities $3,753
    wholesale trade $2,146
    retail trade $4,795
    finance/real estate/insurance $6,689
    services $9,170
    federal, state & local government $8,594

Establishments, by major industry group, 1999
total 42,918
    forestry, fishing & agriculture 90
    mining 566
    construction 4,873
    manufacturing 1,577
    transportation & warehousing 1,088
    wholesale trade 2,163
    retail trade 7,359
    finance & insurance 2,722
    professional/scientific/technical 4,203
    health care/social assistance 3,697
    information 808
    accommodation/food services 3,690

Payroll, by major industry group, 1999
total ($1,000) $13,638,579
    forestry, fishing & agriculture $9,501
    mining $509,306
    construction $1,147,356
    manufacturing $1,218,316
    transportation & warehousing $365,003
    wholesale trade $683,536
    retail trade $1,673,436
    finance & insurance $743,826
    professional/scientific/technical $1,564,701
    health care/social assistance $2,047,007
    information $471,595
    accommodation/food services $698,781

Agriculture
number of farms, 2000 15,000
farm acreage, 2000 44,000,000
acres per farm, 2000 2,895
value of farms, 1997 ($mil) $12,180
farm income, 1999 ($mil)
    net farm income $640
    debt/asset ratio 12.2%
farm marketings, 1999 ($mil)
total $1,953
    crops $513
    livestock $1,441
principal commodities, in order by marketing
receipts, 1999
    Cattle, dairy products, hay, pecans

Federal economic activity in state
expenditures, 2000
    total ($mil) $14,470
    per capita $7,954
    defense ($mil) $1,714
    non-defense ($mil) $12,755
defense department, 2000
    contract awards ($mil) $654
    payroll ($mil) $1,106
    civilian employees (x1,000) 7
    military personnel (x1,000) 11

Fishing, 2000
catch (thousands of pounds) .... NA
value ($1,000) .... $NA

Mining, 2000 ($mil; preliminary)
total non fuel mineral production $812

New Mexico 8

Construction, 1999 ($mil)
total contracts (including
  non-building) $2,378
    residential $914
    non-residential $801

Construction industries, 1997
establishments 4,556
receipts ($1,000) $4,635,238
annual payroll ($1,000) $1,001,815
paid employees 38,990

Manufacturing, 1997
establishments 1,655
value of shipments ($1,000) $18,147,245
annual payroll ($1,000) $1,203,286
paid employees 42,254

Transportation industries, 1997
establishments 1,861
receipts ($1,000) $5,245,148
annual payroll ($1,000) $820,968
paid employees 26,543

Wholesale trade, 1997
establishments 2,640
sales($1,000) $8,408,873
annual payroll ($1,000) $725,940
paid employees 26,259

Retail trade, 1997
establishments 10,176
sales($1,000) $15,585,757
annual payroll ($1,000) $1,787,439
paid employees 135,164

Finance industries
establishments, 1997 4,055
receipts ($1,000), 1997 .... $NA
annual payroll ($1,000), 1997 .... $817,528
paid employees, 1997 30,150
commercial banks, 2000
  number 54
    assets ($bil) $15.4
    deposits ($bil) $11.3

Service industries, 1997 (non-exempt firms only)
establishments 12,347
receipts ($1,000) $8,626,946
annual payroll ($1,000) $3,273,538
paid employees 135,537

COMMUNICATION, ENERGY & TRANSPORTATION

Communication
daily newspapers, 2000 18
households with
  telephones, 1998 .... 87.1%
  computers, 2000 .... 47.6%
  internet access, 2000 .... 35.7%

Energy
consumption, 1999
total (trillion Btu) 635
per capita (million Btu) 365
by source of production (trillion Btu)
  coal 298
  natural gas 225
  petroleum 257
  nuclear electric power .... NA
  hydroelectric power 3
by end-use sector (trillion Btu)
  residential 93
  commercial 106
  industrial 202
  transportation 234
electric energy, 1999
  production (billion kWh) 31.7
  net summer capability (million kW) ... 5.3
gas utilities, 1999
  customers 520,000
  sales (trillion Btu) 58
nuclear plants, 1999 .... na

Transportation, 2000
public road & street mileage
total 59,927
  urban 6,110
  rural 53,817
  interstate 1,000
vehicle miles of travel (mil) 22,760
total motor vehicle registrations 1,528,510
  automobiles 729,727
  motorcycles 28,291
licensed drivers 1,239,043
  per 1,000 driving age population 904
deaths from motor vehicle
  accidents 430

STATE SUMMARY

Capital City . . . . Albany

Governor . . . . George Pataki

Address . . . . STATE CAPITOL
ALBANY, NY 12224
518 474-8390

Admitted as a state 1788

Area (square miles) 54,475

Population, 1980 17,558,072

Population, 1990 17,990,455

Population, 2000 18,976,457

Persons per square mile, 2000 . . . . 401.8

Largest city . . . . New York
  population, 2000 8,008,000

Personal income per capita, 2000
  (in current dollars) $34,547

Gross state product ($mil), 1999 . . . . . . $754,590

Leading industries, 1999 (by payroll)
Finance & Insurance
Health care/Social assistance
Professional/Scientific/Technical

Leading agricultural commodities, 1999
Dairy products, greenhouse, cattle, apples

GEOGRAPHY & ENVIRONMENT

Area, 1990 (square miles)
total 54,475
  land 47,224
  water (includes territorial water) 7,251

Federally owned land, 2000 . . . . 0.7%

Highest point
name . . . . Mt. Marcy
elevation (feet) 5,344

Lowest point
name . . . . Atlantic Ocean
elevation (feet) . . . . sea level

General coastline (miles) 127

Tidal shoreline (miles) 1,850

Capital city . . . . Albany
population, 2000 95,658

Largest city . . . . New York
population, 2000 8,008,000

Number of cities with over 100,000 population
  1980 5
  1990 5
  2000 5

State parks and Recreation areas, 2000
area (acres) 1,016,000
number of visitors 59,126,000
revenues $63,254,000

Natl. forest system land, 1999 (acres) 0

National park acreage, 1984 35,000

DEMOGRAPHICS & CHARACTERISTICS OF THE POPULATION

Population
1970 18,241,391
1980 17,558,072
1990 17,990,455
2000 18,976,457
2015 (projection) 18,916,000
2025 (projection) 19,830,000

Metropolitan area population
1970 16,647,000
1980 15,869,000
2000 17,473,000

Non-metropolitan area population
1970 1,594,000
1980 1,689,000
2000 1,503,000

Change in population, 1990-2000
number 986,002
percent 5.48%

Persons per square mile, 2000 . . . . 401.8

Persons by age, 2000
under 5 years 1,239,417
18 and over 14,286,350
21 and over 13,505,172
65 and over 2,448,352
85 and over 311,488

New York 2

Persons by age, 2025 (projected)
under 5 years 1,393,000
5 to 17 years 3,511,000
65 and over 3,263,000

Median age, 2000 .... 35.9

Race, 2000
One race
White 12,893,689
Black or African American 3,014,385
American Indian and Alaska Native 82,461
Asian Indian 251,724
Chinese 424,774
Filipino 81,681
Japanese 37,279
Korean 119,846
Vietnamese 23,818
Native Hawaiian and other Pacific Islander 8,818
Two or more races 590,182

Race, 2025 (projected)
White 13,813,000
Black 4,048,000

Persons of Hispanic origin, 2000
total Hispanic or Latino 2,867,583
  Mexican 260,889
  Puerto Rican 1,050,293
  Cuban 62,590
  Other Hispanic or Latino 1,493,811

Persons of Hispanic origin, 2025 (proj.) . 4,309,000

Persons by sex, 2000
male 9,146,748
female 9,829,709

Marital status, 1990
males
  15 years & older 6,797,219
    single 2,432,069
    married 3,804,860
      separated 187,868
    widowed 199,610
    divorced 360,680
females
  15 years & older 7,619,289
    single 2,200,191
    married 3,874,584
      separated 302,498

widowed 967,501
divorced 577,013

Households & families, 2000
households 7,056,860
persons per household 2.61
  families 4,639,387
  persons per family 3.22
    married couples 3,289,514
  female householder, no husband
    present 1,038,176
  one person households 1,982,742
households with persons under 18 years 2,466,483
households with persons over 65 years .. 1,767,452

Nativity, 1990
number of persons born in state 12,147,209
percent of total residents 67.5%

Immigration & naturalization, 1998
immigrants admitted 96,559
persons naturalized 47,456
refugees granted resident status 8,430

VITAL STATISTICS & HEALTH

Births
1999
  with low birth weight 7.8%
  to teenage mothers 14.0%
  to unmarried mothers 36.6%
Birth rate, 1999 (per 1,000) 14.0
Birth rate, 2000 (per 1,000) 14.1

Abortions, 1996
total 168,000
rate (per 1,000 women age 15-44) 41.1

Deaths
1998 153,175
1999 159,927
2000 158,137

Infant deaths
1998 1,432
1999 1,532
2000 1,668

Average lifetime, by race, 1989-1991
total .... 74.68 years
  white .... 75.61 years
  black .... 69.33 years

Marriages
1998 115,928
1999 137,153
2000 161,984

Divorces
1998 45,781
1999 61,803
2000 62,794

Physicians, 1999
total 71,840
rate (per 1,000 persons) 3.95

Nurses, 1999
total 170,930
rate (per 1,000 persons) 9.39

Hospitals, 1998
number 222
beds (x 1,000) 68.5
average daily census (x 1,000) 52.5
patients admitted (x1,000) 2,365
average cost per day to hospital, 1995 ...... $909
average cost per stay to hospital, 1995 .... $8,077

EDUCATION

*Educational attainment of all persons
25 years and older, 1990*
less than 9th grade 1,200,827
high school graduates 3,485,686
bachelor's degree 1,561,719
graduate or professional degree 1,172,110

2000
high school graduate or more 82.5%
college graduate or more 28.7%

Public school enrollment, Fall, 1998
total 2,877,143
Kindergarten through grade 8 2,028,167
grades 9 through 12 848,976

Public School Teachers, 2000
total 203,400
elementary 101,700
secondary 101,700
average salaries
elementary $49,800
secondary $51,800

*State receipts & expenditures for public
schools, 2000*
revenue receipts ($mil) $32,094

*State receipts & expenditures for public
schools, 2000 (continued)*
expenditures
total ($mil) $31,829
per capita $1,749
per pupil $10,807

*Graduating high school seniors,
public high schools, 2000 (est.)* 141,800

SAT scores, 2001
verbal 495
math 505
percent graduates taking test 77%

Institutions of higher education, 1999
total 320
public 89
private 231

*Enrollment in institutions of higher
education, Fall, 1998*
total 1,014,271
full-time men 304,488
full-time women 372,319
part-time men 127,654
part-time women 209,810

*Minority enrollment in institutions of higher
education, Fall, 1997*
Black, non-Hispanic 137,711
Hispanic 104,157
Asian/Pacific Islander 68,688

Earned degrees conferred, 1998
Bachelor's 92,489
First professional 7,491
Master's 46,211
Doctor's 4,013

SOCIAL INSURANCE & WELFARE PROGRAMS

Social Security beneficiaries & benefits, 2000
beneficiaries
total 3,006,000
retired and dependents 2,147,000
survivors 416,000
disabled & dependents 443,000
annual benefit payments ($mil)
total $28,691
retired and dependents $19,916
survivors $4,912
disabled & dependents $3,862

New York 4

Medicare, 2000
enrollment (x1,000) 2,694
payments ($mil) $18,653

Medicaid, 1998
recipients (x1,000) 3,073
payments ($mil) $24,299

Federal public aid
Temporary Assistance for Needy Families
(TANF), 2000
    Recipients (x1,000) 723
    Families (x1,000) 258
Supplemental Security Income
    total recipients, 1999 (x1,000) 609

Food Stamp Program
    participants, 2000 (x1,000) 1,439

HOUSING & CONSTRUCTION

Total housing units, 2000 7,679,307
    seasonal or recreational use 235,043
    occupied 7,056,860
        owner occupied 3,739,166
        renter occupied 3,317,694

New privately owned housing units uthorized, 2000
number (x1,000) 44.1
value ($mil) $4,992

New privately owned housing units
    started, 2000 (est.) (x1,000) 34.9

Existing home sales, 2000 (x1,000) 194.7

GOVERNMENT & ELECTIONS

State officials, 2002
    Governor (name/party/term expires)
        GEORGE PATAKI
        Republican - 2002
Lt. Governor ....Mary Donahue
Sec. of State .... Randy Daniels
Atty. General .... Eliott Spitzer
Chief Justice ....Judith Kaye

Governorship
minimum age 30
length of term .... 4 years
number of consecutive
    terms permitted .... not specified
who succeeds .... Lt. Governor

State legislature
name .... Legislature
    upper chamber
        name .... Senate
        number of members 61
        length of term .... 2 years
        party in majority, 2000 .... Republican
    lower chamber
        name .... Assembly
        number of members 150
        length of term .... 2 years
        party in majority, 2000 ....Democratic

State employees March, 2000
total 279,988
March payroll $951,088,438

Local governments, 1997
total 3,413
    county 57
    municipal 615
    township 929
    school districts 686
    special districts 1,126

Voting age population, November, 2000, projected
Total 13,805,000
    male 6,511,000
    female 7,294,000

Vote for president
2000
    Gore 4,108,000
    Bush 2,403,000
1996
    Clinton 3,756,000
    Dole 1,933,000
    Perot 503,000

Federal representation, 2002 (107th Congress)
Senators (name/party/term expires)

        HILLARY CLINTON
        Democrat - 2007
        CHARLES SCHUMER
        Democrat - 2005

Representatives, total 31
    Democrats 19
    Republicans 12
    other................................. 0

Women holding public office, 2001
U.S. Congress 7
statewide elected office 1
state legislature 46

Black elected officials, 1999
total 305
US and state legislatures 32
city/county/regional offices 73
judicial/law enforcement 75
education/school boards 125

Hispanic public officials, 2000
total 76
state executives & legislators 14
city/county/regional offices 16
judicial/law enforcement 8
education/school boards 38

GOVERNMENTAL FINANCE

State government revenues, 1999 ($per capita)
total revenue $5,618.73
total general revenue $4,398.71
intergovernmental revenue $1,729.94
taxes $2,126.81
current charges $241.30
miscellaneous $300.65

State government expenditures, 1999 ($per capita)
total expenditure $5,087.96
total general expenditure $4,326.11
education $1,030.30
public welfare $1,675.44
health $153.56
hospitals $172.77
highways $176.66
police protection $25.43
correction $129.95
natural resources $18.76
governmental administration $189.02
interest on general debt $191.27

State debt, 1999 ($per capita) $4,207.51

Federal government grants to state & local government, 2000 (≈$1,000)
total $30,037,681
Dept. of Education $1,743,521
Environmental Protection Agency . . . $345,506
Health Care Financing Admin. $15,961,598
Dept. Housing & Urban Devel. $4,048,503
Dept. of Labor $372,121
Highway trust fund $1,132,588

CRIME, LAW ENFORCEMENT & COURTS

Crime, 2000 (all rates per 100,000 inhabitants)
total crimes 588,189
overall crime rate 3,099.6
property crimes 483,078
burglaries 87,946
larcenies 340,901
motor vehicle thefts 54,231
property crime rate 2,545.7
violent crimes 105,111
murders 952
forcible rapes 3,530
robberies 40,539
aggravated assaults 60,090
violent crime rate 553.9

Number of police agencies, 2000 412

Arrests, 2000
total 308,480
persons under 18 years of age 50,003

Prisoners under state & federal jurisdiction, 2000
total 70,198
percent change, 1999-2000 . . . . -3.7%
sentenced to more than one year
total 70,198
rate per 100,000 residents 383

Persons under sentence of death, 4/1/2001 6

State's highest court
name . . . . .Court of Appeals
number of members 7
length of term . . . . 14 years
intermediate appeals court? . . . . yes

New York 6

LABOR & INCOME

Civilian labor force, 2000

total	8,941,000
men	4,727,000
women	4,214,000
persons 16-19 years	442,000
white	6,989,000
black	1,386,000

Civilian labor force as a percent of civilian non-institutional population, 2000

total	63.1%
men	71.0%
women	56.1%
persons 16-19 years	NA%
white	63.6%
black	60.5%

Employment, 2000

total	8,533,000
men	4,508,000
women	4,025,000
persons 16-19 years	383,000
white	6,715,000
black	1,276,000

Full-time/part-time labor force, 1998

full-time labor force	7,250,000
working part-time for economic reasons	55,000
part-time labor force	1,620,000

Unemployment rate, 2000

total	4.6%
men	4.6%
women	4.5%
persons 16-19 years	13.3%
white	3.9%
black	7.9%

Unemployed by reason for unemployment (as a percent of total unemployment), 1998

job losers or completed temp jobs	46.6%
job leavers	8.6%
reentrants	36.3%
new entrants	8.4%

Experienced civilian labor force, by occupation, 1998

executive/administrative/managerial	1,248,000
professional/specialty	1,410,000
technicians & related support	269,000
sales	1,092,000
administrative support/clerical	1,345,000
service occupations	1,480,000
precision production/craft/repair	806,000
machine operators/assemblers	415,000
transportation/material moving	334,000
handlers/helpers/laborers	313,000
farming/forestry/fishing	115,000

Experienced civilian labor force, by industry, 1998

construction	361,000
manufacturing	1,013,000
transportation/communication	511,000
wholesale/retail trade	1,682,000
finance/real estate/insurance	703,000
services	2,362,000
government	1,466,000
agriculture	98,000

Average annual pay, 1999	$42,133
change in average annual pay, 1998-1999	3.6%

Hours and earnings of production workers on manufacturing payrolls, 2000

average weekly hours	41.0
average hourly earnings	$14.24
average weekly earnings	$583.84

Labor union membership, 2000 1,958,000

Household income (in 2000 dollars)

median household income, three year average, 1998-2000	$41,605

Poverty

persons below poverty level, three year average, 1998-2000	14.7%

Personal income ($per capita)

2000 (prelim.)	
in current dollars	$34,547
in constant (1996) dollars	$32,179
1999 (preliminary)	
in current dollars	$33,946
in constant (1996) dollars	$32,459

Federal income tax returns, 1999

returns filed	8,417,974
adjusted gross income ($1,000)	$444,100,204
total income tax paid ($1,000)	$76,907,018

ECONOMY, BUSINESS, INDUSTRY & AGRICULTURE

Fortune 500 companies, 2000 55

Business incorporations, 1998
total 72,568
change, 1997-1998 . . . . -2.5%

Business failures, 1998 4,233

Business firm ownership, 1997
Hispanic owned firms 104,189
Black owned firms 86,469
women owned firms 394,014
Asian & Pacific Islander owned firms . . . 123,258
American Indian & Alaska
native owned firms 6,443

Shopping centers, 2000 1,800

Gross state product, 1999 ($mil)
total $754,590
agriculture services, forestry, fisheries . . $3,175
mining $545
construction $22,862
manufacturing--durable goods $38,341
manufacturing--nondurable goods $39,023
transportation, communication &
public utilities $55,123
wholesale trade $45,078
retail trade $52,556
finance/real estate/insurance $247,163
services $173,681
federal, state & local government $77,042

Establishments, by major industry group, 1999
total 485,954
forestry, fishing & agriculture 648
mining 362
construction 39,210
manufacturing 23,071
transportation & warehousing 10,710
wholesale trade 36,868
retail trade 74,912
finance & insurance 28,432
professional/scientific/technical 51,237
health care/social assistance 46,509
information 10,441
accommodation/food services 37,036

Payroll, by major industry group, 1999
total ($1,000) $294,640,576
forestry, fishing & agriculture $125,545
mining $155,439
construction $12,476,260
manufacturing $27,062,534
transportation & warehousing $6,908,103
wholesale trade $19,418,436
retail trade $16,643,704
finance & insurance $62,563,945
professional/scientific/technical $29,324,399
health care/social assistance $36,976,918
information $16,606,722
accommodation/food services $7,241,917

Agriculture
number of farms, 2000 38,000
farm acreage, 2000 8,000,000
acres per farm, 2000 203
value of farms, 1997 ($mil) $10,703
farm income, 1999 ($mil)
net farm income $587
debt/asset ratio 20.5%
farm marketings, 1999 ($mil)
total $3,097
crops $1,054
livestock $2,043
principal commodities, in order by marketing
receipts, 1999
Dairy products, greenhouse, cattle, apples

Federal economic activity in state
expenditures, 2000
total ($mil) $110,333
per capita $5,814
defense ($mil) $5,585
non-defense ($mil) $104,748
defense department, 2000
contract awards ($mil) $3,839
payroll ($mil) $1,776
civilian employees (x1,000) 11.1
military personnel (x1,000) 19.6

Fishing, 2000
catch (thousands of pounds) 41,230
value ($1,000) $59,501

Mining, 2000 ($mil; preliminary)
total non-fuel mineral production $970

Construction, 1999 ($mil)
total contracts (including
    non-building) $19,306
      residential $5,606
      non-residential $8,754

Construction industries, 1997
establishments 35,989
receipts ($1,000) $43,762,820
annual payroll ($1,000) $9,559,421
paid employees 271,483

Manufacturing, 1997
establishments 23,997
value of shipments ($1,000) $168,162,761
annual payroll ($1,000) $30,405,687
paid employees 860,233

Transportation industries, 1997
establishments 18,299
receipts ($1,000) $85,434,885
annual payroll ($1,000) $16,409,597
paid employees 403,558

Wholesale trade, 1997
establishments 41,060
sales($1,000) $328,515,445
annual payroll ($1,000) $18,292,181
paid employees 450,559

Retail trade, 1997
establishments 109,098
sales($1,000) $148,865,467
annual payroll ($1,000) $18,094,333
paid employees 1,181,372

Finance industries
establishments, 1997 54,966
receipts ($1,000), 1997 .... $NA
annual payroll ($1,000), 1997 .... $58,600,613
paid employees, 1997 771,470
commercial banks, 2000
  number 148
    assets ($bil) $1,304.3
    deposits ($bil) $790.7

Service industries, 1997 (non-exempt firms only)
establishments 145,612
receipts ($1,000) $147,920,576
annual payroll ($1,000) $52,238,947
paid employees 1,582,735

COMMUNICATION, ENERGY & TRANSPORTATION

Communication
daily newspapers, 2000 59
households with
  telephones, 1998 .... 95.1%
  computers, 2000 .... 48.7%
  internet access, 2000 .... 39.8%

Energy
consumption, 1999
total (trillion Btu) 4,283
per capita (million Btu) 235
by source of production (trillion Btu)
  coal 188
  natural gas 1,251
  petroleum 1,653
  nuclear electric power 393
  hydroelectric power 265
by end-use sector (trillion Btu)
  residential 1,092
  commercial 1,216
  industrial 995
  ' transportation 980
electric energy, 1999
  production (billion kWh) 97
  net summer capability (million kW) 17.7
gas utilities, 1999
  customers 4,357,000
  sales (trillion Btu) 653
nuclear plants, 1999 6

Transportation, 2000
public road & street mileage
total 112,783
  urban 40,993
  rural 71,790
  interstate 1,667
vehicle miles of travel (mil) 129,057
total motor vehicle registrations 10,234,531
  automobiles 7,501,343
  motorcycles 106,371
licensed drivers 10,871,344
  per 1,000 driving age population 735
deaths from motor vehicle
  accidents 1,458

North Carolina 1

STATE SUMMARY

Capital City . . . . Raleigh

Governor .Michael Easley

Address . . . . . . .STATE CAPITOL
 RALEIGH, NC 27611
 919 733-5811

Admitted as a state 1789

Area (square miles) 53,821

Population, 1980 .5,881,766

Population, 1990 .6,628,637

Population, 2000 .8,049,313

Persons per square mile, 2000 . . . . 165.2

Largest city . . . . .Charlotte
 population, 2000 541,000

Personal income per capita, 2000
 (in current dollars) $27,194

Gross state product ($mil), 1999 . . . . . . $258,592

Leading industries, 1999 (by payroll)
 Manufacturing
 Health care/Social assistance
 Retail trade

Leading agricultural commodities, 1999
 Broilers, hogs, greenhouse, tobacco

GEOGRAPHY & ENVIRONMENT

Area, 1990 (square miles)
total 53,821
 land 48,718
 water (includes territorial water) 5,103

Federally owned land, 2000 . . . . 6.3%

Highest point
name . . . . Mt. Mitchell
elevation (feet) 6,684

Lowest point
name . . . . .Atlantic Ocean
elevation (feet) .sea level

General coastline (miles) 301

Tidal shoreline (miles) 3,375

Capital city . . . . Raleigh
population, 2000 276,000

Largest city . . . . Charlotte
population, 2000 541,000

Number of cities with over 100,000 population
 1980 5
 1990 5
 2000 6

State parks and Recreation areas, 2000
area (acres) 159,000
number of visitors 12,400,000
revenues $3,500,000

Natl. forest system land, 1999 (acres) . . .1,244,000

National park acreage, 1984 377,800

DEMOGRAPHICS & CHARACTERISTICS OF THE POPULATION

Population
1970 5,088,411
1980 5,881,766
1990 6,628,637
2000 8,049,313
2015 (projection) .8,840,000
2025 (projection) .9,349,000

Metropolitan area population
1970 2,755,000
1980 3,204,000
2000 5,437,000

Non-metropolitan area population
1970 2,330,000
1980 2,678,000
2000 2,612,000

Change in population, 1990-2000
number 1,420,676
percent 21.43%

Persons per square mile, 2000 . . . . 165.2

Persons by age, 2000
under 5 years 539,509
18 and over 6,085,266
21 and over 5,733,268
65 and over 969,048
85 and over 105,461

North Carolina 2

Persons by age, 2025 (projected)
under 5 years 510,000
5 to 17 years 1,424,000
65 and over 2,004,000

Median age, 2000 .... 35.3

Race, 2000
One race
White 5,804,656
Black or African American 1,737,545
American Indian and Alaska Native 99,551
Asian Indian 26,197
Chinese 18,984
Filipino 9,592
Japanese 5,664
Korean 12,600
Vietnamese 15,596
Native Hawaiian and other Pacific Islander 3,983
Two or more races 103,260

Race, 2025 (projected)
White 6,824,000
Black 2,244,000

Persons of Hispanic origin, 2000
total Hispanic or Latino 378,963
Mexican 246,545
Puerto Rican 31,117
Cuban 7,389
Other Hispanic or Latino 93,912

Persons of Hispanic origin, 2025 (proj.) .. 210,000

Persons by sex, 2000
male 3,942,695
female 4,106,618

Marital status, 1990
males
15 years & older 2,532,813
single 726,858
married 1,581,394
separated 78,527
widowed 61,149
divorced 163,412
females
15 years & older 2,760,408
single 603,374
married 1,581,108
separated 103,674

widowed 352,110
divorced 223,816

Households & families, 2000
households 3,132,013
persons per household 2.49
families 2,158,869
persons per family 2.98
married couples 1,645,346
female householder, no husband
present 389,997
one person households 795,271
households with persons under 18 years 1,104,659
households with persons over 65 years ... 682,982

Nativity, 1990
number of persons born in state 4,668,539
percent of total residents 70.4%

Immigration & naturalization, 1998
immigrants admitted 6,415
persons naturalized 3,463
refugees granted resident status 422

VITAL STATISTICS & HEALTH

Births
1999
with low birth weight 8.9%
to teenage mothers 14.9%
to unmarried mothers 33.2%
Birth rate, 1999 (per 1,000) 14.9
Birth rate, 2000 (per 1,000) 15.5

Abortions, 1996
total 34,000
rate (per 1,000 women age 15-44) 20.2

Deaths
1998 68,111
1999 69,600
2000 71,995

Infant deaths
1998 1,049
1999 1,065
2000 1,052

Average lifetime, by race, 1989-1991
total .... 74.48 years
white .... 75.89 years
black .... 69.38 years

Marriages
1998 63,798
1999 67,496
2000 65,622

Divorces
1998 36,832
1999 36,739
2000 36,889

Physicians, 1999
total 18,166
rate (per 1,000 persons) 2.37

Nurses, 1999
total 71,550
rate (per 1,000 persons) 9.35

Hospitals, 1998
number 116
beds (x 1,000) 23.3
average daily census (x 1,000) 15.9
patients admitted (x1,000) 908
average cost per day to hospital, 1995 ...... $832
average cost per stay to hospital, 1995 .... $5,631

EDUCATION

*Educational attainment of all persons
    25 years and older, 1990*
less than 9th grade 539,974
high school graduates 1,232,868
bachelor's degree 510,003
graduate or professional degree 229,046

2000
high school graduate or more 79.2%
college graduate or more 23.2%

Public school enrollment, Fall, 1998
total 1,254,821
Kindergarten through grade 8 920,838
grades 9 through 12 333,983

Public School Teachers, 2000
total 79,800
elementary 50,200
secondary 29,600
average salaries
elementary $39,200
secondary $39,700

*State receipts & expenditures for public
    schools, 2000*
revenue receipts ($mil) $8,373

*State receipts & expenditures for public
    schools, 2000 (continued)*
expenditures
total ($mil) $8,227
per capita $1,075
per pupil $6,185

*Graduating high school seniors,
    public high schools, 2000 (est.)* 61,463

SAT scores, 2001
verbal 493
math 499
percent graduates taking test 65%

Institutions of higher education, 1999
total 120
public 73
private 47

*Enrollment in institutions of higher
    education, Fall, 1998*
total 387,407
full-time men 108,107
full-time women 137,048
part-time men 56,476
part-time women 85,776

*Minority enrollment in institutions of higher
    education, Fall, 1997*
Black, non-Hispanic 76,801
Hispanic 5,478
Asian/Pacific Islander 8,046

Earned degrees conferred, 1998
Bachelor's 34,129
First professional 1,902
Master's 8,125
Doctor's 1,083

SOCIAL INSURANCE & WELFARE PROGRAMS

Social Security beneficiaries & benefits, 2000
beneficiaries
total 1,350,000
retired and dependents 906,000
survivors 193,000
disabled & dependents 251,000
annual benefit payments ($mil)
total $11,651
retired and dependents $7,652
survivors $1,977
disabled & dependents $2,021

North Carolina 4

Medicare, 2000
enrollment (x1,000) 1,111
payments ($mil) $5,942

Medicaid, 1998
recipients (x1,000) 1,168
payments ($mil) $4,014

Federal public aid
Temporary Assistance for Needy Families
(TANF), 2000
   Recipients (x1,000) 99
   Families (x1,000) 46
Supplemental Security Income
   total recipients, 1999 (x1,000) 192

Food Stamp Program
   participants, 2000 (x1,000) 488

HOUSING & CONSTRUCTION

Total housing units, 2000 3,523,944
   seasonal or recreational use 134,870
   occupied 3,132,013
      owner occupied 2,172,355
      renter occupied 959,658

New privately owned housing units uthorized, 2000
number (x1,000) 78.4
value ($mil) $8,643

New privately owned housing units
   started, 2000 (est.) (x1,000) 74.8

Existing home sales, 2000 (x1,000) 215.5

GOVERNMENT & ELECTIONS

State officials, 2002
   Governor (name/party/term expires)
      MICHAEL EASLEY
      Democrat - 2005
Lt. Governor . . . . .Beverly Perdue
Sec. of State . . . . Elaine Marshall
Atty. General . . . . Roy Cooper
Chief Justice . . . . I. Beverly Lake, Jr.

Governorship
minimum age 30
length of term . . . . 4 years
number of consecutive
   terms permitted 2
who succeeds . . . . Lt. Governor

State legislature
name . . . . .General Assembly
   upper chamber
      name . . . . Senate
      number of members 50
      length of term . . . . .2 years
      party in majority, 2000 . . . . .Democratic
   lower chamber
      name . . . . House of Representatives
      number of members 120
      length of term . . . . .2 years
      party in majority, 2000 . . . . .Democratic

State employees March, 2000
total 141,581
March payroll $362,400,610

Local governments, 1997
total 952
   county 100
   municipal 527
   township 0
   school districts 0
   special districts 325

Voting age population, November, 2000, projected
Total 5,797,000
   male 2,762,000
   female 3,036,000

Vote for president
2000
   Gore 1,258,000
   Bush 1,631,000
1996
   Clinton 1,108,000
   Dole 1,226,000
   Perot 168,000

Federal representation, 2002 (107th Congress)
Senators (name/party/term expires)

      JESSE A. HELMS
      Republican - 2003
      JOHN EDWARDS
      Democrat - 2005

Representatives, total 12
   Democrats 5
   Republicans 7
   other 0

Women holding public office, 2001
U.S. Congress 2
statewide elected office 4
state legislature 32

Black elected officials, 1999
total 506
US and state legislatures 27
city/county/regional offices 359
judicial/law enforcement 28
education/school boards 92

Hispanic public officials, 2000
total 1
state executives & legislators 1
city/county/regional offices . . . . NA
judicial/law enforcement . . . . NA
education/school boards . . . . NA

GOVERNMENTAL FINANCE

State government revenues, 1999 ($per capita)
total revenue $4,452.34
total general revenue $3,308.42
intergovernmental revenue $995.12
taxes $1,886.90
current charges $261.62
miscellaneous $164.77

State government expenditures, 1999 ($per capita)
total expenditure $3,506.84
total general expenditure $3,216.75
education $1,383.48
public welfare $668.25
health $122.89
hospitals $117.10
highways $288.77
police protection $45.28
correction $117.69
natural resources $59.97
governmental administration $90.85
interest on general debt $57.17

State debt, 1999 ($per capita) $1,075.34

Federal government grants to state & local government, 2000 (x$1,000)
total $7,911,422
Dept. of Education $650,409
Environmental Protection Agency $74,505
Health Care Financing Admin. $3,580,885
Dept. Housing & Urban Devel. $715,819
Dept. of Labor $102,554
Highway trust fund $756,222

CRIME, LAW ENFORCEMENT & COURTS

Crime, 2000 (all rates per 100,000 inhabitants)
total crimes 395,972
overall crime rate 4,919.3
property crimes 355,921
burglaries 97,888
larcenies 232,767
motor vehicle thefts 25,266
property crime rate 4,421.8
violent crimes 40,051
murders 560
forcible rapes 2,181
robberies 12,595
aggravated assaults 24,715
violent crime rate 497.6

Number of police agencies, 2000 349

Arrests, 2000
total 453,693
persons under 18 years of age 48,857

Prisoners under state & federal jurisdiction, 2000
total 31,266
percent change, 1999-2000 . . . . 0.5%
sentenced to more than one year
total 27,043
rate per 100,000 residents 347

Persons under sentence of death, 4/1/2001 . . . 233

State's highest court
name . . . . Supreme Court
number of members 7
length of term . . . . 8 years
intermediate appeals court? . . . . yes

North Carolina 6

LABOR & INCOME

Civilian labor force, 2000
total	3,958,000
men	2,089,000
women	1,869,000
persons 16-19 years	204,000
white	2,928,000
black	891,000

Civilian labor force as a percent of civilian non-institutional population, 2000
total	68.1%
men	75.3%
women	61.6%
persons 16-19 years	NA%
white	67.6%
black	69.9%

Employment, 2000
total	3,814,000
men	2,021,000
women	1,793,000
persons 16-19 years	177,000
white	2,847,000
black	834,000

Full-time/part-time labor force, 1998
full-time labor force	3,258,000
working part-time for economic reasons	45,000
part-time labor force	536,000

Unemployment rate, 2000
total	3.6%
men	3.3%
women	4.1%
persons 16-19 years	13.3%
white	2.8%
black	6.4%

Unemployed by reason for unemployment (as a percent of total unemployment), 1998
job losers or completed temp jobs	43.5%
job leavers	17.6%
reentrants	32.8%
new entrants	6.1%

Experienced civilian labor force, by occupation, 1998
executive/administrative/managerial	484,000
professional/specialty	501,000
technicians & related support	127,000
sales	471,000
administrative support/clerical	457,000
service occupations	446,000
precision production/craft/repair	499,000
machine operators/assemblers	372,000
transportation/material moving	159,000
handlers/helpers/laborers	162,000
farming/forestry/fishing	108,000

Experienced civilian labor force, by industry, 1998
construction	201,000
manufacturing	857,000
transportation/communication	178,000
wholesale/retail trade	716,000
finance/real estate/insurance	178,000
services	784,000
government	498,000
agriculture	112,000

Average annual pay, 1999 .... $29,453
change in average annual pay, 1998-1999	4.5%

Hours and earnings of production workers on manufacturing payrolls, 2000
average weekly hours	41.4
average hourly earnings	$12.79
average weekly earnings	$529.51

Labor union membership, 2000 124,100

Household income (in 2000 dollars)
median household income, three year average, 1998-2000	$38,829

Poverty
persons below poverty level, three year average, 1998-2000	13.2%

Personal income ($per capita)
2000 (prelim.)	
in current dollars	$27,194
in constant (1996) dollars	$25,330
1999 (preliminary)	
in current dollars	$26,220
in constant (1996) dollars	$25,072

Federal income tax returns, 1999
returns filed	3,577,630
adjusted gross income ($1,000)	$146,642,891
total income tax paid ($1,000)	$20,545,430

ECONOMY, BUSINESS, INDUSTRY & AGRICULTURE

Fortune 500 companies, 2000 13

Business incorporations, 1998
total 17,762
change, 1997-1998 .... -6.9%

Business failures, 1998 846

Business firm ownership, 1997
Hispanic owned firms 7,270
Black owned firms 39,901
women owned firms 139,900
Asian & Pacific Islander owned firms 8,050
American Indian & Alaska
  native owned firms 7,148

Shopping centers, 2000 1,649

Gross state product, 1999 ($mil)
total $258,592
  agriculture services, forestry, fisheries .. $3,933
  mining $533
  construction $12,793
  manufacturing--durable goods $25,675
  manufacturing--nondurable goods $36,536
  transportation, communication &
    public utilities $18,273
  wholesale trade $15,875
  retail trade $23,022
  finance/real estate/insurance $47,441
  services $42,305
  federal, state & local government $32,207

Establishments, by major industry group, 1999
total 201,706
  forestry, fishing & agriculture 1,019
  mining 186
  construction 25,935
  manufacturing 11,137
  transportation & warehousing 5,432
  wholesale trade 12,409
  retail trade 35,684
  finance & insurance 11,301
  professional/scientific/technical 17,157
  health care/social assistance 15,877
  information 2,969
  accommodation/food services 14,924

Payroll, by major industry group, 1999
total ($1,000) $92,841,543
  forestry, fishing & agriculture $135,902
  mining $133,719
  construction $6,381,924
  manufacturing $22,753,733
  transportation & warehousing $3,105,973
  wholesale trade $6,640,454
  retail trade $8,111,320
  finance & insurance $5,722,839
  professional/scientific/technical $5,607,275
  health care/social assistance $11,091,971
  information $2,699,757
  accommodation/food services $2,889,347

Agriculture
number of farms, 2000 57,000
farm acreage, 2000 9,000,000
acres per farm, 2000 161
value of farms, 1997 ($mil) $18,450
farm income, 1999 ($mil)
  net farm income $1,966
  debt/asset ratio 15.6%
farm marketings, 1999 ($mil)
total $6,688
  crops $2,838
  livestock $3,850
principal commodities, in order by marketing
receipts, 1999
  Broilers, hogs, greenhouse, tobacco

Federal economic activity in state
expenditures, 2000
  total ($mil) $41,367
  per capita $5,139
  defense ($mil) $5,858
  non-defense ($mil) $35,508
defense department, 2000
  contract awards ($mil) $1,199
  payroll ($mil) $4,653
  civilian employees (x1,000) 15.4
  military personnel (x1,000) 90.9

Fishing, 2000
catch (thousands of pounds) 155,214
value ($1,000) $95,305

Mining, 2000 ($mil; preliminary)
total non-fuel mineral production $779

North Carolina 8

Construction, 1999 ($mil)
total contracts (including
    non-building) $17,080
       residential $9,405
       non-residential $5,656

Construction industries, 1997
establishments 23,413
receipts ($1,000) .... $NA
annual payroll ($1,000) $5,095,496
paid employees 195,189

Manufacturing, 1997
establishments 11,971
value of shipments ($1,000) $163,729,870
annual payroll ($1,000) $21,713,029
paid employees 789,476

Transportation industries, 1997
establishments 7,846
receipts ($1,000) $25,128,003
annual payroll ($1,000) $4,973,419
paid employees 147,158

Wholesale trade, 1997
establishments 14,502
sales($1,000) $103,199,221
annual payroll ($1,000) $6,122,329
paid employees 178,604

Retail trade, 1997
establishments 46,815
sales($1,000) $74,507,525
annual payroll ($1,000) $8,174,994
paid employees 628,124

Finance industries
establishments, 1997 16,843
receipts ($1,000), 1997 .... $NA
annual payroll ($1,000), 1997 .... $6,267,017
paid employees, 1997 170,949
commercial banks, 2000
    number 75
       assets ($bil) $980.7
       deposits ($bil) $645.4

Service industries, 1997 (non-exempt firms only)
establishments 52,222
receipts ($1,000) $37,729,870
annual payroll ($1,000) $14,283,142
paid employees 607,654

COMMUNICATION, ENERGY & TRANSPORTATION

Communication
daily newspapers, 2000 47
households with
    telephones, 1998 .... 93.6%
    computers, 2000 .... 45.3%
    internet access, 2000 .... 35.3%

Energy
consumption, 1999
total (trillion Btu) 2,447
per capita (million Btu) 320
by source of production (trillion Btu)
    coal 708
    natural gas 229
    petroleum 937
    nuclear electric power 399
    hydroelectric power 40
by end-use sector (trillion Btu)
    residential 563
    commercial 440
    industrial 754
    transportation 691
electric energy, 1999
    production (billion kWh) 109.9
    net summer capability (million kW) 21.2
gas utilities, 1999
    customers 920,000
    sales (trillion Btu) 152
nuclear plants, 1999 5

Transportation, 2000
public road & street mileage
total 99,813
    urban 23,628
    rural 76,185
    interstate 1,024
vehicle miles of travel (mil) 89,504
total motor vehicle registrations 6,222,503
    automobiles 3,743,066
    motorcycles 82,302
licensed drivers 5,690,494
    per 1,000 driving age population 905
deaths from motor vehicle
    accidents 1,472

STATE SUMMARY

Capital City . . . . .Bismark

Governor . . . . John Hoeven

Address . . . . STATE CAPITOL
BISMARK, ND 58505
701 328-2200

Admitted as a state 1889

Area (square miles) 70,704

Population, 1980 652,717

Population, 1990 638,800

Population, 2000 642,200

Persons per square mile, 2000 . . . . 9.3

Largest city . . . . .Fargo
population, 2000 90,599

Personal income per capita, 2000
(in current dollars) $25,068

Gross state product ($mil), 1999 . . . . $16,991

Leading industries, 1999 (by payroll)
Health care/Social assistance
Manufacturing
Retail trade

Leading agricultural commodities, 1999
Wheat, cattle, sunflower, soybeans

GEOGRAPHY & ENVIRONMENT

Area, 1990 (square miles)
total 70,704
land 68,994
water (includes territorial water) 1,710

Federally owned land, 2000 . . . . 5.2%

Highest point
name . . . . White Butte (Slope County)
elevation (feet) 3,506

Lowest point
name . . . . Red River
elevation (feet) 750

General coastline (miles) 0

Tidal shoreline (miles) 0

Capital city . . . . .Bismark
population, 2000 55,532

Largest city . . . . .Fargo
population, 2000 90,599

Number of cities with over 100,000 population
1980 0
1990 0
2000 0

State parks and Recreation areas, 2000
area (acres) 20,000
number of visitors 1,111,000
revenues $1,168,000

Natl. forest system land, 1999 (acres) . . . 1,106,000

National park acreage, 1984 71,300

DEMOGRAPHICS & CHARACTERISTICS OF THE POPULATION

Population
1970 617,792
1980 652,717
1990 638,800
2000 642,200
2015 (projection) 704,000
2025 (projection) 729,000

Metropolitan area population
1970 196,000
1980 234,000
2000 284,000

Non-metropolitan area population
1970 422,000
1980 418,000
2000 358,000

Change in population, 1990-2000
number 3,400
percent 0.53%

Persons per square mile, 2000 . . . . 9.3

Persons by age, 2000
under 5 years 39,400
18 and over 481,351
21 and over 447,103
65 and over 94,478
85 and over 14,726

Persons by age, 2025 (projected)
under 5 years 46,000
5 to 17 years 124,000
65 and over 166,000

Median age, 2000 .... 36.2

Race, 2000
One race
White 593,181
Black or African American 3,916
American Indian and Alaska Native 31,329
Asian Indian 822
Chinese 606
Filipino 643
Japanese 186
Korean 411
Vietnamese 478
Native Hawaiian and other Pacific Islander .. 230
Two or more races 7,398

Race, 2025 (projected)
White 654,000
Black 5,000

Persons of Hispanic origin, 2000
total Hispanic or Latino 7,786
  Mexican 4,295
  Puerto Rican 507
  Cuban 250
  Other Hispanic or Latino 2,734

Persons of Hispanic origin, 2025 (proj.) ... 14,000

Persons by sex, 2000
male 320,524
female 321,676

Marital status, 1990
males
  15 years & older 241,899
    single 74,201
    married 148,509
      separated 1,653
    widowed 5,663
    divorced 13,526
females
  15 years & older 248,204
    single 52,711
    married 148,021
      separated 2,116

  widowed 31,525
  divorced 15,947

Households & families, 2000
households 257,152
persons per household 2.41
  families 166,150
  persons per family 3
    married couples 137,433
    female householder, no husband
      present 20,148
    one person households 75,420
households with persons under 18 years .. 83,975
households with persons over 65 years 63,607

Nativity, 1990
number of persons born in state 467,822
percent of total residents 73.2%

Immigration & naturalization, 1998
immigrants admitted 472
persons naturalized 166
refugees granted resident status 183

VITAL STATISTICS & HEALTH

Births
1999
  with low birth weight 6.2%
  to teenage mothers 12.1%
  to unmarried mothers 27.5%
Birth rate, 1999 (per 1,000) 12.1
Birth rate, 2000 (per 1,000) 12.2

Abortions, 1996
total 1,000
rate (per 1,000 women age 15-44) 9.4

Deaths
1998 5,915
1999 6,103
2000 5,860

Infant deaths
1998 57
1999 42
2000 70

Average lifetime, by race, 1989-1991
total .... 77.62 years
  white .... 77.99 years
  black .... NA years

Marriages
1998 4,206
1999 4,277
2000 4,600

Divorces
1998 2,087
1999 2,023
2000 2,024

Physicians, 1999
total 1,420
rate (per 1,000 persons) 2.24

Nurses, 1999
total 7,460
rate (per 1,000 persons) 11.77

Hospitals, 1998
number 43
beds (x 1,000) 4.0
average daily census (x 1,000) 2.4
patients admitted (x1,000) 85
average cost per day to hospital, 1995 ...... $521
average cost per stay to hospital, 1995 .... $5,589

EDUCATION

*Educational attainment of all persons
  25 years and older, 1990*
less than 9th grade 59,354
high school graduates 111,215
bachelor's degree 53,637
graduate or professional degree 18,002

2000
high school graduate or more 85.5%
college graduate or more 22.6%

Public school enrollment, Fall, 1998
total 114,597
Kindergarten through grade 8 76,860
grades 9 through 12 37,737

Public School Teachers, 2000
total 8,000
elementary 5,100
secondary 2,900
average salaries
elementary $29,500
secondary $30,100

*State receipts & expenditures for public
  schools, 2000*
revenue receipts ($mil) $727

*State receipts & expenditures for public
  schools, 2000 (continued)*
expenditures
total ($mil) $574
per capita $905
per pupil $4,621

*Graduating high school seniors,
  public high schools, 2000 (est.)* 8,635

SAT scores, 2001
verbal 592
math 599
percent graduates taking test 4%

Institutions of higher education, 1999
total 21
public 15
private 6

*Enrollment in institutions of higher
  education, Fall, 1998*
total 39,441
full-time men 16,224
full-time women 15,496
part-time men 3,268
part-time women 4,453

*Minority enrollment in institutions of higher
  education, Fall, 1997*
Black, non-Hispanic 340
Hispanic 291
Asian/Pacific Islander 276

Earned degrees conferred, 1998
Bachelor's 4,588
First professional 178
Master's 766
Doctor's 71

SOCIAL INSURANCE &
WELFARE PROGRAMS

Social Security beneficiaries & benefits, 2000
beneficiaries
total 114,000
retired and dependents 81,000
survivors 21,000
disabled & dependents 12,000
annual benefit payments ($mil)
total $972
retired and dependents $645
survivors $232
disabled & dependents $95

North Dakota 4

Medicare, 2000
enrollment (x1,000) 103
payments ($mil) $501

Medicaid, 1998
recipients (x1,000) 62
payments ($mil) $341

Federal public aid
Temporary Assistance for Needy Families
(TANF), 2000
  Recipients (x1,000) 8
  Families (x1,000) 3
Supplemental Security Income
  total recipients, 1999 (x1,000) 8

Food Stamp Program
  participants, 2000 (x1,000) 32

HOUSING & CONSTRUCTION

Total housing units, 2000 289,677
  seasonal or recreational use 8,340
  occupied 257,152
    owner occupied 171,299
    renter occupied 85,853

New privately owned housing units uthorized, 2000
number (x1,000) 2.1
value ($mil) $190

New privately owned housing units
  started, 2000 (est.) (x1,000) 2.7

Existing home sales, 2000 (x1,000) 10.2

GOVERNMENT & ELECTIONS

State officials, 2002
  Governor (name/party/term expires)
        JOHN HOEVEN
        Republican - 2005
Lt. Governor .... Jack Dalrymple
Sec. of State .... Al Jaeger
Atty. General .... Wayne Stenehjen
Chief Justice .... Gerald VandeWalle

Governorship
minimum age 30
length of term .... 4 years
number of consecutive
  terms permitted .... not specified
who succeeds .... Lt. Governor

State legislature
name .... Legislative Assembly
  upper chamber
    name .... Senate
    number of members 49
    length of term .... 4 years
    party in majority, 2000 .... Republican
  lower chamber
    name .... House of Representatives
    number of members 98
    length of term .... 2 years
    party in majority, 2000 .... Republican

State employees March, 2000
total 20,688
March payroll $42,563,938

Local governments, 1997
total 2,758
  county 53
  municipal 363
  township 1,341
  school districts 237
  special districts 764

Voting age population, November, 2000, projected
Total 477,000
  male 235,000
  female 242,000

Vote for president
2000
  Gore 95,000
  Bush 175,000
1996
  Clinton 107,000
  Dole 125,000
  Perot 33,000

Federal representation, 2002 (107th Congress)
Senators (name/party/term expires)

        KENT CONRAD
        Democrat - 2007
        BYRON DORGAN
        Democrat - 2005

Representatives, total 1
  Democrats 1
  Republicans 0
  other 0

Women holding public office, 2001
U.S. Congress 0
statewide elected office 2
state legislature 25

Black elected officials, 1999
total . . . . NA
  US and state legislatures . . . . NA
  city/county/regional offices . . . . NA
  judicial/law enforcement . . . . NA
  education/school boards . . . . NA

Hispanic public officials, 2000
total . . . . NA
  state executives & legislators . . . . NA
  city/county/regional offices . . . . NA
  judicial/law enforcement . . . . NA
  education/school boards . . . . NA

GOVERNMENTAL FINANCE

State government revenues, 1999 ($per capita)
total revenue $4,632.71
  total general revenue $4,026.94
    intergovernmental revenue $1,378.32
    taxes $1,746.19
    current charges $643.79
    miscellaneous $258.65

State government expenditures, 1999 ($per capita)
total expenditure $4,220.71
  total general expenditure $3,880.92
    education $1,361.89
    public welfare $929.82
    health $73.11
    hospitals $0.00
    highways $483.37
    police protection $20.70
    correction $61.30
    natural resources $130.35
    governmental administration $132.21
    interest on general debt $108.44

State debt, 1999 ($per capita) $2,097.95

Federal government grants to state & local government, 2000 (x$1,000)
total $1,154,518
  Dept of Education $116,889
  Environmental Protection Agency $17,439
  Health Care Financing Admin. $320,334
  Dept Housing & Urban Devel. $128,609
  Dept of Labor $30,265
  Highway trust fund $187,421

CRIME, LAW ENFORCEMENT & COURTS

Crime, 2000 (all rates per 100,000 inhabitants)
total crimes 14,694
overall crime rate 2,288.1
  property crimes 14,171
    burglaries 2,093
    larcenies 11,092
    motor vehicle thefts 986
  property crime rate 2,206.6
  violent crimes 523
    murders 4
    forcible rapes 169
    robberies 56
    aggravated assaults 294
  violent crime rate 81.4

Number of police agencies, 2000 61

Arrests, 2000
total 26,869
  persons under 18 years of age 8,085

Prisoners under state & federal jurisdiction, 2000
total 1,076
percent change, 1999-2000 . . . . 14.1%
  sentenced to more than one year
    total 994
    rate per 100,000 residents 158

Persons under sentence of death, 4/1/2001 . . . NA

State's highest court
name . . . . Supreme Court
number of members 5
length of term . . . . 10 years
intermediate appeals court? . . . . no

North Dakota 6

LABOR & INCOME

Civilian labor force, 2000
total 339,000
  men 174,000
  women 164,000
  persons 16-19 years 25,000
  white 322,000
  black .... NA

Civilian labor force as a percent of
civilian non-institutional population, 2000
total 71.0%
  men 75.3%
  women 67.0%
  persons 16-19 years ....NA%
  white 71.7%
  black .... NA%

Employment, 2000
total 329,000
  men 168,000
  women 161,000
  persons 16-19 years 23,000
  white 314,000
  black .... NA

Full-time/part-time labor force, 1998
full-time labor force 274,000
  working part-time for
    economic reasons 5,000
part-time labor force 73,000

Unemployment rate, 2000
total 3.0%
  men 3.6%
  women 2.4%
  persons 16-19 years 8.5%
  white 2.5%
  black .... NA%

Unemployed by reason for unemployment
(as a percent of total unemployment), 1998
job losers or completed temp jobs 36.4%
job leavers 9.1%
reentrants 36.4%
new entrants 9.1%

Experienced civilian labor force, by occupation,
1998
executive/administrative/managerial 39,000
professional/specialty 42,000
technicians & related support ....NA

sales 42,000
administrative support/clerical 44,000
service occupations 54,000
precision production/craft/repair 33,000
machine operators/assemblers 13,000
transportation/material moving 16,000
handlers/helpers/laborers 12,000
farming/forestry/fishing 41,000

Experienced civilian labor force, by industry, 1998
construction 16,000
manufacturing 25,000
transportation/communication 17,000
wholesale/retail trade 73,000
finance/real estate/insurance 14,000
services 78,000
government 57,000
agriculture 40,000

Average annual pay, 1999 .... $23,753
change in average annual pay,
  1998-1999 .... 3.3%

Hours and earnings of production workers
on manufacturing payrolls, 2000
average weekly hours 40.2
average hourly earnings $12.66
average weekly earnings $506.93

Labor union membership, 2000 17,600

Household income (in 2000 dollars)
median household income,
  three year average, 1998-2000 .... $35,349

Poverty
persons below poverty level,
  three year average, 1998-2000 .... 12.7%

Personal income ($per capita)
2000 (prelim.)
  in current dollars $25,068
  in constant (1996) dollars $23,349
1999 (preliminary)
  in current dollars $23,518
  in constant (1996) dollars $22,488

Federal income tax returns, 1999
returns filed 301,559
adjusted gross income ($1,000) $10,111,796
total income tax paid ($1,000) $1,350,378

ECONOMY, BUSINESS, INDUSTRY & AGRICULTURE

Fortune 500 companies, 2000 0

Business incorporations, 1998
total 762
change, 1997-1998 .... -18.3%

Business failures, 1998 144

Business firm ownership, 1997
Hispanic owned firms 444
Black owned firms 99
women owned firms 12,417
Asian & Pacific Islander owned firms 279
American Indian & Alaska
  native owned firms 752

Shopping centers, 2000 87

Gross state product, 1999 ($mil)
total $16,991
  agriculture services, forestry, fisheries $701
  mining $611
  construction $931
  manufacturing--durable goods $931
  manufacturing--nondurable goods $596
  transportation, communication &
    public utilities $1,753
  wholesale trade $1,573
  retail trade $1,747
  finance/real estate/insurance $2,404
  services $3,290
  federal, state & local government $2,455

Establishments, by major industry group, 1999
total 20,380
  forestry, fishing & agriculture 143
  mining 196
  construction 2,045
  manufacturing 717
  transportation & warehousing 959
  wholesale trade 1,568
  retail trade 3,499
  finance & insurance 1,413
  professional/scientific/technical 1,252
  health care/social assistance 1,506
  information 366
  accommodation/food services 1,772

Payroll, by major industry group, 1999
total ($1,000) $5,789,027
  forestry, fishing & agriculture .... $NA
  mining $177,941
  construction $498,380
  manufacturing $685,744
  transportation & warehousing $206,311
  wholesale trade $502,408
  retail trade $684,909
  finance & insurance $409,695
  professional/scientific/technical $244,306
  health care/social assistance $1,122,334
  information $235,856
  accommodation/food services $214,947

Agriculture
number of farms, 2000 30,000
farm acreage, 2000 39,000,000
acres per farm, 2000 1,300
value of farms, 1997 ($mil) $16,482
farm income, 1999 ($mil)
  net farm income $452
  debt/asset ratio 17.9%
farm marketings, 1999 ($mil)
total $2,759
  crops $2,112
  livestock $647
principal commodities, in order by marketing
receipts, 1999
  Wheat, cattle, sunflower, soybeans

Federal economic activity in state
expenditures, 2000
  total ($mil) $5,245
  per capita $8,166
  defense ($mil) $506
  non-defense ($mil) $4,738
defense department, 2000
  contract awards ($mil) $134
  payroll ($mil) $405
  civilian employees (x1,000) 3.3
  military personnel (x1,000) 7.2

Fishing, 2000
catch (thousands of pounds) .... NA
value ($1,000) .... $NA

Mining, 2000 ($mil; preliminary)
total non-fuel mineral production $42

Construction, 1999 ($mil)
total contracts (including
  non-building) $1,391
    residential $252
    non-residential $319

Construction industries, 1997
establishments 2,008
receipts ($1,000) $1,822,852
annual payroll ($1,000) .... $NA
paid employees 15,693

Manufacturing, 1997
establishments 742
value of shipments ($1,000) $5,196,919
annual payroll ($1,000) $627,982
paid employees 23,218

Transportation industries, 1997
establishments 1,431
receipts ($1,000) $2,700,295
annual payroll ($1,000) $467,406
paid employees 16,236

Wholesale trade, 1997
establishments 1,963
sales($1,000) $9,490,288
annual payroll ($1,000) $539,816
paid employees 20,321

Retail trade, 1997
establishments 4,810
sales($1,000) $6,382,015
annual payroll ($1,000) $682,581
paid employees 59,130

Finance industries
establishments, 1997 1,991
receipts ($1,000), 1997 .... $NA
annual payroll ($1,000), 1997 .... $371,627
paid employees, 1997 14,314
commercial banks, 2000
  number 110
    assets ($bil) $17.6
    deposits ($bil) $13.3

Service industries, 1997 (non-exempt firms only)
establishments 4,560
receipts ($1,000) $2,543,573
annual payroll ($1,000) $943,973
paid employees 46,358

COMMUNICATION, ENERGY & TRANSPORTATION

Communication
daily newspapers, 2000 10
households with
  telephones, 1998 .... 97.5%
  computers, 2000 .... 47.5%
  internet access, 2000 .... 37.7%

Energy
consumption, 1999
total (trillion Btu) 366
per capita (million Btu) 577
by source of production (trillion Btu)
  coal 412
  natural gas 59
  petroleum 123
  nuclear electric power .... NA
  hydroelectric power 28
by end-use sector (trillion Btu)
  residential 54
  commercial 43
  industrial 186
  transportation 82
electric energy, 1999
  production (billion kWh) 31.3
  net summer capability (million kW) 4.7
gas utilities, 1999
  customers 117,000
  sales (trillion Btu) 23
nuclear plants, 1999 .... na

Transportation, 2000
public road & street mileage
total 86,609
  urban 1,834
  rural 84,775
  interstate 572
vehicle miles of travel (mil) 7,217
total motor vehicle registrations 693,860
  automobiles 339,237
  motorcycles 17,003
licensed drivers 458,944
  per 1,000 driving age population 914
deaths from motor vehicle
  accidents 86

STATE SUMMARY

Capital City .... Columbus

Governor .... Bob Taft

Address ....STATE HOUSE
COLUMBUS, OH 43215
614 466-2000

Admitted as a state 1803

Area (square miles) 44,828

Population, 1980 10,797,630

Population, 1990 10,847,115

Population, 2000 11,353,140

Persons per square mile, 2000 .... 277.2

Largest city .... Columbus
population, 2000 711,000

Personal income per capita, 2000
(in current dollars) $28,400

Gross state product ($mil), 1999 ...... $361,981

Leading industries, 1999 (by payroll)
Manufacturing
Health care/Social assistance
Retail trade

Leading agricultural commodities, 1999
Soybeans, corn, dairy products, greenhouse

GEOGRAPHY & ENVIRONMENT

Area, 1990 (square miles)
total 44,828
land 40,953
water (includes territorial water) 3,875

Federally owned land, 2000 .... 1.7%

Highest point
name ....Campbell Hill
elevation (feet) 1,549

Lowest point
name .... Ohio River
elevation (feet) 455

General coastline (miles) 0

Tidal shoreline (miles) 0

Capital city .... Columbus
population, 2000 711,000

Largest city .... Columbus
population, 2000 711,000

Number of cities with over 100,000 population
1980 7
1990 6
2000 6

State parks and Recreation areas, 2000
area (acres) 205,000
number of visitors 55,340,000
revenues $26,467,000

Natl. forest system land, 1999 (acres) 229,000

National park acreage, 1984 14,600

DEMOGRAPHICS & CHARACTERISTICS OF THE POPULATION

Population
1970 10,657,423
1980 10,797,630
1990 10,847,115
2000 11,353,140
2015 (projection) 11,588,000
2025 (projection) 11,744,000

Metropolitan area population
1970 8,565,000
1980 8,521,000
2000 9,214,000

Non-metropolitan area population
1970 2,092,000
1980 2,277,000
2000 2,139,000

Change in population, 1990-2000
number 506,025
percent 4.67%

Persons per square mile, 2000 .... 277.2

Persons by age, 2000
under 5 years 754,930
18 and over 8,464,801
21 and over 7,977,101
65 and over 1,507,757
85 and over 176,796

Persons by age, 2025 (projected)
under 5 years 726,000
5 to 17 years 1,960,000
65 and over 2,305,000

Median age, 2000 .... 36.2

Race, 2000
One race
White 9,645,453
Black or African American 1,301,307
American Indian and Alaska Native 24,486
Asian Indian 38,752
Chinese 30,425
Filipino 12,393
Japanese 10,732
Korean 13,376
Vietnamese 9,812
Native Hawaiian and other Pacific Islander 2,749
Two or more races 157,885

Race, 2025 (projected)
White 9,805,000
Black 1,600,000

Persons of Hispanic origin, 2000
total Hispanic or Latino 217,123
  Mexican 90,663
  Puerto Rican 66,269

  Cuban 5,152
  Other Hispanic or Latino 55,039

Persons of Hispanic origin, 2025 (proj.) .. 319,000

Persons by sex, 2000
male 5,512,262
female 5,840,878

Marital status, 1990
males
  15 years & older 4,024,476
    single 1,156,250
    married 2,436,833
      separated 58,248
    widowed 109,520
    divorced 321,873
females
  15 years & older 4,475,533
    single 1,013,457
    married 2,452,698
      separated 82,065

widowed 556,165
divorced 453,213

Households & families, 2000
households 4,445,773
persons per household 2.49
  families 2,993,023
  persons per family 3.04
    married couples 2,285,798
    female householder, no husband
      present 536,878
    one person households 1,215,614
households with persons under 18 years 1,534,008
households with persons over 65 years . . 1,058,224

Nativity, 1990
number of persons born in state 8,038,140
percent of total residents 74.1%

Immigration & naturalization, 1998
immigrants admitted 7,697
persons naturalized 5,859
refugees granted resident status 664

VITAL STATISTICS & HEALTH
Births
1999
  with low birth weight 7.9%
  to teenage mothers 13.6%
  to unmarried mothers 34.1%
Birth rate, 1999 (per 1,000) 13.6
Birth rate, 2000 (per 1,000) .... NA

Abortions, 1996
total 43,000
rate (per 1,000 women age 15-44) 17.0

Deaths
1998 105,709
1999 108,517
2000 .... NA

Infant deaths
1998 1,146
1999 1,330
2000 1,265

Average lifetime, by race; 1989-1991
total .... 75.32 years
  white .... 75.93 years
  black .... 70.15 years

Marriages
1998 85,607
1999 88,638
2000 88,490

Divorces
1998 46,042
1999 45,695
2000 49,272

Physicians, 1999
total 26,731
rate (per 1,000 persons) 2.37

Nurses, 1999
total 103,980
rate (per 1,000 persons) 9.24

Hospitals, 1998
number 172
beds (x 1,000) 35.2
average daily census (x 1,000) 20.0
patients admitted (x1,000) 1,355
average cost per day to hospital, 1995 .... $1,061
average cost per stay to hospital, 1995 .... $6,141

EDUCATION

*Educational attainment of all persons
25 years and older, 1990*
less than 9th grade 546,954
high school graduates 2,515,987
bachelor's degree 767,845
graduate or professional degree 407,491

2000
high school graduate or more 87.0%
college graduate or more 24.6%

Public school enrollment, Fall, 1998
total 1,842,559
Kindergarten through grade 8 1,301,438
grades 9 through 12 541,121

Public School Teachers, 2000
total 114,000
elementary 76,800
secondary 37,200
average salaries
elementary $41,100
secondary $42,100

*State receipts & expenditures for public
schools, 2000*
revenue receipts ($mil) $16,600

*State receipts & expenditures for public
schools, 2000 (continued)*
expenditures
total ($mil) $14,420
per capita $1,281
per pupil $7,152

*Graduating high school seniors,
public high schools, 2000 (est.)* 115,000

SAT scores, 2001
verbal 534
math 539
percent graduates taking test 26%

Institutions of higher education, 1999
total 173
public 63
private 110

*Enrollment in institutions of higher
education, Fall, 1998*
total 542,201
full-time men 158,822
full-time women 186,630
part-time men 79,774
part-time women 116,975

*Minority enrollment in institutions of higher
education, Fall, 1997*
Black, non-Hispanic 51,838
Hispanic 8,201
Asian/Pacific Islander 11,181

Earned degrees conferred, 1998
Bachelor's 49,080
First professional 3,301
Master's 17,013
Doctor's 2,223

SOCIAL INSURANCE &
WELFARE PROGRAMS

Social Security beneficiaries & benefits, 2000
beneficiaries
total 1,918,000
retired and dependents 1,334,000
survivors 327,000
disabled & dependents 257,000
annual benefit payments ($mil)
total $17,724
retired and dependents $11,698
survivors $3,877
disabled & dependents $2,149

Ohio 4

Medicare, 2000
enrollment (x1,000) 1,692
payments ($mil) $9,310

Medicaid, 1998
recipients (x1,000) 1,291
payments ($mil) $6,121

Federal public aid
Temporary Assistance for Needy Families
(TANF), 2000
Recipients (x1,000) 252
Families (x1,000) 100
Supplemental Security Income
total recipients, 1999 (x1,000) 243

Food Stamp Program
participants, 2000 (x1,000) 610

HOUSING & CONSTRUCTION

Total housing units, 2000 4,783,051
seasonal or recreational use 47,239
occupied 4,445,773
owner occupied 3,072,522
renter occupied 1,373,251

New privately owned housing units uthorized, 2000
number (x1,000) 49.7
value ($mil) $6,154

New privately owned housing units
started, 2000 (est.) (x1,000) 45.3

Existing home sales, 2000 (x1,000) 187.9

GOVERNMENT & ELECTIONS

State officials, 2002
Governor (name/party/term expires)
BOB TAFT
Republican - 2002
Lt. Governor ....Maureen O'Conner
Sec. of State .... Kenneth Blackwell
Atty. General .... Betty Dee Montgomery
Chief Justice ....Thomas Moyer

Governorship
minimum age ....not specified
length of term .... 4 years
number of consecutive
terms permitted 2
who succeeds .... Lt. Governor

State legislature
name ....General Assembly
upper chamber
name .... Senate
number of members 33
length of term .... 4 years
party in majority, 2000 .... Republican
lower chamber
name .... House of Representatives
number of members 99
length of term .... 2 years
party in majority, 2000 .... Republican

State employees March, 2000
total 173,716
March payroll $434,583,071

Local governments, 1997
total 3,597
county 88
municipal 941
township 1,310
school districts 666
special districts 592

Voting age population, November, 2000, projected
Total 8,433,000
male 3,997,000
female 4,436,000

Vote for president
2000
Gore 2,184,000
Bush 2,350,000
1996
Clinton 2,148,000
Dole 1,860,000
Perot 483,000

Federal representation, 2002 (107th Congress)
Senators (name/party/term expires)

MIKE DEWINE
Republican - 2007
GEORGE VOINOVITCH
Republican - 2005

Representatives, total 19
Democrats 8
Republicans 11
other 0

Women holding public office, 2001
U.S. Congress 3
statewide elected office 2
state legislature 29

Black elected officials, 1999
total 284
US and state legislatures 18
city/county/regional offices 199
judicial/law enforcement 25
education/school boards 42

Hispanic public officials, 2000
total 7
state executives & legislators . . . . NA
city/county/regional offices 5
judicial/law enforcement 2
education/school boards . . . . NA

GOVERNMENTAL FINANCE

State government revenues, 1999 ($per capita)
total revenue $4,554.92
total general revenue $2,949.98
intergovernmental revenue $826.96
taxes $1,614.93
current charges $298.79
miscellaneous $209.30

State government expenditures, 1999 ($per capita)
total expenditure $3,652.36
total general expenditure $2,956.90
education $1,094.86
public welfare $737.46
health $135.95
hospitals $92.74
highways $245.94
police protection $20.10
correction $128.03
natural resources $29.46
governmental administration $94.92
interest on general debt $75.92

State debt, 1999 ($per capita) $1,329.26

Federal government grants to state & local
government, 2000 (x$1,000)
total $10,559,814
Dept. of Education $910,510
Environmental Protection Agency . . . $141,955
Health Care Financing Admin. $4,704,199
Dept. Housing & Urban Devel. $1,324,454
Dept. of Labor $175,408
Highway trust fund $742,635

CRIME, LAW ENFORCEMENT & COURTS

Crime, 2000 (all rates per 100,000 inhabitants)
total crimes 458,874
overall crime rate 4,041.8
property crimes 420,939
burglaries 88,636
larcenies 293,277
motor vehicle thefts 39,026
property crime rate 3,707.7
violent crimes 37,935
murders 418
forcible rapes 4,271
robberies 15,610
aggravated assaults 17,636
violent crime rate 334.1

Number of police agencies, 2000 271

Arrests, 2000
total 301,000
persons under 18 years of age 56,887

Prisoners under state & federal jurisdiction, 2000
total 45,833
percent change, 1999-2000 . . . . -2.2%
sentenced to more than one year
total 45,833
rate per 100,000 residents 406

Persons under sentence of death, 4/1/2001 . . . 202

State's highest court
name . . . . Supreme Court
number of members 7
length of term . . . . 6 years
intermediate appeals court? . . . . yes

Ohio 6

LABOR & INCOME

Civilian labor force, 2000

total	5,783,000
men	3,029,000
women	2,754,000
persons 16-19 years	410,000
white	5,065,000
black	624,000

Civilian labor force as a percent of
civilian non-institutional population, 2000

total	67.1%
men	73.9%
women	60.9%
persons 16-19 years	NA%
white	67.3%
black	65.0%

Employment, 2000

total	5,546,000
men	2,909,000
women	2,637,000
persons 16-19 years	364,000
white	4,879,000
black	577,000

Full-time/part-time labor force, 1998

full-time labor force	4,587,000
working part-time for economic reasons	45,000
part-time labor force	1,091,000

Unemployment rate, 2000

total	4.1%
men	4.0%
women	4.2%
persons 16-19 years	11.3%
white	3.7%
black	7.6%

Unemployed by reason for unemployment
(as a percent of total unemployment), 1998

job losers or completed temp jobs	45.9%
job leavers	12.8%
reentrants	33.1%
new entrants	8.3%

Experienced civilian labor force, by occupation,
1998

executive/administrative/managerial	766,000
professional/specialty	784,000
technicians & related support	190,000
sales	653,000
administrative support/clerical	750,000
service occupations	810,000
precision production/craft/repair	625,000
machine operators/assemblers	440,000
transportation/material moving	271,000
handlers/helpers/laborers	251,000
farming/forestry/fishing	118,000

Experienced civilian labor force, by industry, 1998

construction	241,000
manufacturing	1,167,000
transportation/communication	267,000
wholesale/retail trade	1,183,000
finance/real estate/insurance	295,000
services	1,357,000
government	672,000
agriculture	106,000

Average annual pay, 1999 ... $31,396

change in average annual pay, 1998-1999	3.3%

Hours and earnings of production workers
on manufacturing payrolls, 2000

average weekly hours	42.9
average hourly earnings	$16.72
average weekly earnings	$717.29

Labor union membership, 2000 ... 879,000

Household income (in 2000 dollars)

median household income, three year average, 1998-2000	$43,894

Poverty

persons below poverty level, three year average, 1998-2000	11.1%

Personal income ($per capita)

2000 (prelim.)

in current dollars	$28,400
in constant (1996) dollars	$26,453

1999 (preliminary)

in current dollars	$27,081
in constant (1996) dollars	$25,895

Federal income tax returns, 1999

returns filed	5,526,890
adjusted gross income ($1,000)	$220,984,028
total income tax paid ($1,000)	$31,439,519

ECONOMY, BUSINESS, INDUSTRY & AGRICULTURE

Fortune 500 companies, 2000 29

Business incorporations, 1998
total 17,134
change, 1997-1998 . . . . -14.8%

Business failures, 1998 2,524

Business firm ownership, 1997
Hispanic owned firms 6,448
Black owned firms 26,970
women owned firms 205,044
Asian & Pacific Islander owned firms 11,398
American Indian & Alaska
  native owned firms 5,124

Shopping centers, 2000 1,741

Gross state product, 1999 ($mil)
total $361,981
  agriculture services, forestry, fisheries . . $2,973
  mining $1,519
  construction $15,645
  manufacturing--durable goods $62,886
  manufacturing--nondurable goods $30,523
  transportation, communication &
    public utilities $26,659
  wholesale trade $25,814
  retail trade $35,102
  finance/real estate/insurance $56,156
  services $66,058
  federal, state & local government $38,648

Establishments, by major industry group, 1999
total 270,766
  forestry, fishing & agriculture 380
  mining 782
  construction 27,299
  manufacturing 17,930
  transportation & warehousing 6,965
  wholesale trade 16,944
  retail trade 43,270
  finance & insurance 16,737
  professional/scientific/technical 23,556
  health care/social assistance 25,109
  information 3,741
  accommodation/food services 22,351

Payroll, by major industry group, 1999
total ($1,000) $148,512,614
  forestry, fishing & agriculture $40,279
  mining $452,207
  construction $8,466,620
  manufacturing $39,124,628
  transportation & warehousing $4,262,420
  wholesale trade $9,929,373
  retail trade $11,401,943
  finance & insurance $10,235,817
  professional/scientific/technical $9,169,635
  health care/social assistance $18,095,398
  information $4,779,900
  accommodation/food services $4,055,199

Agriculture
number of farms, 2000 80,000
farm acreage, 2000 15,000,000
acres per farm, 2000 186
value of farms, 1997 ($mil) $31,861
farm income, 1999 ($mil)
  net farm income $803
  debt/asset ratio 12.4%
farm marketings, 1999 ($mil)
total $4,429
  crops $2,643
  livestock $1,786
principal commodities, in order by marketing
receipts, 1999
  Soybeans, corn, dairy products, greenhouse

Federal economic activity in state
expenditures, 2000
  total ($mil) $57,355
  per capita $5,052
  defense ($mil) $5,099
  non-defense ($mil) $52,256
defense department, 2000
  contract awards ($mil) $3,077
  payroll ($mil) $2,189
  civilian employees (x1 000) 23.4
  military personnel (x1 000) 6.8

Fishing, 2000
catch (thousands of pounds) 3,497
value ($1,000) $2,442

Mining, 2000 ($mil; preliminary)
total non-fuel mineral production $1,060

Construction, 1999 ($mil)
total contracts (including
    non-building) $17,100
       residential $6,938
       non-residential $7,083

Construction industries, 1997
establishments 25,509
receipts ($1,000) ....$NA
annual payroll ($1,000) $6,969,902
paid employees 221,240

Manufacturing, 1997
establishments 17,926
value of shipments ($1,000) $245,502,486
annual payroll ($1,000) $36,849,904
paid employees 1,009,620

Transportation industries, 1997
establishments 10,627
receipts ($1,000) $42,586,412
annual payroll ($1,000) $7,692,590
paid employees 223,638

Wholesale trade, 1997
establishments 20,099
sales($1,000) ....$NA
annual payroll ($1,000) ....$NA
paid employees ....NA

Retail trade, 1997
establishments 63,662
sales($1,000) $107,417,375
annual payroll ($1,000) $12,234,786
paid employees 971,264

Finance industries
establishments, 1997 24,643
receipts ($1,000), 1997 ....$NA
annual payroll ($1,000), 1997 .... $10,227,387
paid employees, 1997 303,312
commercial banks, 2000
    number 211
       assets ($bil) $361.9
       deposits ($bil) $229.8

Service industries, 1997 (non-exempt firms only)
establishments 77,002
receipts ($1,000) $58,945,593
annual payroll ($1,000) $23,350,605
paid employees 950,157

COMMUNICATION, ENERGY & TRANSPORTATION

Communication
daily newspapers, 2000 84
households with
    telephones, 1998 .... 95.8%
    computers, 2000 .... 49.5%
    internet access, 2000 .... 40.7%

Energy
consumption, 1999
total (trillion Btu) 4,323
per capita (million Btu) 384
by source of production (trillion Btu)
    coal 1,379
    natural gas 878
    petroleum 1,340
    nuclear electric power 175
    hydroelectric power 4
by end-use sector (trillion Btu)
    residential 867
    commercial 632
    industrial 1,855
    transportation 969
electric energy, 1999
    production (billion kWh) 140.9
    net summer capability (million kW) 27.1
gas utilities, 1999
    customers 3,133,000
    sales (trillion Btu) 406
nuclear plants, 1999 2

Transportation, 2000
public road & street mileage
total 116,964
    urban 33,545
    rural 83,419
    interstate 1,572
vehicle miles of travel (mil) 105,898
total motor vehicle registrations 10,467,476
    automobiles 6,709,706
    motorcycles 253,842
licensed drivers 8,205,524
    per 1,000 driving age population 934
deaths from motor vehicle
    accidents 1,351

Oklahoma 1

STATE SUMMARY

Capital City .... Oklahoma City

Governor .... Frank Keating

Address .... STATE CAPITOL
OKLAHOMA, CITY 73105
405 521-2342

Admitted as a state 1907

Area (square miles) 69,903

Population, 1980 3,025,290

Population, 1990 3,145,585

Population, 2000 3,450,654

Persons per square mile, 2000 .... 50.2

Largest city .... Oklahoma City
population, 2000 506,000

Personal income per capita, 2000
(in current dollars) $23,517

Gross state product ($mil), 1999 .... $86,382

Leading industries, 1999 (by payroll)
Manufacturing
Health care/Social assistance
Retail trade

Leading agricultural commodities, 1999
Cattle, broilers, wheat, hogs

GEOGRAPHY & ENVIRONMENT

Area, 1990 (square miles)
total 69,903
land 68,679
water (includes territorial water) 1,224

Federally owned land, 2000 .... 3.8%

Highest point
name .... Black Mesa
elevation (feet) 4,973

Lowest point
name .... Little River
elevation (feet) 289

General coastline (miles) 0

Tidal shoreline (miles) 0

Capital city .... Oklahoma City
population, 2000 506,000

Largest city .... Oklahoma City
population, 2000 506,000

Number of cities with over 100,000 population
1980 2
1990 2
2000 2

State parks and Recreation areas, 2000
area (acres) 72,000
number of visitors 16,148,000
revenues $22,804,000

Natl. forest system land, 1999 (acres) 397,000

National park acreage, 1984 9,500

DEMOGRAPHICS & CHARACTERISTICS OF THE POPULATION

Population
1970 2,559,463
1980 3,025,290
1990 3,145,585
2000 3,450,654
2015 (projection) 3,789,000
2025 (projection) 4,057,000

Metropolitan area population
1970 1,432,000
1980 1,724,000
2000 2,098,000

Non-metropolitan area population
1970 1,127,000
1980 1,301,000
2000 1,352,000

Change in population, 1990-2000
number 305,069
percent 9.70%

Persons per square mile, 2000 .... 50.2

Persons by age, 2000
under 5 years 236,353
18 and over 2,558,294
21 and over 2,393,620
65 and over 455,950
85 and over 57,175

Oklahoma 2

Persons by age, 2025 (projected)
under 5 years 245,000
5 to 17 years 677,000
65 and over 888,000

Median age, 2000 .... 35.5

Race, 2000
One race
White 2,628,434
Black or African American 260,968
American Indian and Alaska Native 273,230
Asian Indian 8,502
Chinese 6,964
Filipino 4,028
Japanese 2,505
Korean 5,074
Vietnamese 12,566
Native Hawaiian and other Pacific Islander   2,372
Two or more races 155,985

Race, 2025 (projected)
White 3,166,000
Black 433,000

Persons of Hispanic origin, 2000
total Hispanic or Latino 179,304
Mexican 132,813
Puerto Rican 8,153
Cuban 1,759
Other Hispanic or Latino 36,579

Persons of Hispanic origin, 2025 (proj.) .. 245,000

Persons by sex, 2000
male 1,695,895
female 1,754,759

Marital status, 1990
males
15 years & older 1,170,478
single 291,237
married 744,454
separated 17,573
widowed 29,341
divorced 105,446
females
15 years & older 1,272,570
single 220,159
married 744,704
separated 23,955

widowed 165,735
divorced 141,972

Households & families, 2000
households 1,342,293
persons per household 2.49
families 921,750
persons per family 3.02
married couples 717,611
female householder, no husband
present 152,575
one person households 358,560
households with persons under 18 years . 479,275
households with persons over 65 years ... 319,395

Nativity, 1990
number of persons born in state 1,996,579
percent of total residents 63.5%

Immigration & naturalization, 1998
immigrants admitted 2,273
persons naturalized 613
refugees granted resident status 62

VITAL STATISTICS & HEALTH

Births
1999
with low birth weight 7.4%
to teenage mothers 14.6%
to unmarried mothers 33.2%
Birth rate, 1999 (per 1,000) 14.6
Birth rate, 2000 (per 1,000) 14.8

Abortions, 1996
total 8,000
rate (per 1,000 women age 15-44) 11.8

Deaths
1998 33,750
1999 34,700
2000 35,265

Infant deaths
1998 323
1999 372
2000 392

Average lifetime, by race, 1989-1991
total .... 75.10 years
white .... 75.21 years
black .... 70.85 years

Marriages
1998	25,872
1999	23,304
2000	15,571

Divorces
1998	19,971
1999	19,696
2000	12,352

Physicians, 1999
total	5,614
rate (per 1,000 persons)	1.67

Nurses, 1999
total	20,500
rate (per 1,000 persons)	6.10

Hospitals, 1998
number	109
beds (x 1,000)	11.0
average daily census (x 1,000)	5.9
patients admitted (x1,000)	391
average cost per day to hospital, 1995	$861
average cost per stay to hospital, 1995	$5,188

EDUCATION

Educational attainment of all persons 25 years and older, 1990
less than 9th grade	195,015
high school graduates	607,903
bachelor's degree	236,112
graduate or professional degree	118,857

2000
high school graduate or more	86.1%
college graduate or more	22.5%

Public school enrollment, Fall, 1998
total	628,492
Kindergarten through grade 8	447,906
grades 9 through 12	180,586

Public School Teachers, 2000
total	41,500
elementary	21,600
secondary	19,900
average salaries	
elementary	$31,100
secondary	$31,500

State receipts & expenditures for public schools, 2000
revenue receipts ($mil)	$4,106

State receipts & expenditures for public schools, 2000 (continued)
expenditures	
total ($mil)	$3,717
per capita	$1,107
per pupil	$6,026

Graduating high school seniors, public high schools, 2000 (est.)
	36,759

SAT scores, 2001
verbal	567
math	561
percent graduates taking test	8%

Institutions of higher education, 1999
total	48
public	29
private	19

Enrollment in institutions of higher education, Fall, 1998
total	178,642
full-time men	53,122
full-time women	57,076
part-time men	28,386
part-time women	40,058

Minority enrollment in institutions of higher education, Fall, 1997
Black, non-Hispanic	13,370
Hispanic	4,610
Asian/Pacific Islander	4,801

Earned degrees conferred, 1998
Bachelor's	15,877
First professional	1,026
Master's	5,310
Doctor's	410

SOCIAL INSURANCE & WELFARE PROGRAMS

Social Security beneficiaries & benefits, 2000
beneficiaries	
total	594,000
retired and dependents	408,000
survivors	100,000
disabled & dependents	86,000
annual benefit payments ($mil)	
total	$5,141
retired and dependents	$3,358
survivors	$1,081
disabled & dependents	$703

Oklahoma 4

Medicare, 2000
enrollment (x1,000) 504
payments ($mil) $2,137

Medicaid, 1998
recipients (x1,000) 342
payments ($mil) $1,178

Federal public aid
Temporary Assistance for Needy Families
(TANF), 2000
   Recipients (x1,000) 25
   Families (x1,000) 11
Supplemental Security Income
  total recipients, 1999 (x1,000) 73

Food Stamp Program
  participants, 2000 (x1,000) 253

HOUSING & CONSTRUCTION

Total housing units, 2000 1,514,400
  seasonal or recreational use 32,293
  occupied 1,342,293
   owner occupied 918,259
   renter occupied 424,034

New privately owned housing units uthorized, 2000
number (x1,000) 11.1
value ($mil) $1,204

New privately owned housing units
  started, 2000 (est.) (x1,000) 15.5

Existing home sales, 2000 (x1,000) 91.9

GOVERNMENT & ELECTIONS

State officials, 2002
Governor (name/party/term expires)
      FRANK KEATING
      Republican - 2002
Lt. Governor ....Mary Fallin
Sec. of State .... Mike Hunter
Atty. General ....Drew Edmondson
Chief Justice ....Hardy Summers

Governorship
minimum age 31
length of term ....4 years
number of consecutive
  terms permitted 2
who succeeds .... Lt. Governor

State legislature
name ....Legislature
  upper chamber
    name ....Senate
    number of members 48
    length of term ....4 years
    party in majority, 2000 ....Democratic
  lower chamber
    name .... House of Representatives
    number of members 101
    length of term ....2 years
    party in majority, 2000 ....Democratic

State employees March, 2000
total 80,173
March payroll $176,782,548

Local governments, 1997
total 1,799
  county 77
  municipal 592
  township 0
  school districts 578
  special districts 552

Voting age population, November, 2000, projected
Total 2,531,000
  male 1,214,000
  female 1,316,000

Vote for president
2000
  Gore 474,000
  Bush 744,000
1996
  Clinton 488,000
  Dole 582,000
  Perot 131,000

Federal representation, 2002 (107th Congress)
Senators (name/party/term expires)

      JAMES INHOFE
      Republican - 2003
      DON NICKLES
      Republican - 2005

Representatives, total 6
  Democrats 1
  Republicans 5
  other.................................0

Women holding public office, 2001
U.S. Congress 0
statewide elected office 4
state legislature 15

Black elected officials, 1999
total 105
   US and state legislatures 6
   city/county/regional offices 80
   judicial/law enforcement 3
   education/school boards 16

Hispanic public officials, 2000
total . . . . NA
   state executives & legislators . . . . NA
   city/county/regional offices . . . . NA
   judicial/law enforcement . . . . NA
   education/school boards . . . . NA

GOVERNMENTAL FINANCE

State government revenues, 1999 ($per capita)
total revenue $3,554.18
   total general revenue $2,883.90
   intergovernmental revenue $832.59
   taxes $1,613.21
   current charges $292.97
   miscellaneous $145.12

State government expenditures, 1999 ($per capita)
total expenditure $3,173.12
   total general expenditure $2,754.28
   education $1,244.07
   public welfare $526.12
   health $108.01
   hospitals $50.66
   highways $297.09
   police protection $9.15
   correction $134.37
   natural resources $51.61
   governmental administration $119.00
   interest on general debt $60.73

State debt, 1999 ($per capita) $1,656.85

*Federal government grants to state & local
government, 2000 (x$1,000)*
total $3,586,855
   Dept. of Education $407,366
   Environmental Protection Agency $38,830
   Health Care Financing Admin. $1,292,509
   Dept. Housing & Urban Devel. $396,148
   Dept. of Labor $45,464
   Highway trust fund $320,071

CRIME, LAW ENFORCEMENT & COURTS

Crime, 2000 (all rates per 100,000 inhabitants)
total crimes 157,302
overall crime rate 4,558.6
   property crimes 140,125
    burglaries 31,661
    larcenies 96,116
    motor vehicle thefts 12,348
   property crime rate 4,060.8
   violent crimes 17,177
    murders 182
    forcible rapes 1,422
    robberies 2,615
    aggravated assaults 12,958
   violent crime rate 497.8

Number of police agencies, 2000 302

Arrests, 2000
total 164,613
   persons under 18 years of age 25,618

Prisoners under state & federal jurisdiction, 2000
total 23,181
percent change, 1999-2000 . . . . 3.5%
   sentenced to more than one year
   total 23,181
   rate per 100,000 residents 685

Persons under sentence of death, 4/1/2001 . . . 128

State's highest court
name . . . . Supreme Court*
number of members 9
length of term . . . . 6 years
intermediate appeals court? . . . . yes

Oklahoma 6

LABOR & INCOME

Civilian labor force, 2000

total 1,648,000
  men 882,000
  women 766,000
  persons 16-19 years 107,000
  white 1,419,000
  black 96,000

Civilian labor force as a percent of
civilian non-institutional population, 2000

total 64.4%
  men 72.2%
  women 57.3%
  persons 16-19 years ....NA%
  white 65.2%
  black 57.0%

Employment, 2000

total 1,598,000
  men 854,000
  women 744,000
  persons 16-19 years 96,000
  white 1,384,000
  black 89,000

Full-time/part-time labor force, 1998

full-time labor force 1,345,000
  working part-time for
    economic reasons 15,000
part-time labor force 283,000

Unemployment rate, 2000

total 3.0%
  men 3.2%
  women 2.8%
  persons 16-19 years 10.4%
  white 2.5%
  black 7.2%

Unemployed by reason for unemployment
(as a percent of total unemployment), 1998

job losers or completed temp jobs 43.2%
job leavers 13.5%
reentrants 36.5%
new entrants 5.4%

Experienced civilian labor force, by occupation,
1998

executive/administrative/managerial 205,000
professional/specialty 230,000
technicians & related support 50,000

sales 185,000
administrative support/clerical 234,000
service occupations 223,000
precision production/craft/repair 189,000
machine operators/assemblers 104,000
transportation/material moving 74,000
handlers/helpers/laborers 72,000
farming/forestry/fishing 58,000

Experienced civilian labor force, by industry, 1998

construction 72,000
manufacturing 212,000
transportation/communication 91,000
wholesale/retail trade 332,000
finance/real estate/insurance 71,000
services 353,000
government 264,000
agriculture 55,000

Average annual pay, 1999 .... $25,748
change in average annual pay,
  1998-1999 .... 2.5%

Hours and earnings of production workers
on manufacturing payrolls, 2000

average weekly hours 40.9
average hourly earnings $13.17
average weekly earnings $538.65

Labor union membership, 2000 93,800

Household income (in 2000 dollars)
median household income,
  three year average, 1998-2000 .... $32,445

Poverty
persons below poverty level,
  three year average, 1998-2000 .... 14.1%

Personal income ($per capita)
2000 (prelim.)
  in current dollars $23,517
  in constant (1996) dollars $21,905
1999 (preliminary)
  in current dollars $22,801
  in constant (1996) dollars $21,802

Federal income tax returns, 1999

returns filed 1,444,575
adjusted gross income ($1,000) $51,125,767
total income tax paid ($1,000) $6,865,101

ECONOMY, BUSINESS, INDUSTRY & AGRICULTURE

Fortune 500 companies, 2000 5

Business incorporations, 1998
total 7,349
change, 1997-1998 .... -10.0%

Business failures, 1998 990

Business firm ownership, 1997
Hispanic owned firms 4,349
Black owned firms 5,309
women owned firms 67,481
Asian & Pacific Islander owned firms 3,999
American Indian & Alaska
native owned firms 15,066

Shopping centers, 2000 577

Gross state product, 1999 ($mil)
total $86,382
  agriculture services, forestry, fisheries .. $1,944
  mining $4,257
  construction $3,316
  manufacturing--durable goods $9,054
  manufacturing--nondurable goods $5,551
  transportation, communication &
    public utilities $7,958
  wholesale trade $5,206
  retail trade $9,035
  finance/real estate/insurance $10,564
  services $15,723
  federal, state & local government $13,774

Establishments, by major industry group, 1999
total 84,854
  forestry, fishing & agriculture 197
  mining 2,116
  construction 7,586
  manufacturing 4,017
  transportation & warehousing 2,260
  wholesale trade 5,049
  retail trade 14,296
  finance & insurance 5,652
  professional/scientific/technical 7,801
  health care/social assistance 8,388
  information 1,405
  accommodation/food services 6,277

Payroll by major industry group, 1999
total ($1,000) $29,887,654
  forestry, fishing & agriculture $27,492
  mining $876,345
  construction $1,612,556
  manufacturing $5,457,419
  transportation & warehousing $1,020,604
  wholesale trade $2,001,697
  retail trade $2,786,746
  finance & insurance $1,870,239
  professional/scientific/technical $1,750,030
  health care/social assistance $4,203,599
  information $1,136,341
  accommodation/food services $1,037,470

Agriculture
number of farms, 2000 85,000
farm acreage, 2000 34,000,000
acres per farm, 2000 400
value of farms, 1997 ($mil) $19,380
farm income, 1999 ($mil)
  net farm income $1,150
  debt/asset ratio 17.3%
farm marketings, 1999 ($mil)
  total $3,991
  crops $855
  livestock $3,135
principal commodities, in order by marketing
receipts, 1999
  Cattle, broilers, wheat, hogs

Federal economic activity in state
expenditures, 2000
  total ($mil) $20,613
  per capita $5,974
  defense ($mil) $3,714
  non-defense ($mil) $16,899
defense department, 2000
  contract awards ($mil) $1,401
  payroll ($mil) $2,391
  civilian employees (x1,000) 21.4
  military personnel (x1,000) 24.6

Fishing, 2000
catch (thousands of pounds) .... NA
value ($1,000) .... $NA

Mining, 2000 ($mil; preliminary)
total non-fuel mineral production $453

Oklahoma 8

Construction, 1999 ($mil)
total contracts (including
   non-building) $4,404
     residential $1,878
     non-residential $1,303

Construction industries, 1997
establishments 6,562
receipts ($1,000) $6,459,579
annual payroll ($1,000) $1,242,602
paid employees 49,861

Manufacturing, 1997
establishments 4,210
value of shipments ($1,000) $37,965,344
annual payroll ($1,000) $5,083,001
paid employees 168,926

Transportation industries, 1997
establishments 3,729
receipts ($1,000) $14,678,845
annual payroll ($1,000) $2,096,468
paid employees 62,993

Wholesale trade, 1997
establishments 6,037
sales($1,000) .... $NA
annual payroll ($1,000) .... $NA
paid employees .... NA

Retail trade, 1997
establishments 19,710
sales($1,000) $28,306,597
annual payroll ($1,000) $3,021,070
paid employees 251,502

Finance industries
establishments, 1997 8,351
receipts ($1,000), 1997 .... $NA
annual payroll ($1,000), 1997 .... $2,003,137
paid employees, 1997 67,101
commercial banks, 2000
   number 286
     assets ($bil) $43.2
     deposits ($bil) $33.4

Service industries, 1997 (non-exempt firms only)
establishments 24,148
receipts ($1,000) $14,414,226
annual payroll ($1,000) $5,491,544
paid employees 259,359

COMMUNICATION, ENERGY & TRANSPORTATION

Communication
daily newspapers, 2000 43
households with
   telephones, 1998 .... 89.6%
   computers, 2000 .... 41.5%
   internet access, 2000 .... 34.3%

Energy
consumption, 1999
total (trillion Btu) 1,378
per capita (million Btu) 410
by source of production (trillion Btu)
   coal 334
   natural gas 543
   petroleum 500
   nuclear electric power .... NA
   hydroelectric power 32
by end-use sector (trillion Btu)
   residential 259
   commercial 198
   industrial 518
   transportation 403
electric energy, 1999
   production (billion kWh) 50.3
   net summer capability (million kW) ... 12.9
gas utilities, 1999
   customers 984,000
   sales (trillion Btu) 123
nuclear plants, 1999 .... na

Transportation, 2000
public road & street mileage
total 112,634
   urban 13,361
   rural 99,273
   interstate 930
vehicle miles of travel (mil) 43,355
total motor vehicle registrations 3,014,491
   automobiles 1,587,115
   motorcycles 57,284
licensed drivers 2,295,036
   per 1,000 driving age population ... 861
deaths from motor vehicle
   accidents 652

298

Oregon 1

STATE SUMMARY

Capital City . . . . .Salem

Governor . . . . John Kitzhaber

Address . . . . . . .STATE CAPITOL
SALEM, OR 97310
503 378-3111

Admitted as a state 1859

Area (square miles) 98,386

Population, 1980 .2,633,105

Population, 1990 .2,842,321

Population, 2000 .3,421,399

Persons per square mile, 2000 . . . . 35.6

Largest city . . . . Portland
population, 2000 529,000

**Personal income per capita, 2000
(in current dollars)** $28,350

Gross state product ($mil), 1999 . . . . . . $109,694

Leading industries, 1999 (by payroll)
Manufacturing
Health care/Social assistance
Retail trade

Leading agricultural commodities, 1999
Greenhouse, cattle, dairy products, ryegrass

GEOGRAPHY & ENVIRONMENT

Area, 1990 (square miles)
total 98,386
  land 96,003
  water (includes territorial water) 2,383

Federally owned land, 2000 . . . . 52.5%

Highest point
name . . . . Mt. Hood
elevation (feet) 11,239

Lowest point
name . . . . Pacific Ocean
elevation (feet) .sea level

General coastline (miles) 26

Tidal shoreline (miles) 1,410

Capital city . . . . .Salem
population, 2000 137,000

Largest city . . . . Portland
population, 2000 529,000

Number of cities with over 100,000 population
1980 2
1990 3
2000 3

State parks and Recreation areas, 2000
area (acres) 95,000
number of visitors 38,563,000
revenues $15,254,000

Natl. forest system land, 1999 (acres) . .15,656,000

National park acreage, 1984 194,600

DEMOGRAPHICS & CHARACTERISTICS OF THE POPULATION

Population
1970 2,091,533
1980 2,633,105
1990 2,842,321
2000 3,421,399
2015 (projection) 3,992,000
2025 (projection) 4,349,000

Metropolitan area population
1970 1,415,000
1980 1,763,000
2000 2,502,000

Non-metropolitan area population
1970 676,000
1980 870,000
2000 919,000

Change in population, 1990-2000
number 579,078
percent 20.37%

Persons per square mile, 2000 . . . . 35.6

Persons by age, 2000
under 5 years 223,005
18 and over 2,574,873
21 and over 2,429,348
65 and over 438,177
85 and over 57,431

Oregon 2

Persons by age, 2025 (projected)
under 5 years 246,000
5 to 17 years 661,000
65 and over 1,054,000

Median age, 2000 .... 36.3

Race, 2000
One race
White 2,961,623
Black or African American 55,662
American Indian and Alaska Native 45,211
Asian Indian 9,575
Chinese 20,930
Filipino 10,627
Japanese 12,131
Korean 12,387
Vietnamese 18,890
Native Hawaiian and other Pacific Islander 7,976
Two or more races 104,745

Race, 2025 (projected)
White 3,960,000
Black 101,000

Persons of Hispanic origin, 2000
total Hispanic or Latino 275,314
    Mexican 214,662
    Puerto Rican 5,092
    Cuban 3,091
    Other Hispanic or Latino 52,469

Persons of Hispanic origin, 2025 (proj.) .. 429,000

Persons by sex, 2000
male 1,696,550
female 1,724,849

Marital status, 1990
males
    15 years & older 1,083,101
        single 292,169
        married 660,657
        separated 18,665
        widowed 25,266
        divorced 105,009
females
    15 years & older 1,146,659
        single 222,695
        married 660,289
        separated 23,687

widowed 127,945
divorced 135,730

Households & families, 2000
households 1,333,723
persons per household 2.51
    families 877,671
    persons per family 3.02
        married couples 692,532
        female householder, no husband
            present 130,782
        one person households 347,624
households with persons under 18 years . 445,764
households with persons over 65 years . . . 305,475

Nativity, 1990
number of persons born in state 1,324,179
percent of total residents 46.6%

Immigration & naturalization, 1998
immigrants admitted 5,909
persons naturalized 2,307
refugees granted resident status 760

VITAL STATISTICS & HEALTH

Births
1999
    with low birth weight 5.4%
    to teenage mothers 13.6%
    to unmarried mothers 30.4%
Birth rate, 1999 (per 1,000) 13.6
Birth rate, 2000 (per 1,000) 13.7

Abortions, 1996
total 15,000
rate (per 1,000 women age 15-44) 21.6

Deaths
1998 29,529
1999 29,422
2000 29,562

Infant deaths
1998 265
1999 285
2000 270

Average lifetime, by race, 1989-1991
total .... 76.44 years
    white .... 76.51 years
    black .... NA years

Marriages
1998 26,040
1999 25,721
2000 25,973

Divorces
1998 15,208
1999 15,867
2000 16,695

Physicians, 1999
total 7,519
rate (per 1,000 persons) 2.27

Nurses, 1999
total 29,580
rate (per 1,000 persons) 8.92

Hospitals, 1998
number 60
beds (x 1,000) 6.8
average daily census (x 1,000) 3.8
patients admitted (x1,000) 313
average cost per day to hospital, 1995 .... $1,141
average cost per stay to hospital, 1995 .... $5,325

EDUCATION

*Educational attainment of all persons
25 years and older, 1990*
less than 9th grade 114,724
high school graduates 536,687
bachelor's degree 252,626
graduate or professional degree 129,545

2000
high school graduate or more 88.1%
college graduate or more 27.2%

Public school enrollment, Fall, 1998
total 542,809
Kindergarten through grade 8 379,770
grades 9 through 12 163,039

Public School Teachers, 2000
total 28,400
elementary 19,700
secondary 8,700
average salaries
elementary $40,900
secondary $41,000

*State receipts & expenditures for public
schools, 2000*
revenue receipts ($mil) $5,687

*State receipts & expenditures for public
schools, 2000 (continued)*
expenditures
total ($mil) $5,568
per capita $1,679
per pupil $9,910

*Graduating high school seniors,
public high schools, 2000 (est.) 28,700*

SAT scores, 2001
verbal 526
math 526
percent graduates taking test 55%

Institutions of higher education, 1999
total 54
public 25
private 29

*Enrollment in institutions of higher
education, Fall, 1998*
total 171,153
full-time men 45,600
full-time women 51,092
part-time men 32,389
part-time women 42,072

*Minority enrollment in institutions of higher
education, Fall, 1997*
Black, non-Hispanic 2,894
Hispanic 6,022
Asian/Pacific Islander 10,013

Earned degrees conferred, 1998
Bachelor's 13,652
First professional 1,067
Master's 4,222
Doctor's 458

SOCIAL INSURANCE &
WELFARE PROGRAMS

Social Security beneficiaries & benefits, 2000
beneficiaries
total 568,000
retired and dependents 420,000
survivors 77,000
disabled & dependents 72,000
annual benefit payments ($mil)
total $5,200
retired and dependents $3,684
survivors $908
disabled & dependents $609

Oregon 4

Medicare, 2000
enrollment (x1,000) 484
payments ($mil) $1,853

Medicaid, 1998
recipients (x1,000) 511
payments ($mil) $1,378

Federal public aid
Temporary Assistance for Needy Families
(TANF), 2000
    Recipients (x1,000) 43
    Families (x1,000) 17
Supplemental Security Income
    total recipients, 1999 (x1,000) 51

Food Stamp Program
    participants, 2000 (x1,000) 234

HOUSING & CONSTRUCTION

Total housing units, 2000 1,452,709
    seasonal or recreational use 36,850
    occupied 1,333,723
      owner occupied 856,951
      renter occupied 476,772

New privately owned housing units uthorized, 2000
number (x1,000) 19.9
value ($mil) $2,533

New privately owned housing units
    started, 2000 (est.) (x1,000) 22.2

Existing home sales, 2000 (x1,000) 64

GOVERNMENT & ELECTIONS

State officials, 2002
Governor (name/party/term expires)
    JOHN KITZHABER
    Democrat - 2002
Lt. Governor ....(no Lieutenant Governor)
Sec. of State .... Bill Bradbury
Atty. General .... Hardy Meyers
Chief Justice .... Wallace Carson

Governorship
minimum age 30
length of term .... 4 years
number of consecutive
    terms permitted 2
who succeeds .... Sec. of State

State legislature
name .... Legislature Assembly
  upper chamber
    name .... Senate
    number of members 30
    length of term .... 4 years
    party in majority, 2000 .... Republican
  lower chamber
    name .... House of Representatives
    number of members 60
    length of term .... 2 years
    party in majority, 2000 .... Republican

State employees March, 2000
total 66,088
March payroll $167,221,364

Local governments, 1997
total 1,493
    county 36
    municipal 240
    township 0
    school districts 258
    special districts 959

Voting age population, November, 2000, projected
Total 2,530,000
    male 1,235,000
    female 1,295,000

Vote for president
2000
    Gore 720,000
    Bush 714,000
1996
    Clinton 650,000
    Dole 538,000
    Perot 121,000

Federal representation, 2002 (107th Congress)
Senators (name/party/term expires)

        RON WYDEN
        Democratic - 2005
        GORDON SMITH
        Republican - 2003

Representatives, total 5
    Democrats 4
    Republicans 1
    other 0

Oregon 5

Women holding public office, 2001
U.S. Congress 1
statewide elected office 0
state legislature 30

Black elected officials, 1999
total 7
  US and state legislatures 4
  city/county/regional offices 1
  judicial/law enforcement 2
  education/school boards .... NA

Hispanic public officials, 2000
total 6
  state executives & legislators .... NA
  city/county/regional offices 5
  judicial/law enforcement .... NA
  education/school boards 1

GOVERNMENTAL FINANCE

State government revenues, 1999 ($per capita)
total revenue $4,724.18
  total general revenue $3,585.11
    intergovernmental revenue $1,063.29
    taxes $1,610.72
    current charges $413.28
    miscellaneous $497.82

State government expenditures, 1999 ($per capita)
total expenditure $4,211.13
  total general expenditure $3,508.72
    education $1,294.99
    public welfare $833.48
    health $131.61
    hospitals $154.75
    highways $304.69
    police protection $45.02
    correction $159.48
    natural resources $84.27
    governmental administration $207.25
    interest on general debt $81.82

State debt, 1999 ($per capita) $1,730.18

Federal government grants to state & local government, 2000 (x$1,000)
total $3,596,708
  Dept. of Education $295,437
  Environmental Protection Agency $58,391
  Health Care Financing Admin. $1,418,915
  Dept. Housing & Urban Devel. $324,267
  Dept. of Labor $89,328
  Highway trust fund $287,216

CRIME, LAW ENFORCEMENT & COURTS

Crime, 2000 (all rates per 100,000 inhabitants)
total crimes 165,780
overall crime rate 4,845.4
  property crimes 153,780
    burglaries 25,618
    larcenies 114,230
    motor vehicle thefts 13,932
  property crime rate 4,494.7
  violent crimes 12,000
    murders 70
    forcible rapes 1,286
    robberies 2,888
    aggravated assaults 7,756
  violent crime rate 350.7

Number of police agencies, 2000 140

Arrests, 2000
total 153,693
  persons under 18 years of age 34,061

Prisoners under state & federal jurisdiction, 2000
total 10,630
percent change, 1999-2000 .... 7.8%
  sentenced to more than one year
    total 10,603
    rate per 100,000 residents 316

Persons under sentence of death, 4/1/2001 29

State's highest court
name .... Supreme Court
number of members 7
length of term .... 6 years
intermediate appeals court? .... yes

Oregon 6

LABOR & INCOME

Civilian labor force, 2000

total 1,803,000
  men 973,000
  women 830,000
  persons 16-19 years 107,000
  white 1,693,000
  black .... NA

Civilian labor force as a percent of
civilian non-institutional population, 2000

total 69.1%
  men 76.4%
  women 62.2%
  persons 16-19 years .... NA%
  white 68.8%
  black .... NA%

Employment, 2000

total 1,715,000
  men 921,000
  women 794,000
  persons 16-19 years 93,000
  white 1,611,000
  black .... NA

Full-time/part-time labor force, 1998

full-time labor force 1,391,000
  working part-time for
    economic reasons 23,000
part-time labor force 371,000

Unemployment rate, 2000

total 4.9%
  men 5.4%
  women 4.3%
  persons 16-19 years 12.7%
  white 4.9%
  black .... NA%

Unemployed by reason for unemployment
(as a percent of total unemployment), 1998

job losers or completed temp jobs 49.0%
job leavers 12.2%
reentrants 34.7%
new entrants 4.1%

Experienced civilian labor force, by occupation,
1998

executive/administrative/managerial 241,000
professional/specialty 249,000
technicians & related support 38,000

sales 216,000
administrative support/clerical 234,000
service occupations 260,000
precision production/craft/repair 186,000
machine operators/assemblers 115,000
transportation/material moving 72,000
handlers/helpers/laborers 67,000
farming/forestry/fishing 81,000

Experienced civilian labor force, by industry, 1998

construction 89,000
manufacturing 290,000
transportation/communication 85,000
wholesale/retail trade 335,000
finance/real estate/insurance 82,000
services 390,000
government 235,000
agriculture 74,000

Average annual pay, 1999 .... $30,867
change in average annual pay,
  1998-1999 .... 4.5%

Hours and earnings of production workers
on manufacturing payrolls, 2000

average weekly hours 40.0
average hourly earnings $15.08
average weekly earnings $603.20

Labor union membership, 2000 234,400

Household income (in 2000 dollars)
median household income,
  three year average, 1998-2000 .... $42,440

Poverty
persons below poverty level,
  three year average, 1998-2000 .... 12.8%

Personal income ($per capita)
2000 (prelim.)
  in current dollars $28,350
  in constant (1996) dollars $26,406
1999 (preliminary)
  in current dollars $27,135
  in constant (1996) dollars $25,947

Federal income tax returns, 1999
returns filed 1,533,824
adjusted gross income ($1,000) $65,053,109
total income tax paid ($1,000) $9,160,262

ECONOMY, BUSINESS, INDUSTRY & AGRICULTURE

Fortune 500 companies, 2000 2

Business incorporations, 1998
total 8,393
change, 1997-1998 .... -9.6%

Business failures, 1998 1,109

Business firm ownership, 1997
Hispanic owned firms 6,022
Black owned firms 2,219
women owned firms 80,543
Asian & Pacific Islander owned firms 7,513
American Indian & Alaska
  native owned firms 2,861

Shopping centers, 2000 525

Gross state product, 1999 ($mil)
total $109,694
  agriculture services, forestry, fisheries .. $3,064
  mining $144
  construction $5,797
  manufacturing--durable goods $22,954
  manufacturing--nondurable goods $4,197
  transportation, communication &
    public utilities $7,750
  wholesale trade $8,226
  retail trade $9,484
  finance/real estate/insurance $15,753
  services $19,334
  federal, state & local government $12,992

Establishments, by major industry group, 1999
total 99,945
  forestry, fishing & agriculture 1,607
  mining 145
  construction 12,446
  manufacturing 5,694
  transportation & warehousing 2,713
  wholesale trade 5,870
  retail trade 14,200
  finance & insurance 5,430
  professional/scientific/technical 9,410
  health care/social assistance 9,146
  information 1,747
  accommodation/food services 8,256

Payroll, by major industry group, 1999
total ($1,000) $39,706,937
  forestry, fishing & agriculture $365,617
  mining $73,149
  construction $2,771,523
  manufacturing $7,774,328
  transportation & warehousing $1,407,942
  wholesale trade $3,108,247
  retail trade $3,894,113
  finance & insurance $2,623,571
  professional/scientific/technical $2,577,484
  health care/social assistance $4,395,568
  information $1,517,373
  accommodation/food services $1,447,109

Agriculture
number of farms, 2000 40,000
farm acreage, 2000 17,000,000
acres per farm, 2000 430
value of farms, 1997 ($mil) $17,500
farm income, 1999 ($mil)
  net farm income $323
  debt/asset ratio 14.2%
farm marketings, 1999 ($mil)
total $3,052
  crops $2,262
  livestock $790
principal commodities, in order by marketing
receipts, 1999
  Greenhouse, cattle, dairy products, ryegrass

Federal economic activity in state
expenditures, 2000
  total ($mil) $16,553
  per capita $4,838
  defense ($mil) $824
  non-defense ($mil) $15,729
defense department, 2000

  contract awards ($mil) $284
  payroll ($mil) $556
  civilian employees (x1,000) 3
  military personnel (x1,000) 0.6

Fishing, 2000
catch (thousands of pounds) 262,917
value ($1,000) $79,351

Mining, 2000 ($mil; preliminary)
total non-fuel mineral production $3439

Construction, 1999 ($mil)
total contracts (including
    non-building) $5,907
      residential $2,695
      non-residential $2,029

Construction industries, 1997
establishments 11,480
receipts ($1,000) ....$NA
annual payroll ($1,000) $2,606,024
paid employees 78,985

Manufacturing, 1997
establishments 6,923
value of shipments ($1,000) $50,200,786
annual payroll ($1,000) $7,514,314
paid employees 226,715

Transportation industries, 1997
establishments 4,359
receipts ($1,000) $12,700,161
annual payroll ($1,000) $2,348,640
paid employees 67,456

Wholesale trade, 1997
establishments 6,929
sales($1,000) .... $MA
annual payroll ($1,000) ....$NA
paid employees ....NA

Retail trade, 1997
establishments 20,920
sales($1,000) $34,066,578
annual payroll ($1,000) $4,001,005
paid employees 274,347

Finance industries
establishments, 1997 9,187
receipts ($1,000), 1997 ....$NA
annual payroll ($1,000), 1997 .... $2,897,089
paid employees, 1997 83,852
commercial banks, 2000
    number 43
      assets ($bil) $17.3
      deposits ($bil) $6.5

Service industries, 1997 (non-exempt firms only)
establishments 27,468
receipts ($1,000) $17,910,150
annual payroll ($1,000) $6,690,289
paid employees 275,689

COMMUNICATION, ENERGY & TRANSPORTATION

Communication
daily newspapers, 2000 19
households with
    telephones, 1998 .... 96.0%
    computers, 2000 .... 61.1%
    internet access, 2000 .... 50.8%

Energy
consumption, 1999
total (trillion Btu) 1,109
per capita (million Btu) 335
by source of production (trillion Btu)
    coal 39
    natural gas 219
    petroleum 392
    nuclear electric power...................NA
    hydroelectric power 475
by end-use sector (trillion Btu)
    residential 238
    commercial 191
    industrial 352
    transportation 328
electric energy, 1999
    production (billion kWh) 51.7
    net summer capability (million kW) 10.3
gas utilities, 1999
    customers 640,000
    sales (trillion Btu) 92
nuclear plants, 1999 ....na

Transportation, 2000
public road & street mileage
total 66,902
    urban 11,064
    rural 55,838
    interstate 727
vehicle miles of travel (mil) 35,010
total motor vehicle registrations 3,021,574
    automobiles 1,541,253
    motorcycles 68,598
licensed drivers 2,495,059
    per 1,000 driving age population 933
deaths from motor vehicle
    accidents 451

Pennsylvania 1

STATE SUMMARY

Capital City .... Harrisburg

Governor .... Mark Schweiker

Address .... STATE CAPITOL
        HARRISBURG, PA 17120
        717 787-2500

Admitted as a state 1787

Area (square miles) 46,058

Population, 1980 11,863,895

Population, 1990 11,881,643

Population, 2000 12,281,054

Persons per square mile, 2000 274

Largest city .... Philadelphia
    population, 2000 1,518,000

Personal income per capita, 2000
    (in current dollars) $29,539

Gross state product ($mil), 1999 ...... $382,980

Leading industries, 1999 (by payroll)
        Manufacturing
      Health care/Social assistance
     Professional/Scientific/Technical

Leading agricultural commodities, 1999
  Dairy products, cattle, greenhouse, chicken eggs

GEOGRAPHY & ENVIRONMENT

Area, 1990 (square miles)
total 46,058
  land 44,820
  water (includes territorial water) 1,239

Federally owned land, 2000 .... 2.5%

Highest point
name .... Mt. Davis
elevation (feet) 3,213

Lowest point
name .... Delaware River
elevation (feet) .... sea level

General coastline (miles) 0

Tidal shoreline (miles) 83

Capital city .... Harrisburg
population, 2000 48,950

Largest city .... Philadelphia
population, 2000 1,518,000

Number of cities with over 100,000 population
  1980 4
  1990 4
  2000 4

State parks and Recreation areas, 2000
area (acres) 288,000
number of visitors 36,717,000
revenues $12,612,000

Natl. forest system land, 1999 (acres) 513,000

National park acreage, 1984 40,900

DEMOGRAPHICS & CHARACTERISTICS OF THE POPULATION

Population
1970 11,800,766
1980 11,863,895
1990 11,881,643
2000 12,281,054
2015 (projection) 12,449,000
2025 (projection) 12,683,000

Metropolitan area population
1970 10,102,000
1980 10,038,000
2000 10,392,000

Non-metropolitan area population
1970 1,698,000
1980 1,826,000
2000 1,890,000

Change in population, 1990-2000
number 399,411
percent 3.36%

Persons per square mile, 2000 274

Persons by age, 2000
under 5 years 727,804
18 and over 9,358,833
21 and over 8,842,276
65 and over 1,919,165
85 and over 237,567

Pennsylvania 2

Persons by age, 2025 (projected)
under 5 years 750,000
5 to 17 years 2,034,000
65 and over 2,659,000

Median age, 2000 38

Race, 2000
One race
White 10,484,203
Black or African American 1,224,612
American Indian and Alaska Native 18,348
Asian Indian 57,241
Chinese 50,650
Filipino 14,506
Japanese 6,984
Korean 31,612
Vietnamese 30,037
Native Hawaiian and other Pacific Islander 3,417
Two or more races 142,224

Race, 2025 (projected)
White 10,716,000
Black 1,530,000

Persons of Hispanic origin, 2000
total Hispanic or Latino 394,088
  Mexican 55,178
  Puerto Rican 228,557
  Cuban 10,363
  Other Hispanic or Latino 99,990

Persons of Hispanic origin, 2025 (proj.) .. 639,000

Persons by sex, 2000
male 5,929,663
female 6,351,391

Marital status, 1990
males
  15 years & older 4,494,327
    single 1,376,014
    married 2,707,088
      separated 99,588
    widowed 147,096
    divorced 264,129
females
  15 years & older 5,046,796
    single 1,232,919
    married 2,727,635
      separated 134,770

widowed 716,548
divorced 369,694

Households & families, 2000
households 4,777,003
persons per household 2.48
  families 3,208,388
  persons per family 3.04
    married couples 2,467,673
    female householder, no husband
      present 554,693
  one person households 1,320,941
households with persons under 18 years 1,559,281
households with persons over 65 years .. 1,328,237

Nativity, 1990
number of persons born in state 9,527,402
percent of total residents 80.2%

Immigration & naturalization, 1998
immigrants admitted 11,942
persons naturalized 9,997
refugees granted resident status 711

VITAL STATISTICS & HEALTH

Births
1999
  with low birth weight 7.9%
  to teenage mothers 12.1%
  to unmarried mothers 32.9%
Birth rate, 1999 (per 1,000) 12.1
Birth rate, 2000 (per 1,000) 12.2

Abortions, 1996
total 40,000
rate (per 1,000 women age 15-44) 15.2

Deaths
1998 126,957
1999 130,283
2000 130,814

Infant deaths
1998 933
1999 1,040
2000 1,104

Average lifetime, by race, 1989-1991
total .... 75.38 years
  white .... 76.15 years
  black .... 68.27 years

Marriages
1998	74,198
1999	75,169
2000	73,197

Divorces
1998	38,509
1999	37,829
2000	37,852

Physicians, 1999
total	35,148
rate (per 1,000 persons)	2.93

Nurses, 1999
total	136,360
rate (per 1,000 persons)	11.37

Hospitals, 1998
number	212
beds (x 1,000)	44.7
average daily census (x 1,000)	29.9
patients admitted (x1,000)	1,752
average cost per day to hospital, 1995	$963
average cost per stay to hospital, 1995	$6,482

EDUCATION

Educational attainment of all persons
25 years and older, 1990
less than 9th grade	741,167
high school graduates	3,035,080
bachelor's degree	890,660
graduate or professional degree	522,086

2000
high school graduate or more	85.7%
college graduate or more	24.3%

Public school enrollment, Fall, 1998
total	1,816,414
Kindergarten through grade 8	1,267,226
grades 9 through 12	549,188

Public School Teachers, 2000
total	114,500
elementary	60,000
secondary	54,500
average salaries	
elementary	$48,100
secondary	$48,600

State receipts & expenditures for public
schools, 2000
revenue receipts ($mil)	$15,557

State receipts & expenditures for public
schools, 2000 (continued)
expenditures	
total ($mil)	$13,882
per capita	$1,157
per pupil	$7,823

Graduating high school seniors,
public high schools, 2000 (est.) 114,160

SAT scores, 2001
verbal	500
math	499
percent graduates taking test	71%

Institutions of higher education, 1999
total	250
public	64
private	186

Enrollment in institutions of higher
education, Fall, 1998
total	595,805
full-time men	195,617
full-time women	219,823
part-time men	70,904
part-time women	109,461

Minority enrollment in institutions of higher
education, Fall, 1997
Black, non-Hispanic	49,132
Hispanic	11,876
Asian/Pacific Islander	21,075

Earned degrees conferred, 1998
Bachelor's	63,484
First professional	3,930
Master's	20,756
Doctor's	2,413

SOCIAL INSURANCE & WELFARE PROGRAMS

Social Security beneficiaries & benefits, 2000
beneficiaries	
total	2,357,000
retired and dependents	1,708,000
survivors	371,000
disabled & dependents	279,000
annual benefit payments ($mil)	
total	$22,121
retired and dependents	$15,315
survivors	$4,464
disabled & dependents	$2,342

Pennsylvania 4

Medicare, 2000
enrollment (x1,000) 2,088
payments ($mil) $13,257

Medicaid, 1998
recipients (x1,000) 1,523
payments ($mil) $6,080

Federal public aid
Temporary Assistance for Needy Families
(TANF), 2000
  Recipients (x1,000) 238
  Families (x1,000) 90
Supplemental Security Income
  total recipients, 1999 (x1,000) 278

Food Stamp Program
participants, 2000 (x1,000) 777

HOUSING & CONSTRUCTION

Total housing units, 2000 5,249,750
  seasonal or recreational use 148,230
  occupied 4,777,003
    owner occupied 3,406,337
    renter occupied 1,370,666

New privately owned housing units uthorized, 2000
number (x1,000) 41.1
value ($mil) $4,616

New privately owned housing units
started, 2000 (est.) (x1,000) 37.5

Existing home sales, 2000 (x1,000) 168.3

GOVERNMENT & ELECTIONS

State officials, 2002
  Governor (name/party/term expires)
        MARK SCHWEIKER
        Republican - 2002
Lt. Governor .... Robert Jubelirer
Sec. of State .... Kim Pizzingrilli
Atty. General .... Mike Fisher
Chief Justice .... John P. Flaherty

Governorship
minimum age 30
length of term .... 4 years
number of consecutive
  terms permitted 2
who succeeds .... Lt. Governor

State legislature
name .... General Assembly
  upper chamber
    name .... Senate
    number of members 50
    length of term .... 4 years
    party in majority, 2000 .... Republican
  lower chamber
    name .... House of Representatives
    number of members 203
    length of term .... 2 years
    party in majority, 2000 .... Republican

State employees March, 2000
total 181,292
March payroll $503,792,960

Local governments, 1997
total 5,070
  county 66
  municipal 1,023
  township 1,546
  school districts 516
  special districts 1,919

Voting age population, November, 2000, projected
Total 9,155,000
  male 4,315,000
  female 4,839,000

Vote for president
2000
  Gore 2,486,000
  Bush 2,281,000
1996
  Clinton 2,216,000
  Dole 1,801,000
  Perot 431,000

Federal representation, 2002 (107th Congress)
Senators (name/party/term expires)

        RICK SANTORUM
        Republican - 2007
        ARLEN SPECTER
        Republican - 2005

Representatives, total 21
  Democrats 10
  Republicans 11
  other 0

Pennsylvania 5

Women holding public office, 2001
U.S. Congress 1
statewide elected office 1
state legislature 34

Black elected officials, 1999
total 164
  US and state legislatures 19
  city/county/regional offices 57
  judicial/law enforcement 60
  education/school boards 28

Hispanic public officials, 2000
total 5
  state executives & legislators 1
  city/county/regional offices 2
  judicial/law enforcement 1
  education/school boards 1

GOVERNMENTAL FINANCE

State government revenues, 1999 ($per capita)
total revenue $4,125.53
  total general revenue $3,239.90
    intergovernmental revenue $855.50
    taxes $1,799.96
    current charges $346.04
    miscellaneous $238.41

State government expenditures, 1999 ($per capita)
total expenditure $3,688.24
  total general expenditure $3,211.38
    education $976.52
    public welfare $952.46
    health $118.65
    hospitals $134.77
    highways $268.24
    police protection $63.79
    correction $117.44
    natural resources $41.65
    governmental administration $101.13
    interest on general debt $141.24

State debt, 1999 ($per capita) $1,472.27

Federal government grants to state & local government, 2000 (x$1,000)
total $12,764,734
  Dept. of Education $1,150,297
  Environmental Protection Agency ... $134,284
  Health Care Financing Admin. $5,904,816
  Dept. Housing & Urban Devel. $1,689,403
  Dept. of Labor $213,227
  Highway trust fund $848,361

CRIME, LAW ENFORCEMENT & COURTS

Crime, 2000 (all rates per 100,000 inhabitants)
total crimes 367,858
overall crime rate 2,995.3
  property crimes 316,274
    burglaries 54,080
    larcenies 225,869
    motor vehicle thefts 36,325
  property crime rate 2,575.3
  violent crimes 51,584
    murders 602
    forcible rapes 3,247
    robberies 18,155
    aggravated assaults 29,580
  violent crime rate 420.0

Number of police agencies, 2000 618

Arrests, 2000
total 415,331
  persons under 18 years of age 94,702

Prisoners under state & federal jurisdiction, 2000
total 36,847
percent change, 1999-2000 .... 0.9%
  sentenced to more than one year
    total 36,844
    rate per 100,000 residents 307

Persons under sentence of death, 4/1/2001 ... 242

State's highest court
name .... Supreme Court
number of members 7
length of term .... 10 years
intermediate appeals court? .... yes

Pennsylvania 6

LABOR & INCOME

Civilian labor force, 2000
total	5,972,000
men	3,194,000
women	2,778,000
persons 16-19 years	351,000
white	5,374,000
black	493,000

Civilian labor force as a percent of civilian non-institutional population, 2000
total	64.3%
men	72.2%
women	57.1%
persons 16-19 years	NA%
white	64.6%
black	60.8%

Employment, 2000
total	5,722,000
men	3,054,000
women	2,668,000
persons 16-19 years	302,000
white	5,179,000
black	443,000

Full-time/part-time labor force, 1998
full-time labor force	4,761,000
working part-time for economic reasons	43,000
part-time labor force	1,176,000

Unemployment rate, 2000
total	4.2%
men	4.4%
women	4.0%
persons 16-19 years	13.9%
white	3.6%
black	10.0%

Unemployed by reason for unemployment (as a percent of total unemployment), 1998
job losers or completed temp jobs	50.9%
job leavers	10.5%
reentrants	28.4%
new entrants	9.8%

Experienced civilian labor force, by occupation, 1998
executive/administrative/managerial	798,000
professional/specialty	891,000
technicians & related support	195,000
sales	680,000
administrative support/clerical	864,000
service occupations	831,000
precision production/craft/repair	624,000
machine operators/assemblers	382,000
transportation/material moving	248,000
handlers/helpers/laborers	269,000
farming/forestry/fishing	125,000

Experienced civilian labor force, by industry, 1998
construction	254,000
manufacturing	1,029,000
transportation/communication	333,000
wholesale/retail trade	1,128,000
finance/real estate/insurance	333,000
services	1,655,000
government	634,000
agriculture	107,000

Average annual pay, 1999 .... $32,694
change in average annual pay, 1998-1999	3.5%

Hours and earnings of production workers on manufacturing payrolls, 2000
average weekly hours	42.1
average hourly earnings	$14.60
average weekly earnings	$614.66

Labor union membership, 2000 869,600

Household income (in 2000 dollars)
median household income, three year average, 1998-2000	$43,742

Poverty
persons below poverty level, three year average, 1998-2000	9.9%

Personal income ($per capita)
2000 (prelim.)
in current dollars	$29,539
in constant (1996) dollars	$27,514

1999 (preliminary)
in current dollars	$28,676
in constant (1996) dollars	$27,420

Federal income tax returns, 1999
returns filed	5,724,621
adjusted gross income ($1,000)	$246,544,804
total income tax paid ($1,000)	$37,828,805

ECONOMY, BUSINESS, INDUSTRY & AGRICULTURE

Fortune 500 companies, 2000 25

Business incorporations, 1998
total 18,852
change, 1997-1998 .... -9.8%

Business failures, 1998 2,641

Business firm ownership, 1997
Hispanic owned firms 7,893
Black owned firms 19,791
women owned firms 202,990
Asian & Pacific Islander owned firms 17,397
American Indian & Alaska
native owned firms 5,161

Shopping centers, 2000 1,704

Gross state product, 1999 ($mil)
total $382,980
    agriculture services, forestry, fisheries .. $3,353
    mining $2,593
    construction $16,079
    manufacturing--durable goods $38,124
    manufacturing--nondurable goods $36,325
    transportation, communication &
        public utilities $32,935
    wholesale trade $23,826
    retail trade $34,359
    finance/real estate/insurance $70,566
    services $85,749
    federal, state & local government $39,070

Establishments, by major industry group, 1999
total 293,491
    forestry, fishing & agriculture 642
    mining 913
    construction 28,325
    manufacturing 17,038
    transportation & warehousing 6,663
    wholesale trade 16,909
    retail trade 48,978
    finance & insurance 17,144
    professional/scientific/technical 26,221
    health care/social assistance 31,383
    information 4,626
    accommodation/food services 24,039

Payroll, by major industry group, 1999
total ($1,000) $154,388,369
    forestry, fishing & agriculture $67,338
    mining $721,023
    construction $9,075,867
    manufacturing $29,662,634
    transportation & warehousing $4,871,773
    wholesale trade $9,625,546
    retail trade $11,896,641
    finance & insurance $12,399,714
    professional/scientific/technical $13,915,444
    health care/social assistance $21,207,267
    information $5,487,894
    accommodation/food services $3,914,586

Agriculture
number of farms, 2000 59,000
farm acreage, 2000 8,000,000
acres per farm, 2000 131
value of farms, 1997 ($mil) $20,251
farm income, 1999 ($mil)
    net farm income $627
    debt/asset ratio 12.6%
farm marketings, 1999 ($mil)
total $4,070
    crops $1,193
    livestock $2,877
principal commodities, in order by marketing
receipts, 1999
    Dairy products, cattle, greenhouse, chicken eggs

Federal economic activity in state
expenditures, 2000
    total ($mil) $73,715
    per capita $6,002
    defense ($mil) $6,057
    non-defense ($mil) $67,658
defense department, 2000
    contract awards ($mil) $3,967
    payroll ($mil) $2,217
    civilian employees (x1,000) 25.7
    military personnel (x1,000) 3.1

Fishing, 2000
catch (thousands of pounds) 20
value ($1,000) $29

Mining, 2000 ($mil; preliminary)
total non-fuel mineral production $31,250

Pennsylvania 8

Construction, 1999 ($mil)
total contracts (including
   non-building) $14,188
     residential $4,563
     non-residential $6,083

Construction industries, 1997
establishments 27,046
receipts ($1,000) .... $NA
annual payroll ($1,000) $7,165,776
paid employees 226,488

Manufacturing, 1997
establishments 17,207
value of shipments ($1,000) $177,169,793
annual payroll ($1,000) $28,688,934
paid employees 857,041

Transportation industries, 1997
establishments 10,905
receipts ($1,000) $66,809,682
annual payroll ($1,000) $8,205,631
paid employees 250,499

Wholesale trade, 1997
establishments 20,135
sales($1,000) $166,524,386
annual payroll ($1,000) $9,438,720
paid employees 269,103

Retail trade, 1997
establishments 70,702
sales($1,000) $113,092,636
annual payroll ($1,000) $12,505,713
paid employees 940,957

Finance industries
establishments, 1997 24,944
receipts ($1,000), 1997 .... $NA
annual payroll ($1,000), 1997 .... $12,788,799
paid employees, 1997 342,807
commercial banks, 2000
  number 187
    assets ($bil) $189.6
    deposits ($bil) $138.7

Service industries, 1997 (non-exempt firms only)
establishments 85,488
receipts ($1,000) $70,881,373
annual payroll ($1,000) $27,644,027
paid employees 978,912

COMMUNICATION, ENERGY & TRANSPORTATION

Communication
daily newspapers, 2000 84
households with
  telephones, 1998 .... 96.7%
  computers, 2000 .... 48.4%
  internet access, 2000 .... 40.1%

Energy
consumption, 1999
total (trillion Btu) 3,716
per capita (million Btu) 310
by source of production (trillion Btu)
  coal 1,143
  natural gas 696
  petroleum 1,385
  nuclear electric power 756
  hydroelectric power 16
by end-use sector (trillion Btu)
  residential 859
  commercial 583
  industrial 1,290
  transportation 984
electric energy, 1999
  production (billion kWh) 161.6
  net summer capability (million kW) 25.3
gas utilities, 1999
  customers 2,321,000
  sales (trillion Btu) 313
nuclear plants, 1999 9

Transportation, 2000
public road & street mileage
total 119,642
  urban 34,250
  rural 85,392
  interstate 1,757
vehicle miles of travel (mil) 102,337
total motor vehicle registrations 9,259,967
  automobiles 6,032,058
  motorcycles 214,630
licensed drivers 8,229,490
  per 1,000 driving age population 849
deaths from motor vehicle
  accidents 1,520

Rhode Island 1

STATE SUMMARY

Capital City . . . . Providence

Governor . . . . Lincoln Almond

Address . . . . STATE HOUSE
PROVIDENCE, RI 02903
401 222-2080

Admitted as a state 1790

Area (square miles) 1,545

Population, 1980 947,154

Population, 1990 1,003,464

Population, 2000 1,048,319

Persons per square mile, 2000 . . . . 1,003.20

Largest city . . . . Providence
population, 2000 174,000

Personal income per capita, 2000
(in current dollars) $29,685

Gross state product ($mil), 1999 . . . . $32,546

Leading industries, 1999 (by payroll)
Manufacturing
Health care/Social assistance
Finance & Insurance

Leading agricultural commodities, 1999
Greenhouse, dairy products, sweet corn, potato

GEOGRAPHY & ENVIRONMENT

Area, 1990 (square miles)
total 1,545
land 1,045
water (includes territorial water) 500

Federally owned land, 2000 . . . . 0.5%

Highest point
name . . . . Jerimoth Hill
elevation (feet) 812

Lowest point
name . . . . Atlantic Ocean
elevation (feet) . . . . sea level

General coastline (miles) 40

Tidal shoreline (miles) 384

Capital city . . . . Providence
population, 2000 174,000

Largest city . . . . Providence
population, 2000 174,000

Number of cities with over 100,000 population
1980 1
1990 1
2000 1

State parks and Recreation areas, 2000
area (acres) 9,000
number of visitors 6,231,000
revenues $3,237,000

Natl. forest system land, 1999 (acres) 0

National park acreage, 1984 . . . . NA

DEMOGRAPHICS & CHARACTERISTICS OF THE POPULATION

Population
1970 949,723
1980 947,154
1990 1,003,464
2000 1,048,319
2015 (projection) 1,070,000
2025 (projection) 1,141,000

Metropolitan area population
1970 868,000
1980 878,000
2000 986,000

Non-metropolitan area population
1970 82,000
1980 69,000
2000 62,000

Change in population, 1990-2000
number 44,855
percent 4.47%

Persons per square mile, 2000 . . . . 1,003.20

Persons by age, 2000
under 5 years 63,896
18 and over 800,497
21 and over 748,445
65 and over 152,402
85 and over 20,897

Rhode Island 2

Persons by age, 2025 (projected)
under 5 years 76,000
5 to 17 years 194,000
65 and over 214,000

Median age, 2000 .... 36.7

Race, 2000
One race
White 891,191
Black or African American 46,908
American Indian and Alaska Native 5,121
Asian Indian 2,942
Chinese 4,974
Filipino 2,062
Japanese 784
Korean 1,560
Vietnamese 952
Native Hawaiian and other Pacific Islander .. 567
Two or more races 28,251

Race, 2025 (projected)
White 977,000
Black 91,000

Persons of Hispanic origin, 2000
total Hispanic or Latino 90,820
    Mexican 5,881
    Puerto Rican 25,422
    Cuban 1,128
    Other Hispanic or Latino 58,389

Persons of Hispanic origin, 2025 (proj.) .. 176,000

Persons by sex, 2000
male 503,635
female 544,684

Marital status, 1990
males
    15 years & older 383,935
        single 127,464
        married 219,614
            separated 5,483
        widowed 11,712
        divorced 25,145
females
    15 years & older 429,423
        single 113,671
        married 220,490
            separated 8,668

widowed 57,244
divorced 38,018

Households & families, 2000
households 408,424
persons per household 2.47
    families 265,398
    persons per family 3.07
        married couples 196,757
        female householder, no husband
            present 52,609
        one person households 116,678
households with persons under 18 years . 134,399
households with persons over 65 years ... 107,335

Nativity, 1990
number of persons born in state 636,222
percent of total residents 63.4%

Immigration & naturalization, 1998
immigrants admitted 1,976
persons naturalized 2,642
refugees granted resident status 71

VITAL STATISTICS & HEALTH

Births
1999
    with low birth weight 7.3%
    to teenage mothers 12.5%
    to unmarried mothers 34.3%
Birth rate, 1999 (per 1,000) 12.5
Birth rate, 2000 (per 1,000) 12.5

Abortions, 1996
total 5,000
rate (per 1,000 women age 15-44) 24.4

Deaths
1998 9,602
1999 9,708
2000 10,030

Infant deaths
1998 89
1999 82
2000 89

Average lifetime, by race, 1989-1991
total .... 76.54 years
    white .... 76.80 years
    black .... NA years

Marriages
1998 7,515
1999 7,770
2000 8,010

Divorces
1998 3,165
1999 2,857
2000 3,121

Physicians, 1999
total 3,362
rate (per 1,000 persons) 3.39

Nurses, 1999
total 11,680
rate (per 1,000 persons) 11.79

Hospitals, 1998
number 12
beds (x 1,000) 2.6
average daily census (x 1,000) 1.8
patients admitted (x1,000) 117
average cost per day to hospital, 1995 . . . . $1,092
average cost per stay to hospital, 1995 . . . . $6,202

EDUCATION

Educational attainment of all persons
25 years and older, 1990
less than 9th grade 72,842
high school graduates 194,064
bachelor's degree 88,634
graduate or professional degree 51,526

2000
high school graduate or more 81.3%
college graduate or more 26.4%

Public school enrollment, Fall, 1998
total 154,785
Kindergarten through grade 8 112,483
grades 9 through 12 42,302

Public School Teachers, 2000
total 12,100
elementary 7,100
secondary 5,000
average salaries
elementary $47,000
secondary $47,100

State receipts & expenditures for public
schools, 2000
revenue receipts ($mil) $1,232

State receipts & expenditures for public
schools, 2000 (continued)
expenditures
total ($mil) $1,296
per capita $1,308
per pupil $8,773

Graduating high school seniors,
public high schools, 2000 (est.) 7,498

SAT scores, 2001
verbal 501
math 499
percent graduates taking test 71%

Institutions of higher education, 1999
total 12
public 3
private 9

Enrollment in institutions of higher
education, Fall, 1998
total 73,970
full-time men 22,740
full-time women 25,302
part-time men 9,875
part-time women 16,053

Minority enrollment in institutions of higher
education, Fall, 1997
Black, non-Hispanic 3,352
Hispanic 3,089
Asian/Pacific Islander 2,754

Earned degrees conferred, 1998
Bachelor's 8,169
First professional 231
Master's 1,929
Doctor's 248

SOCIAL INSURANCE & WELFARE PROGRAMS

Social Security beneficiaries & benefits, 2000
beneficiaries
total 192,000
retired and dependents 139,000
survivors 23,000
disabled & dependents 30,000
annual benefit payments ($mil)
total $1,739
retired and dependents $1,237
survivors $259
disabled & dependents $243

Rhode Island 4

Medicare, 2000
enrollment (x1,000) 170
payments ($mil) $1,075

Medicaid, 1998
recipients (x1,000) 153
payments ($mil) $919

Federal public aid
Temporary Assistance for Needy Families
(TANF), 2000
    Recipients (x1,000) 45
    Families (x1,000) 16
Supplemental Security Income
    total recipients, 1999 (x1,000) 27

Food Stamp Program
    participants, 2000 (x1,000) 74

HOUSING & CONSTRUCTION

Total housing units, 2000 439,837
    seasonal or recreational use 12,988
    occupied 408,424
    owner occupied 245,156
    renter occupied 163,268

New privately owned housing units uthorized, 2000
number (x1,000) 2.6
value ($mil) $296

New privately owned housing units
started, 2000 (est.) (x1,000) 2.7

Existing home sales, 2000 (x1,000) 21

GOVERNMENT & ELECTIONS

State officials, 2002
Governor (name/party/term expires)
      LINCOLN ALMOND
      Republican - 2002
Lt. Governor .... Charles Fogarty
Sec. of State .... Edward Inman
Atty. General .... Sheldon Whitehouse
Chief Justice .... Joseph R. Weisberger

Governorship
minimum age .... not specified
length of term .... 4 years
number of consecutive
    terms permitted 2
who succeeds .... Lt. Governor

State legislature
name .... General Assembly
  upper chamber
    name .... Senate
    number of members 50
    length of term .... 2 years
    party in majority, 2000 .... Democratic
  lower chamber
    name .... House of Representatives
    number of members 100
    length of term .... 2 years
    party in majority, 2000 .... Democratic

State employees March, 2000
total 24,047
March payroll $71,392,194

Local governments, 1997
total 119
  county 0
  municipal 8
  township 31
  school districts 4
  special districts 76

Voting age population, November, 2000, projected
Total 753,000
  male 355,000
  female 398,000

Vote for president
2000
  Gore 250,000
  Bush 131,000
1996
  Clinton 233,000
  Dole 105,000
  Perot 44,000

Federal representation, 2002 (107th Congress)
Senators (name/party/term expires)

      LINCOLN CHAFEE
      Republican - 2007
      JOHN REED
      Democrat - 2003

Representatives, total 2
  Democrats 2
  Republicans 0
  other 0

Women holding public office, 2001
U.S. Congress 0
statewide elected office 0
state legislature 34

Black elected officials, 1999
total 10
  US and state legislatures 9
  city/county/regional offices 1
  judicial/law enforcement .... NA
  education/school boards .... NA

Hispanic public officials, 2000
total 3
  state executives & legislators 2
  city/county/regional offices 1
  judicial/law enforcement .... NA
  education/school boards .... NA

GOVERNMENTAL FINANCE

State government revenues, 1999 ($per capita)
total revenue $5,528.94
  total general revenue $4,031.09
    intergovernmental revenue $1,314.60
    taxes $1,912.76
    current charges $308.60
    miscellaneous $495.13

State government expenditures, 1999 ($per capita)
total expenditure $4,418.77
  total general expenditure $3,764.48
    education $1,087.91
    public welfare $1,071.33
    health $129.30
    hospitals $110.94
    highways $234.29
    police protection $32.71
    correction $141.96
    natural resources $34.18
    governmental administration $227.04
    interest on general debt $273.02

State debt, 1999 ($per capita) $5,514.79

Federal government grants to state & local government, 2000 (x$1,000)
total $1,526,108
  Dept. of Education $99,863
  Environmental Protection Agency $23,308
  Health Care Financing Admin. $683,484
  Dept. Housing & Urban Devel. $249,257
  Dept. of Labor $22,738
  Highway trust fund $133,047

CRIME, LAW ENFORCEMENT & COURTS

Crime, 2000 (all rates per 100,000 inhabitants)
total crimes 36,444
overall crime rate 3,476.4
  property crimes 33,323
    burglaries 6,620
    larcenies 22,038
    motor vehicle thefts 4,665
  property crime rate 3,178.7
  violent crimes 3,121
    murders 45
    forcible rapes 412
    robberies 922
    aggravated assaults 1,742
  violent crime rate 297.7

Number of police agencies, 2000 46

Arrests, 2000
total 37,103
  persons under 18 years of age 7,300

Prisoners under state & federal jurisdiction, 2000
total 3,286
percent change, 1999-2000 .... 9.4%
  sentenced to more than one year
    total 1,966
    rate per 100,000 residents 197

Persons under sentence of death, 4/1/2001 ... NA

State's highest court
name .. .. Supreme Court
number of members 5
length of term .... life
intermediate appeals court? .... no

Rhode Island 6

LABOR & INCOME

Civilian labor force, 2000
total 505,000
  men 259,000
  women 246,000
  persons 16-19 years 29,000
  white 465,000
  black 26,000

Civilian labor force as a percent of
civilian non-institutional population, 2000
total 67.0%
  men 74.5%
  women 60.6%
  persons 16-19 years .... NA%
  white 67.2%
  black 71.8%

Employment, 2000
total 484,000
  men 249,000
  women 236,000
  persons 16-19 years 24,000
  white 447,000
  black 24,000

Full-time/part-time labor force, 1998
full-time labor force 399,000
  working part-time for
    economic reasons 4,000
part-time labor force 99,000

Unemployment rate, 2000
total 4.1%
  men 4.0%
  women 4.2%
  persons 16-19 years 16.6%
  white 3.8%
  black 8.3%

Unemployed by reason for unemployment
(as a percent of total unemployment), 1998
job losers or completed temp jobs 45.8%
job leavers 12.5%
reentrants 33.3%
new entrants 8.3%

Experienced civilian labor force, by occupation,
1998
executive/administrative/managerial 67,000
professional/specialty 77,000
technicians & related support 19,000

sales 63,000
administrative support/clerical 67,000
service occupations 72,000
precision production/craft/repair 52,000
machine operators/assemblers 41,000
transportation/material moving 15,000
handlers/helpers/laborers 18,000
farming/forestry/fishing .... NA

Experienced civilian labor force, by industry, 1998
construction 20,000
manufacturing 100,000
transportation/communication 16,000
wholesale/retail trade 101,000
finance/real estate/insurance 34,000
services 135,000
government 55,000
agriculture .... NA

Average annual pay, 1999 .... $31,177
change in average annual pay,
  1998-1999 .... 3.4%

Hours and earnings of production workers
on manufacturing payrolls, 2000
average weekly hours 40.4
average hourly earnings $12.18
average weekly earnings $492.07

Labor union membership, 2000 79,600

Household income (in 2000 dollars)
median household income,
  three year average, 1998-2000 .... $42,973

Poverty
persons below poverty level,
  three year average, 1998-2000 .... 10.0%

Personal income ($per capita)
2000 (prelim.)
  in current dollars $29,685
  in constant (1996) dollars $27,650
1999 (preliminary)
  in current dollars $29,720
  in constant (1996) dollars $28,418

Federal income tax returns, 1999
returns filed 481,564
adjusted gross income ($1,000) $20,682,012
total income tax paid ($1,000) $3,020,656

ECONOMY, BUSINESS, INDUSTRY & AGRICULTURE

Fortune 500 companies, 2000 3

Business incorporations, 1998
total 2,334
change, 1997-1998 .... -11.9%

Business failures, 1998 150

Business firm ownership, 1997
Hispanic owned firms 2,186
Black owned firms 1,269
women owned firms 19,886
Asian & Pacific Islander owned firms 1,110
American Indian & Alaska
   native owned firms 625

Shopping centers, 2000 211

Gross state product, 1999 ($mil)
total $32,546
   agriculture services, forestry, fisheries $214
   mining $12
   construction $1,724
   manufacturing--durable goods $2,745
   manufacturing--nondurable goods $1,353
   transportation, communication &
      public utilities $2,187
   wholesale trade $1,710
   retail trade $2,949
   finance/real estate/insurance $8,678
   services $7,074
   federal, state & local government $3,899

Establishments, by major industry group, 1999
total 28,240
   forestry, fishing & agriculture 49
   mining 28
   construction 3,089
   manufacturing 2,376
   transportation & warehousing 585
   wholesale trade 1,534
   retail trade 4,182
   finance & insurance 1,273
   professional/scientific/technical 2,636
   health care/social assistance 2,706
   information 371
   accommodation/food services 2,639

Payroll, by major industry group, 1999
total ($1,000) $11,842,626
   forestry, fishing & agriculture .... $NA
   mining .... $NA
   construction $696,952
   manufacturing $2,379,201
   transportation & warehousing $184,860
   wholesale trade $702,099
   retail trade $931,283
   finance & insurance $978,526
   professional/scientific/technical $695,406
   health care/social assistance $1,888,124
   information $453,683
   accommodation/food services $424,266

Agriculture
number of farms, 2000 1,000
farm acreage, 2000 .... NA
acres per farm, 2000 86
value of farms, 1997 ($mil) $498
farm income, 1999 ($mil)
   net farm income $12
   debt/asset ratio 10.9%
farm marketings, 1999 ($mil)
total $48
   crops $39
   livestock $8
principal commodities, in order by marketing
receipts, 1999
   Greenhouse, dairy products, sweet corn, potato

Federal economic activity in state
expenditures, 2000
   total ($mil) $6,876
   per capita $6,559
   defense ($mil) $918
   non-defense ($mil) $5,958
defense department, 2000
   contract awards ($mil) $418
   payroll ($mil) $502
   civilian employees (x1,000) 4.3
   military personnel (x1,000) 3.4

Fishing, 2000
catch (thousands of pounds) 119,295
value ($1,000) $72,544

Mining, 2000 ($mil; preliminary)
total non-fuel mineral production $24

Rhode Island 8

Construction, 1999 ($mil)
total contracts (including
 non-building) $1,083
   residential $381
   non-residential $559

Construction industries, 1997
establishments 2,940
receipts ($1,000) .... $NA
annual payroll ($1,000) $542,662
paid employees 16,820

Manufacturing, 1997
establishments 2,506
value of shipments ($1,000) $10,709,098
annual payroll ($1,000) $2,381,199
paid employees 78,452

Transportation industries, 1997
establishments 959
receipts ($1,000) .... $NA
annual payroll ($1,000) .... $NA
paid employees .... NA

Wholesale trade, 1997
establishments 1,802
sales($1,000) $7,991,515
annual payroll ($1,000) $687,749
paid employees 20,487

Retail trade, 1997
establishments 6,474
sales($1,000) $8,207,824
annual payroll ($1,000) $1,001,897
paid employees 75,777

Finance industries
establishments, 1997 2,155
receipts ($1,000), 1997 .... $NA
annual payroll ($1,000), 1997 .... $932,248
paid employees, 1997 26,944
commercial banks, 2000
 number 7
   assets ($bil) $182.1
   deposits ($bil) $114.5

Service industries, 1997 (non-exempt firms only)
establishments 8,296
receipts ($1,000) $5,176,184
annual payroll ($1,000) $2,034,627
paid employees 84,785

COMMUNICATION, ENERGY & TRANSPORTATION

Communication
daily newspapers, 2000 6
households with
 telephones, 1998 .... 94.6%
 computers, 2000 .... 47.9%
 internet access, 2000 .... 38.8%

Energy
consumption, 1999
total (trillion Btu) 261
per capita (million Btu) 264
by source of production (trillion Btu)
 coal .... NA
 natural gas 86
 petroleum 99
 nuclear electric power .... NA
 hydroelectric power 10
by end-use sector (trillion Btu)
 residential 66
 commercial 52
 industrial 77
 transportation 66
electric energy, 1999
 production (billion kWh) .... NA
 net summer capability (million kW) ... NA
gas utilities, 1999
 customers 229,000
 sales (trillion Btu) 27
nuclear plants, 1999 .... na

Transportation, 2000
public road & street mileage
total 6,052
 urban 4,719
 rural 1,333
 interstate 70
vehicle miles of travel (mil) 8,359
total motor vehicle registrations 759,570
 automobiles 538,975
 motorcycles 19,432
licensed drivers 654,035
 per 1,000 driving age population 790
deaths from motor vehicle
 accidents 80

STATE SUMMARY

Capital City .... Columbia

Governor .... Jim Hodges

Address .... STATE HOUSE
COLUMBIA, SC 29211
803 734-2170

Admitted as a state 1788

Area (square miles) 32,007

Population, 1980 3,121,820

Population, 1990 3,486,703

Population, 2000 4,012,012

Persons per square mile, 2000 .... 133.2

Largest city .... Columbia
population, 2000 116,000

Personal income per capita, 2000
(in current dollars) $24,321

Gross state product ($mil), 1999 ...... $106,917

Leading industries, 1999 (by payroll)
Manufacturing
Health care/Social assistance
Retail trade

Leading agricultural commodities, 1999
Broilers, greenhouse, turkeys, tobacco

GEOGRAPHY & ENVIRONMENT

Area, 1990 (square miles)
total 32,007
land 30,111
water (includes territorial water) 1,896

Federally owned land, 2000 .... 5.7%

Highest point
name .... Sassafras Mountain
elevation (feet) 3,560

Lowest point
name .... Atlantic Ocean
elevation (feet) .... sea level

General coastline (miles) 187

Tidal shoreline (miles) 2,876

Capital city .... Columbia
population, 2000 116,000

Largest city .... Columbia
population, 2000 116,000

Number of cities with over 100,000 population
1980 0
1990 0
2000 1

State parks and Recreation areas, 2000
area (acres) 80,000
number of visitors 9,247,000
revenues $16,057,000

Natl. forest system land, 1999 (acres) 613,000

National park acreage, 1984 21,000

DEMOGRAPHICS & CHARACTERISTICS OF THE POPULATION

Population
1970 2,590,713
1980 3,121,820
1990 3,486,703
2000 4,012,012
2015 (projection) 4,369,000
2025 (projection) 4,645,000

Metropolitan area population
1970 1,504,000
1980 1,865,000
2000 2,807,000

Non-metropolitan area population
1970 1,087,000
1980 1,256,000
2000 1,205,000

Change in population, 1990-2000
number 525,309
percent 15.07%

Persons per square mile, 2000 .... 133.2

Persons by age, 2000
under 5 years 264,679
18 and over 3,002,371
21 and over 2,814,131
65 and over 485,333
85 and over 50,269

South Carolina 2

Persons by age, 2025 (projected)
under 5 years 267,000
5 to 17 years 743,000
65 and over 963,000

Median age, 2000 .... 35.4

Race, 2000
One race
White 2,695,560
Black or African American 1,185,216
American Indian and Alaska Native 13,718
Asian Indian 8,356
Chinese 5,967
Filipino 6,423
Japanese 2,448
Korean 3,665
Vietnamese 4,248
Native Hawaiian and other Pacific Islander 1,628
Two or more races 39,950

Race, 2025 (projected)
White 3,174,000
Black 1,402,000

Persons of Hispanic origin, 2000
total Hispanic or Latino 95,076
  Mexican 52,871
  Puerto Rican 12,211
  Cuban 2,875
  Other Hispanic or Latino 27,119

Persons of Hispanic origin, 2025 (proj.) ... 81,000

Persons by sex, 2000
male 1,948,929
female 2,063,083

Marital status, 1990
males
  15 years & older 1,298,504
    single 386,819
    married 793,839
      separated 39,238
    widowed 32,582
    divorced 85,264
females
  15 years & older 1,422,067
    single 330,381
    married 798,571
      separated 56,261

widowed 181,673
divorced 111,442

Households & families, 2000
households 1,533,854
persons per household 2.53
  families 1,072,822
  persons per family 3.02
  married couples 783,142
  female householder, no husband
    present 226,958
  one person households 383,142
households with persons under 18 years . 560,160
households with persons over 65 years ... 346,175

Nativity, 1990
number of persons born in state 2,385,744
percent of total residents 68.4%

Immigration & naturalization, 1998
immigrants admitted 2,125
persons naturalized 1,334
refugees granted resident status 55

VITAL STATISTICS & HEALTH
Births
1999
  with low birth weight 9.8%
  to teenage mothers 14.1%
  to unmarried mothers 39.0%
Birth rate, 1999 (per 1,000) 14.1
Birth rate, 2000 (per 1,000) 14.3

Abortions, 1996
total 10,000
rate (per 1,000 women age 15-44) 11.6

Deaths
1998 34,208
1999 36,053
2000 36,948
Infant deaths
1998 479
1999 493
2000 452

Average lifetime, by race, 1989-1991
total .... 73.51 years
  white .... 75.33 years
  black .... 68.82 years

Marriages
1998 41,494
1999 40,728
2000 42,667

Divorces
1998 14,608
1999 14,496
2000 14,409

Physicians, 1999
total 8,294
rate (per 1,000 persons) 2.13

Nurses, 1999
total 32,410
rate (per 1,000 persons) 8.34

Hospitals, 1998
number 65
beds (x 1,000) 11.5
average daily census (x 1,000) 7.6
patients admitted (x1,000) 475
average cost per day to hospital, 1995 ...... $923
average cost per stay to hospital, 1995 .... $5,935

EDUCATION

Educational attainment of all persons
25 years and older, 1990
less than 9th grade 295,167
high school graduates 639,358
bachelor's degree 243,161
graduate or professional degree 117,672

2000
high school graduate or more 83.0%
college graduate or more 19.0%

Public school enrollment, Fall, 1998
total 664,592
Kindergarten through grade 8 477,850
grades 9 through 12 186,742

Public School Teachers, 2000
total 43,500
elementary 30,500
secondary 13,100
average salaries
elementary $35,800
secondary $36,700

State receipts & expenditures for public
schools, 2000
revenue receipts ($mil) $5,178

State receipts & expenditures for public
schools, 2000 (continued)
expenditures
total ($mil) $4,869
per capita $1,253
per pupil $6,400

Graduating high school seniors
public high schools, 2000 (est) 34,500

SAT scores, 2001
verbal 486
math 488
percent graduates taking test 57%

Institutions of higher education, 1999
total 62
public 33
private 29

Enrollment in institutions of higher
education, Fall, 1998
total 181,353
full-time men 50,953
full-time women 64,737
part-time men 23,779
part-time women 41,884

Minority enrollment in institutions of higher
education, Fall, 1997
Black, non-Hispanic 41,993
Hispanic 1,816
Asian/Pacific Islander 2,316

Earned degrees conferred, 1998
Bachelor's 15,174
First professional 737
Master's 4,615
Doctor's 404

SOCIAL INSURANCE & WELFARE PROGRAMS

Social Security beneficiaries & benefits, 2000
beneficiaries
total 689,000
retired and dependents 448,000
survivors 107,000
disabled & dependents 134,000
annual benefit payments ($mil)
total $5,908
retired and dependents $3,760
survivors $1,060
disabled & dependents $1,088

South Carolina 4

Medicare, 2000
enrollment (x1,000) 555
payments ($mil) $2,947

Medicaid, 1998
recipients (x1,000) 595
payments ($mil) $2,019

Federal public aid
Temporary Assistance for Needy Families
(TANF), 2000
   Recipients (x1,000) 37
   Families (x1,000) 16
Supplemental Security Income
   total recipients, 1999 (x1,000) 108

Food Stamp Program
  participants, 2000 (x1,000) 295

HOUSING & CONSTRUCTION

Total housing units, 2000 1,753,670
  seasonal or recreational use 70,198
  occupied 1,533,854
    owner occupied 1,107,617
    renter occupied 426,237

New privately owned housing units uthorized, 2000
number (x1,000) 32.8
value ($mil) $3,533

New privately owned housing units
  started, 2000 (est.) (x1,000) 33.9

Existing home sales, 2000 (x1,000) 97

GOVERNMENT & ELECTIONS

State officials, 2002
  Governor (name/party/term expires)
        JIM HODGES
        Democrat - 2002
Lt. Governor . . . . Bob Peeler
Sec. of State . . . . James Miles
Atty. General . . . . Charles Condon
Chief Justice . . . . Jean Toal

Governorship
minimum age 30
length of term . . . . 4 years
number of consecutive
  terms permitted 2
who succeeds . . . . Lt. Governor

State legislature
name . . . . General Assembly
  upper chamber
    name . . . . Senate
    number of members 46
    length of term . . . . 4 years
    party in majority, 2000 . . . . .Democratic
  lower chamber
    name . . . . House of Representatives
    number of members 124
    length of term . . . . 2 years
    party in majority, 2000 . . . . Republican

State employees March, 2000
total 90,274
March payroll $211,506,464

Local governments, 1997
total 716
  county 46
  municipal 269
  township 0
  school districts 91
  special districts 310

Voting age population, November, 2000, projected
Total 2,977,000
  male 1,408,000
  female 1,569,000

Vote for president
2000
  Gore 566,000
  Bush 786,000
1996
  Clinton 506,000
  Dole 573,000
  Perot 64,000

Federal representation, 2002 (107th Congress)
Senators (name/party/term expires)

     STROM THURMOND
      Republican - 2003
     ERNEST F. HOLLINGS
      Democrat - 2005

Representatives, total 6
  Democrats 2
  Republicans 3
  vacant 1

Women holding public office, 2001
U.S. Congress 0
statewide elected office 1
state legislature 18

Black elected officials, 1999
total 542
  US and state legislatures 34
  city/county/regional offices 333
  judicial/law enforcement 8
  education/school boards 167

Hispanic public officials, 2000
total ....NA
  state executives & legislators ....NA
  city/county/regional offices ....NA
  judicial/law enforcement ....NA
  education/school boards ....NA

GOVERNMENTAL FINANCE

State government revenues, 1999 ($per capita)
total revenue $3,748.65
  total general revenue $3,185.40
    intergovernmental revenue $999.05
    taxes $1,585.60
    current charges $417.31
    miscellaneous $183.43

State government expenditures, 1999 ($per capita)
total expenditure $3,727.22
  total general expenditure $3,253.30
    education $1,138.51
    public welfare $804.44
    health $166.71
    hospitals $188.23
    highways $247.68
    police protection $47.74
    correction $112.38
    natural resources $49.54
    governmental administration $77.22
    interest on general debt $55.66

State debt, 1999 ($per capita) $1,307.83

Federal government grants to state & local government, 2000 (x$1,000)
total $4,017,245
  Dept. of Education $368,670
  Environmental Protection Agency $54,652
  Health Care Financing Admin. $1,989,153
  Dept. Housing & Urban Devel. $307,906
  Dept. of Labor $66,518
  Highway trust fund $363,429

CRIME, LAW ENFORCEMENT & COURTS

Crime, 2000 (all rates per 100,000 inhabitants)
total crimes 209,482
overall crime rate 5,221.4
  property crimes 177,189
    burglaries 38,888
    larcenies 123,094
    motor vehicle thefts 15,207
  property crime rate 4,416.5
  violent crimes 32,293
    murders 233
    forcible rapes 1,511
    robberies 5,883
    aggravated assaults 24,666
  violent crime rate 804.9

Number of police agencies, 2000 86

Arrests, 2000
total 78,992
  persons under 18 years of age 9,154

Prisoners under state & federal jurisdiction, 2000
total 21,778
percent change, 1999-2000 .... -1.0%
  sentenced to more than one year
    total 21,017
    rate per 100,000 residents 532

Persons under sentence of death, 4/1/2001 73

State's highest court
name .... Supreme Court
number of members 5
length of term .... 10 years
intermediate appeals court? .... yes

South Carolina 6

LABOR & INCOME

Civilian labor force, 2000

total	1,985,000
men	1,013,000
women	973,000
persons 16-19 years	113,000
white	1,486,000
black	471,000

Civilian labor force as a percent of civilian non-institutional population, 2000

total	65.5%
men	72.5%
women	59.5%
persons 16-19 years	NA%
white	65.8%
black	63.9%

Employment, 2000

total	1,909,000
men	976,000
women	933,000
persons 16-19 years	96,000
white	1,440,000
black	442,000

Full-time/part-time labor force, 1998

full-time labor force	1,655,000
working part-time for economic reasons	23,000
part-time labor force	304,000

Unemployment rate, 2000

total	3.9%
men	3.6%
women	4.1%
persons 16-19 years	15.0%
white	3.1%
black	6.3%

Unemployed by reason for unemployment (as a percent of total unemployment), 1998

job losers or completed temp jobs	44.0%
job leavers	16.0%
reentrants	30.7%
new entrants	8.0%

Experienced civilian labor force, by occupation, 1998

executive/administrative/managerial	222,000
professional/specialty	262,000
technicians & related support	63,000
sales	240,000
administrative support/clerical	234,000
service occupations	266,000
precision production/craft/repair	254,000
machine operators/assemblers	202,000
transportation/material moving	87,000
handlers/helpers/laborers	84,000
farming/forestry/fishing	NA

Experienced civilian labor force, by industry, 1998

construction	113,000
manufacturing	436,000
transportation/communication	88,000
wholesale/retail trade	386,000
finance/real estate/insurance	91,000
services	374,000
government	304,000
agriculture	NA

Average annual pay, 1999 .... $27,124

change in average annual pay, 1998-1999 .... 3.7%

Hours and earnings of production workers on manufacturing payrolls, 2000

average weekly hours	42.5
average hourly earnings	$10.96
average weekly earnings	$465.80

Labor union membership, 2000 70,300

Household income (in 2000 dollars)

median household income, three year average, 1998-2000 .... $37,119

Poverty

persons below poverty level, three year average, 1998-2000 .... 11.9%

Personal income ($per capita)

2000 (prelim.)

in current dollars	$24,321
in constant (1996) dollars	$22,654

1999 (preliminary)

in current dollars	$23,496
in constant (1996) dollars	$22,467

Federal income tax returns, 1999

returns filed	1,775,986
adjusted gross income ($1,000)	$66,164,663
total income tax paid ($1,000)	$8,837,273

ECONOMY, BUSINESS, INDUSTRY & AGRICULTURE

Fortune 500 companies, 2000 1

Business incorporations, 1998
total 7,524
change, 1997-1998 .... -7.7%

Business failures, 1998 410

Business firm ownership, 1997
Hispanic owned firms 2,036
Black owned firms 23,216
women owned firms 64,232
Asian & Pacific Islander owned firms 3,530
American Indian & Alaska
  native owned firms 2,229

Shopping centers, 2000 845

Gross state product, 1999 ($mil)
total $106,917
  agriculture services, forestry, fisheries .. $1,164
  mining $177
  construction $6,281
  manufacturing--durable goods $10,412
  manufacturing--nondurable goods $12,488
  transportation, communication &
    public utilities $9,495
  wholesale trade $6,699
  retail trade $11,851
  finance/real estate/insurance $14,650
  services $17,519
  federal, state & local government $16,180

Establishments, by major industry group, 1999
total 96,440
  forestry, fishing & agriculture 676
  mining 76
  construction 11,266
  manufacturing 4,520
  transportation & warehousing 2,325
  wholesale trade 5,099
  retail trade 18,511
  finance & insurance 5,823
  professional/scientific/technical 7,746
  health care/social assistance 7,648
  information 1,185
  accommodation/food services 7,987

Payroll, by major industry group, 1999
total ($1,000) $40,900,431
  forestry, fishing & agriculture $130,292
  mining .... $NA
  construction $3,159,298
  manufacturing $11,192,936
  transportation & warehousing $1,126,462
  wholesale trade $2,161,692
  retail trade $3,769,860
  finance & insurance $2,036,062
  professional/scientific/technical $2,308,272
  health care/social assistance $4,947,153
  information $1,019,328
  accommodation/food services $1,617,812

Agriculture
number of farms, 2000 24,000
farm acreage, 2000 5,000,000
acres per farm, 2000 196
value of farms, 1997 ($mil) $7,000
farm income, 1999 ($mil)
  net farm income $422
  debt/asset ratio 11.8%
farm marketings, 1999 ($mil)
total $1,406
  crops $633
  livestock $773
principal commodities, in order by marketing
receipts, 1999
    Broilers, greenhouse, turkeys, tobacco

Federal economic activity in state
expenditures, 2000
  total ($mil) $22,294
  per capita $5,557
  defense ($mil) $3,499
  non-defense ($mil) $18,796
defense department, 2000
  contract awards ($mil) $1,055
  payroll ($mil) $2,449
  civilian employees (x1,000) 8.9
  military personnel (x1,000) 39.6

Fishing, 2000
catch (thousands of pounds) 15,835
value ($1,000) $30,344

Mining, 2000 ($mil; preliminary)
total non-fuel mineral production $560

South Carolina 8

Construction, 1999 ($mil)
total contracts (including
    non-building) $7,236
      residential $3,854
      non-residential $2,305

Construction industries, 1997
establishments 10,183
receipts ($1,000) ....$NA
annual payroll ($1,000) $2,039,531
paid employees 83,661

Manufacturing, 1997
establishments 4,966
value of shipments ($1,000) $71,550,765
annual payroll ($1,000) $10,552,195
paid employees 353,858

Transportation industries, 1997
establishments 3,537
receipts ($1,000) $11,906,119
annual payroll ($1,000) $2,161,006
paid employees 66,140

Wholesale trade, 1997
establishments 5,965
sales($1,000) $36,680,250
annual payroll ($1,000) $2,083,589
paid employees 67,606

Retail trade, 1997
establishments 24,572
sales($1,000) $34,912,588
annual payroll ($1,000) $3,934,406
paid employees 328,850

Finance industries
establishments, 1997 8,499
receipts ($1,000), 1997 ....$NA
annual payroll ($1,000), 1997 .... $2,191,655
paid employees, 1997 73,899
commercial banks, 2000
  number 79
    assets ($bil) $23.6
    deposits ($bil) $18.4

Service industries, 1997 (non-exempt firms only)
establishments 25,349
receipts ($1,000) $20,635,494
annual payroll ($1,000) $7,380,548
paid employees 325,235

COMMUNICATION, ENERGY & TRANSPORTATION

Communication
daily newspapers, 2000 15
households with
  telephones, 1998 .... 92.6%
  computers, 2000 .... 43.3%
  internet access, 2000 .... 32.0%

Energy
consumption, 1999
total (trillion Btu) 1,493
per capita (million Btu) 384
by source of production (trillion Btu)
  coal 403
  natural gas 163
  petroleum 467
  nuclear electric power 540
  hydroelectric power 7
by end-use sector (trillion Btu)
  residential 288
  commercial 210
  industrial 618
  transportation 376
electric energy, 1999
  production (billion kWh) 87.3
  net summer capability (million kW) ... 17.7
gas utilities, 1999
  customers 511,000
  sales (trillion Btu) 94
nuclear plants, 1999 7

Transportation, 2000
public road & street mileage
total 64,921
  urban 10,621
  rural 54,300
  interstate 829
vehicle miles of travel (mil) 45,538
total motor vehicle registrations 3,094,729
  automobiles 1,924,398
  motorcycles 51,436
licensed drivers 2,842,553
  per 1,000 driving age population 912
deaths from motor vehicle
  accidents 1,065

STATE SUMMARY

Capital City . . . . .Pierre

Governor . . . . William Janklow

Address . . . . STATE CAPITOL
PIERRE, SD 57501
605 773-3212

Admitted as a state 1889

Area (square miles) 77,121

Population, 1980 690,768

Population, 1990 696,004

Population, 2000 754,844

Persons per square mile, 2000 . . . . 9.9

Largest city . . . . Sioux Falls
population, 2000 124,000

Personal income per capita, 2000
(in current dollars) $26,115

Gross state product ($mil), 1999 . . . . $21,631

Leading industries, 1999 (by payroll)
Manufacturing
Health care/Social assistance
Retail trade

Leading agricultural commodities, 1999
Cattle, soybeans, corn, wheat

GEOGRAPHY & ENVIRONMENT

Area, 1990 (square miles)
total 77,121
land 75,898
water (includes territorial water) 1,224

Federally owned land, 2000 . . . . 6.4%

Highest point
name . . . . .Henry Peak
elevation (feet) 7,242

Lowest point
name . . . . Big Stone Lake
elevation (feet) 966

General coastline (miles) 0

Tidal shoreline (miles) 0

Capital city . . . . Pierre
population, 2000 13,876

Largest city . . . . Sioux Falls
population, 2000 124,000

Number of cities with over 100,000 population
1980 0
1990 0
2000 1

State parks and Recreation areas, 2000
area (acres) 93,000
number of visitors 7,033,000
revenues $7,154,000

Natl. forest system land, 1999 (acres) . . . 2,012,000

National park acreage, 1984 183,300

DEMOGRAPHICS & CHARACTERISTICS OF THE POPULATION

Population
1970 666,257
1980 690,768
1990 696,004
2000 754,844
2015 (projection) 840,000
2025 (projection) 866,000

Metropolitan area population
1970 155,000
1980 180,000
2000 261,000

Non-metropolitan area population
1970 512,000
1980 511,000
2000 494,000

Change in population, 1990-2000
number 58,840
percent 8.45%

Persons per square mile, 2000 . . . . 9.9

Persons by age, 2000
under 5 years 51,069
18 and over 552,195
21 and over 515,188
65 and over 108,131
85 and over 16,086

VITAL STATISTICS & HEALTH

Marriages
1998 6,710
1999 6,840
2000 7,060

Divorces
1998 2,591
1999 2,768
2000 2,678

Physicians, 1999
total 1,379
rate (per 1,000 persons) 1.88

Nurses, 1999
total 7,400
rate (per 1,000 persons) 10.09

Hospitals, 1998
number 49
beds (x 1,000) 4.4
average daily census (x 1,000) 2.8
patients admitted (x1,000) 96
average cost per day to hospital, 1995 ..... $476
average cost per stay to hospital, 1995 .... $5,494

EDUCATION

Educational attainment of all persons
  25 years and older, 1990
  less than 9th grade 57,707
  high school graduates 144,990
  bachelor's degree 52,773
  graduate or professional degree 21,118

2000
  high school graduate or more 91.8%
  college graduate or more 25.7%

Public school enrollment, Fall, 1998
total 132,495
  Kindergarten through grade 8 90,887
  grades 9 through 12 41,608

Public School Teachers, 2000
total 9,300
  elementary 6,400
  secondary 2,800
average salaries
  elementary $29,100
  secondary $29,000

State receipts & expenditures for public
  schools, 2000
revenue receipts ($mil) $881

State receipts & expenditures for public
  schools, 2000 (continued)
expenditures
  total ($mil) $814
  per capita $1,111
  per pupil $5,737

Graduating high school seniors,
  public high schools, 2000 (est.) 9,420

SAT scores, 2001
verbal 577
math 582
percent graduates taking test 4%

Institutions of higher education, 1999
total 25
  public 14
  private 11

Enrollment in institutions of higher
  education, Fall, 1998
total 41,545
full-time men 13,982
full-time women 15,370
part-time men 4,626
part-time women 7,567

Minority enrollment in institutions of higher
  education, Fall, 1997
Black, non-Hispanic 275
Hispanic 165
Asian/Pacific Islander 259

Earned degrees conferred, 1998
Bachelor's 4,273
First professional 189
Master's 937
Doctor's 71

SOCIAL INSURANCE & WELFARE PROGRAMS

Social Security beneficiaries & benefits, 2000
beneficiaries
total 136,000
  retired and dependents 97,000
  survivors 23,000
  disabled & dependents 16,000
annual benefit payments ($mil)
total $1,124
  retired and dependents $766
  survivors $240
  disabled & dependents $118

Medicare, 2000
enrollment (x1,000) 119
payments ($mil) $564

Medicaid, 1998
recipients (x1,000) 90
payments ($mil) $356

Federal public aid
Temporary Assistance for Needy Families
(TANF), 2000
   Recipients (x1,000) 7
   Families (x1,000) 3
Supplemental Security Income
   total recipients, 1999 (x1,000) 13

Food Stamp Program
   participants, 2000 (x1,000) 43

HOUSING & CONSTRUCTION

Total housing units, 2000 323,208
   seasonal or recreational use 9,839
   occupied 290,245
      owner occupied 197,940
      renter occupied 92,305

New privately owned housing units uthorized, 2000
number (x1,000) 4.2
value ($mil) $369

New privately owned housing units
   started, 2000 (est.) (x1,000) 3.5

Existing home sales, 2000 (x1,000) 15.4

GOVERNMENT & ELECTIONS

State officials, 2002
Governor (name/party/term expires)
     WILLIAM JANKLOW
     Republican - 2002
Lt. Governor .... Carole Hillard
Sec. of State .... Joyce Hazeltine
Atty. General .... Mark Barnett
Chief Justice .... Dave Gilbertson

Governorship
minimum age .... not specified
length of term .... 4 years
number of consecutive
   terms permitted 2
who succeeds .... Lt. Governor

State legislature
name .... Legislature
   upper chamber
     name .... Senate
     number of members 35
     length of term .... 2 years
     party in majority, 2000 .... Republican
   lower chamber
     name .... House of Representatives
     number of members 70
     length of term .... 2 years
     party in majority, 2000 .... Republican

State employees March, 2000
total 17,174
March payroll $34,779,428

Local governments, 1997
total 1,810
   county 66
   municipal 309
   township 956
   school districts 177
   special districts 302

Voting age population, November, 2000, projected
Total 542,000
   male 263,000
   female 279,000

Vote for president
2000
   Gore 119,000
   Bush 191,000
1996
   Clinton 139,000
   Dole 151,000
   Perot 31,000

Federal representation, 2002 (107th Congress)
Senators (name/party/term expires)

     TIM JOHNSON
     Democrat - 2003
     TOM DASCHLE
     Democrat - 2005

Representatives, total 1
   Democrats 0
   Republicans 1
   other 0

Women holding public office, 2001
U.S. Congress 0
statewide elected office 3
state legislature 16

Black elected officials, 1999
total ....NA
  US and state legislatures ....NA
  city/county/regional offices ....NA
  judicial/law enforcement ....NA
  education/school boards ....NA

Hispanic public officials, 2000
total ....NA
  state executives & legislators ....NA
  city/county/regional offices ....NA
  judicial/law enforcement ....NA
  education/school boards ....NA

GOVERNMENTAL FINANCE

State government revenues, 1999 ($per capita)
total revenue $3,936.34
  total general revenue $2,971.76
    intergovernmental revenue $1,100.78
    taxes $1,187.59
    current charges $275.87
    miscellaneous $407.52

State government expenditures, 1999 ($per capita)
total expenditure $3,098.58
  total general expenditure $2,872.44
    education $903.66
    public welfare $592.02
    health $84.19
    hospitals $60.93
    highways $422.50
    police protection $24.88
    correction $79.66
    natural resources $111.47
    governmental administration $126.05
    interest on general debt $157.85

State debt, 1999 ($per capita) $2,871.05

Federal government grants to state & local government, 2000 (x$1,000)
total $1,131,343
  Dept. of Education $137,041
  Environmental Protection Agency $23,196
  Health Care Financing Admin. $295,558
  Dept. Housing & Urban Devel. $131,412
  Dept. of Labor $18,346
  Highway trust fund $179,601

CRIME, LAW ENFORCEMENT & COURTS

Crime, 2000 (all rates per 100,000 inhabitants)
total crimes 17,511
overall crime rate 2,319.8
  property crimes 16,252
    burglaries 2,896
    larcenies 12,558
    motor vehicle thefts 798
  property crime rate 2,153.0
  violent crimes 1,259
    murders 7
    forcible rapes 305
    robberies 131
    aggravated assaults 816
  violent crime rate 166.8

Number of police agencies, 2000 78

Arrests, 2000
total 38,859
  persons under 18 years of age 9,111

Prisoners under state & federal jurisdiction, 2000
total 2,616
percent change, 1999-2000 .... 4.4%
  sentenced to more than one year
    total 2,613
    rate per 100,000 residents 353

Persons under sentence of death, 4/1/2001 5

State's highest court
name .... Supreme Court
number of members 5
length of term .... 8 years
intermediate appeals court? ....no

South Dakota 6

LABOR & INCOME

Civilian labor force, 2000

total 401,000
  men 210,000
  women 191,000
  persons 16-19 years 34,000
  white 378,000
  black .... NA

Civilian labor force as a percent of
civilian non-institutional population, 2000

total 72.7%
  men 77.8%
  women 67.7%
  persons 16-19 years ....NA%
  white 73.0%
  black .... NA%

Employment, 2000

total 392,000
  men 205,000
  women 187,000
  persons 16-19 years 31,000
  white 371,000
  black .... NA

Full-time/part-time labor force, 1998

full-time labor force ....NA
  working part-time for
    economic reasons 3,000
part-time labor force ....NA

Unemployment rate, 2000

total 2.3%
  men 2.5%
  women 2.0%
  persons 16-19 years 6.5%
  white 1.9%
  black .... NA%

Unemployed by reason for unemployment
(as a percent of total unemployment), 1998

job losers or completed temp jobs .... NA%
job leavers .... NA%
reentrants .... NA%
new entrants.......................... NA%

Experienced civilian labor force, by occupation,
1998

executive/administrative/managerial 44,000
professional/specialty 50,000
technicians & related support ....NA

sales 48,000
administrative support/clerical 48,000
service occupations 65,000
precision production/craft/repair 42,000
machine operators/assemblers 26,000
transportation/material moving ....NA
handlers/helpers/laborers 15,000
farming/forestry/fishing 36,000

Experienced civilian labor force, by industry, 1998

construction 17,000
manufacturing 49,000
transportation/communication 14,000
wholesale/retail trade 79,000
finance/real estate/insurance 24,000
services 79,000
government 67,000
agriculture 36,000

Average annual pay, 1999 .... $23,765
change in average annual pay,
  1998-1999 .... 4.5%

Hours and earnings of production workers
on manufacturing payrolls, 2000

average weekly hours 43.1
average hourly earnings $10.71
average weekly earnings $461.60

Labor union membership, 2000 18,200

Household income (in 2000 dollars)
median household income,
  three year average, 1998-2000 .... $36,172

Poverty
persons below poverty level,
  three year average, 1998-2000 .... 9.3%

Personal income ($per capita)
2000 (prelim.)
  in current dollars $26,115
  in constant (1996) dollars $24,325
1999 (preliminary)
  in current dollars $25,107
  in constant (1996) dollars $24,007

Federal income tax returns, 1999
returns filed 350,533
adjusted gross income ($1,000) $12,631,204
total income tax paid ($1,000) $1,883,004

ECONOMY, BUSINESS, INDUSTRY & AGRICULTURE

Fortune 500 companies, 2000 2

Business incorporations, 1998
total 1,515
change, 1997-1998 .... 5.2%

Business failures, 1998 275

Business firm ownership, 1997
Hispanic owned firms 261
Black owned firms 150
women owned firms 14,121
Asian & Pacific Islander owned firms 303
American Indian & Alaska
  native owned firms 955

Shopping centers, 2000 58

Gross state product, 1999 ($mil)
total $21,631
  agriculture services, forestry, fisheries .. $1,500
  mining $130
  construction $893
  manufacturing--durable goods $2,239
  manufacturing--nondurable goods $797
  transportation, communication &
    public utilities $1,784
  wholesale trade $1,516
  retail trade $2,307
  finance/real estate/insurance $3,923
  services $3,810
  federal, state & local government $2,733

Establishments, by major industry group, 1999
total 23,693
  forestry, fishing & agriculture 99
  mining 57
  construction 2,649
  manufacturing 897
  transportation & warehousing 1,031
  wholesale trade 1,425
  retail trade 4,183
  finance & insurance 1,699
  professional/scientific/technical 1,507
  health care/social assistance 1,977
  information 455
  accommodation/food services 2,201

Payroll, by major industry group, 1999
total ($1,000) $6,857,456
  forestry, fishing & agriculture .... $NA
  mining .... $NA
  construction $452,850
  manufacturing $1,452,244
  transportation & warehousing $181,533
  wholesale trade $475,349
  retail trade $825,341
  finance & insurance $595,071
  professional/scientific/technical $214,413
  health care/social assistance $1,277,121
  information $198,731
  accommodation/food services $272,345

Agriculture
number of farms, 2000 33,000
farm acreage, 2000 44,000,000
acres per farm, 2000 1,354
value of farms, 1997 ($mil) $14,300
farm income, 1999 ($mil)
  net farm income $1,190
  debt/asset ratio 18.1%
farm marketings, 1999 ($mil)
  total $3,539
  crops $1,709
  livestock $1,830
principal commodities, in order by marketing
receipts, 1999
    Cattle, soybeans, corn, wheat

Federal economic activity in state
expenditures, 2000
  total ($mil) $5,138
  per capita $6,807
  defense ($mil) $344
  non-defense ($mil) $4,794
defense department, 2000
  contract awards ($mil) $87
  payroll ($mil) $266
  civilian employees (x1,000) 1.7
  military personnel (x1,000) 3.1

Fishing, 2000
catch (thousands of pounds) .... NA
value ($1,000) .... $NA

Mining, 2000 ($mil; preliminary)
total non-fuel mineral production $260

South Dakota 8

Construction, 1999 ($mil)
total contracts (including
    non-building) $931
      residential $347
      non-residential $274

Construction industries, 1997
establishments 2,375
receipts ($1,000) .... $NA
annual payroll ($1,000) .... $NA
paid employees 14,229

Manufacturing, 1997
establishments 975
value of shipments ($1,000) $12,412,102
annual payroll ($1,000) $1,194,187
paid employees 48,306

Transportation industries, 1997
establishments 1,510
receipts ($1,000) .... $NA
annual payroll ($1,000) .... $NA
paid employees .... NA

Wholesale trade, 1997
establishments 1,796
sales($1,000) $10,357,776
annual payroll ($1,000) $493,062
paid employees 19,329

Retail trade, 1997
establishments 5,752
sales($1,000) $9,872,544
annual payroll ($1,000) $761,528
paid employees 66,008

Finance industries
establishments, 1997 2,303
receipts ($1,000), 1997 .... $NA
annual payroll ($1,000), 1997 .... $NA
paid employees, 1997 .... NA
commercial banks, 2000
   number 97
    assets ($bil) $37.2
    deposits ($bil) $13.5

Service industries, 1997 (non-exempt firms only)
establishments 5,677
receipts ($1,000) $2,655,345
annual payroll ($1,000) $941,726
paid employees 48,237

COMMUNICATION, ENERGY & TRANSPORTATION

Communication
daily newspapers, 2000 11
households with
  telephones, 1998 .... 91.0%
  computers, 2000 .... 50.4%
  internet access, 2000 .... 37.9%

Energy
consumption, 1999
total (trillion Btu) 239
per capita (million Btu) 326
by source of production (trillion Btu)
  coal 46
  natural gas 36
  petroleum 115
  nuclear electric power .... NA
  hydroelectric power 71
by end-use sector (trillion Btu)
  residential 53
  commercial 39
  industrial 62
  transportation 84
electric energy, 1999
  production (billion kWh) 10.6
  net summer capability (million kW) 2.9
gas utilities, 1999
  customers 156,000
  sales (trillion Btu) 22
nuclear plants, 1999 .... na

Transportation, 2000
public road & street mileage
total 83,471
  urban 2,017
  rural 81,454
  interstate 678
vehicle miles of travel (mil) 8,432
total motor vehicle registrations 792,509
  automobiles 380,281
  motorcycles 29,175
licensed drivers 543,817
  per 1,000 driving age population 942
deaths from motor vehicle
  accidents 173

Tennessee 1

STATE SUMMARY

Capital City . . . . Nashville

Governor . . . . Don Sundquist

Address . . . . STATE CAPITOL
NASHVILLE, TN 37219
615 741-2001

Admitted as a state 1796

Area (square miles) 42,146

Population, 1980 4,591,120

Population, 1990 4,877,185

Population, 2000 5,689,283

Persons per square mile, 2000 138

Largest city . . . . Memphis
population, 2000 650,000

Personal income per capita, 2000
(in current dollars) $26,239

Gross state product ($mil), 1999 . . . . . . $170,085

Leading industries, 1999 (by payroll)
Manufacturing
Health care/Social assistance
Retail trade

Leading agricultural commodities, 1999
Cattle, broilers, dairy products, tobacco

GEOGRAPHY & ENVIRONMENT

Area, 1990 (square miles)
total 42,146
land 41,220
water (includes territorial water) 926

Federally owned land, 2000 . . . . 7.9%

Highest point
name . . . . Clingmans Dome
elevation (feet) 6,643

Lowest point
name . . . . Mississippi River
elevation (feet) 178

General coastline (miles) 0

Tidal shoreline (miles) 0

Capital city . . . . Nashville
population, 2000 545,000

Largest city . . . . Memphis
population, 2000 650,000

Number of cities with over 100,000 population
1980 4
1990 4
2000 5

State parks and Recreation areas, 2000
area (acres) 141,000
number of visitors 30,182,000
revenues $28,451,000

Natl. forest system land, 1999 (acres) 634,000

National park acreage, 1984 266,400

DEMOGRAPHICS & CHARACTERISTICS OF THE POPULATION

Population
1970 3,926,018
1980 4,591,120
1990 4,877,185
2000 5,689,283
2015 (projection) 6,365,000
2025 (projection) 6,665,000

Metropolitan area population
1970 2,630,000
1980 3,048,000
2000 3,862,000

Non-metropolitan area population
1970 1,296,000
1980 1,543,000
2000 1,827,000

Change in population, 1990-2000
number 812,098
percent 16.65%

Persons per square mile, 2000 138

Persons by age, 2000
under 5 years 374,880
18 and over 4,290,762
21 and over 4,046,450
65 and over 703,311
85 and over 81,465

Tennessee 2

Persons by age, 2025 (projected)
under 5 years 377,000
5 to 17 years 1,041,000
65 and over 1,355,000

Median age, 2000 .... 35.9

Race, 2000
One race
White 4,563,310
Black or African American 932,809
American Indian and Alaska Native 15,152
Asian Indian 12,835
Chinese 9,426
Filipino 5,426
Japanese 4,304
Korean 7,395
Vietnamese 7,007
Native Hawaiian and other Pacific Islander 2,205
Two or more races 63,109

Race, 2025 (projected)
White 5,332,000
Black 1,223,000

Persons of Hispanic origin, 2000
total Hispanic or Latino 123,838
   Mexican 77,372
   Puerto Rican 10,303
   Cuban 3,695
   Other Hispanic or Latino 32,468

Persons of Hispanic origin, 2025 (proj.) .. 104,000

Persons by sex, 2000
male 2,770,275
female 2,919,008

Marital status, 1990
males
   15 years & older 1,831,058
   single 488,843
   married 1,141,001
      separated 33,320
      widowed 45,612
      divorced 155,602
females
   15 years & older 2,036,246
   single 409,983
   married 1,148,469
      separated 48,119

   widowed 266,366
   divorced 211,428

Households & families, 2000
households 2,232,905
persons per household 2.48
   families 1,547,835
   persons per family 2.99
      married couples 1,173,960
      female householder, no husband
         present 287,899
      one person households 576,401
households with persons under 18 years . 785,816
households with persons over 65 years ... 502,332

Nativity, 1990
number of persons born in state 3,373,365
percent of total residents 69.2%

Immigration & naturalization, 1998
immigrants admitted 2,806
persons naturalized 1,255
refugees granted resident status 331

VITAL STATISTICS & HEALTH

Births
1999
   with low birth weight 9.2%
   to teenage mothers 14.2%
   to unmarried mothers 34.7%
Birth rate, 1999 (per 1,000) 14.2
Birth rate, 2000 (per 1,000) 14.4

Abortions, 1996
total 18,000
rate (per 1,000 women age 15-44) 14.8

Deaths
1998 54,034
1999 53,765
2000 55,318

Infant deaths
1998 688
1999 624
2000 820

Average lifetime, by race, 1989-1991
total .... 74.32 years
   white .... 75.27 years
   black .... 68.97 years

Marriages
1998 81,168
1999 83,162
2000 88,244

Divorces
1998 34,509
1999 32,737
2000 33,842

Physicians, 1999
total 13,626
rate (per 1,000 persons) 2.48

Nurses, 1999
total 49,210
rate (per 1,000 persons) 8.97

Hospitals, 1998
number 122
beds (x 1,000) 20.7
average daily census (x 1,000) 11.8
patients admitted (x1,000) 745
average cost per day to hospital, 1995 ..... $871
average cost per stay to hospital, 1995 .... $5,355

EDUCATION

*Educational attainment of all persons
25 years and older, 1990*
less than 9th grade 500,929
high school graduates 942,865
bachelor's degree 330,742
graduate or professional degree 170,249

2000
high school graduate or more 79.9%
college graduate or more 22.0%

Public school enrollment, Fall, 1998
total 905,442
Kindergarten through grade 8 664,570
grades 9 through 12 240,872

Public School Teachers, 2000
total 55,500
elementary 40,300
secondary 15,200
average salaries
elementary $36,000
secondary $37,300

*State receipts & expenditures for public
schools, 2000*
revenue receipts ($mil) $5,429

*State receipts & expenditures for public
schools, 2000 (continued)*
expenditures
total ($mil) $5,159
per capita $941
per pupil $5,780

*Graduating high school seniors,
public high schools, 2000 (est.)* 41,719

SAT scores, 2001
verbal 562
math 553
percent graduates taking test 13%

Institutions of higher education, 1999
total 84
public 24
private 60

*Enrollment in institutions of higher
education, Fall, 1998*
total 251,410
full-time men 76,655
full-time women 93,957
part-time men 33,246
part-time women 47,552

*Minority enrollment in institutions of higher
education, Fall, 1997*
Black, non-Hispanic 37,708
Hispanic 2,780
Asian/Pacific Islander 1,593

Earned degrees conferred, 1998
Bachelor's 21,538
First professional 1,453
Master's 7,072
Doctor's 687

SOCIAL INSURANCE &
WELFARE PROGRAMS

Social Security beneficiaries & benefits, 2000
beneficiaries
total 996,000
retired and dependents 642,000
survivors 165,000
disabled & dependents 188,000
annual benefit payments ($mil)
total $8,537
retired and dependents $5,332
survivors $1,699
disabled & dependents $1,505

341

Medicare, 2000
enrollment (x1,000) 815
payments ($mil) $4,907

Medicaid, 1998
recipients (x1,000) 1,844
payments ($mil) $3,167

Federal public aid
Temporary Assistance for Needy Families
(TANF), 2000
   Recipients (x1,000) 146
   Families (x1,000) 56
Supplemental Security Income
   total recipients, 1999 (x1,000) 166

Food Stamp Program
   participants, 2000 (x1,000) 496

HOUSING & CONSTRUCTION

Total housing units, 2000 2,439,443
   seasonal or recreational use 36,712
   occupied 2,232,905
      owner occupied 1,561,363
      renter occupied 671,542

New privately owned housing units uthorized, 2000
number (x1,000) 32.2
value ($mil) $3,378

New privately owned housing units
   started, 2000 (est.) (x1,000) 33.9

Existing home sales, 2000 (x1,000) 140.2

GOVERNMENT & ELECTIONS

State officials, 2002
Governor (name/party/term expires)
DON SUNDQUIST
Republican - 2002
Lt. Governor .... John S. Wilder
Sec. of State .... Riley Darnell
Atty. General .... Paul Summers
Chief Justice .... Frank Drowota III

Governorship
minimum age 30
length of term .... 4 years
number of consecutive
   terms permitted 2
who succeeds .... Lt. Governor

State legislature
name .... General Assembly
  upper chamber
     name .... Senate
     number of members 33
     length of term .... 4 years
     party in majority, 2000 .... Democratic
  lower chamber
     name .... House of Representatives
     number of members 99
     length of term .... 2 years
     party in majority, 2000 .... Democratic

State employees March, 2000
total 94,370
March payroll $218,958,956

Local governments, 1997
total 940
   county 93
   municipal 343
   township 0
   school districts 14
   special districts 490

Voting age population, November, 2000, projected
Total 4,221,000
   male 1,998,000
   female 2,224,000

Vote for president
2000
   Gore 982,000
   Bush 1,062,000
1996
   Clinton 909,000
   Dole 864,000
   Perot 106,000

Federal representation, 2002 (107th Congress)
Senators (name/party/term expires)

BILL FRIST
Republican - 2007
FRED THOMPSON
Republican - 2003

Representatives, total 9
   Democrats 4
   Republicans 5
   other 0

Women holding public office, 2001
U.S. Congress 0
statewide elected office 0
state legislature 21

Black elected officials, 1999
total 172
   US and state legislatures 17
   city/county/regional offices 105
   judicial/law enforcement 25
   education/school boards 25

Hispanic public officials, 2000
total .... NA
   state executives & legislators .... NA
   city/county/regional offices .... NA
   judicial/law enforcement .... NA
   education/school boards .... NA

GOVERNMENTAL FINANCE

State government revenues, 1999 ($per capita)
total revenue $3,082.62
   total general revenue $2,668.99
     intergovernmental revenue $1,015.48
     taxes $1,312.56
     current charges $254.15
     miscellaneous $86.79

State government expenditures, 1999 ($per capita)
total expenditure $2,897.76
   total general expenditure $2,717.25
     education $952.62
     public welfare $839.20
     health $106.04
     hospitals $102.87
     highways $257.28
     police protection $20.85
     correction $79.28
     natural resources $34.48
     governmental administration $77.77
     interest on general debt $37.50

State debt, 1999 ($per capita) $605.71

Federal government grants to state & local government, 2000 (x$1,000)
total $6,160,429
   Dept. of Education $482,291
   Environmental Protection Agency $39,717
   Health Care Financing Admin. $3,190,747
   Dept. Housing & Urban Devel. $496,023
   Dept. of Labor $96,719
   Highway trust fund $482,604

CRIME, LAW ENFORCEMENT & COURTS

Crime, 2000 (all rates per 100,000 inhabitants)
total crimes 278,218
overall crime rate 4,890.2
   property crimes 237,985
     burglaries 56,344
     larcenies 154,111
     motor vehicle thefts 27,530
   property crime rate 4,183.0
   violent crimes 40,233
     murders 410
     forcible rapes 2,186
     robberies 9,465
     aggravated assaults 28,172
   violent crime rate 707.2

Number of police agencies, 2000 285

Arrests, 2000
total 187,110
   persons under 18 years of age 19,846

Prisoners under state & federal jurisdiction, 2000
total 22,166
percent change, 1999-2000 .... -1.5%
   sentenced to more than one year
     total 22,166
     rate per 100,000 residents 399

Persons under sentence of death, 4/1/2001 ... 103

State's highest court
name .... Supreme Court
number of members 5
length of term .... 8 years
intermediate appeals court? .... yes

Tennessee 6

LABOR & INCOME

Civilian labor force, 2000

total	2,798,000
men	1,505,000
women	1,294,000
persons 16-19 years	165,000
white	2,356,000
black	414,000

*Civilian labor force as a percent of
civilian non-institutional population, 2000*

total	65.3%
men	71.8%
women	59.1%
persons 16-19 years	NA%
white	65.4%
black	65.7%

Employment, 2000

total	2,688,000
men	1,452,000
women	1,236,000
persons 16-19 years	143,000
white	2,280,000
black	380,000

Full-time/part-time labor force, 1998

full-time labor force	2,320,000
working part-time for economic reasons	28,000
part-time labor force	439,000

Unemployment rate, 2000

total	3.9%
men	3.5%
women	4.5%
persons 16-19 years	13.4%
white	3.2%
black	8.2%

*Unemployed by reason for unemployment
(as a percent of total unemployment), 1998*

job losers or completed temp jobs	46.6%
job leavers	12.9%
reentrants	32.8%
new entrants	6.9%

Experienced civilian labor force, by occupation, 1998

executive/administrative/managerial	390,000
professional/specialty	319,000
technicians & related support	98,000
sales	322,000
administrative support/clerical	391,000
service occupations	344,000
precision production/craft/repair	330,000
machine operators/assemblers	228,000
transportation/material moving	133,000
handlers/helpers/laborers	128,000
farming/forestry/fishing	69,000

Experienced civilian labor force, by industry, 1998

construction	135,000
manufacturing	505,000
transportation/communication	159,000
wholesale/retail trade	510,000
finance/real estate/insurance	150,000
services	601,000
government	366,000
agriculture	NA

Average annual pay, 1999	$29,518
change in average annual pay, 1998-1999	3.7%

*Hours and earnings of production workers
on manufacturing payrolls, 2000*

average weekly hours	40.2
average hourly earnings	$12.92
average weekly earnings	$519.38

Labor union membership, 2000 211,500

Household income (in 2000 dollars)

median household income, three year average, 1998-2000	$33,885

Poverty

persons below poverty level, three year average, 1998-2000	13.3%

Personal income ($per capita)

2000 (prelim.)	
in current dollars	$26,239
in constant (1996) dollars	$24,440
1999 (preliminary)	
in current dollars	$25,581
in constant (1996) dollars	$24,461

Federal income tax returns, 1999

returns filed	2,536,680
adjusted gross income ($1,000)	$99,016,531
total income tax paid ($1,000)	$14,877,181

ECONOMY, BUSINESS, INDUSTRY & AGRICULTURE

Fortune 500 companies, 2000 6

Business incorporations, 1998
total 6,495
change, 1997-1998 . . . . -13.8%

Business failures, 1998 1,369

Business firm ownership, 1997
Hispanic owned firms 3,639
Black owned firms 20,196
women owned firms 99,772
Asian & Pacific Islander owned firms 5,296
American Indian & Alaska
    native owned firms 3,746

Shopping centers, 2000 1,214

Gross state product, 1999 ($mil)
total $170,085
    agriculture services, forestry, fisheries . . $1,492
    mining $510
    construction $7,462
    manufacturing--durable goods $20,736
    manufacturing--nondurable goods $14,656
    transportation, communication &
        public utilities $14,141
    wholesale trade $12,996
    retail trade $19,439
    finance/real estate/insurance $24,019
    services $35,089
    federal, state & local government $19,546

Establishments, by major industry group, 1999
total 131,116
    forestry, fishing & agriculture 354
    mining 228
    construction 11,636
    manufacturing 7,248
    transportation & warehousing 4,163
    wholesale trade 8,125
    retail trade 24,532
    finance & insurance 8,670
    professional/scientific/technical 9,902
    health care/social assistance 12,404
    information 2,344
    accommodation/food services 9,511

Payroll, by major industry group, 1999
total ($1 000) $65,963,770
    forestry, fishing & agriculture $33,116
    mining $148,570
    construction $4,076,994
    manufacturing $15,725,176
    transportation & warehousing $2,954,344
    wholesale trade $4,761,264
    retail trade $5,680,134
    finance & insurance $4,412,318
    professional/scientific/technical $3,661,453
    health care/social assistance $8,482,755
    information $1,735,178
    accommodation/food services $2,126,938

Agriculture
number of farms, 2000 90,000
farm acreage, 2000 12,000,000
acres per farm, 2000 130
value of farms, 1997 ($mil) $19,470
farm income, 1999 ($mil)
    net farm income $141
    debt/asset ratio 10.1%
farm marketings, 1999 ($mil)
total $1,974
    crops $963
    livestock $1,011
principal commodities, in order by marketing
receipts, 1999
    Cattle, broilers, dairy products, tobacco

Federal economic activity in state
expenditures, 2000
    total ($mil) $33,560
    per capita $5,899
    defense ($mil) $2,250
    non-defense ($mil) $31,310
defense department, 2000
    contract awards ($mil) $1,077
    payroll ($mil) $1,165
    civilian employees (x1,000) 6.7
    military personnel (x1,000) 2.4

Fishing, 2000
catch (thousands of pounds) . . . . NA
value ($1,000) . . . . $NA

Mining, 2000 ($mil; preliminary)
total non-fuel mineral production $770

Construction, 1999 ($mil)
total contracts (including
   non-building) $10,101
      residential $4,633
      non-residential $3,976

Construction industries, 1997
establishments 11,124
receipts ($1,000) $16,992,684
annual payroll ($1,000) $3,322,234
paid employees 118,094

Manufacturing, 1997
establishments 7,699
value of shipments ($1,000) $99,789,023
annual payroll ($1,000) $14,679,651
paid employees 495,760

Transportation industries, 1997
establishments 5,869
receipts ($1,000) $15,151,641
annual payroll ($1,000) $3,540,051
paid employees 111,487

Wholesale trade, 1997
establishments 9,673
sales($1,000) $85,925,887
annual payroll ($1,000) $4,351,058
paid employees 135,432

Retail trade, 1997
establishments 32,139
sales($1,000) $52,750,245
annual payroll ($1,000) $5,927,923
paid employees 457,976

Finance industries
establishments, 1997 12,215
receipts ($1,000), 1997 .... $NA
annual payroll ($1,000), 1997 .... $4,247,723
paid employees, 1997 123,091
commercial banks, 2000
  number 197
    assets ($bil) $86.9
    deposits ($bil) $61.9

Service industries, 1997 (non-exempt firms only)
establishments 36,914
receipts ($1,000) $31,225,566
annual payroll ($1,000) $12,005,081
paid employees 487,855

COMMUNICATION, ENERGY & TRANSPORTATION

Communication
daily newspapers, 2000 25
households with
  telephones, 1998 .... 93.4%
  computers, 2000 .... 45.7%
  internet access, 2000 .... 36.3%

Energy
consumption, 1999
total (trillion Btu) 2,071
per capita (million Btu) 378
by source of production (trillion Btu)
  coal 626
  natural gas 286
  petroleum 713
  nuclear electric power 289
  hydroelectric power 74
by end-use sector (trillion Btu)
  residential 442
  commercial 328
  industrial 711
  transportation 590
electric energy, 1999
  production (billion kWh) 89.7
  net summer capability (million kW) 17.3
gas utilities, 1999
  customers 1,028,000
  sales (trillion Btu) 170
nuclear plants, 1999 3

Transportation, 2000
public road & street mileage
total 87,419
  urban 17,740
  rural 69,679
  interstate 1,073
vehicle miles of travel (mil) 65,732
total motor vehicle registrations 4,819,799
  automobiles 2,854,569
  motorcycles 70,846
licensed drivers 4,251,228
  per 1,000 driving age population 956
deaths from motor vehicle
  accidents 1,306

Texas 1

STATE SUMMARY

Capital City . . . . Austin

Governor . . . . Rick Perry

Address . . . . STATE CAPITOL
AUSTIN, TX 78711
512 463-2000

Admitted as a state 1845

Area (square miles) 268,601

Population, 1980 14,229,191

Population, 1990 16,986,510

Population, 2000 20,851,820

Persons per square mile, 2000 . . . . 79.6

Largest city . . . . Houston
population, 2000 1,954,000

Personal income per capita, 2000
(in current dollars) $27,871

Gross state product ($mil), 1999 . . . . . . $687,272

Leading industries, 1999 (by payroll)
Manufacturing
Health care/Social assistance
Professional/Scientific/Technical

Leading agricultural commodities, 1999
Cattle, cotton, greenhouse, broilers

GEOGRAPHY & ENVIRONMENT

Area, 1990 (square miles)
total 268,601
land 261,914
water (includes territorial water) 6,687

Federally owned land, 2000 . . . . 1.4%

Highest point
name . . . . Gaudalupe Peak
elevation (feet) 8,749

Lowest point
name . . . . Gulf of Mexico
elevation (feet) . . . . sea level

General coastline (miles) 367

Tidal shoreline (miles) 3,359

Capital city . . . . Austin
population, 2000 657,000

Largest city . . . . Houston
population, 2000 1,954,000

Number of cities with over 100,000 population
1980 16
1990 17
2000 24

State parks and Recreation areas, 2000
area (acres) 631,000
number of visitors 18,751,000
revenues $21,248,000

Natl. forest system land, 1999 (acres) 755,000

National park acreage, 1984 1,098,700

DEMOGRAPHICS & CHARACTERISTICS OF THE POPULATION

Population
1970 11,198,655
1980 14,229,191
1990 16,986,510
2000 20,851,820
2015 (projection) 24,280,000
2025 (projection) 27,183,000

Metropolitan area population
1970 8,716,000
1980 11,307,000
2000 17,692,000

Non-metropolitan area population
1970 2,483,000
1980 2,922,000
2000 3,160,000

Change in population, 1990-2000
number 3,865,310
percent 22.76%

Persons per square mile, 2000 . . . . 79.6

Persons by age, 2000
under 5 years 1,624,628
18 and over 14,965,061
21 and over 13,981,939
65 and over 2,072,532
85 and over 237,940

Texas 2

Persons by age, 2025 (projected)
under 5 years 2,073,000
5 to 17 years 5,277,000
65 and over 4,364,000

Median age, 2000 .... 32.3

Race, 2000
One race
White 14,799,505
Black or African American 2,404,566
American Indian and Alaska Native 118,362
Asian Indian 129,365
Chinese 105,829
Filipino 58,340
Japanese 17,120
Korean 45,571
Vietnamese 134,961
Native Hawaiian and other Pacific Islander 14,434
Two or more races 514,633

Race, 2025 (projected)
White 22,089,000
Black 3,871,000

Persons of Hispanic origin, 2000
total Hispanic or Latino 6,669,666
  Mexican 5,071,963
  Puerto Rican 69,504
  Cuban 25,705
  Other Hispanic or Latino 1,502,494

Persons of Hispanic origin, 2025 (proj.) 10,230,000

Persons by sex, 2000
male 10,352,910
female 10,498,910

Marital status, 1990
males
  15 years & older 6,279,064
    single 1,822,173
    married 3,830,591
      separated 144,206
    widowed 132,379
    divorced 493,921
females
  15 years & older 6,626,866
    single 1,421,299
    married 3,819,716
      separated 202,639

widowed 705,759
divorced 680,092

Households & families, 2000
households 7,393,354
persons per household 2.74
  families 5,247,794
  persons per family 3.28
    married couples 3,989,741
    female householder, no husband
      present 937,589
    one person households 1,752,141
households with persons under 18 years 3,027,570
households with persons over 65 years .. 1,469,876

Nativity, 1990
number of persons born in state 10,994,794
percent of total residents 64.7%

Immigration & naturalization, 1998
immigrants admitted 44,428
persons naturalized 30,862
refugees granted resident status 982

VITAL STATISTICS & HEALTH

Births
1999
  with low birth weight 7.4%
  to teenage mothers 17.4%
  to unmarried mothers 31.3%
Birth rate, 1999 (per 1,000) 17.4
Birth rate, 2000 (per 1,000) 18.0

Abortions, 1996
total 91,000
rate (per 1,000 women age 15-44) 20.7

Deaths
1998 145,364
1999 146,858
2000 148,554

Infant deaths
1998 2,221
1999 2,168
2000 2,050

Average lifetime, by race, 1989-1991
total .... 75.14 years
  white .... 75.75 years
  black .... 69.79 years

Marriages

1998	188,923
1999	187,370
2000	196,417

Divorces

1998	NA
1999	73,283
2000	82,864

Physicians, 1999

total	41,084
rate (per 1,000 persons)	2.05

Nurses, 1999

total	132,110
rate (per 1,000 persons)	6.59

Hospitals, 1998

number	400
beds (x 1,000)	56.6
average daily census (x 1,000)	32.1
patients admitted (x1,000)	2,227
average cost per day to hospital, 1995	$1,063
average cost per stay to hospital, 1995	$5,879

EDUCATION

Educational attainment of all persons 25 years and older, 1990

less than 9th grade	1,387,528
high school graduates	2,640,162
bachelor's degree	1,428,031
graduate or professional degree	666,874

2000

high school graduate or more	79.2%
college graduate or more	23.9%

Public school enrollment, Fall, 1998

total	3,945,367
Kindergarten through grade 8	2,868,209
grades 9 through 12	1,077,158

Public School Teachers, 2000

total	267,900
elementary	136,600
secondary	131,300
average salaries	
elementary	$37,400
secondary	$38,100

State receipts & expenditures for public schools, 2000

revenue receipts ($mil)	$30,976

State receipts & expenditures for public schools, 2000 (continued)
expenditures

total ($mil)	$29,574
per capita	$1,475
per pupil	$6,588

Graduating high school seniors

public high schools, 2000 (est)	212,966

SAT scores, 2001

verbal	493
math	499
percent graduates taking test	53%

Institutions of higher education, 1999

total	199
public	109
private	90

Enrollment in institutions of higher education, Fall, 1998

total	928,227
full-time men	257,541
full-time women	292,742
part-time men	187,352
part-time women	244,592

Minority enrollment in institutions of higher education, Fall, 1997

Black, non-Hispanic	98,255
Hispanic	209,984
Asian/Pacific Islander	45,851

Earned degrees conferred, 1998

Bachelor's	71,771
First professional	4,821
Master's	23,632
Doctor's	2,815

SOCIAL INSURANCE & WELFARE PROGRAMS

Social Security beneficiaries & benefits, 2000
beneficiaries

total	2,638,000
retired and dependents	1,811,000
survivors	481,000
disabled & dependents	346,000
annual benefit payments ($mil)	
total	$22,883
retired and dependents	$14,963
survivors	$5,139
disabled & dependents	$2,781

Texas 4

Medicare, 2000
enrollment (x1,000) 2,223
payments ($mil) $14,538

Medicaid, 1998
recipients (x1,000) 2,325
payments ($mil) $7,140

Federal public aid
Temporary Assistance for Needy Families
(TANF), 2000
   Recipients (x1,000) 338
   Families (x1,000) 126
Supplemental Security Income
   total recipients, 1999 (x1,000) 408

Food Stamp Program
   participants, 2000 (x1,000) 1,333

HOUSING & CONSTRUCTION

Total housing units, 2000 8,157,575
   seasonal or recreational use 173,149
   occupied 7,393,354
      owner occupied 4,716,959
      renter occupied 2,676,395

New privately owned housing units uthorized, 2000
number (x1,000) 141.2
value ($mil) $15,418

New privately owned housing units
started, 2000 (est.) (x1,000) 148.4

Existing home sales, 2000 (x1,000) 518.5

GOVERNMENT & ELECTIONS

State officials, 2002
   Governor (name/party/term expires)
       RICK PERRY
       Republican - 2002
Lt. Governor .... Bill Ratliff
Sec. of State .... Elton Bomer
Atty. General .... John Cornyn
Chief Justice .... Tom Phillips

Governorship
minimum age 30
length of term .... 4 years
number of consecutive
   terms permitted .... not specified
who succeeds .... Lt. Governor

State legislature
name .... Legislature
   upper chamber
      name .... Senate
      number of members 31
      length of term .... 4 years
      party in majority, 2000 .... Republican
lower chamber
      name .... House of Representatives
      number of members 150
      length of term .... 2 years
      party in majority, 2000 .... Democratic

State employees March, 2000
total 303,795
March payroll $813,300,130

Local governments, 1997
total 4,700
   county 254
   municipal 1,177
   township 0
   school districts 1,087
   special districts 2,182

Voting age population, November, 2000, projected
Total 14,850,000
   male 7,219,000
   female 7,630,000

Vote for president
2000
   Gore 2,434,000
   Bush 3,800,000
1996
   Clinton 2,460,000
   Dole 2,736,000
   Perot 379,000

Federal representation, 2002 (107th Congress)
Senators (name/party/term expires)

      KAY BAILEY HUTCHISON
      Republican - 2007
      PHIL GRAMM
      Republican - 2003

Representatives, total 30
   Democrats 17
   Republicans 13
   other 0

Women holding public office, 2001
U.S. Congress 4
statewide elected office 2
state legislature 34

Black elected officials, 1999
total 479
US and state legislatures 18
city/county/regional offices 319
judicial/law enforcement 42
education/school boards 100

Hispanic public officials, 2000
total 1,828
state executives & legislators 42
city/county/regional offices 768
judicial/law enforcement 280
education/school boards 738

GOVERNMENTAL FINANCE

State government revenues, 1999 ($per capita)
total revenue $3,574.54
total general revenue $2,621.47
intergovernmental revenue $813.69
taxes $1,280.95
current charges $230.27
miscellaneous $296.55

State government expenditures, 1999 ($per capita)
total expenditure $2,732.04
total general expenditure $2,474.08
education $1,026.04
public welfare $587.50
health $73.50
hospitals $130.46
highways $199.50
police protection $16.20
correction $132.69
natural resources $35.53
governmental administration $71.46
interest on general debt $43.46

State debt, 1999 ($per capita) $735.19

Federal government grants to state & local government, 2000 (x$1,000)
total $17,350,136
Dept. of Education $2,031,762
Environmental Protection Agency . . . $164,473
Health Care Financing Admin. $7,067,987
Dept. Housing & Urban Devel. $1,653,549
Dept. of Labor $299,300
Highway trust fund $1,783,411

CRIME, LAW ENFORCEMENT & COURTS

Crime, 2000 (all rates per 100,000 inhabitants)
total crimes 1,033,311
overall crime rate 4,955.5
property crimes 919,658
burglaries 188,975
larcenies 637,522
motor vehicle thefts 93,161
property crime rate 4,410.4
violent crimes 113,653
murders 1,238
forcible rapes 7,856
robberies 30,257
aggravated assaults 74,302
violent crime rate 545.1

Number of police agencies, 2000 901

Arrests, 2000
total 1,145,271
persons under 18 years of age 202,504

Prisoners under state & federal jurisdiction, 2000
total 157,997
percent change, 1999-2000 . . . . -3.2%
sentenced to more than one year
total 150,107
rate per 100,000 residents 730

Persons under sentence of death, 4/1/2001 . . . 450

State's highest court
name . . . . Supreme Court
number of members 9
length of term . . . . 6 years
intermediate appeals court? . . . . yes

Texas 6

LABOR & INCOME

Civilian labor force, 2000
total	10,325,000
men	5,711,000
women	4,613,000
persons 16-19 years	629,000
white	8,836,000
black	1,108,000

Civilian labor force as a percent of civilian non-institutional population, 2000
total	68.2%
men	77.5%
women	59.4%
persons 16-19 years	NA%
white	68.4%
black	67.5%

Employment, 2000
total	9,887,000
men	5,486,000
women	4,401,000
persons 16-19 years	532,000
white	8,499,000
black	1,022,000

Full-time/part-time labor force, 1998
full-time labor force	8,583,000
working part-time for economic reasons	112,000
part-time labor force	1,535,000

Unemployment rate, 2000
total	4.2%
men	3.9%
women	4.6%
persons 16-19 years	15.4%
white	3.8%
black	7.8%

Unemployed by reason for unemployment (as a percent of total unemployment), 1998
job losers or completed temp jobs	39.6%
job leavers	12.9%
reentrants	37.2%
new entrants	10.1%

Experienced civilian labor force, by occupation, 1998
executive/administrative/managerial	1,363,000
professional/specialty	1,455,000
technicians & related support	315,000
sales	1,229,000
administrative support/clerical	1,418,000
service occupations	1,424,000
precision production/craft/repair	1,190,000
machine operators/assemblers	491,000
transportation/material moving	445,000
handlers/helpers/laborers	425,000
farming/forestry/fishing	314,000

Experienced civilian labor force, by industry, 1998
construction	600,000
manufacturing	1,342,000
transportation/communication	691,000
wholesale/retail trade	2,034,000
finance/real estate/insurance	520,000
services	2,285,000
government	1,348,000
agriculture	330,000

Average annual pay, 1999 ... $32,895
change in average annual pay,
1998-1999 ... 4.4%

Hours and earnings of production workers on manufacturing payrolls, 2000
average weekly hours	43.3
average hourly earnings	$12.37
average weekly earnings	$535.62

Labor union membership, 2000 ... 505,400

Household income (in 2000 dollars)
median household income,
three year average, 1998-2000 ... $39,842

Poverty
persons below poverty level,
three year average, 1998-2000 ... 14.9%

Personal income ($per capita)
2000 (prelim.)
in current dollars	$27,871
in constant (1996) dollars	$25,960

1999 (preliminary)
in current dollars	$26,525
in constant (1996) dollars	$25,363

Federal income tax returns, 1999
returns filed	8,837,214
adjusted gross income ($1,000)	$380,232,946
total income tax paid ($1,000)	$62,368,990

ECONOMY, BUSINESS, INDUSTRY & AGRICULTURE

Fortune 500 companies, 2000 45

Business incorporations, 1998
total 38,829
change, 1997-1998 .... -1.2%

Business failures, 1998 6,785

Business firm ownership, 1997
Hispanic owned firms 240,396
Black owned firms 60,427
women owned firms 381,453
Asian & Pacific Islander owned firms 60,226
American Indian & Alaska
  native owned firms 15,668

Shopping centers, 2000 3,045

Gross state product, 1999 ($mil)
total $687,272
  agriculture services, forestry, fisheries .. $9,197
  mining $39,365
  construction $32,288
  manufacturing--durable goods $55,803
  manufacturing--nondurable goods $40,396
  transportation, communication &
    public utilities $75,205
  wholesale trade $54,573
  retail trade $66,107
  finance/real estate/insurance $101,021
  services $136,533
  federal, state & local government $76,783

Establishments, by major industry group, 1999
total 467,087
  forestry, fishing & agriculture 1,373
  mining 5,989
  construction 37,910
  manufacturing 21,724
  transportation & warehousing 13,892
  wholesale trade 32,997
  retail trade 74,023
  finance & insurance 29,885
  professional/scientific/technical 48,058
  health care/social assistance 43,847
  information 8,215
  accommodation/food services 34,398

Payroll, by major industry group, 1999
total ($1,000) $245,163,283
  forestry, fishing & agriculture $218,440
  mining $5,250,251
  construction $15,993,349
  manufacturing $36,485,925
  transportation & warehousing $10,323,133
  wholesale trade $18,333,123
  retail trade $20,152,923
  finance & insurance $16,804,857
  professional/scientific/technical $21,484,372
  health care/social assistance $25,753,776
  information $11,364,240
  accommodation/food services $7,875,038

Agriculture
number of farms, 2000 226,000
farm acreage, 2000 130,000,000
acres per farm, 2000 575
value of farms, 1997 ($mil) $77,400
farm income, 1999 ($mil)
  net farm income $4,650
  debt/asset ratio 12.6%
farm marketings, 1999 ($mil)
  total $13,052
  crops $4,572
  livestock $8,480
principal commodities, in order by marketing
receipts, 1999
  Cattle, cotton, greenhouse, broilers

Federal economic activity in state
expenditures, 2000
  total ($mil) $106,493
  per capita $5,107
  defense ($mil) $20,564
  non-defense ($mil) $85,928
defense department, 2000
  contract awards ($mil) $12,145
  payroll ($mil) $8,659
  civilian employees (x1,000) 39.3
  military personnel (x1,000) 109.9

Fishing, 2000
catch (thousands of pounds) 87,990
value ($1,000) $232,400

Mining, 2000 ($mil; preliminary)
total non-fuel mineral production $2,050

Texas 8

Construction, 1999 ($mil)
total contracts (including
    non-building) $40,157
      residential $15,984
      non-residential $14,830

Construction industries, 1997
establishments 34,198
receipts ($1,000) .... $NA
annual payroll ($1,000) .... $NA
paid employees 420,823

Manufacturing, 1997
establishments 22,458
value of shipments ($1,000) $301,788,258
annual payroll ($1,000) $33,519,948
paid employees 985,731

Transportation industries, 1997
establishments 21,411
receipts ($1,000) $134,303,226
annual payroll ($1,000) $14,930,807
paid employees 423,790

Wholesale trade, 1997
establishments 37,984
sales($1,000) .... $NA
annual payroll ($1,000) .... $NA
paid employees .... NA

Retail trade, 1997
establishments 102,185
sales($1,000) $183,274,112
annual payroll ($1,000) $20,061,530
paid employees 1,464,183

Finance industries
establishments, 1997 45,137
receipts ($1,000), 1997 .... $NA
annual payroll ($1,000), 1997 .... $16,855,122
paid employees, 1997 452,103
commercial banks, 2000
    number 710
      assets ($bil) $166.4
      deposits ($bil) $133.2

Service industries, 1997 (non-exempt firms only)
establishments 143,006
receipts ($1,000) $135,616,651
annual payroll ($1,000) $52,412,361
paid employees 1,968,608

COMMUNICATION, ENERGY & TRANSPORTATION

Communication
daily newspapers, 2000 87
households with
    telephones, 1998 .... 91.6%
    computers, 2000 .... 47.9%
    internet access, 2000 .... 38.3%

Energy
consumption, 1999
total (trillion Btu) 11,501
per capita (million Btu) 574
by source of production (trillion Btu)
    coal 1,535
    natural gas 3,982
    petroleum 5,565
    nuclear electric power 391
    hydroelectric power 13
by end-use sector (trillion Btu)
    residential 1,323
    commercial 1,147
    industrial 6,482
    transportation 2,549
electric energy, 1999
    production (billion kWh) 292.5
    net summer capability (million kW) 65.3
gas utilities, 1999
    customers 3,916,000
    sales (trillion Btu) 631
nuclear plants, 1999 4

Transportation, 2000
public road & street mileage
total 301,035
    urban 82,394
    rural 218,641
    interstate 3,234
vehicle miles of travel (mil) 220,064
total motor vehicle registrations 14,070,096
    automobiles 7,616,183
    motorcycles 181,787
licensed drivers 13,462,023
    per 1,000 driving age population 862
deaths from motor vehicle
    accidents 3,769

STATE SUMMARY

Capital City ....Salt Lake City

Governor ....Mike Leavitt

Address ....STATE CAPITOL
SALT LAKE CITY, UT 84114
801 538-1000

Admitted as a state 1896

Area (square miles) 84,904

Population, 1980 1,461,037

Population, 1990 1,722,850

Population, 2000 2,233,169

Persons per square mile, 2000 ....27.2

Largest city ....Salt Lake City
population, 2000 182,000

Personal income per capita, 2000
(in current dollars) $23,907

Gross state product ($mil), 1999 ....$62,641

Leading industries, 1999 (by payroll)
Manufacturing
Health care/Social assistance
Retail trade

Leading agricultural commodities, 1999
Cattle, dairy products, hay, greenhouse

GEOGRAPHY & ENVIRONMENT

Area, 1990 (square miles)
total 84,904
land 82,168
water (includes territorial water) 2,736

Federally owned land, 2000 ....64.5%

Highest point
name ....Kings Peak
elevation (feet) 13,528

Lowest point
name ....Beaverdam Creek
elevation (feet) 2,000

General coastline (miles) 0

Tidal shoreline (miles) 0

Capital city ....Salt Lake City
population, 2000 182,000

Largest city ....Salt Lake City
population, 2000 182,000

Number of cities with over 100,000 population
1980 1
1990 1
2000 3

State parks and Recreation areas, 2000
area (acres) 114,000
number of visitors 6,737,000
revenues $7,849,000

Natl. forest system land, 1999 (acres) ...8,111,000

National park acreage, 1984 2,022,700

DEMOGRAPHICS & CHARACTERISTICS OF THE POPULATION

Population
1970 1,059,273
1980 1,461,037
1990 1,722,850
2000 2,233,169
2015 (projection) 2,670,000
2025 (projection) 2,883,000

Metropolitan area population
1970 822,000
1980 1,128,000
2000 1,708,000

Non-metropolitan area population
1970 238,000
1980 333,000
2000 525,000

Change in population, 1990-2000
number 510,319
percent 29.62%

Persons per square mile, 2000 ....27.2

Persons by age, 2000
under 5 years 209,378
18 and over 1,514,471
21 and over 1,379,043
65 and over 190,222
85 and over 21,751

Utah 2

Persons by age, 2025 (projected)
under 5 years 225,000
5 to 17 years 605,000
65 and over 495,000

Median age, 2000 .... 27.1

Race, 2000
One race
White 1,992,975
Black or African American 17,657
American Indian and Alaska Native 29,684
Asian Indian 3,065
Chinese 8,045
Filipino 3,106
Japanese 6,186
Korean 3,473
Vietnamese 5,968
Native Hawaiian and other Pacific Islander 15,145
Two or more races 47,195

Race, 2025 (projected)
White 2,672,000
Black 39,000

Persons of Hispanic origin, 2000
total Hispanic or Latino 201,559
  Mexican 136,416
  Puerto Rican 3,977
  Cuban 940
  Other Hispanic or Latino 60,226

Persons of Hispanic origin, 2025 (proj.) .. 265,000

Persons by sex, 2000
male 1,119,031
female 1,114,138

Marital status, 1990
males
  15 years & older 580,050
  single 165,764
  married 366,139
    separated 6,288
  widowed 9,074
  divorced 39,073
females
  15 years & older 605,647
  single 136,825
  married 367,263
    separated 8,478

widowed 48,925
divorced 52,634

Households & families, 2000
households 701,281
persons per household 3.13
  families 535,294
  persons per family 3.57
    married couples 442,931
    female householder, no husband
      present 65,941
  one person households 124,756
households with persons under 18 years . 321,108
households with persons over 65 years ... 130,469

Nativity, 1990
number of persons born in state 1,157,744
percent of total residents 67.2%

Immigration & naturalization, 1998
immigrants admitted 3,360
persons naturalized 1,421
refugees granted resident status 612

VITAL STATISTICS & HEALTH
Births
1999
  with low birth weight 6.8%
  to teenage mothers 21.7%
  to unmarried mothers 16.7%
Birth rate, 1999 (per 1,000) 21.7
Birth rate, 2000 (per 1,000) 21.9

Abortions, 1996
total 4,000
rate (per 1,000 women age 15-44) 7.8

Deaths
1998 11,920
1999 12,058
2000 12,370

Infant deaths
1998 260
1999 230
2000 281

Average lifetime, by race, 1989-1991
total .... 77.70 years
  white .... 77.77 years
  black .... NA years

Marriages
1998 21,547
1999 21,089
2000 24,097

Divorces
1998 8,835
1999 9,455
2000 9,714

Physicians, 1999
total 4,312
rate (per 1,000 persons) 2.02

Nurses, 1999
total 13,870
rate (per 1,000 persons) 6.51

Hospitals, 1998
number 41
beds (x 1,000) 4.0
average daily census (x 1,000) 2.4
patients admitted (x1,000) 192
average cost per day to hospital, 1995 . . . . $1,213
average cost per stay to hospital, 1995 . . . . $5,676

EDUCATION

Educational attainment of all persons
25 years and older, 1990
less than 9th grade 30,379
high school graduates 244,132
bachelor's degree 138,534
graduate or professional degree 61,219

2000
high school graduate or more 90.7%
college graduate or more 26.4%

Public school enrollment, Fall, 1998
total 481,176
Kindergarten through grade 8 328,522
grades 9 through 12 152,654

Public School Teachers, 2000
total 22,200
elementary 11,500
secondary 10,600
average salaries
elementary $34,900
secondary $35,400

State receipts & expenditures for public
schools, 2000
revenue receipts ($mil) $2,418

State receipts & expenditures for public
schools, 2000 (continued)
expenditures
total ($mil) $2,386
per capita $1,120
per pupil $4,282

Graduating high school seniors,
public high schools, 2000 (est.) 32,303

SAT scores, 2001
verbal 575
math 570
percent graduates taking test 5%

Institutions of higher education, 1999
total 21
public 9
private 12

Enrollment in institutions of higher
education, Fall, 1998
total 151,232
full-time men 46,565
full-time women 48,378
part-time men 28,513
part-time women 27,776

Minority enrollment in institutions of higher
education, Fall, 1997
Black, non-Hispanic 909
Hispanic 4,603
Asian/Pacific Islander 3,531

Earned degrees conferred, 1998
Bachelor's 16,670
First professional .379
Master's 3,473
Doctor's 357

SOCIAL INSURANCE & WELFARE PROGRAMS

Social Security beneficiaries & benefits, 2000
beneficiaries
total 242,000
retired and dependents 178,000
survivors 34,000
disabled & dependents 30,000
annual benefit payments ($mil)
total $2,152
retired and dependents $1,530
survivors $386
disabled & dependents $236

Utah 4

Medicare, 2000
enrollment (x1,000) 201
payments ($mil) $918

Medicaid, 1998
recipients (x1,000) 216
payments ($mil) $619

Federal public aid
Temporary Assistance for Needy Families
(TANF), 2000
   Recipients (x1,000) 24
   Families (x1,000) 8
Supplemental Security Income
   total recipients, 1999 (x1,000) 20

Food Stamp Program
   participants, 2000 (x1,000) 82

HOUSING & CONSTRUCTION

Total housing units, 2000 768,594
   seasonal or recreational use 29,685
   occupied 701,281
      owner occupied 501,547
      renter occupied 199,734

New privately owned housing units uthorized, 2000
number (x1,000) 17.6
value ($mil) $2,138

New privately owned housing units
   started, 2000 (est.) (x1,000) 19.5

Existing home sales, 2000 (x1,000) 50.9

GOVERNMENT & ELECTIONS

State officials, 2002
Governor (name/party/term expires)
        MIKE LEAVITT
        Republican - 2000
Lt. Governor . . . . Olene Walker
Sec. of State . . . . (no Secretary of State)
Atty. General . . . . Mike Shirtleffe
Chief Justice . . . . Richard Howe

Governorship
minimum age 30
length of term . . . . 4 years
number of consecutive
   terms permitted 3
who succeeds . . . . Lt. Governor

State legislature
name . . . . Legislature
  upper chamber
     name . . . . Senate
     number of members 29
     length of term . . . . 4 years
     party in majority, 2000 . . . . Republican
  lower chamber
     name . . . . House of Representatives
     number of members 75
     length of term . . . . 2 years
     party in majority, 2000 . . . . Republican

State employees March, 2000
total 59,863
March payroll $135,422,509

Local governments, 1997
total 683
   county 29
   municipal 230
   township 0
   school districts 40
   special districts 384

Voting age population, November, 2000, projected
Total 1,435,000
   male 717,000
   female 748,000

Vote for president
2000
   Gore 203,000
   Bush 515,000
1996
   Clinton 222,000
   Dole 362,000
   Perot 66,000

Federal representation, 2002 (107th Congress)
Senators (name/party/term expires)

       ORRIN G. HATCH
       Republican - 2007
       ROBERT BENNETT
       Republican - 2005

Representatives, total 3
   Democrats 1
   Republicans 2
   other 0

Women holding public office, 2001
U.S. Congress 0
statewide elected office 1
state legislature 23

Black elected officials, 1999
total 1
US and state legislatures .... NA
city/county/regional offices .... NA
judicial/law enforcement 1
education/school boards .... NA

Hispanic public officials, 2000
total 3
state executives & legislators 1
city/county/regional offices 2
judicial/law enforcement .... NA
education/school boards .... NA

GOVERNMENTAL FINANCE

State government revenues, 1999 ($per capita)
total revenue $4,104.63
total general revenue $3,306.88
intergovernmental revenue $857.83
taxes $1,715.52
current charges $492.50
miscellaneous $241.03

State government expenditures, 1999 ($per capita)
total expenditure $3,666.76
total general expenditure $3,387.32
education $1,593.90
public welfare $611.87
health $89.79
hospitals $186.47
highways $282.95
police protection $32.22
correction $102.02
natural resources $68.52
governmental administration $197.82
interest on general debt $83.92

State debt, 1999 ($per capita) $1,775.20

Federal government grants to state & local government, 2000 (x$1,000)
total $1,910,316
Dept. of Education $205,480
Environmental Protection Agency $26,098
Health Care Financing Admin. $635,266
Dept. Housing & Urban Devel. $136,547
Dept. of Labor $42,984
Highway trust fund $230,078

CRIME, LAW ENFORCEMENT & COURTS

Crime, 2000 (all rates per 100,000 inhabitants)
total crimes 99,958
overall crime rate 4,476.1
property crimes 94,247
burglaries 14,348
larcenies 73,438
motor vehicle thefts 6,461
property crime rate 4,220.3
violent crimes 5,711
murders 43
forcible rapes 863
robberies 1,242
aggravated assaults 3,563
violent crime rate 255.7

Number of police agencies, 2000 90

Arrests, 2000
total 98,038
persons under 18 years of age 25,824

Prisoners under state & federal jurisdiction, 2000
total 5,630
percent change, 1999-2000 .... 5.8%
sentenced to more than one year
total 5,526
rate per 100,000 residents 254

Persons under sentence of death, 4/1/2001 11

State's highest court
name .... Supreme Court
number of members 5
length of term .... 10 years
intermediate appeals court? .... no

Utah 6

LABOR & INCOME

Civilian labor force, 2000
total	1,104,000
men	626,000
women	479,000
persons 16-19 years	94,000
white	1,055,000
black	NA

Civilian labor force as a percent of civilian non-institutional population, 2000
total	72.3%
men	82.0%
women	62.7%
persons 16-19 years	NA%
white	72.2%
black	NA%

Employment, 2000
total	1,068,000
men	607,000
women	461,000
persons 16-19 years	86,000
white	1,020,000
black	NA

Full-time/part-time labor force, 1998
full-time labor force	820,000
working part-time for economic reasons	9,000
part-time labor force	243,000

Unemployment rate, 2000
total	3.2%
men	3.0%
women	3.6%
persons 16-19 years	8.8%
white	3.3%
black	NA%

Unemployed by reason for unemployment (as a percent of total unemployment), 1998
job losers or completed temp jobs	40.0%
job leavers	15.0%
reentrants	37.5%
new entrants	5.0%

Experienced civilian labor force, by occupation, 1998
executive/administrative/managerial	140,000
professional/specialty	165,000
technicians & related support	33,000
sales	146,000
administrative support/clerical	165,000
service occupations	123,000
precision production/craft/repair	118,000
machine operators/assemblers	58,000
transportation/material moving	35,000
handlers/helpers/laborers	52,000
farming/forestry/fishing	NA

Experienced civilian labor force, by industry, 1998
construction	71,000
manufacturing	132,000
transportation/communication	52,000
wholesale/retail trade	220,000
finance/real estate/insurance	61,000
services	252,000
government	157,000
agriculture	NA

Average annual pay, 1999
	$27,884
change in average annual pay, 1998-1999	3.8%

Hours and earnings of production workers on manufacturing payrolls, 2000
average weekly hours	39.8
average hourly earnings	$13.69
average weekly earnings	$544.86

Labor union membership, 2000
69,300

Household income (in 2000 dollars)
median household income, three year average, 1998-2000	$45,230

Poverty
persons below poverty level, three year average, 1998-2000	8.1%

Personal income ($per capita)
2000 (prelim.)
in current dollars	$23,907
in constant (1996) dollars	$22,268

1999 (preliminary)
in current dollars	$23,356
in constant (1996) dollars	$22,333

Federal income tax returns, 1999
returns filed	919,417
adjusted gross income ($1,000)	$37,557,772
total income tax paid ($1,000)	$4,806,634

ECONOMY, BUSINESS, INDUSTRY & AGRICULTURE

Fortune 500 companies, 2000 1

Business incorporations, 1998
total 6,864
change, 1997-1998 .... -6.0%

Business failures, 1998 388

Business firm ownership, 1997
Hispanic owned firms 4,740
Black owned firms 440
women owned firms 41,991
Asian & Pacific Islander owned firms 2,379
American Indian & Alaska
  native owned firms 1,428

Shopping centers, 2000 248

Gross state product, 1999 ($mil)
total $62,641
  agriculture services, forestry, fisheries $697
  mining $1,143
  construction $4,092
  manufacturing--durable goods $5,349
  manufacturing--nondurable goods $2,962
  transportation, communication &
    public utilities $5,514
  wholesale trade $3,894
  retail trade $6,708
  finance/real estate/insurance $10,299
  services $12,935
  federal, state & local government $9,047

Establishments, by major industry group, 1999
total 53,809
  forestry, fishing & agriculture 67
  mining 288
  construction 7,931
  manufacturing 2,948
  transportation & warehousing 1,347
  wholesale trade 3,336
  retail trade 7,778
  finance & insurance 4,073
  professional/scientific/technical 5,076
  health care/social assistance 4,532
  information 1,081
  accommodation/food services 3,869

Payroll, by major industry group, 1999
total ($1,000) $23,363,993
  forestry, fishing & agriculture $6,085
  mining $332,755
  construction $1,923,124
  manufacturing $4,074,085
  transportation & warehousing $1,146,923
  wholesale trade $1,512,741
  retail trade $2,174,548
  finance & insurance $1,472,602
  professional/scientific/technical $1,843,017
  health care/social assistance $2,301,681
  information $979,974
  accommodation/food services $768,501

Agriculture
number of farms, 2000 16,000
farm acreage, 2000 12,000,000
acres per farm, 2000 748
value of farms, 1997 ($mil) $8,250
farm income, 1999 ($mil)
  net farm income $280
  debt/asset ratio 7.4%
farm marketings, 1999 ($mil)
total $967
  crops $243
  livestock $724
principal commodities, in order by marketing
receipts, 1999
  Cattle, dairy products, hay, greenhouse

Federal economic activity in state
expenditures, 2000
  total ($mil) $10,037
  per capita $4,494
  defense ($mil) $1,934
  non-defense ($mil) $8,103
defense department, 2000
  contract awards ($mil) $950
  payroll ($mil) $1,044
  civilian employees (x1,000) 13.5
  military personnel (x1,000) 4.8

Fishing, 2000
catch (thousands of pounds) ....NA
value ($1,000) ....$NA

Mining, 2000 ($mil; preliminary)
total non-fuel mineral production $31,420

Utah 8

Construction, 1999 ($mil)
total contracts (including
    non-building) $4,489
       residential $2,106
       non-residential $1,854

Construction industries, 1997
establishments 7,031
receipts ($1,000) ....$NA
annual payroll ($1,000) ....$NA
paid employees 54,881

Manufacturing, 1997
establishments 2,859
value of shipments ($1,000) $24,348,385
annual payroll ($1,000) $3,801,688
paid employees 122,200

Transportation industries, 1997
establishments 2,018
receipts ($1,000) $9,223,166
annual payroll ($1,000) $1,572,680
paid employees 49,333

Wholesale trade, 1997
establishments 3,818
sales($1,000).......................$22,789,697
annual payroll ($1,000) $1,592,842
paid employees 50,823

Retail trade, 1997
establishments 10,509
sales($1,000).......................$20,110,336
annual payroll ($1,000) $2,170,334
paid employees 167,441

Finance industries
establishments, 1997 5,141
receipts ($1,000), 1997 ....$NA
annual payroll ($1,000), 1997 .... $1,462,093
paid employees, 1997 48,569
commercial banks, 2000
    number 56
      assets ($bil) $102.9
      deposits ($bil) $69.7

Service industries, 1997 (non-exempt firms only)
establishments 15,000
receipts ($1,000) $12,233,112
annual payroll ($1,000) $4,680,897
paid employees 207,939

COMMUNICATION, ENERGY & TRANSPORTATION

Communication
daily newspapers, 2000 6
households with
    telephones, 1998 .... 94.6%
    computers, 2000 .... 66.1%
    internet access, 2000 .... 48.4%

Energy
consumption, 1999
total (trillion Btu) 694
per capita (million Btu) 326
by source of production (trillion Btu)
    coal 382
    natural gas 169
    petroleum 262
    nuclear electric power ....NA
    hydroelectric power 13
by end-use sector (trillion Btu)
    residential 128
    commercial 120
    industrial 235
    transportation 211
electric energy, 1999
    production (billion kWh) 36.1
    net summer capability (million kW) 5.1
gas utilities, 1999
    customers 1,255,000
    sales (trillion Btu) 177
nuclear plants, 1999 ....na

Transportation, 2000
public road & street mileage
total 41,852
    urban 7,521
    rural 34,331
    interstate 938
vehicle miles of travel (mil) 22,597
total motor vehicle registrations 1,627,606
    automobiles 866,723
    motorcycles 28,116
licensed drivers 1,463,366
    per 1,000 driving age population 915
deaths from motor vehicle
    accidents 373

Vermont 1

STATE SUMMARY

Capital City .... Montpelier

Governor .... Howard Dean

Address .... STATE CAPITOL
MONTPELIER, VT 05602
802 828-3333

Admitted as a state 1791

Area (square miles) 9,615

Population, 1980 511,456

Population, 1990 562,758

Population, 2000 608,827

Persons per square mile, 2000 .... 65.8

Largest city .... Burlington
population, 2000 38,889

Personal income per capita, 2000
(in current dollars) $26,901

Gross state product ($mil), 1999 .... $17,164

Leading industries, 1999 (by payroll)
Manufacturing
Health care/Social assistance
Retail trade

Leading agricultural commodities, 1999
Dairy products, cattle, greenhouse, hay

GEOGRAPHY & ENVIRONMENT

Area, 1990 (square miles)
total 9,615
land 9,249
water (includes territorial water) 366

Federally owned land, 2000 .... 6.3%

Highest point
name .... Mt. Mansfield
elevation (feet) 4,393

Lowest point
name .... Lake Champlain
elevation (feet) 95

General coastline (miles) 0

Tidal shoreline (miles) 0

Capital city .... Montpelier
population, 2000 8,035

Largest city .... Burlington
population, 2000 38,889

Number of cities with over 100,000 population
1980 0
1990 0
2000 0

State parks and Recreation areas, 2000
area (acres) 84,000
number of visitors 719,000
revenues $5,614,000

Natl. forest system land, 1999 (acres) 368,000

National park acreage, 1984 4,100

DEMOGRAPHICS & CHARACTERISTICS OF THE POPULATION

Population
1970 444,732
1980 511,456
1990 562,758
2000 608,827
2015 (projection) 662,000
2025 (projection) 678,000

Metropolitan area population
1970 99,000
1980 115,000
2000 169,000

Non-metropolitan area population
1970 346,000
1980 396,000
2000 439,000

Change in population, 1990-2000
number 46,069
percent 8.19%

Persons per square mile, 2000 .... 65.8

Persons by age, 2000
under 5 years 33,989
18 and over 461,304
21 and over 433,348
65 and over 77,510
85 and over 9,996

Vermont 2

Persons by age, 2025 (projected)
under 5 years 38,000
5 to 17 years 107,000
65 and over 138,000

Median age, 2000 .... 37.7

Race, 2000
One race
White 589,208
Black or African American 3,063
American Indian and Alaska Native 2,420
Asian Indian 858
Chinese 1,330
Filipino 328
Japanese 403
Korean 669
Vietnamese 980
Native Hawaiian and other Pacific Islander .. 141
Two or more races 7,335

Race, 2025 (projected)
White 659,000
Black 6,000

Persons of Hispanic origin, 2000
total Hispanic or Latino 5,504
  Mexican 1,174
  Puerto Rican 1,374
  Cuban 310
  Other Hispanic or Latino 2,646

Persons of Hispanic origin, 2025 (proj.) ... 12,000

Persons by sex, 2000
male 298,337
female 310,490

Marital status, 1990
males
  15 years & older 213,331
    single 66,171
    married 125,887
      separated 3,166
    widowed 5,039
    divorced 16,234
females
  15 years & older 228,387
    single 55,531
    married 126,511
      separated 4,003

widowed 25,054
divorced 21,291

Households & families, 2000
households 240,634
persons per household 2.44
  families 157,763
  persons per family 2.96
    married couples 126,413
    female householder, no husband
      present 22,272
    one person households 63,112
households with persons under 18 years .. 80,904
households with persons over 65 years 54,149

Nativity, 1990
number of persons born in state 321,704
percent of total residents 57.2%

Immigration & naturalization, 1998
immigrants admitted 513
persons naturalized 360
refugees granted resident status 103

VITAL STATISTICS & HEALTH

Births
1999
  with low birth weight 5.7%
  to teenage mothers 11.1%
  to unmarried mothers 28.9%
Birth rate, 1999 (per 1,000) 11.1
Birth rate, 2000 (per 1,000) 10.9

Abortions, 1996
total 2,000
rate (per 1,000 women age 15-44) 17.1

Deaths
1998 4,836
1999 4,993
2000 5,142

Infant deaths
1998 38
1999 38
2000 39

Average lifetime, by race, 1989-1991
total .... 76.54 years
  white .... 76.50 years
  black .... NA years

Marriages
1998 5,853
1999 6,024
2000 6,088

Divorces
1998 2,559
1999 2,603
2000 5,148

Physicians, 1999
total 1,860
rate (per 1,000 persons) 3.13

Nurses, 1999
total 5,160
rate (per 1,000 persons) 8.69

Hospitals, 1998
number 14
beds (x 1,000) 1.7
average daily census (x 1,000) 1.1
patients admitted (x1,000) 50
average cost per day to hospital, 1995 . . . . . . $714
average cost per stay to hospital, 1995 . . . . $5,883

EDUCATION

*Educational attainment of all persons
25 years and older, 1990*
less than 9th grade 30,945
high school graduates 123,430
bachelor's degree 55,120
graduate or professional degree 31,734

2000
high school graduate or more 90.0%
college graduate or more 28.8%

Public school enrollment, Fall, 1998
total 105,120
Kindergarten through grade 8 73,257
grades 9 through 12 31,863

Public School Teachers, 2000
total 8,500
elementary 4,400
secondary 4,100
average salaries
elementary $38,300
secondary $36,800

*State receipts & expenditures for public
schools, 2000*
revenue receipts ($mil) $912

*State receipts & expenditures for public
schools, 2000 (continued)*
expenditures
total ($mil) $806
per capita $1,358
per pupil $7,352

*Graduating high school seniors,
public high schools, 2000 (est.)* 6,763

SAT scores, 2001
verbal 511
math 506
percent graduates taking test 69%

Institutions of higher education, 1999
total 25
public 6
private 19

*Enrollment in institutions of higher
education, Fall, 1998*
total 37,054
full-time men 12,284
full-time women 13,700
part-time men 3,705
part-time women 7,365

*Minority enrollment in institutions of higher
education, Fall, 1997*
Black, non-Hispanic 413
Hispanic 571
Asian/Pacific Islander 590

Earned degrees conferred, 1998
Bachelor's 4,455
First professional 236
Master's 1,510
Doctor's 62

SOCIAL INSURANCE &
WELFARE PROGRAMS

Social Security beneficiaries & benefits, 2000
beneficiaries
total 105,000
retired and dependents 73,000
survivors 14,000
disabled & dependents 18,000
annual benefit payments ($mil)
total $918
retired and dependents $624
survivors $159
disabled & dependents $135

Vermont 4

Medicare, 2000
enrollment (x1,000) 88
payments ($mil) $315

Medicaid, 1998
recipients (x1,000) 124
payments ($mil) $351

Federal public aid
Temporary Assistance for Needy Families
(TANF), 2000
    Recipients (x1,000) 16
    Families (x1,000) 6
Supplemental Security Income
    total recipients, 1999 (x1,000) 13

Food Stamp Program
    participants, 2000 (x1,000) 41

HOUSING & CONSTRUCTION

Total housing units, 2000 294,382
    seasonal or recreational use 43,060
    occupied 240,634
        owner occupied 169,784
        renter occupied 70,850

New privately owned housing units uthorized, 2000
number (x1,000) 2.5
value ($mil) $319

New privately owned housing units
started, 2000 (est.) (x1,000) 2.4

Existing home sales, 2000 (x1,000) 7.2

GOVERNMENT & ELECTIONS

State officials, 2002
  Governor (name/party/term expires)
        HOWARD DEAN
        Democrat - 2002
Lt. Governor .... Doug Racine
Sec. of State .... Deborah Markowitz
Atty. General .... William Sorrell
Chief Justice .... Jeffery Amestoy

Governorship
minimum age .... not specified
length of term .... 2 years
number of consecutive
    terms permitted .... not specified
who succeeds .... Lt. Governor

State legislature
name .... General Assembly
  upper chamber
    name .... Senate
    number of members 30
    length of term .... 2 years
    party in majority, 2000 .... Democratic
  lower chamber
    name .... House of Representatives
    number of members 150
    length of term .... 2 years
    party in majority, 2000 .... Democratic

State employees March, 2000
total 15,261
March payroll $42,321,010

Local governments, 1997
total 691
  county 14
  municipal 49
  township 237
  school districts 279
  special districts 112

Voting age population, November, 2000, projected
Total 460,000
  male 223,000
  female 237,000

Vote for president
2000
  Gore 149,000
  Bush 120,000
1996
  Clinton 138,000
  Dole 80,000
  Perot 31,000

Federal representation, 2002 (107th Congress)
Senators (name/party/term expires)

        JIM JEFFORDS
        Independent- 2007
        PATRICK J. LEAHY
        Democrat - 2005

Representatives, total 1
  Democrats 0
  Republicans 0
  other 1

Vermont 5

Women holding public office, 2001
U.S. Congress 0
statewide elected office 2
state legislature 50

Black elected officials, 1999
total 1
  US and state legislatures 1
  city/county/regional offices .... NA
  judicial/law enforcement .... NA
  education/school boards .... NA

Hispanic public officials, 2000
total .... NA
  state executives & legislators .... NA
  city/county/regional offices .... NA
  judicial/law enforcement .... NA
  education/school boards .... NA

GOVERNMENTAL FINANCE

State government revenues, 1999 ($per capita)
total revenue $5,144.95
  total general revenue $4,598.42
    intergovernmental revenue $1,402.43
    taxes $2,338.30
    current charges $499.86
    miscellaneous $357.83

State government expenditures, 1999 ($per capita)
total expenditure $4,383.38
  total general expenditure $4,137.16
    education $1,768.71
    public welfare $941.46
    health $85.15
    hospitals $9.04
    highways $403.11
    police protection $41.25
    correction $65.67
    natural resources $100.22
    governmental administration $212.58
    interest on general debt $202.62

State debt, 1999 ($per capita) $3,564.60

Federal government grants to state & local government, 2000 (x$1,000)
total $899,675
  Dept. of Education $80,563
  Environmental Protection Agency $29,829
  Health Care Financing Admin. $350,124
  Dept. Housing & Urban Devel. $76,382
  Dept. of Labor $13,731
  Highway trust fund $115,497

CRIME, LAW ENFORCEMENT & COURTS

Crime, 2000 (all rates per 100,000 inhabitants)
total crimes 18,185
overall crime rate 2,986.9
  property crimes 17,494
    burglaries 3,501
    larcenies 13,184
    motor vehicle thefts 809
  property crime rate 2,873.4
  violent crimes 691
    murders 9
    forcible rapes 140
    robberies 117
    aggravated assaults 425
  violent crime rate 113.5

Number of police agencies, 2000 38

Arrests, 2000
total 14,101
  persons under 18 years of age 2,343

Prisoners under state & federal jurisdiction, 2000
total 1,697
percent change, 1999-2000 .... 10.5%
  sentenced to more than one year
    total 1,313
    rate per 100,000 residents 218

Persons under sentence of death, 4/1/2001 ...NA

State's highest court
name .... Supreme Court
number of members 5
length of term .... 6 years
intermediate appeals court? .... no

Vermont 6

LABOR & INCOME

Civilian labor force, 2000

total 332,000
  men 170,000
  women 161,000
  persons 16-19 years 22,000
  white 326,000
  black .... NA

Civilian labor force as a percent of
civilian non-institutional population, 2000

total 70.4%
  men 76.1%
  women 65.3%
  persons 16-19 years .... NA%
  white 70.4%
  black .... NA%

Employment, 2000

total 322,000
  men 165,000
  women 157,000
  persons 16-19 years 20,000
  white 317,000
  black .... NA

Full-time/part-time labor force, 1998

full-time labor force .... NA
  working part-time for
    economic reasons 3,000
part-time labor force .... NA

Unemployment rate, 2000

total 2.9%
  men 3.0%
  women 2.8%
  persons 16-19 years 7.7%
  white 2.8%
  black .... NA%

Unemployed by reason for unemployment
(as a percent of total unemployment), 1998

job losers or completed temp jobs .... NA%
job leavers .... NA%
reentrants .... NA%
new entrants .... NA%

Experienced civilian labor force, by occupation, 1998

executive/administrative/managerial 44,000
professional/specialty 53,000
technicians & related support .... NA

sales 39,000
administrative support/clerical 47,000
service occupations 42,000
precision production/craft/repair 41,000
machine operators/assemblers 19,000
transportation/material moving 14,000
handlers/helpers/laborers .... NA
farming/forestry/fishing 12,000

Experienced civilian labor force, by industry, 1998

construction 14,000
manufacturing 48,000
transportation/communication .... NA
wholesale/retail trade 63,000
finance/real estate/insurance 14,000
services 96,000
government 36,000
agriculture .... NA

Average annual pay, 1999 .... $27,595
change in average annual pay,
  1998-1999 .... 3.7%

Hours and earnings of production workers
on manufacturing payrolls, 2000

average weekly hours 40.3
average hourly earnings $14.23
average weekly earnings $573.47

Labor union membership, 2000 28,200

Household income (in 2000 dollars)
median household income,
  three year average, 1998-2000 .... $38,150

Poverty
persons below poverty level,
  three year average, 1998-2000 .... 10.1%

Personal income ($per capita)
2000 (prelim.)
  in current dollars $26,901
  in constant (1996) dollars $25,057
1999 (preliminary)
  in current dollars $25,892
  in constant (1996) dollars $24,758

Federal income tax returns, 1999
returns filed 293,581
adjusted gross income ($1,000) $11,520,952
total income tax paid ($1,000) $1,624,288

ECONOMY, BUSINESS, INDUSTRY & AGRICULTURE

Fortune 500 companies, 2000 0

Business incorporations, 1998
total 1,217
change, 1997-1998 .... -14.1%

Business failures, 1998 80

Business firm ownership, 1997
Hispanic owned firms 898
Black owned firms 168
women owned firms 17,030
Asian & Pacific Islander owned firms 304
American Indian & Alaska
  native owned firms 751

Shopping centers, 2000 116

Gross state product, 1999 ($mil)
total $17,164
  agriculture services, forestry, fisheries $374
  mining $47
  construction $754
  manufacturing--durable goods $2,182
  manufacturing--nondurable goods $816
  transportation, communication &
    public utilities $1,298
  wholesale trade $989
  retail trade $1,700
  finance/real estate/insurance $3,043
  services $3,832
  federal, state & local government $2,129

Establishments, by major industry group, 1999
total 21,598
  forestry, fishing & agriculture 155
  mining 55
  construction 2,638
  manufacturing 1,245
  transportation & warehousing 534
  wholesale trade 930
  retail trade 3,968
  finance & insurance 942
  professional/scientific/technical 1,871
  health care/social assistance 1,854
  information 477
  accommodation/food services 1,843

Payroll, by major industry group, 1999
total ($1,000) $6,336,255
  forestry, fishing & agriculture .... $NA
  mining .... $NA
  construction $427,823
  manufacturing $1,546,513
  transportation & warehousing $129,179
  wholesale trade $368,791
  retail trade $700,625
  finance & insurance $382,026
  professional/scientific/technical $384,349
  health care/social assistance $914,439
  information $197,209
  accommodation/food services $318,096

Agriculture
number of farms, 2000 7,000
farm acreage, 2000 1,000,000
acres per farm, 2000 197
value of farms, 1997 ($mil) $2,093
farm income, 1999 ($mil)
  net farm income $141
  debt/asset ratio 14.9%
farm marketings, 1999 ($mil)
  total $541
  crops $66
  livestock $473
principal commodities, in order by marketing
receipts, 1999
    Dairy products, cattle, greenhouse, hay

Federal economic activity in state
expenditures, 2000
  total ($mil) $3,362
  per capita $5,523
  defense ($mil) $346
  non-defense ($mil) $3,017
defense department, 2000
  contract awards ($mil) $243
  payroll ($mil) $96
  civilian employees (x1,000) 0.6
  military personnel (x1,000) .... -

Fishing, 2000
catch (thousands of pounds) .... NA
value ($1,000) .... $NA

Mining, 2000 ($mil; preliminary)
total non-fuel mineral production $43

Vermont 8

Construction, 1999 ($mil)
total contracts (including
    non-building) $648
      residential $253
      non-residential $273

Construction industries, 1997
establishments 2,442
receipts ($1,000) $1,676,945
annual payroll ($1,000) .... $NA
paid employees 12,967

Manufacturing, 1997
establishments 1,409
value of shipments ($1,000) $7,986,254
annual payroll ($1,000) $1,515,461
paid employees 44,648

Transportation industries, 1997
establishments 924
receipts ($1,000) $2,762,902
annual payroll ($1,000) $337,413
paid employees 10,965

Wholesale trade, 1997
establishments 1,200
sales($1,000) .... $NA
annual payroll ($1,000) .... $NA
paid employees .... NA

Retail trade, 1997
establishments 5,277
sales($1,000) $6,018,347
annual payroll ($1,000) $716,044
paid employees 52,529

Finance industries
establishments, 1997 1,564
receipts ($1,000), 1997 .... $NA
annual payroll ($1,000), 1997 .... $NA
paid employees, 1997 .... NA
commercial banks, 2000
    number 18
    assets ($bil) $7.6
    deposits ($bil) $6.3

Service industries, 1997 (non-exempt firms only)
establishments 5,836
receipts ($1,000) $2,745,721
annual payroll ($1,000) $952,644
paid employees 46,922

COMMUNICATION, ENERGY & TRANSPORTATION

Communication
daily newspapers, 2000 8
households with
    telephones, 1998 .... 94.8%
    computers, 2000 .... 53.7%
    internet access, 2000 .... 46.7%

Energy
consumption, 1999
total (trillion Btu) 165
per capita (million Btu) 278
by source of production (trillion Btu)
    coal 2
    natural gas 8
    petroleum 85
    nuclear electric power 43
    hydroelectric power 61
by end-use sector (trillion Btu)
    residential 43
    commercial 29
    industrial 40
    transportation 53
electric energy, 1999
    production (billion kWh) 4.7
    net summer capability (million kW) 0.8
gas utilities, 1999
    customers 39,000
    sales (trillion Btu) 8
nuclear plants, 1999 1

Transportation, 2000
public road & street mileage
total 14,273
    urban 1,379
    rural 12,894
    interstate 320
vehicle miles of travel (mil) 6,811
total motor vehicle registrations 514,883
    automobiles 295,640
    motorcycles 21,740
licensed drivers 506,085
    per 1,000 driving age population 1,056
deaths from motor vehicle
    accidents 79

STATE SUMMARY

Capital City .... Richmond

Governor .... James Gilmore III

Address .... STATE CAPITOL
RICHMOND, VA 23219
804 786-2211

Admitted as a state 1788

Area (square miles) 42,769

Population, 1980 5,346,818

Population, 1990 6,187,358

Population, 2000 7,078,515

Persons per square mile, 2000 .... 178.8

Largest city .... Virginia Beach
population, 2000 425,000

Personal income per capita, 2000
(in current dollars) $31,162

Gross state product ($mil), 1999 ...... $242,221

Leading industries, 1999 (by payroll)
Professional/Scientific/Technical
Manufacturing
Information

Leading agricultural commodities, 1999
Broilers, cattle, dairy products, turkeys

GEOGRAPHY & ENVIRONMENT

Area, 1990 (square miles)
total 42,769
land 39,598
water (includes territorial water) 3,171

Federally owned land, 2000 .... 8.9%

Highest point
name .... Mt. Rogers
elevation (feet) 5,729

Lowest point
name .... Atlantic Ocean
elevation (feet) .... sea level

General coastline (miles) 112

Tidal shoreline (miles) 3,315

Capital city .... Richmond
population, 2000 198,000

Largest city .... Virginia Beach
population, 2000 425,000

Number of cities with over 100,000 population
1980 9
1990 8
2000 8

State parks and Recreation areas, 2000
area (acres) 73,000
number of visitors 5,717,000
revenues $6,477,000

Natl. forest system land, 1999 (acres) ... 1,659,000

National park acreage, 1984 309,600

DEMOGRAPHICS & CHARACTERISTICS OF THE POPULATION

Population
1970 4,651,448
1980 5,346,818
1990 6,187,358
2000 7,078,515
2015 (projection) 7,921,000
2025 (projection) 8,466,000

Metropolitan area population
1970 3,279,000
1980 3,745,000
2000 5,528,000

Non-metropolitan area population
1970 1,373,000
1980 1,601,000
2000 1,550,000

Change in population, 1990-2000
number 891,157
percent 14.40%

Persons per square mile, 2000 .... 178.8

Persons by age, 2000
under 5 years 461,982
18 and over 5,340,253
21 and over 5,039,883
65 and over 792,333
85 and over 87,266

Virginia 2

Persons by age, 2025 (projected)
under 5 years 502,000
5 to 17 years 1,359,000
65 and over 1,515,000

Median age, 2000 .... 35.7

Race, 2000
One race
White 5,120,110
Black or African American 1,390,293
American Indian and Alaska Native 21,172
Asian Indian ....:................. 48,815
Chinese 36,966
Filipino 47,609
Japanese 9,080
Korean 45,279
Vietnamese 37,309
Native Hawaiian and other Pacific Islander 3,946
Two or more races 143,069

Race, 2025 (projected)
White 5,951,000
Black 1,973,000

Persons of Hispanic origin, 2000
total Hispanic or Latino 329,540
  Mexican 73,979
  Puerto Rican 41,131
  Cuban 8,332
  Other Hispanic or Latino 206,098

Persons of Hispanic origin, 2025 (proj.) .. 538,000

Persons by sex, 2000
male 3,471,895
female 3,606,620

Marital status, 1990
males
  15 years & older 2,386,768
    single 733,040
    married 1,447,219
      separated 67,405
      widowed 52,018
      divorced 154,491
females
  15 years & older 2,534,543
    single 598,188
    married 1,445,038
      separated 85,886

  widowed 280,192
  divorced 211,125

Households & families, 2000
households 2,699,173
persons per household 2.54
  families 1,847,796
  persons per family 3.04
    married couples 1,426,044
    female householder, no husband
      present 320,290
    one person households 676,907
households with persons under 18 years . 968,736
households with persons over 65 years ... 565,204

Nativity, 1990
number of persons born in state 3,356,594
percent of total residents 54.2%

Immigration & naturalization, 1998
immigrants admitted 15,686
persons naturalized ...,............. 8,589
refugees granted resident status 1,094

VITAL STATISTICS & HEALTH
Births
1999
  with low birth weight 7.8%
  to teenage mothers 13.9%
  to unmarried mothers 29.7%
Birth rate, 1999 (per 1,000) 13.9
Birth rate, 2000 (per 1,000) 14.2

Abortions, 1996
total 30,000
rate (per 1,000 women age 15-44) 18.9

Deaths
1998 54,274
1999 55,320
2000 56,161

Infant deaths
1998 683
1999 707
2000 646

Average lifetime, by race, 1989-1991
total .... 75.22 years
  white .... 76.34 years
  black .... 70.05 years

Marriages
1998 64,271
1999 64,683
2000 62,411

Divorces
1998 29,965
1999 31,729
2000 30,242

Physicians, 1999
total 16,717
rate (per 1,000 persons) 2.43

Nurses, 1999
total 57,560
rate (per 1,000 persons) 8.37

Hospitals, 1998
number 93
beds (x 1,000) 17.9
average daily census (x 1,000) 11.2
patients admitted (x1,000) 717
average cost per day to hospital, 1995 . . . . . . $901
average cost per stay to hospital, 1995 . . . . $5,423

EDUCATION

Educational attainment of all persons
25 years and older, 1990
less than 9th grade 443,668
high school graduates 1,059,199
bachelor's degree 612,679
graduate or professional degree 360,215

2000
high school graduate or more 86.6%
college graduate or more 31.9%

Public school enrollment, Fall, 1998
total 1,124,022
Kindergarten through grade 8 815,266
grades 9 through 12 308,756

Public School Teachers, 2000
total 87,600
elementary 52,800
secondary 34,700
average salaries
elementary $36,900
secondary $40,100

State receipts & expenditures for public
schools, 2000
revenue receipts ($mil) $7,158

State receipts & expenditures for public
schools, 2000 (continued)
expenditures
total ($mil) $7,932
per capita $1,154
per pupil $6,543

Graduating high school seniors,
public high schools, 2000 (est.) 66,868

SAT scores, 2001
verbal 510
math 501
percent graduates taking test 68%

Institutions of higher education, 1999
total 92
public 39
private 53

Enrollment in institutions of higher
education, Fall, 1998
total 370,142
full-time men 95,957
full-time women 116,128
part-time men 64,108
part-time women 93,949

Minority enrollment in institutions of higher
education, Fall, 1997
Black, non-Hispanic 61,941
Hispanic 9,151
Asian/Pacific Islander 18,291

Earned degrees conferred, 1998
Bachelor's 31,000
First professional 1,953
Master's 10,935
Doctor's 1,083

SOCIAL INSURANCE & WELFARE PROGRAMS

Social Security beneficiaries & benefits, 2000
beneficiaries
total 1,035,000
retired and dependents 704,000
survivors 161,000
disabled & dependents 169,000
annual benefit payments ($mil)
total $9,060
retired and dependents $5,929
survivors $1,741
disabled & dependents $1,390

Virginia 4

Medicare, 2000
enrollment (x1,000) 876
payments ($mil) $4,038

Medicaid, 1998
recipients (x1,000) 653
payments ($mil) $2,118

Federal public aid
Temporary Assistance for Needy Families
(TANF), 2000
   Recipients (x1,000) 71
   Families (x1,000) 31
Supplemental Security Income
   total recipients, 1999 (x1,000) 132

Food Stamp Program
   participants, 2000 (x1,000) 336

HOUSING & CONSTRUCTION

Total housing units, 2000 2,904,192
   seasonal or recreational use 54,696
   occupied 2,699,173
      owner occupied 1,837,939
      renter occupied 861,234

New privately owned housing units uthorized, 2000
number (x1,000) 48.4
value ($mil) $5,052

New privately owned housing units
   started, 2000 (est.) (x1,000) 50.2

Existing home sales, 2000 (x1,000) 131.4

GOVERNMENT & ELECTIONS

State officials, 2002
   Governor (name/party/term expires)
      JAMES S. GILMORE III
      Republican - 2001
   Lt. Governor .... John H. Hager
   Sec. of State .... Anne Petera
   Atty. General .... Randy Beales
   Chief Justice .... Harry L. Carrico

Governorship
minimum age 30
length of term .... 4 years
number of consecutive
   terms permitted .... none
who succeeds .... Lt. Governor

State legislature
name .... General Assembly
   upper chamber
      name .... Senate
      number of members 40
      length of term .... 4 years
      party in majority, 2000 .... Republican
   lower chamber
      name .... House of Delegates
      number of members 100
      length of term .... 2 years
      party in majority, 2000 .... Republican

State employees March, 2000
total 147,462
March payroll $367,528,696

Local governments, 1997
total 483
   county 95
   municipal 231
   township 0
   school districts 1
   special districts 156

Voting age population, November, 2000, projected
Total 5,263,000
   male 2,529,000
   female 2,734,000

Vote for president
2000
   Gore 1,217,000
   Bush 1,437,000
1996
   Clinton 1,091,000
   Dole 1,138,000
   Perot 160,000

Federal representation, 2002 (107th Congress)
Senators (name/party/term expires)

      GEORGE ALLEN
      Republican - 2007
      JOHN W. WARNER
      Republican - 2003

Representatives, total 11
   Democrats 3
   Republicans 7
   other 1

Women holding public office, 2001
U.S. Congress 1
statewide elected office 0
state legislature 23

Black elected officials, 1999
total 251
    US and state legislatures 16
    city/county/regional offices 137
    judicial/law enforcement 16
    education/school boards 82

Hispanic public officials, 2000
total 1
    state executives & legislators .... NA
    city/county/regional offices .... NA
    judicial/law enforcement .... NA
    education/school boards 1

GOVERNMENTAL FINANCE

State government revenues, 1999 ($per capita)
total revenue $3,803.10
    total general revenue $3,036.06
      intergovernmental revenue $588.79
      taxes $1,682.36
      current charges $452.17
      miscellaneous $312.73

State government expenditures, 1999 ($per capita)
total expenditure $3,308.52
    total general expenditure $3,078.04
      education $1,198.82
      public welfare $528.59
      health $84.63
      hospitals $197.62
      highways $348.49
      police protection $55.28
      correction $152.23
      natural resources $24.25
      governmental administration $141.75
      interest on general debt $125.11

State debt, 1999 ($per capita) $1,728.05

Federal government grants to state & local government, 2000 (x$1,000)
total $4,615,448
    Dept. of Education $549,736
    Environmental Protection Agency $55,246
    Health Care Financing Admin. $1,497,876
    Dept. Housing & Urban Devel. $573,246
    Dept. of Labor $91,866
    Highway trust fund $507,026

CRIME, LAW ENFORCEMENT & COURTS

Crime, 2000 (all rates per 100,000 inhabitants)
total crimes 214,348
overall crime rate 3,028.1
    property crimes 194,405
      burglaries 30,434
      larcenies 146,158
      motor vehicle thefts 17,813
    property crime rate 2,746.4
    violent crimes 19,943
      murders 401
      forcible rapes 1,616
      robberies 6,295
      aggravated assaults 11,631
    violent crime rate 281.7

Number of police agencies, 2000 303

Arrests, 2000
total 272,656
    persons under 18 years of age 32,759

Prisoners under state & federal jurisdiction, 2000
total 30,168
percent change, 1999-2000 .... 1.3%
    sentenced to more than one year
      total 29,643
      rate per 100,000 residents 422

Persons under sentence of death, 4/1/2001 28

State's highest court
name .... Supreme Court
number of members 7
length of term .... 12 years
intermediate appeals court? .... no

Virginia 6

LABOR & INCOME

Civilian labor force, 2000
total	3,610,000
men	1,910,000
women	1,700,000
persons 16-19 years	175,000
white	2,765,000
black	696,000

*Civilian labor force as a percent of
civilian non-institutional population, 2000*
total	68.1%
men	75.6%
women	61.3%
persons 16-19 years	NA%
white	68.1%
black	66.9%

Employment, 2000
total	3,530,000
men	1,865,000
women	1,665,000
persons 16-19 years	161,000
white	2,717,000
black	667,000

Full-time/part-time labor force, 1998
full-time labor force	NA
working part-time for economic reasons	28,000
part-time labor force	NA

Unemployment rate, 2000
total	2.2%
men	2.3%
women	2.1%
persons 16-19 years	7.7%
white	1.7%
black	4.2%

*Unemployed by reason for unemployment
(as a percent of total unemployment), 1998*
job losers or completed temp jobs	NA%
job leavers	NA%
reentrants	NA%
new entrants	NA%

Experienced civilian labor force, by occupation, 1998
executive/administrative/managerial	562,000
professional/specialty	609,000
technicians & related support	112,000
sales	408,000
administrative support/clerical	472,000
service occupations	447,000
precision production/craft/repair	394,000
machine operators/assemblers	171,000
transportation/material moving	121,000
handlers/helpers/laborers	122,000
farming/forestry/fishing	NA

Experienced civilian labor force, by industry, 1998
construction	188,000
manufacturing	428,000
transportation/communication	198,000
wholesale/retail trade	636,000
finance/real estate/insurance	239,000
services	923,000
government	585,000
agriculture	NA

Average annual pay, 1999 ... $33,015
change in average annual pay,
1998-1999 ... 5.2%

*Hours and earnings of production workers
on manufacturing payrolls, 2000*
average weekly hours	42.3
average hourly earnings	$13.82
average weekly earnings	$584.59

Labor union membership, 2000 ... 179,100

Household income (in 2000 dollars)
median household income,
three year average, 1998-2000 ... $50,069

Poverty
persons below poverty level,
three year average, 1998-2000 ... 8.1%

Personal income ($per capita)
2000 (prelim.)
in current dollars	$31,162
in constant (1996) dollars	$29,026
1999 (preliminary)
in current dollars	$29,484
in constant (1996) dollars	$28,193

Federal income tax returns, 1999
returns filed	3,261,947
adjusted gross income ($1,000)	$159,154,671
total income tax paid ($1,000)	$25,043,984

ECONOMY, BUSINESS, INDUSTRY & AGRICULTURE

Fortune 500 companies, 2000 16

Business incorporations, 1998
total 17,808
change, 1997-1998 . . . . -4.8%

Business failures, 1998 860

Business firm ownership, 1997
Hispanic owned firms 13,703
Black owned firms 33,539
women owned firms 132,219
Asian & Pacific Islander owned firms 22,441
American Indian & Alaska
native owned firms 3,280

Shopping centers, 2000 1,318

Gross state product, 1999 ($mil)
total $242,221
agriculture services, forestry, fisheries . . $1,994
mining $1,084
construction $11,086
manufacturing--durable goods $12,662
manufacturing--nondurable goods $19,117
transportation, communication &
public utilities $21,679
wholesale trade $13,845
retail trade $20,977
finance/real estate/insurance $41,832
services $54,741
federal, state & local government $43,205

Establishments, by major industry group, 1999
total 173,550
forestry, fishing & agriculture 752
mining 379
construction 20,204
manufacturing 5,949
transportation & warehousing 4,752
wholesale trade 7,935
retail trade 28,803
finance & insurance 10,083
professional/scientific/technical 20,408
health care/social assistance 14,322
information 3,304
accommodation/food services 12,401

Payroll, by major industry group, 1999
total ($1,000) $93,167,636
forestry, fishing & agriculture $93,434
mining $394,763
construction $5,693,590
manufacturing $12,423,621
transportation & warehousing $2,630,825
wholesale trade $4,214,449
retail trade $7,454,836
finance & insurance $5,822,432
professional/scientific/technical $14,413,198
health care/social assistance $8,688,478
information $12,047,561
accommodation/food services $2,733,152

Agriculture
number of farms, 2000 49,000
farm acreage, 2000 9,000,000
acres per farm, 2000 178
value of farms, 1997 ($mil) $17,255
farm income, 1999 ($mil)
net farm income $396
debt/asset ratio 10.6%
farm marketings, 1999 ($mil)
total $2,283
crops $704
livestock $1,580
principal commodities, in order by marketing
receipts, 1999
Broilers, cattle, dairy products, turkeys

Federal economic activity in state
expenditures, 2000
total ($mil) $62,709
per capita $8,859
defense ($mil) $24,543
non-defense ($mil) $38,166
defense department, 2000
contract awards ($mil) $13,637
payroll ($mil) $11,407
civilian employees (x1,000) 79.6
military personnel (x1,000) 133.3

Fishing, 2000
catch (thousands of pounds) 443,197
value ($1,000) $118,336

Mining, 2000 ($mil; preliminary)
total non-fuel mineral production $692

Virginia 8

Construction, 1999 ($mil)
total contracts (including
  non-building) $12,776
    residential $5,762
    non-residential $4,921

Construction industries, 1997
establishments 19,117
receipts ($1,000) $22,569,591
annual payroll ($1,000) $4,732,942
paid employees 176,432

Manufacturing, 1997
establishments 6,633
value of shipments ($1,000) $87,071,056
annual payroll ($1,000) $12,130,687
paid employees 387,576

Transportation industries, 1997
establishments 7,210
receipts ($1,000) $30,186,917
annual payroll ($1,000) $5,166,829
paid employees 138,818

Wholesale trade, 1997
establishments 9,697
sales($1,000) $65,348,420
annual payroll ($1,000) $4,271,495
paid employees 125,191

Retail trade, 1997
establishments 38,588
sales($1,000) $64,575,911
annual payroll ($1,000) $7,513,550
paid employees 555,088

Finance industries
establishments, 1997 15,552
receipts ($1,000), 1997 .... $NA
annual payroll ($1,000), 1997 .... $6,145,840
paid employees, 1997 173,123
commercial banks, 2000
  number 143
    assets ($bil) $59.6
    deposits ($bil) $42.9

Service industries, 1997 (non-exempt firms only)
establishments 53,890
receipts ($1,000) $55,699,728
annual payroll ($1,000) $21,415,115
paid employees 716,667

COMMUNICATION, ENERGY & TRANSPORTATION

Communication
daily newspapers, 2000 28
households with
  telephones, 1998 .... 92.3%
  computers, 2000 .... 53.9%
  internet access, 2000 .... 44.3%

Energy
consumption, 1999
total (trillion Btu) 2,227
per capita (million Btu) 324
by source of production (trillion Btu)
  coal 402
  natural gas 275
  petroleum 864
  nuclear electric power 301
  hydroelectric power .... -6
by end-use sector (trillion Btu)
  residential 494
  commercial 463
  industrial 614
  transportation 656
electric energy, 1999
  production (billion kWh) 65.1
  net summer capability (million kW) ... 15.3
gas utilities, 1999
  customers 956,000
  sales (trillion Btu) 128
nuclear plants, 1999 4

Transportation, 2000
public road & street mileage
total 70,393
  urban 18,938
  rural 51,455
  interstate 1,118
vehicle miles of travel (mil) 74,801
total motor vehicle registrations 6,046,127
  automobiles 3,873,910
  motorcycles 60,463
licensed drivers 4,836,993
  per 1,000 driving age population 875
deaths from motor vehicle
  accidents 930

STATE SUMMARY

Capital City .... Olympia

Governor .... Gary Locke

Address .... STATE CAPITOL
OLYMPIA, WA 98504
360 753-6780

Admitted as a state 1889

Area (square miles) 71,303

Population, 1980 4,132,156

Population, 1990 4,866,692

Population, 2000 5,894,121

Persons per square mile, 2000 .... 88.5

Largest city .... Seattle
population, 2000 563,000

Personal income per capita, 2000
(in current dollars) $31,528

Gross state product ($mil), 1999 ..... $209,258

Leading industries, 1999 (by payroll)
Manufacturing
Health care/Social assistance
Retail trade

Leading agricultural commodities, 1999
Dairy products, apples, cattle, potatoes

GEOGRAPHY & ENVIRONMENT

Area, 1990 (square miles)
total 71,303
land 66,582
water (includes territorial water) 4,721

Federally owned land, 2000 .... 28.5%

Highest point
name .... Mt. Rainier
elevation (feet) 14,410

Lowest point
name .... Pacific Ocean
elevation (feet) .... sea level

General coastline (miles) 157

Tidal shoreline (miles) 3,026

Capital city .... Olympia
population, 2000 42,514

Largest city .... Seattle
population, 2000 563,000

Number of cities with over 100,000 population
1980 3
1990 3
2000 5

State parks and Recreation areas, 2000
area (acres) 259,000
number of visitors 46,444,000
revenues $10,574,000

Natl. forest system land, 1999 (acres) ... 9,202,000

National park acreage, 1984 1,912,700

DEMOGRAPHICS & CHARACTERISTICS OF THE POPULATION

Population
1970 3,413,244
1980 4,132,156
1990 4,866,692
2000 5,894,121
2015 (projection) 7,058,000
2025 (projection) 7,808,000

Metropolitan area population
1970 2,752,000
1980 3,322,000
2000 4,899,000

Non-metropolitan area population
1970 661,000
1980 810,000
2000 995,000

Change in population, 1990-2000
number 1,027,429
percent 21.11%

Persons per square mile, 2000 .... 88.5

Persons by age, 2000
under 5 years 394,306
18 and over 4,380,278
21 and over 4,127,976
65 and over 662,148
85 and over 84,085

Washington 2

Persons by age, 2025 (projected)
under 5 years 483,000
5 to 17 years 1,267,000
65 and over 1,580,000

Median age, 2000 .... 35.3

Race, 2000
One race
White 4,821,823
Black or African American 190,267
American Indian and Alaska Native 93,301
Asian Indian 23,992
Chinese 59,914
Filipino 65,373
Japanese 35,985
Korean 46,880
Vietnamese 46,149
Native Hawaiian and other Pacific Islander 23,953
Two or more races 213,519

Race, 2025 (projected)
White 6,662,000
Black 279,000

Persons of Hispanic origin, 2000
total Hispanic or Latino 441,509
   Mexican 329,934
   Puerto Rican 16,140
   Cuban 4,501
   Other Hispanic or Latino 90,934

Persons of Hispanic origin, 2025 (proj.) .. 797,000

Persons by sex, 2000
male 2,934,300
female 2,959,821

Marital status, 1990
males
   15 years & older 1,862,291
      single 539,893
      married 1,109,090
         separated 30,865
      widowed 38,826
      divorced 174,482
females
   15 years & older 1,928,866
      single 402,111
      married 1,109,215
         separated 40,404

widowed 190,605
divorced 226,935

Households & families, 2000
households 2,271,398
persons per household 2.53
   families 1,499,127
   persons per family 3.07
      married couples 1,181,995
      female householder, no husband
         present 224,618
      one person households 594,325
households with persons under 18 years . 799,102
households with persons over 65 years ... 463,007

Nativity, 1990
number of persons born in state 2,344,187
percent of total residents 48.2%

Immigration & naturalization, 1998
immigrants admitted 16,920
persons naturalized 12,991
refugees granted resident status 2,874

VITAL STATISTICS & HEALTH

Births
1999
   with low birth weight 5.8%
   to teenage mothers 13.8%
   to unmarried mothers 28.1%
Birth rate, 1999 (per 1,000) 13.8
Birth rate, 2000 (per 1,000) 13.9

Abortions, 1996
total 26,000
rate (per 1,000 women age 15-44) 20.9

Deaths
1998 42,432
1999 43,865
2000 43,976

Infant deaths
1998 437
1999 374
2000 422

Average lifetime, by race, 1989-1991
total .... 76.82 years
   white .... 76.92 years
   black .... 71.34 years

Marriages

1998	41,185
1999	42,325
2000	40,891

Divorces

1998	28,786
1999	28,970
2000	27,210

Physicians, 1999

total	13,616
rate (per 1,000 persons)	2.37

Nurses, 1999

total	44,740
rate (per 1,000 persons)	7.77

Hospitals, 1998

number	86
beds (x 1,000)	10.7
average daily census (x 1,000)	6.3
patients admitted (x1,000)	474
average cost per day to hospital, 1995	$1,318
average cost per stay to hospital, 1995	$6,180

EDUCATION

Educational attainment of all persons 25 years and older, 1990

less than 9th grade	171,311
high school graduates	873,150
bachelor's degree	496,866
graduate or professional degree	220,103

2000

high school graduate or more	91.8%
college graduate or more	28.6%

Public school enrollment, Fall, 1998

total	998,053
Kindergarten through grade 8	695,950
grades 9 through 12	302,103

Public School Teachers, 2000

total	50,300
elementary	28,100
secondary	22,200
average salaries	
elementary	$41,100
secondary	$40,900

State receipts & expenditures for public schools, 2000

revenue receipts ($mil)	$7,865

State receipts & expenditures for public schools, 2000 (continued)

expenditures	
total ($mil)	$9,039
per capita	$1,570
per pupil	$6,992

Graduating high school seniors, public high schools, 2000 (est.) 57,246

SAT scores, 2001

verbal	527
math	527
percent graduates taking test	53%

Institutions of higher education, 1999

total	71
public	40
private	31

Enrollment in institutions of higher education, Fall, 1998

total	298,974
full-time men	85,032
full-time women	99,339
part-time men	48,240
part-time women	66,363

Minority enrollment in institutions of higher education, Fall, 1997

Black, non-Hispanic	12,631
Hispanic	13,278
Asian/Pacific Islander	26,267

Earned degrees conferred, 1998

Bachelor's	23,442
First professional	967
Master's	7,417
Doctor's	707

SOCIAL INSURANCE & WELFARE PROGRAMS

Social Security beneficiaries & benefits, 2000

beneficiaries	
total	845,000
retired and dependents	618,000
survivors	114,000
disabled & dependents	114,000
annual benefit payments ($mil)	
total	$7,898
retired and dependents	$5,564
survivors	$1,366
disabled & dependents	$968

Washington 4

Medicare, 2000
enrollment (x1,000) 725
payments ($mil) $2,843

Medicaid, 1998
recipients (x1,000) 1,413
payments ($mil) $2,044

Federal public aid
Temporary Assistance for Needy Families
(TANF), 2000
   Recipients (x1,000) 154
   Families (x1,000) 57
Supplemental Security Income
   total recipients, 1999 (x1,000) 98

Food Stamp Program
   participants, 2000 (x1,000) 295

HOUSING & CONSTRUCTION

Total housing units, 2000 2,451,075
   seasonal or recreational use 60,355
   occupied 2,271,398
      owner occupied 1,467,009
      renter occupied 804,389

New privately owned housing units uthorized, 2000
number (x1,000) 39
value ($mil) $4,426

New privately owned housing units
   started, 2000 (est.) (x1,000) 40.9

Existing home sales, 2000 (x1,000) 189.9

GOVERNMENT & ELECTIONS

State officials, 2002
Governor (name/party/term expires)
        GARY LOCKE
        Democrat - 2001
Lt. Governor .... Brad Owen
Sec. of State .... Sam Reed
Atty. General .... Christine Gregoire
Chief Justice .... Gary Alexander

Governorship
minimum age 18
length of term .... 4 years
number of consecutive
   terms permitted .... not specified
who succeeds .... Lt. Governor

State legislature
name .... Legislature
   upper chamber
      name .... Senate
      number of members 49
      length of term .... 4 years
      party in majority, 2000 .... Democratic
   lower chamber
      name .... House of Representatives
      number of members 98
      length of term .... 2 years
      party in majority, 2000 .... 50/50

State employees March, 2000
total 145,133
March payroll $373,141,773

Local governments, 1997
total 1,812
   county 39
   municipal 275
   township 0
   school districts 296
   special districts 1,202

Voting age population, November, 2000, projected
Total 4,368,000
   male 2,147,000
   female 2,221,000

Vote for president
2000
   Gore 1,248,000
   Bush 1,109,000
1996
   Clinton 1,123,000
   Dole 841,000
   Perot 201,000

Federal representation, 2002 (107th Congress)
Senators (name/party/term expires)

        MARIA CANTWELL
        Democrat - 2007
        PATTY MURRAY
        Democrat - 2005

Representatives, total 9
   Democrats 6
   Republicans 3
   other 0

Women holding public office, 2001
U.S. Congress 3
statewide elected office 2
state legislature 57

Black elected officials, 1999
total 21
  US and state legislatures 2
  city/county/regional offices 9
  judicial/law enforcement 9
  education/school boards 1

Hispanic public officials, 2000
total 12
  state executives & legislators 3
  city/county/regional offices 6
  judicial/law enforcement .... NA
  education/school boards 3

GOVERNMENTAL FINANCE

State government revenues, 1999 ($per capita)
total revenue $4,992.23
  total general revenue $3,516.45
    intergovernmental revenue $815.63
    taxes $2,143.29
    current charges $348.39
    miscellaneous $209.14

State government expenditures, 1999 ($per capita)
total expenditure $4,209.22
  total general expenditure $3,581.49
    education $1,489.08
    public welfare $794.22
    health $200.20
    hospitals $104.26
    highways $275.10
    police protection $38.43
    correction $115.17
    natural resources $91.57
    governmental administration $83.72
    interest on general debt $99.30

State debt, 1999 ($per capita) $1,924.78

Federal government grants to state & local government, 2000 (x$1,000)
total $5,707,329
  Dept. of Education $510,069
  Environmental Protection Agency $57,698
  Health Care Financing Admin. $2,347,728
  Dept. Housing & Urban Devel. $504,251
  Dept. of Labor $135,153
  Highway trust fund $477,468

CRIME, LAW ENFORCEMENT & COURTS

Crime, 2000 (all rates per 100,000 inhabitants)
total crimes 300,932
overall crime rate 5,105.6
  property crimes 279,144
    burglaries 53,476
    larcenies 190,650
    motor vehicle thefts 35,018
  property crime rate 4,736.0
  violent crimes 21,788
    murders 196
    forcible rapes 2,737
    robberies 5,812
    aggravated assaults 13,043
  violent crime rate 369.7

Number of police agencies, 2000 217

Arrests, 2000
total 242,128
  persons under 18 years of age 47,404

Prisoners under state & federal jurisdiction, 2000
total 14,915
percent change, 1999-2000 .... 2.2%
  sentenced to more than one year
    total 14,666
    rate per 100,000 residents 251

Persons under sentence of death, 4/1/2001 15

State's highest court
name .... Supreme Court
number of members 9
length of term .... 6 years
intermediate appeals court? .... yes

Washington 6

LABOR & INCOME

Civilian labor force, 2000
total 3,045,000
  men 1,603,000
  women 1,442,000
  persons 16-19 years 195,000
  white 2,726,000
  black 114,000

Civilian labor force as a percent of
civilian non-institutional population, 2000
total 68.7%
  men 75.2%
  women 62.6%
  persons 16-19 years .... NA%
  white 68.3%
  black 78.2%

Employment, 2000
total 2,888,000
  men 1,520,000
  women 1,368,000
  persons 16-19 years 159,000
  white 2,589,000
  black 105,000

Full-time/part-time labor force, 1998
full-time labor force 2,431,000
  working part-time for
    economic reasons 41,000
part-time labor force 609,000

Unemployment rate, 2000
total 5.2%
  men 5.2%
  women 5.2%
  persons 16-19 years 18.6%
  white 5.0%
  black 8.3%

Unemployed by reason for unemployment
(as a percent of total unemployment), 1998
job losers or completed temp jobs 46.2%
job leavers 11.0%
reentrants 35.9%
new entrants 6.2%

Experienced civilian labor force, by occupation,
1998
executive/administrative/managerial 471,000
professional/specialty 489,000
technicians & related support 115,000

sales 358,000
administrative support/clerical 375,000
service occupations 392,000
precision production/craft/repair 304,000
machine operators/assemblers 140,000
transportation/material moving 140,000
handlers/helpers/laborers 131,000
farming/forestry/fishing 115,000

Experienced civilian labor force, by industry, 1998
construction 177,000
manufacturing 453,000
transportation/communication 159,000
wholesale/retail trade 604,000
finance/real estate/insurance 148,000
services 691,000
government 452,000
agriculture 103,000

Average annual pay, 1999 .... $35,736
change in average annual pay,
  1998-1999 .... 8.0%

Hours and earnings of production workers
on manufacturing payrolls, 2000
average weekly hours 40.7
average hourly earnings $16.76
average weekly earnings $682.13

Labor union membership, 2000 470,800

Household income (in 2000 dollars)
median household income,
  three year average, 1998-2000 .... $42,024

Poverty
persons below poverty level,
  three year average, 1998-2000 .... 9.4%

Personal income ($per capita)
2000 (prelim.)
  in current dollars $31,528
  in constant (1996) dollars $29,367
1999 (preliminary)
  in current dollars $30,295
  in constant (1996) dollars $28,968

Federal income tax returns, 1999
returns filed 2,713,142
adjusted gross income ($1,000) $143,076,231
total income tax paid ($1,000) $25,433,322

ECONOMY, BUSINESS, INDUSTRY & AGRICULTURE

Fortune 500 companies, 2000 11

Business incorporations, 1998
total 12,179
change, 1997-1998 .... -2.5%

Business failures, 1998 2,528

Business firm ownership, 1997
Hispanic owned firms 10,009
Black owned firms 5,553
women owned firms 123,042
Asian & Pacific Islander owned firms 23,309
American Indian & Alaska
  native owned firms 4,689

Shopping centers, 2000 785

Gross state product, 1999 ($mil)
total $209,258
  agriculture services, forestry, fisheries .. $4,365
  mining $383
  construction $10,204
  manufacturing--durable goods $18,041
  manufacturing--nondurable goods $8,260
  transportation, communication &
    public utilities $16,624
  wholesale trade $14,524
  retail trade $20,584
  finance/real estate/insurance $36,420
  services $52,286
  federal, state & local government $27,566

Establishments, by major industry group, 1999
total 162,932
  forestry, fishing & agriculture 1,853
  mining 182
  construction 21,352
  manufacturing 7,741
  transportation & warehousing 4,120
  wholesale trade 9,988
  retail trade 22,582
  finance & insurance 8,894
  professional/scientific/technical 15,628
  health care/social assistance 15,194
  information 2,844
  accommodation/food services 13,051

Payroll, by major industry group, 1999
total ($1,000) $78,711,159
  forestry, fishing & agriculture $538,257
  mining $141,544
  construction $5,753,610
  manufacturing $14,036,573
  transportation & warehousing $2,728,936
  wholesale trade $4,951,201
  retail trade $6,681,229
  finance & insurance $4,446,563
  professional/scientific/technical $5,812,892
  health care/social assistance $8,233,063
  information $5,104,115
  accommodation/food services $2,355,678

Agriculture
number of farms, 2000 40,000
farm acreage, 2000 16,000,000
acres per farm, 2000 393
value of farms, 1997 ($mil) $19,311
farm income, 1999 ($mil)
  net farm income $519
  debt/asset ratio 17.6%
farm marketings, 1999 ($mil)
total $4,933
  crops $3,275
  livestock $1,658
principal commodities, in order by marketing
receipts, 1999
  Dairy products, apples, cattle, potatoes

Federal economic activity in state
expenditures, 2000
  total ($mil) $33,897
  per capita $5,751
  defense ($mil) $6,130
  non-defense ($mil) $27,767
defense department, 2000
  contract awards ($mil) $2,192
  payroll ($mil) $4,035
  civilian employees (x1,000) 23.1
  military personnel (x1,000) 48.9

Fishing, 2000
catch (thousands of pounds) 380,223
value ($1,000) $145,311

Mining, 2000 ($mil; preliminary)
total non-fuel mineral production $691

Washington 8

Construction, 1999 ($mil)
total contracts (including
  non-building) $10,714
    residential $4,645
    non-residential $4,544

Construction industries, 1997
establishments 19,339
receipts ($1,000) $21,101,831
annual payroll ($1,000) . . . . $NA
paid employees . . . . .NA

Manufacturing, 1997
establishments 8,812
value of shipments ($1,000) $82,356,770
annual payroll ($1,000) $13,589,194
paid employees 347,549

Transportation industries, 1997
establishments 6,718
receipts ($1,000) $19,516,018
annual payroll ($1,000) $4,301,090
paid employees 115,980

Wholesale trade, 1997
establishments 11,507
sales($1,000) $79,247,592
annual payroll ($1,000) $4,826,192
paid employees 134,842

Retail trade, 1997
establishments 33,512
sales($1,000) . . . . $NA
annual payroll ($1,000) . . . . $NA
paid employees . . . . .NA

Finance industries
establishments, 1997 15,149
receipts ($1,000), 1997 . . . . $NA
annual payroll ($1,000), 1997 . . . . $4,561,913
paid employees, 1997 127,681
commercial banks, 2000
  number 79
    assets ($bil) $14.9
    deposits ($bil) $12.3

Service industries, 1997 (non-exempt firms only)
establishments 46,202
receipts ($1,000) $37,604,349
annual payroll ($1,000) $13,253,812
paid employees 461,505

COMMUNICATION, ENERGY & TRANSPORTATION

Communication
daily newspapers, 2000 .24
households with
  telephones, 1998 . . . . 95.5%
  computers, 2000 . . . . 60.7%
  internet access, 2000 . . . . 49.7%

Energy
consumption, 1999
total (trillion Btu) 2,241
per capita (million Btu) 389
by source of production (trillion Btu)
  coal 96
  natural gas 277
  petroleum 878
  nuclear electric power 65
  hydroelectric power 988
by end-use sector (trillion Btu)
  residential 436
  commercial 332
  industrial 856
  transportation 617
electric energy, 1999
  production (billion kWh) 112.1
  net summer capability (million kW) 25.2
gas utilities, 1999
  customers 900,000
  sales (trillion Btu) 155
nuclear plants, 1999 1

Transportation, 2000
public road & street mileage
total 80,209
  urban 18,197
  rural 62,012
  interstate 764
vehicle miles of travel (mil) 53,330
total motor vehicle registrations 5,115,866
  automobiles 2,891,430
  motorcycles 117,857
licensed drivers 4,154,501
  per 1,000 driving age population 913
deaths from motor vehicle
  accidents 632

STATE SUMMARY

Capital City .... Charleston

Governor ....Robert Wise, Jr.

Address ....STATE CAPITOL
CHARLESTON, WV 25305
304 558-2000

Admitted as a state 1863

Area (square miles) 24,231

Population, 1980 1,949,644

Population, 1990 1,793,477

Population, 2000 1,808,344

Persons per square mile, 2000 .... 75.1

Largest city .... Charleston
population, 2000 53,421

Personal income per capita, 2000
(in current dollars) $21,915

Gross state product ($mil), 1999 .... $40,685

Leading industries, 1999 (by payroll)
Manufacturing
Health care/Social assistance
Retail trade

Leading agricultural commodities, 1999
Broilers, cattle, dairy products, turkeys

GEOGRAPHY & ENVIRONMENT

Area, 1990 (square miles)
total 24,231
land 24,087
water (includes territorial water) 145

Federally owned land, 2000 .... 7.9%

Highest point
name ....Spruce Knob
elevation (feet) 4,861

Lowest point
name .... Potomac River
elevation (feet) 240

General coastline (miles) 0

Tidal shoreline (miles) 0

Capital city .... Charleston
population, 2000 53,421

Largest city .... Charleston
population, 2000 53,421

Number of cities with over 100,000 population
1980 0
1990 0
2000 0

State parks and Recreation areas, 2000
area (acres) 196,000
number of visitors 7,990,000
revenues $18,036,000

Natl. forest system land, 1999 (acres) ...1,033,000

National park acreage, 1984 3,200

DEMOGRAPHICS & CHARACTERISTICS OF THE POPULATION

Population
1970 1,744,237
1980 1,949,644
1990 1,793,477
2000 1,808,344
2015 (projection) 1,851,000
2025 (projection) 1,845,000

Metropolitan area population
1970 683,000
1980 718,000
2000 766,000

Non-metropolitan area population
1970 1,061,000
1980 1,232,000
2000 1,043,000

Change in population, 1990-2000
number 14,867
percent 0.83%

Persons per square mile, 2000 .... 75.1

Persons by age, 2000
under 5 years 101,805
18 and over 1,405,951
21 and over 1,326,880
65 and over 276,895
85 and over 31,779

West Virginia 2

Persons by age, 2025 (projected)
under 5 years 87,000
5 to 17 years 261,000
65 and over 460,000

Median age, 2000 .... 38.9

Race, 2000
One race
White 1,718,777
Black or African American 57,232
American Indian and Alaska Native 3,606
Asian Indian 2,856
Chinese 1,878
Filipino 1,495
Japanese 887
Korean 857
Vietnamese 379
Native Hawaiian and other Pacific Islander .. 400
Two or more races 15,788

Race, 2025 (projected)
White 1,755,000
Black 66,000

Persons of Hispanic origin, 2000
total Hispanic or Latino 12,279
Mexican 4,347
Puerto Rican 1,609
Cuban 453
Other Hispanic or Latino 5,870

Persons of Hispanic origin, 2025 (proj.) ... 24,000

Persons by sex, 2000
male 879,170
female 929,174

Marital status, 1990
males
15 years & older 675,682
single 174,280
married 429,780
separated 8,422
widowed 21,012
divorced 50,610
females
15 years & older 756,449
single 143,058
married 431,831
separated 11,458

widowed 116,043
divorced 65,517

Households & families, 2000
households 736,481
persons per household 2.4
families 504,055
persons per family 2.9
married couples 397,499
female householder, no husband
present 79,120
one person households 199,587
households with persons under 18 years . 233,906
households with persons over 65 years ... 201,399

Nativity, 1990
number of persons born in state 1,386,139
percent of total residents 77.3%

Immigration & naturalization, 1998
immigrants admitted 375
persons naturalized 265
refugees granted resident status 5

VITAL STATISTICS & HEALTH

Births
1999
with low birth weight 8.0%
to teenage mothers 11.5%
to unmarried mothers 31.7%
Birth rate, 1999 (per 1,000) 11.5
Birth rate, 2000 (per 1,000) 11.6

Abortions, 1996
total 3,000
rate (per 1,000 women age 15-44) 6.6

Deaths
1998 20,890
1999 21,049
2000 21,078

Infant deaths
1998 153
1999 176
2000 158

Average lifetime, by race, 1989-1991
total .... 74.26 years
white .... 74.37 years
black .... 69.75 years

Marriages
1998 11,738
1999 13,549
2000 15,687

Divorces
1998 9,314
1999 8,957
2000 9,336

Physicians, 1999
total 3,962
rate (per 1,000 persons) 2.19

Nurses, 1999
total 16,130
rate (per 1,000 persons) 8.93

Hospitals, 1998
number 58
beds (x 1,000) 8.1
average daily census (x 1,000) 4.9
patients admitted (x1,000) 281
average cost per day to hospital, 1995 . . . . . $763
average cost per stay to hospital, 1995 . . . . $4,974

EDUCATION

*Educational attainment of all persons
25 years and older, 1990*
less than 9th grade 196,319
high school graduates 429,123
bachelor's degree 88,136
graduate or professional degree 56,382

2000
high school graduate or more 77.1%
college graduate or more 15.3%

Public school enrollment, Fall, 1998
total 297,530
Kindergarten through grade 8 205,840
grades 9 through 12 91,690

Public School Teachers, 2000
total 20,900
elementary 14,500
secondary 6,500
average salaries
elementary $34,700
secondary $35,600

*State receipts & expenditures for public
schools, 2000*
revenue receipts ($mil) $2,516

*State receipts & expenditures for public
schools, 2000 (continued)*
expenditures
total ($mil) $2,743
per capita $1,518
per pupil $9,238

*Graduating high school seniors,
public high schools, 2000 (est.)* 19,582

SAT scores, 2001
verbal 527
math 512
percent graduates taking test 18%

Institutions of higher education, 1999
total 33
public 15
private 18

*Enrollment in institutions of higher
education, Fall, 1998*
total 88,107
full-time men 29,580
full-time women 32,884
part-time men 9,398
part-time women 16,245

*Minority enrollment in institutions of higher
education, Fall, 1997*
Black, non-Hispanic 3,706
Hispanic 933
Asian/Pacific Islander 950

Earned degrees conferred, 1998
Bachelor's 8,290
First professional 382
Master's 2,562
Doctor's 158

SOCIAL INSURANCE &
WELFARE PROGRAMS

Social Security beneficiaries & benefits, 2000
beneficiaries
total 390,000
retired and dependents 233,000
survivors 76,000
disabled & dependents 81,000
annual benefit payments ($mil)
total $3,488
retired and dependents $1,947
survivors $837
disabled & dependents $705

West Virginia 4

Medicare, 2000
enrollment (x1,000) 336
payments ($mil) $1,656

Medicaid, 1998
recipients (x1,000) 343
payments ($mil) $1,243

Federal public aid
Temporary Assistance for Needy Families
(TANF), 2000
  Recipients (x1,000) 32
  Families (x1,000) 11
Supplemental Security Income
  total recipients, 1999 (x1,000) 71

Food Stamp Program
  participants, 2000 (x1,000) 227

HOUSING & CONSTRUCTION

Total housing units, 2000 844,623
  seasonal or recreational use 32,757
  occupied 736,481
    owner occupied 553,699
    renter occupied 182,782

New privately owned housing units uthorized, 2000
number (x1,000) 3.8
value ($mil) $360

New privately owned housing units
  started, 2000 (est.) (x1,000) 5.3

Existing home sales, 2000 (x1,000) 21.5

GOVERNMENT & ELECTIONS

State officials, 2002
  Governor (name/party/term expires)
    ROBERT WISE, JR.
    Democrat - 2005
Lt. Governor . . . . (no Lieutenant Governor)
Sec. of State . . . . Joe Manchin
Atty. General . . . . Darrell McGraw
Chief Justice . . . . Warren McGraw

Governorship
minimum age 30
length of term . . . . 4 years
number of consecutive
  terms permitted 2
who succeeds . . . . Pres. of Senate

State legislature
name . . . . Legislature
  upper chamber
    name . . . . Senate
    number of members 34
    length of term . . . . 4 years
    party in majority, 2000 . . . . Democratic
  lower chamber
    name . . . . House of Delegates
    number of members 100
    length of term . . . . 2 years
    party in majority, 2000 . . . . Democratic

State employees March, 2000
total 38,369
March payroll $84,838,470

Local governments, 1997
total 704
  county 55
  municipal 232
  township 0
  school districts 55
  special districts 362

Voting age population, November, 2000, projected
Total 1,416,000
  male 670,000
  female 746,000

Vote for president
2000
  Gore 295,000
  Bush 336,000
1996
  Clinton 328,000
  Dole 234,000
  Perot 72,000

Federal representation, 2002 (107th Congress)
Senators (name/party/term expires)

    ROBERT C. BYRD
    Democrat - 2007
    JAY ROCKEFELLER
    Democrat - 2003

Representatives, total 3
  Democrats 2
  Republicans 1
  other 0

West Virginia 5

Women holding public office, 2001
U.S. Congress 1
statewide elected office 0
state legislature 25

Black elected officials, 1999
total 19
  US and state legislatures 4
  city/county/regional offices 12
  judicial/law enforcement 3
  education/school boards .... NA

Hispanic public officials, 2000
total .... NA
  state executives & legislators .... NA
  city/county/regional offices .... NA
  judicial/law enforcement .... NA
  education/school boards .... NA

GOVERNMENTAL FINANCE

State government revenues, 1999 ($per capita)
total revenue $4,446.38
  total general revenue $3,644.00
  intergovernmental revenue $1,175.12
  taxes $1,827.44
  current charges $331.67
  miscellaneous $309.78

State government expenditures, 1999 ($per capita)
total expenditure $4,059.81
  total general expenditure $3,510.24
  education $1,331.74
  public welfare $921.78
  health $77.42
  hospitals $45.94
  highways $434.74
  police protection $23.20
  correction $69.06
  natural resources $75.75
  governmental administration $175.52
  interest on general debt $112.40

State debt, 1999 ($per capita) $2,041.79

Federal government grants to state & local government, 2000 (x$1,000)
total $2,541,963
  Dept. of Education $228,689
  Environmental Protection Agency $74,708
  Health Care Financing Admin. $1,099,610
  Dept. Housing & Urban Devel. $190,405
  Dept. of Labor $43,598
  Highway trust fund $286,007

CRIME, LAW ENFORCEMENT & COURTS

Crime, 2000 (all rates per 100,000 inhabitants)
total crimes 47,067
overall crime rate 2,602.8
  property crimes 41,344
    burglaries 9,890
    larcenies 28,139
    motor vehicle thefts 3,315
  property crime rate 2,286.3
  violent crimes 5,723
    murders 46
    forcible rapes 331
    robberies 749
    aggravated assaults 4,597
  violent crime rate 316.5

Number of police agencies, 2000 131

Arrests, 2000
total 27,275
  persons under 18 years of age 2,508

Prisoners under state & federal jurisdiction, 2000
total 3,856
percent change, 1999-2000 .... 9.2%
  sentenced to more than one year
  total 3,795
  rate per 100,000 residents 211

Persons under sentence of death, 4/1/2001 ...NA

State's highest court
name .... Supreme Court of Appeals
number of members 5
length of term .... 12 years
intermediate appeals court? .... no

West Virginia 6

LABOR & INCOME

Civilian labor force, 2000
total	825,000
men	432,000
women	393,000
persons 16-19 years	50,000
white	792,000
black	26,000

Civilian labor force as a percent of civilian non-institutional population, 2000
total	57.1%
men	63.5%
women	51.3%
persons 16-19 years	NA%
white	56.8%
black	68.7%

Employment, 2000
total	779,000
men	406,000
women	373,000
persons 16-19 years	40,000
white	750,000
black	24,000

Full-time/part-time labor force, 1998
full-time labor force	652,000
working part-time for economic reasons	8,000
part-time labor force	148,000

Unemployment rate, 2000
total	5.5%
men	6.1%
women	4.9%
persons 16-19 years	18.9%
white	5.3%
black	10.6%

Unemployed by reason for unemployment (as a percent of total unemployment), 1998
job losers or completed temp jobs	41.5%
job leavers	9.4%
reentrants	34.0%
new entrants	13.2%

Experienced civilian labor force, by occupation, 1998
executive/administrative/managerial	84,000
professional/specialty	111,000
technicians & related support	30
sales	103,000
administrative support/clerical	110,000
service occupations	118,000
precision production/craft/repair	95,000
machine operators/assemblers	41,000
transportation/material moving	51,000
handlers/helpers/laborers	35,000
farming/forestry/fishing	14,000

Experienced civilian labor force, by industry, 1998
construction	38,000
manufacturing	89,000
transportation/communication	47,000
wholesale/retail trade	165,000
finance/real estate/insurance	34,000
services	179,000
government	134,000
agriculture	NA

Average annual pay, 1999
Average annual pay, 1999	$26,008
change in average annual pay, 1998-1999	2.9%

Hours and earnings of production workers on manufacturing payrolls, 2000
average weekly hours	41.3
average hourly earnings	$14.60
average weekly earnings	$602.98

Labor union membership, 2000
Labor union membership, 2000	102,900

Household income (in 2000 dollars)
median household income, three year average, 1998-2000	$29,052

Poverty
persons below poverty level, three year average, 1998-2000	15.8%

Personal income ($per capita)
2000 (prelim.)	
in current dollars	$21,915
in constant (1996) dollars	$20,413
1999 (preliminary)	
in current dollars	$20,888
in constant (1996) dollars	$19,973

Federal income tax returns, 1999
returns filed	745,092
adjusted gross income ($1,000)	$24,457,453
total income tax paid ($1,000)	$3,098,445

ECONOMY, BUSINESS, INDUSTRY & AGRICULTURE

Fortune 500 companies, 2000 0

Business incorporations, 1998
total 1,908
change, 1997-1998 .... -7.81%

Business failures, 1998 305

Business firm ownership, 1997
Hispanic owned firms 940
Black owned firms 1,148
women owned firms 30,231
Asian & Pacific Islander owned firms 1,240
American Indian & Alaska
    native owned firms 1,017

Shopping centers, 2000 164

Gross state product, 1999 ($mil)
total $40,685
    agriculture services, forestry, fisheries $261
    mining $2,967
    construction $1,852
    manufacturing--durable goods $2,873
    manufacturing--nondurable goods $3,628
    transportation, communication &
        public utilities $4,609
    wholesale trade $2,223
    retail trade $4,063
    finance/real estate/insurance $4,604
    services $7,283
    federal, state & local government $6,323

Establishments, by major industry group, 1999
total 41,451
    forestry, fishing & agriculture 368
    mining 682
    construction 4,637
    manufacturing 1,510
    transportation & warehousing 1,502
    wholesale trade 1,893
    retail trade 7,883
    finance & insurance 2,150
    professional/scientific/technical 2,854
    health care/social assistance 4,319
    information 680
    accommodation/food services 3,259

Payroll, by major industry group, 1999
total ($1,000) $13,513,976
    forestry, fishing & agriculture $22,075
    mining $893,173
    construction $796,360
    manufacturing $2,590,925
    transportation & warehousing $468,428
    wholesale trade $685,155
    retail trade $1,424,365
    finance & insurance $604,169
    professional/scientific/technical $540,654
    health care/social assistance $2,577,104
    information $373,480
    accommodation/food services $525,362

Agriculture
number of farms, 2000 21,000
farm acreage, 2000 4,000,000
acres per farm, 2000 176
value of farms, 1997 ($mil) $3,700
farm income, 1999 ($mil)
    net farm income $13
    debt/asset ratio 10.5%
farm marketings, 1999 ($mil)
    total $387
        crops $53
        livestock $334
principal commodities, in order by marketing
receipts, 1999
        Broilers, cattle, dairy products, turkeys

Federal economic activity in state
expenditures, 2000
    total ($mil) $11,739
    per capita $6,491
    defense ($mil) $352
    non-defense ($mil) $11,387
defense department, 2000
    contract awards ($mil) $74
    payroll ($mil) $271
    civilian employees (x1,000) 1.8
    military personnel (x1,000) 0.6

Fishing, 2000
catch (thousands of pounds) ....NA
value ($1,000) .... $NA

Mining, 2000 ($mil; preliminary)
total non-fuel mineral production $3182

West Virginia 8

Construction, 1999 ($mil)
total contracts (including
   non-building) $1,537
    residential $231
    non-residential $617

Construction industries, 1997
establishments 4,391
receipts ($1,000) $3,033,608
annual payroll ($1,000) $745,340
paid employees 30,892

Manufacturing, 1997
establishments 1,879
value of shipments ($1,000) $18,545,029
annual payroll ($1,000) $2,528,978
paid employees 76,772

Transportation industries, 1997
establishments 2,311
receipts ($1,000) $6,927,456
annual payroll ($1,000) $1,052,526
paid employees 32,924

Wholesale trade, 1997
establishments 2,385
sales($1,000) $10,979,160
annual payroll ($1,000) $761,823
paid employees 27,352

Retail trade, 1997
establishments 10,652
sales($1,000) $14,639,608
annual payroll ($1,000) $1,580,346
paid employees 129,956

Finance industries
establishments, 1997 3,375
receipts ($1,000), 1997 .... $NA
annual payroll ($1,000), 1997 .... $NA
paid employees, 1997 .... NA
commercial banks, 2000
   number 70
    assets ($bil) $17.5
    deposits ($bil) $13.8

Service industries, 1997 (non-exempt firms only)
establishments 10,676
receipts ($1,000) $6,248,808
annual payroll ($1,000) $2,265,430
paid employees 106,642

COMMUNICATION, ENERGY & TRANSPORTATION

Communication
daily newspapers, 2000 22
households with
   telephones, 1998 .... 93.5%
   computers, 2000 .... 42.8%
   internet access, 2000 .... 34.3%

Energy
consumption, 1999
total (trillion Btu) 735
per capita (million Btu) 407
by source of production (trillion Btu)
   coal 977
   natural gas 147
   petroleum 220
   nuclear electric power .... NA
   hydroelectric power 10
by end-use sector (trillion Btu)
   residential 142
   commercial 101
   industrial 311
   transportation 182
electric energy, 1999
   production (billion kWh) 91.7
   net summer capability (million kW) 14.5
gas utilities, 1999
   customers 368,000
   sales (trillion Btu) 60
nuclear plants, 1999 .... na

Transportation, 2000
public road & street mileage
total 37,277
   urban 3,251
   rural 34,026
   interstate 549
vehicle miles of travel (mil) 19,242
total motor vehicle registrations 1,441,735
   automobiles 795,249
   motorcycles 25,705
licensed drivers 1,347,207
   per 1,000 driving age population 926
deaths from motor vehicle
   accidents 410

STATE SUMMARY

Capital City .... Madison

Governor .... Scott McCallum

Address .... STATE CAPITOL
MADISON, WI 53702
608 266-1212

Admitted as a state 1848

Area (square miles) 65,503

Population, 1980 4,705,767

Population, 1990 4,891,769

Population, 2000 5,363,675

Persons per square mile, 2000 .... 98.8

Largest city .... Milwaukee
population, 2000 597,000

Personal income per capita, 2000
(in current dollars) $28,232

Gross state product ($mil), 1999 ...... $166,481

Leading industries, 1999 (by payroll)
Manufacturing
Health care/Social assistance
Retail trade

Leading agricultural commodities, 1999
Dairy products, cattle, corn, potatoes

GEOGRAPHY & ENVIRONMENT

Area, 1990 (square miles)
total 65,503
land 54,314
water (includes territorial water) 11,190

Federally owned land, 2000 .... 5.2%

Highest point
name .... Timms Hill
elevation (feet) 1,951

Lowest point
name .... Lake Michigan
elevation (feet) 581

General coastline (miles) 0

Tidal shoreline (miles) 0

Capital city .... Madison
population, 2000 208,000

Largest city .... Milwaukee
population, 2000 597,000

Number of cities with over 100,000 population
1980 2
1990 2
2000 3

State parks and Recreation areas, 2000
area (acres) 129,000
number of visitors 15,470,000
revenues $12,855,000

Natl. forest system land, 1999 (acres) ... 1,521,000

National park acreage, 1984 66,400

DEMOGRAPHICS & CHARACTERISTICS OF THE POPULATION

Population
1970 4,417,821
1980 4,705,767
1990 4,891,769
2000 5,363,675
2015 (projection) 5,693,000
2025 (projection) 5,867,000

Metropolitan area population
1970 3,019,000
1980 3,145,000
2000 3,640,000

Non-metropolitan area population
1970 1,399,000
1980 1,561,000
2000 1,723,000

Change in population, 1990-2000
number 471,906
percent 9.65%

Persons per square mile, 2000 .... 98.8

Persons by age, 2000
under 5 years 342,340
18 and over 3,994,919
21 and over 3,751,033
65 and over 702,553
85 and over 95,625

Wisconsin 2

Persons by age, 2025 (projected)
under 5 years 354,000
5 to 17 years 976,000
65 and over 1,200,000

Median age, 2000 36

Race, 2000
One race
White 4,769,857
Black or African American 304,460
American Indian and Alaska Native 47,228
Asian Indian 12,665
Chinese 11,184
Filipino 5,158
Japanese 2,868
Korean 6,800
Vietnamese 3,891
Native Hawaiian and other Pacific Islander   1,630
Two or more races 66,895

Race, 2025 (projected)
White 5,093,000
Black 501,000

Persons of Hispanic origin, 2000
total Hispanic or Latino 192,921
   Mexican 126,719
   Puerto Rican 30,267
   Cuban 2,491
   Other Hispanic or Latino 33,444

Persons of Hispanic origin, 2025 (proj.) .. 236,000

Persons by sex, 2000
male 2,649,041
female 2,714,634

Marital status, 1990
males
   15 years & older 1,833,873
      single 560,190
      married 1,101,329
         separated 21,613
      widowed 47,121
      divorced 125,233
females
   15 years & older 1,967,276
      single 469,094
      married 1,105,905
         separated 29,411

widowed 233,268
divorced 159,009

Households & families, 2000
households 2,084,544
persons per household 2.5
   families 1,386,815
   persons per family 3.05
      married couples 1,108,597
      female householder, no husband
         present 200,300
      one person households 557,875
households with persons under 18 years . 706,399
households with persons over 65 years ... 479,787

Nativity, 1990
number of persons born in state 3,737,602
percent of total residents 76.4%

Immigration & naturalization, 1998
immigrants admitted 3,724
persons naturalized 1,894
refugees granted resident status 418

VITAL STATISTICS & HEALTH

Births
1999
   with low birth weight 6.7%
   to teenage mothers 13.0%
   to unmarried mothers 29.2%
Birth rate, 1999 (per 1,000) 13.0
Birth rate, 2000 (per 1,000) 13.1

Abortions, 1996
total 14,000
rate (per 1,000 women age 15-44) 12.3

Deaths
1998 45,843
1999 46,672
2000 46,519

Infant deaths
1998 481
1999 453
2000 450

Average lifetime, by race, 1989-1991
total .... 76.87 years
   white .... 77.18 years
   black .... 70.96 years

Wisconsin 3

Marriages
1998 35,057
1999 35,864
2000 36,066

Divorces
1998 17,665
1999 17,758
2000 17,616

Physicians, 1999
total 12,167
rate (per 1,000 persons) 2.32

Nurses, 1999
total 47,520
rate (per 1,000 persons) 9.05

Hospitals, 1998
number 123
beds (x 1,000) 16.7
average daily census (x 1,000) 9.4
patients admitted (x1,000) 554
average cost per day to hospital, 1995 ..... $794
average cost per stay to hospital, 1995 .... $5,679

EDUCATION

*Educational attainment of all persons
25 years and older, 1990*
less than 9th grade 294,862
high school graduates 1,147,697
bachelor's degree 375,603
graduate or professional degree 173,367

2000
high school graduate or more 86.7%
college graduate or more 23.8%

Public school enrollment, Fall, 1998
total 879,542
Kindergarten through grade 8 600,703
grades 9 through 12 278,839

Public School Teachers, 2000
total 57,400
elementary 39,300
secondary 18,100
average salaries
elementary $40,900
secondary $41,700

*State receipts & expenditures for public
schools, 2000*
revenue receipts ($mil) $9,016

*State receipts & expenditures for public
schools, 2000 (continued)*
expenditures
total ($mil) $8,294
per capita $1,580
per pupil $8,718

*Graduating high school seniors,
public high schools, 2000 (est.)* 59,438

SAT scores, 2001
verbal 584
math 596
percent graduates taking test 6%

Institutions of higher education, 1999
total 66
public 32
private 34

*Enrollment in institutions of higher
education, Fall, 1998*
total 309,354
full-time men 85,983
full-time women 101,491
part-time men 51,278
part-time women 70,647

*Minority enrollment in institutions of higher
education, Fall, 1997*
Black, non-Hispanic 12,780
Hispanic 6,612
Asian/Pacific Islander 6,565

Earned degrees conferred, 1998
Bachelor's 27,379
First professional 975
Master's 6,729
Doctor's 948

SOCIAL INSURANCE & WELFARE PROGRAMS

Social Security beneficiaries & benefits, 2000
beneficiaries
total 900,000
retired and dependents 665,000
survivors 127,000
disabled & dependents 107,000
annual benefit payments ($mil)
total $8,347
retired and dependents $5,936
survivors $1,522
disabled & dependents $889

Wisconsin 4

Medicare, 2000
enrollment (x1,000) 777
payments ($mil) $3,498

Medicaid, 1998
recipients (x1,000) 519
payments ($mil) $2,206

Federal public aid
Temporary Assistance for Needy Families
(TANF), 2000
   Recipients (x1,000) 38
   Families (x1,000) 17
Supplemental Security Income
   total recipients, 1999 (x1,000) 87

Food Stamp Program
   participants, 2000 (x1,000) 193

HOUSING & CONSTRUCTION

Total housing units, 2000 2,321,144
   seasonal or recreational use 142,313
   occupied 2,084,544
      owner occupied 1,426,361
      renter occupied 658,183

New privately owned housing units uthorized, 2000
number (x1,000) 34.2
value ($mil) $3,917

New privately owned housing units
   started, 2000 (est.) (x1,000) 32.0

Existing home sales, 2000 (x1,000) 94.2

GOVERNMENT & ELECTIONS

State officials, 2002
   Governor (name/party/term expires)
      SCOTT MCCALLUM
      Republican - 2002
Lt. Governor . . . . Margaret Farrow
Sec. of State . . . . Douglas LaFollette
Atty. General . . . . James Doyle
Chief Justice . . . . Shirley Abrahamson

Governorship
minimum age . . . . not specified
length of term . . . . 4 years
number of consecutive
   terms permitted . . . . not specified
who succeeds . . . . Lt. Governor

State legislature
name . . . . Legislature
   upper chamber
      name . . . . Senate
      number of members 33
      length of term . . . . 4 years
      party in majority, 2000 . . . . Democratic
   lower chamber
      name . . . . Assembly
      number of members 99
      length of term . . . . 2 years
      party in majority, 2000 . . . . Republican

State employees March, 2000
total 77,532
March payroll $230,570,128

Local governments, 1997
total 3,059
   county 72
   municipal 583
   township 1,266
   school districts 442
   special districts 696

Voting age population, November, 2000, projected
Total 3,930,000
   male 1,904,000
   female 129026000

Vote for president
2000
   Gore 1,243,000
   Bush 1,237,000
1996
   Clinton 1,072,000
   Dole 845,000
   Perot 227,000

Federal representation, 2002 (107th Congress)
Senators (name/party/term expires)

      HERBERT KOHL
      Democrat - 2007
      RUSSELL FEINGOLD
      Democrat - 2005

Representatives, total 9
   Democrats 5
   Republicans 4
   other 0

Women holding public office, 2001
U.S. Congress 1
statewide elected office 2
state legislature 32

Black elected officials, 1999
total 31
   US and state legislatures 8
   city/county/regional offices 14
   judicial/law enforcement 4
   education/school boards 5

Hispanic public officials, 2000
total 12
   state executives & legislators 1
   city/county/regional offices 6
   judicial/law enforcement 3
   education/school boards 2

GOVERNMENTAL FINANCE

State government revenues, 1999 ($per capita)
total revenue $5,396.52
   total general revenue $3,668.67
   intergovernmental revenue $813.40
   taxes $2,214.63
   current charges $376.51
   miscellaneous $264.13

State government expenditures, 1999 ($per capita)
total expenditure $3,897.91
   total general expenditure $3,488.22
   education $1,328.99
   public welfare $635.33
   health $104.08
   hospitals $102.23
   highways $258.05
   police protection $20.67
   correction $139.81
   natural resources $61.94
   governmental administration $104.63
   interest on general debt $125.20

State debt, 1999 ($per capita) $2,137.94

Federal government grants to state & local government, 2000 (x$1,000)
total $4,503,678
   Dept. of Education $468,913
   Environmental Protection Agency $56,715
   Health Care Financing Admin. $2,078,095
   Dept. Housing & Urban Devel. $435,551
   Dept. of Labor $88,176
   Highway trust fund $172,080

CRIME, LAW ENFORCEMENT & COURTS

Crime, 2000 (all rates per 100,000 inhabitants)
total crimes 172,124
overall crime rate 3,209.1
   property crimes 159,424
      burglaries 25,183
      larcenies 119,605
      motor vehicle thefts 14,636
   property crime rate 2,972.3
   violent crimes 12,700
      murders 169
      forcible rapes 1,165
      robberies 4,537
      aggravated assaults 6,829
   violent crime rate 236.8

Number of police agencies, 2000 . . . . na

Arrests, 2000
total . . . . NA
   persons under 18 years of age . . . . na

Prisoners under state & federal jurisdiction, 2000
total 20,612
percent change, 1999-2000 . . . . 1%
   sentenced to more than one year
   total 20,013
   rate per 100,000 residents 376

Persons under sentence of death, 4/1/2001 . . . NA

State's highest court
name . . . . Supreme Court
number of members 7
length of term . . . . 10 years
intermediate appeals court? . . . . yes

Wisconsin 6

LABOR & INCOME

Civilian labor force, 2000

total	2,935,000
men	1,563,000
women	1,372,000
persons 16-19 years	210,000
white	2,728,000
black	137,000

Civilian labor force as a percent of civilian non-institutional population, 2000

total	72.8%
men	77.3%
women	68.3%
persons 16-19 years	NA%
white	73.2%
black	67.9%

Employment, 2000

total	2,831,000
men	1,508,000
women	1,323,000
persons 16-19 years	190,000
white	2,645,000
black	123,000

Full-time/part-time labor force, 1998

full-time labor force	2,342,000
working part-time for economic reasons	28,000
part-time labor force	609,000

Unemployment rate, 2000

total	3.5%
men	3.6%
women	3.5%
persons 16-19 years	9.2%
white	3.0%
black	9.9%

Unemployed by reason for unemployment (as a percent of total unemployment), 1998

job losers or completed temp jobs	47.5%
job leavers	11.1%
reentrants	36.4%
new entrants	6.1%

Experienced civilian labor force, by occupation, 1998

executive/administrative/managerial	401,000
professional/specialty	406,000
technicians & related support	NA
sales	307,000
administrative support/clerical	429,000
service occupations	380,000
precision production/craft/repair	355,000
machine operators/assemblers	252,000
transportation/material moving	129,000
handlers/helpers/laborers	135,000
farming/forestry/fishing	NA

Experienced civilian labor force, by industry, 1998

construction	147,000
manufacturing	645,000
transportation/communication	116,000
wholesale/retail trade	564,000
finance/real estate/insurance	173,000
services	641,000
government	386,000
agriculture	NA

Average annual pay, 1999 .... $29,597
change in average annual pay, 1998-1999 .... 3.7%

Hours and earnings of production workers on manufacturing payrolls, 2000

average weekly hours	41.5
average hourly earnings	$14.85
average weekly earnings	$616.28

Labor union membership, 2000 446,000

Household income (in 2000 dollars)
median household income, three year average, 1998-2000 .... $45,349

Poverty
persons below poverty level, three year average, 1998-2000 .... 8.8%

Personal income ($per capita)
2000 (prelim.)
  in current dollars $28,232
  in constant (1996) dollars $26,297
1999 (preliminary)
  in current dollars $27,412
  in constant (1996) dollars $26,212

Federal income tax returns, 1999

returns filed	2,560,400
adjusted gross income ($1,000)	$109,497,163
total income tax paid ($1,000)	$15,478,573

ECONOMY, BUSINESS, INDUSTRY & AGRICULTURE

Fortune 500 companies, 2000 10

Business incorporations, 1998
total 7,049
change, 1997-1998 .... -11.5%

Business failures, 1998 1,005

Business firm ownership, 1997
Hispanic owned firms 3,020
Black owned firms 4,848
women owned firms 89,284
Asian & Pacific Islander owned firms 3,752
American Indian & Alaska
    native owned firms 2,338

Shopping centers, 2000 637

Gross state product, 1999 ($mil)
total $166,481
    agriculture services, forestry, fisheries .. $3,162
    mining $226
    construction $7,830
    manufacturing--durable goods $26,126
    manufacturing--nondurable goods $17,730
    transportation, communication &
        public utilities $11,858
    wholesale trade $10,682
    retail trade $15,626
    finance/real estate/insurance $25,953
    services $29,639
    federal, state & local government $17,648

Establishments, by major industry group, 1999
total 139,646
    forestry, fishing & agriculture 653
    mining 159
    construction 15,952
    manufacturing 10,005
    transportation & warehousing 5,237
    wholesale trade 7,941
    retail trade 21,409
    finance & insurance 8,271
    professional/scientific/technical 10,512
    health care/social assistance 12,282
    information 2,049
    accommodation/food services 12,934

Payroll, by major industry group, 1999
total ($1,000) $69,270,659
    forestry, fishing & agriculture $61,141
    mining $124,988
    construction $4,806,911
    manufacturing $20,805,044
    transportation & warehousing $2,223,794
    wholesale trade $4,339,305
    retail trade $5,569,946
    finance & insurance $5,260,385
    professional/scientific/technical $3,462,298
    health care/social assistance $8,336,764
    information $1,754,068
    accommodation/food services $1,830,330

Agriculture
number of farms, 2000 77,000
farm acreage, 2000 16,000,000
acres per farm, 2000 210
value of farms, 1997 ($mil) $21,000
farm income, 1999 ($mil)
    net farm income $879
    debt/asset ratio 19.8%
farm marketings, 1999 ($mil)
total $5,596
    crops $1,447
    livestock $4,149
principal commodities, in order by marketing
receipts, 1999
    Dairy products, cattle, corn, potatoes

Federal economic activity in state
expenditures, 2000
    total ($mil) $24,300
    per capita $4,531
    defense ($mil) $1,231
    non-defense ($mil) $23,069
defense department, 2000
    contract awards ($mil) $768
    payroll ($mil) $456
    civilian employees (x1,000) 3
    military personnel (x1,000) 0.6

Fishing, 2000
catch (thousands of pounds) 5,549
value ($1,000) $6,792

Mining, 2000 ($mil; preliminary)
total non-fuel mineral production $349

Wisconsin 8

Construction, 1999 ($mil)
total contracts (including
    non-building) $7,472
      residential $3,331
      non-residential $2,937

Construction industries, 1997
establishments 14,760
receipts ($1,000) $16,872,393
annual payroll ($1,000) $3,837,291
paid employees 114,490

Manufacturing, 1997
establishments 10,373
value of shipments ($1,000) $118,860,895
annual payroll ($1,000) $19,094,326
paid employees 575,318

Transportation industries, 1997
establishments 7,203
receipts ($1,000) $17,821,818
annual payroll ($1,000) $3,501,127
paid employees 112,086

Wholesale trade, 1997
establishments 9,663
sales($1,000) $61,464,527
annual payroll ($1,000) $4,267,164
paid employees 128,690

Retail trade, 1997
establishments 32,260
sales($1,000) $51,066,574
annual payroll ($1,000) $5,636,864
paid employees 453,927

Finance industries
establishments, 1997 12,581
receipts ($1,000), 1997 .... $NA
annual payroll ($1,000), 1997 .... $5,357,920
paid employees, 1997 152,563
commercial banks, 2000
  number 315
    assets ($bil) $78.8
    deposits ($bil) $58.8

Service industries, 1997 (non-exempt firms only)
establishments 36,188
receipts ($1,000) $24,660,249
annual payroll ($1,000) $9,557,053
paid employees 416,814

COMMUNICATION, ENERGY & TRANSPORTATION

Communication
daily newspapers, 2000 35
households with
  telephones, 1998 .... 96.4%
  computers, 2000 .... 50.9%
  internet access, 2000 .... 40.6%

Energy
consumption, 1999
total (trillion Btu) 1,811
per capita (million Btu) 345
by source of production (trillion Btu)
  coal 472
  natural gas 379
  petroleum 668
  nuclear electric power 122
  hydroelectric power 23
by end-use sector (trillion Btu)
  residential 376
  commercial 285
  industrial 717
  transportation 432
electric energy, 1999
  production (billion kWh) 54.7
  net summer capability (million kW) 12.1
gas utilities, 1999
  customers 1,411,000
  sales (trillion Btu) 256
nuclear plants, 1999 3

Transportation, 2000
public road & street mileage
total 112,359
  urban 16,650
  rural 95,709
  interstate 743
vehicle miles of travel (mil) 57,266
total motor vehicle registrations 4,365,525
  automobiles 2,526,849
  motorcycles 178,897
licensed drivers 3,770,453
  per 1,000 driving age population 907
deaths from motor vehicle
  accidents 799

Wyoming 1

STATE SUMMARY

Capital City .... Cheyenne

Governor .... Jim Geringer

Address ....STATE CAPITOL
CHEYENNE, WY 82002
307 777-7434

Admitted as a state 1890

Area (square miles) 97,818

Population, 1980 469,557

Population, 1990 453,588

Population, 2000 493,782

Persons per square mile, 2000 .... 5.1

Largest city .... Cheyenne
population, 2000 53,011

Personal income per capita, 2000
(in current dollars) $27,230

Gross state product ($mil), 1999 ...... $17,448

Leading industries, 1999 (by payroll)
Mining
Health care/Social assistance
Retail trade

Leading agricultural commodities, 1999
Cattle, sugar beets, hay, sheep/lambs

GEOGRAPHY & ENVIRONMENT

Area, 1990 (square miles)
total 97,818
land 97,105
water (includes territorial water) 714

Federally owned land, 2000 .... 49.8%

Highest point
name ....Gannett Peak
elevation (feet) 13,804

Lowest point
name .... Belle Fourche River
elevation (feet) 3,009

General coastline (miles) 0

Tidal shoreline (miles) 0

Capital city .... Cheyenne
population, 2000 53,011

Largest city .... Cheyenne
population, 2000 53,011

Number of cities with over 100,000 population
1980 0
1990 0
2000 0

State parks and Recreation areas, 2000
area (acres) 121,000
number of visitors 2,538,000
revenues $1,067,000

Natl. forest system land, 1999 (acres) ...9,238,000

National park acreage, 1984 2,392,400

DEMOGRAPHICS & CHARACTERISTICS OF THE POPULATION

Population
1970 332,416
1980 469,557
1990 453,588
2000 493,782
2015 (projection) 641,000
2025 (projection) 694,000

Metropolitan area population
1970 108,000
1980 141,000
2000 148,000

Non-metropolitan area population
1970 225,000
1980 329,000
2000 346,000

Change in population, 1990-2000
number 40,194
percent 8.86%

Persons per square mile, 2000 .... 5.1

Persons by age, 2000
under 5 years 30,940
18 and over 364,909
21 and over 340,803
65 and over 57,693
85 and over 6,735

Wyoming 2

Persons by age, 2025 (projected)
under 5 years 45,000
5 to 17 years 124,000
65 and over 145,000

Median age, 2000 .... 36.2

Race, 2000
One race
White 454,670
Black or African American 3,722
American Indian and Alaska Native 11,133
Asian Indian 354
Chinese 609
Filipino 472
Japanese 485
Korean 412
Vietnamese 100
Native Hawaiian and other Pacific Islander . . 302
Two or more races 8,883

Race, 2025 (projected)
White 648,000
Black 11,000

Persons of Hispanic origin, 2000
total Hispanic or Latino 31,669
Mexican 19,963
Puerto Rican 575
Cuban 160
Other Hispanic or Latino 10,971

Persons of Hispanic origin, 2025 (proj.) ... 74,000

Persons by sex, 2000
male 248,374
female 245,408

Marital status, 1990
males
15 years & older 168,395
single 43,086
married 105,963
separated 1,700
widowed 3,533
divorced 15,813
females
15 years & older 170,879
single 30,469
married 105,665
separated 2,109

widowed 17,013
divorced 17,732

Households & families, 2000
households 193,608
persons per household 2.48
families 130,497
persons per family 3
married couples 106,179
female householder, no husband
present 16,837
one person households 50,980
households with persons under 18 years .. 67,742
households with persons over 65 years 40,335

Nativity, 1990
number of persons born in state 193,436
percent of total residents 42.6%

Immigration & naturalization, 1998
immigrants admitted 159
persons naturalized 121
refugees granted resident status ....

VITAL STATISTICS & HEALTH

Births
1999
with low birth weight 8.4%
to teenage mothers 12.8%
to unmarried mothers 29.0%
Birth rate, 1999 (per 1,000) 12.8
Birth rate, 2000 (per 1,000) 13.0

Abortions, 1996
total ....
rate (per 1,000 women age 15-44) 2.7

Deaths
1998 3,883
1999 4,042
2000 3,918

Infant deaths
1998 27
1999 38
2000 20

Average lifetime, by race; 1989-1991
total .... 76.21 years
white .... 76.34 years
black .... NA years

Marriages
1998	4,656
1999	4,845
2000	4,939

Divorces
1998	2,834
1999	2,824
2000	2,821

Physicians, 1999
total	825
rate (per 1,000 persons)	1.72

Nurses, 1999
total	5,030
rate (per 1,000 persons)	10.49

Hospitals, 1998
number	25
beds (x 1,000)	1.9
average daily census (x 1,000)	1.0
patients admitted (x1,000)	44
average cost per day to hospital, 1995	$545
average cost per stay to hospital, 1995	$4,817

EDUCATION

Educational attainment of all persons 25 years and older, 1990
less than 9th grade	15,919
high school graduates	92,081
bachelor's degree	36,354
graduate or professional degree	15,841

2000
high school graduate or more	90.0%
college graduate or more	20.6%

Public school enrollment, Fall, 1998
total	95,241
Kindergarten through grade 8	63,940
grades 9 through 12	31,301

Public School Teachers, 2000
total	6,800
elementary	3,300
secondary	3,500
average salaries	
elementary	$34,100
secondary	$34,100

State receipts & expenditures for public schools, 2000
revenue receipts ($mil)	$807

State receipts & expenditures for public schools, 2000 (continued)
expenditures	
total ($mil)	$740
per capita	$1,543
per pupil	$7,391

Graduating high school seniors, public high schools, 2000 (est.)
	6,300

SAT scores, 2001
verbal	547
math	545
percent graduates taking test	11%

Institutions of higher education, 1999
total	9
public	8
private	1

Enrollment in institutions of higher education, Fall, 1998
total	29,707
full-time men	8,435
full-time women	8,672
part-time men	4,589
part-time women	8,011

Minority enrollment in institutions of higher education, Fall, 1997
Black, non-Hispanic	275
Hispanic	1,284
Asian/Pacific Islander	265

Earned degrees conferred, 1998
Bachelor's	1,706
First professional	60
Master's	387
Doctor's	64

SOCIAL INSURANCE & WELFARE PROGRAMS

Social Security beneficiaries & benefits, 2000
beneficiaries	
total	77,000
retired and dependents	56,000
survivors	10,000
disabled & dependents	11,000
annual benefit payments ($mil)	
total	$690
retired and dependents	$485
survivors	$118
disabled & dependents	$87

Wyoming 4

Medicare, 2000
enrollment (x1,000) 64
payments ($mil) $247

Medicaid, 1998
recipients (x1,000) 46
payments ($mil) $192

Federal public aid
Temporary Assistance for Needy Families
(TANF), 2000
  Recipients (x1,000) 1
  Families (x1,000) 1
Supplemental Security Income
  total recipients, 1999 (x1,000) 6

Food Stamp Program
  participants, 2000 (x1,000) 22

HOUSING & CONSTRUCTION

Total housing units, 2000 223,854
  seasonal or recreational use 12,389
  occupied 193,608
    owner occupied 135,514
    renter occupied 58,094

New privately owned housing units uthorized, 2000
number (x1,000) 1.6
value ($mil) $314

New privately owned housing units
  started, 2000 (est.) (x1,000) 1.8

Existing home sales, 2000 (x1,000) 13.5

GOVERNMENT & ELECTIONS

State officials, 2002
  Governor (name/party/term expires)
    JIM GERINGER
    Republican - 2002
Lt. Governor . . . . (no Lieutenant Governor)
Sec. of State . . . . Joe Meyer
Atty. General . . . . H. M. MacMillan
Chief Justice . . . . Larry Lehman

Governorship
minimum age 30
length of term . . . . 4 years
number of consecutive
  terms permitted 2
who succeeds . . . . Sec. of State

State legislature
name . . . . Legislature
  upper chamber
    name . . . . Senate
    number of members 30
    length of term . . . . 4 years
    party in majority, 2000 . . . . Republican
  lower chamber
    name . . . . House of Representatives
    number of members 64
    length of term . . . . 2 years
    party in majority, 2000 . . . . Republican

State employees March, 2000
total 13,703
March payroll $28,436,795

Local governments, 1997
total 654
  county 23
  municipal 97
  township 0
  school districts 56
  special districts 478

Voting age population, November, 2000, projected
Total 358,000
  male 179,000
  female 180,000

Vote for president
2000
  Gore 60,000
  Bush 148,000
1996
  Clinton 78,000
  Dole 105,000
  Perot 26,000

Federal representation, 2002 (107th Congress)
Senators (name/party/term expires)

    CRAIG THOMAS
    Republican - 2007
    MICHAEL ENZI
    Republican - 2003

Representatives, total 1
  Democrats 0
  Republicans 1
  other 0

Wyoming 5

Women holding public office, 2001
U.S. Congress 1
statewide elected office 2
state legislature 14

Black elected officials, 1999
total .... NA
  US and state legislatures .... NA
  city/county/regional offices .... NA
  judicial/law enforcement .... NA
  education/school boards .... NA

Hispanic public officials, 2000
total 4
  state executives & legislators 1
  city/county/regional offices 3
  judicial/law enforcement .... NA
  education/school boards .... NA

GOVERNMENTAL FINANCE

State government revenues, 1999 ($per capita)
total revenue $6,447.55
  total general revenue $4,617.59
    intergovernmental revenue $1,892.86
    taxes $1,692.34
    current charges $220.47
    miscellaneous $811.92

State government expenditures, 1999 ($per capita)
total expenditure $4,947.71
  total general expenditure $4,392.99
    education $1,575.10
    public welfare $511.22
    health $186.52
    hospitals $79.79
    highways $681.57
    police protection $47.87
    correction $158.63
    natural resources $259.18
    governmental administration $207.98
    interest on general debt $126.99

State debt, 1999 ($per capita) $2,180.58

*Federal government grants to state & local
government, 2000 (x$1,000)*
total $1,014,391
  Dept. of Education $88,440
  Environmental Protection Agency $13,853
  Health Care Financing Admin. $150,775
  Dept. Housing & Urban Devel. $48,042
  Dept. of Labor $18,017
  Highway trust fund $180,753

CRIME, LAW ENFORCEMENT & COURTS

Crime, 2000 (all rates per 100,000 inhabitants)
total crimes 16,285
overall crime rate 3,298.0
  property crimes 14,969
    burglaries 2,078
    larcenies 12,318
    motor vehicle thefts 573
  property crime rate 3,031.5
  violent crimes 1,316
    murders 12
    forcible rapes 160
    robberies 70
    aggravated assaults 1,074
  violent crime rate 266.5

Number of police agencies, 2000 65

Arrests, 2000
total 36,409
  persons under 18 years of age 8,156

Prisoners under state & federal jurisdiction, 2000
total 1,680
percent change, 1999-2000 .... -1.9%
  sentenced to more than one year
    total 1,680
    rate per 100,000 residents 349

Persons under sentence of death, 4/1/2001 2

State's highest court
name .... Supreme Court
number of members 5
length of term .... 8 years
intermediate appeals court? .... no

Wyoming 6

LABOR & INCOME

Civilian labor force, 2000

total 267,000
  men 144,000
  women 122,000
  persons 16-19 years 20,000
  white 260,000
  black .... NA

Civilian labor force as a percent of
civilian non-institutional population, 2000

total 72.0%
  men 79.0%
  women 65.1%
  persons 16-19 years .... NA%
  white 72.0%
  black .... NA%

Employment, 2000

total 257,000
  men 139,000
  women 118,000
  persons 16-19 years 18,000
  white 250,000
  black .... NA

Full-time/part-time labor force, 1998

full-time labor force 202,000
  working part-time for
    economic reasons 3,000
part-time labor force 56,000

Unemployment rate, 2000

total 3.9%
  men 4.0%
  women 3.7%
  persons 16-19 years 10.7%
  white 3.8%
  black .... NA%

Unemployed by reason for unemployment
(as a percent of total unemployment), 1998

job losers or completed temp jobs 41.7%
job leavers 16.7%
reentrants 41.7%
new entrants 8.3%

Experienced civilian labor force, by occupation,
1998

executive/administrative/managerial 31,000
professional/specialty 31,000
technicians & related support 6,000

sales 27,000
administrative support/clerical 32,000
service occupations 40,000
precision production/craft/repair 35,000
machine operators/assemblers 8,000
transportation/material moving 18,000
handlers/helpers/laborers 10,000
farming/forestry/fishing 19,000

Experienced civilian labor force, by industry, 1998

construction 15,000
manufacturing 13,000
transportation/communication 16,000
wholesale/retail trade 49,000
finance/real estate/insurance 8,000
services 44,000
government 50,000
agriculture 18,000

Average annual pay, 1999 .... $25,639
change in average annual pay,
  1998-1999 .... 3.7%

Hours and earnings of production workers
on manufacturing payrolls, 2000

average weekly hours 39.2
average hourly earnings $15.76
average weekly earnings $617.79

Labor union membership, 2000 17,900

Household income (in 2000 dollars)

median household income,
  three year average, 1998-2000 .... $39,026

Poverty

persons below poverty level,
  three year average, 1998-2000 .... 11.0%

Personal income ($per capita)

2000 (prelim.)
  in current dollars $27,230
  in constant (1996) dollars $25,363
1999 (preliminary)
  in current dollars $26,003
  in constant (1996) dollars $24,864

Federal income tax returns, 1999

returns filed 232,131
adjusted gross income ($1,000) $9,965,395
total income tax paid ($1,000) $1,673,159

ECONOMY, BUSINESS, INDUSTRY & AGRICULTURE

Fortune 500 companies, 2000 0

Business incorporations, 1998
total 1,897
change, 1997-1998 .... -16.3%

Business failures, 1998 166

Business firm ownership, 1997
Hispanic owned firms 1,239
Black owned firms 232
women owned firms 11,148
Asian & Pacific Islander owned firms 294
American Indian & Alaska
  native owned firms 477

Shopping centers, 2000 53

Gross state product, 1999 ($mil)
total $17,448
  agriculture services, forestry, fisheries $443
  mining $3,831
  construction $936
  manufacturing--durable goods $269
  manufacturing--nondurable goods $875
  transportation, communication &
    public utilities $2,585
  wholesale trade $709
  retail trade $1,346
  finance/real estate/insurance $1,968
  services $2,029
  federal, state & local government $2,455

Establishments, by major industry group, 1999
total 17,909
  forestry, fishing & agriculture 97
  mining 627
  construction 2,291
  manufacturing 559
  transportation & warehousing 620
  wholesale trade 781
  retail trade 2,897
  finance & insurance 801
  professional/scientific/technical 1,443
  health care/social assistance 1,422
  information 334
  accommodation/food services 1,712

Payroll, by major industry group, 1999
total ($1,000) $4,288,227
  forestry, fishing & agriculture .... $NA
  mining $763,100
  construction $440,766
  manufacturing $307,888
  transportation & warehousing $152,203
  wholesale trade $190,159
  retail trade $490,266
  finance & insurance $224,504
  professional/scientific/technical $183,142
  health care/social assistance $587,007
  information $109,281
  accommodation/food services $258,744

Agriculture
number of farms, 2000 9,000
farm acreage, 2000 35,000,000
acres per farm, 2000 3,761
value of farms, 1997 ($mil) $7,612
farm income, 1999 ($mil)
  net farm income $173
  debt/asset ratio 11.4%
farm marketings, 1999 ($mil)
total $852
  crops $172
  livestock $680
principal commodities, in order by marketing
receipts, 1999
  Cattle sugar beets, hay, sheep/lambs

Federal economic activity in state
expenditures, 2000
  total ($mil) $3,220
  per capita $6,521
  defense ($mil) $326
  non-defense ($mil) $2,894
defense department, 2000
  contract awards ($mil) $100
  payroll ($mil) $226
  civilian employees (x1,000) 1
  military personnel (x1,000) 3.3

Fishing, 2000
catch (thousands of pounds) .... NA
value ($1,000) .... $NA

Mining, 2000 ($mil; preliminary)
total non-fuel mineral production $922

Wyoming 8

Construction, 1999 ($mil)
total contracts (including
non-building) $721
   residential $227
   non-residential $161

Construction industries, 1997
establishments 2,138
receipts ($1,000) $1,550,334
annual payroll ($1,000) $340,248
paid employees 13,703

Manufacturing, 1997
establishments 610
value of shipments ($1,000) $3,032,066
annual payroll ($1,000) $280,185
paid employees 9,763

Transportation industries, 1997
establishments 1,008
receipts ($1,000) . . . . $NA
annual payroll ($1,000) . . . . $NA
paid employees . . . . NA

Wholesale trade, 1997
establishments 991
sales($1,000) . . . . $NA
annual payroll ($1,000) . . . . $NA
paid employees . . . . NA

Retail trade, 1997
establishments 4,009
sales($1,000) . . . . $NA
annual payroll ($1,000) . . . . $NA
paid employees . . . . NA

Finance industries
establishments, 1997 1,357
receipts ($1,000), 1997 . . . . $NA
annual payroll ($1,000), 1997 . . . . $NA
paid employees, 1997 . . . . NA
commercial banks, 2000
  number 46
    assets ($bil) $7.5
    deposits ($bil) $5.7

Service industries, 1997 (non-exempt firms only)
establishments 4,845
receipts ($1,000) $2,012,731
annual payroll ($1,000) $645,479
paid employees 33,771

COMMUNICATION, ENERGY & TRANSPORTATION

Communication
daily newspapers, 2000 9
households with
  telephones, 1998 . . . . 94.0%
  computers, 2000 . . . . 58.2%
  internet access, 2000 . . . . 44.1%

Energy
consumption, 1999
total (trillion Btu) 422
per capita (million Btu) 879
by source of production (trillion Btu)
  coal 495
  natural gas 102
  petroleum 156
  nuclear electric power . . . . NA
  hydroelectric power 12
by end-use sector (trillion Btu)
  residential 36
  commercial 42
  industrial 224
  transportation 120
electric energy, 1999
  production (billion kWh) 43
  net summer capability (million kW) 6
gas utilities, 1999
  customers 156,000
  sales (trillion Btu) 25
nuclear plants, 1999 . . . . na

Transportation, 2000
public road & street mileage
total 27,326
  urban 2,298
  rural 25,028
  interstate 913
vehicle miles of travel (mil) 8,090
total motor vehicle registrations 585,690
  automobiles 215,110
  motorcycles 19,121
licensed drivers 370,740
  per 1,000 driving age population 971
deaths from motor vehicle
  accidents 152

US Summary 1

STATE SUMMARY

Capital City .... Washington, DC

Governor ....

Address ....

Admitted as a state ....

Area (square miles) 3,787,425

Population, 1980 226,546,000

Population, 1990 248,709,873

Population, 2000 281,421,906

Persons per square mile, 2000 .... 79.6

Largest city .... New York
    population, 2000 8,008,000

Personal income per capita, 2000
    (in current dollars) $29,676

Gross state product ($mil), 1999 ..... $9,308,983

Leading industries, 1999 (by payroll)
        Manufacturing
        Health care/Social assistance
        Finance & Insurance

Leading agricultural commodities, 1999
        Cattle, dairy products, broilers, corn

GEOGRAPHY & ENVIRONMENT

Area, 1990 (square miles)
total 3,787,425
    land 3,536,342
    water (includes territorial water) 251,083

Federally owned land, 2000 .... 28.0%

Highest point
name .... Mt. McKinley
elevation (feet) 20,320

Lowest point
name .... Death Valley
elevation (feet) .... -282

General coastline (miles) 12,383

Tidal shoreline (miles) 88,633

Capital city .... Washington, DC
population, 2000 572,000

Largest city .... New York
population, 2000 8,008,000

Number of cities with over 100,000 population
    1980 172
    1990 190
    2000 239

State parks and Recreation areas, 2000
area (acres) 12,807,000
number of visitors 786,610,000
revenues $677,911,000

Natl. forest system land, 1999 (acres) . 191,910,000

National park acreage, 1984 74,897,800

DEMOGRAPHICS & CHARACTERISTICS OF THE POPULATION

Population
1970 203,320,000
1980 226,546,000
1990 248,709,873
2000 281,421,906
2015 (projection) 310,134,000
2025 (projection) 335,050,000

Metropolitan area population
1970 155,832,000
1980 172,335,000
2000 225,968,000

Non-metropolitan area population
1970 47,470,000
1980 54,211,000
2000 55,453,000

Change in population, 1990-2000
number 32,712,033
percent 13.15%

Persons per square mile, 2000 .... 79.6

Persons by age, 2000
under 5 years 19,175,798
18 and over 209,128,094
21 and over 196,899,193
65 and over 34,991,753
85 and over 4,239,587

411

US Summary 2

Persons by age, 2025 (projected)
under 5 years 22,498,000
5 to 17 years 58,286,000
65 and over 61,952,000

Median age, 2000 .... 35.3

Race, 2000
One race
White 211,460,626
Black or African American 34,658,190
American Indian and Alaska Native ... 2,475,956
Asian Indian 1,678,765
Chinese 2,432,585
Filipino 1,850,314
Japanese 796,700
Korean 1,076,872
Vietnamese 1,122,528
Native Hawaiian and other Pacific Islander 398,835
Two or more races 6,826,228

Race, 2025 (projected)
White 262,227,000
Black 47,539,000

Persons of Hispanic origin, 2000
total Hispanic or Latino 35,305,818
  Mexican 20,640,711
  Puerto Rican 3,406,178
  Cuban 1,241,685
  Other Hispanic or Latino 10,017,244

Persons of Hispanic origin, 2025 (proj.) 58,930,000

Persons by sex, 2000
male 138,053,563
female 143,368,343

Marital status, 1990
males
  15 years & older 93,817,315
    single 28,804,618
    married 55,677,642
      separated 1,896,397
    widowed 2,377,589
    divorced 6,957,466
females
  15 years & older 101,324,687
    single 23,755,235
    married 55,820,936
      separated 2,676,840

widowed 12,121,939
divorced 9,626,577

Households & families, 2000
households 105,480,101
persons per household 2.59
  families 71,787,347
  persons per family 3.14
    married couples 54,493,232
    female householder, no husband
      present 12,900,103
    one person households 27,230,075
households with persons under 18 years 38,022,115
households with persons over 65 years . 24,672,708

Nativity, 1990
number of persons born in state 153,684,685
percent of total residents 61.8%

Immigration & naturalization, 1998
immigrants admitted 660,477
persons naturalized 463,060
refugees granted resident status 54,645

VITAL STATISTICS & HEALTH

Births
1999
  with low birth weight 7.6%
  to teenage mothers 14.5%
  to unmarried mothers 33.0%
Birth rate, 1999 (per 1,000) 14.5
Birth rate, 2000 (per 1,000) 14.8

Abortions, 1996
total 1,366,000
rate (per 1,000 women age 15-44) 22.9

Deaths
1998 2,331,000
1999 2,391,399
2000 2,404,598

Infant deaths
1998 27,600
1999 27,100
2000 28,045

Average lifetime, by race, 1989-1991
total .... 75.37 years
  white .... 76.13 years
  black .... 69.16 years

Marriages
1998 2,244,000
1999 2,358,000
2000 2,329,000

Divorces
1998 1,135,000
1999 . . . . NA
2000 . . . . NA

Physicians, 1999
total 693,345
rate (per 1,000 persons) 2.54

Nurses, 1999
total 2,271,340
rate (per 1,000 persons) 8.33

Hospitals, 1998
number 5,015
beds (x 1,000) 840.0
average daily census (x 1,000) 524.5
patients admitted (x1,000) 31,812
average cost per day to hospital, 1995 . . . . . . $968
average cost per stay to hospital, 1995 . . . . $6,216

EDUCATION

Educational attainment of all persons
25 years and older, 1990
less than 9th grade 16,502,211
high school graduates 47,642,763
bachelor's degree 20,832,567
graduate or professional degree 11,477,686

2000
high school graduate or more 84.1%
college graduate or more 25.6%

Public school enrollment, Fall, 1998
total 46,534,687
Kindergarten through grade 8 33,343,787
grades 9 through 12 13,190,900

Public School Teachers, 2000
total 2,886,000
elementary 1,720,000
secondary 1,165,000
average salaries
elementary $41,500
secondary $42,400

State receipts & expenditures for public
schools, 2000
revenue receipts ($mil) $378,575

State receipts & expenditures for public
schools, 2000 (continued)
expenditures
total ($mil) $360,303
per capita $1,321
per pupil $7,146

Graduating high school seniors,
public high schools, 2000 (est.) 2,545,317

SAT scores, 2001
verbal 506
math 514
percent graduates taking test 45%

Institutions of higher education, 1999
total 4,070
public 1,688
private 2,382

Enrollment in institutions of higher
education, Fall 1998
total 14,549,189
full-time men 3,941,098
full-time women 4,640,445
part-time men 2,445,460
part-time women 3,552,186

Minority enrollment in institutions of higher
education, Fall, 1997
Black, non-Hispanic 1,551,044
Hispanic 1,218,493
Asian/Pacific Islander 859,206

Earned degrees conferred, 1998
Bachelor's 1,184,406
First professional 78,598
Master's 430,164
Doctor's 46,010

SOCIAL INSURANCE & WELFARE PROGRAMS

Social Security beneficiaries & benefits, 2000
beneficiaries
total 44,324,000
retired and dependents 31,090,000
survivors 6,763,000
disabled & dependents 6,471,000
annual benefit payments ($mil)
total $401,044
retired and dependents $271,185
survivors $76,233
disabled & dependents $53,625

US Summary 4

Medicare, 2000
enrollment (x1,000) 38,286
payments ($mil) $213,555

Medicaid, 1998
recipients (x1,000) 39,666
payments ($mil) $142,058

Federal public aid
Temporary Assistance for Needy Families
(TANF), 2000
   Recipients (x1,000) 5,785
   Families (x1,000) 2,230
Supplemental Security Income
   total recipients, 1999 (x1,000) 6,556

Food Stamp Program
   participants, 2000 (x1,000) 17,125

HOUSING & CONSTRUCTION

Total housing units, 2000 115,904,641
   seasonal or recreational use 3,578,718
   occupied 105,480,101
      owner occupied 69,815,753
      renter occupied 35,664,348

New privately owned housing units uthorized, 2000
number (x1,000) 1,592.30
value ($mil) $185,744

New privately owned housing units
   started, 2000 (est.) (x1,000) 1,535.0

Existing home sales, 2000 (x1,000) 5,842

GOVERNMENT & ELECTIONS

State officials, 2002
   Governor (name/party/term expires)

Lt. Governor . . . .
Sec. of State . . . .
Atty. General . . . .
Chief Justice . . . .

Governorship
minimum age . . . .
length of term . . . .
number of consecutive
   terms permitted . . . .
who succeeds . . . .

State legislature
name . . . .
   upper chamber
      name . . . .
      number of members . . . .
      length of term . . . .
      party in majority, 2000 . . . .
   lower chamber
      name . . . .
      number of members . . . .
      length of term . . . .
      party in majority, 2000 . . . .

State employees March, 2000
total 4,877,420
March payroll $13,279,135,982

Local governments, 1997
total 87,453
   county 3,043
   municipal 19,372
   township 16,629
   school districts 13,726
   special districts 34,683

Voting age population, November, 2000, projected
Total 205,813,000
   male 98,947,000
   female 106,865,000

Vote for president
2000
   Gore 50,992,000
   Bush 50,455,000
1996
   Clinton 47,401,000
   Dole 39,197,000
   Perot 8,085,000

Federal representation, 2002 (107th Congress)
Senators (name/party/term expires)

Representatives, total 435
   Democrats 211
   Republicans 221
   other 3

US Summary 5

Women holding public office, 2001
U.S. Congress 73
statewide elected office 88
state legislature 1,663

Black elected officials, 1999
total 8,896
  US and state legislatures 618
  city/county/regional offices 5,354
  judicial/law enforcement 997
  education/school boards 1,927

Hispanic public officials, 2000
total 5,205
  state executives & legislators 223
  city/county/regional offices 1,846
  judicial/law enforcement 454
  education/school boards 2,682

GOVERNMENTAL FINANCE

State government revenues, 1999 ($per capita)
total revenue $4,235.82
  total general revenue $3,329.06
    intergovernmental revenue $932.10
    taxes $1,836.87
    current charges $291.39
    miscellaneous $268.70

State government expenditures, 1999 ($per capita)
total expenditure $3,668.14
  total general expenditure $3,268.07
    education $1,170.59
    public welfare $812.60
    health $139.65
    hospitals $110.20
    highways $251.01
    police protection $32.31
    correction $120.67
    natural resources $53.21
    governmental administration $123.31
    interest on general debt $102.09

State debt, 1999 ($per capita) $1,875.60

Federal government grants to state & local government, 2000 (x$1,000)
total $291,942,541
  Dept. of Education $26,653,590
  Environmental Protection Agency .. $3,628,507
  Health Care Financing Admin. .. $119,307,867
  Dept. Housing & Urban Devel. $32,363,791
  Dept. of Labor $5,148,546
  Highway trust fund $24,148,983

CRIME, LAW ENFORCEMENT & COURTS

Crime, 2000 (all rates per 100,000 inhabitants)
total crimes 11,605,751
overall crime rate 4,124.0
  property crimes 10,181,462
    burglaries 2,049,946
    larcenies 6,965,957
    motor vehicle thefts 1,165,559
  property crime rate 3,617.9
  violent crimes 1,424,289
    murders 15,517
    forcible rapes 90,186
    robberies 407,842
    aggravated assaults 910,744
  violent crime rate 506.1

Number of police agencies, 2000 11,639

Arrests, 2000
total 13,980,297
  persons under 18 years of age 1,554,802

Prisoners under state & federal jurisdiction, 2000
total 1,381,892
percent change, 1999-2000 .... 1.3%
  sentenced to more than one year
    total 1,321,137
    rate per 100,000 residents 478

Persons under sentence of death, 4/1/2001 . 3,711

State's highest court
name ....
number of members ....
length of term ....
intermediate appeals court? ....

US Summary 6

LABOR & INCOME

Civilian labor force, 2000
```
total ........................... 140,863,000
  men ........................ 75,247,000
  women ...................... 65,616,000
  persons 16-19 years ............. 8,369,000
  white ...................... 117,574,000
  black ...................... 16,603,000
```

Civilian labor force as a percent of
civilian non-institutional population, 2000
```
total ............................... 67.2%
  men ............................ 74.7%
  women .......................... 60.2%
  persons 16-19 years ............... NA%
  white .......................... 67.4%
  black .......................... 65.8%
```

Employment, 2000
```
total ........................... 135,208,000
  men ........................ 72,293,000
  women ...................... 62,915,000
  persons 16-19 years ............. 7,276,000
  white ...................... 113,475,000
  black ...................... 15,334,000
```

Full-time/part-time labor force, 1998
```
full-time labor force .............. 113,236,000
  working part-time for
    economic reasons .............. 1,323,000
part-time labor force .............. 24,579,000
```

Unemployment rate, 2000
```
total ............................... 4.0%
  men ............................ 3.9%
  women .......................... 4.1%
  persons 16-19 years .............. 13.1%
  white .......................... 3.5%
  black .......................... 7.6%
```

Unemployed by reason for unemployment
(as a percent of total unemployment), 1998
```
job losers or completed temp jobs ....... 45.5%
job leavers .......................... 11.8%
reentrants .......................... 34.4%
new entrants ......................... 8.4%
```

Experienced civilian labor force, by occupation,
1998
```
executive/administrative/managerial .. 19,418,000
professional/specialty .............. 20,287,000
technicians & related support ......... 4,362,000
```

```
sales ........................... 16,614,000
administrative support/clerical ....... 19,141,000
service occupations ................. 19,075,000
precision production/craft/repair ..... 15,054,000
machine operators/assemblers ........ 8,292,000
transportation/material moving ....... 5,646,000
handlers/helpers/laborers ........... 5,639,000
farming/forestry/fishing ............. 3,749,000
```

Experienced civilian labor force, by industry, 1998
```
construction ...................... 7,049,000
manufacturing .................... 21,062,000
transportation/communication ........ 7,541,000
wholesale/retail trade ............. 26,930,000
finance/real estate/insurance ......... 7,992,000
services ......................... 33,366,000
government ......................... NA
agriculture ........................ NA
```

```
Average annual pay, 1999 ............. $33,313
change in average annual pay,
  1998-1999 .......................... 4.3%
```

Hours and earnings of production workers
on manufacturing payrolls, 2000
```
average weekly hours ................... 41.5
average hourly earnings .............. $14.38
average weekly earnings .............. $596.77
```

Labor union membership, 2000 16,258,200

Household income (in 2000 dollars)
```
median household income,
  three year average, 1998-2000 ........ $42,148
```

Poverty
```
persons below poverty level,
  three year average, 1998-2000 .......... 11.9%
```

Personal income ($per capita)
```
2000 (prelim.)
  in current dollars .................. $29,676
  in constant (1996) dollars ........... $27,642
1999 (preliminary)
  in current dollars .................. $28,518
  in constant (1996) dollars ........... $27,269
```

Federal income tax returns, 1999
```
returns filed ..................... 127,667,890
adjusted gross income ($1,000) ... $5,813,855,173
total income tax paid ($1,000) ...... $918,602,005
```

ECONOMY, BUSINESS, INDUSTRY & AGRICULTURE

Fortune 500 companies, 2000 500

Business incorporations, 1998
total 760,925
change, 1997-1998 . . . . -4.7%

Business failures, 1998 71,857

Business firm ownership, 1997
Hispanic owned firms 1,199,896
Black owned firms 823,499
women owned firms 5,417,034
Asian & Pacific Islander owned firms . . . 912,960
American Indian & Alaska
 native owned firms 197,300

Shopping centers, 2000 45,115

Gross state product, 1999 ($mil)
total $9,308,983
 agriculture services, forestry, fisheries $125,441
 mining $111,797
 construction $416,354
 manufacturing--durable goods $877,756
 manufacturing--nondurable goods . . . $623,050
 transportation, communication &
  public utilities $779,647
 wholesale trade $643,284
 retail trade $856,364
 finance/real estate/insurance $1,792,090
 services $1,986,918
 federal, state & local government . . . $1,096,282

Establishments, by major industry group, 1999
total 7,008,444
 forestry, fishing & agriculture 26,926
 mining 23,699
 construction 698,541
 manufacturing 360,244
 transportation & warehousing 187,339
 wholesale trade 450,030
 retail trade 1,111,260
 finance & insurance 418,337
 professional/scientific/technical 704,779
 health care/social assistance 649,846
 information 126,510
 accommodation/food services 539,576

Payroll, by major industry group, 1999
total ($1,000) $3,554,692,909
 forestry, fishing & agriculture $4,812,649
 mining $20,975,962
 construction $219,087,088
 manufacturing $625,536,131
 transportation & warehousing $116,682,214
 wholesale trade $249,997,598
 retail trade $281,946,316
 finance & insurance $313,245,188
 professional/scientific/technical . . . $311,238,501
 health care/social assistance $409,223,160
 information $170,282,356
 accommodation/food services $116,924,965

Agriculture
number of farms, 2000 2,172,000
farm acreage, 2000 943,000,000
acres per farm, 2000 434
value of farms, 1997 ($mil) $912,344
farm income, 1999 ($mil)
 net farm income $43,398
 debt/asset ratio 15.8%
farm marketings, 1999 ($mil)
total $188,610
 crops $93,146
 livestock $95,463
principal commodities, in order by marketing
receipts, 1999
 Cattle, dairy products, broilers, corn

Federal economic activity in state
expenditures, 2000
 total ($mil) $1,637,170
 per capita $5,740
 defense ($mil) $238,224
 non-defense ($mil) $1,398,947
defense department, 2000
 contract awards ($mil) . . . . $NA
 payroll ($mil) . . . . $NA
 civilian employees (x1,000) . . . . NA
 military personnel (x1,000) . . . . na

Fishing, 2000
catch (thousands of pounds) 9,068,982
value ($1,000) $3,549,481

Mining, 2000 ($mil; preliminary)
total non-fuel mineral production $40,100

US Summary 8

Construction, 1999 ($mil)
total contracts (including
  non-building) $444,080
    residential $194,762
    non-residential $167,933

Construction industries, 1997
establishments 639,482
receipts ($1,000) $834,794,940
annual payroll ($1,000) $170,962,019
paid employees 5,567,052

Manufacturing, 1997
establishments 377,776
value of shipments ($1,000) $3,958,050,434
annual payroll ($1,000) $595,685,786
paid employees 17,557,008

Transportation industries, 1997
establishments 293,575
receipts ($1,000) $1,143,936,913
annual payroll ($1,000) $199,706,592
paid employees 5,689,138

Wholesale trade, 1997
establishments 521,127
sales($1,000) $4,235,400,325
annual payroll ($1,000) $234,516,934
paid employees 6,509,333

Retail trade, 1997
establishments 1,561,195
sales($1,000) $2,545,881,473
annual payroll ($1,000) $290,525,257
paid employees 21,165,862

Finance industries
establishments, 1997 661,388
receipts ($1,000), 1997 .... $2,474,943,634
annual payroll ($1,000), 1997 ...... $308,154,498
paid employees, 1997 7,314,321
commercial banks, 2000
  number 8,297
    assets ($bil) $6,185.4
    deposits ($bil) $4,146.0

Service industries, 1997 (non-exempt firms only)
establishments 2,077,666
receipts ($1,000) $1,843,791,887
annual payroll ($1,000) $688,873,138
paid employees 25,278,399

COMMUNICATION, ENERGY & TRANSPORTATION

Communication
daily newspapers, 2000 1,480
households with
  telephones, 1998 .... 94.1%
  computers, 2000 .... 51.0%
  internet access, 2000 .... 41.5%

Energy
consumption, 1999
total (trillion Btu) 95,682
per capita (million Btu) 351
by source of production (trillion Btu)
  coal 20,498
  natural gas 22,295
  petroleum 37,960
  nuclear electric power 7,736
  hydroelectric power 3,449
by end-use sector (trillion Btu)
  residential 18,382
  commercial 15,059
  industrial 335,917
  transportation 26,325
electric energy, 1999
  production (billion kWh) 3,173.7
  net summer capability (million kW) 639.3
gas utilities, 1999
  customers 61,869,000
  sales (trillion Btu) 8,747
nuclear plants, 1999 104

Transportation, 2000
public road & street mileage
total 3,936,229
  urban 852,241
  rural 3,083,988
  interstate 46,427
vehicle miles of travel (mil) 2,749,803
total motor vehicle registrations 221,475,173
  automobiles 133,621,420
  motorcycles 4,303,762
licensed drivers 190,625,023
  per 1,000 driving age population 878
deaths from motor vehicle
  accidents 41,821

Comparative Tables

1. Total Area (square miles)

* UNITED STATES	3,787,425
1. Alaska	656,424
2. Texas	268,601
3. California	163,707
4. Montana	147,046
5. New Mexico	121,598
6. Arizona	114,006
7. Nevada	110,567
8. Colorado	104,100
9. Oregon	98,386
10. Wyoming	97,818
11. Michigan	96,810
12. Minnesota	86,943
13. Utah	84,904
14. Idaho	83,574
15. Kansas	82,282
16. Nebraska	77,358
17. South Dakota	77,121
18. Washington	71,303
19. North Dakota	70,704
20. Oklahoma	69,903
21. Missouri	69,709
22. Florida	65,758
23. Wisconsin	65,503
24. Georgia	59,441
25. Illinois	57,918
26. Iowa	56,276
27. New York	54,475
28. North Carolina	53,821
29. Arkansas	53,182
30. Alabama	52,423
31. Louisiana	51,843
32. Mississippi	48,434
33. Pennsylvania	46,058
34. Ohio	44,828
35. Virginia	42,769
36. Tennessee	42,146
37. Kentucky	40,411
38. Indiana	36,420
39. Maine	35,387
40. South Carolina	32,007
41. West Virginia	24,231
42. Maryland	12,407
43. Hawaii	10,932
44. Massachusetts	10,555
45. Vermont	9,615
46. New Hampshire	9,351
47. New Jersey	8,722
48. Connecticut	5,544
49. Delaware	2,489
50. Rhode Island	1,545
51. District of Columbia	68

2. Federally Owned Land, 2000

1. Nevada	83.0%
2. Utah	64.5
3. Idaho	62.5
4. Alaska	60.4
5. Oregon	52.5
6. Wyoming	49.8
7. California	47.8
8. Arizona	44.5
9. Colorado	36.3
10. New Mexico	34.2
11. Montana	29.4
12. Washington	28.5
* UNITED STATES	28.0
13. District of Columbia	23.2
14. Hawaii	15.6
15. New Hampshire	13.2
16. Florida	13.2
17. Michigan	11.2
18. Missouri	10.8
19. Arkansas	10.1
20. Virginia	8.9
21. Minnesota	8.2
22. Tennessee	7.9
23. West Virginia	7.9
24. South Dakota	6.4
25. Vermont	6.3
26. North Carolina	6.3
27. South Carolina	5.7
28. Kentucky	5.7
29. Mississippi	5.5
30. Georgia	5.4
31. Wisconsin	5.2
32. North Dakota	5.2
33. Louisiana	4.2
34. Alabama	4.1
35. Oklahoma	3.8
36. New Jersey	2.6
37. Maryland	2.6
38. Pennsylvania	2.5
39. Indiana	2.2
40. Ohio	1.7
41. Illinois	1.6
42. Texas	1.4
43. Massachusetts	1.4
44. Nebraska	1.3
45. Kansas	1.3
46. Delaware	1.2
47. Maine	0.9
48. New York	0.7
49. Iowa	0.6
50. Rhode Island	0.5
51. Connecticut	0.5

3. Cities with over 100,000 Population, 2000		4. 1970 Population	
* UNITED STATES	239	* UNITED STATES	203,320,000
1. California	56	1. California	19,971,069
2. Texas	24	2. New York	18,241,391
3. Florida	13	3. Pennsylvania	11,800,766
4. Arizona	9	4. Texas	11,198,655
5. Colorado	8	5. Illinois	11,110,285
6. Michigan	8	6. Ohio	10,657,423
7. Virginia	8	7. Michigan	8,881,826
8. Illinois	7	8. New Jersey	7,171,112
9. North Carolina	6	9. Florida	6,791,418
10. Ohio	6	10. Massachusetts	5,689,170
11. Connecticut	5	11. Indiana	5,195,392
12. Georgia	5	12. North Carolina	5,088,411
13. Indiana	5	13. Missouri	4,677,623
14. Massachusetts	5	14. Virginia	4,651,448
15. New York	5	15. Georgia	4,587,930
16. Tennessee	5	16. Wisconsin	4,417,821
17. Washington	5	17. Tennessee	3,926,018
18. Alabama	4	18. Maryland	3,923,897
19. Kansas	4	19. Minnesota	3,806,103
20. Louisiana	4	20. Louisiana	3,644,637
21. Missouri	4	21. Alabama	3,444,354
22. Nevada	4	22. Washington	3,413,244
23. New Jersey	4	23. Kentucky	3,220,711
24. Pennsylvania	4	24. Connecticut	3,032,217
25. Oregon	3	25. Iowa	2,825,368
26. Utah	3	26. South Carolina	2,590,713
27. Wisconsin	3	27. Oklahoma	2,559,463
28. Iowa	2	28. Kansas	2,249,071
29. Kentucky	2	29. Mississippi	2,216,994
30. Minnesota	2	30. Colorado	2,209,596
31. Nebraska	2	31. Oregon	2,091,533
32. Oklahoma	2	32. Arkansas	1,923,322
33. Alaska	1	33. Arizona	1,775,399
34. Arkansas	1	34. West Virginia	1,744,237
35. District of Columbia	1	35. Nebraska	1,485,333
36. Hawaii	1	36. Utah	1,059,273
37. Idaho	1	37. New Mexico	1,017,055
38. Maryland	1	38. Maine	993,722
39. Mississippi	1	39. Rhode Island	949,723
40. New Hampshire	1	40. Hawaii	769,913
41. New Mexico	1	41. District of Columbia	756,668
42. Rhode Island	1	42. New Hampshire	737,681
43. South Carolina	1	43. Idaho	713,015
44. South Dakota	1	44. Montana	694,409
45. Delaware	0	45. South Dakota	666,257
46. Maine	0	46. North Dakota	617,792
47. Montana	0	47. Delaware	548,107
48. North Dakota	0	48. Nevada	488,738
49. Vermont	0	49. Vermont	444,732
50. West Virginia	0	50. Wyoming	332,416
51. Wyoming	0	51. Alaska	302,583

5. 1980 Population

* UNITED STATES		226,546,000
1.	California	23,667,902
2.	New York	17,558,072
3.	Texas	14,229,191
4.	Pennsylvania	11,863,895
5.	Illinois	11,426,518
6.	Ohio	10,797,630
7.	Florida	9,746,324
8.	Michigan	9,262,078
9.	New Jersey	7,364,823
10.	North Carolina	5,881,766
11.	Massachusetts	5,737,037
12.	Indiana	5,490,224
13.	Georgia	5,463,105
14.	Virginia	5,346,818
15.	Missouri	4,916,686
16.	Wisconsin	4,705,767
17.	Tennessee	4,591,120
18.	Maryland	4,216,975
19.	Louisiana	4,205,900
20.	Washington	4,132,156
21.	Minnesota	4,075,970
22.	Alabama	3,893,800
23.	Kentucky	3,660,777
24.	South Carolina	3,121,820
25.	Connecticut	3,107,576
26.	Oklahoma	3,025,290
27.	Iowa	2,913,808
28.	Colorado	2,889,964
29.	Arizona	2,718,215
30.	Oregon	2,633,105
31.	Mississippi	2,520,638
32.	Kansas	2,363,679
33.	Arkansas	2,286,435
34.	West Virginia	1,949,644
35.	Nebraska	1,569,825
36.	Utah	1,461,037
37.	New Mexico	1,302,894
38.	Maine	1,124,660
39.	Hawaii	964,691
40.	Rhode Island	947,154
41.	Idaho	943,935
42.	New Hampshire	920,610
43.	Nevada	800,493
44.	Montana	786,690
45.	South Dakota	690,768
46.	North Dakota	652,717
47.	District of Columbia	638,333
48.	Delaware	594,338
49.	Vermont	511,456
50.	Wyoming	469,557
51.	Alaska	401,851

6. 1990 Population

* UNITED STATES		248,709,873
1.	California	29,760,021
2.	New York	17,990,455
3.	Texas	16,986,510
4.	Florida	12,937,926
5.	Pennsylvania	11,881,643
6.	Illinois	11,430,602
7.	Ohio	10,847,115
8.	Michigan	9,295,297
9.	New Jersey	7,730,188
10.	North Carolina	6,628,637
11.	Georgia	6,478,216
12.	Virginia	6,187,358
13.	Massachusetts	6,016,425
14.	Indiana	5,544,159
15.	Missouri	5,117,073
16.	Wisconsin	4,891,769
17.	Tennessee	4,877,185
18.	Washington	4,866,692
19.	Maryland	4,781,468
20.	Minnesota	4,375,099
21.	Louisiana	4,219,973
22.	Alabama	4,040,587
23.	Kentucky	3,685,296
24.	Arizona	3,665,228
25.	South Carolina	3,486,703
26.	Colorado	3,294,394
27.	Connecticut	3,287,116
28.	Oklahoma	3,145,585
29.	Oregon	2,842,321
30.	Iowa	2,776,755
31.	Mississippi	2,573,216
32.	Kansas	2,477,574
33.	Arkansas	2,350,725
34.	West Virginia	1,793,477
35.	Utah	1,722,850
36.	Nebraska	1,578,385
37.	New Mexico	1,515,069
38.	Maine	1,227,928
39.	Nevada	1,201,833
40.	New Hampshire	1,109,252
41.	Hawaii	1,108,229
42.	Idaho	1,006,749
43.	Rhode Island	1,003,464
44.	Montana	799,065
45.	South Dakota	696,004
46.	Delaware	666,168
47.	North Dakota	638,800
48.	District of Columbia	606,900
49.	Vermont	562,758
50.	Alaska	550,043
51.	Wyoming	453,588

7. 2000 Population

*	UNITED STATES	281,421,906
1.	California	33,871,648
2.	Texas	20,851,820
3.	New York	18,976,457
4.	Florida	15,982,378
5.	Illinois	12,419,293
6.	Pennsylvania	12,281,054
7.	Ohio	11,353,140
8.	Michigan	9,938,444
9.	New Jersey	8,414,350
10.	Georgia	8,186,453
11.	North Carolina	8,049,313
12.	Virginia	7,078,515
13.	Massachusetts	6,349,097
14.	Indiana	6,080,485
15.	Washington	5,894,121
16.	Tennessee	5,689,283
17.	Missouri	5,595,211
18.	Wisconsin	5,363,675
19.	Maryland	5,296,486
20.	Arizona	5,130,632
21.	Minnesota	4,919,479
22.	Louisiana	4,468,976
23.	Alabama	4,447,100
24.	Colorado	4,301,261
25.	Kentucky	4,041,769
26.	South Carolina	4,012,012
27.	Oklahoma	3,450,654
28.	Oregon	3,421,399
29.	Connecticut	3,405,565
30.	Iowa	2,926,324
31.	Mississippi	2,844,658
32.	Kansas	2,688,418
33.	Arkansas	2,673,400
34.	Utah	2,233,169
35.	Nevada	1,998,257
36.	New Mexico	1,819,046
37.	West Virginia	1,808,344
38.	Nebraska	1,711,263
39.	Idaho	1,293,953
40.	Maine	1,274,923
41.	New Hampshire	1,235,786
42.	Hawaii	1,211,537
43.	Rhode Island	1,048,319
44.	Montana	902,195
45.	Delaware	783,600
46.	South Dakota	754,844
47.	North Dakota	642,200
48.	Alaska	626,932
49.	Vermont	608,827
50.	District of Columbia	572,059
51.	Wyoming	493,782

8. 2025 Projected Population

*	UNITED STATES	335,050,000
1.	California	49,285,000
2.	Texas	27,183,000
3.	Florida	20,710,000
4.	New York	19,830,000
5.	Illinois	13,440,000
6.	Pennsylvania	12,683,000
7.	Ohio	11,744,000
8.	Michigan	10,078,000
9.	Georgia	9,869,000
10.	New Jersey	9,558,000
11.	North Carolina	9,349,000
12.	Virginia	8,466,000
13.	Washington	7,808,000
14.	Massachusetts	6,902,000
15.	Tennessee	6,665,000
16.	Indiana	6,546,000
17.	Arizona	6,412,000
18.	Maryland	6,274,000
19.	Missouri	6,250,000
20.	Wisconsin	5,867,000
21.	Minnesota	5,510,000
22.	Alabama	5,224,000
23.	Colorado	5,188,000
24.	Louisiana	5,133,000
25.	South Carolina	4,645,000
26.	Oregon	4,349,000
27.	Kentucky	4,314,000
28.	Oklahoma	4,057,000
29.	Connecticut	3,739,000
30.	Mississippi	3,142,000
31.	Kansas	3,108,000
32.	Arkansas	3,055,000
33.	Iowa	3,040,000
34.	Utah	2,883,000
35.	New Mexico	2,612,000
36.	Nevada	2,312,000
37.	Nebraska	1,930,000
38.	West Virginia	1,845,000
39.	Hawaii	1,812,000
40.	Idaho	1,739,000
41.	New Hampshire	1,439,000
42.	Maine	1,423,000
43.	Rhode Island	1,141,000
44.	Montana	1,121,000
45.	Alaska	885,000
46.	South Dakota	866,000
47.	Delaware	861,000
48.	North Dakota	729,000
49.	Wyoming	694,000
50.	Vermont	678,000
51.	District of Columbia	655,000

9. Metropolitan Area Population, 2000		10. Non-Metropolitan Population, 2000	
* UNITED STATES	225,968,000	* UNITED STATES	55,453,000
1. California	32,750,000	1. Texas	3,160,000
2. Texas	17,692,000	2. North Carolina	2,612,000
3. New York	17,473,000	3. Georgia	2,520,000
4. Florida	14,837,000	4. Ohio	2,139,000
5. Illinois	10,542,000	5. Kentucky	2,069,000
6. Pennsylvania	10,392,000	6. Pennsylvania	1,890,000
7. Ohio	9,214,000	7. Illinois	1,878,000
8. New Jersey	8,414,000	8. Tennessee	1,827,000
9. Michigan	8,169,000	9. Mississippi	1,821,000
10. Massachusetts	6,088,000	10. Missouri	1,800,000
11. Georgia	5,667,000	11. Michigan	1,769,000
12. Virginia	5,528,000	12. Wisconsin	1,723,000
13. North Carolina	5,437,000	13. Indiana	1,691,000
14. Maryland	4,911,000	14. Iowa	1,600,000
15. Washington	4,899,000	15. Virginia	1,550,000
16. Arizona	4,527,000	16. New York	1,503,000
17. Indiana	4,390,000	17. Minnesota	1,456,000
18. Tennessee	3,862,000	18. Arkansas	1,352,000
19. Missouri	3,795,000	19. Oklahoma	1,352,000
20. Wisconsin	3,640,000	20. Alabama	1,338,000
21. Colorado	3,608,000	21. South Carolina	1,205,000
22. Minnesota	3,463,000	22. Kansas	1,167,000
23. Louisiana	3,370,000	23. Florida	1,145,000
24. Connecticut	3,257,000	24. California	1,121,000
25. Alabama	3,109,000	25. Louisiana	1,099,000
26. South Carolina	2,807,000	26. West Virginia	1,043,000
27. Oregon	2,502,000	27. Washington	995,000
28. Oklahoma	2,098,000	28. Oregon	919,000
29. Kentucky	1,973,000	29. Nebraska	811,000
30. Nevada	1,748,000	30. Maine	803,000
31. Utah	1,708,000	31. Idaho	785,000
32. Kansas	1,521,000	32. New Mexico	784,000
33. Iowa	1,326,000	33. Colorado	694,000
34. Arkansas	1,321,000	34. Arizona	604,000
35. New Mexico	1,035,000	35. Montana	597,000
36. Mississippi	1,024,000	36. Utah	525,000
37. Rhode Island	986,000	37. New Hampshire	456,000
38. Nebraska	900,000	38. South Dakota	494,000
39. Hawaii	876,000	39. Vermont	439,000
40. West Virginia	766,000	40. Maryland	385,000
41. New Hampshire	740,000	41. Alaska	367,000
42. Delaware	627,000	42. North Dakota	358,000
43. District of Columbia	572,000	43. Wyoming	346,000
44. Idaho	508,000	44. Hawaii	335,000
45. Maine	467,000	45. Massachusetts	261,000
46. Montana	306,000	46. Nevada	251,000
47. North Dakota	284,000	47. Delaware	157,000
48. South Dakota	261,000	48. Connecticut	149,000
49. Alaska	260,000	49. Rhode Island	62,000
50. Vermont	169,000	50. District of Columbia	0
51. Wyoming	148,000	51. New Jersey	0

11. Change in Population, 1990-2000

1. Nevada	66.27%
2. Arizona	39.98
3. Colorado	30.56
4. Utah	29.62
5. Idaho	28.53
6. Georgia	26.37
7. Florida	23.53
8. Texas	22.76
9. North Carolina	21.43
10. Washington	21.11
11. Oregon	20.37
12. New Mexico	20.06
13. Delaware	17.63
14. Tennessee	16.65
15. South Carolina	15.07
16. Virginia	14.40
17. Alaska	13.98
18. California	13.82
19. Arkansas	13.73
* UNITED STATES	13.15
20. Montana	12.91
21. Minnesota	12.44
22. New Hampshire	11.41
23. Maryland	10.77
24. Mississippi	10.55
25. Alabama	10.06
26. Oklahoma	9.70
27. Indiana	9.67
28. Kentucky	9.67
29. Wisconsin	9.65
30. Missouri	9.34
31. Hawaii	9.32
32. Wyoming	8.86
33. New Jersey	8.85
34. Illinois	8.65
35. Kansas	8.51
36. South Dakota	8.45
37. Nebraska	8.42
38. Vermont	8.19
39. Michigan	6.92
40. Louisiana	5.90
41. Massachusetts	5.53
42. New York	5.48
43. Iowa	5.39
44. Ohio	4.67
45. Rhode Island	4.47
46. Maine	3.83
47. Connecticut	3.60
48. Pennsylvania	3.36
49. West Virginia	0.83
50. North Dakota	0.53
51. District of Columbia	-5.74

12. Persons per Square Mile, 2000

1. District of Columbia	9,316.90
2. New Jersey	1,134.20
3. Rhode Island	1,003.20
4. Massachusetts	810
5. Connecticut	702.9
6. Maryland	541.8
7. New York	401.8
8. Delaware	400.8
9. Florida	296.3
10. Ohio	277.2
11. Pennsylvania	274
12. Illinois	223.4
13. California	217.2
14. Hawaii	188.6
15. Virginia	178.8
16. Michigan	174.9
17. Indiana	169.5
18. North Carolina	165.2
19. Georgia	141.3
20. Tennessee	138
21. New Hampshire	137.8
22. South Carolina	133.2
23. Louisiana	102.6
24. Kentucky	101.7
25. Wisconsin	98.8
26. Washington	88.5
27. Alabama	87.6
28. Missouri	81.2
* UNITED STATES	79.6
29. Texas	79.6
30. West Virginia	75.1
31. Vermont	65.8
32. Minnesota	61.8
33. Mississippi	60.6
34. Iowa	52.4
35. Arkansas	51.3
36. Oklahoma	50.2
37. Arizona	45.1
38. Colorado	41.5
39. Maine	41.3
40. Oregon	35.6
41. Kansas	32.9
42. Utah	27.2
43. Nebraska	22.3
44. Nevada	18.2
45. Idaho	15.6
46. New Mexico	15
47. South Dakota	9.9
48. North Dakota	9.3
49. Montana	6.2
50. Wyoming	5.1
51. Alaska	1.1

13. Households, 1990

* UNITED STATES	91,947,410
1. California	10,381,206
2. New York	6,639,322
3. Texas	6,070,937
4. Florida	5,134,869
5. Pennsylvania	4,495,966
6. Illinois	4,202,240
7. Ohio	4,087,546
8. Michigan	3,419,331
9. New Jersey	2,794,711
10. North Carolina	2,517,026
11. Georgia	2,366,615
12. Virginia	2,291,830
13. Massachusetts	2,247,110
14. Indiana	2,065,355
15. Missouri	1,961,206
16. Washington	1,872,431
17. Tennessee	1,853,725
18. Wisconsin	1,822,118
19. Maryland	1,748,991
20. Minnesota	1,647,853
21. Alabama	1,506,790
22. Louisiana	1,499,269
23. Kentucky	1,379,782
24. Arizona	1,368,843
25. Colorado	1,282,489
26. South Carolina	1,258,044
27. Connecticut	1,230,479
28. Oklahoma	1,206,135
29. Oregon	1,103,313
30. Iowa	1,064,325
31. Kansas	944,726
32. Mississippi	911,374
33. Arkansas	891,179
34. West Virginia	688,557
35. Nebraska	602,363
36. New Mexico	542,709
37. Utah	537,273
38. Nevada	466,297
39. Maine	465,312
40. New Hampshire	411,186
41. Rhode Island	377,977
42. Idaho	360,723
43. Hawaii	356,267
44. Montana	306,163
45. South Dakota	259,034
46. District of Columbia	249,634
47. Delaware	247,497
48. North Dakota	240,878
49. Vermont	210,650
50. Alaska	188,915
51. Wyoming	168,839

14. Households, 2000

* UNITED STATES	105,480,101
1. California	11,502,870
2. Texas	7,393,354
3. New York	7,056,860
4. Florida	6,337,929
5. Pennsylvania	4,777,003
6. Illinois	4,591,779
7. Ohio	4,445,773
8. Michigan	3,785,661
9. North Carolina	3,132,013
10. New Jersey	3,064,645
11. Georgia	3,006,369
12. Virginia	2,699,173
13. Massachusetts	2,443,580
14. Indiana	2,336,306
15. Washington	2,271,398
16. Tennessee	2,232,905
17. Missouri	2,194,594
18. Wisconsin	2,084,544
19. Maryland	1,980,859
20. Arizona	1,901,327
21. Minnesota	1,895,127
22. Alabama	1,737,080
23. Colorado	1,658,238
24. Louisiana	1,656,053
25. Kentucky	1,590,647
26. South Carolina	1,533,854
27. Oklahoma	1,342,293
28. Oregon	1,333,723
29. Connecticut	1,301,670
30. Iowa	1,149,276
31. Mississippi	1,046,434
32. Arkansas	1,042,696
33. Kansas	1,037,891
34. Nevada	751,165
35. West Virginia	736,481
36. Utah	701,281
37. New Mexico	677,971
38. Nebraska	666,184
39. Maine	518,200
40. New Hampshire	474,606
41. Idaho	469,645
42. Rhode Island	408,424
43. Hawaii	403,240
44. Montana	358,667
45. Delaware	298,736
46. South Dakota	290,245
47. North Dakota	257,152
48. District of Columbia	248,338
49. Vermont	240,634
50. Alaska	221,600
51. Wyoming	193,608

## 15. Persons Born in State of Residence, 1990		## 16. Physicians per 1,000 persons, 1999	
1. Pennsylvania	80.2%	1. District of Columbia	7.58
2. Louisiana	79.0	2. Massachusetts	4.22
3. Iowa	77.6	3. New York	3.95
4. Kentucky	77.4	4. Maryland	3.79
5. West Virginia	77.3	5. Connecticut	3.61
6. Mississippi	77.3	6. Rhode Island	3.39
7. Wisconsin	76.4	7. Vermont	3.13
8. Alabama	75.9	8. New Jersey	3.01
9. Michigan	74.9	9. Pennsylvania	2.93
10. Ohio	74.1	10. Hawaii	2.69
11. Minnesota	73.6	11. Illinois	2.63
12. North Dakota	73.2	* UNITED STATES	2.54
13. Indiana	71.1	12. Minnesota	2.54
14. North Carolina	70.4	13. Louisiana	2.51
15. South Dakota	70.2	14. California	2.48
16. Nebraska	70.2	15. Tennessee	2.48
17. Missouri	69.6	16. Colorado	2.44
18. Tennessee	69.2	17. Florida	2.43
19. Illinois	69.1	18. Virginia	2.43
20. Massachusetts	68.7	19. Delaware	2.38
21. Maine	68.5	20. North Carolina	2.37
22. South Carolina	68.4	21. Ohio	2.37
23. New York	67.5	22. Washington	2.37
24. Utah	67.2	23. New Hampshire	2.34
25. Arkansas	67.1	24. Maine	2.32
26. Texas	64.7	25. Missouri	2.32
27. Georgia	64.5	26. Wisconsin	2.32
28. Oklahoma	63.5	27. Oregon	2.27
29. Rhode Island	63.4	28. Michigan	2.26
* UNITED STATES	61.8	29. North Dakota	2.24
30. Kansas	61.3	30. Nebraska	2.21
31. Montana	58.9	31. West Virginia	2.19
32. Vermont	57.2	32. New Mexico	2.14
33. Connecticut	57.0	33. South Carolina	2.13
34. Hawaii	56.1	34. Kentucky	2.12
35. New Jersey	54.8	35. Georgia	2.11
36. Virginia	54.2	36. Texas	2.05
37. New Mexico	51.7	37. Kansas	2.04
38. Idaho	50.6	38. Arizona	2.03
39. Delaware	50.2	39. Utah	2.02
40. Maryland	49.8	40. Alabama	2.00
41. Washington	48.2	41. Indiana	1.98
42. Oregon	46.6	42. Arkansas	1.92
43. California	46.4	43. Montana	1.91
44. New Hampshire	44.1	44. South Dakota	1.88
45. Colorado	43.3	45. Nevada	1.77
46. Wyoming	42.6	46. Iowa	1.75
47. District of Columbia	39.3	47. Wyoming	1.72
48. Arizona	34.2	48. Alaska	1.70
49. Alaska	34.0	49. Oklahoma	1.67
50. Florida	30.5	50. Mississippi	1.64
51. Nevada	21.8	51. Idaho	1.55

17. Nurses per 1,000 persons, 1999

1. District of Columbia	15.97
2. Alaska	11.86
3. Massachusetts	11.80
4. Rhode Island	11.79
5. North Dakota	11.77
6. Pennsylvania	11.37
7. Delaware	11.20
8. Iowa	10.88
9. Minnesota	10.88
10. Maine	10.85
11. Wyoming	10.49
12. South Dakota	10.09
13. Connecticut	9.95
14. Missouri	9.85
15. New York	9.39
16. North Carolina	9.35
17. Ohio	9.24
18. Illinois	9.09
19. Wisconsin	9.05
20. New Hampshire	9.04
21. Nebraska	8.97
22. Tennessee	8.97
23. West Virginia	8.93
24. Oregon	8.92
25. Kansas	8.91
26. Montana	8.89
27. Florida	8.72
28. Vermont	8.69
29. Maryland	8.55
30. Michigan	8.45
31. Kentucky	8.38
32. Virginia	8.37
33. South Carolina	8.34
* UNITED STATES	8.33
34. Indiana	8.31
35. Louisiana	8.09
36. New Jersey	8.07
37. Hawaii	8.05
38. Mississippi	7.84
39. Arkansas	7.80
40. Washington	7.77
41. Alabama	7.71
42. Colorado	7.70
43. Arizona	7.67
44. Georgia	7.28
45. New Mexico	7.24
46. Texas	6.59
47. Utah	6.51
48. Nevada	6.31
49. Oklahoma	6.10
50. Idaho	6.01
51. California	5.32

18. Hospitals-Average Cost per Day, 1995 (to hospital)

1. District of Columbia	$1,346
2. Alaska	1,341
3. Washington	1,318
4. California	1,315
5. Connecticut	1,264
6. Utah	1,213
7. Arizona	1,191
8. Massachusetts	1,157
9. Oregon	1,141
10. Rhode Island	1,092
11. New Mexico	1,073
12. Nevada	1,072
13. Colorado	1,069
14. Maryland	1,064
15. Texas	1,063
16. Ohio	1,061
17. Delaware	1,058
18. Illinois	1,050
19. Florida	1,004
20. Michigan	994
* UNITED STATES	968
21. Missouri	967
22. Pennsylvania	963
23. Indiana	963
24. New Jersey	962
25. Hawaii	956
26. South Carolina	923
27. Maine	916
28. New Hampshire	915
29. New York	909
30. Louisiana	902
31. Virginia	901
32. Tennessee	871
33. Oklahoma	861
34. Georgia	836
35. North Carolina	832
36. Alabama	819
37. Kentucky	795
38. Wisconsin	794
39. West Virginia	763
40. Minnesota	736
41. Kansas	732
42. Idaho	719
43. Vermont	714
44. Arkansas	704
45. Iowa	702
46. Nebraska	661
47. Mississippi	584
48. Wyoming	545
49. North Dakota	521
50. Montana	493
51. South Dakota	476

19. Hospitals-Average Cost per Stay, 1995 (to hospital)		20. Persons with Less Than 9 Years of School, 1990	
1. District of Columbia	$8,632	* UNITED STATES	16,502,211
2. Hawaii	8,445	1. California	2,085,905
3. Alaska	8,282	2. Texas	1,387,528
4. New York	8,077	3. New York	1,200,827
5. Connecticut	7,358	4. Florida	842,811
6. Delaware	7,298	5. Illinois	750,932
7. California	7,111	6. Pennsylvania	741,167
8. Massachusetts	7,099	7. Ohio	546,954
9. New Jersey	7,007	8. North Carolina	539,974
10. Illinois	6,584	9. Tennessee	500,929
11. Pennsylvania	6,482	10. New Jersey	486,210
12. Colorado	6,289	11. Georgia	483,755
13. Minnesota	6,241	12. Michigan	452,893
14. Missouri	6,228	13. Virginia	443,668
15. Michigan	6,218	14. Kentucky	442,579
* UNITED STATES	6,216	15. Missouri	380,613
16. Rhode Island	6,202	16. Louisiana	372,913
17. New Hampshire	6,188	17. Alabama	348,848
18. Washington	6,180	18. Massachusetts	317,943
19. Ohio	6,141	19. Indiana	297,423
20. Maine	6,083	20. South Carolina	295,167
21. Florida	6,040	21. Wisconsin	294,862
22. Nevada	6,014	22. Maryland	246,505
23. South Carolina	5,935	23. Mississippi	240,267
24. Maryland	5,899	24. Minnesota	239,322
25. Vermont	5,883	25. Arkansas	227,633
26. Nebraska	5,880	26. Arizona	207,509
27. Texas	5,879	27. West Virginia	196,319
28. Wisconsin	5,679	28. Oklahoma	195,015
29. Utah	5,676	29. Connecticut	185,213
30. North Carolina	5,631	30. Washington	171,311
31. Georgia	5,618	31. Iowa	163,335
32. Arizona	5,613	32. Kansas	120,951
33. Louisiana	5,612	33. Colorado	118,252
34. Indiana	5,610	34. Oregon	114,724
35. North Dakota	5,589	35. New Mexico	105,362
36. South Dakota	5,494	36. Nebraska	79,925
37. Virginia	5,423	37. Rhode Island	72,842
38. New Mexico	5,358	38. Hawaii	71,806
39. Tennessee	5,355	39. Maine	70,153
40. Oregon	5,325	40. North Dakota	59,354
41. Kansas	5,308	41. South Dakota	57,707
42. Oklahoma	5,188	42. Nevada	47,771
43. Montana	5,184	43. New Hampshire	47,691
44. Iowa	5,049	44. Idaho	44,219
45. Alabama	5,028	45. Montana	41,144
46. West Virginia	4,974	46. District of Columbia	39,107
47. Kentucky	4,838	47. Delaware	31,009
48. Wyoming	4,817	48. Vermont	30,945
49. Idaho	4,686	49. Utah	30,379
50. Arkansas	4,459	50. Alaska	16,621
51. Mississippi	4,265	51. Wyoming	15,919

21. High School Graduates, 1990*

* UNITED STATES	47,642,763
1. California	4,167,897
2. New York	3,485,686
3. Pennsylvania	3,035,080
4. Florida	2,679,285
5. Texas	2,640,162
6. Ohio	2,515,987
7. Illinois	2,187,342
8. Michigan	1,887,449
9. New Jersey	1,606,555
10. Indiana	1,333,093
11. North Carolina	1,232,868
12. Georgia	1,192,935
13. Massachusetts	1,178,509
14. Wisconsin	1,147,697
15. Missouri	1,090,940
16. Virginia	1,059,199
17. Tennessee	942,865
18. Minnesota	913,265
19. Maryland	878,432
20. Washington	873,150
21. Louisiana	803,328
22. Alabama	749,591
23. Kentucky	741,012
24. Iowa	684,368
25. Connecticut	648,366
26. South Carolina	639,358
27. Oklahoma	607,903
28. Arizona	601,440
29. Colorado	558,312
30. Oregon	536,687
31. Kansas	514,177
32. Arkansas	489,570
33. West Virginia	429,123
34. Mississippi	423,624
35. Nebraska	345,778
36. Maine	295,074
37. New Mexico	264,943
38. Nevada	248,968
39. Utah	244,132
40. New Hampshire	226,267
41. Hawaii	203,893
42. Rhode Island	194,064
43. Idaho	182,892
44. Montana	170,070
45. South Dakota	144,990
46. Delaware	140,030
47. Vermont	123,430
48. North Dakota	111,215
49. Alaska	92,925
50. Wyoming	92,081
51. District of Columbia	86,756

*Persons 25 years and older with high school
diplomas

22. Persons Holding Bachelor's Degree, 1990

* UNITED STATES	20,832,567
1. California	2,858,107
2. New York	1,561,719
3. Texas	1,428,031
4. Florida	1,062,649
5. Illinois	989,808
6. Pennsylvania	890,660
7. New Jersey	826,887
8. Ohio	767,845
9. Massachusetts	657,161
10. Michigan	638,267
11. Virginia	612,679
12. Georgia	519,613
13. North Carolina	510,003
14. Washington	496,866
15. Maryland	486,695
16. Minnesota	431,381
17. Missouri	383,678
18. Colorado	379,150
19. Wisconsin	375,603
20. Connecticut	356,289
21. Tennessee	330,742
22. Indiana	321,278
23. Arizona	306,554
24. Louisiana	267,055
25. Alabama	258,231
26. Oregon	252,626
27. South Carolina	243,161
28. Oklahoma	236,112
29. Kansas	221,016
30. Iowa	207,269
31. Kentucky	189,539
32. Mississippi	149,109
33. Utah	138,534
34. Arkansas	132,712
35. Nebraska	130,172
36. New Hampshire	117,260
37. New Mexico	111,957
38. Hawaii	111,837
39. Maine	100,788
40. Rhode Island	88,634
41. West Virginia	88,136
42. Nevada	79,693
43. Idaho	74,443
44. Montana	71,610
45. District of Columbia	65,892
46. Delaware	58,615
47. Vermont	55,120
48. North Dakota	53,637
49. South Dakota	52,773
50. Alaska	48,617
51. Wyoming	36,354

23. Average Secondary Teachers' Salaries, 2000

1. New Jersey	$54,200
2. Connecticut	53,300
3. New York	51,800
4. Illinois	51,300
5. California	50,000
6. Michigan	48,700
7. Pennsylvania	48,600
8. Alaska	47,300
9. Rhode Island	47,100
10. District of Columbia	46,400
11. Massachusetts	46,300
12. Maryland	45,000
13. Delaware	44,600
* UNITED STATES	42,400
14. Ohio	42,100
15. Georgia	41,800
16. Indiana	41,800
17. Wisconsin	41,700
18. Oregon	41,000
19. Washington	40,900
20. Hawaii	40,600
21. Virginia	40,100
22. Nevada	39,800
23. North Carolina	39,700
24. Minnesota	39,200
25. Colorado	39,000
26. Kansas	38,500
27. Texas	38,100
28. Kentucky	37,700
29. New Hampshire	37,700
30. Tennessee	37,300
31. Vermont	36,800
32. Alabama	36,700
33. Florida	36,700
34. South Carolina	36,700
35. Iowa	36,500
36. Missouri	36,300
37. Maine	36,100
38. Arizona	35,700
39. West Virginia	35,600
40. Utah	35,400
41. Idaho	35,100
42. Arkansas	34,300
43. Wyoming	34,100
44. Nebraska	33,300
45. New Mexico	33,200
46. Louisiana	33,100
47. Montana	32,900
48. Mississippi	32,500
49. Oklahoma	31,500
50. North Dakota	30,100
51. South Dakota	29,000

24. Expenditures for Public Schools, per capita, 2000

1. Alaska	$2,129
2. Connecticut	1,864
3. New York	1,749
4. Oregon	1,679
5. Minnesota	1,673
6. Wisconsin	1,580
7. New Jersey	1,579
8. Washington	1,570
9. Wyoming	1,543
10. West Virginia	1,518
11. Texas	1,475
12. Massachusetts	1,449
13. Michigan	1,422
14. Nevada	1,389
15. Maine	1,368
16. Maryland	1,361
17. Vermont	1,358
18. Indiana	1,336
* UNITED STATES	1,321
19. Delaware	1,318
20. District of Columbia	1,317
21. Rhode Island	1,308
22. Georgia	1,307
23. California	1,283
24. Ohio	1,281
25. Kansas	1,254
26. South Carolina	1,253
27. Montana	1,230
28. New Mexico	1,227
29. New Hampshire	1,223
30. Illinois	1,222
31. Hawaii	1,198
32. Iowa	1,191
33. Idaho	1,184
34. Pennsylvania	1,157
35. Florida	1,156
36. Kentucky	1,154
37. Virginia	1,154
38. Nebraska	1,143
39. Missouri	1,132
40. Arkansas	1,124
41. Colorado	1,124
42. Utah	1,120
43. South Dakota	1,111
44. Oklahoma	1,107
45. Louisiana	1,106
46. North Carolina	1,075
47. Arizona	1,024
48. Alabama	1,016
49. Mississippi	974
50. Tennessee	941
51. North Dakota	905

25. Expenditures for Public Schools, per pupil, 2000

1. New York	$10,807
2. Alaska	10,711
3. New Jersey	10,504
4. Connecticut	10,286
5. District of Columbia	9,933
6. Oregon	9,910
7. Massachusetts	9,366
8. West Virginia	9,238
9. Rhode Island	8,773
10. Wisconsin	8,718
11. Delaware	8,653
12. Maine	8,173
13. Michigan	8,099
14. Minnesota	8,015
15. Pennsylvania	7,823
16. Maryland	7,704
17. Wyoming	7,391
18. Vermont	7,352
19. Indiana	7,254
20. Ohio	7,152
21. Kansas	7,149
* UNITED STATES	7,146
22. Kentucky	7,053
23. Washington	6,992
24. New Hampshire	6,840
25. Montana	6,801
26. Hawaii	6,777
27. Illinois	6,720
28. Texas	6,588
29. Nebraska	6,576
30. Virginia	6,543
31. Florida	6,536
32. New Mexico	6,513
33. South Carolina	6,400
34. Georgia	6,387
35. Iowa	6,386
36. Nevada	6,283
37. Missouri	6,234
38. California	6,232
39. North Carolina	6,185
40. Louisiana	6,039
41. Oklahoma	6,026
42. Tennessee	5,780
43. Idaho	5,756
44. South Dakota	5,737
45. Colorado	5,695
46. Arkansas	5,625
47. Alabama	5,118
48. Mississippi	4,905
49. Arizona	4,866
50. North Dakota	4,621
51. Utah	4,282

26. Social Security Beneficiaries, 2000

* UNITED STATES	44,324,000
1. California	4,208,000
2. Florida	3,193,000
3. New York	3,006,000
4. Texas	2,638,000
5. Pennsylvania	2,357,000
6. Ohio	1,918,000
7. Illinois	1,842,000
8. Michigan	1,645,000
9. New Jersey	1,352,000
10. North Carolina	1,350,000
11. Georgia	1,106,000
12. Massachusetts	1,064,000
13. Virginia	1,035,000
14. Missouri	1,005,000
15. Tennessee	996,000
16. Indiana	994,000
17. Wisconsin	900,000
18. Washington	845,000
19. Alabama	827,000
20. Arizona	791,000
21. Kentucky	739,000
22. Minnesota	739,000
23. Maryland	723,000
24. Louisiana	711,000
25. South Carolina	689,000
26. Oklahoma	594,000
27. Connecticut	579,000
28. Oregon	568,000
29. Iowa	540,000
30. Colorado	535,000
31. Arkansas	517,000
32. Mississippi	516,000
33. Kansas	440,000
34. West Virginia	390,000
35. Nevada	287,000
36. Nebraska	284,000
37. New Mexico	281,000
38. Maine	251,000
39. Utah	242,000
40. New Hampshire	200,000
41. Idaho	194,000
42. Rhode Island	192,000
43. Hawaii	184,000
44. Montana	158,000
45. South Dakota	136,000
46. Delaware	135,000
47. North Dakota	114,000
48. Vermont	105,000
49. Wyoming	77,000
50. District of Columbia	74,000
51. Alaska	55,000

27. Medicare Enrollment, 2000*

* UNITED STATES	38,286
1. California	3,837
2. Florida	2,771
3. New York	2,694
4. Texas	2,223
5. Pennsylvania	2,088
6. Ohio	1,692
7. Illinois	1,629
8. Michigan	1,389
9. New Jersey	1,195
10. North Carolina	1,111
11. Massachusetts	954
12. Georgia	898
13. Virginia	876
14. Missouri	854
15. Indiana	845
16. Tennessee	815
17. Wisconsin	777
18. Washington	725
19. Alabama	677
20. Arizona	658
21. Minnesota	648
22. Maryland	635
23. Kentucky	615
24. Louisiana	597
25. South Carolina	555
26. Connecticut	512
27. Oklahoma	504
28. Oregon	484
29. Iowa	476
30. Colorado	458
31. Arkansas	436
32. Mississippi	414
33. Kansas	389
34. West Virginia	336
35. Nebraska	252
36. Nevada	229
37. New Mexico	229
38. Maine	213
39. Utah	201
40. Rhode Island	170
41. New Hampshire	167
42. Hawaii	162
43. Idaho	161
44. Montana	135
45. South Dakota	119
46. Delaware	110
47. North Dakota	103
48. Vermont	88
49. District of Columbia	76
50. Wyoming	64
51. Alaska	40

*x1,000

28. Medicaid Recipients, 1998*

* UNITED STATES	39,666
1. California	7,082
2. New York	3,073
3. Texas	2,325
4. Florida	1,905
5. Tennessee	1,844
6. Pennsylvania	1,523
7. Washington	1,413
8. Illinois	1,364
9. Michigan	1,363
10. Ohio	1,291
11. Georgia	1,222
12. North Carolina	1,168
13. Massachusetts	908
14. New Jersey	813
15. Missouri	734
16. Louisiana	721
17. Virginia	653
18. Kentucky	644
19. Indiana	607
20. South Carolina	595
21. Maryland	561
22. Minnesota	538
23. Alabama	527
24. Wisconsin	519
25. Oregon	511
26. Arizona	508
27. Mississippi	486
28. Arkansas	425
29. Connecticut	381
30. Colorado	345
31. West Virginia	343
32. Oklahoma	342
33. New Mexico	329
34. Iowa	315
35. Kansas	242
36. Utah	216
37. Nebraska	211
38. Hawaii	185
39. Maine	170
40. District of Columbia	166
41. Rhode Island	153
42. Nevada	128
43. Vermont	124
44. Idaho	123
45. Delaware	101
46. Montana	101
47. New Hampshire	94
48. South Dakota	90
49. Alaska	75
50. North Dakota	62
51. Wyoming	46

*x1,000

29. Shopping Centers, 2000

* UNITED STATES	45,115
1. California	6,044
2. Florida	3,452
3. Texas	3,045
4. Illinois	2,175
5. New York	1,800
6. Ohio	1,741
7. Pennsylvania	1,704
8. North Carolina	1,649
9. Georgia	1,644
10. Virginia	1,318
11. New Jersey	1,279
12. Tennessee	1,214
13. Arizona	1,062
14. Michigan	1,056
15. Massachusetts	1,008
16. Maryland	940
17. Indiana	926
18. Missouri	903
19. South Carolina	845
20. Connecticut	800
21. Washington	785
22. Colorado	777
23. Louisiana	710
24. Alabama	651
25. Wisconsin	637
26. Kentucky	625
27. Oklahoma	577
28. Oregon	525
29. Kansas	493
30. Minnesota	483
31. Mississippi	444
32. Nevada	382
33. Arkansas	381
34. Iowa	326
35. New Mexico	311
36. Nebraska	277
37. Utah	248
38. New Hampshire	229
39. Rhode Island	211
40. Maine	203
41. Hawaii	190
42. Idaho	168
43. West Virginia	164
44. Delaware	149
45. Vermont	116
46. Montana	97
47. District of Columbia	87
48. North Dakota	87
49. Alaska	68
50. South Dakota	58
51. Wyoming	53

30. Federal Govt. Grants to State & Local Government, 2000*

* UNITED STATES	$291,942,541
1. California	33,157,559
2. New York	30,037,681
3. Texas	17,350,136
4. Pennsylvania	12,764,734
5. Florida	11,675,656
6. Illinois	11,270,857
7. Ohio	10,559,814
8. Michigan	9,486,173
9. New Jersey	8,212,241
10. North Carolina	7,911,422
11. Massachusetts	7,499,910
12. Georgia	7,192,114
13. Tennessee	6,160,429
14. Washington	5,707,329
15. Missouri	5,671,188
16. Maryland	5,538,103
17. Louisiana	5,247,616
18. Indiana	5,141,961
19. Kentucky	4,719,614
20. Virginia	4,615,448
21. Minnesota	4,599,300
22. Alabama	4,569,788
23. Wisconsin	4,503,678
24. Arizona	4,500,535
25. South Carolina	4,017,245
26. Connecticut	3,770,947
27. Oregon	3,596,708
28. Oklahoma	3,586,855
29. Mississippi	3,420,424
30. Colorado	3,272,542
31. District of Columbia	2,962,504
32. New Mexico	2,773,983
33. Arkansas	2,657,353
34. Iowa	2,639,454
35. West Virginia	2,541,963
36. Kansas	2,314,551
37. Alaska	2,260,169
38. Utah	1,910,316
39. Maine	1,849,710
40. Nebraska	1,682,451
41. Rhode Island	1,526,108
42. Montana	1,438,862
43. Nevada	1,244,481
44. Idaho	1,229,225
45. Hawaii	1,221,151
46. North Dakota	1,154,518
47. South Dakota	1,131,343
48. New Hampshire	1,115,854
49. Wyoming	1,014,391
50. Vermont	899,675
51. Delaware	817,675

* x1,000

31. Crime Rate, per 100,000 persons, 2000

1. District of Columbia	7,276.5
2. Arizona	5,829.5
3. Florida	5,694.7
4. New Mexico	5,518.9
5. Louisiana	5,422.8
6. South Carolina	5,221.4
7. Hawaii	5,198.9
8. Washington	5,105.6
9. Texas	4,955.5
10. North Carolina	4,919.3
11. Tennessee	4,890.2
12. Oregon	4,845.4
13. Maryland	4,816.1
14. Georgia	4,751.1
15. Oklahoma	4,558.6
16. Alabama	4,545.9
17. Missouri	4,527.8
18. Delaware	4,478.1
19. Utah	4,476.1
20. Kansas	4,408.8
21. Illinois	4,286.2
22. Nevada	4,268.6
23. Alaska	4,249.4
* UNITED STATES	4,124.0
24. Arkansas	4,115.3
25. Michigan	4,109.9
26. Nebraska	4,095.5
27. Ohio	4,041.8
28. Mississippi	4,004.4
29. Colorado	3,982.6
30. Indiana	3,751.9
31. California	3,739.7
32. Montana	3,533.4
33. Minnesota	3,488.4
34. Rhode Island	3,476.4
35. Wyoming	3,298.0
36. Iowa	3,233.7
37. Connecticut	3,232.7
38. Wisconsin	3,209.1
39. Idaho	3,186.2
40. New Jersey	3,160.5
41. New York	3,099.6
42. Virginia	3,028.1
43. Massachusetts	3,026.1
44. Pennsylvania	2,995.3
45. Vermont	2,986.9
46. Kentucky	2,959.7
47. Maine	2,619.8
48. West Virginia	2,602.8
49. New Hampshire	2,433.1
50. South Dakota	2,319.8
51. North Dakota	2,288.1

32. Violent Crime Rate, per 100,000 persons, 2000

1. District of Columbia	1,507.9
2. Florida	812.0
3. South Carolina	804.9
4. Maryland	786.6
5. New Mexico	757.9
6. Tennessee	707.2
7. Delaware	684.4
8. Louisiana	681.1
9. Illinois	656.8
10. California	621.6
11. Alaska	566.9
12. Michigan	555.0
13. New York	553.9
14. Texas	545.1
15. Arizona	531.7
16. Nevada	524.2
* UNITED STATES	506.1
17. Georgia	504.7
18. Oklahoma	497.8
19. North Carolina	497.6
20. Missouri	490.0
21. Alabama	486.2
22. Massachusetts	476.1
23. Arkansas	445.3
24. Pennsylvania	420.0
25. Kansas	389.4
26. New Jersey	383.8
27. Washington	369.7
28. Mississippi	360.9
29. Oregon	350.7
30. Indiana	349.1
31. Ohio	334.1
32. Colorado	334.0
33. Nebraska	327.6
34. Connecticut	324.7
35. West Virginia	316.5
36. Rhode Island	297.7
37. Kentucky	294.5
38. Virginia	281.7
39. Minnesota	280.8
40. Wyoming	266.5
41. Iowa	266.4
42. Utah	255.7
43. Idaho	252.5
44. Hawaii	243.8
45. Montana	240.6
46. Wisconsin	236.8
47. New Hampshire	175.4
48. South Dakota	166.8
49. Vermont	113.5
50. Maine	109.6
51. North Dakota	81.4

33. Incarceration Rate, 2000*

1. District of Columbia	971
2. Louisiana	801
3. Texas	730
4. Mississippi	688
5. Oklahoma	685
6. Georgia	550
7. Alabama	549
8. South Carolina	532
9. Nevada	518
10. Arizona	515
11. Delaware	513
12. Missouri	494
13. Michigan	480
* UNITED STATES	478
14. California	474
15. Florida	462
16. Arkansas	458
17. Idaho	430
18. Maryland	429
19. Virginia	422
20. Ohio	406
21. Colorado	403
22. Tennessee	399
23. Connecticut	398
24. New York	383
25. Wisconsin	376
26. Kentucky	373
27. Illinois	371
28. New Jersey	362
29. South Dakota	353
30. Wyoming	349
31. Montana	348
32. North Carolina	347
33. Alaska	341
34. Indiana	335
35. Oregon	316
36. Kansas	312
37. Pennsylvania	307
38. Hawaii	302
39. New Mexico	279
40. Iowa	276
41. Utah	254
42. Massachusetts	252
43. Washington	251
44. Nebraska	228
45. Vermont	218
46. West Virginia	211
47. Rhode Island	197
48. New Hampshire	185
49. North Dakota	158
50. Maine	129
51. Minnesota	128

*The number of prisoners sentenced to more than one year, per 100,000 residents

34. Civilian Labor Force, 2000

* UNITED STATES	140,863,000
1. California	17,091,000
2. Texas	10,325,000
3. New York	8,941,000
4. Florida	7,490,000
5. Illinois	6,419,000
6. Pennsylvania	5,972,000
7. Ohio	5,783,000
8. Michigan	5,201,000
9. New Jersey	4,188,000
10. Georgia	4,173,000
11. North Carolina	3,958,000
12. Virginia	3,610,000
13. Massachusetts	3,237,000
14. Indiana	3,084,000
15. Washington	3,045,000
16. Wisconsin	2,935,000
17. Missouri	2,930,000
18. Maryland	2,805,000
19. Tennessee	2,798,000
20. Minnesota	2,739,000
21. Arizona	2,347,000
22. Colorado	2,276,000
23. Alabama	2,154,000
24. Louisiana	2,030,000
25. South Carolina	1,985,000
26. Kentucky	1,982,000
27. Oregon	1,803,000
28. Connecticut	1,746,000
29. Oklahoma	1,648,000
30. Iowa	1,563,000
31. Kansas	1,411,000
32. Mississippi	1,326,000
33. Arkansas	1,238,000
34. Utah	1,104,000
35. Nevada	986,000
36. Nebraska	924,000
37. New Mexico	833,000
38. West Virginia	825,000
39. Maine	689,000
40. New Hampshire	686,000
41. Idaho	658,000
42. Hawaii	595,000
43. Rhode Island	505,000
44. Montana	479,000
45. Delaware	409,000
46. South Dakota	401,000
47. North Dakota	339,000
48. Vermont	332,000
49. Alaska	322,000
50. District of Columbia	279,000
51. Wyoming	267,000

35. Unemployment Rate, 2000

1. Alaska	6.6
2. District of Columbia	5.8
3. Mississippi	5.7
4. Louisiana	5.5
5. West Virginia	5.5
6. Washington	5.2
7. California	4.9
8. Idaho	4.9
9. Montana	4.9
10. New Mexico	4.9
11. Oregon	4.9
12. Alabama	4.6
13. New York	4.6
14. Arkansas	4.4
15. Illinois	4.4
16. Hawaii	4.3
17. Pennsylvania	4.2
18. Texas	4.2
19. Kentucky	4.1
20. Nevada	4.1
21. Ohio	4.1
22. Rhode Island	4.1
* UNITED STATES	4.0
23. Delaware	4.0
24. Arizona	3.9
25. Maryland	3.9
26. South Carolina	3.9
27. Tennessee	3.9
28. Wyoming	3.9
29. New Jersey	3.8
30. Georgia	3.7
31. Kansas	3.7
32. Florida	3.6
33. Michigan	3.6
34. North Carolina	3.6
35. Maine	3.5
36. Missouri	3.5
37. Wisconsin	3.5
38. Minnesota	3.3
39. Indiana	3.2
40. Utah	3.2
41. Nebraska	3.0
42. North Dakota	3.0
43. Oklahoma	3.0
44. Vermont	2.9
45. New Hampshire	2.8
46. Colorado	2.7
47. Iowa	2.6
48. Massachusetts	2.6
49. Connecticut	2.3
50. South Dakota	2.3
51. Virginia	2.2

36. Average Annual Pay, 1999

1. District of Columbia	$50,742
2. Connecticut	42,653
3. New York	42,133
4. Massachusetts	40,331
5. California	37,564
6. Illinois	36,279
7. Washington	35,736
8. Michigan	35,734
9. Delaware	35,102
10. Maryland	34,472
11. Colorado	34,192
12. Alaska	34,034
13. Minnesota	33,487
* UNITED STATES	33,313
14. Virginia	33,015
15. Texas	32,895
16. Pennsylvania	32,694
17. Georgia	32,339
18. New Hampshire	32,139
19. Ohio	31,396
20. Nevada	31,213
21. Rhode Island	31,177
22. Oregon	30,867
23. Arizona	30,523
24. Indiana	30,027
25. Missouri	29,958
26. Hawaii	29,771
27. Wisconsin	29,597
28. Tennessee	29,518
29. North Carolina	29,453
30. Florida	28,911
31. Alabama	28,069
32. Kansas	28,029
33. Utah	27,884
34. Kentucky	27,748
35. Vermont	27,595
36. Louisiana	27,221
37. South Carolina	27,124
38. Iowa	26,939
39. Maine	26,887
40. Nebraska	26,633
41. New Mexico	26,270
42. Idaho	26,042
43. West Virginia	26,008
44. Oklahoma	25,748
45. Wyoming	25,639
46. Arkansas	25,371
47. Mississippi	24,392
48. South Dakota	23,765
49. North Dakota	23,753
50. Montana	23,253
51. New Jersey	NA

37. Average Hourly Earnings of Production Workers, 2000

1. Michigan	$19.20
2. Washington	16.76
3. Ohio	16.72
4. Delaware	16.54
5. Indiana	15.83
6. Wyoming	15.76
7. Connecticut	15.69
8. District of Columbia	15.57
9. Louisiana	15.57
10. New Jersey	15.47
11. Oregon	15.08
12. Maryland	14.99
13. Minnesota	14.99
14. Kansas	14.98
15. Wisconsin	14.85
16. Kentucky	14.82
17. Colorado	14.76
18. Iowa	14.66
19. Massachusetts	14.65
20. Pennsylvania	14.60
21. West Virginia	14.60
22. Missouri	14.40
23. Illinois	14.39
* UNITED STATES	14.38
24. Montana	14.34
25. Maine	14.28
26. California	14.25
27. New York	14.24
28. Vermont	14.23
29. Idaho	14.17
30. Nevada	13.84
31. Virginia	13.82
32. Utah	13.69
33. Hawaii	13.58
34. New Hampshire	13.41
35. New Mexico	13.34
36. Oklahoma	13.17
37. Georgia	13.01
38. Alabama	12.94
39. Nebraska	12.93
40. Tennessee	12.92
41. North Carolina	12.79
42. Arizona	12.77
43. North Dakota	12.66
44. Alaska	12.45
45. Texas	12.37
46. Florida	12.28
47. Rhode Island	12.18
48. Arkansas	11.98
49. Mississippi	11.64
50. South Carolina	10.96
51. South Dakota	10.71

38. Average Weekly Earnings of Production Workers, 2000

1. Michigan	$837.12
2. Delaware	717.84
3. Ohio	717.29
4. Washington	682.13
5. Connecticut	668.39
6. Indiana	666.44
7. Louisiana	666.40
8. New Jersey	648.19
9. Kentucky	623.92
10. Wyoming	617.79
11. District of Columbia	616.57
12. Wisconsin	616.28
13. Colorado	615.49
14. Pennsylvania	614.66
15. Massachusetts	613.84
16. Maryland	611.59
17. Minnesota	611.59
18. Iowa	609.86
19. Kansas	608.19
20. Oregon	603.20
21. West Virginia	602.98
22. Illinois	597.19
* UNITED STATES	596.77
23. Missouri	596.16
24. California	594.23
25. Maine	589.76
26. Nevada	586.82
27. Virginia	584.59
28. New York	583.84
29. Vermont	573.47
30. Idaho	555.46
31. Montana	552.09
32. Alaska	551.54
33. New Hampshire	547.13
34. Utah	544.86
35. Alabama	542.19
36. Oklahoma	538.65
37. Georgia	536.01
38. Texas	535.62
39. Nebraska	535.30
40. North Carolina	529.51
41. Hawaii	520.11
42. Tennessee	519.38
43. Arizona	515.91
44. Florida	514.53
45. New Mexico	509.59
46. North Dakota	506.93
47. Rhode Island	492.07
48. Arkansas	491.18
49. Mississippi	473.75
50. South Carolina	465.80
51. South Dakota	461.60

39. Median Household Income, three year average, 1998-2000

1. Maryland	$51,695
2. New Jersey	51,032
3. Minnesota	50,865
4. Alaska	50,746
5. Connecticut	50,360
6. Delaware	50,154
7. Virginia	50,069
8. New Hampshire	48,928
9. Colorado	48,506
10. Hawaii	48,026
11. Missouri	47,462
12. Massachusetts	46,947
13. California	46,802
14. Illinois	46,435
15. Michigan	46,181
16. Wisconsin	45,349
17. Utah	45,230
18. Nevada	44,755
19. Ohio	43,894
20. Pennsylvania	43,742
21. Iowa	42,993
22. Rhode Island	42,973
23. Georgia	42,887
24. Oregon	42,440
* UNITED STATES	42,148
25. Washington	42,024
26. New York	41,605
27. Maine	41,597
28. Arizona	41,456
29. Texas	39,842
30. Indiana	39,717
31. Wyoming	39,026
32. North Carolina	38,829
33. District of Columbia	38,752
34. Nebraska	38,574
35. Vermont	38,150
36. Florida	37,998
37. Kansas	37,705
38. Idaho	37,462
39. Kentucky	37,186
40. South Carolina	37,119
41. South Dakota	36,172
42. North Dakota	35,349
43. New Mexico	35,254
44. Tennessee	33,885
45. Alabama	33,105
46. Oklahoma	32,445
47. Montana	32,045
48. Mississippi	31,528
49. Arkansas	30,293
50. Louisiana	30,219
51. West Virginia	29,052

40. Persons Below Poverty Level, three year average, 1998-2000

1. New Mexico	19.3%
2. Louisiana	18.6
3. District of Columbia	17.3
4. Montana	16.0
5. Arkansas	15.8
6. West Virginia	15.8
7. Mississippi	15.5
8. Texas	14.9
9. New York	14.7
10. Alabama	14.6
11. Oklahoma	14.1
12. California	14.0
13. Arizona	13.6
14. Idaho	13.3
15. Tennessee	13.3
16. North Carolina	13.2
17. Oregon	12.8
18. North Dakota	12.7
19. Georgia	12.6
20. Kentucky	12.5
21. Florida	12.1
* UNITED STATES	11.9
22. South Carolina	11.9
23. Ohio	11.1
24. Wyoming	11.0
25. Nebraska	10.6
26. Hawaii	10.5
27. Illinois	10.5
28. Kansas	10.4
29. Massachusetts	10.2
30. Michigan	10.2
31. Vermont	10.1
32. Nevada	10.0
33. Rhode Island	10.0
34. Pennsylvania	9.9
35. Delaware	9.8
36. Maine	9.8
37. Missouri	9.7
38. Washington	9.4
39. South Dakota	9.3
40. Wisconsin	8.8
41. Colorado	8.5
42. Alaska	8.3
43. Indiana	8.2
44. New Jersey	8.1
45. Utah	8.1
46. Virginia	8.1
47. Iowa	7.9
48. Minnesota	7.8
49. Connecticut	7.6
50. New Hampshire	7.4
51. Maryland	7.3

41. Personal Income, per capita, in current dollars, 2000

1. Connecticut	$40,640
2. Massachusetts	37,992
3. District of Columbia	37,383
4. New Jersey	36,983
5. New York	34,547
6. Maryland	33,872
7. New Hampshire	33,332
8. Colorado	32,949
9. California	32,275
10. Illinois	32,259
11. Minnesota	32,101
12. Washington	31,528
13. Delaware	31,255
14. Virginia	31,162
15. Nevada	30,529
16. Alaska	30,064
17. Rhode Island	29,685
* UNITED STATES	29,676
18. Michigan	29,612
19. Pennsylvania	29,539
20. Ohio	28,400
21. Oregon	28,350
22. Wisconsin	28,232
23. Hawaii	28,221
24. Florida	28,145
25. Georgia	27,940
26. Texas	27,871
27. Nebraska	27,829
28. Kansas	27,816
29. Missouri	27,445
30. Wyoming	27,230
31. North Carolina	27,194
32. Indiana	27,011
33. Vermont	26,901
34. Iowa	26,723
35. Tennessee	26,239
36. South Dakota	26,115
37. Maine	25,623
38. Arizona	25,578
39. North Dakota	25,068
40. South Carolina	24,321
41. Kentucky	24,294
42. Idaho	24,180
43. Utah	23,907
44. Oklahoma	23,517
45. Alabama	23,471
46. Louisiana	23,334
47. Montana	22,569
48. Arkansas	22,257
49. New Mexico	22,203
50. West Virginia	21,915
51. Mississippi	20,993

42. Personal Income, per capita, in constant (1996) dollars, 2000

1. Connecticut	$37,854
2. Massachusetts	35,387
3. District of Columbia	34,820
4. New Jersey	34,448
5. New York	32,179
6. Maryland	31,550
7. New Hampshire	31,047
8. Colorado	30,690
9. California	30,062
10. Illinois	30,048
11. Minnesota	29,900
12. Washington	29,367
13. Delaware	29,112
14. Virginia	29,026
15. Nevada	28,436
16. Alaska	28,003
17. Rhode Island	27,650
* UNITED STATES	27,642
18. Michigan	27,582
19. Pennsylvania	27,514
20. Ohio	26,453
21. Oregon	26,406
22. Wisconsin	26,297
23. Hawaii	26,286
24. Florida	26,216
25. Georgia	26,025
26. Texas	25,960
27. Nebraska	25,921
28. Kansas	25,909
29. Missouri	25,564
30. Wyoming	25,363
31. North Carolina	25,330
32. Indiana	25,159
33. Vermont	25,057
34. Iowa	24,891
35. Tennessee	24,440
36. South Dakota	24,325
37. Maine	23,866
38. Arizona	23,825
39. North Dakota	23,349
40. South Carolina	22,654
41. Kentucky	22,629
42. Idaho	22,522
43. Utah	22,268
44. Oklahoma	21,905
45. Alabama	21,862
46. Louisiana	21,734
47. Montana	21,022
48. Arkansas	20,731
49. New Mexico	20,681
50. West Virginia	20,413
51. Mississippi	19,554

43. Business Failures, 1998

* UNITED STATES	71,857
1. California	17,679
2. Texas	6,785
3. New York	4,233
4. Illinois	3,291
5. Pennsylvania	2,641
6. Washington	2,528
7. Ohio	2,524
8. Colorado	2,483
9. Florida	2,047
10. New Jersey	2,024
11. Minnesota	1,711
12. Michigan	1,551
13. Tennessee	1,369
14. Missouri	1,321
15. Maryland	1,283
16. Arizona	1,225
17. Massachusetts	1,200
18. Kansas	1,140
19. Oregon	1,109
20. Wisconsin	1,005
21. Oklahoma	990
22. Virginia	860
23. North Carolina	846
24. Georgia	800
25. Hawaii	781
26. Arkansas	748
27. Nevada	677
28. New Mexico	585
29. Alabama	546
30. Connecticut	530
31. Indiana	473
32. Idaho	441
33. South Carolina	410
34. Utah	388
35. Nebraska	383
36. Louisiana	377
37. New Hampshire	322
38. West Virginia	305
39. South Dakota	275
40. Kentucky	270
41. Maine	259
42. Iowa	244
43. Montana	201
44. Alaska	177
45. Mississippi	177
46. Wyoming	166
47. Rhode Island	150
48. North Dakota	144
49. Vermont	80
50. District of Columbia	75
51. Delaware	28

44. Fortune 500 Companies, 2000

* UNITED STATES	500
1. New York	55
2. California	55
3. Texas	45
4. Illinois	39
5. Ohio	29
6. Pennsylvania	25
7. New Jersey	22
8. Michigan	19
9. Virginia	16
10. Minnesota	16
11. Georgia	15
12. North Carolina	13
13. Missouri	13
14. Massachusetts	13
15. Connecticut	13
16. Florida	12
17. Washington	11
18. Wisconsin	10
19. Maryland	7
20. Alabama	7
21. Tennessee	6
22. Oklahoma	5
23. Nebraska	5
24. Indiana	5
25. Arkansas	5
26. Arizona	5
27. Kentucky	4
28. Colorado	4
29. Rhode Island	3
30. Nevada	3
31. Idaho	3
32. Delaware	3
33. South Dakota	2
34. Oregon	2
35. Kansas	2
36. Iowa	2
37. District of Columbia	2
38. Utah	1
39. South Carolina	1
40. Mississippi	1
41. Louisiana	1
42. Wyoming	0
43. West Virginia	0
44. Vermont	0
45. North Dakota	0
46. New Mexico	0
47. New Hampshire	0
48. Montana	0
49. Maine	0
50. Hawaii	0
51. Alaska	0

45. Gross State Product, 1999*

* UNITED STATES	$9,308,983
1. California	1,229,098
2. New York	754,590
3. Texas	687,272
4. Illinois	445,666
5. Florida	442,895
6. Pennsylvania	382,980
7. Ohio	361,981
8. New Jersey	331,544
9. Michigan	308,310
10. Georgia	275,719
11. Massachusetts	262,564
12. North Carolina	258,592
13. Virginia	242,221
14. Washington	209,258
15. Indiana	182,202
16. Maryland	174,710
17. Minnesota	172,982
18. Missouri	170,470
19. Tennessee	170,085
20. Wisconsin	166,481
21. Colorado	153,728
22. Connecticut	151,779
23. Arizona	143,683
24. Louisiana	128,959
25. Alabama	115,071
26. Kentucky	113,539
27. Oregon	109,694
28. South Carolina	106,917
29. Oklahoma	86,382
30. Iowa	85,243
31. Kansas	80,843
32. Nevada	69,864
33. Arkansas	64,773
34. Mississippi	64,286
35. Utah	62,641
36. District of Columbia	55,832
37. Nebraska	53,744
38. New Mexico	51,026
39. New Hampshire	44,229
40. Hawaii	40,914
41. West Virginia	40,685
42. Delaware	34,669
43. Maine	34,064
44. Idaho	34,025
45. Rhode Island	32,546
46. Alaska	26,353
47. South Dakota	21,631
48. Montana	20,636
49. Wyoming	17,448
50. Vermont	17,164
51. North Dakota	16,991

*millions of dollars

46. Number of Farms, 2000

* UNITED STATES	2,172,000
1. Texas	226,000
2. Missouri	109,000
3. Iowa	95,000
4. Kentucky	90,000
5. Tennessee	90,000
6. California	88,000
7. Oklahoma	85,000
8. Ohio	80,000
9. Minnesota	79,000
10. Illinois	78,000
11. Wisconsin	77,000
12. Indiana	64,000
13. Kansas	64,000
14. Pennsylvania	59,000
15. North Carolina	57,000
16. Nebraska	54,000
17. Michigan	52,000
18. Georgia	50,000
19. Virginia	49,000
20. Arkansas	48,000
21. Alabama	47,000
22. Florida	44,000
23. Mississippi	43,000
24. Oregon	40,000
25. Washington	40,000
26. New York	38,000
27. South Dakota	33,000
28. Louisiana	30,000
29. North Dakota	30,000
30. Colorado	29,000
31. Montana	28,000
32. Idaho	25,000
33. South Carolina	24,000
34. West Virginia	21,000
35. Utah	16,000
36. New Mexico	15,000
37. Maryland	12,000
38. New Jersey	10,000
39. Wyoming	9,000
40. Arizona	8,000
41. Maine	7,000
42. Vermont	7,000
43. Hawaii	6,000
44. Massachusetts	6,000
45. Connecticut	4,000
46. Delaware	3,000
47. Nevada	3,000
48. New Hampshire	3,000
49. Alaska	1,000
50. Rhode Island	1,000
51. District of Columbia	NA

47. Value of Farms, 1997*

* UNITED STATES	$912,344
1. Texas	77,400
2. California	75,300
3. Illinois	61,880
4. Iowa	54,780
5. Nebraska	31,960
6. Ohio	31,861
7. Indiana	31,323
8. Minnesota	30,992
9. Missouri	30,199
10. Kansas	27,485
11. Florida	23,690
12. Wisconsin	21,000
13. Pennsylvania	20,251
14. Kentucky	20,155
15. Tennessee	19,470
16. Oklahoma	19,380
17. Washington	19,311
18. Colorado	19,175
19. North Carolina	18,450
20. Montana	18,178
21. Oregon	17,500
22. Virginia	17,255
23. Georgia	16,874
24. Michigan	16,800
25. North Dakota	16,482
26. Arkansas	14,948
27. Arizona	14,868
28. Alabama	14,356
29. South Dakota	14,300
30. Idaho	12,960
31. New Mexico	12,180
32. Mississippi	11,875
33. New York	10,703
34. Louisiana	10,455
35. Maryland	8,400
36. Utah	8,250
37. Wyoming	7,612
38. South Carolina	7,000
39. New Jersey	6,881
40. West Virginia	3,700
41. Massachusetts	3,534
42. Nevada	3,080
43. Connecticut	2,850
44. Vermont	2,093
45. Delaware	1,791
46. Maine	1,742
47. New Hampshire	1,118
48. Rhode Island	498
49. Alaska	NA
50. District of Columbia	NA
51. Hawaii	NA

*millions of dollars

48. Net Farm Income, 1999*

* UNITED STATES	$43,398
1. California	4,986
2. Texas	4,650
3. Florida	2,815
4. Georgia	2,099
5. North Carolina	1,966
6. Arkansas	1,831
7. Nebraska	1,651
8. Kansas	1,548
9. Alabama	1,450
10. Iowa	1,450
11. Minnesota	1,257
12. South Dakota	1,190
13. Oklahoma	1,150
14. Illinois	1,007
15. Mississippi	949
16. Colorado	923
17. Wisconsin	879
18. Idaho	874
19. Kentucky	847
20. Ohio	803
21. Arizona	708
22. Michigan	659
23. New Mexico	640
24. Pennsylvania	627
25. New York	587
26. Louisiana	565
27. Washington	519
28. Montana	482
29. North Dakota	452
30. South Carolina	422
31. Indiana	421
32. Missouri	405
33. Virginia	396
34. Maryland	337
35. Oregon	323
36. Utah	280
37. Wyoming	173
38. Tennessee	141
39. Vermont	141
40. Connecticut	139
41. New Jersey	127
42. Delaware	121
43. Maine	98
44. Massachusetts	65
45. Nevada	65
46. Hawaii	63
47. New Hampshire	25
48. Alaska	20
49. West Virginia	13
50. Rhode Island	12
51. District of Columbia	NA

*millions of dollars

49. Farm Marketings, 1999*		50. Total Non-fuel Mineral Production, 2000 (preliminary)*	
* UNITED STATES	$188,610	* UNITED STATES	$40,100
1. California	24,801	1. Nevada	32,800
2. Texas	13,052	2. Utah	31,420
3. Iowa	9,716	3. Pennsylvania	31,250
4. Nebraska	8,555	4. Oregon	3439
5. Kansas	7,616	5. California	3,350
6. Florida	7,066	6. West Virginia	3182
7. Minnesota	7,061	7. Maine	3102
8. Illinois	6,757	8. Connecticut	3100
9. North Carolina	6,688	9. Arizona	2,550
10. Wisconsin	5,596	10. Texas	2,050
11. Arkansas	5,259	11. Florida	1,920
12. Georgia	5,241	12. Michigan	1,670
13. Washington	4,933	13. Georgia	1,660
14. Ohio	4,429	14. Minnesota	1,570
15. Indiana	4,373	15. Missouri	1,320
16. Colorado	4,354	16. Alaska	1,140
17. Missouri	4,256	17. Alabama	1,070
18. Pennsylvania	4,070	18. Ohio	1,060
19. Oklahoma	3,991	19. New York	970
20. South Dakota	3,539	20. Wyoming	922
21. Michigan	3,470	21. Illinois	907
22. Kentucky	3,456	22. New Mexico	812
23. Alabama	3,438	23. North Carolina	779
24. Idaho	3,347	24. Tennessee	770
25. Mississippi	3,174	25. Indiana	729
26. New York	3,097	26. Virginia	692
27. Oregon	3,052	27. Washington	691
28. North Dakota	2,759	28. Kansas	624
29. Virginia	2,283	29. Montana	582
30. Arizona	2,178	30. Colorado	566
31. Tennessee	1,974	31. South Carolina	560
32. New Mexico	1,953	32. Iowa	510
33. Louisiana	1,848	33. Arkansas	506
34. Montana	1,716	34. Kentucky	497
35. Maryland	1,481	35. Oklahoma	453
36. South Carolina	1,406	36. Louisiana	404
37. Utah	967	37. Idaho	398
38. Wyoming	852	38. New Hampshire	359
39. New Jersey	740	39. Maryland	357
40. Delaware	718	40. Wisconsin	349
41. Vermont	541	41. Delaware	312
42. Hawaii	533	42. New Jersey	286
43. Maine	515	43. South Dakota	260
44. Connecticut	482	44. Massachusetts	210
45. Massachusetts	396	45. Nebraska	170
46. West Virginia	387	46. Mississippi	157
47. Nevada	334	47. Hawaii	91
48. New Hampshire	153	48. Vermont	43
49. Alaska	48	49. North Dakota	42
50. Rhode Island	48	50. Rhode Island	24
51. District of Columbia	NA	51. District of Columbia	NA

*millions of dollars

*millions of dollars

51. Value of Manufacturing Shipments, 1997*

* UNITED STATES	$3,958,050,434
1. California	390,321,123
2. Texas	301,788,258
3. Ohio	245,502,486
4. Michigan	218,202,588
5. Illinois	205,420,843
6. Pennsylvania	177,169,793
7. New York	168,162,761
8. North Carolina	163,729,870
9. Indiana	143,606,930
10. Georgia	126,678,011
11. Wisconsin	118,860,895
12. New Jersey	101,328,913
13. Tennessee	99,789,023
14. Missouri	96,452,153
15. Kentucky	88,437,375
16. Virginia	87,071,056
17. Massachusetts	82,603,724
18. Washington	82,356,770
19. Florida	82,022,637
20. Louisiana	81,385,399
21. Minnesota	78,725,094
22. South Carolina	71,550,765
23. Alabama	69,694,695
24. Iowa	63,640,436
25. Oregon	50,200,786
26. Connecticut	48,699,736
27. Kansas	48,611,181
28. Arkansas	46,398,118
29. Arizona	44,093,719
30. Colorado	41,931,225
31. Mississippi	40,608,792
32. Maryland	38,281,223
33. Oklahoma	37,965,344
34. Nebraska	28,357,769
35. Utah	24,348,385
36. New Hampshire	20,196,331
37. West Virginia	18,545,029
38. New Mexico	18,147,245
39. Idaho	17,608,486
40. Maine	15,184,255
41. Delaware	13,516,996
42. South Dakota	12,412,102
43. Rhode Island	10,709,098
44. Vermont	7,986,254
45. Nevada	6,673,683
46. Montana	5,222,699
47. North Dakota	5,196,919
48. Alaska	3,760,829
49. Hawaii	3,416,655
50. Wyoming	3,032,066
51. District of Columbia	2,443,911

* (x 1,000)

52. Manufacturing Payroll, 1997*

* UNITED STATES	595,685,786
1. California	68,097,248
2. Ohio	36,849,904
3. Michigan	34,937,673
4. Texas	33,519,948
5. Illinois	32,953,527
6. New York	30,405,687
7. Pennsylvania	28,688,934
8. Indiana	22,476,650
9. North Carolina	21,713,029
10. Wisconsin	19,094,326
11. Massachusetts	17,445,834
12. New Jersey	16,479,211
13. Georgia	16,051,302
14. Tennessee	14,679,651
15. Florida	14,199,437
16. Minnesota	13,759,547
17. Washington	13,589,194
18. Missouri	12,300,024
19. Virginia	12,130,687
20. Connecticut	10,862,423
21. South Carolina	10,552,195
22. Alabama	10,497,421
23. Kentucky	9,416,025
24. Iowa	7,849,890
25. Oregon	7,514,314
26. Arizona	6,957,158
27. Kansas	6,772,450
28. Colorado	6,634,727
29. Louisiana	6,259,067
30. Maryland	6,220,818
31. Arkansas	5,967,308
32. Mississippi	5,745,062
33. Oklahoma	5,083,001
34. Utah	3,801,688
35. New Hampshire	3,461,347
36. Nebraska	3,165,556
37. Maine	2,755,677
38. West Virginia	2,528,978
39. Rhode Island	2,381,199
40. Idaho	2,231,139
41. Vermont	1,515,461
42. Delaware	1,505,099
43. Nevada	1,241,068
44. New Mexico	1,203,286
45. South Dakota	1,194,187
46. North Dakota	627,982
47. Montana	626,561
48. District of Columbia	569,906
49. Hawaii	470,626
50. Alaska	422,169
51. Wyoming	280,185

* (x 1,000)

53. Commercial Bank Deposits, 2000*

* UNITED STATES	$4,146.0
1. New York	790.7
2. North Carolina	645.4
3. Illinois	249.4
4. California	238.5
5. Ohio	229.8
6. Pennsylvania	138.7
7. Texas	133.2
8. Alabama	129.9
9. Minnesota	122.6
10. Rhode Island	114.5
11. Georgia	109.3
12. Michigan	97.7
13. New Jersey	80.0
14. Delaware	77.8
15. Massachusetts	72.6
16. Utah	69.7
17. Tennessee	61.9
18. Wisconsin	58.8
19. Indiana	54.6
20. Missouri	52.4
21. Florida	47.7
22. Virginia	42.9
23. Louisiana	41.9
24. Kentucky	39.5
25. Colorado	37.3
26. Maryland	35.6
27. Iowa	34.3
28. Oklahoma	33.4
29. Kansas	31.0
30. Arizona	30.7
31. Mississippi	26.4
32. Nebraska	23.7
33. Arkansas	21.5
34. South Carolina	18.4
35. Hawaii	17.5
36. New Hampshire	16.4
37. West Virginia	13.8
38. South Dakota	13.5
39. Nevada	13.3
40. North Dakota	13.3
41. Washington	12.3
42. New Mexico	11.3
43. Montana	8.8
44. Oregon	6.5
45. Vermont	6.3
46. Wyoming	5.7
47. Maine	5.4
48. Alaska	4.1
49. Connecticut	2.8
50. Idaho	2.1
51. District of Columbia	0.6

*billions of dollars

54. Motorcycle Registrations, 2000

* UNITED STATES	4,303,762
1. California	434,257
2. Ohio	253,842
3. Florida	249,276
4. Pennsylvania	214,630
5. Illinois	195,443
6. Michigan	182,213
7. Texas	181,787
8. Wisconsin	178,897
9. Arizona	164,279
10. Minnesota	142,799
11. Iowa	126,421
12. Washington	117,857
13. Indiana	117,331
14. New Jersey	111,430
15. Massachusetts	106,715
16. New York	106,371
17. Colorado	98,218
18. Georgia	86,988
19. North Carolina	82,302
20. Tennessee	70,846
21. Oregon	68,598
22. Missouri	60,897
23. Virginia	60,463
24. Oklahoma	57,284
25. Alabama	54,359
26. Connecticut	53,742
27. South Carolina	51,436
28. Kansas	49,548
29. Maryland	49,296
30. New Hampshire	48,651
31. Louisiana	47,736
32. Kentucky	43,990
33. Idaho	42,001
34. Mississippi	31,845
35. South Dakota	29,175
36. Maine	28,791
37. New Mexico	28,291
38. Utah	28,116
39. Montana	26,402
40. West Virginia	25,705
41. Arkansas	24,998
42. Nevada	24,445
43. Vermont	21,740
44. Nebraska	20,881
45. Hawaii	19,772
46. Rhode Island	19,432
47. Wyoming	19,121
48. North Dakota	17,003
49. Alaska	16,063
50. Delaware	10,952
51. District of Columbia	1,127